CASES AND MATERIALS

EUROPEAN COMMUNITY LAW

CASES AND MATERIALS

EUROPEAN COMMUNITY LAW

Second Edition

Elspeth Deards LLB, Solicitor
Senior Lecturer in Law, Nottingham Law School

Sylvia Hargreaves BA, LLM, PhD, Solicitor
Senior Lecturer in Law, Nottingham Law School

b BLACKSTONE
PRESS LIMITED

First published in Great Britain 1996 by Blackstone Press Limited,
Aldine Place, London W12 8AA.   Telephone 0181–740 2277

© Nottingham Law School, Nottingham Trent University, 1996

First edition 1996
Reprinted 1997
Second edition 1998

ISBN: 1 85431 822 5

British Library Cataloguing in Publication Data
A CIP catalogue record for this book is available from the British Library.

Typeset by Style Photosetting Limited, Mayfield, East Sussex
Printed by Livesey Limited, Shrewsbury, Shropshire

FOREWORD

The books in the LLB series have been written for students studying law at undergraduate level. There are two books for each subject. The first is the *Learning Text* which is designed to teach you about the particular subject in question. However, it does much more than that. By means of Activities, Self Assessment, and End of Chapter Questions, the *Learning Text* allows you to test your knowledge and understanding as you work. Each chapter starts with 'Objectives' which indicate what you should be able to do by the end of it. You should use these Objectives in your learning — check them frequently and ask yourself whether you have attained them.

The second book is a volume of *Cases and Materials*. This is cross-referenced from the *Learning Text*. It contains the primary sources of law such as statutes and cases plus subsidiary sources such as extracts from journals, law reform papers and textbooks. This is your portable library. Although each volume can stand alone, they are designed to be complementary.

The two-volume combination aims to support your learning by challenging you to demonstrate your mastery of the principles and application of the law. They are appropriate whatever your mode of study — full-time or part-time.

CONTENTS

1.1 The Economic Origins of the Community — 1.2 The Political Origins of the Community — 1.3 The Community — 1.4 The Single European Act — 1.5 Later Developments — 1.6 End of Chapter Assessment Question — 1.7 End of Chapter Assessment Outline Answer

2.1 The 'Big Five' Institutions — 2.2 The Other Institutions — 2.3 End of Chapter Assessment Question — 2.4 End of Chapter Assessment Outline Answer

3.1 Sovereignty — 3.2 Federalism — 3.3 Attribution of Powers to the Community — 3.4 Sources of Community Law — 3.5 Legislative Procedures — 3.6 End of Chapter Assessment Question — 3.7 End of Chapter Assessment Outline Answer

4.1 The European Union — 4.2 Key Provisions of the TEU — 4.3 End of Chapter Assessment Question — 4.4 End of Chapter Assessment Outline Answer

5.1 Direct Effect — 5.2 Indirect Effect — 5.3 Member State Liability — 5.4 Remedies Available — 5.5 End of Chapter Assessment Question — 5.6 End of Chapter Assessment Outline Answer

6.1 Issues which may be Referred — 6.2 The Status of the National Court — 6.3 Discretionary References — 6.4 Mandatory References — 6.5 Misuse of Article 177 — 6.6 Issues of Validity — 6.7 The Effect of a Ruling — 6.8 Conclusion — 6.9 End of Chapter Assessment Question — 6.10 End of Chapter Assessment Outline Answer

ACKNOWLEDGMENTS

Nottingham Law School and the publishers would like to thank to following for permission to reproduce copyright material:

Blackwell Publishers for extracts from *Modern Law Review*.

The British Institute of International and Comparative Law for extracts from *The Role and Future of the European Court of Justice*.

Butterworths & Co. (Publishers) Ltd for extracts from the *All England Law Reports*.

Hart Publishing for extracts from *New Directions in European Public Law*, 'Taking Article 215 EC Treaty Seriously', W. Van Gerven.

The Incorporated Council of Law Reporting for England & Wales for extracts from the *Weekly Law Reports*.

Kluwer Law International for 'Editorial Comments — The Treaty of Amsterdam; Neither a Bang Nor a Whimper' [1997] CMLR 34.

David Perry on behalf of the Office for Official Publications of the European Community for permission to quote from the *Official Journal of the European Communities, European Parliament: The Week* and *European Community Bulletin*.

Sweet & Maxwell Ltd for extracts from the *Common Market Law Reports* and the *European Law Review*.

TABLE OF CASES

Cases reported in full are shown in heavy type. The page at which the report is printed is shown in heavy type.

Court of Justice of the European Communities

Cases have been arranged in alphabetical order. See page xix for a chronological list of ECJ cases by case number and year.

*Cases have been arranged in chronological order by case number and year. See page xi for the
alphabetical list of ECJ cases.*

Commission Decisions

Council Decisions

TABLE OF LEGISLATION

Treaties, and articles thereof, which are set out in full or in part are shown in heavy type. The page at which the Treaty or article is printed is also shown in heavy type.

CHAPTER ONE

ORIGINS OF THE COMMUNITY

1.1   The Economic Origins of the Community

THE TREATY OF ROME

Article 2 (prior to SEA and TEU amendments)
The Community shall have as its task, by establishing a common market and progressively approximating the economic policies of Member States, to promote throughout the
Community a harmonious development of economic activities, a continuous and balanced expansion, an increase in stability, an accelerated raising of the standard of living
and closer relations between the States belonging to it.

THE TREATY OF ROME

Article 3 (prior to SEA and TEU amendments)
For the purposes set out in Article 2, the activities of the Community shall include, as
provided in this Treaty and in accordance with the timetable set out therein:

(a)   the elimination, as between Member States, of customs duties and of quantitative
restrictions on the import and export of goods, and of all other measures having
equivalent effect;
(b)   the establishment of a common customs tariff and of a common commercial policy
towards third countries;
(c)   the abolition, as between Member States, of obstacles to freedom of movement for
persons, services and capital;
(d)   the adoption of a common policy in the sphere of agriculture;
(e)   the adoption of a common policy in the sphere of transport;
(f)   the institution of a system ensuring that competition in the common market is not
distorted;
(g)   the application of procedures by which the economic policies of Member States
can be coordinated and disequilibria in their balances of payments remedied;
(h)   the approximation of the laws of Member States to the extent required for the
proper functioning of the common market;
(i)   the creation of a European Social Fund in order to improve employment
opportunities for workers and to contribute to the raising of their standard of living;
(j)   the establishment of a European Investment Bank to facilitate the economic
expansion of the Community by opening up fresh resources;
(k)   the association of the overseas countries and territories in order to increase trade
and to promote jointly economic and social development.

1.1.1   THE CURRENT ECONOMIC STATUS OF THE COMMUNITY

Editorial Comments (1995) 32 CML Rev 673

Schengen: The pros and cons
On 26 March 1995, the area of free circulation set up by the Schengen Agreement of 14
June 1985 and the Implementing Convention of 19 June 1990 entered into force. Seven

countries have implemented Schengen: Belgium, France, Germany, Luxembourg, The Netherlands, Portugal and Spain. The Convention did not enter into force for the other parties to Schengen, Italy and Greece, which have implementation problems both as regards their immigration controls and procedures, and the establishment of data protection legislation which would comply with the requirements of the Implementing Convention. It is understood that Austria intends to accede shortly to the Convention, though entry into force for Austria may be delayed.

Of the other Member States, the United Kingdom and Ireland have shown no interest in adhering to Schengen, the former presumably because of its long-stated opposition to the abolition of internal frontier controls, and the latter presumably because of the common travel area which it shares with the United Kingdom. Denmark, Sweden and Finland have the still unresolved problem of how to reconcile adhesion to Schengen with the existence of the Nordic travel area.

The problems and defects of the Schengen Convention have been dealt with extensively elsewhere, and it is not intended to re-examine them here. The positive aspect of Schengen is that, for the seven countries in respect of which it has entered into force, the promise of the free circulation of persons within an area without internal frontiers, as required by Article 7A of the EC Treaty, has been realized. The Commission has thus been justified in its oft-repeated assertion that Schengen is a laboratory experiment to see what can be achieved in the area of the free circulation of persons.

Schengen is now a concrete example of the two-speed Europe. It is outside the Union framework but it is within the Union orbit in the sense that all of its members are members of the Union and the Implementing Convention makes specific reference to the aim of the EEC Treaty in creating an area without internal frontiers; Article 134 of the Convention provides that '[T]he provisions of this Convention shall apply only in so far as they are compatible with Community law'. The aim of Schengen, an area with free circulation of persons, is the aim of Article 7A of the Treaty, but it is a goal which has been achieved by only 7 out of 15 Member States.

. . .

Inevitably, the question which comes to mind is whether the Schengen free circulation area is worth all this; is the game worth the candle? Is the dispensation from the requirement to show a travel document to an immigration officer, but which is factually necessary to prove one's identity and perhaps to board a plane, so important as to justify the expense, the different regimes and the possible conflicts with, if not the letter, at least the spirit of Community law? Proponents of free movement and free circulation will answer affirmatively, as they see Schengen as the precursor to the full implementation of Article 7A of the EC Treaty and the realization of the internal market in persons. Others may not be so sure. Insofar as Schengen is largely the model upon which the Union is basing its own efforts in this area, such as the draft Convention on the crossing of the external frontiers of the Member States, the draft visa regulation, resolutions on asylum and the institution of a European Information System, it seems likely that the Union framework for free circulation could share the defects of Schengen. If the Union does not modify certain aspects of the Schengen model, these defects will be perpetuated.

That controls are necessary is beyond doubt. The growth of international organized crime, the problem of drugs and terrorists, and other issues such as illegal immigration, are reasons for compensatory measures to replace internal border controls at least. However, the abolition of internal border controls should not lead to the establishment of a system which is potentially more intrusive on the rights of the individual than internal border controls ever were, with new threats to privacy and the rights of asylum-seekers and others; nor should it lack effective parliamentary and judicial control at national or supranational levels. The fundamental problem may be the equation of goods with persons which is made in Article 7A of the EC Treaty. Whereas the abolition of internal border controls on goods is clearly necessary in order to achieve the internal market in goods, it has not been convincingly shown that this is the case for persons, where the benefits of the abolition of internal border controls may not genuinely counter-balance the necessary compensatory measures and the lack of effective parliamentary and judicial control. One hopes that these problems may be overcome in time.

2.1.2 ECONOMIC INTEGRATION AND THE TREATY OF ROME

THE TREATY OF ROME

Article 2

The Community shall have as its task, by establishing a common market and an economic and monetary union and by implementing the common policies of activities referred to in Articles 3 and 3a, to promote throughout the Community a harmonious and balanced development of economic activities, sustainable and non-inflationary growth respecting the environment, a high degree of convergence of economic performance, a high level of employment and of social protection, the raising of the standard of living and quality of life, and economic and social cohesion and solidarity among Member States.

THE TREATY OF ROME

Article 3

For the purposes set out in Article 2, the activities of the Community shall include, as provided in this Treaty and in accordance with the timetable set out therein:

    (a)   the elimination, as between Member States, of customs duties and quantitative restrictions on the import and export of goods, and of all other measures having equivalent effect;

    (b)   a common commercial policy;

    (c)   an internal market characterised by the abolition, as between Member States, of obstacles to the free movement of goods, persons, services and capital;

    (d)   measures concerning the entry and movement of persons in the internal market as provided for in Article 100c;

    (e)   a common policy in the sphere of agriculture and fisheries;

    (f)   a common policy in the sphere of transport;

    (g)   a system ensuring that competition in the internal market is not distorted;

    (h)   the approximation of the laws of Member States to the extent required for the functioning of the common market;

    (i)   a policy in the social sphere comprising a European Social Fund;

    (j)   the strengthening of economic and social cohesion;

    (k)   a policy in the sphere of the environment;

    (l)   the strengthening of the competitiveness of Community industry;

    (m) the promotion of research and technological development;

    (n)   encouragement for the establishment and development of trans-European networks;

    (o)   a contribution to the attainment of a high level of health protection;

    (p)   a contribution to education and training of quality and to the flowering of the cultures of the Member States;

    (q)   a policy in the sphere of development cooperation;

    (r)   the association of the overseas countries and territories in order to increase trade and promote jointly economic and social development;

    (s)   a contribution to the strengthening of consumer protection;

    (t)   measures in the spheres of energy, civil protection and tourism.

1.2 The Political Origins of the Community

1.2.1 THE EUROPEAN COAL AND STEEL COMMUNITY

THE TREATY ESTABLISHING THE EUROPEAN COAL AND STEEL COMMUNITY

Preamble

THE PRESIDENT OF THE FEDERAL REPUBLIC OF GERMANY, HIS ROYAL HIGHNESS THE PRINCE ROYAL OF BELGIUM, THE PRESIDENT OF THE FRENCH REPUBLIC, THE PRESIDENT OF THE ITALIAN REPUBLIC, HER ROYAL HIGHNESS THE GRAND DUCHESS OF LUXEMBOURG, HER MAJESTY THE QUEEN OF THE NETHERLANDS,

CONSIDERING that world peace can be safeguarded only by creative efforts commensurate with the dangers that threaten it,

CONVINCED that the contribution which an organised and vital Europe can make to civilisation is indispensable to the maintenance of peaceful relations,

RECOGNISING that Europe can be built only through practical achievements which will first of all create real solidarity, and through the establishment of common bases for economic development,

ANXIOUS to help, by expanding their basic production, to raise the standard of living and further the works of peace,

RESOLVED to substitute for age-old rivalries the merging of their essential interests; to create, by establishing an economic community, the basis for a broader and deeper community among peoples long divided by bloody conflicts; and to lay the foundations for institutions which will give direction to a destiny henceforward shared,

HAVE DECIDED to create a European Coal and Steel Community and to this end have designated as their plenipotentiaries:

. . .

1.2.2   THE CREATION OF THE COMMUNITY

THE TREATY OF ROME

Preamble

HIS MAJESTY THE KING OF THE BELGIANS, THE PRESIDENT OF THE FEDERAL REPUBLIC OF GERMANY, THE PRESIDENT OF THE FRENCH REPUBLIC, THE PRESIDENT OF THE ITALIAN REPUBLIC, HER ROYAL HIGHNESS THE GRAND DUCHESS OF LUXEMBOURG, HER MAJESTY THE QUEEN OF THE NETHERLANDS,

DETERMINED to lay the foundations of an ever closer union among the peoples of Europe,

RESOLVED to ensure the economic and social progress of their countries by common action to eliminate the barriers which divide Europe,

AFFIRMING as the essential objective of their efforts the constant improvement of the living and working conditions of their peoples,

RECOGNISING that the removal of existing obstacles calls for concerted action in order to guarantee steady expansion, balanced trade and fair competition,

ANXIOUS to strengthen the unity of their economies and to ensure their harmonious development by reducing the differences existing between the various regions and the backwardness of the less favoured regions,

DESIRING to contribute, by means of a common commercial policy, to the progressive abolition of restrictions on international trade,

INTENDING to confirm the solidarity which binds Europe and the overseas countries and desiring to ensure the development of their prosperity, in accordance with the principles of the Charter of the United Nations,

RESOLVED by thus pooling their resources to preserve and strengthen peace and liberty, and calling upon the other peoples of Europe who share their ideal to join in their efforts,

HAVE DECIDED to create a European Economic Community and to this end have designated as their Plenipotentiaries:

1.3   The Community

1.3.1   THE EARLY YEARS OF THE COMMUNITY

THE LUXEMBOURG ACCORDS

At the extraordinary Council session of 28 and 29 January 1966 the Six reached agreement and the following statements were issued:

. . .

(b)   Majority voting procedure

I.   Where, in the case of decisions which may be taken by majority vote on a proposal of the Commission, very important interests of one or more partners are at stake, the

Members of the Council will endeavour, within a reasonable time, to reach solutions which can be adopted by all the Members of the Council while respecting their mutual interests and those of the Community, in accordance with Article 2 of the Treaty.

II. With regard to the preceding paragraph, the French delegation considers that where very important interests are at stake the discussion must be continued until unanimous agreement is reached.

III. The six delegations note that there is a divergence of views on what should be done in the event of a failure to reach complete agreement.

IV. The six delegations nevertheless consider that this divergence does not prevent the Community's work being resumed in accordance with the normal procedure.

The members of the Council agreed that decisions on the following should be by common consent:

    (a) The financial regulation for agriculture;
    (b) Extensions to the market organisation for fruit and vegetables;
    (c) The regulation on the organisation of sugar markets;
    (d) The regulation on the organisation of markets for oils and fats;
    (e) The fixing of common prices for milk, beef and veal, rice, sugar, olive oil and oil seeds. . . .

1.3.2 A PERIOD OF STAGNATION FOR THE COMMUNITY

See *Commission* v *Council (ERTA)* (**3.3**), *Van Duyn* v *Home Office* (**5.1.4**) *Amministrazino delle Finanze dello Stato* v *Simmenthal SpA, (Simmenthal II)* (**3.1.2.2**) and *SA Roquette Frères* v *Council* (**7.1.4**).

1.4 The Single European Act

1.4.1 AMENDMENTS TO THE TREATY OF ROME TO ENSURE COMPLETION OF THE SINGLE INTERNAL MARKET BY THE END OF 1992

THE TREATY OF ROME

Article 7a
The Community shall adopt measures with the aim of progressively establishing the internal market over a period expiring on 31 December 1992, in accordance with the provisions of this Article and of Articles 7b, 7c, 28, 57(2), 59, 70(1), 84, 99, 100a and 100b and without prejudice to the other provisions of this Treaty.

The internal market shall comprise an area without internal frontiers in which the free movement of goods, persons, services and capital is ensured in accordance with the provisions of this Treaty.

1.4.2 PROVISIONS (OPERATING OUTSIDE THE TREATY OF ROME) OF EUROPEAN POLITICAL CO-OPERATION

THE SINGLE EUROPEAN ACT

Article 30
European co-operation in the sphere of foreign policy shall be governed by the following provisions:

1. The High Contracting Parties, being members of the European Communities, shall endeavour jointly to formulate and implement a European foreign policy.

2. (a) The High Contracting Parties undertake to inform and consult each other on any foreign policy matters of general interest so as to ensure that their combined influence is exercised as effectively as possible through co-ordination, the convergence of their positions and the implementation of joint action.

    (b) Consultations shall take place before the High Contracting Parties decide on their final position.

(c)   In adopting its positions and in its national measures each High Contracting Party shall take full account of the positions of the other partners and shall give due consideration to the desirability of adopting and implementing common European positions.

In order to increase their capacity for joint action in the foreign policy field, the High Contracting Parties shall ensure that common principles and objectives are gradually developed and defined.

The determination of common positions shall constitute a point of reference for the policies of the High Contracting Parties.

(d)   The High Contracting Parties shall endeavour to avoid any action or position which impairs their effectiveness as a cohesive force in international relations or within international organisations.

3.   (a)   The Ministers for Foreign Affairs and a member of the Commission shall meet at least four times a year within the framework of European Political Co-operation. They may also discuss foreign policy matters within the framework of Political Co-operation on the occasion of meetings of the Council of the European Communities.

(b)   The Commission shall be fully associated with the proceedings of political co-operation.

(c)   In order to ensure the swift adoption of common positions and the implementation of joint action, the High Contracting Parties shall, as far as possible, refrain from impeding the formation of a consensus and the joint action which this could produce.
. . .

7.   (a)   In international institutions and at international conferences which they attend, the High Contracting Parties shall endeavour to adopt common positions on the subjects covered by this Title.

(b)   In international institutions and at international conferences in which not all the High Contracting Parties participate, those who do participate shall take full account of positions agreed in European political co-operation.

1.5   Later Developments

THE TREATY OF ROME

Article 118a
1.   Member States shall pay particular attention to encouraging improvements, especially in the working environment, as regards the health and safety of workers, and shall set as their objective the harmonisation of conditions in this area, while maintaining the improvements made.

2.   In order to help achieve the objective laid down in the first paragraph, the Council, acting in accordance with the procedure referred to in Article 189c, and after consulting the Economic and Social Committee, shall adopt by means of directives, minimum requirements for gradual implementation, having regard to the conditions and technical rules obtaining in each of the Member States.

Such directives shall avoid imposing administrative, financial and legal constraints in a way which would hold back the creation and development of small and medium-sized undertakings.

3.   The provisions adopted pursuant to this Article shall not prevent any Member State from maintaining or introducing more stringent measures for the protection of working conditions compatible with this Treaty.

THE TREATY OF ROME

Article 119
Each Member State shall during the first stage ensure and subsequently maintain the application of the principle that men and women should receive equal pay for equal work.

For the purpose of this Article, 'pay' means the ordinary basic or minimum wage or salary and any other consideration, whether in cash or in kind, which the worker receives, directly or indirectly, in respect of his employment from his employer.

Equal pay without discrimination based on sex means:
   (a) that pay for the same work at piece rates shall be calculated on the basis of the same unit of measurement;
   (b) that pay for work at time rates shall be the same for the same job.

Editorial, 'The Treaty of Amsterdam: Neither a bang nor a whimper' (1997) 34 CML Rev 767

The Treaty that emerged from the European Council of Amsterdam is likely to have as few admirers as its predecessor of Maastricht. This will not be the fault of the technicians who have shown their customary talent for bridging seemingly unbridgeable political differences, or at all events papering them over. The leaders of the European Union were simply not ready to take enough of the hard decisions that will be necessary before the impending enlargement. We can only hope they make a better showing as salesmen of the new text to their parliaments and electorates, than they did during the ratification process of the Maastricht Treaty – another technical triumph, though a near political disaster. It is a text which does indeed have some worrying features but still quite a lot to recommend it.

The 'pillared' structure erected by Maastricht has been preserved, but with a significant shift of matters relating to the treatment of third country nationals from Title VI of the TEU ('the third pillar') to a new EC Treaty Title on the free movement of persons, asylum and immigration. That Title will establish a legal basis for legislation aimed at ensuring, within five years, the complete abolition of controls on persons, whatever their nationality, when crossing the Union's internal frontiers. In addition, legal bases will be provided for the 'flanking' measures needed to make a reality of internal free movement – on things such as external border controls, asylum and immigration. Judicial cooperation in civil matters will also pass into the Community sphere, whereas police cooperation and judicial cooperation in criminal matters remain under Title VI, though their scope is to be notably enhanced.

Those provisions, aimed at creating 'an area of freedom, security and justice', have as their corollary the integration of the so-called 'Schengen *acquis*' into the framework of the European Union. The Protocol on Schengen is a clever – perhaps too clever – piece of drafting, over which many litres of academic ink are likely to be spilt. However, the basic idea is a simple one. The provisions or decisions which constitute the *acquis* are to be consigned, by the Council acting unanimously, to the legal bases, found either in the EC Treaty or in Title VI of the TEU, which are appropriate to their subject-matter. A Declaration to the Final Act will call for the necessary preparatory work to be done in good time to allow the adoption of the requisite Council measures on the date of entry into force of the Amsterdam Treaty; though, as a fail-safe, it is provided that, in the absence of such measures, the Schengen provisions and decisions are to be regarded, in their entirety, as acts based on Title VI.

At this point, the *leitmotif* that sounds persistently throughout the draft Treaty – flexibility or, as we must learn to call it, 'closer cooperation' – can no longer be ignored. It was Maastricht that made respectable what was then lumpishly, but less tendentiously, known as 'variable geometry', the idea that all of the Member States need not be committed, even in principle, sooner or later to participate fully in all Union activities: the notorious example of this technique, soon to be consigned to history, was the Social Protocol; more interesting and lasting examples are the derogations from EMU and the arrangements under Article J.4 of the TEU on decisions having defence implications. The novelty of Amsterdam-style flexibility lies in the insertion into the Common Provisions of the TEU of a *general* flexibility clause, complemented by similar clauses in the EC Treaty and in Title VI. These are enabling provisions available, under specified conditions, to authorize closer cooperation between certain Member States, in fields which need not have been identified in advance at the level of the Treaties themselves.

The mechanism is, accordingly, one of 'secondary flexibility', allowing new fields of activity to be opened up, through differentiated arrangements established under internal legislation. A first question that arises is whether such a mechanism is compatible with the principle of the attribution of powers, now enshrined in Article 3B of the EC Treaty. The intention is, apparently, that it should be, since one of the conditions laid down by the new Article 5A EC is that any proposed cooperation 'remains within the limits of the powers conferred upon the Community by this Treaty'. In other words, an existing legal basis in the Treaty will have to be found for closer cooperation proposals. But could the mechanism be used to modify the procedure provided for by the chosen legal basis: for instance, to create for the participating Member States the possibility of harmonizing indirect taxation by qualified majority decision? Presumably not, since the attribution principle has traditionally been regarded as having both substantive and procedural aspects. All that may be reassuring, but it leaves room for wondering just how useful, in practice, the new mechanism is likely to be.

A thoroughly unreassuring feature of closer cooperation, however, is the rule in Article 5A(2) that, if a member of the Council declares that, for important and stated reasons of national policy, it intends to oppose the granting of an authorization by qualified majority, a vote shall not be taken; in which case, the Council may, by a qualified majority, request that the matter be referred to the European Council for decisions by unanimity. Predictions of the demise of the Luxembourg Compromise were thus distinctly premature: it has been given a new lease of life, no longer in the *demi-monde* of political deals but as part of the legal machinery of the EC Treaty. True, the goodwill costs of invoking the rule will be high, and it will seldom, perhaps never, be resorted to: the worry is that, once legally baptized, the Luxembourg Compromise may start popping up in other places. Indeed, its reception into the EC Treaty may have been facilitated by the acceptance, at an earlier stage of the IGC, of a similar rule in the context of the common foreign and security policy (as to which, more below). it would have been less subversive of the Community order to have stuck to the unanimity rule.

Returning to Schengen, one of the clevernesses of the Amsterdam text is to treat the *acquis* as a particular case of closer cooperation. That was necessary, because Ireland and the United Kingdom have not acceded to the Schengen Agreement and have, moreover, negotiated an opt-out from the new free movement Title of the EC Treaty. A rather alarming impression of the far-reaching implications of flexibility can be gathered from Article 2 of the opting-out Protocol. According to that Article, Ireland and the United Kingdom will be immune not only from the provisions of the new Treaty Title but also from measures adopted, or the provisions of international agreements concluded, pursuant to that Title and from decisions of the Court of Justice interpreting any such provision or measure. What is more, 'no such provision measure or decision shall in any way affect the *acquis communautaire* nor form part of Community law as they apply to the United Kingdom or Ireland'. Maintaining the unity of the constitutional order under such conditions will be an uphill task.

Truly bizarre are the specific arrangements applicable to Denmark. Though a party to the Schengen Agreement, that country will enjoy an opt-out from the free movement Title of the EC Treaty; and it will also stand aside from the incorporation of the Schengen *acquis*, so far as elements of the latter are determined to have legal bases in that Title. If, pursuant to Article 5 of the relevant Protocol, Denmark decides to apply in its national law a Council measure building on the Schengen *acquis*, its decision to do so will generate an obligation of *international* law, not of Community law. This gives a new twist to flexibility: Denmark will be a participating Member State in the field covered by Schengen, and yet the rules by which it is bound will have a different legal character from those binding the other Member States. There is no objective justification for this, as there is in terms of geography for the British/Irish opt-out.

It would be wrong, though, to go on too long about possible threats the Amsterdam Treaty may pose to the constitutional order of the polity built up over the past 40 years. In fact, there is much in the Treaty that readers of this Review should feel able to applaud.

First and foremost, perhaps, is the stronger emphasis given to the fundamental values of the Union and the establishment of new machinery to ensure that they are respected. The procedure for the suspension of a Member State's rights, in the face of serious and persistent breaches of the principles spelt out in the new Article F(1), may never, in practice, be used; but it is nevertheless timely, with countries pressing for membership of the Union, where democracy and the rule of law are still a recent and tender growth. It is good news, too, that the Council will have power under the new Article 6A of the EC Treaty to legislate against a much wider range of discrimination; and that equal treatment between men and women will receive an explicit mention in both Article 2 and Article 3.

Surely, also, the new Article K.7 must count as a gain. The Court of Justice is to have jurisdiction to give preliminary rulings on law-making acts adopted under Title VI of the TEU – though admittedly only if the Member State of the referring court has made a declaration accepting such jurisdiction. Regrettably, the Court's jurisdiction is to be excluded, here as well as under Article H of the free movement Title of the EC Treaty, in respect of measures or decisions relating to the maintenance of law and order and the safeguarding of internal security; but the interpretation of that restrictive provision will be a matter for the Court itself.

As for the decision-making procedures of the institutions, significant progress was made towards simplifying and rationalizing the legislative process. Except in the domain of EMU, which was untouchable, the cooperation procedure is to disappear; and more streamlined co-decision will provide the standard way of enacting most measures of a genuinely legislative nature. However, it is indeed a pity that the Heads of State and Government ran out of steam over the issue of reweighting the qualified majority. The changes in CFSP procedures are broadly welcome, too. It was pie in the sky to suppose that qualified majority voting would become the rule in an area of such acute political sensitivity. The constructive abstention mechanism is a good – because realistic – compromise solution; and, in fact, there should be considerable scope for majority decisions, on matters covered by a common strategy or when a joint action or common position is being implemented – a shame, though, that the Luxembourg Compromise was allowed to creep into the new Article J.13.

So all is not doom and gloom. Except perhaps for the negotiators, who will have to reassemble all too soon to complete their unfinished business.

1.6   End of Chapter Assessment Question

(a)   (i)   Explain the underlying philosophy behind the formation of the Community.

(ii)   How has this philosophy changed?

(b)   Why was the Single European Act necessary and how does it provide for the achievement of its objectives?

1.7   End of Chapter Assessment Outline Answer

(a)(i)   The philosophies underlying the formation of the Community were both economic and political. The economies of Europe had been devastated by the Second World War and the best hope of recovery seemed to lie in a pooling of resources and the creation of a trading bloc to compete with the USA and the USSR. The union of the coal and steel industries of six countries (the ECSC) had proved to be a success and its members felt that co-operation over a wider sphere would bring them greater prosperity. It was also felt that a European union would lessen the likelihood of another European war and enable its members to withstand military pressure from the Soviet bloc. The Preamble stressed the intention to lay the foundations of an ever closer union of peoples and to strengthen peace and liberty.

(ii)   The original impetus was towards the creation of a common or single market in goods, services, labour and capital. The ambit of the Community has now taken in full economic and monetary union, with a single currency and a single policy for the Member States, and its activities as listed in Article 3 of the Treaty of Rome now include, *inter alia*, an environmental policy, the strenthening of consumer protection and the promotion of research and development.

In addition, the Community now forms part of the EU which has limited competence in the areas of foreign policy and home affairs.

(b)   By the early 1980s it was clear that radical new steps had to be taken if the Community was to be rejuvenated. The deadline for the creation of a common market had passed without fulfilment and few measures of importance had been taken for over a decade while the Member States contemplated their domestic woes.

The SEA set out to achieve this rejuvenation, paying particular attention to the objective of a Single Market. A new and more detailed definition of the Single Market was provided, together with a new law-making power to be applied to provisions to achieve the Single Market. New areas of competence for the Community were estab-lished, although these merely reflected de facto extensions of the Community's powers over previous years. Foreign policy co-operation was also mentioned for the first time although it was not incorporated into the Treaty of Rome.

The SEA succeeded in reviving interest in the Community and promoting the importance of the Community to future European development. In particular the completion of the Single Market, albeit later than the original deadline of the end of 1992, has made it possible for the Member States to contemplate full economic integration in the Community.

CHAPTER TWO

THE INSTITUTIONS OF THE COMMUNITY

2.1   The 'Big Five' Institutions

2.1.1   THE COMMISSION

THE TREATY OF ROME

Article 157

1.   The Commission shall consist of 20 members, who shall be chosen on the grounds of their general competence and whose independence is beyond doubt.

The number of members of the Commission may be altered by the Council, acting unanimously.

Only nationals of Member States may be members of the Commission.

The Commission must include at least one national of each of the Member States, but may not include more than two members having the nationality of the same State.

2.   The members of the Commission shall, in the general interest of the Community, be completely independent in the performance of their duties.

In the performance of these duties, they shall neither seek nor take instructions from any government or from any other body. They shall refrain from any action incompatible with their duties. Each Member State undertakes to respect this principle and not to seek to influence the members of the Commission in the performance of their tasks.

The members of the Commission may not, during their term of office, engage in any other occupation, whether gainful or not. When entering upon their duties they shall give a solemn undertaking that, both during and after their term of office, they will respect the obligations arising therefrom and in particular their duty to behave with integrity and discretion as regards the acceptence, after they have ceased to hold office, of certain appointments or benefits. In the event of any breach of these obligations, the Court of Justice may, on application by the Council or the Commission, rule that the member concerned be, according to the circumstances, either compulsorily retired in accordance with Article 160 or deprived of his right to a pension or other benefits in its stead.

THE TREATY OF ROME

Article 163

The Commission shall act by a majority of the number of members provided for in Article 157.

A meeting of the Commission shall be valid only if the number of members laid down in its rules of procedure is present.

THE TREATY OF ROME

Article 155

In order to ensure the proper functioning and development of the common market, the Commission shall:

— ensure that the provisions of this Treaty and the measures taken by the institutions pursuant thereto are applied;

— formulate recommendations or deliver opinions on matters dealt with in this Treaty, if it expressly so provides or if the Commission considers it necessary;

— have its own power of decision and participate in the shaping of measures taken by the Council and by the European Parliament in the manner provided for in this Treaty;

— exercise the powers conferred on it by the Council for the implementation of the rules laid down by the latter.

2.1.1.1   Guardianship of the Treaty of Rome

THE TREATY OF ROME

Article 169   Actions by Commission against Member State

If the Commission considers that a Member State has failed to fulfil an obligation under the Treaty, it shall deliver a reasoned opinion on the matter after giving the State concerned the opportunity to submit its observations.

If the State concerned does not comply with the opinion within the time laid down by the Commission, the latter may bring the matter before the Court of Justice.

THE TREATY OF ROME

Article 170

A Member State which considers that another Member State has failed to fulfil an obligation under this Treaty may bring the matter before the Court of Justice.

Before a Member State brings an action against another Member State for an alleged infringement of an obligation under this Treaty, it shall bring the matter before the Commission.

The Commission shall deliver a reasoned opinion after each of the States concerned has been given the opportunity to submit its own case and its observations on the other party's case both orally and in writing.

If the Commission has not delivered an opinion within three months of the date on which the matter was brought before it, the absence of such opinion shall not prevent the matter from being brought before the Court of Justice.

COMMISSION v FRANCE (Joined Cases 24 & 87/80)
[1980] ECR 1319, Court of Justice

The Commission brought enforcement proceedings against France under Article 169 of the Treaty. The facts and the judgment appear in the extract below.

1.   The Court in its judgment of 25 September 1979 in Case 232/78 (*Commission of the European Communities* v *French Republic* [1979] ECR 2729) declared that by continuing to apply after 1 January 1978 its restrictive national system to the importation of mutton and lamb from the United Kingdom the French Republic had failed to fulfil its obligations under Articles 12 and 30 of the EEC Treaty.

2.   The Commission by applications lodged at the Court Registry on 14 January and 13 March 1980 has brought two actions before the Court for declarations that the French Republic by neglecting to take the necessary steps to comply with the above-mentioned judgment has failed to fulfil its obligations under Article 171 of the EEC Treaty.

3.   The first application (Case 24/80) requests the Court to 'declare that the French Republic, by continuing to apply after 25 September 1979 its restrictive national system to the importation of mutton and lamb from the United Kingdom, has failed to fulfill its obligations under Article 171 of the EEC Treaty'.

4.   The second application (Case 97/80) requests the court to 'declare that the French Republic, by continuing to levy after 25 September 1979 a charge on imports of mutton and lamb from the United Kingdom, has failed to fulfil its obligations under Article 171 of the EEC Treaty'.

5.   The French Republic lodged its defence in Case 24/80 on 22 February 1980. It contended that the action should be dismissed, its principal submission being that Article

171 implies that Member States are allowed for the purpose of taking the necessary steps to comply with a judgment of the Court a 'reasonable period of time' which varies with each case and that this period has not been exceeded in this case.

6. The Commission pursuant to Article 186 of the EEC Treaty and Article 83 of the Rules of Procedure of the Court, on 13 March 1980, subsequent to the lodging of its application in Case 97/80, made an application for the adoption of interim measures in both cases, in which it asks the Court to 'order the French Republic to desist forthwith from applying any restriction and/or levying any charge on imports of mutton and lamb from the United Kingdom'.

7. The two cases were joined by an order of the Court dated 24 March 1980.

8. The French Republic, whilst acknowledging that the judgment of the Court of 25 September 1979 imposes upon it the obligation to discontinue its national organization of the market in mutton and lamb, has submitted that there are obstacles of a political and economic nature impeding the immediate enforcement of that judgment. The French Government has also maintained that the order sought by the Commission is not covered by Article 186 and that in any case the conditions laid down by the case law of the Court for the application of interim measures are not present. The French Republic has therefore contended that the application for the adoption of interim measures should be dismissed.

9. The Commission replies that the period which has elapsed since the delivery by the Court of its judgment in Case 232/78 exceeds the 'reasonable period' for the adoption of the requisite measures for ensuring that the judgment of the Court is enforced. The Commission therefore considers that, owing to the serious damage which has flowed from the French Republic's maintaining in force measures restricting imports of mutton and lamb from the United Kingdom, it is a matter of urgency to order by way of interim measures the repeal of the said measures.

10. Article 171 of the Treaty states that 'If the Court of Justice finds that a Member State has failed to fulfil an obligation under this Treaty, the State shall be required to take the necessary measures to comply with the judgment of the Court of Justice'.

11. As provided for in Article 155 of the Treaty it is for the Commission to 'ensure that the provisions of this Treaty and the measures taken by the institutions pursuant thereto are applied'; the Commission is therefore under a duty to ensure also that Member States comply with the judgments delivered by the Court of Justice.

12. The Commission in the exercise of this power may bring actions pursuant to Article 169 of the Treaty if it considers that a Member State has not taken the necessary steps to ensure compliance with a judgment or that any measures taken for this purpose do not comply with the obligations arising out of the latter. In the context of such an action the possibility cannot be ruled out that the Court be asked to prescibe such interim measures as may be necessary pursuant to Article 186 of the Treaty and Article 36 of the Protocol on the Statute of the Court of Justice of the EEC provided that the conditions laid down by those provisions and by Article 83 of the Rules of Procedure are present. It is for the Court to determine in each individual case the need for such interim measures in accordance with the criteria laid down by the said provisions.

13. In the present case this need must be assessed by taking into account, on the one hand, the legal considerations arising from the above-mentioned judgment of the Court of 25 September 1979 and, on the other hand, the aim of the two actions brought successively by the Commission against the French Republic for failure to fulfil its obligations under Article 171 of the Treaty.

14. In the light of these considerations it is necessary first to recall the terms of the judgment of 25 September 1979. Although it is true that the Court stated that it was aware of 'the genuine problems which the French authorities have to solve in the sector under consideration and of the desirability of achieving the establishment, in the shortest possible time, of a common organisation of the market in mutton and lamb', it nevertheless pointed out that 'after the expiration of the transitional period of the EEC Treaty, and, as far as the new Member States are concerned, after the expiration of the time-limits for the transition specifically provided for in the Act of Accession, a national organisation of the market must no longer operate in such a way as to prevent the Treaty provisions relating to the elimination of restrictions on intra-Community trade from having full force and effect'.

15. Although the Court stressed in its judgment that 'it is for the competent institutions and for them alone to adopt within the appropriate periods the requisite measures with a view to finding, in a Community context, a comprehensive solution of the problem of the market in mutton and lamb and of the special difficulties which arise in this connexion in certain areas, it stated that the fact that the work done by the Community institutions with a view to establishing a common organisation of the market in the sector under consideration has not yet been successful 'is not a sufficient justification for the maintenance by a Member State of a national organisation of the market which includes features which are incompatible with the requirements of the Treaty relating to the free movement of goods, such as bans on imports and levying dues on imported products, under any designation whatsoever'.

16. As the Court held in its judgment of 13 July 1972 in Case 48/71, *Commission of the European Communities* v *Italian Republic* [1972] ECR 527 the finding in a judgment having the force of res judicata that the Member State concerned has failed to fulfil its obligations under Community law amounts to 'a prohibition having the full force of law on the competent national authorities against applying a national rule recognized as incompatible with the Treaty and, if the circumstances so require, an obligation on them to take all appropriate measures to enable Community law to be fully applied'. It follows that by reason solely of the judgment declaring the Member State to be in default, the State concerned is required to take the necessary measures to remedy its default and may not create any impediment whatsoever.

17. The French Republic is therefore required, by virtue of Articles 12 and 30 of the Treaty, as declared in the judgment of 25 September 1979, to desist from applying any restrictive measure of any kind whatsoever to the importation of mutton and lamb from the United Kingdom; as was stated in that judgment, that obligation was effective as from 1 January 1978.

18. It must moreover be borne in mind that the purpose of the applications in Joined Cases 24 and 97/80 is to obtain a declaration that the French Republic, by continuing to apply its restrictive scheme after the judgment of 25 September 1979 has failed to fulfil its obligations under Article 171 of the Treaty.

19. The Commission, by requesting the Court in an application for the adoption of interim measures to order the French Republic to desist forthwith from applying its restrictive scheme, is asking the Court for an order the purpose of which would in substance be the same as that of the judgment of 25 September 1979. It follows that the interim measures which the Commission has asked the Court to order are not in the present circumstances within the meaning of Article 186 of the Treaty.

20. There are therefore no grounds for ordering the interim measures requested by the Commission.

2.1.1.2   Formulation of policy

THE TREATY OF ROME

Article 118
Without prejudice to the other provisions of this Treaty and in conformity with its general objectives, the Commission shall have the task of promoting close co-operation between Member States in the social field, particularly in matters relating to:
– employment;
– labour law and working conditions;
– basic and advanced vocational training;
– social security;
– prevention of occupational accidents and diseases;
– occupational hygiene;
– the right of association, and collective bargaining between employers and workers.
To this end, the Commission shall act in close contact with Member States by making studies, delivering opinions and arranging consultations both on problems arising at national level and on those of concern to international organisations.

Before delivering the opinions provided for in this Article, the Commission shall consult the Economic and Social Committee.

GERMANY v COMMISSION (MIGRATION POLICY) (Cases 281/85 etc.)
[1987] ECR 3203, Court of Justice

A number of Member States challenged the power of the Commission to take certain Decisions pursuant to Article 118 of the Treaty of Rome (see above) and requested annulment of these Decisions under Article 173 of the Treaty.

It was held that the Decisions were validly taken.

27.   Since the contested decision falls only partly outside the social field covered by Article 118, it must be considered whether the second paragraph of Article 118 which provides that the Commission is to act, inter alia, by arranging consultations, gives it the power to adopt a binding decision with a view to the arrangement of such consultations.

28.   In that connection it must be emphasized that where an article of the EEC Treaty – in this case Article 118 – confers a specific task on the Commission it must be accepted, if that provision is not to be rendered wholly ineffective, that it confers on the Commission necessarily and per se the powers which are indispensable in order to carry out that task. Accordingly, the second paragraph of Article 118 must be interpreted as conferring on the Commission all the powers which are necessary in order to arrange the consultations. In order to perform the task of arranging consultations the Commission must necessarily be able to require the Member States to notify essential information, in the first place in order to identify the problems and in the second place in order to pinpoint the possible guidelines for any future joint action on the part of the Member States; likewise it must be able to require them to take part in consultations.

29.   Indeed, the collaboration between Member States required by Article 118 is only possible within the framework of organized consultations. In the absence of any action to initiate it that collaboration might remain a dead letter, even though provision is made for it in the Treaty. Since the Commission was specifically given the task of promoting such collaboration and arranging it, it is entitled to initiate consultation procedures within the social field referred to in Article 118.

30.   It must be borne in mind that that power of the Commission must be confined to arranging a procedure for the notification of information and consultation and that in the present stage of development of Community law the subject-matter of the notification and consultation falls within the competence of the Member States. It must also be pointed out that the power which the Commission seeks to exercise under Article 118 is simply a procedural one to set up the notification and consultation machinery which is to result in the adoption of a common position on the part of the Member States.

31.   Consequently, since Article 118 provides a specific basis for the Commission's decision there is no need to consider whether the outcome sought by the decision in question might have been achieved through other general provisions of the Treaty or other procedures necessitating action on the part of other institutions.

2.1.2   THE COUNCIL

THE TREATY OF ROME

Article 148
1.   Save as otherwise provided in this Treaty, the Council shall act by a majority of its members.

2.   Where the Council is required to act by a qualified majority, the votes of its members shall be weighted as follows:

Belgium	5	Luxembourg	2
Denmark	3	Netherlands	5
Germany	10	Austria	4
Greece	5	Portugal	5
Spain	8	Finland	3
France	10	Sweden	4
Ireland	3	United Kingdom	10
Italy	10		

For their adoption, acts of the Council shall require at least:
- 62 votes in favour where this Treaty requires them to be adopted on a proposal from the Commission,
- 62 votes in favour, cast by at least 10 members, in other cases.

3. Abstentions by members present in person or represented shall not prevent the adoption by the Council of acts which required unanimity.

2.1.3 THE PARLIAMENT

THE TREATY OF ROME

Article 137
The European Parliament, which shall consist of representatives of the peoples of the States brought together in the Community, shall exercise the powers conferred upon it by this Treaty.

Article 138
(Paragraphs 1 and 2 lapsed on 17 July 1979 in accordance with Article 14 of the Act concerning the election of the representatives of the European Parliament)
[See Article 1 of that Act which reads as follows:
1. The representatives in the European Parliament of the peoples of the States brought together in the Community shall be elected by direct universal suffrage.]
[See Article 2 of that Act which reads as follows:
2. The number of representatives elected in each Member State is as follows:

Belgium	25	Luxembourg	6
Denmark	16	Netherlands	31
Germany	99	Austria	21
Greece	25	Portugal	25
Spain	64	Finland	16
France	87	Sweden	22
Ireland	15	United Kingdom	87.]
Italy	87		

3. The European Parliament shall draw up proposals for elections by direct universal suffrage in accordance with a uniform procedure in all Member States.

The Council shall, acting unanimously after obtaining the assent of the European Parliament, which shall act by a majority of its component members, lay down the appropriate provisions, which it shall recommend to Member States for adoption in accordance with their respective constitutional requirements.

Article 138a
Political parties at European level are important as a factor for integration within the Union. They contribute to forming a European awareness and to expressing the political will of the citizens of the Union.

Article 138b
In so far as provided in this Treaty, the European Parliament shall participate in the process leading up to the adoption of Community acts by exercising its powers under the procedures laid down in Articles 189b and 189c and by giving its assent or delivering advisory opinions.

The European Parliament may, acting by a majority of its members, request the Commission to submit any appropriate proposal on matters on which it considers that a Community act is required for the purpose of implementing this Treaty.

Article 138c
In the course of its duties, the European Parliament may, at the request of a quarter of its members, set up a temporary Committee of Inquiry to investigate, without prejudice to the powers conferred by this Treaty on other institutions or bodies, alleged contraventions or maladministration in the implementation of Community law, except where the

alleged facts are being examined before a court and while the case is still subject to legal proceedings.

The temporary Committee of Inquiry shall cease to exist on the submission of its report.

The detailed provisions governing the exercise of the right of inquiry shall be determined by common accord of the European Parliament, the Council and the Commission.

Article 138d

Any citizen of the Union, and any natural or legal person residing or having its registered office in a Member State, shall have the right to address, individually or in association with other citizens or persons, a petition to the European Parliament on a matter which comes within the Community's fields of activity and which affects him, her or it directly.

Article 138e

1. The European Parliament shall appoint an Ombudsman empowered to receive complaints from any citizen of the Union or any natural or legal person residing or having its registered office in a Member State concerning instances of maladministration in the activities of the Community institutions or bodies, with the exception of the Court of Justice and the Court of First Instance acting in their judicial role.

In accordance with his duties, the Ombudsman shall conduct inquiries for which he finds grounds, either on his own initiative or on the basis of complaints submitted to him direct or through a member of the European Parliament, except where the alleged facts are or have been the subject of legal proceedings. Where the Ombudsman establishes an instance of maladministration, he shall refer the matter to the institution concerned, which shall have a period of three months in which to inform him of its views. The Ombudsman shall then forward a report to the European Parliament and the institution concerned. The person lodging the complaint shall be informed of the outcome of such inquiries.

The Ombudsman shall submit an annual report to the European Parliament on the outcome of his inquiries.

2. The Ombudsman shall be appointed after each election of the European Parliament for the duration of its term of office. The Ombudsman shall be eligible for reappointment.

The Ombudsman may be dismissed by the Court of Justice at the request of the European Parliament if he no longer fulfils the conditions required for the performance of his duties or if he is guilty of serious misconduct.

3. The Ombudsman shall be completely independent in the performance of his duties. In the performance of those duties he shall neither seek nor take instructions from any body. The Ombudsman may not, during his term of office, engage in any other occupation, whether gainful or not.

4. The European Parliament shall, after seeking an opinion from the Commission and with the approval of the Council acting by a qualified majority, lay down the regulations and general conditions governing the performance of the Ombudsman's duties.

Article 139

The European Parliament shall hold an annual session. It shall meet, without requiring to be convened, on the second Tuesday in March.

The European Parliament may meet in extraordinary session at the request of a majority of its members or at the request of the Council or of the Commission.

Article 140

The European Parliament shall elect its President and its officers from among its members.

Members of the Commission may attend all meetings and shall, at their request, be heard on behalf of the Commission.

The Commission shall reply orally or in writing to questions put to it by the European Parliament or by its members.

The Council shall be heard by the European Parliament in accordance with the conditions laid down by the Council in its rules of procedure.

Article 141

Save as otherwise provided in this Treaty, the European Parliament shall act by an absolute majority of the votes cast.

The rules of procedure shall determine the quorum.

Article 142

The European Parliament shall adopt its rules of procedure, acting by a majority of its members.

The proceedings of the European Parliament shall be published in the manner laid down in its rules of procedure.

Article 143

The European Parliament shall discuss in open session the annual general report submitted to it by the Commission.

Article 144

If a motion of censure on the activities of the Commission is tabled before it, the European Parliament shall not vote thereon until at least three days after the motion has been tabled and only by open vote.

If the motion of censure is carried by a two-third majority of the votes cast, representing a majority of the members of the European Parliament, the members of the Commission shall resign as a body. They shall continue to deal with current business until they are replaced in accordance with Article 158. In this case, the term of office of the members of the Commission appointed to replace them shall expire on the date on which the term of office of the members of the Commission obliged to resign as a body would have expired.

2.1.3.1 Powers

Supervisory

THE TREATY OF ROME

Article 8a

1. Every citizen of the Union shall have the right to move and reside freely within the territory of the Member States, subject to the limitations and conditions laid down in this Treaty and by the measures adopted to give it effect.

2. The Council may adopt provisions with a view to facilitating the exercise of the rights referred to in paragraph 1; save as otherwise provided in this Treaty, the Council shall act unanimously on a proposal from the Commission and after obtaining the assent of the European Parliament.

Other powers

THE TREATY OF ROME

Article 105

6. The Council may, acting unanimously on a proposal from the Commission and after consulting the ECB and after receiving the assent of the European Parliament, confer upon the ECB specific tasks concerning policies relating to the prudential supervision of credit institutions and other financial institutions with the exception of insurance undertakings.

2.1.4 THE EUROPEAN COURT OF JUSTICE

THE TREATY OF ROME

Article 165

The Court of Justice shall consist of 15 judges.

The Court of Justice shall sit in plenary session. It may, however, form chambers, each consisting of three or five judges, either to undertake certain preparatory inquiries or to adjudicate on particular categories of cases in accordance with rules laid down for these purposes.

The Court of Justice shall sit in plenary session when a Member State or a Community institution that is a party to the proceedings so requests.

Should the Court of Justice so request, the Council may, acting unanimously, increase the number of judges and make the necessary adjustments to the second and third paragraphs of this Article and to the second paragraph of Article 167.

The Role and Future of the European Court of Justice, **British Institute of International and Comparative Law, 1996**

Use of chambers and plenum

(a) Increased use of chambers and curtailing the use of the plenum in the ECJ

Although the ECJ consists of 15 judges, only cases which raise important issues of principle are heard by all the judges. The full Court normally sits in a *petit* plenum of 11 judges (the quorum is nine). It also works in 6 chambers of 3 or 5 in the simpler or more technical cases.

Undoubtedly the tendency for chambers to become the normal organ of judgment and for the Court to sit in plenary session only exceptionally saves considerable time for the Court. The amendments made by the Maastricht Treaty have already provided greater scope for the use of chambers: whereas the ECJ was previously required to sit in plenary session in all cases brought by a Member State or a Community institution, it is now required to do so only when a Member State or institution which is a party to the proceedings so requests. Whether Member States should have the right to request a plenary session needs to be considered. The Court should in fact be able to refer all cases to a chamber where no new principle of law is involved. To give the ECJ this flexibility, an amendment of Article 165 of the Treaty would be necessary.

With regard to the number of chambers, the accession of Greece in 1981 and of Spain and Portugal in 1986 resulted in the creation of new chambers. This contributed to a reduction in the workload of the full Court. By contrast, following the recent round of enlargement by the accession of 3 new Member States, the number of chambers has not been increased but remains 6. Instead of moving to 7 chambers (with 3 'large' chambers of 5 judges), there are now still only two large chambers (but of 7 judges, sitting as 5) and four small chambers of 3 judges.

It should be recalled at this point that encouraging the use of chambers does not automatically mean an increase in the number of chambers and a consequent increase in the number of judges. As discussed above, such a development has its disadvantages. The fear has been expressed that the proliferation in the number of chambers could endanger the consistency of the ECJs case-law and, therefore, paradoxically require the Court to sit more frequently in plenary session in order to preserve it. That danger can be averted by the judicious selection of the cases which are sent to chambers and by the constant vigilance of the President of the Court and the Presidents of the Chambers, as under the present system. But the problem remains that a plenary session made up of 20 or more judges would be an unmanageable structure. It is already liable to be difficult to draft a collegiate judgment in a controversial case with 13 or 15 judges.

In the light of the foregoing, the balance between use of the chambers and of the plenary session seems to work efficiently as long as the size of the ECJ is kept much as it is at present. The frequent use of the *petit* plenum of 11 judges also seems to work well. Any further increase beyond the present number of judges may therefore cause more problems than it would apparently solve.

A different question is whether the efficiency of the Court might be improved by the creation of specialised chambers formally constituted. Although such a system in a large national supreme court appears to work well, it is much more difficult in EC law to impose rigid divisions between specialist matters. Rather than formalising the specialisation of chambers in the ECJ, it seems preferable to have a system with some degree of flexibility, where the President of the Court takes into account the accumulated experience of a particular chamber when allocating a case.

(b) Chambers and single judges within the CFI

The CFI has rarely sat in plenary session although it has the power to do so. The consistency of the case-law is preserved by the ECJ on appeal.

The creation of specialised chambers within the Court of First Instance should be encouraged. For instance, a particular group of judges of the CFI could be assigned, for the time being, to anti-dumping cases. Such an approach would help to prevent the development of different lines of authority emanating from different chambers. The creation of specialised chambers must however be distinguished from the proposal to create specialised courts or tribunals, which is discussed below. Under the present proposal, judges of the CFI could be assigned to a particular specialist chamber (e.g. 'anti-dumping') for a limited period of time, and could then move to a different chamber (e.g. 'competition' or 'state aids'). A judge would not therefore necessarily be faced with the prospect of deciding a particular category of case for his or her entire judicial career.

Consideration should also be given to the possibility of assigning certain 'technical' cases for decision by a single judge rather than a chamber. The possibility of referring a difficult case to a chamber, together with possible review by the ECJ on points of law, would reduce any risks of inconsistency in the case-law. As outlined above, the involvement of assistant *rapporteurs* in cases dealt with by a single judge may also be attractive.

COMMISSION v BELGIUM (Case 77/69) [1970] ECR 237, Court of Justice

The Belgian government was prevented, by the dissolution of the Belgian Parliament, from enacting legislation to amend a law which had been declared contrary to Community law by the Court of Justice. The Commission brought enforcement proceedings against Belgium under Article 173 of the Treaty.

It was held that this was not a valid defence.

COMMISSION OF THE EUROPEAN COMMUNITIES, represented by its Legal Adviser, Cesare Maestripieri, acting as Agent, with an address for service in Luxembourg at the offices of its Legal Adviser, Emile Reuter, 4, boulevard Royal,

applicant,

v

KINGDOM OF BELGIUM, represented by Gilbert de Klerck, acting Director of Administration at the Ministry for Foreign Affairs and External Trade, acting as Agent, with an address for service in Luxembourg at the Belgian Embassy,

defendant

Application for a declaration that the Kingdom of Belgium has failed to fulfil its obligations under Article 95 of the EEC Treaty in respect of the flat-rate transference duty on wood,

THE COURT

composed of: R. Lecourt, President, R. Monaco and P. Pescatore (Rapporteur) Presidents of Chambers, A. M. Donner, A. Trabucchi, W. Strauß and J. Mertens de Wilmars, Judges,

Advocate-General: J. Gand
Registrar: A. Van Houtte

gives the following

JUDGMENT

Issues of fact and of law

I – Facts

In Belgium, in application of Article 31–14(1) of the Règlement Général sur les Taxes Assimilées au Timbre (the General Regulation on Duties assimilated to Stamp Duties)

(Royal Decree of 3 March 1927, amended by Royal Decree of 27 December 1965), a single flat-rate duty of 14% *ad valorem* is levied on the transference of home-grown wood transferred standing or felled, as well as on a certain number of products resulting from the processing of wood and imported into Belgium.

Under Article 31–14(3) of the said General Regulation the said flat-rate duty is paid on sale by the producer in respect of home-grown wood transferred standing or felled and on declaration of entry for home use in respect of imported products.

Nevertheless, when a producer of home-grown wood subjects it to processing the flat-rate duty is paid on the price of the product when sold (Article 31–14(4)).

As the price of processed wood is appreciably higher than that of standing or felled wood, the Commission has considered since 1963 that the application of Article 31–14 of the General Regulation on Duties assimilated to Stamp Duties had the effect, in numerous cases, of imposing on products imported from other Member States into Belgium a duty higher than that borne by similar home-grown products.

In the opinion of the Commission, duty imposed at the same rate on standing wood and on wood after processing amounts to an infringement of Article 95 of the EEC Treaty, according to which no Member State may impose on the products of other Member States any internal taxation of any kind in excess of that imposed on similar domestic products.

In response to the first approaches of the Commission in 1963, the Belgian Government did not dispute the existence of discrimination, in respect of the flat-rate transference duty, as regards certain types of imported wood and undertook to study measures capable of putting an end to it.

By letter of 14 October 1966 the permanent representative of Belgium accredited to the Communities informed the Commission that the Belgian Government considered that it was appropriate, for the calculation of the duties imposed on home-grown wood, to take into account the provincial taxes imposed in the provinces of Luxembourg, Liège and Namur at the rate of 3% or 2%, either on the sale of cut wood or on the use of such cut wood by the owner for commercial or industrial purposes.

On 14 February 1967 the Commission informed the Belgian Government that the provincial taxes could not be the subject of compensation on imports, in particular because they were imposed only on a part of the domestic production of wood. In its opinion, in the opposite case, because provincial taxes were not imposed on the wood produced in six of the nine Belgian provinces, imported wood was more heavily taxed than certain types of domestic wood, which was incompatible with Article 95 of the Treaty as interpreted by the Court in its judgment of 1 December 1965 in Case 45/64.

The Commission insisted that the Belgian Government should as rapidly as possible bring into force measures enabling it to conform to the Treaty.

On 2 June 1967 the Commission was informed of the measures which the Belgian Government intended to put into force to 'eliminate the discrimination which the system of the flat-rate transference duty applicable to wood involves to the detriment of foreign products':

(a) in respect of the transference duty, the Belgian Government intended by a Royal Decree to fix rates differentiated in accordance with the category of the products: a rate of 18% for standing trees transferred in Belgium, of 15.5% for undressed wood (wood with bark) transferred in Belgium by a producer or importer and of 12.5% for wood sawn or otherwise processed, on importation;

(b) in respect of registration fees, it was intended to abolish the duty of 5% imposed on public sales of trees, the collection of which excluded that of the flat-rate transference duty; the Belgian Government undertook to table the necessary draft law to carry out the latter measure as soon as it had been considered by the Conseil d'État and to endeavour to obtain its adoption by Parliament as soon as possible;

(c) the alterations in the system of the flat-rate duty and the abolition of registration fees were to enter into force simultaneously at the beginning of September 1967.

The Commission informed the Belgian Government by letter of 13 March 1968 that an examination of calculations on the basis of which the new rates settled for the transference duty had been established had shown that, contrary to its observations of

14 February 1967, the rates intended to be collected on the import of round wood and sawn wood had been fixed taking into account the average weighted incidence on the sale prices of such wood in Belgium of the provincial taxes levied by the provinces of Luxembourg, Liège and Namur. The Commission did not therefore consider that the arrangement which the Belgian Government proposed to make in respect of the taxation system on imported wood was capable of putting an end to the infringements found, and it commenced the procedure provided for in Article 169 of the Treaty against the Kingdom of Belgium.

On 25 April 1968 the permanent representative of Belgium accredited to the Communities informed the Commission that:

(a) the necessary draft law for the abolition of the registration fee on the public sale of trees had been introduced into the Chamber of Representatives on 27 June 1967, but that on the dissolution of the Chambers it had lapsed and that it would be for a future Government to reintroduce it into Parliament;

(b) in respect of the observations of the Commission concerning the provincial taxes, it would be necessary for the new Government to review the problem at the time of the Royal Decree intended to introduce the necessary amendments to the system of transference duty after the vote on the law abolishing the registration fee on public sales.

On 28 November 1968 the Commission delivered a reasoned opinion under Article 169 of the Treaty, in which it first justified the finding of a failure by the Kingdom of Belgium to comply with its obligations under Articles 95 and 97 of the EEC Treaty, and then called upon it to take the necessary measures to conform to the reasoned opinion within a period of one month, such period being capable of being extended so far as necessary for compliance with parliamentary procedures.

On 26 February 1969 the permanent representatives of Belgium accredited to the Communities informed the Commission that the draft law of 27 June 1967, which was intended to amend the system complained of, had been saved from lapsing by a law of 20 December 1968 and that the Council of Ministers had decided that the parliamentary procedure would be continued in respect of the said draft law and that account would no longer be taken of the provincial taxes when the new rates of transference duty were subsequently fixed. By letter of 2 April 1969 the Commission noted with satisfaction the procedure commenced by the Belgian Government to end the infringement which was the subject of its reasoned opinion but pointed out that for the suppression of the disputed taxes it could no longer agree to a period extending beyond 30 June 1969.

By an application lodged on 22 December 1969 the Commission brought before the Court the failures of the Kingdom of Belgium to fulfil its obligations under Article 95 of the EEC Treaty of which it complains in respect of the general transference duty on wood.

II – Procedure

The written procedure followed the normal course.

However, the Commission refrained from lodging a reply.

On hearing the preliminary report of the Judge-Rapporteur and the views of the Advocate-General the Court decided to open the oral procedure without a preparatory inquiry. The parties presented oral argument at the hearing on 10 March 1970. The Advocate-General delivered his opinion at the hearing on 14 April 1970.

III – Conclusions of the parties

The *Commission* claims that the Court should:

— declare that the Kingdom of Belgium, by applying the same rate laid down by Article 31-14 of the General Regulation on Duties assimilated to Stamp Duties (Royal Decree of 3 March 1927) to home-grown wood transferred standing or felled and to imported wood, calculated on the value at the time of the declaration of entry for home use, has failed to fulfil its obligations under Article 95 of the EEC Treaty;

— order the Kingdom of Belgium to pay the costs.

The *Kingdom of Belgium* stated that it relied upon the wisdom of the Court.

IV – Submissions and arguments of the parties

The submissions and arguments of the parties may be summarized as follows:

The *Commission*, after recalling the facts of the case and the voluminous correspondence exchanged with the defendant, states that the system of the flat-rate transference duty, as applied in Belgium to wood, constitutes an infringement of Article 95 of the EEC Treaty and that the infringement has been continuing for an unreasonable time.

In respect of the provincial taxes, the Commission points out that they are levied only in three provinces of Belgium and that even in these provinces they are not imposed on all cut wood, as cutting done in the State forests is not subject to them.

Furthermore cutting done in the provinces of Luxembourg, Liège and Namur represents only 84% of Belgian production.

As to the economic incidence of the disputed taxation, the Commission points out that in 1968 Belgium imported from other Member States of the Community 729 metric tons of wood of an approximate value of 850 million francs, which was only very slightly less than national production. As a matter of principle, the Commission states that it attaches the greatest importance to the complete achievement of the internal market; for this purpose it is important that examples of tax discrimination such as that of which it complains to Belgium in the present case should be eliminated.

The *Kingdom of Belgium* does not dispute that the contested regulations impose higher duties on imported wood than are imposed on home-grown wood.

It recalls that in order to remedy this state of affairs the Government on 27 June 1967 introduced into the Chamber of Representatives a draft law amending the code of registration, mortgage and court fees. Its statement of reasons shows clearly that this draft law is intended to ensure conformity with Article 95 of the EEC Treaty in the sector of wood.

As to the problem of provincial taxes, the Council of Ministers agreed with the reasoned opinion of the Commission and decided that account would not be taken of them when the new rates of transference duty were subsequently fixed. The Royal Decree to be introduced for this purpose would be closely linked to the law to repeal the provision relating to the registration fee of 5% and would enter into force at the same time as that law. The Belgian Government on two occasions reminded the President of the Finance Committee of the Chamber of Representatives of its interest in seeing the draft law – saved from lapsing in 1968 – come to fruition as soon as possible. Under the principle of the separation of powers the Belgian Government has no other means of action; it finds itself facing a situation of *force majeure*.

Grounds of Judgment

1. By an application lodged at the Registry on 22 December 1969, the Commission made an application to the Court under Article 169 of the Treaty for a declaration 'that the Kingdom of Belgium, by applying the same rate laid down in Article 31-14 of the General Regulation on Duties assimilated to Stamp Duties (Royal Decree of 3 March 1927) to home-grown wood transferred standing or felled and to imported wood calculated on its value at the time of the declaration of entry for home use, has failed to fulfil its obligations under Article 95 of the Treaty establishing the European Economic Community'.

2. Under Article 31–14 of the Royal Decree of 3 March 1927 introducing the General Regulation on Duties assimilated to Stamp Duties as amended in particular by the Royal Decree of 27 December 1965, a single flat-rate duty of 14% is levied on the transfer of home-grown or imported wood.

3. Although the rate of tax is uniform for all wood whatever its origin, the basis and the detailed methods of levying the duty are different for home-grown wood and for products coming from abroad

4. In respect of the former, the flat-rate is paid, according to Article 31–14(1) (1) and Article 31–14(3) of the Royal Decree of 3 March 1927, at the time of sale by the producer of wood transferred standing or felled.

5. On the other hand, in respect of imported products, assessment takes place, in accordance with paragraph 3(1) of the same article, at the time of the declaration of entry for home use, taking into account the more or less advanced state of processing, defined by paragraph 1(2)(a) to (j).

6.   According to the wording of paragraph 3(1), 'the flat-rate duty shall cover all subsequent transfers until the arrival of the goods in the hands of the consumer or the person who submits them to an industrial process', it being understood however that 'processing of one of the products enumerated in paragraph 1 into another of those products shall not be regarded as industrial processing'.

7.   It follows from this system that, because of the fact that the flat-rate duty is paid at the time of the transfer of standing or felled wood, home-grown wood is exempted from all subsequent charges arising out of the increase in value due to the processing defined by the Royal Decree.

8.   The same treatment is not extended to imported wood which, under the terms of the same decree, is taxed in relation to its more advanced state of processing and assessed consequently on the basis of a higher value than that of wood transferred standing or felled.

9.   The system established by Article 31–14 of the Royal Decree of 3 March 1927 thus has, as a result of this differentiation in the basis of the single flat-rate duty, the effect of taxing imported wood, if it has already undergone processing, more heavily than national products in a similar stage of processing.

10.   It appears consequently that, although the rate of tax is apparently a uniform one, the scheme brought into force by the Royal Decree of 3 March 1927 results in discrimination between home-grown and imported wood contrary to the prohibition of the first paragraph of Article 95 of the Treaty.

11.   The defendant does not dispute the existence of discrimination resulting from the provisions which form the subject-matter of the proceedings.

12.   Following a series of steps taken by the Commission the first of which dates back to 1963, the Belgian Government has shown its willingness to take the necessary measures with a view to eliminating the discrimination complained of.

13.   A draft law intended to make possible a revision of the disputed scheme was put before Parliament in 1967 and provisions were later adopted in order to revive this draft law which had lapsed owing to the dissolution of the Belgian Parliament in the meanwhile.

14.   In these circumstances the Belgian Government considers that the delay in enacting the law amounts as far as it is concerned to a 'case of *force majeure*'.

15.   The obligations arising from Article 95 of the Treaty devolve upon States as such and the liability of a Member State under Article 169 arises whatever the agency of the State whose action or inaction is the cause of the failure to fulfil its obligations, even in the case of a constitutionally independent institution.

16.   The objection raised by the defendant cannot therefore be sustained.

17.   In these circumstances, by applying a duty at the same rate, as laid down by Article 31-14 of the Royal Decree of 3 March 1927 as amended, to home-grown wood transferred standing or felled and to imported wood calculated on its value at the time of the declaration of entry for home use, the Kingdom of Belgium has failed to fulfil its obligations under Article 95 of the Treaty.

Costs

18.   Under the terms of Article 69 (2) of the Rules of Procedure the unsuccessful party shall be ordered to pay the costs.

19.   The defendant has failed in its submissions.

On those grounds,

Upon reading the pleadings;
Upon hearing the report of the Judge-Rapporteur;
Upon hearing the parties;
Upon hearing the opinion of the Advocate-General;
Having regard to the Treaty establishing the European Economic Community, especially Articles 95, 169 and 171;
Having regard to the Protocol on the Statute of the Court of Justice of the European Economic Community.
Having regard to the Rules of Procedure of the Court of Justice of the European Communities.

THE COURT

hereby:

1.   Declares that, by applying a duty at the same rate, as laid down by Article 31–14 of the Royal Decree of 3 March 1927 as amended by the Royal Decree of 3 March 1927 as amended by the Royal Decree of 27 December 1965, to home-grown wood transferred standing or felled and to imported wood calculated on its value at the time of the declaration of entry for home use, the Kingdom of Belgium has failed to fulfil its obligations under Article 95 of the EEC Treaty;

2.   Orders the defendant to pay the costs.

	Lecourt		Monaco		Pescatore	
Donner		Trabucchi		Strauß		Mertens de Wilmars

Delivered in open court in Luxembourg on 5 May 1970.

A. Van Houtte   R. Lecourt
Registrar   President

OPINION OF MR ADVOCATE-GENERAL GAND DELIVERED ON 14 APRIL 1970

Mr President,
Members of the Court
The Court has today to decide on a case – I dare not say a dispute – which arises in unusual circumstances. The Commission of the European Communities, acting in accordance with the conditions laid down in Article 169 of the EEC Treaty, has asked you to hold that, in applying a flat-rate transfer price duty at the same rate to home-grown wood and to imported wood calculated on the value of such wood at the time of its declaration of entry for home use, the Kingdom of Belgium has failed to fulfil its obligations under Article 95. Without disputing that allegation, the Belgian Government in its statement of defence relies on the wisdom of the Court; at the oral procedure it maintained that position although indicating briefly the situation of *force majeure* in which it is placed.

Although the last remark calls for certain observations on my part, my opinion can be brief, because the report of the hearing sets out very fully the situation in law and fact which led to the present application.

I

1.   The system criticized, which is still in force at the present time, may be summarized in the following manner.

For home-grown wood the flat-rate transference duty is applied at the rate of 14% on the sale of standing trees (Article 31–14 of the General Regulation on Duties assimilated to Stamp Duties); in the case of a public sale, a registration fee of 5%, which excludes liability to transference duty, is levied. But the payment of that duty, like the registration fee, covers the transfer of products derived from wood such as planks, beams, sheets of veneer and packing cases.

Let me add for the sake of completeness that in the three provinces of Liège, Luxembourg and Namur, which account for a little less than 85% of domestic wood production, cut wood is subject in addition to a provincial tax of 2% or 3%.

For imported wood the flat-rate duty is payable, still at the rate of 14%, on goods in the state in which they are brought into the country; as the price of processed wood is clearly higher than that of standing or cut wood, the duty imposed on imported products is necessarily greater than that imposed on corresponding domestic products, which constitutes an infringement of Article 95 of the Treaty.

2.   That was the observation made by the Commission in a letter of 9 March 1964 which marked the beginning of a long exchange of memoranda between the parties.

The Belgian Government accepted the existence of inequality between domestic and foreign products from the beginning and stated that it was prepared to eliminate it, but two difficulties arose.

In the first place, although it was in agreement concerning the diversification of the rates of the transference duty to which sales of standing trees and imports of undressed or sawn wood are subject, it intended to take into account, in the calculation of the new rates, the existence of special taxes levied in certain provinces. Such a method was certainly open to criticism because, although these taxes were compensated for on importation, imported wood would be more heavily taxed than certain types of domestic wood grown in the other provinces. On that point the Belgian Government finally deferred to the objections contained in the reasoned opinion of the Commission and informed it by letter of 26 February 1969 that it would no longer take into account the provincial taxes when new rates of transference duty were subsequently fixed.

On the other hand – and this was the second difficulty – it was not sufficient to diversify these rates in order to put an end to all inequality. It was necessary in addition to remove public sales of standing trees from liability to registration fees in order to subject them to tax, and on that point the intervention of Parliament was necessary. That was the object of the draft law which was introduced in June 1967 and lapsed following the dissolution of Parliament, but was then revived by the law of 20 December 1968, and is still pending. During the oral procedure the Agent of the Belgian Government emphasized that it had twice drawn the attention of the Chairman of the Financial Committee of the Chamber of Representatives to this matter and to the importance which it attached to having the draft law passed in the shortest time. The constitutional principle of separation of powers, he added, did not allow more to be done.

II

It was then that the concept of *force majeure* was raised. No doubt it was a reference made in passing; nevertheless, if it is necessary to give it a more exact significance, that would, it appears, be the following: the disregard of Article 95 is accepted but the situation can be redressed only with the agreement of Parliament which is constitutionally separated from the executive and, as the executive had used all the means of action in its power, there cannot be a failure within the meaning of Article 169 or at least there is no reason for the Court to hold that there has been such a failure.

Such reasoning ignores that the subjects of rights – or of obligations – are the Member States of the Community. It is they who under Article 5 must take 'all appropriate measures, whether general or particular' necessary for ensuring the execution of the obligations resulting from the Treaty. The undertaking which they have thus contracted extends to the most diverse spheres and may consequently necessitate on their part very varied legal measures: it may be a matter of instituting, amending or repealing legislation or regulations of general scope, or equally of taking decisions of individual scope intended to ensure the execution of the Treaty and of the provisions implementing it. To know whether in a particular case such execution requires the agreement of only one or of several of the powers which constitute the structure of the State is a question the solution of which depends upon the constitutional system of that State but it cannot modify the extent of the obligations which must apply equally to all and the organs of the Community must not take cognizance of it. No doubt the latter, in accordance with the traditional practices of international relations, are answerable only to the Governments, but it does not follow that only the acts or omissions of the executive and of the departments put under its control amount to failures to fulfil obligations within the meaning of Article 169 of the Treaty. These may arise as soon as the Member State fails to carry out the obligations incumbent upon it, without any need to consider which of its agencies are responsible for the failure complained of.

The necessity to appeal to Parliament, the duties of which are increasing, may, it is true, complicate and delay the redressing of a situation contrary to the Treaty. That is a point to which the Commission is not indifferent, since Article 169 refers to it. Thus in the present case – as in all the others which raise a similar problem – the Commission, when giving a time-limit to the Kingdom of Belgium by which to conform to the reasoned opinion, added that on receipt of a request before the expiration of that period it could be extended 'in so far as is necessary to conform to the parliamentary procedures which are required by the national law in force'. That was on 28 November 1968, and the matter has not progressed since then.

Also, without there being any need to consider who is responsible for that situation, the Commission is correct in its view that persistent prolongation of the situation amounts to a failure on the part of the Kingdom of Belgium to fulfil its obligations under Article 95 of the Treaty.

Might one say lastly that the finding to which you will come will be merely theoretical? One might believe on the contrary that the authority of your judgment will give the various powers concerned a clearer understanding of the extent of their obligations in respect of the Community and will allow the termination of a procedure which is delayed not because of any ill will but because of the slowness of political machinery.

In my opinion it should be declared that the Kingdom of Belgium, by applying the same rate provided for in Article 31-14 of the General Regulations on Duties assimilated to Stamp Duties to home-grown wood transferred standing or felled and to imported wood calculated on its value at the time of the declaration of its entry for home use, fails to fulfil its obligations under Article 95 of the EEC Treaty and that the costs should be paid by the Kingdom of Belgium.

D. Edward, 'How the Court of Justice Works' (1995) 20 EL Rev 539

Dissenting opinions

The argument usually advanced against dissenting opinions is that Community judges would be compromised if they were seen to decide in favour of their Member State of origin or, conversely, if they did not do so. Given the recent attitude of certain Member States, this danger may be greater than it used to be. On the other hand, the Advocates General regularly deliver Opinions which may be unwelcome to their Member State of origin and there is not the slightest evidence of their being compromised.

There are, however, other problems. In the common world, the possibility of dissent normally arises only in appeals, where there has already been a judgment in the court below and the arguments have been fully canvassed in oral debate. The issues are pretty clear at that stage, and the minority know what they are dissenting from.

By contrast, except in appeals, the Court of Justice is acting as a court of first and last instance. As has been explained above, the point at issue often becomes clear only in deliberation and it is important that all judges participate until the point has been identified.

So it would not be possible for a conscientious judge to decide whether to dissent until the judgment had reached its final form. Moreover, he would have to write his dissenting opinion in such a way as not to reveal how the arguments developed in the course of the deliberation. This would take time and a great deal of care.

Introduction of dissenting opinions would also involve a change of style for the majority judgment since the majority would wish to explain their position vis-à-vis the dissenter(s). The majority judgment would therefore take longer to agree and longer to translate. Delivery of the judgment would have to be delayed until both the majority and dissenting opinions were ready and translated.

It is not self-evident, to the present writer at any rate, that the merits of dissenting opinions and their contribution to the evolution of the Court's case law would outweigh the disadvantages of further serious delay in producing judgments, particularly in references.

Presumably these difficulties could be avoided if dissenting judges were to take no part in the deliberation after the vote in which they were defeated. They could then get on with preparing their dissenting opinion(s) while the majority prepared theirs. But this would seriously affect, if not destroy, the collegiate character of the Court and its decision-making process. The Court would, sooner or later, divide into publicly identi-fied camps or factions ('liberal' and 'conservative', 'activist' and 'abstentionist' and so on) in the style of some other courts.

This has not happened so far. Indeed, to a relative newcomer, one of the most impressive, and in some ways most unexpected, features of the Court has been its relaxed, non-confrontational way of working. Every deliberation in a difficult case produces some surprises in the attitudes and votes of colleagues – the predictable does not happen and the unpredictable does.

2.1.4.1   Jurisdiction

THE TREATY OF ROME

Article 164

The Court of Justice shall ensure that in the interpretation and application of this Treaty the law is observed.

Disputes about the obligations of Member States

THE TREATY OF ROME

Article 169

If the Commission considers that a Member State has failed to fulfil an obligation under this Treaty, it shall deliver a reasoned opinion on the matter after giving the State concerned the opportunity to submit its observations.

If the State concerned does not comply with the opinion within the period laid down by the Commission, the latter may bring the matter before the Court of Justice.

THE TREATY OF ROME

Article 170

A Member State which considers that another Member State has failed to fulfil an obligation under this Treaty may bring the matter before the Court of Justice.

Before a Member State brings an action against another Member State for an alleged infringement of an obligation under this Treaty, it shall bring the matter before the Commission.

The Commission shall deliver a reasoned opinion after each of the States concerned has been given the opportunity to submit its own case and its observations on the other party's case both orally and in writing.

If the Commission has not delivered an opinion within three months of the date on which the matter was brought before it, the absence of such opinion shall not prevent the matter from being brought before the Court of Justice.

THE TREATY OF ROME

Article 171

1.   If the Court of Justice finds that a Member State has failed to fulfil an obligation under this Treaty, the State shall be required to take the necessary measures to comply with the judgment of the Court of Justice.

2.   If the Commission considers that the Member State concerned has not taken such measures it shall, after giving that State opportunity to submit its observations, issue a reasoned opinion specifying the points on which the Member State concerned has not complied with the judgment of the Court of Justice.

If the Member State concerned fails to take the necessary measures to comply with the Court's judgment within the time-limit laid down by the Commission, the latter may bring the case before the Court of Justice. In so doing it shall specify the amount of the lump sum or penalty payment to be paid by the Member State concerned which it considers appropriate in the circumstances.

If the Court of Justice finds that the Member State concerned has not complied with its judgment it may impose a lump sum or penalty payment on it.

This procedure shall be without prejudice to Article 170.

A. Arnull, 'Judging The New Europe' (1994) 19 EL Rev 3

The price of success

The Court has therefore shown few signs of being inhibited by the increased effectiveness of the political institutions following the demise of the Luxembourg Compromise or by the growing maturity of the Community system, which might have been expected to reduce the scope for judicial creativity. Moreover, by ruling in late 1991 that the original version of the agreement creating a European Economic Area was incompatible with the EEC Treaty, the Court demonstrated its determination to protect the fundamental principles of the system it had done so much to create.

Indications had begun to emerge, however, of a growing reluctance among the Member States to bow to the wisdom of the Court. The Council's 1988 decision establishing a Court of First Instance departed in a number of significant respects from the proposal of the Court of Justice. A decision taken by the Court in 1989 that some of its judgments should be published in summary form only had to be reversed following objections from a number of Member States. A proposal by the Court that it be given the power to respond to requests for preliminary rulings by reasoned order in clear cases was amended by the Council. The result is that the Court may only respond to such requests in this way where the question referred is *'manifestly identical* to a question on which the Court has already ruled' (emphasis added). Chancellor Kohl publicly criticised the Court for exceeding its powers and its authority was further weakened by its apparent failure to foresee some of the implications of controversial rulings on Sunday trading and on pensions.

To add to the growing tension between the Court on the one hand and the other institutions and the Member States on the other, a new problem began to emerge during the 1980s, that of coping with the Court's apparently ever-increasing work load. Indeed, this problem – in some ways a measure of the Court's success – has become one of its major preoccupations. In 1980, it took the Court on average nine months to deal with a reference for preliminary ruling and 18 months to dispose of a direct action. By 1988, those figures had risen to 18 months and 24 months respectively. The establishment of the Court of First Instance, which started to hear cases in late 1989, provided temporary respite, but by the end of 1992 it was taking the Court of Justice as long to deal with cases as it took before the Court of First Instance was established. Moreover, the number of cases pending before the Court by the end of 1992 had reached alarming proportions. The delay in responding to requests for preliminary rulings is particularly serious, as the time spent before the Court of Justice has to be added to the time spent in the national forum.

One of the principal causes of delay in proceedings before the Court is the volume of documents which have to be translated into other languages during the course of the procedure. This problem will be exacerbated by the accession of new Member States. One solution is to appoint more translators, but they have to be legally qualified and are not easy to find.

However, one advantage of the multi-lingual character of proceedings before the Court is that it sometimes provides moments of light relief. Visitors to the Court always enjoy watching the gesticulations of the interpreters. Something which causes interpreters particular difficulty is jokes, since these often only make sense in the language in which they are told. One quick-witted interpreter got round this problem by saying : 'Counsel is in the process of telling a joke. It is completely impossible to translate. However, I think it would be polite to laugh . . . now!' The Judges dutifully chuckled at the appropriate moment and counsel could be seen preening himself on his wit.

The Court has taken steps to address some of the other causes of delay. In late 1991, it proposed a significant extension in the jurisdiction of the Court of First Instance. In addition, it has sought to streamline its own procedures. For example, the Court now has the power, with the consent of the parties to a case, to dispense with a hearing. But the benefits of these changes are liable to be outweighed by other factors. Major sources of future growth in the Court's work load are likely to be the vast body of legislation adopted to implement the Single Market programme and the growing familiarity of courts in some of the newer Member States with the preliminary rulings procedure. And then there is Maastricht.

2.1.5 THE COURT OF AUDITORS

Court of Auditors' Annual Report concerning Financial Year 1993 OJ (94/C327/01)

INTRODUCTION

0.1.   Overall, it would be fair to say that the development of Community activities has not been accompanied, either in the Commission or in the Member States, by a commensurate development of the necessary financial management and control systems and that insufficient resources, both in quantity and in quality, have been allocated to ensuring the best use of public money and accountability for it.

0.2.   Comparing findings in this report with those of the Court's Annual Report for 1983 and with the observations in its report in response to the conclusions of the European Council of 18 June 1983, it is clear that many of the problems then identified in accounting and financial management of the most important areas of Community expenditure have not yet been overcome. Although the Commission has undoubtedly made efforts to correct the weaknesses in accounting and financial management systems to which successive reports of the Court have drawn attention, it has failed to secure the enforcement of the proper level of financial management and control necessary in the complex environment of Community finances. The Commission might well point out that its problems have increased with the entry of additional Member States and the considerable increase in the Community budget during the period. Nevertheless, despite repeated assurances of remedial action, the Commission has not managed to achieve the results desired by the budgetary authorities in the field of financial control.

0.3.   Agricultural management measures are still failing to achieve balanced markets. This report shows how aids for distillation, appropriate for a temporary production surplus, have been made into a permanent encouragement to the production of unsaleable wine, and how the effects of measures for the permanent abandonment of vineyards are offset by others which encourage investment in the sector.

0.4.   Member State authorities continue to issue incorrect certificates for Structural Funds expenditure, in some cases covering expenditure which has not really been incurred or is ineligible for aid. They have generally failed to monitor the aid or to ensure that it is properly accounted for. The Commission needs to pay more attention to the reliability of certificates issued by national authorities, given their importance in determining Community expenditure.

0.5.   Administration and control systems for the EAGGF-Guarantee paying agencies still display serious inadequacies, for which the national authorities and the Commission share responsibility. Structural shortcomings in the conception, functioning and surveillance of internal control systems result in lack of proper protection of the financial interests of the Community against fraud and other irregularities. In this same general context, the Court's Special Reports Nos 7/93, 8/93 and 1/94 drew public attention to the dangers of inadequate internal controls in specific areas and to the very unsatisfactory situations which had arisen.

0.6.   Weak internal control systems together with legislation that is often complex and far too open to misinterpretation facilitate fraud, whilst permitting other irregularities to go undetected. Simplification of legislation, and better, more detailed stipulations for accounting, financial management and control are the key to considerable economies of public funds. Where systems of administration and control in Member States are found to be inadequate the flow of funds through them should be halted until remedial action has been taken.

0.7.   The audit of matters which are the exclusive concern of the Commission also reveals some of the same problems in 1993 as the Court has raised since 1983. Authorizing officers fail to ensure that expenditure is preceded by the fixing of clear objectives and criteria. Prior appraisal is often inadequate, while monitoring and *ex post* evaluation do not provide the feedback necessary for improvements to be made. The same criticisms apply to the Structural Funds where the Community support frameworks agreed with the Member States generally fail to specify the clearly defined and quantified objectives required by Article 2 of the Financial Regulation against which progress could be measured.

0.8.   The audit continues to discover breaches of the rules governing the placing of contracts with third parties. Occasional, but significant cases are still found where financial decisions have been taken without proper delegated authority. The Financial Controller's department has sometimes accepted that expenditure be charged to the wrong account or that a single operation be covered by several small private-treaty contracts instead of one large contract which would have to be put out to tender. There is a real risk of confusion in accounting between administrative and operational expenditure, particularly with regard to aid to Eastern Europe and the former Soviet Union.

0.9. The Commission's central accounting system is supported by inadequate documentation which fails to provide a clear 'audit trail'. The ongoing computerization of bank reconciliations should allow further improvement of this basic safeguard in the accounting department.

0.10. There are also signs of an increasing tendency for the Commission to delegate its financial management responsibilities not only to national administrations, but also to third parties (consultants or bureaux which act as intermediaries between the Commission and aid beneficiaries). Such delegation has led to loss of control over the proper use of Community funds.

0.11. In view of the situation described above and the numerous weaknesses in accounting and financial management mentioned throughout this report, the Commission needs to devote a significantly larger proportion of its staff resources to securing the necessary improvements in the performance of its own services and of those in Member States which handle Community funds. Community and national civil servants must be made more accountable for the way in which funds are spent.

Presentation to Parliament of the Court of Auditors' Annual Report for 1993 ('European Parliament: The Week' 14–18 November 1994)

Court of Auditors' annual report – Commission under attack

Tuesday, 15 November. Presenting the Court of Auditor's annual report for 1993, the Court's President André Middelhoek took the Commission to task for its management of the Union's finances. 'The Commission has largely failed to achieve the level of financial control needed', he said, pointing out that many of the criticisms made as long ago as 1983 were still valid today.

He then proceeded to analyse deficiencies and weaknesses of financial management in the various sectors beginning with agricultural spending where, he said, the responsible authorities had failed to achieve balanced markets.

In addition, aid had been inadequately monitored with the responsibility shared between the Commission and the national authorities. Moreover, there were shortcomings in the measures taken to safeguard against fraud as pointed out in the Court's special sectoral reports. He particularly singled out the tobacco sector and the area of export refunds.

He then recommended blocking the flow of funds to those Member States who had failed to take appropriate action to control maladministration.

Other weaknesses identified included the poor monitoring of expenditure and the lack of prior appraisal of projects financed. Rules were systematically broken and no follow up taken.

One problem with the management of the Commission's budget was the tendency to subcontract to consultants which made it even more difficult to check on expenditure. More staff were needed to carry out controls, he said.

Other specific sectoral problems concerned the allocation of milk quotas to Italy and Spain without a proper legal base and inadequate 'buy back' arrangements. He was however heartened by what he saw as Council's response now being prepared to accept the Court's comments. Administrative procedures in the German Länder where, he said, there were too many paying agencies were also criticised.

The wine sector was another area under fire where, he said, the present rules amounted to an incentive to produce for intervention or distillation. Neither were the rules controlling the addition of sugar sufficient to safeguard against fraud while export refunds had been paid without proof of reliability.

In other areas the complexity of the payments system meant that national administrations were unable to monitor procedures properly.

Turning to regional spending, he said there were delays in programming while no Member State was in a position to check that all the payments were correct. There was a need for rigorous evaluation of regional expenditure, he said. Indeed the report points to a lack of co-ordination between different bodies responsible for spending.

On the Social Fund there was a widespread breach of the rules. Certain lines of expenditure were incorrectly based while agencies in the Member States held on to money earmarked for programmes for far too long.

The report points out that in some cases EU expenditure is used merely to reimburse the national authorities for expenditure already incurred while spot checks revealed that projects ineligible, because of incompatibility with national aid regulations or carried out before being submitted to the Commission and amounting to 1.6m ECU, had been backed.

On Eastern Europe there was no evaluation or precious little control of the PHARE and TACIS programmes while the TEMPUS programme had not been adapted to the needs of those concerned.

The European Development Fund was another area where there were weaknesses with the presentation of the accounts and advances were cleared without proper authorization. It was doubtful if all projects were eligible. The report draws attention to another problem – the immobilisation of funds – which could have been used for other development projects, as a result of the Commission's failure to respond to an absence of final accounts being presented when due.

Neither was Mr Middelhoek satisfied with procedures relating to the construction of Parliament's new building in Brussels. The absence of a proper tendering procedure was not an example that should be set to the European taxpayer, he said, although he noted this issue had now been taken up by the budgetary control committee.

Concluding, he said there was a need for more resources and staffing to tackle financial management, a proper fixing of objectives and greater use made of 'risk analysis'.

For the Commission, Peter Schmidhuber made a spirited response to the criticisms. Improvements had been made, more staff hired to combat fraud and legislative proposals made to the Council who held the responsibility for taking the political decisions, he said.

Replying to the debate, Mr Middelhoek said the Court of Auditor's criticism of the Commission was intended to be constructive. As far as he was concerned financial management had not kept pace with the expansion of EU tasks or the increase of the size of the EU budget. He then made a number of suggestions for improving financial efficiency including the simplification of EU rules, improvement to financial management in both the Commission and the member states, better control powers for the Commission, wider use of penalties, greater co-operation between Member States in tracing fraud and the use of more staff in financial control.

Court of Auditors' Annual Report concerning Financial Year 1993 OJ (95/C303/38)

The General Context of the 1994 Annual Report

0.1.   This report is being published as the first year of the new Commission draws to a close, a year of enlargement of the Community and of a 12% increase in the size of the budget. At its first meeting on 25 January 1995, the incoming Commission decided to initiate a reform of its internal management, with the necessary analysis and reflection in three phases (consolidation and rationalization of the existing system; reform of structures and rules; search for closer partnership with Member States), each to be followed by concrete proposals. The Court welcomes this financial management improvement programme and, while recognizing that a particular corporate culture cannot be changed overnight, finds the initial steps taken within the Commission's services encouraging. The third stage envisaged (implying measures to improve Member States' management of EC funds) may take longer to achieve significant progress, but it is equally vital. The examples of waste and mismanagement of EC funds that are to be found in numerous Court audit reports are ample evidence for the need for a concerted effort to complete the Commission's improvement programme and convert a rather lax 'spend the budget' approach into one which emphasizes value for money and rigorous financial and accounting management with clear attribution of responsibility for success and failure.
. . .

Principal Findings of the 1994 Audit

0.4.   Throughout this 1994 annual report the Court mentions examples of financial management weaknesses that are often closely similar to those mentioned in its previous reports, even though many of the examples are drawn from audits of specific measures which have not previously, or at least not recently, been audited by the Court. This is further evidence of the need for substantial change in what might be termed 'the financial management culture' which administers and controls the collection and utilization of budgetary resources, at Commission and Member State levels.

0.5. Evidence of the problems to which this financial management culture gives rise can be seen in budgetary planning far in excess of the Commission's real ability to plan and; in weak management of available funds (which are paid out without regard to the legislator's objectives and or without sufficiently clear targets being specified for achievement through the expenditure in question, and often without sufficient attention to cost-effectiveness); and in failure to act quickly and vigorously to recover funds wrongly paid or overpaid.

0.6. There is a striking example of underspending in the Structural Funds, which results mainly from failure to anticipate difficulties in the first year of a reformed approach, despite such difficulties having occurred at the time of the last such reform six years previously.

0.7. The employment of funds without policy objectives being achieved is described in most of the chapters of the report. This situation arises both where – as in the areas of agricultural guarantee and development aid – it is the Commission's exclusive responsibility to specify the objectives of expenditure, and where – as in the case of the Structural Funds – the objectives have to be agreed between the Commission and the member governments sponsoring the programme. In Chapter 2 the inadequate results of the common market organization for fruit and vegetables are mentioned. Chapter 3 concludes that aid for tunny fishing has no clear justification. Chapter 4 shows that the Interreg programme has not significantly stimulated cross-border partnership in frontier areas, while Chapter 5 demonstrates that the results of European Social Fund actions in favour of small and medium-sized enterprises, where they can be measured at all, fall far short of the objectives.

0.8. With regard to development aid from both the budget (structural adjustment support programmes in four Arab countries) and the European Development Fund (regional cooperation), the Court concludes that objectives fixed were so vague or general that it is very difficult to make satisfactory comparisons between what has been done and what was intended. In various areas of expenditure on the Community budget, the Court has found that imprecise regulations (which are generally silent as regards requirements for accounting and financial management) have enabled Member States to interpret differently eligibility criteria which should be equally applicable to all. Such imprecision inhibits effective monitoring and audit of programmes by national authorities, the Commission and the Court.

0.9 Cases where management had failed to take timely and vigorous action with a view to the recovery of funds owing to the Community are reported in Chapters 1, 2, 4, 5, 6, 8 and 10. Failure to take such action may make it difficult or impossible subsequently to recover the amount due from the debtor.

0.10. This report, like its predecessors, draws attention to significant weaknesses in mechanisms for planning, approving, monitoring, controlling and evaluating Community actions. The audit of the common market organization for fresh and processed fruit and vegetables revealed that Member State inspection and approval of producer organizations, which play a major role in market management, were very weak and that many producer organizations, despite nearly 30 years of encouragement and assistance, had insufficient working capital for intervention purposes.

. . .

0.14. In a significant number of the Regional Fund programmes' projects audited, irregularities found underline the extent to which, six years after a major reform, improvements are still needed to ensure the legality and regularity of Structural Funds operations. Member State declarations of expenditure should be better presented and controlled. The Commission needs to insist on more rigorous application of the funds regulations and the financial regulation; it should also define more clearly the criteria for eligibility for aid. Weaknesses in contract award procedures for public sector infrastructure increase the risk of irregularity, while the Commission could do more to check that environmental aspects are properly considered during both planning and execution of programmes.

. . .

0.16.   The Social Fund chapter of this report again draws attention to the way in which the accounts by regarding advance payments as definitive expenditures overstate the real impact of expenditure on the underlying operations. It also mentions that whenever checks conclude that an action undertaken is ineligible for Community financing, the Member State can simply substitute some other action, often for retrospective financing, so that there are no effective sanctions against Member State authorities which fail to ensure that Community funds are used only for approved purposes and within the terms of previously agreed plans.
. . .

Benefits from Improved Financial Management
0.25.   There is clearly considerable potential for improving the way Community finances are managed in all the main areas of activity mentioned above and thus ensuring that public money is being properly used to achieve, in an efficient and effective way, the objectives laid down by the legislator. It is, of course, not possible to quantify with any certainty the real benefits that could result from more efficient and better targeted financing. There are, however, throughout this report, mentions of specific audit findings which give some indication of the scale of potential benefits which more rigorous financial management and control could achieve, in terms of amounts which should be recovered, payments for activities which were not eligible for aid or expenditures which were not demonstrably useful in achieving policy objectives, even if they could not be considered as entirely irregular. Given the limited extent to which the Court, with the number of auditors at its disposal, can audit financial management in any one year, it is clear that there is great scope for improvement and that any costs incurred in securing such improvement would be recovered in a very short time.

Implications of the Statement of Assurance
0.26.   The Statement of Assurance for 1994, issued at the same time as this report is published, contains significant reservations concerning the reliability of the accounts (mainly about presentation and disclosure) and draws attention to many errors affecting the legality and regularity of the underlying transactions for payments. This result represents further evidence of inadequate financial administration, by both the Commission and Member State bodies, of a significant part of the Community budget, in a wide variety of areas. The application of the principle of subsidiarity does not, of course, imply any diminution of the Commission's responsibility for the proper execution of the budget. A serious, concerted effort by the Commission and Member State authorities is urgently needed in order to raise the quality of the performance of responsible management at all levels.
. . .

The Court of Auditors' Role with regard to Fraud
0.29.   The Essen European Council concluded that fraud, waste and mismanagement of Community resources needed to be tackled with the utmost vigour and recalling that the Treaty on European Union had given new powers to the European Parliament, the Council, the Commission and the European Court of Auditors, called for concerted action by these institutions and the Member States.
0.30.   The primary responsibility for prevention, detection and investigation of fraud lies with those who manage and supervise policy execution in the Commission and the Member States. They have to ensure the existence of adequate systems of internal control, including segregation of duties, proper authorization procedures and an effective internal audit function and ensure that intentional irregularities (whether fraud or gross negligence) are detected, investigated and sanctioned.
0.31.   The Court, as external auditor, has to review critically the arrangements made by management. It has always done this to an appreciable extent and Court annual or special reports have consistently drawn attention to weaknesses in legislation, in accounting and in financial management systems and indicated the risks involved as well as concrete cases involved. Although the Court, like other audit institutions, does not have the power to investigate crime (a task for the police and judicial authorities) but it plays its part by paying due attention to the prevention and deterrence of irregularities in general (whether intentional or not) and stimulating effective action by the appropriate

authorities when audit indicates that some fraud may have possibly occurred or circumstances have arisen which are particularly favourable to the potential fraudster.

Presentation to Parliament of the Court of Auditors' Annual Report for 1994 ('European Parliament: The Week' 13–17 November 1995)

Court of Auditors' annual report

Tuesday, 14 November – Presenting the Court of Auditors' annual report for 1994, the Court's President André Middelhoek said the report revealed 'many examples of financial management weaknesses' which are similar to previous years. These, he said, demonstrated the continuing need for better management at Commission and member state levels. He said: 'The problems of this "financial management culture" are reflected in poor budgetary planning, in weak management of available funds and in lack of urgency in recovering amounts wrongly paid'.

The report concludes: 'The total of these amounts, for cases mentioned in this report, is more than 500m ECU'.

Mr Middelhoek then proceeded to analyse the problems of various sectors, beginning with structural funds, where, he said, the considerable underspending in 1994 resulted mainly from a failure to anticipate difficulties in the first year of the reforms. He said that the INTERREG programme had not significantly stimulated cross-border partnership in frontier areas, while actions under the Social Fund in favour of small firms fell far short of objectives.

Furthermore, irregularities in regional programmes underlined the fact that improvements were still needed to ensure the legality of structural fund operations, he stressed. He called for contract award procedures for public sector infrastructures to be strengthened and he also urged the Commission to do more to check that environmental aspects were properly considered in the planning and implementation of programmes. Mr Middelhoek added that the Social Fund continued to be adversely affected by 'imprecise eligibility criteria, insufficient verification and unreliable certification of expenditure by national authorities'.

Turning to agricultural expenditure, Mr Middelhoek criticised the management of the fruit and vegetable sectors, saying that controls on citrus and tomato processing were so weak that there could be no assurance that aid was justified. He said there was overpayment of aid for nuts while aid for dried grapes was not subject to any independent check. He said: 'Control of aid per hectare without a land register and with a very large number of growers is impossible'.

. . .

Before Commissioner Erkki Liikanen took the floor to reply, Liberal Group leader Gijs de Vries (Nl) objected to the absence of Council from the debate.

The Commissioner emphasised his intention to cooperate fully with the Court. Improvements had been made, he said, accepting, however, that there was still some way to go. But the principle of sound financial management was, he said, one of the aims of the new Commission, which he felt had, on balance, been vindicated by the Court's comments in the Statement of Assurance that 'the accounts of the Community are fundamentally in order'. Similarly, with regard to the comments on supervising expenditure and the EU's revenues, the Court had given the Commission a clean bill of health.

. . .

The other errors discovered by the Court in relation to payments were mainly the fault of the member states and this, Commission Liikanen recognised, was a worrying area for concern that could only be tackled through increased cooperation between the Commission and national administrations.

Turning to other general criticism such as poor budgetary planning, weak management and lack of urgency in recovering amounts wrongly paid, Mr Liikanen defended the Commission's actions by pointing out that it had to respect the financial perspectives and the introduction of more multi-annual programmes. And, he added, its record was no worse than in the member states. Furthermore, improvements were being activated in the area of financial management. He accepted, however, that in many cases it was difficult to recover payments wrongly made owing to the absence of the necessary legislation.

. . .

2.2   The Other Institutions

2.2.1   THE EUROPEAN COUNCIL

THE TREATY ON EUROPEAN UNION

Article D
The European Council shall provide the Union with the necessary impetus for its development and shall define the general political guidelines thereof.

The European Council shall bring together the Heads of State or Government of the Member States and the President of the Commission. They shall be assisted by the Ministers for Foreign Affairs of the Member States and by a Member of the Commission. The European Council shall meet at least twice a year, under the chairmanship of the Head of State or Government of the Member State which holds the Presidency of the Council.

The Euorpean Council shall submit to the European Parliament a report after each of its meetings and a yearly written report on the progress achieved by the Union.

2.2.2   THE COURT OF FIRST INSTANCE

The Role and Future of the European Court of Justice, **The British Institute of International and Comparative Law, 1996**

Court of First Instance

(a)   Should its jurisdiction be extended? If so, how?
Cases brought before the Community Courts can be classified in many ways, in particular, according to:

— the parties (Member States, third countries, institutions, legal persons, individuals, staff etc.);
— the type of procedure and the article of the EC Treaty (or other treaties) under which they are brought;
— the subject matter (agriculture, State aids, competition, dumping, staff cases etc.);
— their degree of difficulty (facts, law, policy, institutional conflict, constitutional importance, external implications etc.).

The jurisdiction of the CFI is determined by unanimous decision of the Council, acting under Article 168a of the EC Treaty. As matters now stand, that jurisdiction encompasses all actions brought by natural or legal persons; the recent amendments to Article 168a have however made possible an extension to all categories of cases other than preliminary references.

When the CFI was first established, its jurisdiction was confined to staff cases, actions for the annulment of Commission decisions in competition cases, and certain matters under the ECSC Treaty. That limited jurisdiction corresponded to the original rationale for establishing a Court of First Instance – namely the 'release [of the ECJ] from the duty of examining the facts and hearing evidence' as opposed to deciding points of law. The extension of jurisdiction made in 1993 was inspired by similar considerations.

In short, the cases which up till now have been considered suitable for the CFI are cases which:

— are factually complicated (e.g. competition and dumping cases);
— by reason of the parties, are less likely to raise issues of constitutional importance; or
— are specialised cases within a limited ambit (e.g. staff cases);

and which more generally are susceptible to being treated in the first tier of a two-tier jurisdiction.

Thus the Council continues to take the view that the CFI is the appropriate forum for the detailed scrutiny of factual issues, and that the tasks of constitutional adjudication and the preservation of the uniformity of Community law (by means of the Article 177 procedure) should continue to be the preserve of the ECJ. As a result of that approach the present jurisdiction of the CFI excludes actions brought by the institutions (including infringement cases) and Member States and preliminary references. In addition to the above-mentioned factors, an element of prestige and sensitivity may attach to having direct access to the ECJ.

Any further extension of the jurisdiction of the CFI should therefore take into account the fact that the ECJ should continue to act as a constitutional court and should therefore retain its present jurisdiction in respect of cases which often involve issues of a genuinely constitutional nature (the distribution of powers between the Community and the Member States and between the various institutions, fundamental principles of the Treaties and human rights, uniform interpretation of Community law). Bearing this consideration in mind, the following categories of cases are examined with a view to considering whether the balance of jurisdiction between the ECJ and the CFI should be changed.

Preliminary references

The question arises whether some or all preliminary references should be given to the CFI. The arguments in favour might be:

— many preliminary references raise relatively simple points of law or relate to technical areas of Community law, which it would be quite convenient for the CFI to handle;
— such references might fit quite conveniently with other areas of work handled by the CFI, such as competition and dumping cases, and would allow the special knowledge of the chambers of the CFI to be exploited to the best advantage.

The arguments against are:

— the role of the ECJ in the preliminary reference procedure is to ensure the uniform interpretation and application of Community law; such uniformity can be best attained by one court assuming this function;
— although it would be possible to allow appeals from the CFI in preliminary reference cases (as an aid to uniformity), such a system is not desirable as it would prolong the preliminary reference procedure (already too long) and would be incompatible with the basic function of this procedure;
— although some preliminary references may be relatively simple, in practice the referring national court has taken the view that a difficult point of Community law is involved to which the answer is not obvious or settled by previous case-law.

Is there some half-way-house between these positions, such as identifying certain categories of preliminary reference as suitable for the CFI or evolving a procedure for allocating certain references to the CFI?

In order to identify categories of cases suitable for the CFI, a first possibility would be to categorise preliminary references by subject matter. But such an exercise would not in general be useful, as within one subject area a case may be easy or difficult and have narrow or wide repercussions in Community law. Nor would categorising the references according to the referring court be satisfactory as the same problem applies. There are however certain areas of Community law of a highly specialised and technical nature which might lend themselves to such treatment (e.g. cases concerned with classification under the Common Customs Tariff), but these categories would need to be defined as clearly as possible.

It should also be remembered that references come to the ECJ not only directly via the Article 177 procedure, but also by virtue of provisions in international agreements concluded by the Member States. Those conventions deal with specialised and technical areas of the law and they could be treated in a similar way to the CCT cases.

A further possibility would be to permit the President of the ECJ to delegate cases to the CFI on a case-by-case basis. There are, however, formal and practical objections to such a course. Formally it might be regarded as incompatible with the principle of the *juge légal* or *gesetzlicher Richter*. (This principle is that the jurisdiction of Courts must be settled in advance in abstract and general terms. Changes in the jurisdiction of the Courts is possible, but the changes must be made in similar terms and apply for the future. Nevertheless, a certain discretion does exist in jurisdictions which apply the principle. For example a State prosecutor in Germany may have the choice between State or regional courts depending on the sentence which he wishes to obtain and several courts may have jurisdiction, in which case the plaintiff can choose.) The application of that principle to the Community legal order has been doubted, but the existence of the principle in the jurisdictions of certain Member States would make this idea hard for those Member States to accept, unless an objective criterion could be found (such as cases which do not involve a new point of law). But in any case the idea suffers from practical drawbacks. It would require members of the ECJ to study all incoming cases to decide whether they were suitable for the CFI and the preparation of an order of the President. Thus the overall workload on the Community Courts would increase.

Another suggestion may be examined: if it were indeed to be decided to extend the jurisdiction of the CFI in certain specialised fields, the CFI should perhaps be given a discretion to decline jurisdiction in favour of the ECJ, wherever it considered that the case raised important questions of law/main issues requiring examination by the ECJ. This follows the precedent of the European Court of Human Rights, where chambers can relinquish jurisdiction if they consider that the case is of general importance. However, this solution does not seem appropriate, because, wherever such power exists, it causes needless complexity and delay, nowhere more clearly than in the ECHR. The 'option to opt out', i.e. relinquishing jurisdiction should therefore be avoided.

The objections to a transfer of preliminary references, or certain categories of preliminary references, to the CFI, are convincing. It is extremely difficult to provide a clear and precise definition of the areas which could be transferred; and a power on the part of the CFI to relinquish jurisdiction to the ECJ would also cause complexities and delays.

2.3 End of Chapter Assessment Question

(a) Outline the composition and functions of:

  (i) the European Council;

  (ii) the Council of the European Union.

(b) The Commission has been said to have 'a vocation to further the interests of the Community as a whole'.
(Wyatt and Dashwood, *European Community Law*, 3rd edn.)
In the light of its composition and powers, to what extent do you consider this proposition to be true?

2.4 End of Chapter Assessment Outline Answer

(a)(i) The composition and functions of the European Council are to be found in Article D of the TEU. It is composed of the Heads of State or Government of all 15 Member States and is required to meet twice a year to give political impetus to, and guidelines for, the EU, including the Community. Although it is perhaps too soon to comment on this role, reference can be made to the European Council's pre-TEU success in assisting in the resolution of the UK's dispute over its contribution to the Community budget, and to its contribution to the Community budget, and to its more recent responses in foreign affairs, such as its declarations on the peace process in the Middle East.

(ii) The 'basic' Council consists of the foreign ministers from the 15 Member States, but membership is not fixed and the Council therefore consists, as necessary, of the ministers with national responsibility for the area under discussion, for example agriculture. It is generally the ultimate decision-making body of the Community, although it may request the Commission to submit proposals and can delegate the implementation of its decisions to the Commission. It is also responsible for the co-ordination of the economic policies of the Member States. The Member State holding the Presidency of the Council (a six-monthly rotating post) is in effect the President of the Community and may have a key influence on Community affairs during its term.

(b) The Commission consists of 20 Commissioners, one from each Member State, with two from the larger States, appointed by common accord of the Member States. They are required to possess general competence and to be independent of their Member States, although they may be influenced by the fact that their re-appointment is partly a matter of national discretion. They meet weekly and take decisions by majority vote. The requirement of independence together with the weekly meetings and full-time status of Commissioners has led to the emergence of a cohesive and European-minded body which is often in the forefront of European integration, both political and economic.

The power of the Commission to represent the Community abroad, albeit often in tandem with the Community Presidency, allows it to represent itself to the outside world, as well as in domestic headlines, as the bonding element and driving force of the Community.

However, its powers to formulate policy are restricted in most (although not all) areas since decisions ultimately lie with the Council, which tends to represent the interests of individual Member States. Its powers to implement policy are similarly restricted in many areas by the practice of comitology, whereby the representatives of individual Member States scrutinise the work of the Commission. Finally, as guardian of the Treaty, the Commission plays a vital role in upholding Community law, and in particular, in keeping Member States on the Community path.

CHAPTER THREE

SOVEREIGNTY AND SOURCES OF LAW

3.1 Sovereignty

3.1.1 THE POLITICAL PROBLEM

J. Kellett *European Business*, London: Hodder & Stoughton, 1995 p. 28

Leaving The Union

It is conceivable that as EU controls grow the people of Britain may decide to leave the Union. Between 1990 and 1994, according to MORI opinion polls, the percentage of the population wanting to leave rose from 28 per cent to 36 per cent and this figure could continue to increase. Greenland actually did leave the EU in 1985 and it would be quite easy for the UK to withdraw. Under our constitution, by rushing a brief Act through Parliament repealing the European Communities Act 1972 which the Queen would then sign, it would be possible to withdraw in less than 24 hours. All that would be necessary to complete the process would be for the British Ambassador to Italy to deliver a withdrawal document to the Italian government which is the guardian of the Treaty of Rome. This act would have a number of both direct and immediate consequences.

Advantages
1   Food prices would fall as a result of withdrawing from the CAP.
2   British fishermen would once again be able to claim sole use of our fishing grounds.
3   Taxes would fall as contributions to the EU budget would be reduced.
4   Industry would benefit from reduced costs as a result of abandoning the Social Charter and other legislation.
5   The British government would once again be in sole control of its defence and foreign policies.

Disadvantages
1   Europe would impose tariffs and quotas on British goods.
2   Britain's existing trade deficit with Europe would grow.
3   The EU might declare the withdrawal illegal and take the case to the European Parliament or impose penalties.
4   American and Japanese companies would transfer their plants to Holland and other member states in order to obtain entry to the EU market.
5   The UK would be isolated from a Europe rapidly growing in power and unity as a result of Britain's withdrawal and could no longer expect diplomatic support from the US and the Commonwealth nations in time of trouble.

In practice it would be very difficult for any government to withdraw from Europe without first holding a referendum containing three options:

1   Should Britain leave the Union?
2   Should Britain remain a full member of the Union?
3   Should Britain opt to move into the slow free trade lane and out of the fast federal
    Europe track?

Supporters of escaping from the Union need to be warned. The attempt by South
Carolina in 1860 to withdraw from the US led to the American Civil War. The attempt
by the Boers at the end of the nineteenth century to settle in the Transvaal and the Orange
Free State by withdrawing from South Africa led to two wars. Slovenia's rush to
withdraw from Yugoslavia in recent times led to a whole string of wars which have
involved Serbs, Croats and Muslims all fighting each other at the same time.

While it is unlikely that Britain could once again be involved in a European war the
people of the United Kingdom will have to expect difficult times if the withdrawal takes
place. If the country eventually decides to remain within the Union it is also possible to
make certain predictions about future developments, particularly as a result of the
planned 1996 conference when the member states will agree on a strategy for the
twenty-first century.

N. MacCormick, 'Beyond the Sovereign State' (1993) 56 MLR 1

There is widespread, but perhaps misguided, belief that there are a lot of sovereign states
in the world, that this is a good thing, that the United Kingdom is one, and that it will
be a bad thing if the UK ceases to be so. It is also a majority view that if the United
Kingdom has a constitution at all, its central pillar is the principle of the sovereignty of
Parliament. No sovereignty, no constitution; no constitution, no UK. There are perhaps
a few wobbles as to where exactly sovereignty resides. Has not the Prime Minister
recently assured the House of Commons that the 'Sovereignty of this House' is in no way
infringed by the Maastricht Treaty? But anyway, sovereignty is thought mightily
important, and always somewhere to be found on the legal-political stage. The only issue
is where.

A different view would be that sovereignty and sovereign states, and the inexorable
linkage of law with sovereignty and the state, have been but the passing phenomena of
a few centuries, that their passing is by no means regrettable, and that current
developments in Europe exhibit the possibility of going beyond all that. On this view,
our passing beyond the sovereign state is to be considered a good thing, an entirely
welcome development in the history of legal and political ideas. This will be the view
stated in the present lecture. The order of presentation will be through consideration of
five connected points.

. . .

My fourth question was to be, and is, whether there actually are any sovereign states
now. My answer is to be a negative one so far as concerns Western Europe, and is so
notwithstanding the *Daily Telegraph's* first leader on the day of this lecture's first delivery.
In this leading article, the Chancellor of the Exchequer, Mr Lamont, was praised for his
absolute adherence to the principle of 'fiscal sovereignty' while exhibiting sensible
flexibility about some process of harmonisation of taxes to a sensible degree within the
Community.

Taking the view of the sovereign state which I suggested, or any reasonable variant on
its terms, it seems obvious that no state in Western Europe any longer is a sovereign state.
None is in a position such that all the power exercised internally in it, whether politically
or legally, derives from purely internal sources. Equally, of course, it is not true that all
the power which is exercised either politically or normatively is exercised by, or through,
or on the grant of, one or more organs of the European Community. Nor has the
Community as such the plenitude of power politically or normatively that could permit
it remotely to resemble in itself a sovereign state or sovereign federation of states. The
observation that there are no remaining sovereign states in the Community does not in
any way entail the proposition that therefore there must instead be a sovereign
Community. In legal orders, the presence or absence of sovereignty in its legal sense is
contingent, and the presupposition of sovereignty in its political sense is also unnecessary in logical terms and unproven in an evidentiary sense. Where at some time past there

were, or may have been, sovereign states, there has now been a pooling or a fusion within the communitarian normative order of some of the states' powers of legislation, adjudication and implementation of law in relation to a wide but restricted range of subjects. Some matters fall to be handled within one normative system or normative order, while other parts remain rooted or based in other normative systems or normative orders, with arrangements designed (so far, rather successfully) to prevent incompatibility in areas of overlap. We must not envisage sovereignty as the object of some kind of zero sum game, such that the moment X loses it Y necessarily has it. Let us think of it rather more as of virginity, which can in at least some circumstances be lost to the general satisfaction without anybody else gaining it.

At least for the moment, and notwithstanding dramatic demonstrations of independence of judgment over proposals for further development such as evidenced in the Danes' referendum over the Maastrict Treaty, even if it is the case there are no sovereign states left within the European Community, this does not make it true that there is instead a sovereign super-state, a sovereign Community.

In a whole variety of ways, to do as you would expect of someone with my personal political stance or attitude, this seems to me to be a good thing and a great historic opportunity for many things which I personally would regard as good. But another issue is that to which I come by way of my fifth and final point, whether this diffusion of power is just the phenomenon of a passing moment. Perhaps it is just a matter of happenstance that at this very moment no one can quite say where final sovereignty rests in Europe. That could be momentarily so, yet fated to be ephemeral. Is sovereignty such that it might be submerged for a while, yet be as certain as anything to fetch up somewhere in due and early course? Do politics or law always have to resolve distributions of power in favour ultimately (perhaps after moments of diffusion) of some absolute and final centralised authority on everything, subject to doubt only on the number of power centres there are to be? If that is true, and a lot of people speak as though it is true, it makes the future seem even more puzzling and worrying than if it is false.

If it is true, we can only either go forward or go back – lateral thinking or movement will be out of the question. Either we are fated to go forward to a situation in which there is a massively centralised European Community which takes over the dominant place in legal imagination. Then, in twenty years' time, Roger Cotterrell's successors will be saying to mine, 'Why do you people always assume that there is only one paradigm of law, the law of the European Community with the states and their ''law'' just being a kind of forgotten extra?' (You hear this said today about state as against federal constitutional law in the USA, as we should not forget.) That we may call the way forward. The other way would be the way back. No doubt many are tempted by it. Their siren voices urge us to go back to the good old world in which we did not face the loss of sovereignty through its being granted somewhere else. The quest is to go back to a European order of fully sovereign states, with no link stronger than those of treaties which bind only *rebus sic stantibus*.

As for that, I am unwaveringly opposed to the road back. One of the main upshots of universal sovereign statehood was two disasters – world wars, one of which dominates my own earlier memories, the other of which scarred the lives of my parents' generation, only for the medicine to be repeated, yet worse, twenty-one years later. So what about the sideways move? Can we think of a world in which our normative existence and our practical life are anchored in, or related to, a variety of institutional systems, each of which has validity or operation in relation to some range of concerns, none of which is absolute over all the others, and all of which, for most purposes, can operate without serious mutual conflict in areas of overlap? If this is as possible practically as it clearly is conceptually, it would involve a diffusion of political power centres as well as of legal authorities. It would depend on a high degree of relatively willing co-operation and a relatively low degree of coercion in its direct and naked forms. It would create space for a real and serious debate about the demands of subsidiarity.

This would no doubt call for some substantial revision of basic concepts in the constitutional tradition within the UK, above all the doctrine or dogma (perhaps always overstated anyway) of Parliamentary sovereignty. But this would merely be a challenge to a more realistic view of the actual UK constitution, connected as our legal systems are beyond present unilateral revocability with both European Community and European Human Rights institutions. In abandoning the dogma of absolute Parliamentary sovereignty, one might well reconsider with it the possibility of further diffusing legal authority inside the UK to the constituent nations or other subdivisions where subsidiarity makes this seem sound. Could our constitution and politics evolve on those lines, and people still be able to carry on practical lives with the same sort of relative assurance of peace, physical protection and normative security that they have now? Surely if that were possible, it would be better than either a European mega-sovereignty or a return to the old polycentric sovereignties of Europe in the nineteenth and twentieth centuries.

3.1.2 THE LEGAL PROBLEM

3.1.2.1 Parliamentary sovereignty

EUROPEAN COMMUNITIES ACT 1972

Section 2(4)
The provision that may be made under subsection (2) above includes, subject to Schedule 2 to this Act, any such provision (of any such extent) as might be made by Act of Parliament, and any enactment passed or to be passed, other than one contained in this Part of this Act, shall be construed and have effect subject to the foregoing provisions of this section; but, except as may be provided by any Act passed after this Act, Schedule 2 shall have effect in connection with the powers conferred by this and the following sections of this Act to make Orders in Council and regulations.

3.1.2.2 The role of the European Court of Justice

THE TREATY OF ROME

Article 5
Member States shall take all appropriate measures, whether general or particular, to ensure fulfilment of the obligations arising out of this Treaty or resulting from action taken by the institutions of the Community. They shall facilitate the achievement of the Community's tasks.

They shall abstain from any measure which could jeopardise the attainment of the objectives of this Treaty.

COSTA v *ENEL* (Case 6/64) [1964] ECR 585, Court of Justice

Costa argued that the nationalisation of the Italian electricity industry was contrary to a number of provisions of Community law, although it was in accordance with a later Italian law. The Italian court made a reference as to the interpretation of these provisions to the Court of Justice under Article 177 of the Treaty. The Italian government argued that the reference was inappropriate since, in any case, the Italian court was obliged to apply national law.

It was held that the Italian court was obliged to apply Community law in preference to later, inconsistent national law.

On the submission that the court was obliged to apply the national law
The Italian Government submits that the request of the Giudice Conciliatore is 'absolutely inadmissible', inasmuch as a national court which is obliged to apply a national law cannot avail itself of Article 177.

By contrast with ordinary international treaties, the EEC Treaty has created its own legal system which, on the entry into force of the Treaty, became an integral part of the legal systems of the Member States and which their courts are bound to apply.

By creating a Community of unlimited duration, having its own institutions, its own personality, its own legal capacity and capacity of representation on the international plane and, more particularly, real powers stemming from a limitation of sovereignty or a transfer of powers from the States to the Community, the Member States have limited their sovereign rights, albeit within limited fields, and have thus created a body of law which binds both their nationals and themselves.

The integration into the laws of each Member State of provisions which derive from the Community, and more generally the terms and the spirit of the Treaty, make it impossible for the States, as a corollary, to accord precedence to a unilateral and subsequent measure over a legal system accepted by them on a basis of reciprocity. Such a measure cannot therefore be inconsistent with that legal system. The executive force of Community law cannot vary from one State to another in deference to subsequent domestic laws, without jeopardizing the attainment of the objectives of the Treaty set out in Article 5(2) and giving rise to the discrimination prohibited by Article 7.

The obligations undertaken under the Treaty establishing the Community would not be unconditional, but merely contingent, if they could be called in question by subsequent legislative acts of the signatories. Wherever the Treaty grants the States the right to act unilaterally, it does this by clear and precise provisions (for example Articles 15, 93(3), 223, 224 and 225). Applications, by Member States for authority to derogate from the Treaty are subject to a special authorization procedure (for example Articles 8(4), 17(4), 25, 26, 73, the third subparagraph of Article 93(2), and 226) which would lose their purpose if the Member States could renounce their obligations by means of an ordinary law.

The precedence of Community law is confirmed by Article 189, whereby a regulation 'shall be binding' and 'directly applicable in all Member States'. This provision, which is subject to no reservation, would be quite meaningless if a State could unilaterally nullify its effects by means of a legislative measure which could prevail over Community law.

It follows from all these observations that the law stemming from the Treaty, an independent source of law, could not, because of its special and original nature, be overridden by domestic legal provisions, however framed, without being deprived of its character as Community law and without the legal basis of the Community itself being called into question.

The transfer by the States from their domestic legal system to the Community legal system of the rights and obligations arising under the Treaty carries with it a permanent limitation of their sovereign rights, against which a subsequent unilateral act incompatible with the concept of the Community cannot prevail. Consequently Article 177 is to be applied regardless of any domestic law, whenever questions relating to the interpretation of the Treaty arise.

AMMINISTRAZIONE DELLE FINANZE DELLO STATO v SIMMENTHAL SPA (SIMMENTHAL II) (Case 106/77) [1978] ECR 629, Court of Justice

An Italian fee levied on certain imports was declared to be contrary to Community law by the Court of Justice. The Amministrazione appealed against the subsequent order by the Italian court that it repay Simmenthal. Under Italian law the legality of the law imposing the fee had then to be referred to the Italian Constitutional Court. The Italian court asked the Court of Justice for a preliminary ruling under Article 177 of the Treaty as to what it was obliged to do.

It was held that in order for Community law to be fully effective, the Italian court must disapply the Italian law itself, without waiting for the decision of the Constitutional Court.

The substance of the case

13. The main purpose of the first question is to ascertain what consequences flow from the direct applicability of a provision of Community law in the event of incompatibility with a subsequent legislative provision of a Member State.

14. Direct applicability in such circumstances means that rules of Community law must be fully and uniformly applied in all the Member States from the date of their entry into force and for so long as they continue in force.

15. These provisions are therefore a direct source of rights and duties for all those affected thereby, whether Member States or individuals, who are parties to legal relationships under Community law.

16. This consequence also concerns any national court whose task it is as an organ of a Member State to protect, in a case within its jurisdiction, the rights conferred upon individuals by Community law.

17.   Furthermore, in accordance with the principle of the precedence of Community law, the relationship between provisions of the Treaty and directly applicable measures of the institutions on the one hand and the national law of the Member States on the other is such that those provisions and measures not only by their entry into force render automatically inapplicable any conflicting provision of current national law but – in so far as they are an integral part of, and take precedence in, the legal order applicable in the territory of each of the Member States – also preclude the valid adoption of new national legislative measures to the extent to which they would be incompatible with Community provisions.

18.   Indeed any recognition that national legislative measures which encroach upon the field within which the Community exercises its legislative power or which are otherwise incompatible with the provisions of Community law had any legal effect would amount to a corresponding denial of the effectiveness of obligations undertaken unconditionally and irrevocably by Member States pursuant to the Treaty and would thus imperil the very foundations of the Community.

19.   The same conclusion emerges from the structure of Article 177 of the Treaty which provides that any court or tribunal of a Member State is entitled to make a reference to the Court whenever it considers that a preliminary ruling on a question of interpretation or validity relating to Community law is necessary to enable it to give judgment.

20.   The effectiveness of that provision would be impaired if the national court were prevented from forthwith applying Community law in accordance with the decision or the caselaw of the Court.

21.   It follows from the foregoing that every national court must, in a case within its jurisdiction, apply Community law in its entirety and protect rights which the latter confers on individuals and must accordingly set aside any provision of national law which may conflict with it, whether prior or subsequent to the Community rule.

22.   Accordingly any provision of a national legal system and any legislative, administrative or judicial practice which might impair the effectiveness of Community law by withholding from the national court having jurisdiction to apply such law the power to do everything necessary at the moment of its application to set aside national legislative provisions which might prevent Community rules from having full force and effect are incompatible with those requirements which are the very essence of Community law.

23.   This would be the case in the event of a conflict between a provision of Community law and a subsequent national law if the solution of the conflict were to be reserved for an authority with a discretion of its own, other than the court called upon to apply Community law, even if such an impediment to the full effectiveness of Community law were only temporary.

24.   The first question should therefore be answered to the effect that a national court which is called upon, within the limits of its jurisdiction, to apply provisions of Community law is under a duty to give full effect to those provisions, if necessary refusing of its own motion to apply any conflicting provision of national legislation, even if adopted subsequently, and it is not necessary for the court to request or await the prior setting aside of such provision by legislative or other constitutional means.
. . .

R v SECRETARY OF STATE FOR TRANSPORT, EX PARTE FACTORTAME LTD (FACTORTAME I)
(Case C-213/89) [1989] 3 CMLR 1, House of Lords and [1990] ECR I–2433, Court of Justice

A number of Spanish fishermen alleged that certain provisions of the Merchant Shipping Act 1988 were contrary to Community law and therefore invalid. They applied to have these provisions suspended while awaiting a final ruling on their validity from the Court of Justice.

It was held by the House of Lords that the remedy was not available under English law, but in the light of conflicting Court of Justice case law on an interim measures a reference would be made to the Court of Justice under Article 177 of the Treaty concerning the award of interim protection.

LORD BRIDGE:

[13]   By virtue of s. 2(4) of the 1972 Act, Part II of the 1988 Act is to be construed and take effect subject to directly enforceable Community rights and those rights are, by

section 2(1) of the Act of 1972, to be 'recognised and available in law, and . . . enforced, allowed and followed accordingly . . .'. This has precisely the same effect as if a section were incorporated in Part II of the Act of 1988 which in terms enacted that the provisions with respect to registration of British fishing vessels were to be without prejudice to the directly enforceable Community rights of nationals of any member State of the EEC. Thus it is common ground that, in so far as the applicants succeed before the ECJ in obtaining a ruling in support of the Community rights which they claim, those rights will prevail over the restrictions imposed on registration of British fishing vessels by Part II of the Act of 1988 and the Divisional Court will, in the final determination of the application for judicial review, be obliged to make appropriate declarations to give effect to those rights. . . .

[37]   I turn finally to consider the submission made on behalf of the appellants that, irrespective of the position under national law, there is an overriding principle of Community law which imposes an obligation on the national court to secure effective interim protection of rights having direct effect under Community law where a seriously arguable claim is advanced to be entitled to such rights and where the rights claimed will in substance be rendered nugatory or will be irremediably impaired if not effectively protected during any interim period which must elapse pending determination of a dispute as to the existence of those rights. The basic propositions of Community law on which the appellants rely in support of this submission may be quite shortly summarised. Directly enforceable Community rights are part of the legal heritage of every citizen of a member State of the EEC. They arise from the Treaty of Rome itself and not from any judgment of the ECJ declaring their existence. Such rights are automatically available and must be given unrestricted retroactive effect. The persons entitled to the enjoyment of such rights are entitled to direct and immediate protection against possible infringement of them. The duty to provide such protection rests with the national court. The remedy to be provided against infringement must be effective, not merely symbolic or illusory. The rules of national law which render the exercise of directly enforceable Community rights excessively difficult or virtually impossible must be overridden.

[38]   Mr. Vaughan, in a most impressive argument presented in opening this appeal, traced the progressive development of these principles of the jurisprudence of the ECJ through long series of reported decisions on which he relies. I must confess that at the conclusion of his argument I was strongly inclined to the view that, if English law could provide no effective remedy to secure the interim protection of the rights claimed by the appellants, it was nevertheless our duty under Community law to devise such a remedy. But the Solicitor General, in his equally impressive reply, and in his careful and thorough analysis of the case law, has persuaded me that none of the authorities on which Mr. Vaughan relies can properly be treated as determinative of the difficult question, which arises for the first time in the instant case, of providing interim protection of putative and disputed rights in Community law before their existence has been established. This is because the relevant decisions of the ECJ from which the propositions of Community law asserted by Mr. Vaughan are derived, were all made by reference to rights which the ECJ was itself then affirming or by reference to the protection of rights the existence of which had already been established by previous decisions of the ECJ.

The Court of Justice held that the Act should be suspended pending a conclusive ruling on its validity.

17.   It is clear from the information before the Court, and in particular from the judgment making the reference and, as described above, the course taken by the proceedings in the national courts before which the case came at first and second instance, that the preliminary question raised by the House of Lords seeks essentially to ascertain whether a national court which, in a case before it concerning Community law, considers that the sole obstacle which precludes it from granting interim relief is a rule of national law, must disapply that rule.

18.   For the purpose of replying to that question, it is necessary to point out that in its judgment of 9 March 1978 in Case 106/77 *Amministrazione delle finanze dello Stato* v *Simmenthal SpA* [1978] ECR 629 the Court held that directly applicable rules of Community law 'must be fully and uniformly applied in all the Member States from the date of

their entry into force and for so long as they continue in force' (paragraph 14) and that 'in accordance with the principle of the precedence of Community law, the relationship between provisions of the Treaty and directly applicable measures of the institutions on the one hand and the national law of the Member States on the other is such that those provisions and measures . . . by their entry into force render automatically inapplicable any conflicting provision of . . . national law' (paragraph 17).

19. In accordance with the case law of the Court, it is for the national courts, in application of the principle of co-operation laid down in Article 5 of the EEC Treaty, to ensure the legal protection which persons derive from the direct effect of provisions of Community law (see, most recently, the judgments of 10 July 1980 in Case 811/79 *Ariete SpA* v *Amministrazione delle finanze dello Stato* [1980] ECR 2545 and Case 826/79 *Mireco* v *Amministrazione delle finanze dello Stato* [1980] ECR 2559).

20. The Court has also held that any provision of a national legal system and any legislative, administrative or judicial practice which might impair the effectiveness of Community law by withholding from the national court having jurisdiction to apply such law the power to do everything necessary at the moment of its application to set aside national legislative provisions which might prevent, even temporarily, Community rules from having full force and effect are incompatible with those requirements, which are the very essence of Community law (judgment of 9 March 1978 in *Simmenthal*, cited above, paragraphs 22 and 23).

21. It must be added that the full effectiveness of Community law would be just as much impaired if a rule of national law could prevent a court seised of a dispute governed by Community law from granting interim relief in order to ensure the full effectiveness of the judgment to be given on the existence of the rights claimed under Community law. It follows that a court which in those circumstances would grant interim relief, if it were not for a rule of national law, is obliged to set aside that rule.

22. That interpretation is reinforced by the system established by Article 177 of the EEC Treaty whose effectiveness would be impaired if a national court, having stayed proceedings pending the reply by the Court of Justice to the question referred to it for a preliminary ruling, were not able to grant interim relief until it delivered its judgment following the reply given by the Court of Justice.

23. Consequently, the reply to the question raised should be that Community law must be interpreted as meaning that a national court which, in a case before it concerning Community law, considers that the sole obstacle which precludes it from granting interim relief is a rule of national law must set aside that rule.

3.2 Federalism

J. C. Piris, 'After Maastricht are the Community Institutions More Efficacious, More Democratic and More Transparent?' (1994) 19 EL Rev 449

Conclusion
In short, do the institutional changes decided at Maastricht amount to a move towards a Europe of nation states or towards a United States of Europe?

The current institutional configuration of the Community, after Maastricht, is far from that of a super-state. It is an emergent construction *sui generis* uniting states which remain sovereign, but which have agreed to share their sovereignty in certain areas, sometimes in a more federal way than in the United States and sometimes through traditional governmental co-operation. This construction *sui generis* cannot be assimilated to the model of a state: 'The Union shall respect the national identities of its Member States', in the words of the Treaty.

Will this situation be altered when the treaties are next revised? Probably not.

The Treaty on European Union contains a single revision clause for all the Treaties (EC, ECSC, EAEC, TEU). The article in question provides for a conference of representatives of the governments of the Member States to be convened in 1996 to examine those provisions of the TEU for which revision is explicitly provided. These provisions are:
- those relating to the common foreign and security policy;
- those which determine the scope of the co-decision procedure;

– the possible establishment of an 'appropriate' hierarchy between the different categories of Community acts.

The existence of these provisions does not mean that the Member States will not be able to amend other provisions of the Treaty in 1996, any more than it means, of course, that they will be able necessarily to agree on these subjects in 1996.

However, a widespread enlargement of the European Union towards certain central and eastern European countries would create very strong pressure for the nature of this construction to be more clearly defined.

If such enlargement is not to result in diluting the Community, far-reaching institutional reform will be required. To preserve the construction of Europe, let alone ensuring its efficacy and any further progress, would require a decisive reinforcement of its institutions, commensurate with enlargement, without which the construction of the Community would lose momentum. The ability of the Communities to withstand the crises which have beset them has been largely due to the solidity of their institutions. In addition, a strong and stable European Union is necessary for the equilibrium of Europe; if enlargement towards eastern Europe were to weaken the Union, what would be the benefits for these new members?

However, such institutional reinforcement is far from guaranteed by 1996; in any case, this is a date which might prove premature in this respect.

Such reinforcement will certainly come up against extremely powerful obstacles:

(1)   the deep attachment of public opinion to national sovereignty and independence: greater certitude that national identities will continue to exist would perhaps help to reassure it;

(2)   the problems of political balance between more or less populated states: while most of the least populated states might be *a priori* those most attached to European integration, they are also those least keen on institutional changes which, at the very least, the more populated states would consider were appropriate to such integration if it was to be more realistic and democratic;

(3)   the mediocre economic and social situation: historically, institutional progress in the Community has only been made in periods of growth;

(4)   the bad psychological-political situation following the trials and tribulations of the ratification of the Maastricht Treaty: to restore confidence will require time, especially if there is continuing uncertainty as to the ultimate purpose of European integration;

(5)   the lack of political will on the part of some governments.

This makes it very difficult to predict future development.

At most we can note that if enlargement towards the East were to become desirable, if not inevitable for political reasons, it would be difficult to put the choice off again.

The success of the Union will clearly then depend on its ability to address realities: the more the institutions lose sight of reality, the less chance they will have of succeeding. These realities cannot be ignored: the 20 or 25 states in question are more or less populated, their economies are more or less efficient, their inhabitants are more or less keen to move fast and far along the path of European integration. This could therefore result in different arrangements for participation at different speeds.

Perhaps consideration will be given to incorporating both schools side by side, the integrationist and the intergovernmental, by creating a 'variable-geometry Europe' with a hard core of a small number of Member States participating in all the policies of the Union, while the other Member States would have the option of taking part, at their own speed, in an à la carte network of policy areas: economic and monetary union? social policy? environmental protection? industrial policy? common foreign and security policy? home affairs and justice?

Such a format would raise difficult problems:

– how to operate the institutions?

– could the small number of Member States of the hard core put up without active solidarity from their partners on foreign policy or comparable social anti-dumping rules, or environmental protection or respect for monetary balances?

The fate of the construction of the Community will be decided or, rather, will be reflected in institutional matters over the coming 10 years. The institutions of a European

Union of 25 Member States cannot be the same as those of a European Community of 12. They must be different. The problem will be, not only to preserve the qualities of efficacy, democracy and transparency which these institutions have undeniably acquired, but also to reinforce them in order to win over the full and wholehearted support of the people.

3.3 Attribution of Powers to the Community

THE TREATY OF ROME

Article 130s.

1.   The Council, acting in accordance with the procedure referred to in Article 189c and after consulting the Economic and Social Committee, shall decide what action is to be taken by the Community in order to achieve the objectives referred to in Article 130r.

2.   By way of derogation from the decision-making procedure provided for in paragraph 1 and without prejudice to Article 100a, the Council, acting unanimously on a proposal from the Commission and after consulting the European Parliament and the Economic and Social Committee, shall adopt:
– provisions primarily of a fiscal nature;
– measures concerning town and country planning, land use with the exception of waste management and measures of a general nature, and management of water resources;
– measures significantly affecting a Member State's choice between different energy sources and the general structure of its energy supply.

The Council may, under the conditions laid down in the preceding subparagraph, define those matters referred to in this paragraph on which decisions are to be taken by a qualified majority.

3.   In other areas, general action programmes setting out priority objectives to be attained shall be adopted by the Council, acting in accordance with the procedure referred to in Article 189b and after consulting the Economic and Social Committee.

The Council, acting under the terms of paragraph 1 or paragraph 2 according to the case, shall adopt the measures necessary for the implementation of these programmes.

4.   Without prejudice to certain measures of a Community nature, the Member States shall finance and implement the environment policy.

5.   Without prejudice to the principle that the polluter should pay, if a measure based on the provisions of paragraph 1 involves costs deemed disproportionate for the public authorities of a Member State, the Council shall, in the act adopting that measure, lay down appropriate provisions in the form of:
– temporary derogations and/or
– financial support from the Cohesion Fund to be set up no later than 31 December 1993 pursuant to Article 130d.

Article 130r.

1.   Community policy on the environment shall contribute to pursuit of the following objectives:
   – preserving, protecting and improving the quality of the environment;
   – protecting human health;
   – prudent and rational utilisation of natural resources;
   – promoting measures at international level to deal with regional or worldwide environmental problems.

2.   Community policy on the environment shall aim at a high level of protection taking into account the diversity of situations in the various regions of the Community. It shall be based on the precautionary principle and on the principles that preventive action should be taken, that environmental damage should as a priority be rectified at source and that the polluter should pay. Environmental protection requirements must be integrated into the definition and implementation of other Community policies.

In this context, harmonisation measures answering these requirements shall include, where appropriate, a safeguard clause allowing Member States to take provisional measures, for non-economic environmental reasons, subject to a Community inspection procedure.

3.   In preparing its policy on the environment, the Community shall take account of:
– available scientific and technical data;
– environmental conditions in the various regions of the Community;
– the potential benefits and costs of action or lack of action;
– the economic and social development of the Community as a whole and the balanced development of its regions.

4.   Within their respective spheres of competence, the Community and the Member States shall cooperate with third countries and with the competent international organisations. The arrangements for Community cooperation may be the subject of agreements between the Community and the third parties concerned, which shall be negotiated and concluded in accordance with Article 228.

The previous subparagraph shall be without prejudice to Member States' competence to negotiate in international bodies and to conclude international agreements.

THE TREATY OF ROME

Article 235.

If action by the Community should prove necessary to attain, in the course of the operation of the common market, one of the objectives of the Community and this Treaty has not provided the necessary powers, the Council shall, acting unanimously on a proposal from the Commission and after consulting the European Parliament, take the appropriate measures.

COMMISSION v *COUNCIL (ERTA)* (Case 22/70) [1971] ECR 263, Court of Justice

The Member States in Council discussed their position with regard to the European Road Transport Agreement (ERTA) and concluded the ERTA in accordance with this position. The Commission alleged that ERTA should be negotiated by the Community, rather than by the Member States individually. It applied for annulment of the Council agreement under Article 173 of the Treaty, arguing that the Member States had acted independently of the Community.

It was held that the Community had sole power to conclude the agreement but the Member States in Council had properly acted in accordance with their Community obligations.

1   The initial question

6.   The Commission takes the view that Article 75 of the Treaty, which conferred on the Community powers defined in wide terms with a view to implementing the common transport policy, must apply to external relations just as much as to domestic measures in the sphere envisaged.

7.   It believes that the full effect of this provision would be jeopardized if the powers which it confers, particularly that of laying down 'any appropriate provisions', within the meaning of subparagraph (1) (c) of the article cited, did not extend to the conclusion of agreements with third countries.

8.   Even if, it is argued, this power did not originally embrace the whole sphere of transport, it would tend to become general and exclusive as and where the common policy in this field came to be implemented.

9.   The Council, on the other hand, contends that since the Community only has such powers as have been conferred on it, authority to enter into agreements with third countries cannot be assumed in the absence of an express provision in the Treaty.

10.   More particularly, Article 75 relates only to measures internal to the Community, and cannot be interpreted as authorizing the conclusion of international agreements.

11.   Even if it were otherwise, such authority could not be general and exclusive, but at the most concurrent with that of the Member States.

12.   In the absence of specific provisions of the Treaty relating to the negotiation and conclusion of international agreements in the sphere of transport policy – a category into which, essentially, the AETR falls – one must turn to the general system of Community Law in the sphere of relations with third countries.

13.   Article 210 provides that 'The Community shall have legal personality'.

14.   This provision, placed at the head of Part Six of the Treaty, devoted to 'General and Final Provisions', means that in its external relations the Community enjoys the capacity to establish contractual links with third countries over the whole field of objectives defined in Part One of the Treaty, which Part Six supplements.

15.   To determine in a particular case the Community's authority to enter into international agreements, regard must be had to the whole scheme of the Treaty no less than to its substantive provisions.

16.   Such authority arises not only from an express conferment by the Treaty – as is the case with Articles 113 and 114 for tariff and trade agreements and with Article 238 for association agreements – but may equally flow from other provisions of the Treaty and from measures adopted, within the framework of those provisions, by the Community institutions.

17.   In particular, each time the Community, with a view to implementing a common policy envisaged by the Treaty, adopts provisions laying down common rules, whatever form these may take, the Member States no longer have the right, acting individually or even collectively, to undertake obligations with third countries which affect those rules.

18.   As and when such common rules come into being, the Community alone is in a position to assume and carry out contractual obligations towards third countries affecting the whole sphere of application of the Community legal system.

19.   With regard to the implementation of the provisions of the Treaty the system of internal Community measures may not therefore be separated from that of external relations.

20.   Under Article 3(e), the adoption of a common policy in the sphere of transport is specially mentioned amongst the objectives of the Community.

21.   Under Article 5, the Member States are required on the one hand to take all appropriate measures to ensure fulfilment of the obligations arising out of the Treaty or resulting from action taken by the institutions and, on the other hand, to abstain from any measure which might jeopardize the attainment of the objectives of the Treaty.

22.   If these two provisions are read in conjunction, it follows that to the extent to which Community rules are promulgated for the attainment of the objectives of the Treaty, the Member States cannot, outside the framework of the Community institutions, assume obligations which might affect those rules or alter their scope.

23.   According to Article 74, the objectives of the Treaty in matters of transport are to be pursued within the framework of a common policy.

24.   With this in view, Article 75 (1) directs the Council to lay down common rules and, in addition, 'any other appropriate provisions'.

25.   By the terms of subparagraph (a) of the same provision, those common rules are applicable 'to international transport to or from the territory of a Member State or passing across the territory of one or more Member States'.

26.   This provision is equally concerned with transport from or to third countries, as regards that part of the journey which takes place on Community territory.

27.   It thus assumes that the powers of the Community extend to relationships arising from international law, and hence involve the need in the sphere in question for agreements with the third countries concerned.

28.   Although it is true that Articles 74 and 75 do not expressly confer on the Community authority to enter into international agreements, nevertheless the bringing into force, on 25th March 1969, of Regulation No. 543/69 of the Council on the harmonization of certain social legislation relating to road transport (OJ L 77, p. 49) necessarily vested in the Community power to enter into any agreements with third countries relating to the subject–matter governed by that regulation.

29.   This grant of power is moreover expressly recognized by Article 3 of the said regulation which prescribes that: 'The Community shall enter into any negotiations with third countries which may prove necessary for the purpose of implementing this regulation.'

30.   Since the subject-matter of the AETR falls within the scope of Regulation No. 543/69, the Community has been empowered to negotiate and conclude the agreement in question since the entry into force of the said regulation.

31.   These Community powers exclude the possibility of concurrent powers on the part of Member States, since any steps taken outside the framework of the Community

institutions would be incompatible with the unity of the Common Market and the uniform application of Community law.

32.   This is the legal position in the light of which the question of admissibility has to be resolved.

3.4   Sources of Community Law

3.4.1   THE TREATIES

EUROPEAN COMMUNITIES ACT 1972

Section 2.

1.   All such rights, powers, liabilities, obligations and restrictions from time to time created or arising by or under the Treaties, and all such remedies and procedures from time to time provided for by or under the Treaties, as in accordance with the Treaties are without further enactment to be given legal effect or used in the United Kingdom shall be recognised and available in law, and be enforced, allowed and followed accordingly; and the expression 'enforceable Community right' and similar expressions shall be read as referring to one to which this subsection applies.

3.4.2   SECONDARY LEGISLATION

THE TREATY OF ROME

Article 189.

In order to carry out their task and in accordance with the provisions of this Treaty, the European Parliament acting jointly with the Council, the Council and the Commission shall make regulations and issue directives, take decisions, make recommendations or deliver opinions.

A regulation shall have general application. It shall be binding in its entirety and directly applicable in all Member States.

A directive shall be binding, as to the result to be achieved, upon each Member State to which it is addressed, but shall leave to the national authorities the choice of form and methods.

A decision shall be binding in its entirety upon those to whom it is addressed.

Recommendations and opinions shall have no binding force.

3.5   Legislative Procedures

A. Dashwood, 'Community Legislative Procedures in the era of the Treaty on European Union' (1994) 19 EL Rev 343

The main purpose of this article has been to provide a detailed, and perhaps at times somewhat technical, analysis of the set of legislative procedures available under the EC Treaty, following its amendment by the Treaty on European Union. However, it may be thought appropriate to conclude with some remarks of a more general character.

A first remark would be that the Treaty on European Union has rendered an already complicated system of decision-making, under the EEC Treaty as amended by the SEA, very considerably more so. Not only has the Treaty on European Union introduced the Article 189b procedure and extended the assent procedure into the legislative sphere; it also provides for a bewildering number of variants within the main procedures, notably as regards the bodies whose opinions must be obtained, the legal form in which the Commission exercises its rights of initiative and the definition of the qualified majority. All of this unavoidably reflects the complexity of the political bargain that was struck at Maastricht; but it must surely be one of the objectives of the review of institutional arrangements in 1996 to simplify and rationalise the Community's legislative procedures, so as to make them intelligible to the citizens of the European Union.

A second remark is that the Treaty on European Union has brought about a major transformation in the role of the European Parliament in Community law-making. Under the consultation and co-operation procedures, the Parliament's best chance of helping to determine the shape of the act in question is by putting political pressure on the Commission to take up some or all of its proposed amendments. By contrast, the Article 189b procedure enables the Parliament directly to influence the final outcome, though face-to-face negotiation with the Council in the Conciliation Committee or, *in extremis*, through use of its veto. Even more radically, as we have seen, measures that are subject to the assent procedure can only be enacted if they are positively approved by the Parliament as well as by the Council. Thus it is no longer the case, where the Article 189b or assent procedures apply, that the Council in alliance with the Commission, or acting on its own by unanimity, can always override the will of the European Parliament.

A final remark concerns the future. One of the issues likely to be on the agenda in 1996 is what further reform of the legislative process should be undertaken to redress the 'democratic deficit' perceived by some critics of the present constitutional order. It is a serious question whether that objective would best be served by inventing ingenious new procedures designed to modify, once again, the institutional balance of the European Union. An alternative would be to seek ways of achieving a freer flow of information and democratic pressures between Union institutions and the political systems of the Member States, accepting that for the foreseeable future democracy will, on the whole, continue to be a game played at the national level.

3.5.1 CO-OPERATION PROCEDURE

THE TREATY OF ROME

Article 189c.
Where reference is made in this Treaty to this Article for the adoption of an act, the following procedures shall apply:

(a)   The Council, acting by a qualified majority on a proposal from the Commission and after obtaining the opinion of the European Parliament, shall adopt a common position.

(b)   The Council's common position shall be communicated to the European Parliament. The Council and the Commission shall inform the European Parliament fully of the reasons which led the Council to adopt its common position and also of the Commission's position.

If, within three months of such communication, the European Parliament approves this common position or has not taken a decision within that period the Council shall definitively adopt the act in question in accordance with the common position.

(c)   The European Parliament may, within the period of three months, referred to in point (b), by an absolute majority of its component members, propose amendments to the Council's common position. The European Parliament may also, by the same majority, reject the Council's common position. The result of the proceedings shall be transmitted to the Council and the Commission.

If the European Parliament has rejected the Council's common position, unanimity shall be required for the Council to act on a second reading.

(d)   The Commission shall, within a period of one month, re-examine the proposal on the basis of which the Council adopted its common position, by taking into account the amendments proposed by the European Parliament.

The Commission shall forward to the Council, at the same time as its re-examined proposal, the amendments of the European Parliament which it has not accepted, and shall express its opinion on them. The Council may adopt these amendments unanimously.

(e)   The Council, acting by a qualified majority, shall adopt the proposal as re-examined by the Commission.

Unanimity shall be required for the Council to amend the proposal as re-examined by the Commission.

(f)   In the cases referred to in points (c), (d) and (e), the Council shall be required to act within a period of three months. If no decision is taken within this period, the Commission proposal shall be deemed not to have been adopted.

(g)   The periods referred to in points (b) and (f) may be extended by a maximum of one month by common accord between the Council and the European Parliament.

3.5.2   CO-DECISION PROCEDURE

THE TREATY OF ROME

Article 189b.

1.   Where reference is made in this Treaty to this Article for the adoption of an act, the following procedure shall apply.

2.   The Commission shall submit a proposal to the European Parliament and the Council.

The Council, acting by a qualified majority after obtaining the opinion of the European Parliament, shall adopt a common position. The common position shall be communicated to the European Parliament. The Council shall inform the European Parliament fully of the reasons which led it to adopt its common position. The Commission shall inform the European Parliament fully of its position.

If within three months of such communication, the European Parliament:

(a)   approves the common position, the Council shall definitively adopt the act in question in accordance with that common position;

(b)   has not taken a decision, the Council shall adopt the act in question in accordance with its common position;

(c)   indicates, by an absolute majority of its component members, that it intends to reject the common position, it shall immediately inform the Council. The Council may convene a meeting of the Conciliation Committee referred to in paragraph 4 to explain further its position. The European Parliament shall thereafter either confirm, by an absolute majority of its component members, its rejection of the common position, in which event the proposed act shall be deemed not to have been adopted, or propose amendments in accordance with subparagraph (d) of this paragraph;

(d)   proposes amendments to the common position by an absolute majority of its component members, the amended text shall be forwarded to the Council and to the Commission, which shall deliver an opinion on those amendments.

3.   If, within three months of the matter being referred to it, the Council, acting by a qualified majority, approves all the amendments of the European Parliament, it shall amend its common position accordingly and adopt the act in question; however, the Council shall act unanimously on the amendments on which the Commission has delivered a negative opinion. If the Council does not approve the act in question, the President of the Council, in agreement with the President of the European Parliament, shall forthwith convene a meeting of the Conciliation Committee.

4.   The Conciliation Committee, which shall be composed of the members of the Council or their representatives and an equal number of representatives of the European Parliament, shall have the task of reaching agreement on a joint text, by a qualified majority of the members of the Council or their representatives and by a majority of the representatives of the European Parliament. The Commission shall take part in the Conciliation Committee's proceedings and shall take all the necessary initiatives with a view to reconciling the positions of the European Parliament and the Council.

5.   If, within six weeks of its being convened, the Conciliation Committee approves a joint text, the European Parliament, acting by an absolute majority of the votes cast, and the Council, acting by a qualified majority, shall have a period of six weeks from that approval in which to adopt the act in question in accordance with the joint text. If one of the two institutions fails to approve the proposed act, it shall be deemed not to have been adopted.

6.   Where the Conciliation Committee does not approve a joint text, the proposed act shall be deemed not to have been adopted unless the Council, acting by a qualified majority within six weeks of expiry of the period granted to the Conciliation Committee, confirms the common position to which it agreed before the conciliation procedure was initiated, possibly with amendments proposed by the European Parliament. In this case, the act in question shall be finally adopted unless the European Parliament, within six weeks of the date of confirmation by the Council, rejects the text by an absolute majority

of its component members, in which case the proposed act shall be deemed not to have been adopted.

7.   The periods of three months and six weeks referred to in this Article may be extended by a maximum of one month and two weeks respectively by common accord of the European Parliament and the Council. The period of three months referred to in paragraph 2 shall be automatically extended by two months where paragraph 2(c) applies.

8.   The scope of the procedure under this Article may be widened, in accordance with the procedure provided for in Article N(2) of the Treaty on European Union, on the basis of a report to be submitted to the Council by the Commission by 1996 at the latest.

3.6   End of Chapter Assessment Question

(a)   Explain the impact of Community membership on British Parliamentary sovereignty.

(b)

   (i)   Briefly outline the main sources of Community law.

   (ii)   Explain the importance of the decisions of the Court of Justice and give three principles which it has developed.

3.7   End of Chapter Assessment Outline Answer

(a)   The doctrine of Parliamentary sovereignty in the UK, in effect establishes Parliament as the supreme law-making body in the UK. The validity of Parliamentary legislation cannot be questioned by the courts and Parliament may make or unmake any law. Since the acts of Parliament are supreme, any previous legislation which is inconsistent with new legislation will be impliedly repealed despite any statement in the earlier legislation that it should not be (as was the situation in *Vauxhall Estates* v *Liverpool Corporation* and *Ellen Street Estates* v *The Ministry of Housing*).

Parliamentary sovereignty has now been curtailed by the accession of the UK to the European Community. As the Court of Justice recognised in the case of *Costa* v *ENEL*, Community membership entailed a transfer of sovereignty to the Community, including the full integration of Community law into the national legal system. If a Member State were able to repeal Community legislation simply by passing conflicting legislation of its own, the uniform system of Community law would be destroyed.

The Court of Justice has also ruled that Article 5, which provides that Member States are under a duty to take all appropriate measures to comply with their Treaty obligations, requires the national courts to question the validity of conflicting national law, and if necessary, to refuse to apply it. The Court of Justice confirmed in *Simmenthal II* that the national court need not wait for the legislature to repeal the offending law before disapplying it.

Although it would, in theory, be possible for the UK Parliament to repeal the European Communities Act 1972, and restore its sovereignty, the current position is that, in areas of Community competence, absolute Parliamentary sovereignty has been lost.

(b)(i)   The main sources of Community law are the Treaties (the ECSC Treaty, the Treaty of Rome and the Euratom Treaty), as amended by later Treaties; secondary legislation, in particular, Regulations (which have binding force throughout the Community), Directives (which apply to named Member States) and Decisions (which may be addressed to anyone); and decisions of the Court of Justice and the general principles of Community law which the Court has developed.

(ii)   The decisions of the Court of Justice provide the authoritative interpretation of the Treaties and secondary legislation. The Court of Justice is also able to rule on the validity of Community law and of national implementing legislation. It has implied a number of legal principles from the Treaty and has also made use of those which are part of the legal traditions of the Member States. These include proportionality, non-discrimination (on grounds of sex or nationality) and solidarity between Member States (including the duty to fulfil Treaty obligations).

CHAPTER FOUR

THE TREATY ON EUROPEAN UNION

4.1 The European Union

4.1.1 OBJECTIVES

THE TREATY ON EUROPEAN UNION

Article B

The Union shall set itself the following objectives:

– to promote economic and social progress which is balanced and sustainable, in particular through the creation of an area without internal frontiers, through the strengthening of economic and social cohesion and through the establishment of economic and monetary union, ultimately including a single currency in accordance with the provisions of this Treaty;

– to assert its identity on the international scene, in particular through the implementation of a common foreign and security policy including the eventual framing of a common defence policy, which might in time lead to a common defence;

– to strengthen the protection of the rights and interests of the nationals of its Member States through the introduction of a citizenship of the Union;

– to develop close co-operation on justice and home affairs;

– to maintain in full the *acquis communautaire* and build on it with a view to considering, through the procedure referred to in Article N (2), to what extent the policies and forms of co-operation introduced by this Treaty may need to be revised with the aim of ensuring the effectiveness of the mechanisms and the institutions of the Community.

The objectives of the Union shall be achieved as provided in this Treaty and in accordance with the conditions and the timetable set out therein while respecting the principle of subsidiarity as defined in Article 3b of the Treaty establishing the European Community.

THE TREATY ON EUROPEAN UNION

Article F

1. The Union shall respect the national identities of its Member States, whose systems of government are founded on the principles of democracy.

2. The Union shall respect fundamental rights, as guaranteed by the European Convention for the Protection of Human Rights and Fundamental Freedoms signed in Rome on 4 November 1950 and as they result from the constitutional traditions common to the Member States, as general principles of Community law.

3. The Union shall provide itself with the means necessary to attain its objectives and carry through its policies.

4.2   Key Provisions of the TEU

4.2.1   ARTICLE 3b OF THE TREATY OF ROME (AS INSERTED BY ARTICLE G(3) OF THE TEU)

THE TREATY OF ROME

Article 3b

The Community shall act within the limits of the powers conferred upon it by this Treaty and of the objectives assigned to it therein.

In areas which do not fall within its exclusive competence, the Community shall take action, in accordance with the principle of subsidiarity, only if and in so far as the objectives of the proposed action cannot be sufficiently achieved by the Member States and can therefore, by reason of the scale or effects of the proposed action, be better achieved by the Community.

Any action by the Community shall not go beyond what is necessary to achieve the objectives of this Treaty.

4.2.1.1   Subsidiarity

Conclusions of the Presidency at the Edinburgh European Council Meeting 11–12 December 1992 (Bull. EC 12–1992)

Annex 2 to Part A

Subsidiarity – Examples of the review of pending proposals and existing legislation

I.23.   The Birmingham European Council agreed that, to flesh out the subsidiarity principle, it would examine at Edinburgh the initial outcome of a Commission review of exiting community legislation, with examples.

The Commission has proceeded along three lines:

- in October it gave the other institutions the fruits of its reflections on subsidiarity in the form of a political, technical and legal analysis;
- it proposed broad lines for an interinstitutional agreement, which was substantially accepted by Parliament and well received by the Member States: the subsidiarity principle has an impact on all the three institutions involved in their respective ways in the decision-making and legislative process;
- the Commission, for its part, embarked on a review of pending proposals, an initial analysis of existing legislation, and deeper reflection on a number of initiatives that it was planning; in accordance with the conclusions of the Lisbon European Council the Commission will supplement this with a report to the December 1993 European Council on the results of its review of certain Community rules with a view to adapting them to the subsidiarity principle.

The Commission's first priority was to review all proposals pending before the Council and Parliament in the light of the subsidiarity principle.

It reviewed each proposal in terms both of the need-for-action criterion and of the intensity criterion – proportionality of resources deployed to objectives pursued.

The Commission has come to the conclusion that certain of its proposals were not fully warranted in terms either of value added by Community action or of comparative efficiency in relation to other possibilities of action in national or international contexts.

In this spirit it recently withdrew three proposals for Directives:

- compulsory indication of nutritional values on the packaging of foodstuffs;
- radio frequencies for land-based telecommunications with aircraft; and
- radio frequencies for remote-processing facilities in road transport.

After the proper contacts, notably with Parliament, it is further considering withdrawing the following proposals:

- measures proposed at the time of the Gulf crisis in the event of oil supply and stock difficulties in the Community;

- conditions in which animals are kept in zoos (there will be a proposal for a recommendation on this subject at a later date);
- radio frequencies for the co-ordinated introduction of digital short-range communications (DSRR);
- indirect taxation on transactions in securities;
- indirect taxation on capital accumulations;
- amendments to the Sixth VAT Directive;
- higher tax-free allowances for fuel in the tanks of utility vehicles;
- VAT on ships' supplies;
- temporary importation of motor vehicles;
- classification of documents of Community institutions;
- network of information centres on argricultural markets and quality standards.

The Commission has also concluded, notably following debates in Parliament and the Council, that certain pending proposals tend to go into excessive detail in relation to the objective pursued.

It is accordingly planning to revise a number of them so that they establish general principles to be given more detailed form by the Member States:

- public takeover bids;
- common definition of the concept of Community shipowner;
- comparative advertising;
- labelling of shoes;
- liability of suppliers of services;
- protection of natural persons in relation to data processed via digital telecommunications networks.

The Commission has also identified several families of existing rules and regulations which it intends to scrutinize as part of its programme for 1993.

As far as technical standards are concerned, a series of directives embodying excessively detailed specifications could be streamlined and replaced, under the new approach to harmonization, by minimum requirements to be met by products circulating freely within the Community. The directives in question relate in the main to foodstuffs (preserves, natural mineral waters, honey, coffee extracts, fruit juices). The Commission will also propose that the scope of certain directives be clarified. Although adopted under the new approach to harmonization, these texts (the low tension and machinery directives for instance) present problems of overlapping.

In the area of qualifications, the Commission will review the already quite old directives on certain regulated occupations to facilitate implementation and reinforce mutual recognition.

On the environment, the Commission intends to simplify, consolidate and update existing texts, particularly those on air and water, to take new knowledge and technical progress into account.

On agriculture, with particular reference to the clearance of accounts, the Commission intends to give national authorities more responsibility for applying Community legislation by allowing them, under certain conditions, to negotiate settlements with individuals.

As to animal welfare, accession by all the Member States to the European Convention on the Protection of Animals kept for Farming Purposes means that there is no point in retaining the Council directives introducing very strict standards, at Parliament's request, for the protection of pigs, calves and laying hens. However, minimum Community rules on animal welfare will be needed to guarantee fair competition and freedom of movement.

Turning to social policy, the Commission considers that the group of directives based on Article 118a of the Treaty is too recent to warrant re-examination. Instead its priority will be to supplement them by implementing all the provisions of the Charter of the Fundamental Social Rights of Workers. However, early steps will have to be taken to simplify and codify the body of older regulations on the free movement of workers.

Finally, the Commission can say that, following consultations with interested parties, it intends to abandon certain initiatives that had been planned.

It will not, for instance, be going ahead with proposals on the harmonization of vehicle number plates or the regulation of gambling.

Similarly, the Commission sees no need to continue preparatory work on the harmonization of certain technical standards (for instance, on dietary foods, second-hand machinery, structures and equipment for funfairs and theme parks, mechnical fixing and bolts in particular).

In more general terms the Commission is tending to use its monopoly of the right of initiative by declining to accept requests made by the Council at informal meetings that it make proposals for directives. In the same spirit it will be tougher about rejecting amendments proposed by the Council and Parliament that run counter to the proportionality rule or would unnecessarily complicate directives or recommendations that are in fact justified under the need-for-action criterion.

FREIGHT TRANSPORT ASSOCIATION LTD AND OTHERS v LONDON BOROUGHS TRANSPORT COMMITTEE [1991] 3 All ER 915, House of Lords

Two Directives imposed restrictions on vehicle brake and exhaust systems and stated that use of a vehicle which complied with these Directives could not be prohibited on grounds relating to its brakes or exhaust system. By UK statutory instrument, heavy goods vehicles were banned from using residential streets in London at night-time, unless they were fitted with a noise suppressor. The FTA challenged this condition on the ground that it contravened Community law.

It was held that the condition in the statutory instrument was valid.

LORD TEMPLEMAN (at p. 923c–924b and 927c–928c): The distinction between the control of vehicles and the regulation of traffic is fully recognised by Community law. Article 30 of the EEC Treaty provides: 'Quantitative restrictions on imports and all measures having equivalent effect shall . . . be prohibited . . .'. Article 130r deals with the environment and so far as relevant directs:

1. Action by the Community relating to the environment shall have the following objectives: (i) to preserve, protect and improve the quality of the environment; (ii) to contribute towards protecting human health; (iii) to ensure a prudent and rational utilization of natural resources.

2. Action by the Community relating to the environment shall be based on the principles that preventive action should be taken, that environmental damage should as a priority be rectified at source, and that the polluter should pay. Environmental protection requirements shall be a component of the Community's other policies . . .

4. The Community shall take action relating to the environment to the extent to which the objectives referred to in paragraph 1 can be attained better at Community level than at the level of the individual Member States. Without prejudice to certain measures of a Community nature, the Member States shall finance and implement the other measures . . .

Article 100 provides:

The Council shall, acting unanimously on a proposal from the Commission, issue directives for the approximation of such provisions laid down by law, regulation or administrative action in Member States as directly affect the establishment or functioning of the common market . . .

Pursuant to Art 100 the Council has issued 140 directives prescibing technical requirements and safety and environmental standards for vehicles, their components and spare parts so that national requirements and standards shall not infringe Art 30 or obstruct the free flow of goods and services throughout the Community. But paragraph 4 of Art 130r recognises that London's environmental traffic problems cannot be solved, although they can be ameliorated by Council directives to control every vehicle at all times throughout the Community.

The attainment of the Community object of preserving, protecting and improving the quality of the environment requires action at the level of individual Member States. A vehicle which complies with all the weight, size, sound level and other technical requirements and standards of directives issued by the Council pursuant to Art 100 and is therefore entitled to be used in every Member State throughout the Community is not thereby entitled to be driven on every road, on every day, at every hour throughout the Community. In the interests of the environment the traffic authorities of Santiago de Compostela may ban all or some Community vehicles from medieval streets. The traffic authorities of Greater London may ban all or some Community vehicles from residential streets at night. The ban may be limited to loud vehicles; the ban may be limited to some vehicles which are louder than others. Condition 11 bans some vehicles which are unnecessarily louder than others.

. . .

Finally the respondents sought a reference to the Court of Justice of the European Communities for a ruling under Article 177 of the EEC Treaty. It was said that a reference was necessary because the Court of Appeal had held that condition 11 infringed the brake directive and the sound level directive. Neill LJ, with whom the other members of the court agreed, mentioned the appellants' argument that the two directives—

> did not impinge on measures introduced by member states relating to the control of the movement of traffic or the protection of the environment, except to the extent that any such measures could be regarded as an indirect attempt to place a restriction on trade.

(See [1991] RTR 13 at 21.) Neill LJ attempted to deal with this argument by referring to the ruling of the Court of Justice in *Commission* v *UK* (Case 60/86) [1988] ECR 3921 (the *Dim-Dip* case), and also by referring to Art 2A of the brake directive and the sound level directive (see [1991] RTR 13 at 21).

My Lords, in my opinion, the Court of Appeal failed to recognise the fundamental distinction between the control of vehicles, necessarily subject to harmonisation by Community legislation, and the regulation of local traffic, which, as I have indicated and as the Commission has recognised, can only be carried out by local authorities. In the *Dim-Dip* case [*Re Dim-Dip Car Lights; Commission* v *United Kingdom* [1988] 3 CMLR 437] the minister had by the Road Vehicles Lighting Regulations 1984, SI 1984/812, prohibited the use of motor vehicles which were not equipped with the dim-dip lighting device. The European Court held that this regulation was inconsistent with a Community Directive relating to the installation of lighting and light signalling devices on motor vehicles and held that motor vehicles which complied with the directive must be able to move freely within the Common Market. The *Dim-Dip* case was concerned with the control of vehicles throughout the United Kingdom at all times, in all places, and was not concerned with the regulation of local traffic. The 1985 order and condition 11 do not interfere with the free movement of vehicles within the Common Market save to the extent that any traffic regulation proposed in the interests of the environment prevents some vehicles from operating on some roads at some times. The Court of Appeal was also wrong in thinking that Art 2A of the brake directive and the sound level directive inhibits the exercise by the appellants of their powers to regulate traffic in Greater London by banning certain traffic from roads at certain times in the interests of the environment and, in particular, for the purpose of reducing noise. The respondents concede that the 1985 order which imposed a ban on heavy commercial vehicles for the purpose of reducing noise at night was valid under Community law and was not affected by any directives. My Lords, the appellants were entitled to relax that admittedly valid ban in favour of some vehicles which were not so loud as other vehicles because they were fitted with noise suppressors. The air brakes of category (B) vehicles which are subject to the ban create a serious brake nuisance. The appellants were entitled to relax the ban on category (B) vehicles which are fitted with a suppressor and to maintain the ban on those category (B) vehicles which do not comply with the appellants' reasonable requirement to fit suppressors. Since the Court of Appeal did not appreciate the fundamental distinction between the control of vehicles and the regulation of local traffic I do not attach significance to its decision on Community law. In my opinion it is clear that the 1985 order and condition 11 are concerned solely with the regulation of local traffic. No plausible grounds have been advanced for a reference to the European Court.

I would allow this appeal, quash the orders made by the Court of Appeal and the Divisional Court, dismiss the respondents' action and order the respondents to pay the cost of the appellants in this House and in the courts below.

A. G. Toth, 'Is Subsidiarity Justiciable?' (1994) 19 EL Rev 268

Substantive assessment of subsidiarity

Whichever way the issue of subsidiarity comes before the Court of Justice, it involves the Court in assessing either an act of a Community institution (usually the Council) or a piece of national legislation or administrative action, from the point of view of its compatibility with Article 3b EC.

. . .

As seen above, Article 3b expressly provides that the principle of subsidiarity applies only 'in areas which do not fall within (the Community's) exclusive competence.' In areas which fall within its exclusive competence, only the Community can take action, not the Member States. Therefore, whenever an issue of subsidiarity comes before the Court, the Court necessarily has to decide two different questions in the following order:

First, does the matter with which the Community act or national legislation is concerned fall within exclusive or non-exclusive Community competence? If it falls within exclusive competence, the principle of subsidiarity cannot apply and that is the end of the matter.

Secondly, if the matter falls within non-exclusive competence, can the objectives of the Community act or national legislation in question be better achieved by the Community or by the Member States? In the first case the Community, in the second case the Member States, have power to act.

There can be hardly any doubt that the first question is a purely legal one and is therefore clearly justiciable. What is more, since competences are conferred by the Treaty, it involves Treaty interpretation and as such falls ultimately within the exclusive jurisdiction of the Court of Justice rather than being the subject of political agreement between the other institutions.

. . .

While the first question facing the Court in subsidiarity cases is always a purely legal one, the second is not. It involves the Court in assessing whether the objectives of a particular Community act (or national legislation) can be better achieved at the Community or at the national level. It is at this stage that the real difficulties begin. This requires a mainly political/economic assessment which exceeds the proper judicial function.

To understand the problem properly, it is necessary to go back to the very nature of the Court of Justice's jurisdiction. Following a well-known distinction made in French administrative law, in actions involving judicial review (such as actions for annulment or actions for failure to act) the Court may only exercise what is called 'limited jurisdiction', while in other actions (for example, actions for damages or actions against penalties) its jurisdiction is said to be 'unlimited' or 'plenary'. Limited jurisdiction means that the Court's power is restricted to reviewing the objective legality of the acts (or omissions) of the institutions, *i.e.* whether they are in conformity with the Treaty and other mandatory rules and principles of Community law. But, subject to certain exceptions, the Court may not review the appropriateness or expediency of the act in question, nor the underlying considerations involving questions of economic policy in the light of which it has been taken. The Court has only one power: to annul; but cannot substitute its own decision for the challenged act, nor vary or correct its terms. The Court cannot even indicate, still less prescribe, to the political institutions what particular act to take in compliance with its judgment.

The Court's powers are further restricted when reviewing acts taken by the institutions in exercise of their (sometimes very wide) discretionary powers, particularly when formulating or implementing economic policies. The exercise of these powers involves an evaluation of complex economic facts and market conditions and the choice of the appropriate means of action. In reviewing the exercise of such wide discretion, the Court's power is restricted to examining whether an act contains a manifest error in the evaluation of the economic, etc., situation or constitutes a misuse of powers, or whether the institutions did not clearly exceed the bounds of their discretion. But the Court is not entitled to enter the actual area of the discretion itself, *i.e.* the sphere of suitability or expediency. It cannot examine whether the measure is good, appropriate or adequate. Nor can the Court substitute its own assessment of the economic situation for that of the institutions. By so doing, the Court would replace the legislative discretion of the Council and the Commission by its own views and, under the disguise of judicial review, it would assume the role of the supreme legislature in the Community. Besides, the Court is not equipped in terms of staff, facilities and expertise to undertake the necessary research to make complex economic and political judgments of this kind.

If these principles apply generally, they must apply *a fortiori* when the Court is confronted with issues of subsidiarity. How can the Court verify whether or not the objectives of sometimes complex measures which may involve policy decisions (for example, in the field of environmental protection) can be sufficiently achieved by the Member States, and whether or not they can be better achieved by the Community? The Court's task is made even more impossible by the European Council's view of subsidiarity as 'a dynamic concept (which) allows Community action to be expanded where circumstances so require, and conversely, to be restricted or discontinued where it is no longer justified.' This obviously creates an ill-defined, ever-changing boundary between Community and Member State powers in areas of shared competence which is subject to very subjective interpretation. But even if the Court could undertake such a task (which is doubtful, given its lack of staff, expertise and facilities), and would annul a Community act on subsidiarity grounds, would this not mean that the Court has substituted itself for the Council as the chief legislator? Therefore, in accordance with the above principles, all that the Court may be expected to do in cases involving the application of Article 3b in areas of shared competence is to examine whether in arriving at its decision the Council has not committed a manifest error or a misuse of powers or has not patently exceeded the bounds of its discretion. These are the ultimate limits of justiciability of subsidiarity.

In carrying out its review within the above limits, the Court will have particular regard to the statement of reasons of the Community act concerned and in particular to the legal basis of the act. This is the main means whereby the Court can control the institutions' discretionary powers. In accordance with the European Council's guidelines and the Interinstitutional Agreement of October 25, 1993, the preamble to an act must always contain a recital justifying the relevance of the act with regard to the subsidiarity principle. While Article 3b alone cannot form the legal basis of an act, insufficient reference to it may serve as a ground for annulment as it may be regarded by the Court as a lack of adequate reasoning.

The Court will also look very carefully at the legal basis of the act (the Treaty Article on which the act is based). In the context of subsidiarity, control of the proper choice of the legal basis will play an important part of judicial review. The reason is that there are many situations in which an act may possibly be adopted on two different legal bases, one of which may indicate exclusive competence (for example, Article 130s EC concerning environmental protection). If an act is adopted on the first basis, this excludes the application of subsidiarity. If it is adopted on the second basis, then the principle of subsidiarity applies to it. In a number of cases, the Court has said that the choice of the legal basis may not depend simply on an institution's conviction as to the objectives pursued but must be based on objective factors which are amenable to judicial review. Those factors include in particular the aim and content of the measure.

Therefore, in examining whether a measure satisfies Article 3b, the Court will look into the objectives of the measure to see if it pursues an aim (for example, the establishment of the internal market) which may be lawfully pursued under a Treaty Article which creates exclusive competence (for example, Article 100a). If so, subsidiarity does not apply. If it pursues an aim which may be lawfully pursued under another Article which creates non-exclusive competence (for example, Article 130s), the measure may only be adopted if this aim can be better achieved at Community level.

The choice of the proper legal basis was the main issue in the *Titanium Dioxide* case. There, the Commission proposed a directive harmonizing the programmes for the reduction and eventual elimination of pollution caused by waste from the titanium dioxide industry. The Commission chose Article 100a as a legal basis, but the Council adopted the directive on the basis of Article 130s. Article 100a deals with the establishment of the internal market, requires recourse to the co-operation procedure and the Council acts by a qualified majority. Article 130s deals with the protection of the environment, requires mere consultation of the European Parliament and the Council can act only unanimously. For reasons which need not be gone into here, the Court of Justice held that Article 100a was the proper legal basis and annulled the directive for that reason.

While the case did not raise issues of subsidiarity directly (it was decided in June 1991), it does show the importance of the correct legal basis. If in this case the main issue had been whether the directive fell within the scope of subsidiarity, the Court would probably have given a negative answer on grounds of exclusive competence generated by Article 100a, in spite of the fact that the directive was an environmental policy measure which is an area prima facie governed by subsidiarity.

THE TREATY OF ROME

Article 74

The objectives of this Treaty shall, in matters governed by this Title, be pursued by Member States within the framework of a common transport policy.

THE TREATY OF ROME

Article 100c

1. The Council, acting unanimously on a proposal from the Commission and after consulting the European Parliament, shall determine the third countries whose nationals must be in possession of a visa when crossing the external borders of the Member States.

2. However, in the event of an emergency situation in a third country posing a threat of a sudden inflow of nationals from that country into the Community, the Council, acting by a qualified majority on a recommendation from the Commission, may introduce, for a period not exceeding six months, a visa requirement for nationals from the country in question. The visa requirements established under this paragraph may be extended in accordance with the procedure referred to in paragraph 1.

3. From 1 January 1996, the Council shall adopt the decisions referred to in paragraph 1 by a qualified majority. The Council shall, before this date, acting by a qualified majority on a proposal from the Commission and after consulting the European Parliament, adopt measures relating to a uniform format for visas.

4. In the areas referred to in this Article, the Commission shall examine any request made by a Member State that it submit a proposal to the Council.

5. This Article shall be without prejudice to the exercise of the responsibilities incumbent upon the Member States with regard to the maintenance of law and order and the safeguarding of internal security.

6. This Article shall apply to other areas if so decided pursuant to Article K.9 of the provisions of the Treaty on European Union which relate to co-operation in the fields of justice and home affairs, subject to the voting conditions determined at the same time.

7. The provisions of the conventions in force between the Member States governing areas covered by this Article shall remain in force until their content has been replaced by directives or measures adopted pursuant to this Article.

THE TREATY OF ROME

Article 7a

The Community shall adopt measures with the aim of progressively establishing the internal market over a period expiring on 31 December 1992, in accordance with the provisions of this Article and of Articles 7b, 7c, 28, 57(2), 59, 70(1), 84, 99,100a and 100b and without prejudice to the other provisions of this Treaty.

The internal market shall comprise an area without internal frontiers in which the free movement of goods, persons, services and capital is ensured in accordance with the provisions of this Treaty.

4.2.2 CITIZENSHIP

THE TREATY OF ROME

Article 8

1. Citizenship of the Union is hereby established.

Every person holding the nationality of a Member State shall be a citizen of the Union.

2.   Citizens of the Union shall enjoy the rights conferred by this Treaty and shall be subject to the duties imposed thereby.

THE TREATY OF ROME

Article 8b
1.   Every citizen of the Union residing in a Member State of which he is not a national shall have the right to vote and to stand as a candidate at municipal elections in the Member State in which he resides, under the same conditions as nationals of that State. This right shall be exercised subject to detailed arrangements to be adopted before 31 December 1994 by the Council, acting unanimously on a proposal from the Commission and after consulting the European Parliament; these arrangements may provide for derogations where warranted by problems specific to a Member State.
2.   Without prejudice to Article 138(3) and to the provisions adopted for its implementation, every citizen of the Union residing in a Member State of which he is not a national shall have the right to vote and to stand as a candidate in elections to the European Parliament in the Member State in which he resides, under the same conditions as nationals of that State. This right shall be exercised subject to detailed arrangements to be adopted before 31 December 1993 by the Council, acting unanimously on a proposal from the Commission and after consulting the European Parliament; these arrangements may provide for derogations where warranted by problems specific to a Member State.

THE TREATY OF ROME

Article 8c
Every citizen of the Union shall, in the territory of a third country in which the Member State of which he is a national is not represented, be entitled to protection by the diplomatic or consular authorities of any Member State, on the same conditions as the nationals of that State. Before 31 December 1993, Member States shall establish the necessary rules among themselves and start the international negotiations required to secure this protection.

THE TREATY OF ROME

Article 8d.
Every citizen of the Union shall have the right to petition the European Parliament in accordance with Article 138d.
    Every citizen of the Union may apply to the Ombudsman established in accordance with Article 138e.

E. Marias, 'The Right to Petition the European Parliament after Maastricht' (1994) EL Rev 169

The Committee on Petitions and the European Ombudsman
According to Article 138e EC, the European Ombudsman is empowered to receive complaints concerning instances of maladministration in the activities of the Community institutions or bodies with the exception of the Court of Justice and the Court of First Instance acting in their judicial role. As these complaints also fall under the competence of the Committee on Petitions the danger of an overlap in the competences of these two bodies is quite evident. In its search for a compromise on the issue after the establishment of the European Ombudsman, the Committee on Petitions emphasised its role as a link between the Ombudsman and the European Parliament and stated in its opinion regarding the duties of the European Ombudsman for the Committee of Institutional Affairs, that the activities of these two respective bodies should complement each other. Accordingly, political matters will essentially be dealt with by the Committee on Petitions as will the political assessment of an instance of maladministration. Parliament could also forward to the European Ombudsman those petitions which it considers could be dealt more effectively by him. On his part, the European Ombudsman could refer to the Committee on Petitions those complaints which he considers as being outside his jurisdiction.
    In conclusion, we would like to state that any overlap of competences between these two bodies should not be to the detriment of the citizens of the Union. To the contrary,

the collaboration of the Committee on Petitions with the European Ombudsman and *vice versa* is essential for the protection of the rights of the European citizen.

The work of the Committee on Petitions and its political significance
According to the Annual Reports of the Committee on Petitions of the European Parliament the number of petitions submitted to it is continually rising.
. . .

There has been a significant increase in mass petitions. Petition No. 280/91, submitted by the British Union for the Abolition of Vivisection, opposing the testing of cosmetic products on animals, was signed by 2,500,000 petitioners. Also Petition No. 250/91 regarding cruelty to animals was signed by 1,000,000 petitioners. Petitions are important for the European Parliament as they constitute a permanent link with the citizens of the Union. It is a means of contact with the Union's citizens which allows them to gain a better understanding of the institution's roles and workings. Petitions are also a very effective means for the European Parliament of verifying the application of Community law and of resolving the problems brought to light. In this respect its strengthens the role of the European Parliament in the institutional framework and reinforces its powers to exercise control.

As a democratically elected body, the Parliament uses petitions as a means to establish a permanent dialogue with the citizens of the Union and as an opportunity to demonstrate its willingness to listen to their problems. At the same time, the citizens, by submitting petitions, have the chance to participate directly in the political life of the Community.

As the content of petitions often points to genuine needs or expresses a general feeling of unease, the European Parliament has emphasised the need that each citizen of the Union must be made fully aware of this right and the conditions under which it can be exercised.

4.2.3   ECONOMIC AND SOCIAL COHESION

PROTOCOL ON ECONOMIC AND SOCIAL COHESION

THE HIGH CONTRACTING PARTIES,
  RECALLING that the Union has set itself the objective of promoting economic and social progress, inter alia, through the strengthening of economic and social cohesion;
  RECALLING that Article 2 of this Treaty includes the task of promoting economic and social cohesion and solidarity between Member States and that the strengthening of economic and social cohesion figures among the activities of the Community listed in Article 3;
  RECALLING that the provisions of Part Three, Title XIV, on economic and social cohesion as a whole provide the legal basis for consolidating and further developing the Community's action in the field of economic and social cohesion, including the creation of a new fund;
  RECALLING that the provisions of Part Three, Title XII on trans-European networks and Title XVI on environment envisage a Cohesion Fund to be set up before 31 December 1993;
  STATING their belief that progress towards Economic and Monetary Union will contribute to the economic growth of all Member States;
  NOTING that the Community's Structural Funds are being doubled in real terms between 1987 and 1993, implying large transfers, especially as a proportion of GDP of the less prosperous Member States;
  NOTING that the EIB is lending large and increasing amounts for the benefit of the poorer regions;
  NOTING the desire for greater flexibility in the arrangements for allocations from the Structural Funds;
  NOTING the desire for modulation of the levels of Community participation in programmes and projects in certain countries;
  NOTING the proposal to take greater account of the relative prosperity of Member States in the system of own resources;
  REAFFIRM that the promotion of economic and social cohesion is vital to the full development and enduring success of the Community, and underline the importance of the inclusion of economic and social cohesion in Articles 2 and 3 of this Treaty;

REAFFIRM their conviction that the Structural Funds should continue to play a considerable part in the achievement of Community objectives in the field of cohesion;

REAFFIRM their conviction that the European Investment Bank should continue to devote the majority of its resources to the promotion of economic and social cohesion, and declare their willingness to review the capital needs of the European Investment Bank as soon as this is necessary for that purpose;

REAFFIRM the need for a thorough evaluation of the operation and effectiveness of the Structural Funds in 1992, and the need to review, on that occasion, the appropriate size of these Funds in the light of the tasks of the Community in the area of economic and social cohesion;

AGREE that the Cohesion Fund to be set up before 31 December 1993 will provide Community financial contributions to projects in the field of environment and trans-European networks in Member States with a per capita GNP of less than 90% of the Community average which have a programme leading to the fulfilment of the conditions of economic convergence as set out in Article 104c;

DECLARE their intention of allowing a greater margin of flexibility in allocating financing from the Structural Funds to specific needs not covered under the present Structural Funds regulations;

DECLARE their willingness to modulate the levels of Community participation in the context of programmes and projects of the Structural Funds, with a view to avoiding excessive increases in budgetary expenditure in the less prosperous Member States;

RECOGNISE the need to monitor regularly the progress made towards achieving economic and social cohesion and state their willingness to study all necessary measures in this respect;

DECLARE their intention of taking greater account of the contributive capacity of individual Member States in the system of own resources, and of examining means of correcting, for the less prosperous Member States, regressive elements existing in the present own resources system;

AGREE to annex this Protocol to this Treaty.

4.2.4   ECONOMIC AND MONETARY UNION

THE TREATY OF ROME

Article 3a

1.   For the purposes set out in Article 2, the activities of the Member States and the Community shall include, as provided in this Treaty and in accordance with the timetable set out therein, the adoption of an economic policy which is based on the close co-ordination of Member States' economic policies, on the internal market and on the definition of common objectives, and conducted in accordance with the principle of an open market economy with free competition.

2.   Concurrently with the foregoing, and as provided in this Treaty and in accordance with the timetable and the procedures set out therein, these activities shall include the irrevocable fixing of exchange rates leading to the introduction of a single currency, the ECU, and the definition and conduct of a single monetary policy and exchange rate policy the primary objective of both of which shall be to maintain price stability and, without prejudice to this objective, to support the general economic policies in the Community, in accordance with the principle of an open market economy with free competition.

3.   These activities of the Member States and the Community shall entail compliance with the following guiding principles; stable prices, sound public finances and monetary conditions and a sustainable balance of payments.

4.2.4.1   The convergence criteria for entry into the third stage

THE TREATY OF ROME

Article 109j

1.   The Commission and the EMI [European Monetary Institute] shall report to the Council on the progress made in the fulfilment by the Member States of their obligations

regarding the achievement of economic and monetary union. These reports shall include an examination of the compatibility between each Member State's national legislation, including the statutes of its national central bank, and Articles 107 and 108 of this Treaty and the Statute of the ESCB. The reports shall also examine the achievement of a high degree of sustainable convergence by reference to the fulfilment by each Member State of the following criteria:

– the achievement of a high degree of price stability; this will be apparent from a rate of inflation which is close to that of, at most, the three best performing Member States in terms of price stability;

– the sustainability of the government financial position; this will be apparent from having achieved a government budgetary position without a deficit that is excessive as determined in accordance with Article 104c(6);

– the observance of the normal fluctuation margins provided for by the Exchange Rate Mechanism of the European Monetary System, for at least two years, without devaluing against the currency of any other Member State;

– the durability of convergence achieved by the Member State and of its participation in the Exchange Rate Mechanism of the European Monetary System being reflected in the long-term interest rate levels.

The four criteria mentioned in this paragraph and the relevant periods over which they are to be respected are developed further in a Protocol annexed to this Treaty. The reports of the Commission and the EMI shall also take account of the development of the ECU, the results of the integration of markets, the situation and development of the balances of payments on current account and an examination of the development of unit labour costs and other price indices.

2.　On the basis of these reports, the Council, acting by a qualified majority on a recommendation from the Commission, shall assess:

– for each Member State, whether it fulfils the necessary conditions for the adoption of a single currency;

– whether a majority of the Member States fulfil the necessary conditions for the adoption of a single currency,

and recommended its findings to the Council, meeting in the composition of the Heads of State or of Government. The European Parliament shall be consulted and forward its opinion to the Council, meeting in the composition of the Heads of State or of Government.

3.　Taking due account of the reports referred to in paragraph 1 and the opinion of the European Parliament referred to in paragraph 2, the Council, meeting in the composition of Heads of State or of Government, shall, acting by a qualified majority, not later than 31 December 1996:

– decide, on the basis of the recommendations of the Council referred to in paragraph 2, whether a majority of the Member States fulfil the necessary conditions for the adoption of a single currency;

– decide whether it is appropriate for the Community to enter the third stage,
and if so;

– set the date for the beginning of the third stage.

4.　If by the end of 1997 the date for the beginning of the third stage has not been set, the third stage shall start on 1 January 1999. Before 1 July 1998, the Council, meeting in the composition of Heads of State or of Government, after a repetition of the procedure provided for in paragraphs 1 and 2, with the exception of the second indent of paragraph 2, taking into account the reports referred to in paragraph 1 and the opinion of the European Parliament, shall, acting by a qualified majority and on the basis of the recommendations of the Council referred to in paragraph 2, confirm which Member States fulfil the necessary conditions for the adoption of a single currency.

4.2.4.2　The second stage of EMU

THE TREATY OF ROME

Article 104

1.　Overdraft facilities or any other type of credit facility with the ECB or with the central banks of the Member States (hereinafter referred to as 'national central banks') in favour of Community institutions or bodies, central governments, regional, local or other public authorities, other bodies governed by public law, or public undertakings of Member States shall be prohibited, as shall the purchase directly from them by the ECB or national central banks of debt instruments.

2. Paragraph 1 shall not apply to publicly-owned credit institutions which, in the context of the supply of reserves by central banks, shall be given the same treatment by national central banks and the ECB as private credit institutions.

THE TREATY OF ROME

Article 104a

1. Any measure, not based on prudential considerations, establishing privileged access by Community institutions or bodies, central governments, regional, local or other public authorities, other bodies governed by public law, or public undertakings of Member States to financial institutions shall be prohibited.

2. The Council, acting in accordance with the procedure referred to in Article 189c, shall, before 1 January 1994, specify definitions for the application of the prohibition referred to in paragraph 1.

THE TREATY OF ROME

Article 104b

1. The Community shall not be liable for or assume the commitments of central governments, regional, local or other public authorities, other bodies governed by public law, or public undertakings of any Member State, without prejudice to mutual financial guarantees for the joint execution of a specific project. A Member State shall not be liable for or assume the commitments of central governments, regional, local or other public authorities, other bodies governed by public law or public undertakings of another Member State, without prejudice to mutual financial guarantees for the joint execution of a specific project.

2. If necessary, the Council, acting in accordance with the procedure referred to in Article 189c, may specify definitions for the application of the prohibition referred to in Article 104 and in this Article.

4.2.4.3 The third stage of EMU

THE TREATY OF ROME

Article 104c

1. Member States shall avoid excessive government deficits.

. . .

9. If a Member State persists in failing to put into practice the recommendations of the Council, the Council may decide to give notice to the Member State to take, within a specified time limit, measures for the deficit reduction which is judged necessary by the Council in order to remedy the situation.

In such case, the Council may request the Member State concerned to submit reports in accordance with a specific timetable in order to examine the adjustment efforts of that Member State.

. . .

11. As long as a Member State fails to comply with a decision taken in accordance with paragraph 9, the Council may decide to apply or, as the case may be, intensify one or more of the following measures:
– to require the Member State concerned to publish additional information to be specified by the Council, before issuing bonds and securities;
– to invite the European Investment Bank to reconsider its lending policy towards the Member State concerned;
– to require the Member State concerned to make a non-interest-bearing deposit of an appropriate size with the Community until the excessive deficit has, in the view of the Council, been corrected;

– to impose fines of an appropriate size.

The President of the Council shall inform the European Parliament of the decisions taken.

THE TREATY OF ROME

Article 105

1.   The primary objective of the ESCB shall be to maintain price stability. Without prejudice to the objective of price stability, the ESCB shall support the general economic policies in the Community with a view to contributing to the achievement of the objectives of the Community as laid down in Article 2. The ESCB shall act in accordance with the principle of an open market economy with free competition, favouring an efficient allocation of resources, and in compliance with the principles set out in Article 3a.

2.   The basic tasks to be carried out through the ESCB shall be:

– to define and implement the monetary policy of the Community;

– to conduct foreign exchange operations consistent with the provisions of Article 109;

– to hold and manage the official foreign reserves of the Member States;

– to promote the smooth operation of payment systems.

3.   The third indent of paragraph 2 shall be without prejudice to the holding and management by the governments of Member States of foreign exchange working balances.

4.   The ECB shall be consulted:

– on any proposed Community act in its field of competence;

– by national authorities regarding any draft legislative provision in its fields of competence, but within the limits and under the conditions set out by the Council in accordance with the procedure laid down in Article 106(6).

The ECB may submit opinions to the appropriate Community institutions or bodies or to national authorities on matters within its field of competence.

5.   The ESCB shall contribute to the smooth conduct of policies pursued by the competent authorities relating to the prudential supervision of credit institutions and the stability of the financial system.

6.   The Council may, acting unanimously on a proposal from the Commission and after consulting the ECB and after receiving the assent of the European Parliament, confer upon the ECB specific tasks concerning policies relating to the prudential supervision of credit institutions and other financial institutions with the exception of insurance undertakings.

4.2.4.4

THE TREATY OF ROME

Article 109k

1.   If the decision has been taken to set the date in accordance with Article 109j(3), the Council shall, on the basis of its recommendations referred to in Article 109j(2), acting by a qualified majority on a recommendation from the Commission, decide whether any, and if so which, Member States shall have a derogation as defined in paragraph 3 of this Article. Such Member States shall in this Treaty be referred to as 'Member States with a derogation'.

If the Council has confirmed which Member States fulfil the necessary conditions for the adoption of a single currency, in accordance with Article 109j(4), those Member States which do not fulfil the conditions shall have a derogation as defined in paragraph 3 of this Article. Such Member States shall in this Treaty be referred to as 'Member States with a derogation'.

2.   At least once every two years, or at the request of a Member State with a derogation, the Commission and the ECB shall report to the Council in accordance with the procedure laid down in Article 109j(1). After consulting the European Parliament and after discussion in the Council, meeting in the composition of the Heads of State or of Government, the Council shall, acting by a qualified majority on a proposal from the

Commission, decide which Member States with a derogation fulfil the necessary conditions on the basis of the critia set out in Article 109j(1), and abrogate the derogations of the Member States concerned.

3. A derogation referred to in paragraph 1 shall entail that the following Articles do not apply to the Member States concerned: Articles 104c(9) and (11), 105(1), (2), (3) and (5), 105a, 108a, 109, and 109a(2)(b). The exclusion of such a Member State and its national central bank from the rights and obligations within the ESCB is laid down in Chapter IX of the Statute of the ESCB.

4. In Articles 105(1), (2) and (3), 105a, 108a, 109, and 109a(2)(b), 'Member States' shall be read as 'Member States without a derogation'.

5. The voting rights of Member States with a derogation shall be suspended for the Council decisions referred to in the Articles of this Treaty mentioned in paragraph 3. In that case, by way of derogation from Articles 148 and 189a(1), a qualified majority shall be defined as two thirds of the votes of the representatives of the Member States without a derogation weighted in accordance with Article 148(2), and unanimity of those Member States shall be required for an act requiring unanimity.

6. Articles 109h and 109i shall continue to apply to a Member State with a derogation.

PROTOCOL ON CERTAIN PROVISIONS RELATING TO THE UNITED KINGDOM OF GREAT BRITAIN AND NORTHERN IRELAND

THE HIGH CONTRACTING PARTIES,

RECOGNISING that the United Kingdom shall not be obliged or committed to move to the third stage of Economic and Monetary Union without a separate decision to do so by its government and Parliament,

NOTING the practice of the government of the United Kingdom to find its borrowing requirement by the sale of debt to the private sector,

HAVE AGREED the following provisions, which shall be annexed to the Treaty establishing the European Community:

1. The United Kingdom shall notify the Council whether it intends to move to the third stage before the Council makes it assessment under Article 109j(2) of this Treaty.

Unless the United Kingdom notifies the Council that it intends to move to the third stage, it shall be under no obligation to do so.

If no date is set for the beginning of the third stage under Article 109j(3) of this Treaty, the United Kingdom may notify its intention to move to the third stage before 1 January 1998.

2. Paragraphs 3 and 9 shall have effect if the United Kingdom notifies the Council that it does not intend to move to the third stage.

3. The United Kingdom shall not be included among the majority of Member States which fulfil the necessary conditions referred to in the second indent of Article 109j(2) and the first indent of Article 109j(3) of this Treaty.

4. The United Kingdom shall retain its powers in the field of monetary policy according to national law.

5. Articles 3a(2), 104c(1), (9) and (11), 105(1) to (5), 105a, 107, 108, 108a, 109, 109a(1) and (2)(b) and 109i(4) and (5) of this Treaty shall not apply to the United Kingdom. In these provisions references to the Community or the Member States shall not include the United Kindom and references to national central banks shall not include the Bank of England.

6. Articles 109e(4) and 109h and i of this Treaty shall continue to apply to the United Kingdom. Articles 109c(4) and 109m shall apply to the United Kingdom as if it had a derogation.

7. The voting rights of the United Kingdom shall be suspended in respect of acts of the Council referred to in the Articles listed in paragraph 5. For this purpose the weighted votes of the United Kingdom shall be excluded from any calculation of a qualified majority under Article 109k(5) of this Treaty.

The United Kingdom shall also have no right to participate in the appointment of the President, the Vice-President and the other members of the Executive Board of the ECB under Articles 109a(2)(b) and 109i(1) of this Treaty.

8.   Articles 3, 4, 6, 7, 9.2, 10.1, 10.3, 11.2, 12.1, 14, 16, 18 to 20, 22, 23, 26, 27, 30 to 34, 50 and 52 of the Protocol on the Statute of the European System of Central Banks and of the European Central Bank ('the Statute') shall not apply to the United Kingdom.

In those Articles, references to the Community or the Member States shall not include the United Kingdom and references to national central banks or shareholders shall not include the Bank of England.

References in Articles 10.3 and 30.2 of the Statute to 'subscribed capital of the ECB' shall not include capital subscribed by the Bank of England.

9.   Article 109i(3) of this Treaty and Articles 44 to 48 of the Statute shall have effect, whether or not there is any Member State with a derogation, subject to the following amendments:

(a)   References in Article 44 to the tasks of the ECB and the EMI shall include those tasks that still need to be performed in the third stage owing to any decision of the United Kingdom not to move to that stage.

(b)   In addition to the tasks referred to in Article 47 the ECB shall also give advice in relation to and contribute to the preparation of any decision of the Council with regard to the United Kingdom taken in accordance with paragraphs 10(a) and 10(c).

(c)   The Bank of England shall pay up its subscription to the capital of the ECB as a contribution to its operational costs on the same basis as national central banks of Member States with a derogation.

10.   If the United Kingdom does not move to the third stage, it may change its notification at any time after the beginning of that stage. In that event:

(a)   The United Kingdom shall have the right to move to the third stage provided only that it satisfies the necessary conditions. The council, acting at the request of the United Kingdom and under the conditions and in accordance with the procedure laid down in Article 109k(2) of this Treaty, shall decide whether it fulfils the necessary conditions.

(b)   The Bank of England shall pay up its subscribed capital, transfer to the ECB foreign reserve assets and contribute to its reserves on the same basis as the national central bank of a Member State whose derogation has been abrogated.

(c)   The Council, acting under the conditions and in accordance with the procedure laid down in Article 109i(5) of this Treaty, shall take all other necessary decisions to enable the United Kingdom to move to the third stage.

If the United Kingdom moves to the third stage pursuant to the provisions of this protocol, paragraphs 3 to 9 shall cease to have effect.

11.   Notwithstanding Articles 104 and 109e(3) of this Treaty and Article 21.1 of the Statute, the government of the United Kingdom may maintain its Ways and Means facility with the Bank of England if and so long as the United Kingdom does not move to the third stage.

R. O'Rourke, 'Changing to Eurocurrency' (1998) 148 NLJ 82

In the aftermath of Chancellor Gordon Brown's Commons Statement at the end of October concerning the United Kingdom's position on the EURO currency, attention in Britain has turned to the more practical aspects of how a single currency will be established on January 1, 2002. In many ways, the Chancellor, although pointing out that the United Kingdom would not join in the first wave of countries in 2002, left the door open for the United Kingdom to join at a later stage in 2002 or early 2003. More recently, the Chancellor and the Prime Minister won a pyrrhic victory at the Luxembourg Summit, by ensuring that an economic consideration body between countries of the EURO zone, to be called Euro-X, would permit the presence of the United Kingdom when issues affecting sterling would be discussed. As the debate at the most recent ECOFIN Council on December 1 showed, the EURO is going ahead and other Member States, in particular France and Germany, will not countenance measures to obstruct its introduction. The Chancellor and the Prime Minister discovered that the UK will get no special treatment in relation to the EURO; it will simply be a question of whether the UK wants to join or not.

Whatever arguments one might read in the financial newspapers about the likely list of countries that will be able to participate in the Single Currency, in line with the various

Maastricht criteria for entry, the United Kingdom could be said, at this juncture, to be in the preparatory stage towards the introduction of the EURO. The Government's urgency in this area is shown by the fact that on November 25 it invited the main UK banks and the four big accountancy firms to a meeting in 11 Downing Street to discuss preparations for the EURO and in particular to ensure that the public information campaigns being prepared by these accountancy firms/banks were accurate. In September a National Westminster survey showed that only 7% of UK firms have established a strategic plan to prepare for the EURO; while 60% of firms have done nothing in terms of preparation for the likely introduction of a single currency after January 1, 2002.

In Brussels, despite the fact that a considerable amount of time, both in the European Council and the European Commission, is taken up in analysing the likely countries that will participate in the single currency in the year 2002, the EU institutions have not forgotten about the practical aspects of the introduction of a single currency. Much of the political debate about the EURO deals with the likelihood of the establishment of the currency in the first place but consumers and businesses who will have to work in the Single Market/Single Currency area should be investigating this issue in order to prepare adequately for this major development in the very near future. In this context, the European Commission published a Communication in October 1997 entitled *Practical Aspects of the Introduction of the EURO*, where they deal with many of these issues. Four particular questions need to be answered in order to assist in the transformation towards a European currency in 1999/2002. The questions are:

• **When to put coins and bank notes in EUROs, into circulation?** The European Council in Madrid set the date at January 1, 2002 but the Commission is coming under considerable pressure to change the date for the introduction of coins and bank notes, due to the fact that retailers in all the 15 Member States believe this date is inconvenient for working patterns. The start date January 1, 2002 is too close to the busiest time of the year, the Christmas/January sales, for retailers to prepare adequately for such a major transformation in their monetary transactions.

• **How long will the simultaneous circulation of national currencies and EUROs last?** The European Council in Madrid, in December 1995, set this period at six months which is written into the Maastricht treaty but this seems somewhat long. The Commission, therefore, is now returning to its initial idea of limiting this period to a few weeks.

• **How to assist consumers and retailers adapt to the new pricing policy under a EURO currency?** Dual labelling is obviously a useful instrument in assisting consumers in this area but the European Commission is at present investigating whether this labelling should be compulsory, whether it should cover all items and whether it should include denominations such as price per kilo/unit.

• **How will the banks be invoicing the services they will provide in the transitional period from 1999 to 2001?** The Commission is concerned about the possible costs of conversions both of bank accounts in the period 1999 to 2001 and coins during the final exchange period, following the introduction of legal tender in 2002.

Following a Round Table Conference in Brussels, in May 1997, on the political aspects of the changeover to the EURO and the publication of the Commission's October Communication, the Commission subsequently established four expert consultative groups to consider some of the technical issues on which further work is required. The plan was that these groups would complete their work by Christmas. The Commission is then planning to hold another Round Table in the early part of 1998 and hopes to be able to make an announcement about decisions in these areas at the same time that the participating members are chosen next Spring. The original idea had been that the Commission would have been able to make all these decisions by the end of 1997. But some of the practical issues are far more difficult to solve than was at first thought by the Commission. The European Parliament is also putting pressure on the Commission to make decisions on these issues as soon as possible. It adopted a report and Resolution on Stage III of EMU at its plenary aspects of the changeover to the EURO.

In terms of the four expert consultative groups, one of them is considering banking and conversion charges, a second is advising on the dual pricing, a third is looking at help for consumers adjusting to the EURO. The fourth group is dealing with the role of information campaigns and SMEs and the EURO. These four groups are organised and co-ordinated by DGXV (Financial Services and Internal Market) and each group consists of ten recognised experts from eight different Member States, drawn from both the banking and financial sectors and from user groups including consumers, small and medium-sized enterprises and large firms. The members of these groups are participating in a personal capacity rather than as representatives of their organisations/Member State. The European Monetary Institute also agreed to participate at these meetings. The groups met on a fortnightly basis in Brussels last autumn and various European trade associations with links to banks, consumers and enterprises have been asked to give both oral and written presentations to the various groups.

In the last few years, the EU institutions and European politicians in general, have concentrated to an extraordinary degree on the question of whether a single currency is viable, rather than asking how a single currency will work in practice, both for businesses and consumers. The European Commission is slowly coming round to the idea that in order to ensure the viability of the EURO it is necessary to make decisions quickly on a number of issues and in particular on the four questions raised, such as dual pricing and the actual date for the introduction of legal tender. Because UK businesses, accountancy firms and by implication legal firms seem to be unprepared for any of these changes, it is most important that time should be made up in the coming months to ensure that whenever the United Kingdom joins following 2002, businesses are aware of what trading with a single currency area will entail. The United Kingdom's transitional period will be longer than most countries, since it could be said that the country is going through that stage now. On the other hand, when the United Kingdom finally decides to join the EURO, the period of dual currencies is likely to be even shorter than the time allotted for the members joining on January 1, 2002—thereby adding pressure on UK companies to adopt more quickly than their continental counterparts to the EURO in order to ensure that they gain all the advantages of trading in a single currency area immediately.

Many decisions have still to be made, both in Brussels and London but there is little doubt that those who remain on the sidelines in the hope that the entire single currency project may falter, are indulging in a very risky strategy. There is little doubt that the single currency will go forward, beginning on January 1, 1999 with the introduction of legal tender in the year 2002, although there are still many practical issues on the introduction of the currency to be ironed out. It is therefore all the more necessary for businesses, consumers and lawyers in the UK to prepare not only for a single currency but also, prepare to trade for a short to medium term period with a single currency area. The UK will therefore have the additional problems involved in preparing for a two dimensional relationship with the EURO Currency—an early stage trading with a single currency area and a later stage actually participating within the single currency itself. Unless UK businesses take the lead from the new Labour Government and prepare adequately for these two scenarios, there is every likelihood that the United Kingdom will, by staying on the sidelines, repeat the mistakes it made earlier in terms of membership of the EU, which could have detrimental effects on its national economic interests.

4.2.5 COMMON FOREIGN AND SECURITY POLICY

THE TREATY ON EUROPEAN UNION

Article J.1

1. The Union and its Member States shall define and implement a common foreign and security policy, governed by the provisions of this Title and covering all areas of foreign and security policy.

2. The objectives of the common foreign and security policy shall be:

– to safeguard the common values, fundamental interests and independence of the Union;

– to strengthen the security of the Union and its Member States in all ways;

– to preserve peace and strengthen international security, in accordance with the principles of the United Nations Charter as well as the principles of the Helsinki Final Act and the objectives of the Paris Charter;

– to promote international cooperation;

– to develop and consolidate democracy and the rule of law, and respect for human rights and fundamental freedoms.

3.   The Union shall pursue these objectives:

– by establishing systematic cooperation between Member States in the conduct of policy, in accordance with Article J.2;

– by gradually implementing, in accordance with Article J.3, joint action in the areas in which the Member States have important interests in common.

4.   The Member States shall support the Union's external and security policy actively and unreservedly in a spirit of loyalty and mutual solidarity. They shall refrain from an action which is contrary to the interests of the Union or likely to impair its effectiveness as a cohesive force in international relations. The Council shall ensure that these principles are complied with.

Article J.2

1.   Member States shall inform and consult one another within the Council on any matter of foreign and security policy of general interest in order to ensure that their combined influence is exerted as effectively as possible by means of concerted and convergent action.

2.   Whenever it deems it necessary, the Council shall define a common position.

Member States shall ensure that their national policies shall conform to the common positions.

3.   Member States shall co-ordinate their action in international organizations and at international conferences. They shall uphold the common positions in such forums.

In international organizations and at international conferences where not all the Member States participate, those which do take part shall uphold the common positions.

Article J.3

The procedure for adopting joint action in matters covered by the foreign and security policy shall be the following:

1.   The Council shall decide, on the basis of general guidelines from the European Council, that a matter should be the subject of joint action.

Whenever the Council decides on the principle of joint action, it shall lay down the specific scope, the Union's general and specific objectives in carrying out such action, if necessary its duration, and the means, procedures and conditions for its implementation.

2.   The Council shall, when adopting the joint action and at any stage during its development, define those matters on which decisions are to be taken by a qualified majority.

Where the Council is required to act by a qualified majority pursuant to the preceding subparagraph, the votes of its members shall be weighted in accordance with Article 148(2) of the Treaty establishing the European Community, and for their adoption, acts of the Council shall require at least 62 votes in favour, cast by at least 10 members.

3.   If there is a change in circumstances having a substantial effect on a question subject to joint action, the Council shall review the principles and objectives of that action and take the necessary decisions. As long as the Council has not acted, the joint action shall stand.

4.   Joint actions shall commit the Member States in the positions they adopt and in the conduct of their activity.

5.   Whenever there is any plan to adopt a national position or take national action pursuant to a joint action, information shall be provided in time to allow, if necessary, for prior consultations within the Council. The obligation to provide prior information shall not apply to measures which are merely a national transposition of Council decisions.

6.   In cases of imperative need arising from changes in the situation and failing a Council decision, Member States may take the necessary measures as a matter of urgency having regard to the general objectives of the joint action. The Member State concerned shall inform the Council immediately of any such measures.

7.   Should there by any major difficulties in implementing a joint action, a Member State shall refer them to the Council which shall discuss them and seek appropriate solutions. Such solutions shall not run counter to the objectives of the joint action or impair its effectiveness.

COUNCIL DECISION 94/672 of 10 October 1994 (OJ L 266/10)

On the Common Position Defined on the Basis of Article J.2 of the Treaty on European Union and Concerning the Reduction of Economic and Financial Relations with Those Parts of the Territory of the Republic of Bosnia-Herzegovina Under the Control of the Bosnian Serb Forces

THE COUNCIL OF THE EUROPEAN UNION,
Having regard to the Treaty on European Union, and in particular Article J.2 thereof,
Having regard to Resolution 942 (1994) adopted by the United Nations Security Council on September 23, 1994,
HAS DECIDED AS FOLLOWS:

ARTICLE 1

Economic and financial relations with those parts of the territory of the Republic of Bosnia-Herzegovina under the control of the Bosnian Serb forces will be reduced in accordance with the relevant provisions of Resolution 942 (1994) adopted by the United Nations Security Council on September 23, 1994.

ARTICLE 2

This decision shall be published in the Official Journal.
Done at Luxembourg, October 10, 1994.

4.2.6   CO-OPERATION ON JUSTICE AND HOME AFFAIRS

THE TREATY ON EUROPEAN UNION

Article K.1

For the purposes of achieving the objectives of the Union, in particular the free movement of persons, and without prejudice to the powers of the European Community, Member States shall regard the following areas as matters of common interest:

(1)   asylum policy;

(2)   rules governing the crossing by persons of the external borders of the Member States and the exercise of controls thereon;

(3)   immigration policy and policy regarding nationals of third countries:

   (a)   conditions of entry and movement by nationals of third countries on the territory of Member States;

   (b)   conditions of residence by nationals of third countries on the territory of Member States, including family reunion and access to employment;

   (c)   combating unauthorized immigration, residence and work by nationals of third countries on the territory of Member States;

(4)   combating drug addiction in so far as this is not covered by (7) to (9);

(5)   combating fraud on an international scale in so far as this is not covered by (7) to (9);

(6)   judicial co-operation in civil matters;

(7)   judicial co-operation in criminal matters;

(8)   customs co-operation;

(9)   police co-operation for the purposes of preventing and combating terrorism, unlawful drug trafficking and other serious forms of international crime, including if necessary certain aspects of customs co-operation, in connection with the organization of a Union-wide system for exchanging information within a European Police Office (Europol).

Article K.3

1.   In the areas referred to in Article K.1, Member States shall inform and consult one another within the Council with a view to coordinating their action. To that end, they shall establish collaboration between the relevant departments of their administrations.

2.   The Council may:

– on the initiative of any Member State or of the Commission, in the areas referred to in Article K.1(1) to (6);

– on the initiative of any Member State, in the area referred to in Article K.1(7) to (9):

(a)   adopt joint positions and promote, using the appropriate form and procedures, any cooperation contributing to the pursuit of the objectives of the Union;

(b)   adopt joint action in so far as the objectives of the Union can be attained better by joint action than by the Member State acting individually on account of the scale or effects of the action envisaged; it may decide that measures implementing joint action are to be adopted by a qualified majority;

(c)   without prejudice to Article 220 of the Treaty establishing the European Community, draw up conventions which it shall recommend to the Member States for adoption in accordance with their respective constitutional requirements.

Unless otherwise provided by such conventions, measures implementing them shall be adopted within the Council by a majority of two-thirds of the High Contracting Parties.

Such conventions may stipulate that the Court of Justice shall have jurisdiction to interpret their provisions and to rule on any disputes regarding their application, in accordance with such arrangements as they may lay down.

4.2.7   PROCEDURES RELATING TO FOREIGN AND SECURITY POLICY AND TO JUSTICE AND HOME AFFAIRS

J. C. Piris, 'After Maastricht, are the Community Institutions More Efficacious, More Democratic and More Transparent?' (1994) EL Rev 449

Common foreign and security policy and home affairs and justice
Efficacy. The fact that, in principle, all decisions must be taken unanimously is obviously an extremely important factor for producing inefficacy, despite the fact that the Council can unanimously define matters relating to a common action on which decisions may be taken by a qualified majority. Nevertheless, the progress which has been made since the Single Act is far from negligible. All decisions are taken within a single institutional framework; all the working groups of the former Political Co-operation are to be merged with the working parties of the Council of the Communities; the General Secretariat of the Council has a role to play in all areas of policy. It must also be stressed that from now on the Council may adopt decisions which are legally binding on the Member States and whose financing it may charge to the Community budget.

Democracy. The European Parliament could hardly hope to play a larger role in foreign and security policy than that which is enjoyed by the national parliaments in some Member States. Foreign policy is largely a matter for the executive branch of government. However, the role given to the European Parliament is home affairs and justice, matters which have a close bearing on human rights and individual freedoms, could doubtless have been more extensive. Some national parliaments are concerned about this situation and have promised to keep whatever is proposed to be done in Brussels under close scrutiny, as far as these areas are concerned.

Transparency. The matters under discussion cannot but be shrouded in at least some secrecy or confidentiality. Moreover, for political reasons the beginnings of a common foreign policy could not have been made subject to review by the Court of Justice, which has acquired more and more of a reputation over the years for being integrationist. On the other hand, it seems difficult to contemplate significant progress in home affairs and justice without a proper system of judicial review; as matters stand, such review remains in the hands of national jurisdictions, thus precluding harmonisation.

4.2.8   THE PROTOCOLS

THE TREATY OF ROME

(See **1.5** above.)

4.3   End of Chapter Assessment Question

Summarise the significance of the TEU.

4.4   End of Chapter Assessment Outline Answer

The most significant developments introduced by the TEU are as follows:

(i)   Subsidiarity
The principle of subsidiarity as defined in Article 3b of the Treaty of Rome states that where the Community does **not** have exclusive competence to act, it may act **only** if the objectives of the proposed measure can be better achieved by the Community than by the Member States.

The Community itself, when drafting and issuing measures, must have first concluded that they are in accordance with subsidiarity. Whether a measure may now be challenged on ground of subsidiarity depends on whether the principle of subsidiarity is justiciable, that is to say, capable of definition and application by the courts. Since neither the TEU nor the draft Treaty of Amsterdam suggests that the measure is justiciable, and since in the six years since the principle was introduced the Court of Justice has not given a ruling suggesting that it is justiciable, it seems likely that it is not. However, the possibility nonetheless exists, and indeed was argued in *UK* v *Council (Working Time Directive)* (Case C-84/94) [1996] 3 CMLR 671, although the Court found that the principle had not been breached and was thus not obliged to rule on the legal consequences of any breach.

Firstly, the Court of Justice may use subsidiarity as an aid to the interpretation of Community law. For example, a Directive standardising the size and shape of apples across the Community, if subsidiarity is taken into account, can be interpreted as applying only to apples intended for export, since it is at least arguable that Member States can equally well govern the standard of apples produced and consumed domestically. The House of Lords appeared to take this approach in the *Freight Transport Association* case when it construed certain vehicle Directives as not applying to vehicles in London. However, it is really a matter, potentially, for the ECJ in the interests of uniformity.

Secondly, and in the alternative, the Court of Justice may use subsidiarity as a test of the validity of Community law. For example, the fictitious Directive on apples referred to above might be considered to concern matters wholly appropriate for Member States to deal with and therefore to have been adopted in contravention of subsidiarity. Directive 999/95 would therefore be annulled on the basis that the composition and conditions of cream are better dealt with by individual Member States. It is perhaps more likely that it would annul only the part of Directive 94/440 relating to conditions at retail outlets, since this has no effect on the Single Market and would be equally well or better dealt with by the Member States. The Court of Justice might agree with the Community legislators that the composition of cream has an effect on the trade in cream within the Community, and thus on the Single Market, and so should properly be dealt with by the Community.

As mentioned above, the principle of subsidiarity does not apply where the Community has exclusive competence to act. Cases such as *Commission* v *Council (ERTA)* have established that once the Community has taken action in a particular policy area, it assumes exclusive competence in that area and Member States can no longer act.

This definition of exclusive competence may not be appropriate in respect of subsidiarity since it would mean that subsidiarity would gradually apply to fewer and fewer areas of policy. However, the Single Market and citizenship must logically be areas of exclusive Community competence.

(ii)   Citizenship
The new concept of EU citizenship gives nationals of Member States certain rights, namely the right of free movement and residence throughout the Community, the right

to vote and stand in local and Community elections in the Member State in which they reside, the right to diplomatic protection abroad by the representatives of other Member States, and the right to petition the Parliament and its Ombudsman.

The first point to be made is that EU citizenship, and thus the ability to claim these rights, is dependent on being a national of a Member State, a status which is determined by the Member States, rather than the Community. The second point is that although the concept of citizenship is new, few of these rights are new.

(iii) Economic and monetary union

The TEU provides that the Community shall adopt an economic policy conducted in accordance with free competition and based on common objectives, the co-ordination of national policies and the Single Market; and a single monetary policy based on fixed exchange rates leading to a single currency.

The TEU also provides a timetable for the achievement of these objectives, and it is on this timetable that concern as to the achievement of EMU has focused. During the second, current, stage, Member States had to avoid excessive budget deficits, provisions for public budget discipline came into force and preparations for the European System of Central Banks (ESCB), composed of the national central banks and a new European Central Bank, were made.

In the third stage, excessive deficits must be avoided and monetary policy will be under the control of the ESCB, and the EU will become the single currency. The third stage will begin in 1999 for those Member States which fulfil the convergence criteria (low inflation, low budget deficit, stable exchange rate and low long-term interest rates).

Whether a two-tier EU is viable, and whether provision will be made for the second tier states to enter into full EMU, remains to be seen.

(iv) Common foreign and security policy

The Common Foreign and Security Policy requires Member States to inform and consult each other on any foreign or security matter of common interest and to defend any common position adopted by the Community. Joint action in these areas and a common defence policy are also envisaged for the future. This pillar is currently of limited significance, but its potential significance in the future is clearly considerable.

(v) Co-operation on Justice and Home Affairs

Co-operation on Justice and Home Affairs requires Member States to inform and consult each other, and establish systems for collaboration, over certain areas, including immigration policy and combating drugs trafficking. Joint action may be taken and a joint police information system, Europol, is already in place. Clearly the establishment of common immigration and asylum policies is vital to European political integration, and the potential exists for the Community to play a significant role in combating international criminal activities.

A further, and at first sight less obvious, significance of both (iv) and (v) is that action is taken by the Council alone and is not subject to Parliamentary or judicial scrutiny. It may be that as the Member States become used to co-operation in these areas, the normal Community legislative procedures will be applied, but it may equally be a sign that there are certain powers which Member States may never be prepared to see exercised by the less nationalistic Community institutions.

CHAPTER FIVE

COMMUNITY LAW IN NATIONAL COURTS

5.1 Direct Effect

5.1.1 TREATY PROVISIONS

VAN GEND EN LOOS v NEDERLANDSE ADMINISTRATIE DER BELASTINGEN
(Case 26/62) [1963] ECR 1, Court of Justice

An importer alleged that an increase in Dutch import duties was contrary to Article 12 of the Treaty of Rome. The Dutch court referred to the Court of Justice (under Article 177 of the Treaty) the question of whether a litigant before a national court could rely directly on the Treaty of Rome, in particular on Article 12.

It was held that those Treaty obligations which were clear, unconditional, and not subject to intervening action by Member States, such as Article 12, could be relied upon in national courts.

On the substance of the cases (at pp. 11–13)

The first question of the Tariefcommissie is whether Article 12 of the Treaty has direct application in national law in the sense that nationals of Member States may on the basis of this Article lay claim to rights which the national court must protect.

To ascertain whether the provisions of an international treaty extend so far in their effects it is necessary to consider the spirit, the general scheme and the wording of those provisions.

The objective of the EEC Treaty, which is to establish a Common Market, the functioning of which is of direct concern to interested parties in the Community, implies that this Treaty is more than an agreement which merely creates mutual obligations between the contracting states. This view is confirmed by the preamble to the Treaty which refers not only to governments but to peoples. It is also confirmed more specifically by the establishment of institutions endowed with sovereign rights, the exercise of which affects Member States and also their citizens. Furthermore, it must be noted that the nationals of the states brought together in the Community are called upon to cooperate in the functioning of this Community through the intermediary of the European Parliament and the Economic and Social Committee.

In addition the task assigned to the Court of Justice under Article 177, the object of which is to secure uniform interpretation of the Treaty by national courts and tribunals, confirms that the states have acknowledged that Community law has an authority which can be invoked by their nationals before those courts and tribunals.

The conclusion to be drawn from this is that the Community constitutes a new legal order of international law for the benefit of which the states have limited their sovereign rights, albeit within limited fields, and the subjects of which comprise not only Member States but also their nationals. Independently of the legislation of Member States, Community law therefore not only imposes obligations on individuals but is also intended to confer upon them rights which become part of their legal heritage. These rights arise not only where they are expressly granted by the Treaty, but also by reason of obligations which the Treaty imposes in a clearly defined way upon individuals as well as upon the Member States and upon the institutions of the Community.

With regard to the general scheme of the Treaty as it relates to customs duties and charges having equivalent effect it must be emphasized that Article 9, which bases the Community upon a customs union, includes as an essential provision the prohibition of these customs duties and charges. This provision is found at the beginning of the part of the Treaty which defines the 'Foundations of the Community'. It is applied and explained by Article 12.

The wording of Article 12 contains a clear and unconditional prohibition which is not a positive but a negative obligation. This obligation, moreover, is not qualified by any reservation on the part of states which would make its implementation conditional upon a positive legislative measure enacted under national law. The very nature of this prohibition makes it ideally adapted to produce direct effects in the legal relationship between Member States and their subjects.

The implementation of Article 12 does not require any legislative intervention on the part of the states. The fact that under this Article it is the Member States who are made the subject of the negative obligation does not imply that their nationals cannot benefit from this obligation.

In addition the argument based on Articles 169 and 170 of the Treaty put forward by the three Governments which have submitted observations to the Court in their statements of case is misconceived. The fact that these Articles of the Treaty enable the Commission and the Member States to bring before the Court a State which has not fulfilled its obligations does not mean that individuals cannot plead these obligations, should the occasion arise, before a national court, any more than the fact that the Treaty places at the disposal of the Commission ways of ensuring that obligations imposed upon those subject to the Treaty are observed, precludes the possibility, in actions between individuals before a national court, of pleading infringements of these obligations.

A restriction of the guarantees against an infringement of Article 12 by Member States to the procedures under Article 169 and 170 would remove all direct legal protection of the individual rights of their nationals. There is the risk that recourse to the procedure under these Articles would be ineffective if it were to occur after the implementation of a national decision taken contrary to the provisions of the Treaty.

The vigilance of individuals concerned to protect their rights amounts to an effective supervision in addition to the supervision entrusted by Articles 169 and 170 to the diligence of the Commission and of the Member States.

It follows from the foregoing considerations that, according to the spirit, the general scheme and the wording of the Treaty, Article 12 must be interpreted as producing direct effects and creating individual rights which national courts must protect.

THE TREATY OF ROME

Article 12
Member States shall refrain from introducing between themselves any new customs duties on imports or exports or any charges having equivalent effect, and from increasing those which they already apply in their trade with each other.

Article 71
Member States shall endeavour to avoid introducing within the Community any new exchange restrictions on the movement of capital and current payments connected with such movements, and shall endeavour not to make existing rules more restrictive.

They declare their readiness to go beyond the degree of liberalisation of capital movements provided for in the preceding Articles in as far as their economic situation, in particular the situation of their balance of payments, so permits.

The Commission may, after consulting the Monetary Committee, make recommendations to Member States on this subject.

CASATI (Case 203/80) [1981] ECR 2595, Court of Justice

Casati was fined under an Italian law which restricted the movement of capital. He alleged that this law was contrary to Article 71 of the Treaty. The Italian court made a reference to the Court of Justice under Article 177 of the Treaty.

It was held that Article 71 was not directly effective.

18.   According to the first paragraph of Article 71, the Member States must endeavour to avoid introducing within the Community any new exchange restrictions on the movement of capital and must endeavour not to make existing rules more restrictive.

19.   By using the term 'shall endeavour', the wording of that provision departs noticeably from the more imperative forms of wording employed in other similar provisions concerning restrictions on the free movement of goods, persons and services. It is apparent from that wording that, in any event, the first paragraph of Article 71 does not impose on the Member States an unconditional obligation capable of being relied upon by individuals.

DEFRENNE v *SABENA* (Case 43/75) [1976] ECR 455, Court of Justice

Belgian legislation concerning the provision of retirement pensions for civil aviation air crews excluded air hostesses from the pension scheme in question. Ms Defrenne, an air hostess employed by SABENA airlines, claimed that this exclusion infringed the principle of equality contained in Article 119. The Belgian court made a reference, *inter alia*, as to the effect of Article 119 to the Court of Justice under Article 177 of the Treaty.

It was held that Article 119 was directly effective. This judgment would not be applied retrospectively, except in respect of cases already pending.

The first question (direct effect of Article 119)

4.   The first question asks whether Article 119 of the Treaty introduces 'directly into the national law of each Member State of the European Community the principle that men and women should receive equal pay for equal work and does it therefore, independently of any national provision, entitle workers to institute proceedings before national courts in order to ensure its observance?'

5.   If the answer to this question is in the affirmative, the question further enquires as from what date this effect must be recognised.

6.   The reply to the final part of the first question will therefore be given with the reply to the second question.

7.   The question of the direct effect of Article 119 must be considered in the light of the nature of the principle of equal pay, the aim of this provision and its place in the scheme of the Treaty.

8.   Article 119 pursues a double aim.

9.   First, in the light of the different stages of the development of social legislation in the various Member States, the aim of Article 119 is to avoid a situation in which undertakings established in States which have actually implemented the principle of equal pay suffer a competitive disadvantage on intra-Community competition as compared with undertakings established in States which have not yet eliminated discrimination against women workers as regards pay.

10.   Secondly, this provision forms part of the social objectives of the Community, which is not merely an economic union, but is at the same time intended, by common action, to ensure social progress and seek the constant improvement of the living and working conditions of their peoples, as it is emphasised by the Preamble to the Treaty.

11.   This aim is accentuated by the insertion of Article 119 into the body of a chapter devoted to social policy whose preliminary provision, Article 117 marks 'the need to promote improved working conditions and an improved standard of living for workers, so as to make possible their harmonisation while the improvement is being maintained.'

12.   This double aim, which is at once economic and social, shows that the principle of equal pay forms part of the foundations of the Community.

13.   Furthermore, this explains why the Treaty has provided for the complete implementation of this principle by the end of the first stage of the transitional period.

14.   Therefore, in interpreting this provision, it is impossible to base any argument on the dilatoriness and resistance which have delayed the actual implementation of this basic principle in certain Member States.

15.   In particular, since Article 119 appears in the context of the harmonisation of working conditions while the improvement is being maintained, the objection that the terms of this Article may be observed in other ways than by raising the lowest salaries may be set aside.

16.   Under the terms of the first paragraph of Article 119, the Member States are bound to ensure and maintain 'the application of the principle that men and women should receive equal pay for equal work'.

17.   The second and third paragraphs of the same Article add a certain number of details concerning the concepts of pay and work referred to in the first paragraph.

18.   For the purposes of the implementation of these provisions a distinction must be drawn within the whole area of application of Article 119 between, first, direct and overt discrimination which may be identified solely with the aid of the criteria based on equal work and equal pay referred to by the Article in question and, secondly, indirect and disguised discrimination which can only be identified by reference to more explicit implementing provisions of a Community or national character.

19.   It is impossible not to recognise that the complete implementation of the aim pursued by Article 119, by means of the elimination of all discrimination, direct or indirect, between men and women workers, not only as regards individual undertakings but also entire branches of industry and even of the economic system as a whole, may in certain cases involve the elaboration of criteria whose implementation necessitates the taking of appropriate measures at Community and national level.

20.   This view is all the more essential in the light of the fact that the Community measures on this question, to which reference will be made in answer to the second question, implement Article 119 from the point of view of extending the narrow criterion of 'equal work', in accordance in particular with the provisions of Convention No. 100 on equal pay concluded by the International Labour Organisation in 1951, Article 2 of which establishes the principle of equal pay for work 'of equal value'.

21.   Among the forms of direct discrimination which may be identified solely by reference to the criteria laid down by Article 119 must be included in particular those which have their origin in legislative provisions or in collective labour agreements and which may be detected on the basis of a purely legal analysis of the situation.

22.   This applies even more in cases where men and women receive unequal pay for equal work carried out in the same establishment or service, whether public or private.

23.   As is shown by the very findings of the judgment making the reference, in such a situation the court is in a position to establish all the facts which enable it to decide whether a woman worker is receiving lower pay than a male worker performing the same tasks.

24.   In such situation, at least, Article 119 is directly applicable and may thus give rise to individual rights which the courts must protect.

25.   Furthermore, as regards equal work, as a general rule, the national legislative provisions adopted for the implementation of the principle of equal pay as a rule merely reproduce the substance of the terms of Article 119 as regards the direct forms of discrimination.

26.   Belgian legislation provides a particularly apposite illustration of this point, since Article 14 of Royal Decree 40 of 24 October 1967 on the employment of women merely sets out the right of any female worker to institute proceedings before the relevant court for the application of the principle of equal pay set out in Article 119 and simply refers to that Article.

27.   The terms of Article 119 cannot be relied on to invalidate this conclusion.

28.   First of all, it is impossible to put forward an argument against its direct effect based on the use in this article of the word 'principle', since, in the language of the Treaty, this term is specifically used in order to indicate the fundamental nature of certain provisions, as is shown, for example, by the heading of the first part of the Treaty which is devoted to 'Principles' and by Article 113, according to which the commercial policy of the Community is to be based on 'uniform principles'.

29.   If this concept were to be attenuated to the point of reducing it to the level of vague declaration, the very foundations of the Community and the coherence of its external relations would be directly affected.

30.   It is also impossible to put forward arguments based on the fact that Article 119 only refers expressly to 'Member States'.

31.   Indeed, as the Court has already found in other contexts, the fact that certain provisions of the Treaty are formally addressed to the Member States does not prevent rights from being conferred at the same time on any individual who has an interest in the performance of the duties thus laid down.

32.   The very wording of Article 119 shows that it imposes on States a duty to bring about a specific result to be mandatorily achieved within a fixed period.

33.   The effectiveness of this provision cannot be affected by the fact that the duty imposed by the Treaty has not been discharged by certain Member States and that the joint institutions have not reacted sufficiently energetically against this failure to act.

34.   To accept the contrary view would be to risk raising the violation of the right to the status of a principle of interpretation, a position the adoption of which would not be consistent with the task assigned to the Court by Article 164 of the Treaty.

35.   Finally, in its reference to 'Member States' in Article 119 is alluding to those States in the exercise of all those of their functions which may usefully contribute to the implementation of the principle of equal pay.

36.   Thus, contrary to the statements made in the course of the proceedings this provision is far from merely referring the matter to the powers of the national legislative authorities.

37.   Therefore, the reference to 'Member States' in Article 119 cannot be interpreted as excluding the intervention of the courts in direct application of the Treaty.

38.   Furthermore, it is not possible to sustain any objection that the application by national courts of the principle of equal pay would amount to modifying independent agreements concluded privately or in the sphere of industrial relations such as individual contracts and collective labour agreements.

39.   In fact, since Article 119 is mandatory in nature, the prohibition on discrimination between men and women applies not only to the action of public authorities, but also extends to all agreements which are intended to regulate paid labour collectively, as well as to contracts between individuals.

40.   The reply to the first question must therefore be that the principle of equal pay contained in Article 119 may be relied upon before the national courts and that these courts have a duty to ensure the protection of the rights which this provision vests in individuals, in particular as regards those types of discrimination arising directly from legislative provisions or collective labour agreements, as well as in cases in which men and women receive unequal pay for equal work which is carried out in the same establishment or service, whether private or public.

5.1.2   REGULATIONS

POLITI SAS v MINISTERO DELLE FINANZE (Case 43/71) [1971] ECR 1039,
Court of Justice

Italy levied import taxes on pork, contrary to the provisions of a Regulation. An importer, Politi, sought to rely on the Regulation. The Italian court made a reference to the Court of Justice under Article 177 of the Treaty.

It was held that Regulations such as this could be directly effective.

8.   The court is next asked whether the provisions of Articles 14(1) and 18(1) of Regulation No. 20, as well as the first indent of Article 17(2) and the first indent of 19(1) of Regulation No. 121/67 are immediately applicable within the national legal system and produce and, as such, create individual rights which national courts must protect.

9.   Under the terms of the second paragraph of Article 189 regulations 'shall have general application' and 'shall be . . . directly applicable in all Member States'.

Therefore, by reason of their nature and of their function in the system of the sources of Community law, regulations have direct effect and are as such, capable of creating individual rights which national courts must protect.

The effect of regulations, as provided for in Article 189, is therefore to prevent the application of any legislative measure, even if it is enacted subsequently, which is incompatible with its provisions.

This applies to the provisions in question.

5.1.3 DECISIONS

GRAD v FINANZAMT TRAUNSTEIN (Case 9/70) [1970] ECR 825, Court of Justice

A Decision provided for the replacement of national freight taxes by a common Community freight tax. A freight transporter sought to rely on the Decision to challenge a German freight tax. The German court made a reference to the Court of Justice under Article 177 of the Treaty.

It was held that Decisions could be directly effective but, on the facts this Decision had not yet come into force, and therefore had not yet become directly effective.

The first question

2.   With its first question the Finanzgericht asks the Court for a decision as to whether Article 4(2) of the Decision in conjunction with Article 1(4) of the Directive produces a direct effect on the legal relations between the Member States and individuals and whether these provisions create rights for individuals to which the national courts must give effect.

3.   The question concerns the total effect of provisions contained in a decision or a directive. According to Article 189 of the EEC Treaty a decision is binding in its entirety upon those whom it designates. Furthermore, according to this Article a directive is binding, in respect of the aim to be achieved, on every Member State to which it is directed although it leaves the choice of forms and methods to the internal national authorities.

4.   The German Government in its submissions maintains that Article 189 by distinguishing between the effects of regulations on the one hand and of decisions and directives on the other hand thus precludes the possibility of decisions and directives producing the effects mentioned in the question; it claims that such effects are on the contrary reserved to regulations.

5.   It is true that by Article 189 regulations are directly applicable and may therefore certainly produce direct effects by virtue of their nature as law. However, it does not follow from this that other categories of legal measures mentioned in that Article could never produce similar effects. The provision that decisions are binding in their entirety on those to whom they are addressed especially enables the question to be posed as to whether the obligation created by the decision can only be invoked by the organs of the Community as against the addressee or whether such a right in a given case is attributed to all those who have an interest in the fulfilment of this obligation. It would be incompatible with the binding effect attributed to decisions by Article 189 to exclude in principle the possibility that persons affected might invoke the obligation imposed by a decision. Particularly in cases where, for example, the Community organs impose an obligation on a Member State or all the Member States by decision to undertake certain conduct, the useful effect of such a measure would be weakened if the nationals of this State could not invoke it in the courts and the national courts could not take it into consideration as part of Community law. Although the effects of a decision may be different from those of a provision contained in a regulation this difference does not prevent the end-result, namely the right of the individual to invoke the measure in the courts, from being the same in a given case as that in the case of a directly applicable provision of a regulation.

6.   Article 177, whereby the national courts are empowered to submit to the Court all questions regarding the validity and interpretation of all measures of the organs without distinction, also pre-supposes that individuals may invoke such measures in the national courts. Therefore, in each particular case, one must examine whether the provision in question, by its legal nature, lay-out and wording, is capable of creating direct effects on the legal relations between the addressee of the measure and third parties.

7.   The Council's Decision of 13 May 1965 addressed to all the Member States is based in particular on Article 75 of the Treaty which empowers the Council to make 'common rules', 'licence conditions' and 'all other appropriate provisions' to implement a common transport policy. The Council therefore has a very wide scope in the choice of the

measures to be instituted. The Decision in question, seen as a whole, lays down the aims pursued in the scope of a policy to harmonise national provisions and the time-table for their realisation. In view of these aims Article 4(1) of the Decision provides that as soon as a common turnover tax system has been determined by the Council and brought into force in the Member States, the Member States shall be obliged to apply it to freight transport in rail, road and inland water traffic, in accordance with methods that have yet to be determined. Paragraph (2) of this Article provides that this common turnover tax system, on or before its entry into force, shall replace the specific taxes imposed instead of turnover tax to the extent that freight transport by the carriers mentioned is subject to such taxes.

8.   Thus this provision imposes two obligations on the Member States: first, to apply the common turnover tax system to freight transport in rail, road and inland water traffic not later than from a certain date, and then, to permit this system to replace the specific taxes within the meaning of paragraph (2) not later than upon its entry into force. This second obligation obviously includes the prohibition on introducing or re-introducing such taxes whereby it is intended to prevent the common turnover tax system from coinciding in the field of transport with similar additional tax systems.

9.   According to the documents submitted by the Finanzgericht the question relates, in particular to the second obligation. The second obligation is by nature binding and general, although the provision leaves the determination of the date on which it becomes effective open. It expressly prohibits the Member States from cumulating the common turnover tax system with specific taxes which are imposed instead of turnover taxes. This obligation is unconditional and sufficiently clear and precise to be capable of creating direct effect in the legal relations between the Member States and individuals.

10.   The date on which this obligation becomes effective was laid down by the Council's Directives on the harmonisation of the legal provisions relating to turnover tax; it is determined therein by the latest date by which the Member States must introduce the common added value tax system. The fact that this date was determined by a directive does not deprive this provision of any of its binding force. Thus the obligation created by Article 4(2) of the Decision of 13 May 1965 was completed by the First Directive. Therefore this provision imposes obligations on the Member States, in particular the obligation from a certain date no longer to cumulate the common added value tax system with the specific taxes mentioned, which are capable of producing direct effects in the legal relations between the Member States and individuals and of creating the right for the latter to invoke these obligations in the courts.

5.1.4   DIRECTIVES

VAN DUYN v *HOME OFFICE* (Case 41/74) [1974] ECR 1337, Court of Justice

Miss Van Duyn, a Dutch national, applied for permission to enter the UK to work for the Church of Scientology. Under Article 48, Member States could exclude an applicant on grounds of public policy, but under Directive 63/22, they could only take into account the individual's personal conduct. The UK sought to exclude Miss Van Duyn on account of her membership of this particular organisation, and she attempted to rely on the Directive, which had not been implemented by the UK. The UK court made a reference to the Court of Justice under Article 177 of the Treaty.

It was held that it was possible to rely directly on an unimplemented Directive (such as Directive 63/22) if it was sufficiently clear. (On the facts, the personal conduct of an individual included membership of any organisations.)

Second question

9.   The second question asks the Court to say whether Council Directive No. 64/221 of 25 February 1964 on the co-ordination of special measures concerning the movement and residence of foreign nationals which are justified on grounds of public policy, public security or public health is directly applicable so as to confer on individuals rights enforceable by them in the courts of a Member State.

10.   It emerges from the order making the reference that the only provision of the Directive which is relevant is that contained in Article 3(1) which provides that 'measures

taken on grounds of public policy or public security shall be based exclusively on the personal conduct of the individual concerned'.

11.   The United Kingdom observes that, since Article 189 of the Treaty distinguishes between the effects ascribed to regulations, directives and decisions, it must therefore be presumed that the Council, in issuing a directive rather than making a regulation, must have intended that the directive should have an effect other than that of a regulation and accordingly that the former should not be directly applicable.

12.   If, however, by virtue of the provisions of Article 189 regulations are directly applicable and, consequently, may by their very nature have direct effects, it does not follow from this that other categories of acts mentioned in that Article can never have similar effects. It would be incompatible with the binding effect attributed to a directive by Article 189 to exclude, in principle, the possibility that the obligation which it imposes may be invoked by those concerned. In particular, where the Community authorities have, by directive, imposed on Member States the obligation to pursue a particular course of conduct, the useful effect of such an act would be weakened if individuals were prevented from relying on it before their national courts and if the latter were prevented from taking it into consideration as an element of Community law. Article 177, which empowers national courts to refer to the Court questions concerning the validity and interpretation of all acts of the Community institutions, without distinction, implies furthermore that these acts may be invoked by individuals in the national courts. It is necessary to examine, in every case, whether the nature, general scheme and wording of the provision in question are capable of having direct effects on the relations between Member States and individuals.

13.   By providing that measures taken on grounds of public policy shall be based exclusively on the personal conduct of the individual concerned, Article 3(1) of Directive No. 64/221 is intended to limit the discretionary power which national laws generally confer on the authorities responsible for the entry and expulsion of foreign nationals. First, the provision lays down an obligation which is not subject to any exception or condition and which, by its very nature, does not require the intervention of any act on the part either of the institutions of the Community or of Member States. Secondly, because Member States are thereby obliged, in implementing a clause which derogates from one of the fundamental principles of the Treaty in favour of individuals, not to take account of factors extraneous to personal conduct, legal certainty for the persons concerned requires that they should be able to rely on this obligation even though it has been laid down in a legislative act which has no automatic direct effect in its entirety.

14.   If the meaning and exact scope of the provision raise questions of interpretation, these questions can be resolved by the courts, taking into account also the procedure under Article 177 of the Treaty.

15.   Accordingly, in reply to the second question, Article 3(1) of Council Directive No. 64/221 of 25 February 1964 confers on individuals rights which are enforceable by them in the courts of a Member State and which the national courts must protect.

MARSHALL v SOUTHAMPTON AND SOUTH WEST AREA HEALTH AUTHORITY (TEACHING) (No. 1) (Case 152/84) [1986] ECR 723, Court of Justice

Miss Marshall was compulsorily retired by her employer, an Area Health Authority, in accordance with their retirement policy which applied an age of 60 in respect of female employees and 65 for male employees. She sought to rely on Directive 76/207 which had not been properly implemented by the UK, and which prohibited discrimination at work on grounds of sex. The UK court made a reference to the Court of Justice under Article 177 of the Treaty.

It was held that Miss Marshall was entitled to rely on the direct effect of the Directive against a Member State or an emanation of a Member State, such as the Area Health Authority.

42.   The Commission is of the opinion that the provisions of Article 5(1) of Directive 76/207 are sufficiently clear and unconditional to be relied upon before a national court. They may therefore be set up against section 6(4) of the Sex Discrimination Act, which, according to the decisions of the Court of Appeal, has been extended to the question of

compulsory retirement and has therefore become ineffective to prevent dismissals based upon the difference in retirement ages for men and women.

43. The respondent and the United Kingdom propose, conversely, that the second question should be answered in the negative. They admit that a directive may, in certain specific circumstances, have direct effect as against a Member State in so far as the latter may not rely on its failure to perform its obligations under the directive. However, they maintain that a directive can never impose obligations directly on individuals and that it can only have direct effect against a Member State *qua* public authority and not against a Member State *qua* employer. As an employer a State is no different from a private employer. It would not therefore be proper to put persons employed by the State in a better position than those who are employed by a private employer.

44. With regard to the legal position of the respondent's employees the United Kingdom states that they are in the same position as the employees of a private employer. Although according to United Kingdom constitutional law the health authorities, created by the National Health Service Act 1977, as amended by the Health Services Act 1980 and other legislation, are Crown bodies and their employees are Crown Servants, nevertheless the administration of the National Health Service by the health authorities is regarded as being separate from the Government's central administration and its employees are not regarded as civil servants.

45. Finally, both the respondent and the United Kingdom take the view that the provisions of Directive 76/207 are neither unconditional nor sufficiently clear and precise to give rise to direct effect. The directive provides for a number of possible exceptions, the details of which are to be laid down by the Member States. Furthermore, the wording of Article 5 is quite imprecise and requires the adoption of measures for its implementation.

46. It is necessary to recall that, according to a long line of decisions of the Court (in particular its judgment in Case 8/81, *Becker* v *Finanzamt Münster-Innenstadt* [1982] ECR 53), wherever the provisions of a directive appear, as far as their subject-matter is concerned, to be unconditional and sufficiently precise, those provisions may be relied upon by an individual against the State where that State fails to implement the directive in national law by the end of the period prescribed or where it fails to implement the directive correctly.

47. That view is based on the consideration that it would be incompatible with the binding nature which Article 189 confers on the directive to hold as a matter of principle that the obligation imposed thereby cannot be relied on by those concerned. From that the Court deduced that a Member State which has not adopted the implementing measures required by the directive within the prescribed period may not plead, as against individuals, its own failure to perform the obligations which the directive entails.

48. With regard to the argument that a directive may not be relied upon against an individual, it must be emphasised that according to Article 189 of the EEC Treaty the binding nature of a directive, which constitutes the basis for the possibility of relying on the directive before a national court, exists only in relation to 'each Member State to which it is addressed'. It follows that a directive may not of itself impose obligations on an individual and that a provision of a directive may not be relied upon as such against such a person. It must therefore by examined whether, in this case, the respondent must be regarded as having acted as an individual.

49. In that respect it must be pointed out that where a person involved in legal proceedings is able to rely on a directive as against the State he may do so regardless of the capacity in which the latter is acting, whether as employer or public authority. In either case it is necessary to prevent the State from taking advantage of its own failure to comply with Community law.

50. It is for the national court to apply those considerations to the circumstances of each case; the Court of Appeal has, however, stated in the order for reference that the respondent, Southampton and South West Hampshire Area Health Authority (Teaching), is a public authority.

51. The argument submitted by the United Kingdom that the possibility of relying on provisions of the directive against the respondent *qua* organ of the State would give rise to an arbitrary and unfair distinction between the rights of State employees and those of private employees does not justify any other conclusion. Such a distinction may easily

be avoided if the Member State concerned has correctly implemented the directive in national law.

52. Finally, with regard to the question whether the provision contained in Article 5(1) of Directive 76/207, which implements the principle of equality of treatment set out in Article 2(1) of the directive, may be considered, as far as its contents are concerned, to be unconditional and sufficiently precise to be relied upon by an individual as against the State, it must be stated that the provision, taken by itself, prohibits any discrimination on grounds of sex with regard to working conditions, including the conditions governing dismissal, in a general manner and in unequivocal terms. The provision is therefore sufficiently precise to be relied on by an individual and to be applied by the national courts.

53. It is necessary to consider next whether the prohibition of discrimination laid down by the directive may be regarded as unconditional, in the light of the exceptions contained therein and of the fact that according to Article 5(2) thereof the Member States are to take the measures necessary to ensure the application of the principle of equality of treatment in the context of national law.

54. With regard, in the first place, to the reservation contained in Article 1(2) of Directive 76/207 concerning the application of the principle of equality of treatment in matters of social security, it must be observed that, although the reservation limits the scope of the directive *ratione materiae*, it does not lay down any condition on the application of that principle in its field of operation and in particular in relation to Article 5 of the directive. Similarly, the exceptions to Directive 76/207 provided for in Article 2 thereof are not relevant to this case.

55. It follows that Article 5 of Directive 76/207 does not confer on the Member States the right to limit the application of the principle of equality of treatment in its field of operation or to subject it to conditions and that that provision is sufficiently precise and unconditional to be capable of being relied upon by an individual before a national court in order to avoid the application of any national provision which does not conform to Article 5(1).

56. Consequently, the answer to the second question must be that Article 5(1) of Council Directive 76/207, which prohibits any discrimination on grounds of sex with regard to working conditions, including the conditions governing dismissal, may be relied upon as against a State authority acting in its capacity as employer, in order to avoid the application of any national provision which does not conform to Article 5(1).

DIRECTIVE 76/207

COUNCIL DIRECTIVE OF 9 FEBRUARY 1976 ON THE IMPLEMENTATION OF THE PRINCIPLE OF EQUAL TREATMENT FOR MEN AND WOMEN AS REGARDS ACCESS TO EMPLOYMENT, VOCATIONAL TRAINING AND PROMOTION, AND WORKING CONDITIONS (76/207/EEC)
[OJ 1976, L 39/40]

[*Preamble omitted*]

Article 1

1. The purpose of this Directive is to put into effect in the Member States the principle of equal treatment for men and women as regards access to employment, including promotion, and to vocational training and as regards working conditions and, on the conditions referred to in paragraph 2, social security. This principle is hereinafter referred to as 'the principle of equal treatment'.

2. With a view to ensuring the progressive implementation of the principle of equal treatment in matters of social security, the Council, acting on a proposal from the Commission, will adopt provisions defining its substance, its scope and the arrangements for its application.

Article 2

1. For the purposes of the following provisions, the principle of equal treatment shall mean that there shall be no discrimination whatsoever on grounds of sex either directly or indirectly by reference in particular to marital or family status.

2.   This Directive shall be without prejudice to the right of Member States to exclude from its field of application those occupational activities and, where appropriate, the training leading thereto, for which, by reason of their nature or the context in which they are carried out, the sex of the worker constitutes a determining factor.

3.   This Directive shall be without prejudice to provisions concerning the protection of women, particularly as regards pregnancy and maternity.

4.   This Directive shall be without prejudice to measures to promote equal opportunity for men and women, in particular by removing existing inequalities which affect women's opportunities in the areas referred to in Article 1(1).

Article 3

1.   Application of the principle of equal treatment means that there shall be no discrimination whatsoever on grounds of sex in the conditions, including selection criteria, for access to all jobs or posts, whatever the sector or branch of activity, and to all levels of the occupational hierarchy.

2.   To this end, Member States shall take the measures necessary to ensure that:

(a)   any laws, regulations and administrative provisions contrary to the principle of equal treatment shall be abolished;

(b)   any provisions contrary to the principle of equal treatment which are included in collective agreements, individual contracts of employment, internal rules of undertakings or in rules governing the independent occupations and professions shall be, or may be declared, null and void or may be amended;

(c)   those laws, regulations and administrative provisions contrary to the principle of equal treatment when the concern for protection which originally inspired them is no longer well founded shall be revised; and that where similar provisions are included in collective agreements labour and management shall be requested to undertake the desired revision.

Article 4

Application of the principle of equal treatment with regard to access to all types and to all levels, of vocational guidance, vocational training, advanced vocational training and retaining, means that Member States shall take all necessary measure to ensure that:

(a)   any laws, regulations and administrative provisions contrary to the principle of equal treatment shall be abolished;

(b)   any provisions contrary to the principle of equal treatment which are included in collective agreements, individual contracts of employment, internal rules of undertakings or in rules governing the independent occupations and professions shall be, or may be declared, null and void or may be amended;

(c)   without prejudice to the freedom granted in certain Member States to certain private training establishments, vocational guidance, vocational training, advanced vocational training and retraining shall be accessible on the basis of the same criteria and at the same levels without any discrimination on grounds of sex.

Article 5

1.   Application of the principle of equal treatment with regard to working conditions, including the conditions governing dismissal, means that men and women shall be guaranteed the same conditions without discrimination on grounds of sex.

2.   To this end, Member States shall take the measures necessary to ensure that:

(a)   any laws, regulations and administrative provisions contrary to the principle of equal treatment shall be abolished;

(b)   any provisions contrary to the principle of equal treatment which are included in collective agreements, individual contracts of employment, internal rules of undertakings or in rules governing the independent occupations and professions shall be, or may be declared, null and void or may be amended;

(c)   those laws, regulations and administrative provisions contrary to the principle of equal treatment when the concern for protection which originally inspired them is no longer well founded shall be revised; and that where similar provisions are included in collective agreements labour and management shall be requested to undertake the desired revision.

Article 6
Member States shall introduce into their national legal systems such measures as are necessary to enable all persons who consider themselves wronged by failure to apply to them the principle of equal treatment within the meaning of Articles 3, 4 and 5 to pursue their claims by judicial process after possible recourse to other competent authorities.

Article 7
Member States shall take the necessary measures to protect employees against dismissal by the employer as a reaction to a complaint within the undertaking or to any legal proceedings aimed at enforcing compliance with the principle of equal treatment.

(*All remaining provisions omitted*)

FOSTER AND OTHERS v *BRITISH GAS PLC* (Case C–188/89) [1990] ECR I–3313, Court of Justice

Mrs Foster was compulsorily retired by her employer, British Gas, at the age of 60, in accordance with their retirement policy which also applied a retirement age of 65 to her male colleagues. She sought to rely on Directive 76/207 which had not been properly implemented by the UK, and which prohibited discrimination at work on grounds of sex.

It was held that the Directive could be relied upon against British Gas, since it was an emanation of the State.

14. The question what effects measures adopted by Community institutions have and in particular whether those measures may be relied on against certain categories of persons necessarily involves interpretation of the articles of the Treaty concerning measures adopted by the institutions and the Community measure in issue.

15. It follows that the Court of Justice has jurisdiction in proceedings for a preliminary ruling to determine the categories of persons against whom the provisions of a directive may be relied on. It is for the national courts, on the other hand, to decide whether a party before them falls within one of the categories so defined.

Reliance on the provisions of the directive against a body such as the BGC

16. As the Court has consistently held (see *Becker* v *Finanzamt Münster-Innenstadt* (Case 8/81) [1982] ECR 53) where the Community authorities have, by means of a directive, placed Member States under a duty to adopt a certain course of action, the effectiveness of such a measure would be diminished if persons were prevented from relying upon it in proceedings before a court and national courts were prevented from taking it into consideration as an element of Community law. Consequently, a Member State which has not adopted the implementing measures required by the directive within the prescribed period may not plead, as against individuals, its own failure to perform the obligations which the directive entails. Thus, wherever the provisons of a directive appear, as far as their subject–matter is concerned, to be unconditional and sufficiently precise, those provisions may, in the absence of implementing measures adopted within the prescribed period, be relied upon as against any national provision which is incompatible with the directive or in so far as the provisions define rights which individuals are able to assert against the State.

17. The Court further held in *Marshall*, at paragraph 49, that where a person is able to rely on a directive as against the State he may do so regardless of the capacity in which the latter is acting, whether as employer or as public authority. In either case it is necessary to prevent the State from taking advantage of its own failure to comply with Community law.

18. On the basis of those considerations, the Court has held in a series of cases that unconditional and sufficiently precise provisions of a directive could be relied on against organisations or bodies which were subject to the authority or control of the State or had special powers beyond those which result from the normal rules applicable to relations between individuals.

19. The Court has accordingly held that provisions of a directive could be relied on against tax authorities (Case 8/81, *Becker*, and 22 February 1990 in Case C–221/88, *ECSC*

v *Acciaierie E Ferriere Busseni* [1990] ECR I-495), local or regional authorities (Case 103/88, *Fratelli Costanzo* v *Comune Di Milano* [1989] ECR 1839), constitutionally independent authorities responsible for the maintenance of public order and safety (Case 222/84, *Johnston* v *Chief Constable of the Royal Ulster Constabulary* [1986] ECR 1651), and public authorities providing public health services (Case 152/84, *Marshall*).

20.   It follows from the foregoing that a body, whatever its legal form, which has been made responsible, pursuant to a measure adopted by the State, for providing a public sevice under the control of the State and has for that purpose special powers beyond those which result from the normal rules applicable in relations between individuals is included in any event among the bodies against which the provisions of a directive capable of having direct effect may be relied upon.

21.   With regard to Article 5(1) of Directive 76/207 it should be observed that in Case 152/84, *Marshall* at paragraph 52, the Court held that that provision was unconditional and sufficiently precise to be relied on by an individual and to be applied by the national courts.

22.   The answer to the question referred by the House of Lords must therefore be that Article 5(1) of Council Directive 76/207 of 9 February 1976 may be relied upon in a claim for damages against a body, whatever its legal form, which has been made responsible, pursuant to a measure adopted by the State, for providing a public service under the control of the State and has for that purpose special powers beyond those which result from the normal rules applicable in relations between individuals.

DOUGHTY v ROLLS ROYCE PLC [1992] 1 CMLR 1045, Court of Appeal

Mrs Doughty was compulsorily retired by her employer, Rolls Royce, at the age of 60, in accordance with their retirement policy which applied a retirement age of 65 to her male colleagues. She sought to rely on Directive 76/207 which had not been properly implemented by the UK, and which prohibited discrimination at work on grounds of sex.

It was held that the Directive could not be directly effective against Rolls Royce because it was not an emanation of the Member State.

[10]   Returning to the question posed at an earlier stage, I confess that it would have seemed to me clear in the absence of guidance that on these facts the doctrine of *Becker* and *Marshall* does not apply, for I would be unable to see how the maintenance by the respondent company of a discriminatory pension policy could be regarded as a breach by the United Kingdom of its obligations under the directive. It is axiomatic that an individual cannot rely on the directive merely by asserting rights against another individual which would be secured to him if the European legislation had been domestically put into effect. It is the fact that the Member State is itself relying on the disconformity as against the individual which brings the doctrine into play. So long as this distinction persists – and it will continue to persist until such time, if ever, as it becomes Community law that the European institutions are empowered to legislate directly for all individuals in the Community – it must follow that the doctrine can be relied upon in a case such as the present only if the acts of the entity against which the individual proceeds are in some sense to be regarded as the acts of the Member State. Unassisted I would have found it hard to see how the maintenance by the respondent company of its pension policy could in any sense be regarded as an act of, or as an act attributable to, or whatever other turn of phrase is preferred, the United Kingdom in such a manner as to cause the United Kingdom (through the respondent) to be relying on its own default.

. . .

[25]   So we must begin by seeing whether the three criteria established by the formula in *Foster* are satisfied in the case of the respondent. For this purpose I am prepared to assume that the second criterion, namely that whatever 'service' the respondent pro-vided was at the material time 'under the control of the State', was fulfilled by Rolls Royce at the time in question; although if this requirement had been crucial to a decision of the present appeal I would have wished to examine it much more closely. To my mind, however, the position is quite different in regard to the other two criteria. As to the first, I am unable to see how it could be said that the respondent 'was made responsible,

pursuant to a measure adopted by the State for providing a public service . . .'. The respondent was a commercial undertaking which as part of its business traded with the State on terms which were negotiated at arm's length. It is true that this trading connection was of importance to the defence of the realm, an activity peculiar to the State, and was liable to become even more so in time of war; and the importance of this was manifested not only by the closeness of the watch kept on the trading relationship but also by the importance attached by officers of state to ensuring that the respondent kept its trading capacity fully in being. Nevertheless, on the evidence before the Industrial Tribunal the 'services' of the respondent were provided to the State, and not to the public for purposes which were of benefit to the State.

[26] Nor can I see any evidence that the respondent possessed or claimed to exercise any 'special powers' of the type enjoyed by the British Gas Corporation, and indeed counsel for the appellant scarcely sought to contend that this requirement was satisfied. What counsel did suggest was that the third requirement was alternative, rather than cumulative, to the others, and he relied for this purpose on the use of the word 'or', rather than 'and', in paragraph 18 of the European Court's judgment, cited above. I am by no means convinced that there is any really disconformity between paragraph 18 on the one hand, and the test prescribed in paragraph 20 of the formal ruling on the other, since paragraph 18 is presented only as a summary of the jurisprudence to date, and not as an authoritative exposition of the way in which cases like *Foster* were to be approached. But if such a disconformity does exist the formal ruling must surely prevail.

[27] For these reasons I consider that the respondent did not at the material time fulfil the requirements of the ruling. As I have suggested, this does not mean that the appellant's claim based on the Directive must inevitably fail, but I would need to find some strong additional reason special to this case before concluding that the Directive can be relied upon by the individual appellant against the respondent. I can see none at all.

FRATELLI COSTANZO v COMUNE DI MILANO (Case C-103/88) [1989] ECR I-1839, Court of Justice

The fourth question

28. In the fourth question the national court asks whether administrative authorities, including municipal authorities, are under the same obligation as a national court to apply the provisions of Article 29(5) of Council Directive 71/305 and to refrain from applying provisions of national law which conflict with them.

29. In its judgments of 19 January 1982 in *Becker* v *Finanzamt Münster-Innenstadt* (Case 8/81) [1982] ECR 53, at p. 71 and 26 February 1986 in *Marshall* v *Southampton and South-West Hampshire Area Health Authority* (Case 152/84) [1986] ECR 723, at p. 748, the Court held that wherever the provisions of a directive appear, as far as their subject-matter is concerned, to be unconditional and sufficiently precise, those provisions may be relied upon by an individual against the State where that State has failed to implement the directive in national law by the end of the period prescribed or where it has failed to implement the Directive correctly.

30. It is important to note that the reason for which an individual may, in the circumstances described above, rely on the provisions of a directive in proceedings before the national courts is that the obligations arising under those provisions are binding upon all the authorities of the Member States.

31. It would, moreover, be contradictory to rule that an individual may rely upon the provisions of a directive which fulfil the conditions defined above in proceedings before the national courts seeking an order against the administrative authorities, and yet to hold that those authorities are under no obligation to apply the provisions of the directive and refrain from applying provisions of national law which conflict with them. It follows that when the conditions under which the Court has held that individuals may rely on the provisions of a directive before the national courts are met, all organs of the administration, including decentralized authorities such as municipalities, are obliged to apply those provisions.

32. With specific regard to Article 29(5) of Directive 71/305, it is apparent from the discussion of the first question that it is unconditional and sufficiently precise to be relied

upon by an individual against the State. An individual may therefore plead that provision before the national courts and, as is clear from the foregoing, all organs of the administration, including decentralized authorities such as municipalities, are obliged to apply it.

33.   The answer to the fourth question must therefore be that administrative authorities, including municipal authorities, are under the same obligation as a national court to apply the provisions of Article 29(5) of Council Directive 71/305/EEC and to refrain from applying provisions of national law which conflict with them.

JOHNSTON v CHIEF CONSTABLE OF THE ROYAL ULSTER CONSTABULARY (Case 222/84) [1986] ECR 1651, Court of Justice

54.   In the event that, having regard to the foregoing, the question should still arise whether an individual may rely on the directive as against a derogation laid down by national legislation, reference should be made to the established case-law of the Court (see in particular its judgment of 19 January 1982 in *Becker* v *Finanzamt Münster-Innenstadt* (Case 8/81) [1982] ECR 53). More particularly, the Court recently held in its judgment delivered on 26 February 1986 in *Marshall* v *Southampton and South West Hampshire Area Health Authority* (Case 152/84) [1986] ECR 723 that certain provisions of Directive No. 76/207 are, as far as their subject-matter is concerned, unconditional and sufficiently precise and that they may be relied upon by individuals as against a Member State where it fails to implement it correctly.

55.   That statement was made, in the aforesaid judgment of 26 February 1986, with regard to the application of the principle of equal treatment laid down in Article 2(1) of the directive to the conditions governing dismissal referred to in Article 5(1). The same applies as regards the application of the principle contained in Article 2(1) to the conditions governing access to jobs and access to vocational training and advanced vocational training referred to in Articles 3(1) and 4 which are in question in this case.

56.   The Court also held in the aforesaid judgment that individuals may rely on the directive as against an organ of the State whether it acts *qua* employer or *qua* public authority. As regards an authority like the Chief Constable, it must be observed that, according to the Industrial Tribunal's decision, the Chief Constable is an official responsible for the direction of the police service. Whatever its relations may be with other organs of the State, such a public authority, charged by the State with the maintenance of public order and safety, does not act as a private individual. It may not take advantage of the failure of the State, of which it is an emanation, to comply with Community law.

57.   The answer to the sixth question should therefore be that individuals may claim the application, as against a State authority charged with the maintenance of public order and safety acting in its capacity of an employer, of the principle of equal treatment for men and women laid down in·Article 2(1) of Directive No. 76/207 to the matters referred to in Articles 3(1) and 4 concerning the conditions for access to posts and to vocational training and advanced vocational training in order to have a derogation from that principle under national legislation set aside in so far as it exceeds the limits of the exceptions permitted by Article 2(2).

PUBBLICO MINISTERO v RATTI (Case 148/78) [1979] ECR 1629, Court of Justice

Ratti's company complied with a Directive as to the information to be supplied on labels on chemicals, but did not comply with the relevant Italian laws, which were stricter. The Directive had not yet been implemented in Italy and Ratti was prosecuted under Italian law. The Italian court made a reference to the Court of Justice under Article 177 of the Treaty.

It was held that Ratti could not rely on the Directive.

The interpretation of Council Directive No. 77/728/EEC of 7 November 1977

39.   In a fifth question the national court asks whether Council Directive No. 77/728 of 7 November 1977, in particular Article 9 thereof, is immediately and directly applicable with regard to the obligations imposed on Member States to refrain from

action as from the date of notification of that directive in a case where a person, acting upon a legitimate expectation, has complied with the provisions of that directive before the expiry of the period within which the Member State must comply with the said directive.

40.   The objective of that directive is analogous to that of Directive No. 73/173 in that it lays down similar rules for preparations intended to be used as paints, varnishes, printing ink, adhesives and similar products, and containing dangerous substances.

41.   Article 12 of that directive provides that Member States must implement it within 24 months of its notification, which took place on 9 November 1977.

42.   That period has not yet expired and the States to which the directive was addressed have until 9 November 1979 to incorporate the provisions of Directive No. 77/728 into their internal legal orders.

43.   It follows that, for the reasons expounded in the grounds of the answer to the national court's first question, it is only at the end of the prescribed period and in the event of the Member State's default that the directive – and in particular Article 9 thereof – will be able to have the effects described in the answer to the first question.

44.   Until that date is reached the Member States remain free in that field.

5.1.5   RECOMMENDATIONS AND OPINIONS

GRIMALDI v FONDS DES MALADIES PROFESSIONNELLES (Case C–322/88)
[1989] ECR 4407, Court of Justice

Grimaldi suffered from a disease which was classified under a Recommendation as an occupational disease. Under French law, however, it was not so classified, and therefore under French law, Grimaldi was not entitled to any compensation. Grimaldi sought to rely on the Recommendation. The French court made a reference to the Court of Justice under Article 177 of the Treaty.

It was held that Recommendations could not be directly effective, but they could be taken into consideration when interpreting other measures.

7.   In so far as the preliminary question concerns the interpretation of recommendations, which, according to the fifth paragraph of Article 189 of the EEC Treaty, have no binding force, it is necessary to consider whether, under Article 177 of the Treaty, the Court has jurisdiction to give a ruling.

8.   It is sufficient to state in that respect that, unlike Article 173 of the EEC Treaty, which excludes review by the Court of acts in the nature of recommendations, Article 177 confers on the Court jurisdiction to give a preliminary ruling on the validity and interpretation of all acts of the institutions of the Community without exception.

9.   Moreover, in proceedings under Article 177 the Court has already ruled on several occasions on the interpretation of recommendations adopted on the basis of the EEC Treaty (see judgments of 15 June 1976 in Case 113/75 *Frecassetti* v *Amministrazione delle finanze dello Stato* [1976] ECR 983, and of 9 June 1977 in Case 90/76 *Van Ameyde* v *UCI* [1977] ECR 1091). It is therefore necessary to consider the question submitted to the Court.

10.   It appears from the documents before the Court that although the question refers only to the recommendation of 23 July 1962, it also seeks to ascertain the effects under national law of Recommendation 66/462 of 20 July 1966. The question must therefore be understood as asking whether, in the absence of any national measure to implement them, those recommendations confer on individuals rights upon which they may rely before national courts.

11.   In the first place, the Court has consistently decided that whilst under Article 189 regulations are directly applicable and, consequently, by their nature capable of producing direct effects, that does not mean that other categories of measures covered by that article can never produce similar effects (see, in particular, judgment of 19 January 1982 in *Becker* v *Finanzamt Münster-Innenstadt* (Case 8/81) [1982] ECR 53).

12.   In order to establish whether the two recommendations may confer rights on individuals, however, it is necessary first to ascertain whether they can produce binding effects.

13.   Recommendations, which according to the fifth paragraph of Article 189 of the Treaty are not binding, are generally adopted by the institutions of the Community when they do not have the power under the Treaty to adopt binding measures or when they consider that it is not appropriate to adopt more mandatory rules.

14.   Since it follows from the settled case law of the Court (see, in particular, judgment of 29 January 1985 in Case 147/83 *Binderer* v *Commission* [1985] ECR 257) that the choice of form cannot alter the nature of a measure, it must nevertheless be ascertained whether the content of a measure is wholly consistent with the form attributed to it.

15.   As regards the two recommendations at issue in these proceedings, it must be stated that in the statement of the reasons on which they are based reference is made to Article 155 of the EEC Treaty, which confers on the Commission a general power to formulate recommendations, and to Articles 117 and 118 of the Treaty. As the Court held in its judgment of 9 July 1987 in Joined Cases 281, 283, 284, 285 and 287/85 *Federal Republic of Germany, France, the Netherlands, Denmark and the United Kingdom* v *Commission* [1987] ECR 3203, Article 118 does not encroach upon the Member States' powers in the social field in so far as the latter is not covered by the other provisions of the Treaty and provided that those powers are exercised in the framework of co-operation between Member States, which is to be organized by the Commission.

16.   In these circumstances there is no reason to doubt that the measures in question are true recommendations, that is to say measures which, even as regards the persons to whom they are addressed, are not intended to produce binding effects. Consequently, they cannot create rights upon which individuals may rely before a national court.

17.   In this regard, the fact that more than 25 years have elapsed since the first of the recommendations in question was adopted, without its having been implemented by all Member States, cannot alter its legal effect.

18.   However, in order to give a comprehensive reply to the question asked by the national court, it must be stressed that the measures in question cannot therefore be regarded as having no legal effect. The national courts are bound to take recommendations into consideration in order to decide disputes submitted to them, in particular where they cast light on the interpretation of national measures adopted in order to implement them or where they are designed to supplement binding Community provisions.

19.   The reply to the question asked by the tribunal du travail, Brussels, must therefore be that in the light of the fifth paragraph of Article 189 of the EEC Treaty, the Commission Recommendation of 23 July 1962 concerning the adoption of a European schedule of occupational diseases and Commission Recommendation 64/462 of 20 July 1966 on the conditions for granting compensation to persons suffering from occupational diseases cannot in themselves confer rights on individuals upon which the latter may rely before national courts. However, national courts are bound to take those recommendations into consideration in order to decide disputes submitted to them, in particular where they are capable of casting light on the interpretation of other provisions of national or Community law.

5.2   Indirect Effect

VON COLSON AND KAMANN v LAND NORDRHEIN-WESTFALEN (Case 14/83)
[1984] ECR 1891, Court of Justice

Two women applied for jobs as social workers, and when two men were appointed, the women alleged that they had been discriminated against contrary to Directive 76/207 which prohibited discrimination at work on grounds of sex. The German court made a reference to the Court of Justice under Article 177 of the Treaty.

It was held that the applicants could not rely on the direct effect of this Directive, but the relevant national law should be interpreted in the light of its provisions.

26.   However, the Member States' obligation arising from a directive to achieve the result envisaged by the directive and their duty under Article 5 of the Treaty to take all appropriate measures, whether general or particular, to ensure the fulfilment of that

obligation, is binding on all the authorities of Member States including, for matters within their jurisdiction, the courts. It follows that, in applying the national law and in particular the provisions of a national law specifically introduced in order to implement Directive No. 76/207, national courts are required to interpret their national law in the light of the wording and the purpose of the directive in order to achieve the result referred to in the third paragraph of Article 189.

27.   On the other hand, as the above considerations show, the directive does not include any unconditional and sufficiently precise obligation as regards sanctions for discrimination which, in the absence of implementing measures adopted in good time may be relied on by individuals in order to obtain specific compensation under the directive, where that is not provided for or permitted under national law.

LITSTER AND OTHERS v FORTH DRY DOCK AND ENGINEERING CO. LTD AND ANOTHER [1989] 1 All ER 1134, House of Lords

The facts appear in the extract below.

It was held that the regulation must be interpreted in the light of the Directive so as to give a remedy to the applicant.

LORD TEMPLEMAN (at pp. 1138j–1140q): The appellants were dismissed at 3.30 pm on 6 February by Forth Dry Dock and the business was transferred to Forth Estuary at 4.30 pm on the same day. It is argued on behalf of Forth Estuary that despite the directive and the regulations they are not liable to the appellants in respect of their unfair dismissal because reg. 5(3) provides:

Any reference in paragraph (1) . . . above to a person employed in an undertaking or part of one transferred by a relevant transfer is a reference to a person so employed immediately before the transfer, including, where the transfer is effected by a series of two or more transactions, a person so employed immediately before any of those transactions.

Thus, it is said, since the workforce of Forth Dry Dock were dismissed at 3.30 pm they were not employed immediately before the transfer at 4.30 pm and therefore reg. 5(1) did not transfer any liability for the workforce from Forth Dry Dock to Forth Estuary. The argument is inconsistent with the directive. In *P Bork International A/S (in liq)* v *Foreningen af Arbejdsledere i Danmark* Case 101/87 [1989] IRLR 41 at 44 (paras. 17–18) the Court of Justice of the European Communities ruled:

. . . the only workers who may invoke Directive 77/187 are those who have current employment relations or a contract of employment at the date of the transfer. The question whether or not a contract of employment or employment relationship exists at that date must be assessed under national law, subject, however, to the observance of the mandatory rules of the Directive concerning the protection of workers against dismissal by reason of the transfer. It follows that the workers employed by the undertaking whose contract of employment or employment relationship has been terminated with effect on a date before that of the transfer, in breach of Article 4(1) of the Directive, must be considered as still employed by the undertaking on the date of transfer with the consequence, in particular, that the obligations of an employer towards them are fully transferred from the transferor to the transferee, in accordance with Article 3(1) of the Directive . . .

In *von Colson* v *Land Nordrhein-Westfalen* (Case 14/83) [1984] ECR 1891 at 1909 (para. 26) the European Court, dealing with EC Council Directive 76/207 forbidding discrimination on grounds of sex regarding access to employment, ruled:

. . . the Member States' obligation arising from a directive to achieve the result envisaged by the directive and their duty under Article 5 of the Treaty to take all appropriate measures, whether general or particular, to ensure the fulfilment of that obligation, is binding on all the authorities of the Member States including, for matters within their jurisdiction, the courts. It follows that, in applying the national law and in particular the provisions of a national law specifically introduced in order to implement Directive No. 76/207, national courts are required to interpret their national law in the light of the wording and the purpose of the directive in order to achieve the result referred to in the third paragraph of Article 189.

Thus the courts of the United Kingdom are under a duty to follow the practice of the European Court by giving a purposive construction to directives and to regulations issued for the purpose of complying with directives. In *Pickstone* v *Freemans plc* [1988] 2 All ER 803, [1989] AC 66 this House implied words in a regulation designed to give effect to EC Council Directive 75/117 dealing with equal pay for women doing work of equal value. If this House had not been able to make the necessary implication the Equal Pay (Amendment) Regulations 1983, SI 1983/1794, would have failed in their object and the United Kingdom would have been in breach of its treaty obligations to give effect to directives. In the present case, in the light of EC Council Directive 77/187 and in the light of the ruling of the European Court in *Bork's* case [1989] IRLR 41, it seems to me, following the suggestion of my noble and learned friend Lord Keith, that reg. 5(3) of the 1981 Regulations was not intended and ought not to be construed so as to limit the operation of reg. 5 to persons employed immediately before the transfer in point of time. Regulation 5(3) must be construed on the footing that it applies to a person employed immediately before the transfer or who would have been so employed if he had not been unfairly dismissed before the transfer for a reason connected with the transfer. It would, of course, still be open for a new owner to show that the employee had been dismissed for an 'economic, technical or organisational reason entailing changes in the workforce', but no such reason could be advanced in the present case where there was no complaint against the workers, they were not redundant and there were no relevent reasons entailing changes in the workforce. I would therefore allow the appeal.

MARLEASING SA v LA COMERCIAL INTERNACIONAL DE ALIMENTACIÓN SA
(Case C–106/89) [1990] ECR I–4135, Court of Justice

Spanish law laid down a number of grounds on which a company could be struck off the register, including lack of cause. Spain had failed to implement a later Directive which did not include this particular ground. The Spanish court made a reference to the Court of Justice under Article 177 of the Treaty.

It was held that Spanish law must be interpreted in accordance with the Directive and therefore a company could not be struck off for lack of cause.

7. However, it is apparent from the documents before the Court that the national court seeks in substance to ascertain whether a national court hearing a case which falls within the scope of Directive 68/151 is required to interpret its national law in the light of the wording and the purpose of that directive in order to preclude a declaration of nullity of a public limited company on a ground other than those listed in Article 11 of the directive.

8. In order to reply to that question, it should be observed that, as the Court pointed out in its judgment in Case 14/83 *Von Colson and Kamann* v *Land Nordrhein-Westfalen* [1984] ECR 1891, paragraph 26, the Member States' obligation arising from a directive to achieve the result envisaged by the directive and their duty under Article 5 of the Treaty to take all appropriate measures, whether general or particular, to ensure the fulfilment of that obligation, is binding on all the authorities of Member States including, for matters within their jurisdiction, the courts. It follows that, in applying national law, whether the provisions in question were adopted before or after the directive, the national court called upon to interpret it is required to do so, as far as possible, in the light of the wording and the purpose of the directive in order to achieve the result pursued by the latter and thereby comply with the third paragraph of Article 189 of the Treaty.

9. It follows that the requirement that national law must be interpreted in comformity with Article 11 of Directive 68/151 precludes the interpretation of provisions of national law relating to public limited companies in such a manner that the nullity of a public

limited company may be ordered on grounds other than those exhaustively listed in Article 11 of the directive in question.

WAGNER MIRET v *FONDO DE GARANTÍA SALARIAL* (Case C-334/92) [1993] 2 CMLR 49, Court of Justice

Wagner was a senior manager in a Spanish company which became insolvent. Directive 80/987 obliged Member States to set up a fund to recompense employees whose employers became insolvent, but the existing Spanish fund did not cover senior managers. The Spanish court made a reference to the Court of Justice under Article 177 of the Treaty.

It was held that the Spanish state was liable in damages to Wagner for its failure to implement fully the Directive.

15.   By the third question, the national court in essence asks whether higher management staff are entitled, by virtue of the directive on the insolvency of employers, to request the payment of amounts owing to them by way of salary from the guarantee body established by national law for the other categories of employee or, if this is not the case, whether they are entitled to request the Member State concerned to make good the loss and damage sustained as a result of the failure to implement the directive in their respect.

16.   It should first be observed that Spain has established no guarantee institution other than the *Fondo de Garantía Salarial*.

17.   Secondly, in its judgment of 19 November 1991, (Cases C-6 & 9/90) *Francovich* v *Republic* [1991] 1 ECR 5357, the Court held that under Article 5 of the directive on the insolvency of employers, the Member States have a broad discretion with regard to the organisation, operation and financing of the guarantee institutions. The Court concluded that even though the provisions of the directive are sufficiently precise and unconditional as regards the determination of the persons entitled to the guarantee and as regards the content of that guarantee, those elements are not sufficient to enable individuals to rely, as against the State, on those provisions before the national courts.

18.   With regard, more particularly, to the problem raised by the national court, it should be pointed out that the directive on the insolvency of employers does not oblige the Member States to set up a single guarantee institution for all categories of employee, and consequently to bring higher management staff within the ambit of the guarantee institution established for the other categories of employee. Article 3(1) leaves it to the Member States to adopt the measures necessary to ensure that guarantee institutions guarantee payment of employees' outstanding claims.

19.   From the discretion thus given to the Member States it must therefore be concluded that higher management staff cannot rely on the directive in order to request the payment of amounts owing by way of salary from the guarantee institution established for the other categories of employee.

20.   Thirdly, it should be borne in mind that when it interprets and applies national law, every national court must presume that the State had the intention of fulfilling entirely the obligations arising from the directive concerned. As the Court held in *Marleasing SA* v *La Comercial Internacional de Alimentación SA* Case C-106/89, in applying national law, whether the provisions in question were adopted before or after the directive, the national court called upon to interpret it is required to do so, so far as possible, in the light of the wording and the purpose of the directive in order to achieve the result pursued by the latter and thereby comply with the third paragraph of **Article 189** of the Treaty.

21.   The principle of interpretation in conformity with directives must be followed in particular where a national court considers, as in the present case, that the pre-existing provisions of its national law satisfy the requirements of the directive concerned.

22.   It would appear from the order for reference that the national provisions cannot be interpreted in a way which conforms with the directive on the insolvency of employers and therefore do not permit higher management staff to obtain the benefit of the guarantees for which it provides. If that is the case, it follows from the *Francovich* judgment, cited above, that the Member State concerned is obliged to make good the loss

and damage sustained as a result of the failure to implement the directive in their respect.

23.   The reply to the third question must therefore be that (a) higher management staff are not entitled, under Directive 80/987, to request payment of amounts owing to them by way of salary from the guarantee institution established by national law for the other categories of employee, and (b) in the event that, even when interpreted in the light of that directive, national law does not enable higher management staff to obtain the benefit of the guarantees for which it provides, such staff are entitled to request the State concerned to make good the loss and damage sustained as a result of the failure to implement the directive in their respect.

WEBB v EMO AIR CARGO (UK) LTD [1992] 4 All ER 929, House of Lords

Webb was employed to cover the absence of another employee on maternity leave, but was dismissed when she herself became pregnant. She argued that her dismissal was in breach of the Sex Discrimination Act 1975 and Directive 76/207.

It was held that the dismissal was not contrary to the Sex Discrimination Act, since had a male employee in the same job been unavailable for work at the same time, he would also have been dismissed. The question of whether the dismissal was contrary to the Directive would be referred to the Court of Justice under Article 177 of the Treaty.

LORD KEITH OF KINKEL (at pp. 939c-g and 940b-j):
Directive 76/207 does not have direct effect upon the relationship between a worker and an employer who is not the state or an emanation of the state, but nevertheless it is for a United Kingdom court to construe domestic legislation in any field covered by a Community directive so as to accord with the interpretation of the directive as laid down by the European Court, if that can be done without distorting the meaning of the domestic legislation: see *Duke v GEC Reliance Ltd* [1988] 1 All ER 626 at 636, [1988] AC 618 at 639–640 per Lord Templeman. This is so whether the domestic legislation came after or, as in this case, preceded the directive: see *Marleasing SA v La Comercial Internacional de Alimentación SA* (Case C-106/89) [1990] ECR I-4135. That was a case where a Spanish company had been founded with the alleged purpose of defrauding the creditors of one of its founders. A provision of the Spanish Civil Code on the validity of contracts laid down that contracts lacking cause or whose cause was unlawful should have no legal effect. A creditor of the company relied upon this provision in order to obtain a declaration that the instrument incorporating the company was invalid. The company relied in its defence upon Article 11 of Council Directive (EEC) 68/151, which contained an exhaustive list of the cases in which the nullity of a company might be declared. The list did not include lack of lawful cause. The article had not been implemented into Spanish national law. The European Court held that the Spanish courts must not interpret the relevant provision of the Civil Code in such a manner that the nullity of a public limited company might be ordered on grounds other than those listed in Article 11 of the directive.
. . .
It is to be observed that the provision of Spanish law in issue in that case was of a general character capable of being construed either widely or narrowly. It did not refer specifically to the grounds upon which the nullity of a public limited company might be ordered. If it had done so, and had included among such grounds the case where the company had been formed with the purpose of defrauding creditors of one of the corporators, the Spanish court would have been entitled and bound to give effect to it notwithstanding the terms of the directive. As the European Court said, a national court must construe a domestic law to accord with the terms of a directive in the same field only if it is possible to do so. That means that the domestic law must be open to an interpretation consistent with the directive whether or not it is also open to an interpretation inconsistent with it.

The European Court did not, in *Dekker's* case and the *Hertz* case, have to consider the situation where a woman, on account of her pregnancy, will not be able to carry out, at the time when her services are required, the particular job for which she is applying or for which she has been engaged. The two decisions do not give any clear indication whether in such a situation the court would regard the fundamental reason for the refusal to engage the woman or for dismissing her as being her unavailability for the job and not her pregnancy. In the event of the court arriving at a decision that the latter and not the former is the correct view for the purposes of the Directive 76/207, it would be necessary for this House to consider whether it is possible to construe the relevant provisions of the 1975 Act in such a way as to accord with such a decision. Further, it is not impossible to envisage that the sort of situation which existed in the present case might arise in circumstances where the Directive 76/707 has direct application, namely where the employer is the state or an emanation of the state. So I think it appropriate that before final judgment is given on this appeal there should be referred to the European Court the following question:

> Is it discrimination on grounds of sex contrary to Directive 76/207 for an employer to dismiss a female employee ('the appellant') (a) whom he engaged for the specific purpose of replacing (after training) another female employee during the latter's forthcoming maternity leave, (b) when, very shortly after appointment, the employer discovers that the appellant herself will be absent on maternity leave during the maternity leave of the other employee, and the employer dismisses her because he needs the job holder to be at work during that period, (c) had the employer known of the pregnancy of the appellant at the date of appointment, she would not have been appointed, and (d) the employer would similarly have dismissed a male employee engaged for this purpose who required leave of absence at the relevant time for medical or other reasons?

I understand that all your Lordships agree that there should be a reference accordingly, and that final disposal of the appeal should be postponed until the decision of the European Court has been made available.

WEBB v EMO AIR CARGO (UK) LTD (NO. 2) [1995] 4 All ER 577, House of Lords

For the facts of this case see *Webb v EMO Air Cargo (UK) Ltd* above. The question of whether Webb's dismissal was contrary to Directive 76/207 had been referred to the Court of Justice. The Court of Justice had ruled ((Case C-32/93) [1994] 2 CMLR 729) that it was.

The House of Lords held that relevant provisions of the Sex Discrimination Act 1975 would be interpreted, in this case, so as to reflect the ruling of the Court of Justice as to the meaning of Directive 76/207. According to this interpretation, Webb's dismissal was discriminatory and illegal.

LORD KEITH OF KINKEL (at p. 582a-h):
The provisions of the 1975 Act which your Lordships must endeavour to construe, so as to accord if at all possible with the ruling of the European Court, are ss. 1(1)(a) and 5(3).
    Section 1(1)(a) provides:

> A person discriminates against a woman in any circumstances relevant for the purposes of any provision of this Act if – (a) on the ground of her sex he treats her less favourably than he treats or would treat a man . . .

Section 5(3) provides:

> A comparison of the cases of persons of different sex or marital status under section 1(1) or 3(1) must be such that the relevant circumstances in the one case are the same, or not materially different, in the other.

The reasoning in my speech in the earlier proceedings was to the effect that the relevant circumstance which existed in the present case and which should be taken to be present in the case of the hypothetical man was unavailability for work at the time when the worker was particularly required, and that the reason for the unavailability was not a relevant circumstance (see [1994] 4 All ER 929 at 933–935, [1993] 1 WLR 49 at 53–55). So it was not relevant that the reason for the woman's unavailability was pregnancy, a condition which could not be present in a man.

The ruling of the European Court proceeds on an interpretation of the broad principles dealt with in art. 2(1) and 5(1) of Directive 76/207. Sections 1(1)(a) and 5(3) of the 1975 Act set out a more precise test of unlawful discrimination, and the problem is how to fit the terms of that test into the ruling. It seems to me that the only way of doing so is to hold that, in a case where a woman is engaged for an indefinite period, the fact that the reason why she will be temporarily unavailable for work at a time when to her knowledge her services will be particularly required is pregnancy is a circumstance relevant to her case, being a circumstance which could not be present in the case of the hypothetical man. It does not necessarily follow that pregnancy would be a relevant circumstance in the situation where the woman is denied employment for a fixed period in the future during the whole of which her pregnancy would make her unavailable for work, nor in the situation where after engagement for such a period the discovery of her pregnancy leads to cancellation of the engagement.

My Lords, for these reasons I would allow the appeal and remit the case to the industrial tribunal to assess compensation.

5.3   Member State Liability

5.3.1   *FRANCOVICH* LIABILITY

FRANCOVICH AND OTHERS v *ITALIAN REPUBLIC* (Cases C–6/90 & C–9/90) [1991] ECR I–5357, Court of Justice

Francovich had no remedy under Italian law for unpaid wages when his employer became insolvent because Italy had failed to implement a Directive which required the State to set up a scheme to compensate such employees. The Italian court made a reference to the Court of Justice under Article 177 of the Treaty.

It was held that the Italian state must make good the loss caused to Francovich by its failure to implement the Directive.

26.   Accordingly, even though the provisions of the directive in question are sufficiently precise and unconditional as regards the determination of the persons entitled to the guarantee and as regards the content of that guarantee, those elements are not sufficient to enable individuals to rely on those provisions before the national courts. Those provisions do not identify the person liable to provide the guarantee, and the State cannot be considered liable on the sole ground that it has failed to take transposition measures within the prescribed period.

27.   The answer to the first part of the first question must therefore be that the provisions of Directive 80/987 which determine the rights of employees must be interpreted as meaning that the persons concerned cannot enforce those rights against the State before the national courts where no implementing measures are adopted within the prescribed period.

Liability of the State for loss and damage resulting from breach of its obligations under Community law

28.   In the second part of the first question the national court seeks to determine whether a Member State is obliged to make good loss and damage suffered by individuals as a result of the failure to transpose Directive 80/987.

29.   The national court thus raises the issue of the existence and scope of a State's liability for loss and damage resulting from breach of its obligations under Community law.

30.   That issue must be considered in the light of the general system of the Treaty and its fundamental principles.

(a)   *The existence of State liability as a matter of principle*

31.   It should be borne in mind at the outset that the EEC Treaty has created its own legal system, which is integrated into the legal systems of the Member States and which

their courts are bound to apply. The subjects of that legal system are not only the Member States but also their nationals. Just as it imposes burdens on individuals, Community law is also intended to give rise to rights which become part of their legal patrimony. Those rights arise not only where they are expressly granted by the Treaty but also by virtue of obligations which the Treaty imposes in a clearly defined manner both on individuals and on the Member States and the Community institutions (see the judgments in Case 26/62 *Van Gend en Loos* [1963] ECR 1 and Case 6/64 *Costa* v *ENEL* [1964] ECR 585).

32. Furthermore, it has been consistently held that the national courts whose task it is to apply the provisions of Community law in areas within their jurisdiction must ensure that those rules take full effect and must protect the rights which they confer on individuals (see in particular the judgments in Case 106/77 *Amministrazione delle Finanze dello Stato* v *Simmenthal* [1978] ECR 629, paragraph 16, and Case C–213/89 *Factortame* [1990] ECR I–2433, paragraph 19).

33. The full effectiveness of Community rules would be impaired and the protection of the rights which they grant would be weakened if individuals were unable to obtain redress when their rights are infringed by a breach of Community law for which a Member State can be held responsible.

34. The possibility of obtaining redress from the Member State is particularly indispensable where, as in this case, the full effectiveness of Community rules is subject to prior action on the part of the State and where, consequently, in the absence of such action, individuals cannot enforce before the national courts the rights conferred upon them by Community law.

35. It follows that the principle whereby a State must be liable for loss and damage caused to individuals as a results of breaches of Community law for which the State can be held responsible is inherent in the system of the Treaty.

36. A further basis for the obligation of Member States to make good such loss and damage is to be found in Article 5 of the Treaty, under which the Member States are required to take all appropriate measures, whether general or particular, to ensure fulfilment of their obligations under Community law. Among these is the obligation to nullify the unlawful consequences of a breach of Community law (see, in relation to the analogous provision of Article 86 of the ECSC Treaty, the judgment in Case 6/60 *Humblet* v *Belgium* [1990] ECR 559).

37. It follows from all the foregoing that it is a principle of Community law that the Member States are obliged to make good loss and damage caused to individuals by breaches of Community law for which they can be held responsible.

(b) *The conditions for State liability*

38. Although State liability is thus required by Community law, the conditions under which that liability gives rise to a right to reparation depend on the nature of the breach of Community law giving rise to the loss and damage.

39. Where, as in this case, a Member State fails to fulfil its obligation under the third paragraph of Article 189 of the Treaty to take all the measures necessary to achieve the result prescribed by a directive, the full effectiveness of that rule of Community law requires that there should be a right to reparation provided that three conditions are fulfilled.

40. The first of those conditions is that the result prescribed by the directive should entail the grant of rights to individuals. The second condition is that it should be possible to identify the content of those rights on the basis of the provisions of the directive. Finally, the third condition is the existence of a causal link between the breach of the State's obligation and the loss and damage suffered by the injured parties.

41. Those conditions are sufficient to give rise to a right on the part of individuals to obtain reparation, a right founded directly on Community law.

42. Subject to that reservation, it is on the basis of the rules of national law on liability that the State must make reparation for the consequences of the loss and damage caused. In the absence of Community legislation, it is for the internal legal order of each Member State to designate the competent courts and lay down the detailed procedural rules for legal proceedings intended fully to safeguard the rights which individuals derive from Community law (see the judgments in Case 60/75 *Russo* v *AIMA* [1976] ECR 45, Case

33/76 *Rewe* v *Landwirstschaftskammer Saarland* [1976] ECR 1989 and Case 158/80 *Rewe* v *Hauptzollamt Kiel* [1981] ECR 1805).

43.   Further, the substantive and procedural conditions for reparation of loss and damage laid down by the national law of the Member States must not be less favourable than those relating to similar domestic claims and must not be so framed as to make it virtually impossible or excessively difficult to obtain reparation (see, in relation to the analogous issue of the repayment of taxes levied in breach of Community law, *inter alia* the judgment in Case 199/82 *Amministrazione delle Finanze dello Stato* v *San Giorgio* [1983] ECR 3595).

44.   In this case, the breach of Community law by a Member State by virtue of its failure to transpose Directive 80/987 within the prescribed period has been confirmed by a judgment of the Court. The result required by that directive entails the grant to employees of a right to a guarantee of payment of their unpaid wage claims. As is clear from the examination of the first part of the first question, the content of that right can be identified on the basis of the provisions of the directive.

45.   Consequently, the national court must, in accordance with the national rules on liability, uphold the right of employees to obtain reparation of loss and damage caused to them as a result of failure to transpose the directive.

46.   The answer to be given to the national court must therefore be that a Member State is required to make good loss and damage caused to individuals by failure to transpose Directive 80/987.

J. Steiner, 'From direct effects to *Francovich*: shifting means of enforcement of Community law' (1993) 18 EL Rev 3

Assessment of Francovich

The decision in *Francovich* is undoubtedly consistent with, and a natural and logical extension of, the Court's case law. Having established that Community law can give rise to rights for individuals, and that national courts are obliged to ensure the full effectiveness of such provisions it was but a small step to guarantee their full effect by holding states liable in damages for infringements of those rights for which they were responsible.

The breakthrough in *Francovich* lay not so much in the fact that individuals were held entitled to claim damages against the State – in the context of actions based on directly effective Community law against 'public' bodies that had long been possible – but that their claim to compensation was *independent* of the principle of direct effects. Provided the criteria for *Francovich* are met the individual may now proceed against the State for breach not of substantive, directly effective Community provisions, but for the State's *primary* failure to comply with its obligation to implement Community law. Although the Court found that the relevant provisions of Directive 80/987 were not directly effective, the criteria for liability under *Francovich* as regards the nature and content of the rights infringed are close to those for direct effects. The Court could without difficulty have found the provisions in question sufficiently precise and unconditional for direct effects, at least as regards the end to be achieved. It is submitted that it did not do so because it wished to establish a remedy for Member States' infringements of Community law which did not depend on the need to prove direct effects. In this way, the problems associated with directives arising from their lack of horizontal effect would be largely circumvented. If Community rights could not be enforced against private parties, compensation would at least be provided for individuals wrongfully deprived of their Community rights. At the same time the prospect of liability to *all* parties suffering damage as a result of their failures to implement Community law would provide States with a powerful incentive fully to comply with their community obligations.

A principle of State liability as applied in *Francovich* is arguably more legitimate as a means of enforcement of Community law than the principle of direct effects. Under the latter principle, Treaty provisions, the scope of which may not be clear (for example, Art. 119), may be enforced against the legitimate expectations of 'private' parties. The majority of 'public' bodies, against which directives may be invoked, can hardly be seen as responsible for non-implementation. The element of public authority or control to which they are subject simply renders them liable-by-association. If that authority or control should have ensured compliance by the defendant organisation with the obligations imposed by directives and failed to do so, the fault lies less with the local authority or public enterprise than with the central authorities, the legislative or executive organs of the State.

If more legitimate than the principle of direct effects, a principle of State liability on the basis of *Francovich* is undoubtedly more legitimate than a principle of indirect effects. Given the nature of directives, as binding on, and requiring implementation by, the State, it can be argued that individuals should not be required to comply with their provisions (albeit by means of 'interpretation' rather than direct effect) until they are implemented into national law. Only where domestic law is ambiguous, and compatible with the directive, or has been expressly introduced in order to implement the directive should it be permissible to give indirect effect to Community law. The principles of direct and indirect effects were simply expedients designed to secure the enforcement of Community law precisely because States had failed to fulfil their obligations. The primary fault for non-compliance has always lain with the State. Since a principle of non-contractual liability of public authorities is recognised in all the Member States and under Community law there seems no good reason why, in a case such as *Francovich*, the State should not be liable to individuals suffering damage as a result of its own failure to comply with Community law.

5.3.2   *FACTORTAME III* LIABILITY

JOINED CASES C-46/93 AND C-48/93 *BRASSERIE DU PÊCHEUR SA* v *FEDERAL REPUBLIC OF GERMANY* AND *R* v *SECRETARY OF STATE FOR TRANSPORT, EX PARTE FACTORTAME LTD AND OTHERS (FACTORTAME III)* [1996] 1 CMLR 889

Spanish fishermen claimed damages after certain provisions of the Merchant Shipping Act 1988, which prevented them fishing in UK waters, were declared contrary to Community law and therefore invalid by the Court of Justice.

The Court of Justice held that the UK government could be sued for damages for its breach of Community law in enacting the invalid Act.

State Liability for Acts and Omissions of the National Legislature Contrary to Community Law (First Question in both Case C-46/93 and Case C-48/93)

. . .

17.   In Joined Cases C-6/90 and 9/90 *Francovich and Others* [1991] ECR I-5357, paragraph 37, the Court held that it is a principle of Community law that Member States are obliged to make good loss and damage caused to individuals by breaches of Community law for which they can be held responsible.

18.   The German, Irish and Netherlands Governments contend that Member States are required to make good loss or damage caused to individuals only where the provisions breached are not directly effective: in *Francovich and Others* the Court simply sought to fill a lacuna in the system for safeguarding rights of individuals. In so far as national law affords individuals a right of action enabling them to assert their rights under directly effective provisions of Community law, it is unnecessary, where such provisions are breached, also to grant them a right to reparation founded directly on Community law.

19.   That argument cannot be accepted.

20.   The Court has consistently held that the right of individuals to rely on the directly effective provisions of the Treaty before national courts is only a minimum guarantee and is not sufficient in itself to ensure the full and complete implementation of the Treaty (see, in particular, Case 168/85 *Commission* v *Italy* [1986] ECR 2945, [1988] 1 CMLR 580, paragraph 11, Case C-120/88 *Commission* v *Italy* [1991] ECR I-621, paragraph 10, and C-119/89 *Commission* v *Spain* [1991] ECR I-641, [1993] 1 CMLR 41, paragraph 9). The purpose of that right is to ensure that provisions of Community law prevail over national provisions. It cannot, in every case, secure for individuals the benefit of the rights conferred on them by Community law and, in particular, avoid their sustaining damage as a result of a breach of Community law attributable to a Member State. As appears from paragraph 33 of the judgment in *Francovich and Others*, the full effectiveness of

Community law would be impaired if individuals were unable to obtain redress when their rights were infringed by a breach of Community law.

21.   This will be so where an individual who is a victim of the non-transposition of a directive and is precluded from relying on certain of its provisions directly before the national court because they are insufficiently precise and unconditional, brings an action for damages against the defaulting Member State for breach of the third paragraph of Article 189 of the Treaty. In such circumstances, which obtained in the case of *Francovich and Others*, the purpose of reparation is to redress the injurious consequences of a Member State's failure to transpose a directive as far as beneficiaries of that directive are concerned.

22.   It is all the more so in the event of infringement of a right directly conferred by a Community provision upon which individuals are entitled to rely before the national courts. In that event, the right to reparation is the necessary corollary of the direct effect of the Community provision whose breach caused the damage sustained.

23.   In this case, it is undisputed that the Community provisions at issue, namely Article 30 of the Treaty in Case C-46/93 and Article 52 in Case C-48/93, have direct effect in the sense that they confer on individuals rights upon which they are entitled to rely directly before the national courts. Breach of such provisions may give rise to reparation.

. . .

25.   It must, however, be stressed that the existence and extent of State liability for damage ensuing as a result of a breach of obligations incumbent on the State by virtue of Community law are questions of Treaty interpretation which fall within the jurisdiction of the Court.

26.   In this case, as in *Francovich and Others*, those questions of interpretation have been referred to the Court by national courts pursuant to Article 177 of the Treaty.

27.   Since the Treaty contains no provision expressly and specifically governing the consequences of breaches of Community law by Member States, it is for the Court, in pursuance of the task conferred on it by Article 164 of the Treaty of ensuring that in the interpretation and application of the Treaty the law is observed, to rule on such a question in accordance with generally accepted methods of interpretation, in particular by reference to the fundamental principles of the Community legal system and, where necessary, general principles common to the legal systems of the Member States.

28.   Indeed, it is to the general principles common to the laws of the Member States that the second paragraph of Article 215 of the Treaty refers as the basis of the non-contractual liability of the Community for damage caused by its institutions or by its servants in the performance of their duties.

29.   The principle of the non-contractual liability of the Community expressly laid down in Article 215 of the Treaty is simply an expression of the general principle familiar to the legal systems of the Member States that an unlawful act or omission gives rise to an obligation to make good the damage caused. That provision also reflects the obligation on public authorities to make good damage caused in the performance of their duties.

30.   In any event, in many national legal systems the essentials of the legal rules governing State liability have been developed by the courts.

31.   In view of the foregoing considerations, the Court held in *Francovich and Others*, at paragraph 35, that the principle of State liability for loss and damage caused to individuals as a result of breaches of Community law for which it can be held responsible is inherent in the system of the Treaty.

32.   It follows that that principle holds good for any case in which a Member State breaches Community law, whatever be the organ of the State whose act or omission was responsible for the breach.

. . .

36.   Consequently, the reply to the national courts must be that the principle that Member States are obliged to make good damage caused to individuals by breaches of Community law attributable to the State is applicable where the national legislature was responsible for the breach in question.

Conditions under which the State may Incur Liability for Acts and Omissions of the National Legislature Contrary to Community Law (Second Question in Case C-46/93 and First Question in Case C-48/93)

. . .

38.   Although Community law imposes State liability, the conditions under which that liability gives rise to a right to reparation depend on the nature of the breach of Community law giving rise to the loss and damage (*Francovich and Others*, paragraph 38).

39.   In order to determine those conditions, account should first be taken of the principles inherent in the Community legal order which form the basis for State liability, namely, first, the full effectiveness of Community rules and the effective protection of the rights which they confer and, second, the obligation to cooperate imposed on Member States by Article 5 of the Treaty (*Francovich and Others*, paragraphs 31 to 36).

40.   In addition, as the Commission and the several governments which submitted observations have emphasized, it is pertinent to refer to the Court's case-law on non-contractual liability on the part of the Community.

41.   First, the second paragraph of Article 215 of the Treaty refers, as regards the non-contractual liability of the Community, to the general principles common to the laws of the Member States, from which, in the absence of written rules, the Court also draws inspiration in other areas of Community law.

42.   Second, the conditions under which the State may incur liability for damage caused to individuals by a breach of Community law cannot, in the absence of particular justification, differ from those governing the liability of the Community in like circumstances. The protection of the rights which individuals derive from Community law cannot vary depending on whether a national authority or a Community authority is responsible for the damage.

43.   The system of rules which the Court has worked out with regard to Article 215 of the Treaty, particularly in relation to liability for legislative measures, takes into account, *inter alia*, the complexity of the situations to be regulated, difficulties in the application or interpretation of the texts and, more particularly, the margin of discretion available to the author of the act in question.

44.   Thus, in developing its case-law on the non-contractual liability of the Community, in particular as regards legislative measures involving choices of economic policy, the Court has had regard to the wide discretion available to the institutions in implementing Community policies.

45.   The strict approach taken towards the liability of the Community in the exercise of its legislative activities is due to two considerations. First, even where the legality of measures is subject to judicial review, exercise of the legislative function must not be hindered by the prospect of actions for damages whenever the general interest of the Community requires legislative measures to be adopted which may adversely affect individual interests. Second, in a legislative context characterized by the exercise of a wide discretion, which is essential for implementing a Community policy, the Community cannot incur liability unless the institution concerned has manifestly and gravely disregarded the limits on the exercise of its powers (Joined Cases 83, 94/76, and 4, 15, & 40/77 *HNL and Others* v *Council and Commission* [1978] ECR 1209, paragraphs 5 and 6).

46.   That said, the national legislature – like the Community institutions – does not systematically have a wide discretion when it acts in a field governed by Community law. Community law may impose upon it obligations to achieve a particular result or obligations to act or refrain from acting which reduce its margin of discretion, sometimes to a considerable degree. This is so, for instance, where, as in the circumstances to which the judgment in *Francovich and Others* relates, Article 189 of the Treaty places the Member State under an obligation to take, within a given period, all the measures needed in order to achieve the result required by a directive. In such a case, the fact that it is for the national legislature to take the necessary measures has no bearing on the Member State's liability for failing to transpose the directive.

47.   In contrast, where a Member State acts in a field where it has a wide discretion, comparable to that of the Community institutions in implementing Community policies, the conditions under which it may incur liability must, in principle, be the same as those under which the Community institutions incur liability in a comparable situation.

48.   In the case which gave rise to the reference in Case C-46/93, the German legislature had legislated in the field of foodstuffs, specifically beer. In the absence of Community harmonization, the national legislature had a wide discretion in that sphere in laying down rules on the quality of beer put on the market.

49.   As regards the facts of Case C-48/93, the United Kingdom legislature also had a wide discretion. The legislation at issue was concerned, first, with the registration of vessels, a field which, in view of the state of development of Community law, falls within the jurisdiction of the Member States and, secondly, with regulating fishing, a sector in which implementation of the common fisheries policy leaves a margin of discretion to the Member States.

50.   Consequently, in each case the German and United Kingdom legislatures were faced with situations involving choices comparable to those made by the Community institutions when they adopt legislative measures pursuant to a Community policy.

51.   In such circumstances, Community law confers a right to reparation where three conditions are met: the rule of law infringed must be intended to confer rights on individuals; the breach must be sufficiently serious; and there must be a direct causal link between the breach of the obligation resting on the State and the damage sustained by the injured parties.

52.   Firstly, those conditions satisfy the requirements of the full effectiveness of the rules of Community law and of the effective protection of the rights which those rules confer.

53.   Secondly, those conditions correspond in substance to those defined by the Court in relation to Article 215 in its case law on liability of the Community for damage caused to individuals by unlawful legislative measures adopted by its institutions.

54.   The first condition is manifestly satisfied in the case of Article 30 of the Treaty, the relevant provision in Case C-46/93, and in the case of Article 52, the relevant provision in Case C-48/93. Whilst Article 30 imposes a prohibition on Member States, it nevertheless gives rise to rights for individuals which the national courts must protect (Case 74/76 *Iannelli & Volpi* v *Meroni* [1977] ECR 557, [1977] 2 CMLR 688, paragraph 13). Likewise, the essence of Article 52 is to confer rights on individuals (Case 2/74 *Reyners* [1974] ECR 631, [1974] 2 CMLR 305, paragraph 25).

55.   As to the second condition, as regards both Community liability under Article 215 and Member State liability for breaches of Community law, the decisive test for finding that a breach of Community law is sufficiently serious is whether the Member State or the Community institution concerned manifestly and gravely disregarded the limits on its discretion.

56.   The factors which the competent court may take into consideration include the clarity and precision of the rule breached, the measure of discretion left by that rule to the national or Community authorities, whether the infringement and the damage caused was intentional or involuntary, whether any error of law was excusable or inexcusable, the fact that the position taken by a Community institution may have contributed towards the omission, and the adoption or retention of national measures or practices contrary to Community law.

57.   On any view, a breach of Community law will clearly be sufficiently serious if it has persisted despite a judgment finding the infringement in question to be established, or a preliminary ruling or settled case-law of the Court on the matter from which it is clear that the conduct in question constituted an infringement.

58.   While, in the present cases, the Court cannot substitute its assessment for that of the national courts, which have sole jurisdiction to find the facts in the main proceedings and decide how to characterize the breaches of Community law at issue, it will be helpful to indicate a number of circumstances which the national courts might take into account.
. . .

61.   The decision of the United Kingdom legislature to introduce in the Merchant Shipping Act 1988 provisions relating to the conditions for the registration of fishing vessels has to be assessed differently in the case of the provisions making registration subject to a nationality condition, which constitute direct discrimination manifestly contrary to Community law, and in the case of the provisions laying down residence and domicile conditions for vessel owners and operators.

62.   The latter conditions are prima facie incompatible with Article 52 of the Treaty in particular, but the United Kingdom sought to justify them in terms of the objectives of the common fisheries policy. In the judgment in *Factortame II*, cited above, the Court rejected that justification.

63.   In order to determine whether the breach of Article 52 thus committed by the United Kingdom was sufficiently serious, the national court might take into account, *inter alia*, the legal disputes relating to particular features of the common fisheries policy, the

attitude of the Commission, which made its position known to the United Kingdom in good time, and the assessments as to the state of certainty of Community law made by the national courts in the interim proceedings brought by individuals affected by the Merchant Shipping Act.

64. Lastly, consideration should be given to the assertion made by Rawlings (Trawling) Ltd, the 37th claimant in Case C-48/93, that the United Kingdom failed to adopt immediately the measures needed to comply with the Order of the President of the Court of 10 October 1989 in *EC Commission* v *United Kingdom* (cited above), and that this needlessly increased the loss it sustained. If this allegation – which was certainly contested by the United Kingdom at the hearing – should prove correct, it should be regarded by the national court as constituting in itself a manifest and, therefore, sufficiently serious breach of Community law.

65. As for the third condition, it is for the national courts to determine whether there is a direct causal link between the breach of the obligation borne by the State and the damage sustained by the injured parties.

66. The aforementioned three conditions are necessary and sufficient to found a right in individuals to obtain redress, although this does not mean that the State cannot incur liability under less strict conditions on the basis of national law.

67. As appears from paragraphs 41, 42 and 43 of *Francovich and Others*, cited above, subject to the right to reparation which flows directly from Community law where the conditions referred to in the preceding paragraph are satisfied, the State must make reparation for the consequences of the loss and damage caused in accordance with the domestic rules on liability, provided that the conditions for reparation of loss and damage laid down by national law must not be less favourable than those relating to similar domestic claims and must not be such as in practice to make it impossible or excessively difficult to obtain reparation (see also *Amministrazione delle Finanze dello Stato* v *San Giorgio* (Case 199/82) [1983] ECR 3595).

68. In that regard, restrictions that exist in domestic legal systems as to the non-contractual liability of the State in the exercise of its legislative function may be such as to make it impossible in practice or excessively difficult for individuals to exercise their right to reparation, as guaranteed by Community law, of loss or damage resulting from the breach of Community law.

. . .

70. While the imposition of such restrictions may be consistent with the requirement that the conditions laid down should not be less favourable than those relating to similar domestic claims, it is still to be considered whether such restrictions are not such as in practice to make it impossible or excessively difficult to obtain reparation.

. . .

73. Likewise, any condition that may be imposed by English law on State liability requiring proof of misfeasance in public office, such an abuse of power being inconceivable in the case of the legislature, is also such as in practice to make it impossible or extremely difficult to obtain effective reparation for loss or damage resulting from a breach of Community law where the breach is attributable to the national legislature.

74. Accordingly, the reply to the questions from the national courts must be that, where a breach of Community law by a Member State is attributable to the national legislature acting in a field in which it has a wide discretion to make legislative choices, individuals suffering loss or injury thereby are entitled to reparation where the rule of Community law breached is intended to confer rights upon them, the breach is sufficiently serious and there is a direct causal link between the breach and the damage sustained by the individuals. Subject to that reservation, the State must make good the consequences of the loss or damage caused by the breach of Community law attributable to it, in accordance with its national law on liability. However, the conditions laid down by the applicable national laws must not be less favourable than those relating to similar domestic claims or framed in such a way as in practice to make it impossible or excessively difficult to obtain reparation.

The Possibility of Making Reparation Conditional upon the Existence of Fault (Third Question in Case C-46/93)

. . .

77.   Next, it follows from the reply to the preceding question that, where a breach of Community law is attributable to a Member State acting in a field in which it has a wide discretion to make legislative choices, a finding of a right to reparation on the basis of Community law will be conditional, *inter alia*, upon the breach having been sufficiently serious.

78.   So, certain objective and subjective factors connected with the concept of fault under a national legal system may well be relevant for the purpose of determining whether or not a given breach of Community law is serious (see the factors mentioned in paragraphs 56 and 57 above).

79.   The obligation to make reparation for loss or damage caused to individuals cannot, however, depend upon a condition based on any concept of fault going beyond that of a sufficiently serious breach of Community law. Imposition of such a supplementary condition would be tantamount to calling in question the right to reparation founded on the Community legal order.

80.   Accordingly, the reply to the question from the national court must be that, pursuant to the national legislation which it applies, reparation of loss or damage cannot be made conditional upon fault (intentional or negligent) on the part of the organ of the State responsible for the breach, going beyond that of a sufficiently serious breach of Community law.

TREATY OF ROME

Article 52

Within the framework of the provisions set out below, restrictions on the freedom of establishment of nationals of a Member State in the territory of another Member State shall be abolished by progressive stages in the course of the transitional period. Such progressive abolition shall also apply to restrictions on the setting up of agencies, branches or subsidiaries by nationals of any Member State established in the territory of any Member State.

Freedom of estalishment shall include the right to take up and pursue activities as self-employed persons and to set up and manage undertakings, in particular companies or firms within the meaning of the second paragraph of Article 58, under the conditions laid down for its own nationals by the law of the country where such establishment is effected, subject to the provisions of the Chapter relating to capital.

R v HM TREASURY, EX PARTE BRITISH TELECOMMUNICATIONS PLC
(Case C-392/93) [1996] 2 CMLR 217, Court of Justice

Question 4

[37]   By its fourth question, the Divisional Court seeks to ascertain whether a Member State which, in transposing the directive into national law, has itself determined which services of a contracting entity are to be excluded from its scope pursuant to Article 8, is required by Community law to compensate that undertaking for any loss suffered by it as a result of the error committed by the State.

[38]   It should be recalled, as a preliminary point, that the principle of State liability for loss and damage caused to individuals as a result of breaches of Community law for which the State can be held responsible is inherent in the system of the Treaty (judgments in *Francovich and Others* (Joined Cases C-6 & 9/90), [1993] 2 CMLR 66 and in *Brasserie du Pêcheur* and *Factortame* (Joined Cases C-46 & 48/93) [1996] 1 CMLR 889). It follows that that principle holds good for any case in which a Member State breaches Community law (*Brasserie du Pêcheur* and *Factortame*).

[39]   In the latter judgment the Court also ruled, with regard to a breach of Community law for which a Member State, acting in a field in which it has a wide discretion in taking legislative decisions, can be held responsible, that Community law confers a right to reparation where three conditions are met: the rule of law infringed must be intended to confer rights on individuals; the breach must be sufficiently serious; and there must be a direct causal link between the breach of the obligation resting on the State and the damage sustained by the injured parties.

[40]   Those same conditions must be applicable to the situation, taken as its hypothesis by the national court, in which a Member State incorrectly transposes a Community

directive into national law. A restrictive approach to State liability is justified in such a situation, for the reasons already given by the Court to justify the strict approach to non-contractual liability of Community institutions or Member States when exercising legislative functions in areas covered by Community law where the institution or State has a wide discretion – in particular, the concern to ensure that the exercise of legislative functions is not hindered by the prospect of actions for damages whenever the general interest requires the institutions or Member States to adopt measures which may adversely affect individual interests (see, in particular, (Joined Cases 83/76, 94/76, 4/77, 15/77 and 40/77), *HNL and Others* v *EC Council and EC Commission* [1978] ECR 1209, and in *Brasserie du Pêcheur* and *Factortame*).

[41]   Whilst it is in principle for the national courts to verify whether or not the conditions governing State liability for a breach of Community law are fulfilled, in the present case the Court has all the necessary information to assess whether the facts amount to a sufficiently serious breach of Community law.

[42]   According to the case law of the Court, a breach is sufficiently serious where, in the exercise of its legislative powers, an institution or a Member State has manifestly and gravely disregarded the limits on the exercise of its powers (judgments in *HNL and Others* v *EC Council and EC Commission*, and in *Brasserie du Pêcheur* and *Factortame*). Factors which the competent court may take into consideration include the clarity and precision of the rule breached (*Brasserie du Pêcheur* and *Factortame*).

[43]   In the present case, Article 8(1) is imprecisely worded and was reasonably capable of bearing, as well as the construction applied to it by the Court in this judgment, the interpretation given to it by the United Kingdom in good faith and on the basis of arguments which are not entirely devoid of substance. That interpretation, which was also shared by other Member States, was not manifestly contrary to the wording of the directive or to the objective pursued by it.

[44]   Moreover, no guidance was available to the United Kingdom from case law of the Court as to the interpretation of the provision at issue, nor did the Commission raise the matter when the 1992 Regulations were adopted. ·

[45]   In those circumstances, the fact that a Member State, when transposing the directive into national law, thought it necessary itself to determine which services were to be excluded from its scope in implementation of Article 8, albeit in breach of that provision, cannot be regarded as a sufficiently serious breach of Community law of the kind intended by the Court in its judgment in *Brasserie du Pêcheur* and *Factortame*.

[46]   The answer to Question 4 must therefore be that Community law does not require a Member State which, in transposing the directive into national law, has itself determined which services of a contracting entity are to be excluded from its scope in implementation of Article 8, to compensate that entity for any loss suffered by it as a result of the error committed by the State.

R v *MINISTRY OF AGRICULTURE, FISHERIES AND FOOD, EX PARTE HEDLEY LOMAS (IRELAND) LTD* (Case C-5/94)
[1996] 2 CMLR 391, Court of Justice

The third question

[23]   By its third question the national court asks the Court to state the conditions under which a Member State is obliged to make good damage caused to an individual by its refusal to issue an export licence in breach of Article 34 of the Treaty.

[24]   The principle of State liability for loss and damage caused to individuals as a result of breaches of Community law for which the State can be held responsible is inherent in the system of the Treaty *Francovich and Others* (Joined Cases C-6 & 9/90) [1993] 2 CMLR 66, and *Brasserie du Pêcheur* and *Factortame* (Joined Cases C-46 & 48/93) [1996] 1 CMLR 889). Furthermore, the conditions under which State liability gives rise to a right to reparation depend on the nature of the breach of Community law giving rise to the loss or damage (*Francovich and Others, Brasserie du Pêcheur* and *Factortame*).

[25]   In the case of a breach of Community law attributable to a Member State acting in a field in which it has a wide discretion to make legislative choices the Court has held, at paragraph [51] of its judgment in *Brasserie du Pêcheur* and *Factortame*, that such a right to reparation must be recognised where three conditions are met: the rule of law infringed must be intended to confer rights on individuals; the breach must be

sufficiently serious; and there must be a direct causal link between the breach of the obligation resting on the State and the damage sustained by the injured parties.

[26]   Those three conditions are also applicable in the circumstances of this case.

[27]   As regards the first condition, as is clear from the answer given to the first question, the United Kingdom's refusal to issue an export licence to Hedley Lomas constituted a quantitative restriction on exports contrary to Article 34 of the Treaty which could not be justified under Article 36. Whilst Article 34 imposes a prohibition on Member States, it also creates rights for individuals which the national courts must protect (*Pigs Marketing Board* v *Redmond* (Case 83/78) [1978] ECR 2347).

[28]   As regards the second condition, where, at the time when it committed the infringement, the Member State in question was not called upon to make any legislative choices and had only considerably reduced, or even no, discretion, the mere infringement of Community law may be sufficient to establish the existence of a sufficiently serious breach.

[29]   In that respect, in this particular case, the United Kingdom was not even in a position to produce any proof of non-compliance with the Directive by the slaughter-house to which the animals for which the export licence was sought were destined.

[30]   As regards the third condition, it is for the national court to determine whether there is a direct causal link between the breach of the obligation resting on the State and the damage sustained by the applicant in the main proceedings.

[31]   As appears from paragraphs [41]-[43] of *Francovich and Others*, subject to the right to reparation which flows directly from Community law where the three conditions referred to above are satisfied, the State must make reparation in accordance with its domestic law on liability for the consequences of the loss and damage caused. However, the conditions for reparation for loss and damage laid down by domestic law must not be less favourable than those relating to similar domestic claims and must not be such as in practice to make it impossible or excessively difficult to obtain reparation (see also *Brasserie du Pêcheur* and *Factortame*).

[32]   The answer to the third question must therefore be that a Member State has an obligation to make reparation for the damage caused to an individual by a refusal to issue an export licence in breach of Article 34 of the Treaty where the rule of Community law infringed is intended to confer rights on individuals, the breach is sufficiently serious and there is a direct causal link between the breach and the damage sustained by the individuals. Subject to that reservation, the State must make good the consequences of the loss or damage caused by a breach of Community law attributable to it, in accordance with its domestic law on liability. However, the conditions laid down by the applicable domestic laws must not be less favourable than those relating to similar domestic claims or framed in such a way as in practice to make it impossible or excessively difficult to obtain reparation.

R v SECRETARY OF STATE FOR THE HOME DEPARTMENT, EX PARTE GALLAGHER
[1996] 2 CMLR 951, Court of Appeal

[16]   The main issue between the parties was whether the United Kingdom's violation of Community law of which Mr Gallagher complained had caused (or directly caused) the damage for which he now sought to amend to claim damages.

[17]   Mr Allen submitted that the United Kingdom's failure to implement the Directive fully and correctly had deprived Mr Gallagher of fundamental procedural safeguards and had caused his exclusion from the United Kingdom in circumstances in which, had he enjoyed those safeguards, he might well not have been excluded. Mr Allen accepted that even if the Directive had been fully and correctly reflected in domestic law, as it now was in the 1996 Regulations, Mr Gallagher might nonetheless have been excluded. But he would (it was argued) have stood a better chance of securing a favourable result had he been able to make representations and be interviewed before the Home Secretary had made a decision, and he was entitled to be compensated for the chance which he had lost of securing a better result. In evaluating Mr Gallagher's chances of obtaining a favourable result, the Court was entitled to take account of the fact that Mr Gallagher had not been shown the report written by the nominated person (as he should have been), that the name of the nominated person had not been disclosed (as it should have been) and that the Home Secretary had adduced no evidence which would enable the Court to determine that the nominated person was (as he should have been)

wholly independent and immune from any control by the Home Secretary. In support of this last point Mr Allen referred to the judgment of the Court of Justice in the present case:

[25] As regards the form of the opinion of the competent authority, the objectives of the system provided for by the directive require that the opinion be duly notified to the person concerned, but the directive does not require the opinion to identify by name the members of the authority or indicate their professional status (*Adoui and Cornuaille*) since such identification is relevant only for the purpose of enabling the national court to determine whether the members of the authority are independent and impartial.

[26] The answer to the second question must therefore be that Article 9(1) of the directive does not preclude the competent authority referred to in that provision from being appointed by the same administrative authority as takes the decision ordering expulsion, provided that the competent authority can perform its duties in absolute independence and is not subject to any control by the authority empowered to take the measures provided for in the directive. It is for the national court to determine in each case whether those requirements have been met.

In this case, Mr Allen submitted, the court was being invited to act on the basis of mere assertion by the Home Secretary.

[18] To these points Mr Pannick gave what are in our judgment convincing answers.

[19] There is nothing whatever to suggest that the Home Secretary's decision would have been any different had he awaited receipt of Mr Gallagher's representations and the report of the nominated person before making an exclusion order. The evidence is clear that after receiving the report and learning the effect of the representations the Home Secretary considered the case *de novo*, which must be taken to mean that he had an open mind. It was because of the unlikelihood that the order of events could have made any substantial difference to the outcome that the members of the Court of Appeal in February 1994, with varying degrees of emphasis, regarded Mr Gallagher's complaint as being, or at least appearing, technical. Had the nominated person favoured revocation and the Home Secretary exclusion, it might be plausible to suggest that the nominated person's opinion would have been more influential if it had preceded the making of any decision; but here the nominated person and the Home Secretary were of one mind. It is in our view clear that even if the procedure prescribed in the current Regulations had been followed, the outcome would have been the same; it is, however, probable that in such event Mr Gallagher would have been detained longer.

[20] This is not a case in which Mr Gallagher is entitled to be compensated for the loss of a chance of securing a favourable result. Causation, as Lord Ackner pointed out in *Hotson v East Berkshire Area Health Authority* [1987] AC 750, is an issue to be decided on the balance of probabilities. The plaintiff must show on the balance of probabilities that the injury for which he seeks compensation was caused by the unlawful conduct of which he complains. In *Hotson's* case, the defendant was negligent but such negligence was not shown on the balance of probabilities to have caused any but a minimal part of the plaintiff's injury. So here: Mr Gallagher has established a breach of Community law, but he cannot show that that breach probably caused him to be excluded from the United Kingdom when he would not otherwise have been excluded.

[21] Nothing in the Directive, or in the 1989 Act, or in the judgment of the Court of Justice entitled Mr Gallagher to receive a copy of the report made by the nominated person. In its previous decision the Court of Appeal, in the light of evidence that Mr Gallagher had been given all the information which he could be given without prejudice to interests of national security, rejected a complaint that the Home Secretary had wrongfully failed to give Mr Gallagher adequate information of the grounds upon which the exclusion order was made. It is obvious that the report of the nominated person, to be of value to the Home Secretary, is likely to make reference to sources of intelligence information which could not be disclosed to the person against whom all order might be made without prejudice to those sources. In ruling that the opinion of the nominated person should be 'duly notified' to the person concerned the Court of Justice meant no more than that the effect of the opinion should be communicated. Any other ruling would be inconsistent with the recognition in Article 48 of the Treaty and in the Directive itself that considerations of national security must be respected.

. . .

[26]   If, as we have concluded, it is necessary for Mr Gallagher to show that the United Kingdom's breach in failing correctly to transpose the Directive into domestic law was 'sufficiently serious', we conclude that he has failed to do so. McCullough J at first instance and Hirst LJ in the Court of Appeal did not consider it arguable that Schedule 2 of the 1989 Act in its unamended form violated Community law. In the Court of Appeal Farquharson LJ regarded Mr Gallagher's complaint as technical, and Steyn LJ went no further than to say that he did not regard it as self-evident that the argument advanced on behalf of Mr Gallagher should necessarily be regarded as technical. There is nothing to suggest that the United Kingdom wilfully deprived suspects of rights which the Directive was intended to confer, and the original statutory procedure (if operated fairly and in good faith) was one which could well be thought to give effective protection. While the chronology in Schedule 2 departed from that prescribed in the Directive, and could thus be described as 'manifest', we do not think the departure can be described as 'grave': the subject of an order was not obviously worse off as a result, and might be better; although notified to the Commission no objection had been taken to the United Kingdom measure; and three judges held there was no violation of Community law. There was authority of the Court of Justice which showed that expulsion should not precede reference to the competent authority (*Pecastaing* v *Belgium* (Case 98/79) [1980] ECR 691), but under Schedule 2 in its unamended form the subject of an order could, if he exercised his statutory rights, avoid expulsion until his case had been duly reconsidered.

[27]   After the argument in this appeal had been concluded, the Court of Justice gave judgment in *R* v *Ministry of Agriculture, Fisheries and Food, ex parte Hedley Lomas (Ireland) Limited* (Case C-5/94) [1996] All ER (EC) 493. The background to the case was a Council directive prescribing minimum standards for the humane slaughter of cattle. The Ministry refused Hedley Lomas a licence to export sheep for slaughter in a named Spanish slaughterhouse, thereby admittedly imposing a quantitative restriction on exports, on the ground that some Spanish slaughterhouses did not comply with the standards required by the Directive. This was held to be a breach of Community law, and the question of compensation accordingly arose.

[28]   The Court held that the three conditions laid down in *Brasserie du Pêcheur* and *Factortame* applied in this case also. With reference to the second 'sufficiently serious' condition, the Court said:

> As regards the second condition, where, at the time when it committed the infringement, the Member State in question was not called upon to make any legislative choices and had only considerably reduced, or even no, discretion, the mere infringement of Community law may be sufficient to establish the existence of a sufficiently serious breach.

With reference to the facts of that case, the Court continued:

> In that respect, in this particular case, the United Kingdom was not even in a position to produce any proof of non-compliance with the Directive by the slaughterhouse to which the animals for which the export licence was sought were destined.

[29]   The contrast with the present case is in our view obvious. Here, the United Kingdom certainly was called upon to make a legislative choice, and certainly did enjoy a measure of discretion. The choice made, although wrong, was not obviously wrong in substance. It was not, as in *Hedley Lomas*, committing what was on its face a blatant breach of the Treaty, without any evidence on which it could rely to justify its conduct. The present case was not one of 'mere infringement'.

5.3.3   CONCLUSION ON MEMBER STATE LIABILITY

DILLENKOFER AND OTHERS v GERMANY (Joined Cases C-178–179/94 & C-188-190/94) [1996] 3 CMLR 469, Court of Justice

Conditions under which a Member State incurs liability (Questions 8, 9, 10, 11 and 12)

[15]   Questions 8, 9, 10, 11 and 12, concerning the conditions under which a State incurs liability towards individuals where a directive has not been transposed within the prescribed period, will be examined first.

[16]   The crux of these questions is whether a failure to transpose a directive within the prescribed period is sufficient per se to afford individuals who have suffered injury a right to reparation or whether other conditions must also be taken into consideration.

[17]   More specifically, the national Court raises the question of the importance to be attached to the German Government's contention that the period prescribed for transposition of the Directive proved inadequate (Question 8). It asks, further, whether State liability requires a serious, that is to say, a manifest and grave, breach of Community obligations (Question 9), whether the breach must have been established in infringement proceedings before the loss or damage occurred (Question 10), whether liability presupposes the existence of fault, of either commission or omission, in the adoption of legislative measures by the Member State (Question 11) and, lastly, in the event that Question 11 is answered in the affirmative, whether liability can be excluded by reason of a judgment such as the 'advance payment' judgment of the Bundesgerichtshof referred to in Question 7 (Question 12).

[18]   The German, Netherlands and United Kingdom Governments have submitted in particular that a State can incur liability for late transposition of a directive only if there has been a serious, that is to say, a manifest and grave, breach of Community law for which it can be held responsible. According to those Governments, this depends on the circumstances which caused the period for transposition to be exceeded.

[19]   In order to reply to those questions, reference must first be made to the court's case law on the individual's right to reparation of damage caused by a breach of Community law for which a Member State can be held responsible.

[20]   The court has held that the principle of State liability for loss and damage caused to individuals as a result of breaches of Community law for which the State can be held responsible is inherent in the system of the Treaty (*Francovich, Brasserie du Pêcheur* and *Factortame* [1996] 1 CMLR 889 (Joined Cases C-46 & 48/93); *British Telecommunications* (Case C-392/93) [1996] 2 CMLR 217; and *Hedley Lomas* (Case C-5/94) [1996] 2 CMLR 391). Furthermore, the Court has held that the conditions under which State liability gives rise to a right to reparation depend on the nature of the breach of Community law giving rise to the loss and damage (*Francovich; Brasserie du Pêcheur* and *Factortame* and *Hedley Lomas*).

[21]   In *Brasserie du Pêcheur* and *Factortame, British Telecommunications* and *Hedley Lomas*, the court, having regard to the circumstances of the case, held that individuals who have suffered damage have a right to reparation where three conditions are met: the rule of law infringed must have been intended to confer rights on individuals; the breach must be sufficiently serious; and there must be a direct causal link between the breach of the obligation resting on the State and the damage sustained by the injured parties.

[22]   Moreover, it is clear from the *Francovich* case which, like these cases, concerned non-transposition of a directive within the prescribed period, that the full effectiveness of the third paragraph of Article 189 of the Treaty requires that there should be a right to reparation where the result prescribed by the directive entails the grant of rights to individuals, the content of those rights is identifiable on the basis of the provisions of the directive and a causal link exists between the breach of the State's obligation and the loss and damage suffered by the injured parties.

[23]   In substance, the conditions laid down in that group of judgments are the same, since the condition that there should be a sufficiently serious breach, although not expressly mentioned in *Francovich*, was nevertheless evident from the circumstances of that case.

[24]   When the court held that the conditions under which State liability gives rise to a right to reparation depended on the nature of the breach of Community law causing the damage, that meant that those conditions are to be applied according to each type of situation.

[25]   On the one hand, a breach of Community law is sufficiently serious if a Community institution or a Member State, in the exercise of its rule-making powers, manifestly and gravely disregards the limits on those powers (see *HNL and Others v EC Council and EC Commission* (Joined Cases 83 & 94/76, 4, 15 & 40/77) [1978] ECR 1209, *Brasserie du Pêcheur* and *Factortame;* and *British Telecommunications*). On the other hand, if, at the time when it committed the infringement, the Member State in question was not called upon to make any legislative choices and had only considerably reduced, or even

no, discretion, the mere infringement of Community law may be sufficient to establish the existence of a sufficiently serious breach (see *Hedley Lomas*).

[26]   So where, as in *Francovich*, a Member State fails, in breach of the third paragraph of Article 189 of the Treaty, to take any of the measures necessary to achieve the result prescribed by a directive within the period it lays down, that Member State manifestly and gravely disregards the limits on its discretion.

[27]   Consequently, such a breach gives rise to a right to reparation on the part of individuals if the result prescribed by the directive entails the grant of rights to them, the content of those rights is identifiable on the basis of the provisions of the directive and a causal link exists between the breach of the State's obligation and the loss and damage suffered by the injured parties: no other conditions need be taken into consideration.

[28]   In particular, reparation of that loss and damage cannot depend on a prior finding by the court of an infringement of Community law attributable to the State (see *Brasserie du Pêcheur*), nor on the existence of intentional fault or negligence on the part of the organ of the State to which the infringement is attributable.

[29]   The reply to Questions 8, 9, 10, 11 and 12 must therefore be that failure to take any measure to transpose a directive in order to achieve the result it prescribes within the period laid down for that purpose constitutes per se a serious breach of Community law and consequently gives rise to a right of reparation for individuals suffering injury if the result prescribed by the directive entails the grant to individuals of rights whose content is identifiable and a causal link exists between the breach of the State's obligation and the loss and damage suffered.

5.4   Remedies Available

5.4.1   PRINCIPLES GOVERNING THE AWARD OF A REMEDY

EMMOTT v MINISTER FOR SOCIAL WELFARE AND ANOTHER (Case C–208/90) [1991] ECR I-4269, Court of Justice

Ireland failed to comply with a Directive on disability benefits for two years after the implementation deadline and Mrs Emmott claimed compensation for underpaid benefit during this time. The Irish authorities alleged that her claim was outside the three-month time limit set by Irish law and the Irish court made a reference to the Court of Justice under Article 177 of the Treaty.

It was held that Mrs Emmott's action was admissible.

16.   As the Court has consistently held (see, in particular, the judgments in Case 33/76, *Rewe-Zentralfinanz eG and Rewe-Zentral AG* v *Landwirtschaftskammer für das Saarland* [1976] ECR 1989 and Case 199/82, *Amministazione delle Finanze dello Stato* v *San Giorgio SpA* [1983] ECR 3595), in the absence of Community rules on the subject, it is for the domestic legal system of each Member State to determine the procedural conditions governing actions at law intended to ensure the protection of the rights which individuals derive from the direct effect of Community law, provided that such conditions are not less favourable than those relating to similar actions of a domestic nature nor framed so as to render virtually impossible the exercise of rights conferred by Community law.

17.   Whilst the laying down of reasonable time-limits which, if unobserved, bar proceedings, in principle satisfies the two conditions mentioned above, account must nevertheless be taken of the particular nature of directives.

18.   According to Article 189 of the EEC Treaty, a directive is to be binding, as to the result to be achieved, upon each Member State to which it is addressed, but is to leave to the national authorities the choice of form and methods. Although that provision leaves Member States free to choose the ways and means of ensuring that a directive is implemented, that freedom does not affect the obligation, imposed on all the Member States to which a directive is addressed, to adopt, within the framework of their national legal systems, all the measures necessary to ensure that the directive is fully effective, in

accordance with the objective which it pursues (see judgment in Case 14/83, *Sabine von Colson and Elisabeth Kamann* v *Land Nordrhein-Westfalen* [1984] ECR 1891).

19. In this regard it must be borne in mind that the Member States are required to ensure the full application of directives in a sufficiently clear and precise manner so that, where directives are intended to create rights for individuals, they can ascertain the full extent of those rights and, where necessary, rely on them before the national courts (see, in particular, judgment in Case 363/85, *Commission* v *Italy* [1987] ECR 1733).

20. Only in specific circumstances, in particular where a Member State has failed to take the implementing measures required or has adopted measures which are not in conformity with a directive, has the Court recognised the right of persons affected thereby to rely, in judicial proceedings, on a directive as against a defaulting Member State. This minimum guarantee, arising from the binding nature of the obligation imposed on the Member States by the effect of directives, cannot justify a Member State absolving itself from taking in due time implementing measures appropriate to the purpose of each directive (see judgment in Case 102/79, *Commission* v *Belgium* [1980] ECR 1473).

21. So long as a directive has not been properly transposed into national law, individuals are unable to ascertain the full extent of their rights. That state of uncertainty for individuals subsists even after the Court has delivered a judgment finding that the Member State in question has not fulfilled its obligations under the directive and even if the Court has held that a particular provision or provisions of the directive are sufficiently precise and unconditional to be relied upon before a national court.

22. Only the proper transposition of the directive will bring that state of uncertainty to an end and it is only upon that transposition that the legal certainty which must exist if individuals are to be required to assert their rights is created.

23. It follows that, until such time as a directive has been properly transposed, a defaulting Member State may not rely on an individual's delay in initiating proceedings against it in order to protect rights conferred upon him by the provisions of the directive and that a period laid down by national law within which proceedings must be initiated cannot begin to run before that time.

24. The answer to the question referred to the Court must therefore be that Community law precludes the competent authorities of a Member State from relying, in proceedings brought against them by an individual before the national courts in order to protect rights directly conferred upon him by Article 4(1) of Directive 79/7, on national procedural rules relating to time-limits for bringing proceedings so long as that Member State has not properly transposed that directive into its domestic legal system.

MARSHALL v SOUTHAMPTON AND SOUTH WEST AREA HEALTH AUTHORITY (No. 2) (Case C–271/91) [1993] 3 CMLR 293, Court of Justice

For the facts, see *Marshall* v *Southampton and South West AHA* (*No. 1*) at **5.1.4.1**. The amount of damages which could be awarded in respect of a discriminatory dismissal was restricted by the Sex Discrimination Act 1975. The UK Court made a reference to the Court of Justice under Article 177 of the Treaty.

It was held that a limit on damages which was unrelated to the loss suffered could not be applied.

[22] Article 6 of the Directive puts member states under a duty to take the necessary measures to enable all persons who consider themselves wronged by discrimination to pursue their claims by judicial process. Such obligation implies that the measures in question should be sufficiently effective to achieve the objective of the Directive and should be capable of being effectively relied upon by the persons concerned before national courts.

[23] As the Court held in the judgment in Case 14/83 *Von Colson and Kamann* v *Land Nordrhein-Westfalen* [1984] ECR 1891, at paragraph 18, Article 6 does not prescribe a specific measure to be taken in the event of a breach of the prohibition of discrimination, but leaves Member States free to choose between the different solutions suitable for achieving the objective of the Directive, depending on the different solutions which may arise.

[24]   However, the objective is to arrive at real equality of opportunity and cannot therefore be attained in the absence of measures appropriate to restore such equality when it has not been observed. As the Court stated in paragraph [23] of the judgment in *Von Colson and Kamann*, cited above, those measures must be such as to guarantee real and effective judicial protection and have a real deterrent effect on the employer.

[25]   Such requirements necessarily entail that the particular circumstances of each breach of the principle of equal treatment should be taken into account. In the event of discriminatory dismissal contrary to Article 5(1) of the Directive, a situation of equality could not be restored without either reinstating the victim of discrimination or, in the alternative, granting financial compensation for the loss and damage sustained.

[26]   Where financial compensation is the measure adopted in order to achieve the objective indicated above, it must be adequate in that it must enable the loss and damage actually sustained as a result of the discriminatory dismissal to be made good in full accordance with the applicable national rules.

The first and second questions

[27]   In its first question, the House of Lords seeks to establish whether it is contrary to Article 6 of the Directive for national provisions to lay down an upper limit on the amount of compensation recoverable by a victim of discrimination.

[28]   In its second question, the House of Lords asks whether Article 6 requires (a) that the compensation for the damage sustained as a result of the illegal discrimination should be full and (b) that it should include an award of interest on the principal amount from the date of the unlawful discrimination to the date when compensation is paid.

[29]   The Court's interpretation of Article 6 as set out above provides a direct reply to the first part of the second question relating to the level of compensation required by that provision.

[30]   It also follows from that interpretation that the fixing of an upper limit of the kind at issue in the main proceedings cannot, by definition, constitute proper implementation of Article 6 of the Directive, since it limits the amount of compensation *a priori* to a level which is not necessarily consistent with the requirement of ensuring real equality of opportunity through adequate reparation for the loss and damage sustained as a result of discriminatory dismissal.

[31]   With regard to the second part of the second question relating to the award of interest, suffice it to say that full compensation for the loss and damage sustained as a result of discriminatory dismissal cannot leave out of account factors, such as the effluxion of time, which may in fact reduce its value. The award of interest, in accordance with the applicable national rules, must therefore be regarded as an essential component of compensation for the purposes of restoring real equality of treatment.

[32]   Accordingly, the reply to be given to the first and second questions is that the interpretation of Article 6 of the Directive must be that reparation of the loss and damage sustained by a person injured as a result of discriminatory dismissal may not be limited to an upper limit fixed *a priori* or by excluding an award of interest to compensate for the loss sustained by the recipient of the compensation as a result of the effluxion of time until the capital sum awarded is actually paid.

The third question

[33]   In its third question, the House of Lords seeks to establish whether a person who has been injured as a result of discriminatory dismissal may rely, as against an authority of the State acting in its capacity as employer, on Article 6 of the Directive in order to contest the application of national rules which impose limits on the amount of compensation recoverable by way of reparation.

[34]   It follows from the considerations set out above as to the meaning and scope of Article 6 of the Directive, that that provision is an essential factor for attaining the fundamental objective of equal treatment for men and women, in particular as regards working conditions, including the conditions governing dismissal, referred to in Article 5(1) of the Directive, and that, where, in the event of discriminatory dismissal, financial compensation is the measure adopted in order to restore that equality, such compensation must be full and may not be limited a priori in terms of its amount.

[35]   Accordingly, the combined provisions of Article 6 and Article 5 of the Directive give rise, on the part of a person who has been injured as a result of discriminatory dismissal, to rights which that person must be able to rely upon before the national courts as against the State and authorities which are an emanation of the State.

[36]   The fact that Member States may choose among different solutions in order to achieve the objective pursued by the Directive depending on the situations which may arise, cannot result in an individual's being prevented from relying on Article 6 in a situation such as that in the main proceedings where the national authorities have no degree of discretion in applying the chosen solution.

[37]   It should be pointed out in that connection that, as appears in particular from the judgment in Joined Cases C–6/90 and C–9/90 *Francovich and Others* v *Italy* [1991] I-ECR 5357 the right of a State to choose among several possible means of achieving the objectives of a directive does not exclude the possibility for individuals of enforcing before national courts rights whose content can be determined sufficiently precisely on the basis of the provisions of the directive alone.

[38]   Accordingly, the reply to be given to the third question is that a person who has been injured as a result of discriminatory dismissal may rely on the provisions of Article 6 of the Directive as against an authority of the State acting in its capacity as an employer in order to set aside a national provision which imposes limits on the amount of compensation recoverable by way of reparation.

REWE HANDELSGESELLSCHAFT NORD GMBH AND REWE-MARKT STEFFEN v *HAUPTZOLLAMT KIEL* (Case 158/80) [1981] ECR 1005, Court of Justice

Cruises which went beyond German territorial waters were organised by certain retailers so that goods could be technically 'exported', traded and 'imported' again, thus incurring certain customs and tax advantages. Land based retailers claimed that this practice was in breach of Community law. The German court made a reference to the Court of Justice under Article 177 of the Treaty on the interpretation and validity of the Community law in question and on the remedies which should be available for any breach.

It was held that all actions available to enforce national law, must be available to enforce Community law, but new actions need not be created. The remedies available for breach of Community law in this instance depended on provisions of German law.

Third, fifth and eighth questions (remedies conferred upon persons by the Regulations and the Directives in question).

39.   These three questions concerned the question whether a person whose interests are adversely affected either by national legislation incompatible with Community law or by the application of an unlawful Community measure may take action before the national courts in order to have measures contrary to Community law declaration inoperative.

40.   In its order the Finanzgericht states that, according to the case law of the Bundesverfassungsgericht [Federal Constitutional Court] and of the Bundesverwaltungsgericht [Federal Administrative Court], laws controlling the economy which are passed to further the interests of individual groups and which alter the situation with regard to competition are in breach of the principle of equality if they are not required in the public interest and if the interests of other persons which merit protection are arbitrarily prejudiced. In such a case under German law the person affected has a right of action. Placed in that context, the questions raised by the national court are intended in substance to establish whether that right of action may be exercised in similar conditions within the framework of the Community legal system in particular in the sense that if the economic interests of a person to whom Community law applies are adversely affected by the non-application of a Community provision to a third party, either through the action of a Member State or of the Community authorities that person may institute proceedings before the courts of a Member State in order to compel the national authorities to apply the provisions in question or to refrain from infringing them.

41.   It should be remarked first of all that under Article 189 of the Treaty a regulation 'shall be binding in its entirety and directly applicable in all Member States'. A directive 'shall be binding, as to the result to be achieved', but leaves to the national authorities

the choice of form and methods. According to the case-law of the Court the binding effect of a directive implies that a national authority may not apply to an individual a national legislative or administrative measure which is not in accordance with a provision of the directive which has all the characteristics necessary to render possible its application by the court.

42.   It follows from these considerations that a person may rely before the national courts on his rights under the regulation.

43.   Likewise, a national authority may not apply to a person legislative or administrative measures which are not in accordance with an unconditional and sufficiently clear obligation imposed by the directive.

44.   With regard to the right of a trader to request the courts to require the authorities of a Member State to compel a third party to comply with obligations arising from Community rules in a given legal situation in which that trader is not involved but is economically adversely affected by the failure to observe Community law, it must be remarked first of all that, although the Treaty has made it possible in a number of instances for private persons to bring a direct action, where appropriate, before the Court of Justice, it was not intended to create new remedies in the national courts to ensure the observance of Community law other than those already laid down by national law. On the other hand the system of legal protection established by the Treaty, as set out in Article 177 in particular, implies that it must be possible for every type of action provided for by national law to be available for the purpose of ensuring observance of Community provisions having direct effect, on the same conditions concerning the admissibility and procedure as would apply were it a question of ensuring observance of national law.

45.   With regard more particularly to Regulation No. 3023/77, it should be noted that that regulation in itself does not confer any exemption. It merely conferred upon the national authorities power to grant a restricted exemption. It accordingly follows from the fact that the regulation is invalid that national measures taken on the basis thereof are not in accordance with Community law.

46.   The reply to the third, fifth and eighth questions should accordingly be as follows:

The system of legal protection established by the Treaty, as set out in Article 177 in particular, implies that it must be possible for every type of action provided for by national law to be available before the national courts for the purpose of ensuring observance of Community provisions having direct effect, on the same conditions concerning admissibility and procedure as would apply were it a question of ensuring observance of national law.

DEKKER v VJV CENTRUM
(Case C-177/88) [1990] ECR 1–3941, Court of Justice

Dekker was rejected for a job after she informed the employer (VJV) that she was pregnant, because his insurance would not cover the cost of a replacement worker during her maternity leave. She sought to rely on Directive 76/207 which prohibited discrimination at work on grounds of sex. Under Dutch law, Dekker was required to prove that the employer was at fault and therefore that his justification was invalid. The Dutch court made a reference to the Court of Justice under Article 177 of the Treaty.

It was held that the Directive imposed liability purely on the basis of discrimination, and therefore the extra requirement under Dutch law could not be applied.

Report for the Hearing (at p. 3945)

. . .

In view of the phrasing of the third question submitted by the Hoge Raad, it is also appropriate to set out the wording of Articles 1401 and 1402 of the Netherlands Civil Code. Article 1401 of the Code provides that 'any unlawful human act causing harm to another obliges the person through whose fault the harm has occurred to make it good', while Article 1402 further provides that 'every person is liable for the harm he causes, not only through his acts but also through his negligence or carelessness'.

Judgment
. . .

19. The third question relates to whether it is contrary to Articles 2 and 3 of the Directive for a legal action in damages based on breach of the principle of equal treatment to be capable of succeeding only if it is also proved that the employer is at fault and cannot avail himself of any ground exempting him from liability.

20. Mrs Dekker, the Netherlands Government and the United Kingdom all take the view that, once an infringement of the principle of equal treatment is established, that infringement must be sufficient to make the employer liable.

21. For its part, the VJV notes that the distinction drawn in the two limbs of the third question between fault attributable to the employer and the possible absence of any ground exempting him from liability is partly linked to the national law applicable to the main proceedings, which provides different legal consequences, according to the case. The VJV claims that the Directive allows an answer to be given only to the question whether an infringement of the principle of equal treatment may be justified in any given case.

22. It must be observed in this regard that Article 2(2), (3) and (4) of the Directive provide for exceptions to the principle of equal treatment set out in Article 2(1), but that the Directive does not make liability on the part of the person guilty of discrimination conditional in any way on proof of fault or on the absence of any ground discharging such liability.

23. Article 6 of the Directive recognizes the existence of rights vesting in the victims of discrimination which can be pleaded in legal proceedings. Although full implementation of the Directive does not require any specific form of sanction for unlawful discrimination, it does entail that that sanction be such as to guarantee real and effective protection (judgment in Case 14/83 *Von Colson and Kamann* v *Land Nordrhein-Westfalen* [1984] ECR 1891, paragraph 23). It must, furthermore, have a real deterrent effect on the employer.

24. It must be observed that, if the employer's liability for infringement of the principle of equal treatment were made subject to proof of a fault attributable to him and also to there being no ground of exemption recognized by the applicable national law, the practical effect of those principles would be weakened considerably.

25. It follows that when the sanction chosen by the Member State is contained within the rules governing an employer's civil liability, any breach of the prohibition of discrimination must, in itself, be sufficient to make the employer liable, without there being any possibility of invoking the grounds of exemption provided by national law.

26. Accordingly, the answer must be that, although Directive 76/207 gives the Member States, in penalizing infringement of the prohibition of discrimination, freedom to choose between the various solutions appropriate for achieving its purpose, it nevertheless requires that, where a Member State opts for a sanction forming part of the rules on civil liability, any infringement of the prohibition of discrimination suffices in itself to make the person guilty of it fully liable, and no regard may be had to the grounds of exemption envisaged by national law.

5.5   End of Chapter Assessment Question

Alf works for Humber plc, a company created to build and operate a railway bridge across the Humber estuary. It is authorised to do so under s. 1 of the (fictitious) Estuary Bridges Act 1990, which also gives it powers to regulate the connecting train service.

(Fictitious) Directive 3/91 requires Member States to take all measures necessary to ensure that bridge workers are provided with appropriate safety equipment, including hard hats. The deadline for implementation of the Directive has passed without UK compliance. The Estuary Bridges Act merely provides that licence holders must ensure that their employees are aware of safety hazards and advised to wear appropriate clothing.

Alf sustained a serious head injury when a cable fell on him during construction of the bridge, and as a result is unfit to work. He claims that his injury was caused by the company's failure to provide workers with hard hats. Humber plc claims that it had made Alf aware of the risks and had advised him to wear a hard hat, although the company was unable to provide them itself. It argues that the Act requires only the provision of information and advice.

(a)   Advise Alf as to whether he has any cause of action against Humber plc.

(b)   Would it make any difference to your answer if the company did not have the power to regulate the train service referred to above but was wholly owned by the State?

5.6   End of Chapter Assessment Outline Answer

2.(a)   Alf clearly has no cause of action under the Act, since Humber plc has fully complied with its provisions, and has no cause of action under any measure implementing the Directive, since the UK has failed to pass such a measure. His only possible cause of action is therefore under the Directive itself. The Directive will, according to the case of *Van Duyn* v *Home Office*, be directly effective if it is clear and unconditional and has not been adequately implemented by the Member State.

In the case of *Defrenne* v *SABENA*, the Court of Justice accepted that if part of a measure was sufficiently clear, that part could be directly effective, even if other parts of the measure were too uncertain. Since the Directive specifically states that hard hats must be provided by the licence holder to its employees, it is sufficiently clear and unconditional in respect of these obligations to establish direct effect. In *Pubblico Minstero* v *Ratti*, the Court of Justice indicated that such direct effect could arise only after the deadline for the implementation of the measure had passed. The deadline for the Directive in question has passed and therefore it has direct effect.

However, the Court of Justice made clear in *Marshall* v *Southampton AHA* that direct effect may be relied upon only against the State or an emanation of the State. In *Foster* v *British Gas* the Court stated that for an organisation to be an emanation of the State, it should be responsible for providing a public service under State control, and to have special powers to do so. Humber plc is providing a public service (the railway bridge), under State control (authorised by the Act) and has special powers (regulation of trains). Alf therefore has a course of action against Humber plc.

(b)   In the case of *Doughty* v *Rolls Royce*, the Court of Appeal indicated that all elements of the *Foster* test (see above) for an emanation of the State must be complied with. If Humber plc does not have any special powers, it fails the test. The fact that it is wholly owned by the State is insufficient, according to *Doughty*, to make it an emanation of the State.

Alf may instead seek to rely on the indirect effect of the Directive, that is to say, its effect on the interpretation of relevant national law such as the Estuary Bridges Act. This concept was recognised by the Court of Justice in *Von Colson*, and by the English courts in *Litster*. The fact that the Act predates the Directive, and therefore could not originally have been intended to reflect the Directive, is no obstacle to the application of indirect effect; *Marleasing*, *Webb* v *EMO*.

Applying this concept to the facts, 'appropriate clothing' could be interpreted as including hard hats, but it is more difficult to construe Humber's duty to **advise** on appropriate clothing as involving a duty to **provide** such clothing. In *Marleasing*, the Court of Justice construed Spanish law as meaning the exact opposite of what it appeared to mean in order to bring it into line with the appropriate Directive; and if such a construction were to be used here, Alf would clearly have a remedy. However, Humber might well seek to rely on the Court of Justice judgment in *Wagner Miret* and the comment of the Court of Justice in *Marleasing* that national legislation need only be construed consistently with a Directive 'as far as possible' in order to allege that a consistent construction is not possible here, and that therefore the word 'advised' in the Act should be given its ordinary, natural meaning. The case of *Webb* v *EMO* indicates that the House of Lords will interpret national legislation according to a Directive even where this interpretation would not be the most obvious one, but in Alf's case, 'provide' is not really one of the interpretations which could be applied to 'advise'. Although it is impossible to give a definite answer to Alf's chances of success, they do not appear to be good.

[It is not necessary to discuss the possibility of Alf bringing a claim against the UK government under *Francovich*, since you are only asked to advise on his cause(s) of action against Humber.]

CHAPTER SIX

PRELIMINARY REFERENCES

6.1 Issues which may be Referred

THE TREATY OF ROME

Article 177.
The Court of Justice shall have jurisdiction to give preliminary rulings concerning:
  (a) the interpretation of this Treaty;
  (b) the validity and interpretation of acts of the institutions of the Community and of the ECB;
  (c) the interpretation of the statutes of bodies established by an act of the Council, where those statutes so provide.

Where such a question is raised before any court or tribunal of a Member State, that court or tribunal may, if it considers that a decision on the question is necessary to enable it to give judgment, request the Court of Justice to give a ruling thereon.

Where any such question is raised in a case pending before a court or tribunal of a Member State against whose decisions there is no judicial remedy under national law, that court or tribunal shall bring the matter before the Court of Justice.

6.2 The Status of the National Court

MAGNAVISION v *GENERAL OPTICAL COUNCIL* (No. 2) [1987] 2 CMLR 262,
Queen's Bench Division

In the main action, a Belgian company had been fined for marketing spectacles contrary to the Opticians Act. It had argued that the Act was in breach of Community law, but the High Court had declined to make a reference to the Court of Justice. Leave to appeal was refused whereupon counsel for the Belgian company argued that a reference must now be made.
It was held that a reference would not be made because the meaning of the Community legislation was clear.

WATKINS LJ: [6] Now that judgments have been delivered, we are in this position. We were invited, at the conclusion of giving judgment, to certify points of law for consideration by the House of Lords. Having looked at the drafts of those points, we had no hesitation in coming to the conclusion that they did not call for certification by us. So we rejected the application therefor. There is no appeal against the refusal by this Court, in a criminal cause or matter, to certify a point of law for consideration by the House of Lords. There is, therefore, nothing a disappointed appellant, or repondent for that matter, can do if he applies for such a certificate and fails. It is, to put it in homely language, 'the end of the road' for him.

  [7] I am bound to say that when we annouced that decision, I thought it was the end of the road for us. But my Lord and I were soon disabused of such a notion, for Mr

Bellamy was once again on his feet, this time making what I regard as a most daring application. The purport of that was that although we had decided the appeal, and refused to certify points of law for the consideration of the House of Lords, we should, notwithstanding all that, refer the point which he had canvassed during argument in the course of the appeal to the European Court for the purpose of obtaining the opinion of that Court upon it.

[8]   As he said, and he was right, so far as I know that was the first time that an application of such a nature had been made, at the time when it was made.

[9]   He has very helpfully set out for us, in a series of carefully argued, written submissions, the reasons why he asserts that not only are we competent at this stage to make a reference to the European Court, but that our reasons for giving judgment as we did call for a reconsideration of the issues involved in declining to make a reference. There are powerful arguments he maintains for doing this. He has, he acknowledges, to surmount the hurdle created by the fact that judgment has been given. We are, it might be said, *functus*. He maintains that he can surmount that because, seeing that the order which we made has not been drawn up, we remain seised of this matter.

[10]   He has referred us to authority to the effect that until the order of the Court is drawn up, it is open to a judge to alter his judgment. That, upon the authorities to which he has referred us, and from my own experience, is true. But it is only true to this extent; that there are circumstances, albeit they are rare, in which a judge may correct an error or even to a limited extent alter an expressed view as to a matter referred to in his judgment; but that he can, in a wholesale way, almost destroy the basis of the judgment already given is unthinkable. That is what Mr. Bellamy, it seems to me, is inviting this Court to do. Having heard argument on the question whether we should make reference to the European Court and declined to, he, to all intents and purposes, invites us to turn a somersault. He has not advanced any good reason, in my judgment, why we should go through so inelegant a manoeuvre.

[11]   Whilst recognising the power of a court in, as I say, rare circumstances, before its order is drawn up, to alter a judgment, I can see no justification whatever for saying that this is an appropriate case for that to be done, having regard to the nature of the application which is made for that purpose.

[12]   His second argument is that by refusing to certify a point or points of law, we have turned ourselves into a final court, that is a court of final decision. In a sense, I agree with that. There is no appeal now from our decision to any other court in this country or elsewhere. Consequently, he submits that the prospect looms, if we do not make a reference to the European Court now, of the matter of which he complains being taken up either by the Commission of the European Community, or by a Member State of it. That may happen. But such a prospect cannot be permitted to sway this Court away from considering the application now made to it otherwise than strictly in accordance with the law of this country. Likewise, when deciding to make a reference during the hearing of a case.

R v THE PHARMACEUTICAL SOCIETY OF GREAT BRITAIN, EX PARTE THE ASSOCIATION OF PHARMACEUTICAL IMPORTERS [1987] 3 CMLR 951, Court of Appeal

UK law prohibited the dispensing of products which were identical to those prescribed, but were of a different brand. A pharmaceutical association alleged that this was contrary to Article 30.

It was held that the Court of Appeal would exercise its discretion to refer this issue to the Court of Justice.

KERR LJ: [23]   The present case falls within the penultimate paragraph of Article 177, since it is not 'a case pending before a court . . . against whose decision there is no judicial remedy'. There is a judicial remedy against a decision of this Court by applying for leave to appeal to the House of Lords, first to this Court and then to the House of Lords itself if necessary. A court or tribunal below the House of Lords can only fall within the last paragraph where there is no possibility of any further appeal from it.

HAGEN v FRATELLI D. & G. MORETTI J.N.C. AND MOLNAR MACHINERY LIMITED
[1980] 3 CMLR 253, Court of Appeal

Under UK law, the holder of a patent was entitled to have products which infringed this patent excluded from the UK. A defendant in such proceedings alleged that this law was contrary to Article 30 and appealed against a decision that he could not amend his original defence to include this point.

It was held that the amendment should be allowed. Leave to appeal to the House of Lords was given.

BUCKLEY LJ: Article 177 of the Treaty provides that 'The Court of Justice' – that is to say, the European Court – 'shall have jurisdiction to give preliminary rulings concerning: (a) the interpretation of this Treaty' and various other matters. Then it goes on to provide: 'Where such a question is raised before any court or tribunal of a Member State, that court or tribunal may, if it considers that a decision on the question is necessary to enable it to give judgment, request the Court of Justice to give a ruling thereon. Where any such question is raised in a case pending before a court or tribunal of a Member State, against whose decisions there is no judicial remedy under national law, that court or tribunal shall bring the matter before the Court of Justice'. So that when a case reaches the ultimate court of appeal in any domestic jurisdiction – and that, in the case of this country, is either this court if leave to appeal to the House of Lords is not obtainable, or the House of Lords – and when any such court decides a question of interpretation of the Treaty, the party who is dissatisfied with the decision can require that court to refer the matter to the European court and the domestic court is bound to make the reference.

6.3   Discretionary References

6.3.1   COURT OF JUSTICE GUIDELINES

DA COSTA EN SCHAAKE N.V., JACOB MEIJER N.V., AND HOECHST-HOLLAND N.V.
v
NEDERLANDSE BELASTINGADMINISTRATIE **(Cases 28-30/62)[1963] ECR 31,**
Court of Justice

A Dutch chemical exporter alleged that certain Dutch import taxes were contrary to Community law. The Dutch court made a reference on this question to the Court of Justice.

It was held that the existence of a prior ruling on the point did not preclude a reference.

[At pp. 37–8] The Commission, appearing by virtue of the provisions of Article 20 of the Statute of the Court of Justice of the EEC, urges that the request should be dismissed for lack of substance, since the questions on which an interpretation is requested from the Court in the present cases have already been decided by the judgment of 5 February 1963 in Case 26/62, which covered identical questions raised in a similar case.

This contention is not justified. A distinction should be made between the obligation imposed by the third paragraph of Article 177 upon national courts or tribunals of last instance and the power granted by the second paragraph of Article 177 to every national court or tribunal to refer to the Court of the Communities a question on the interpretation of the Treaty. Although the third paragraph of Article 177 unreservedly requires courts or tribunals of a Member State against whose decisions there is no judicial remedy under national law – like the Tariefcommissie – to refer to the Court every question of interpretation raised before them, the authority of an interpretation under Article 177 already given by the Court may deprive the obligation of its purpose and thus empty it of its substance. Such is the case especially when the question raised is materially identical with a question which has already been the subject of a preliminary ruling in a similar case.

When it gives an interpretation of the Treaty in a specific action pending before a national court, the Court limits itself to deducing the meaning of the Community rules from the wording and spirit of the Treaty, it being left to the national court to apply in the particular case the rules which are thus interpreted. Such an attitude conforms with the function assigned to the Court by Article 177 of ensuring unity of interpretation of Community law within the six Member States. If Article 177 had not such a scope, the procedural requirements of Article 20 of the Statute of the Court of Justice, which provides for the participation in the hearing of the Member States and the Community institutions, and of the third paragraph of Article 165 of the Treaty, which requires the Court to sit in plenary session, would not be justified. This aspect of the activity of the Court within the framework of Article 177 is confirmed by the absence of parties, in the proper sense of the word, which is characteristic of this procedure.

It is no less true that Article 177 always allows a national court, if it considers it desirable, to refer questions of interpretation to the Court again. This follows from Article 20 of the Statute of the Court of Justice, under which the procedure laid down for the settlement of preliminary questions is automatically set in motion as soon as such a question is referred by a national court.

RHEINMÜHLEN-DÜSSELDORF v *EINFÜHR-UND VORRATSSTELLE FÜR GETREIDE UND FUTTERMITTEL* (Joined Cases 146 & 166/73) [1974] ECR 33, Court of Justice

A German appeal court ruled that the withdrawal of exports refunds from a barley exporter was contrary to Community law, and the case was referred back to the lower court, which had reached a different decision, to reconsider. The lower court attempted to make a reference under Article 177. Under German law, the lower court was bound by the decision of the higher court. The higher court referred to the Court of Justice the question of whether the lower court could make a reference despite the national rules of precedent.

It was held that the lower court was not precluded from making a reference to the Court of Justice.

2. Article 177 is essential for the preservation of the Community character of the law established by the Treaty and has the object of ensuring that in all circumstances this law is the same in all States of the Community.

Whilst it thus aims to avoid divergences in the interpretation of Community law which the national courts have to apply, it likewise tends to ensure this application by making available to the national judge a means of eliminating difficulties which may be occasioned by the requirement of giving Community law its full effect within the framework of the judicial systems of the Member States.

Consequently any gap in the system so organized could undermine the effectiveness of the provisions of the Treaty and of the secondary Community law.

The provisions of Article 177, which enable every national court or tribunal without distinction to refer a case to the Court for a preliminary ruling when it considers that a decision on the question is necessary to enable it to give judgment, must be seen in this light.

3. The provisions of Article 177 are absolutely binding on the national judge and, in so far as the second paragraph is concerned, enable him to refer a case to the Court of Justice for a preliminary ruling on interpretation or validity.

This Article gives national courts the power and, where appropriate, imposes on them the obligation to refer a case for a preliminary ruling, as soon as the judge perceives either of his own motion or at the request of the parties that the litigation depends on a point referred to in the first paragraph of Article 177.

4. It follows that national courts have the widest discretion in referring matters to the Court of Justice if they consider that a case pending before them raises questions involving interpretation, or consideration of the validity, of provisions of Community law, necessitating a decision on their part.

It follows from these factors that a rule of national law whereby a court is bound on points of law by the rulings of a superior court cannot deprive the inferior courts of their power to refer to the Court questions of interpretation of Community law involving such rulings.

It would be otherwise if the questions put by the inferior court were substantially the same as questions already put by the superior court.

On the other hand the inferior court must be free, if it considers that the ruling on law made by the superior court could lead it to give a judgment contrary to Community law, to refer to the Court questions which concern it.

If inferior courts were bound without being able to refer matters to the Court, the jurisdiction of the latter to give preliminary rulings and the application of Community law at all levels of the judicial systems of the Member States would be compromised.

5.   The reply must therefore be that the existence of a rule of domestic law whereby a court is bound on points of law by the rulings of the court superior to it cannot of itself take away the power provided for by Article 177 of referring cases to the Court.

IRISH CREAMERY MILK SUPPLIERS ASSOCIATION v *IRELAND*
(Joined Cases 36 & 71/80) [1981] ECR 735, Court of Justice

Agricultural producers argued that an Irish levy on agricultural products was contrary to Community law. The Irish government wished to delay the making of a reference under Article 177 until the facts had been established. The Irish Court made a reference on this question to the Court of Justice.

It was held that it was for the national court to decide on the most appropriate time to make a reference.

First question
4.   The first question raised by the High Court of Ireland is worded as follows:

Was the decision by the High Court, at this stage of the hearing, to refer to the European Court under Article 177 of the Treaty, the question set out in paragraph 2 below a correct exercise on the part of the High Court of its discretion pursuant to the said article?

5.   Before an answer is given to that question it should be recalled that Article 177 of the Treaty establishes a framework for close co-operation between the national courts and the Court of Justice based on the assignment to each of different functions. The second paragraph of that article makes it clear that it is for the national court to decide at what stage in the proceedings it is appropriate for that court to refer a question to the Court of Justice for a preliminary ruling.

6.   The need to provide an interpretation of Community law which will be of use to the national court makes it essential, as the Court has already stated in its judgment of 12 July 1979 (Cases 244/78 *Union Laitière Normande* [1979] ECR 2663) to define the legal context in which the interpretation requested should be placed. From that aspect it might be convenient, in certain circumstances, for the facts in the case to be established and for questions of purely national law to be settled at the time the reference is made to the Court of Justice so as to enable the latter to take cognizance of all the features of fact and of law which may be relevant to the interpretation of Community law which it is called upon to give.

7.   However, those considerations do not in any way restrict the discretion of the national court, which alone has a direct knowledge of the facts of the case and of the arguments of the parties, which will have to take responsibility for giving judgment in the case and which is therefore in the best position to appreciate at what stage in the proceedings it requires a preliminary ruling from the Court of Justice.

8.   Hence it is clear that the national court's decision when to make a reference under Article 177 must be dictated by considerations of procedural organization and efficiency to be weighed by that court.

9.   The reply to the first question which has been raised should therefore be that under Article 177 the decision at what stage in proceedings before it a national court should refer a question to the Court of Justice for a preliminary ruling is a matter for the discretion of the national court.

DZODZI v *BELGIAN STATE* (Joined Cases C–297/88 & C–197/89) [1990] ECR I–3763,
Court of Justice

A Togolese widow of a Belgian national claimed the right to reside in Belgium on the basis of a Belgian law which gave the spouses of Belgian nationals the same residency rights as Community nationals. The Belgian government argued that since the case turned on the meaning of Belgian law, a reference to the Court of Justice was unnecessary. The Belgian court made a reference on this question to the Court of Justice.

It was held that although it was for the Belgian court to determine the relevance of Community law in these circumstances, if a ruling was requested, the Court of Justice had jurisdiction.

15.   Accordingly, a distinction must be drawn between the questions submitted by the national courts in so far as, on the one hand, they refer to Community law alone and in so far as, on the other hand, they are based on Article 40 of the aforesaid national law, for the purposes of justifying their requests for an interpretation of Community law. The two points will be considered in turn in the light of the Community legislation applicable at the material time; account will not be taken in particular of the later provisions of Council Directive 90/364 of 28 June 1990 on the right of residence (Official Journal 1990 L 180, p. 26) or Council Directive 90/365 of 28 June 1990 on the right of residence for employees and self-employed people who have ceased their occupational activity (Official Journal 1990 L 180, p. 28).

. . .

Questions on the interpretation of Community law made applicable by Article 40 of the Belgian Law of 15 December 1990 (third question submitted by the Tribunal de première instance and the questions submitted by the Cour d'appel)

Jurisdiction of the Court

29.   The Belgian State and the Commission contend that it is only the application of domestic Belgian law which is at issue, and the Commission argues in particular that a provision of the kind contained in Article 40 of the national law has no effect on the determination of the field of application of Community law. The Belgian State asks the Court to rule that it has no jurisdiction to answer these questions.

30.   In contrast, Mrs Dzodzi argues that, owing to Article 40 of the national law, the dispute before the national courts puts Community provisions in contention. It is for the Court to rule on questions of interpretation raised in such disputes in order to avoid divergence developing between the case law on the interpretation of Community provisions of the Court of Justice and that of national courts.

31.   Under Article 177 of the Treaty the Court has jurisdiction to give preliminary rulings concerning the interpretation of the Treaty and the acts of the institutions of the Community.

32.   The second and third paragraphs of Article 177 provide that, where a question concerning the interpretation of a provision of Community law is raised before any court or tribunal of a Member State, that court or tribunal may – or in the case of a court tribunal against whose decisions there is no remedy under national law, must – request the Court to give a ruling, if it considers that a decision on the question is necessary to enable it to give judgment.

33.   The procedure provided for in Article 177 of the Treaty is therefore an instrument for co-operation between the Court of Justice and the national courts, whereby the Court of Justice provides the national courts with the criteria for the interpretation of Community law which they need in order to dispose of the disputes which they are called upon to resolve.

34.   It follows that it is solely for the national courts before which the dispute has been brought, and which must bear the responsibility for the subsequent judicial decision, to determine in the light of the special features of each case both the need for a preliminary ruling in order to enable them to deliver judgment and the relevance of the questions which they submit to the Court.

35. Accordingly, since the questions submitted by the national courts concern the interpretation of a provision of Community law, the Court is, in principle, obliged to give a ruling.

36. It does not appear either from the wording of Article 177 or from the aim of the procedure introduced by that article that the authors of the Treaty intended to exclude from the jurisdiction of the Court requests for a preliminary ruling on a Community provision in the specific case where the national law of a Member State refers to the content of that provision in order to determine rules applicable to a situation which is purely internal to that State.

37. On the contrary, it is manifestly in the interest of the Community legal order that, in order to forestall future differences of interpretation, every Community provision should be given a uniform interpretation irrespective of the circumstances in which it is to be applied.

38. Since the jurisdiction of the Court under Article 177 is designed to ensure uniform interpretation in all Member States of the provisions of Community law, the Court merely deduces from the letter and the spirit of those provisions the meaning of the Community rules at issue. Thereafter it is for the national courts alone to apply the Community provisions thus interpreted in the light of the factual and legal circumstances of the case before them.

39. Consequently, in accordance with the division of judicial tasks between the national courts and the Court of Justice pursuant to Article 177, the Court gives its preliminary ruling without, in principle, having to look into the circumstances in which the national courts were prompted to submit the questions and envisage applying the provision of Community law which they have asked the Court to interpret.

40. The matter would be different only if it were apparent either that the procedure provided for by Article 177 had been diverted from its true purpose and sought in fact to lead the Court to give a ruling by means of a contrived dispute, or that the provision of Community law referred to the Court for interpretation was manifestly incapable of applying.

41. Where Community law is made applicable by national provisions, it is for the national court alone to assess the precise scope of that reference to Community law. If it takes the view that the content of a provision of Community law is applicable, by virtue of that reference, to the purely internal situation underlying the dispute brought before it, the national court is entitled to request the Court for a preliminary ruling on the terms laid down by the provisions of Article 177 as a whole, as they have been interpreted in the case law of the Court of Justice.

42. Nevertheless, the jurisdiction of the Court is confined to considering provisions of Community law only. In its reply to the national court, the Court of Justice cannot take account of the general scheme of the provisions of domestic law which, while referring to Community law, define the extent of that reference. Consideration of the limits which the national legislature may have placed on the application of Community law to purely internal situations, to which it is applicable only through the operation of the national legislation, is a matter for domestic law and hence falls within the exclusive jurisdiction of the courts of the Member State.

43. In the present case it must be observed that the questions set out above do not relate to provisions of Belgian domestic law but exclusively to provisions of the abovementioned regulations and directive on the right of residence and the right to remain in the territory of a Member State of spouses of Community workers and to Directive 64/221 of 25 February 1964, cited above. Accordingly, for those reasons and within the limits defined above, the Court has jurisdiction to rule on those questions.

6.3.2 CASELAW OF THE UK COURTS

H.P. BULMER LTD AND ANOTHER v J. BOLLINGER S.A. AND OTHERS **[1974] 2 CMLR 91, Court of Appeal**

UK producers of 'champagne cider' applied for a declaration that they could use the description 'champagne'. French producers argued that this contravened Community law on the origin of wines and requested an Article 177 reference. The judge at first instance refused to make a reference until the case had been fully heard and the French producers appealed on this point.

In the Court of Appeal Lord Denning laid down a number of guidelines as to whether a decision was 'necessary' and as to the use of the discretion to refer 'necessary' questions. The court concluded that a reference was not necessary in this case.

LORD DENNING MR: . . .

8. *The condition precedent to a reference. It must be 'necessary'*

[23] Whenever any English court thinks it would be helpful to get the view of the European court – on the interpretation of the Treaty – there is a *condition precedent* to be fulfilled. It is a condition which applies to the House of Lords as well as to the lower courts. It is contained in the same paragraph of Article 177(2) and applies in Article 177(3) as well. It is this: An English court can only refer the matter to the European court '*if it considers* that a decision on the question is necessary to enable it to give judgment'. Note the words 'if *it* considers'. That is, 'if the *English court* considers'. On this point again the opinion of the English courts is final, just as it is on the matter of discretion. An English judge can say either 'I consider it necessary' or 'I do not consider it necessary'. His discretion in that respect is final. Let me take the two in order.

[24] (i) If the English judge considers it *necessary* to refer the matter, no one can gainsay it save the Court of Appeal. The European Court will accept his opinion. It will not go into the grounds on which he based it. The European Court so held in *van Gend en Loos* (Case 26/62) [1963] CMLR 105, 128–129 and *Albatros* v *SOPECO* (Case 20/64) [1965] CMLR 159, 177. It will accept the question as he formulates it: *Fratelli Grassi* v *Amministrazione delle Finanze* (Case 5/72) [1973] CMLR 322, 335. It will not alter it or send it back. Even if it is a faulty question, it will do the best it can with it (see *Deutsche Grammophon Geselschaft mbH v Metro-SB-Grossmärkte GmbH* (Case 78/70) [1971] CMLR 631, 656). The European Court treats it as a matter between the English courts and themselves – to be dealt with in a spirit of co-operation – in which the parties have no place save that they are invited to be heard. It was so held in *Hessische Knappschaft* v *Maison Singer et Fils* (Case 44/65) [1966] CMLR 82, 94.

[25] (ii) If the English judge considers it '*not necessary*' to refer a question of interpretation to the European Court – but instead decides it himself – that is the end of the matter. It is no good a party going off to the European Court. They would not listen to him. They are conscious that the Treaty gives the final word in this respect to the English courts. From all I have read of their cases, they are very careful not to exceed their jurisdiction. They never do anything to trespass on any ground which is properly the province of the national courts.

9. *The guide lines*

[26] Seeing that these matters of 'necessary' and 'discretion' are the concern of the English courts, it will fall to the English judges to rule upon them. Likewise the national courts of other member states have to rule on them. They are matters on which guidance is needed. It may not be out of place, therefore, to draw attention to the way in which other national courts have dealt with them.

(1) *Guide lines as to whether a decision is necessary*

(i) *The point must be conclusive*

[27] The English Court has to consider whether 'a decision on the question is *necessary* to enable them to give *judgment*'. That means judgment in the very case which is before the Court. The judge must have got to the stage when he says to himself: 'This clause of the Treaty is capable of two or more meanings. If it means *this*, I give judgment for the plaintiff. If it means *that*, I give judgment for the defendant'. In short, the point must be such that, whichever way the point is decided, it is conclusive of the case. Nothing more remains but to give judgment. The Hamburg Court stressed the necessity in *In re Adjustment Tax on Petrol* [1966] CMLR 409, 416 (Finanzgericht). In *Van Duyn* v *Home Office* [1974] 1 CMLR 347, in England the Vice-Chancellor Sir John Pennycuick said: 'It would be quite impossible to give judgment without such a decision'.

(ii) *Previous ruling*

[28] In some cases, however, it may be found that the same point – or substantially the same point – has already been decided by the European Court in a previous case. In

that event it is not necessary for the English Court to decide it. It can follow the previous decision without troubling the European Court. But, as I have said, the European Court is *not* bound by its previous decisions. So if the English Court thinks that a previous decision of the European Court may have been wrong – or if there are new factors which ought to be brought to the notice of the European Court – the English Court may consider it *necessary* to re-submit the point to the European Court. In that event, the European Court will consider the point again. It was so held by the European Court itself in the *Da Costa* case (Cases 28 & 30/62) [1963] CMLR 224, in Holland in *Vereniging van Fabrikanten en Importeurs van FIVA* v *Mertens (No. 1)* [1963] CMLR 141 and in Germany in *Import of Powdered Milk (No. 3)* [1967] CMLR 326, 336.

(iii) *Acte clair*

[29]   In other cases the English Court may consider the point is reasonably clear and free from doubt. In that event there is no need to interpret the Treaty but only to apply it: and that is the task of the English Court. It was so submitted by the Advocate General to the European Court of Justice in the *Da Costa* case (Cases 28 & 30/62) [1963] CMLR 224, 234. It has been so held by the highest courts in France; by the Conseil d'Etat in *re Shell-Berre* [1964] CMLR 462, 481, and by the Cour de Cassation in *State* v *Cornet* [1967] CMLR 351 and *Lapeyre* v *Administration des Douanes* [1967] CMLR 362, 368; also by a superior court in Germany in the *French Widows Pension Settlement* [1971] CMLR 20 (Bundessozialgericht).

(iv) *Decide the facts first*

[30]   It is to be noticed, too, that the word is 'necessary'. This is much stronger than 'desirable' or 'convenient'. There are some cases where the point, if decided one way, would shorten the trial greatly. But, if decided the other way, it would mean that the trial would have to go its full length. In such a case it might be 'convenient' or 'desirable' to take it as a preliminary point because it might save much time and expense. But it would not be 'necessary' at that stage. When the facts were investigated, it might turn out to have been quite unnecessary. The case would be determined on another ground altogether. As a rule you cannot tell whether it is necessary to decide a point until all the facts are ascertained. So in general it is best to decide the facts first.

(2) *Guide lines as to the exercise of discretion*

[31]   Assuming that the condition about 'necessary' is fulfilled, there remains the matter of discretion. This only applies to the trial judge or the Court of Appeal, not to the House of Lords. The English Court has a discretion either to decide the point itself or to refer it to the European Court. The national courts of the various member countries have had to consider how to exercise this discretion. The cases show that they have taken into account such matters as the following:

(i) *The time taken to get a ruling*

[32]   The length of time which may elapse before a ruling can be obtained from the European Court. This may take months and months. The lawyers have to prepare their briefs; the Advocate-General has to prepare his submissions; the case has to be argued; the court has to give its decision. The average length of time at present seems to be between six and nine months. Meanwhile, the whole action in the English Court is stayed until the ruling is obtained. This may be very unfortunate, especially in a case where an injunction is sought or there are other reasons for expedition. This was very much in the mind of the German Court of Appeal of Frankfurt in the *Export of Oat Flakes* case [1969] CMLR 85, 97. It said that it was important 'to prevent undue protraction of both the proceedings before the Court of Justice and trial before the national courts'. On that ground it decided a point of interpretation itself, rather than submit it to the European Court.

(ii) *Do not overload the court*

[33]   The importance of not overwhelming the European Court by references to it. If it were overloaded, it could not get through its work. There are nine judges of that court. All nine must sit in plenary sessions on these cases, as well as many other important

cases (see **Article 165**). They cannot split up into divisions of three or five judges. All nine must sit. So do not put too much on them. The Court of Appeal in Frankfurt took this view pointedly in *Import Licence for Oats* [1968] CMLR 103, 117:

> ... the European Court must not be overwhelmed by requests for rulings ... [Courts should] exercise their right sparingly. A reference to the European Court must not become an automatic reaction, and ought only to be made if serious difficulties of interpretation occur ...

(iii)   *Formulate the question clearly*
[34]   The need to formulate the question clearly. It must be a question of *interpretation only* of the Treaty. It must not be mixed up with the facts. It is the task of the national courts to find the facts and apply the Treaty. The European Court must not take that task on themselves. In fairness to them, it is desirable to find the facts and state them clearly before referring the question. That appears from the *Salgoil SpA* case (Case 13/68) [1969] CMLR 181, 193 and the *Sirena* case (Case 40/70) [1971] CMLR 260. In any case, the task of interpretation is better done with the facts in mind rather than in ignorance of them.

(iv)   *Difficulty and importance*
[35]   The difficulty and importance of the point. Unless the point is really difficult and important, it would seem better for the English judge to decide it himself. For in so doing, much delay and expense will be saved. So far the English judges have not shirked their responsibilities. They have decided several points of interpretation on the Treaty to the satisfaction, I hope, of the parties. At any rate, there has been no appeal from them. I refer to the decision of Whitford J in *Lerose Ltd* v *Hawick Jersey International Ltd* [1973] CMLR 83, Graham J in *Minnesota Mining & Manufacturing Co.* v *Geerpres Europe Ltd* [1973] CMLR 259, Bridge J in *Esso Petroleum* v *Kingswood Motors (Addlestone) Ltd* [1973] CMLR 665, Graham J in *Löwenbräu München* v *Grunhalle Lager International Ltd* [1974] 1 CMLR 1 and Mr. Suenson-Taylor QC in *Processed Vegetable Growers Association Ltd* v *Commissioners of Customs and Excise* [1974] 1 CMLR 113 (Leeds VAT Tribunal).

(v)   *Expense*
[36]   The expense to the parties of getting a ruling from the European Court. That influenced a Nuremberg Court in the case of *re Potato Flour Tax* [1964] CMLR 96, 106 (Finanzgericht). On request for interpretation, the European Court does not as a rule award costs, and for a simple reason. It does not decide the case. It only gives advice on the meaning of the Treaty. If either party wishes to get the costs of the reference, he must get it from the English Court, when it eventually decides the case: see *Sociale Verzekeringsbank* v *Van der Vecht* (Case 19/67) [1968] CMLR 151, 167.

(vi)   *Wishes of the parties*
[37]   The wishes of the parties. If both parties want the point to be referred to the European Court, the English Court should have regard to their wishes, but it should not give them undue weight. The English Court should hesitate before making a reference against the wishes of one of the parties, seeing the expense and delay which it involves.

The Role and Future of the European Court of Justice, **The British Institute of International and Comparative Law, 1996**

(c)   **Encouraging national courts to decide more questions of Community law without references to the ECJ**
In the early days of the Community, national courts needed to be encouraged to identify questions of Community law in cases before them and to refer them to the ECJ. Now, however, a substantial body of case law has built up and national courts and practitioners have become familiar with Community law issues. The problem is now the overload rather than the lack of cases referred to the ECJ.

National courts generally have a discretion whether to refer questions to the ECJ, but courts of last instance are under an obligation to do so. In appropriate cases it is fully consistent with Article 177 for national courts to decide Community law questions without making a reference to the ECJ and it is not necessary or desirable to amend Article 177 to this effect.

The practice of national courts deciding questions of Community law has now increased. The question therefore arises whether that development should be further encouraged; if so, it might ultimately result in the suggestion of curtailing the right of the lower national courts and the duty of the highest national courts to make references.

(i)   lower national courts

Ordinarily, national courts at first instance should be encouraged to decide Community law questions themselves. These include cases:

— where the issue in question is clearly covered by an earlier ruling of the ECJ;
— where the relevant principles have already been established in rulings of the ECJ and the point in issue involves the application of the principles to the facts of the particular case;
— where time or cost constraints render a reference undesirable in the interests of justice.

However, if the right of lower national courts to make a preliminary reference were to be abolished, the consequence would be that the unsuccessful party would be bound to appeal its case where a reference could be made to the ECJ. This would prolong the litigation and add to the expense. On the other hand, where the parties had not the means or patience to litigate far up the national hierarchy of courts, important questions of Community law might remain unresolved. In the field of the Brussels Convention, where the right to make preliminary references is reserved to the appeal courts, the absence of the right to make preliminary references is on occasions regretted by courts of first instance.

Lower national courts appear to be reluctant to resolve the Community questions themselves. For instance, in *R* v *Pharmaceutical Society of Great Britain, ex parte The Association of Pharmaceutical Importers* [1978] 3 CMLR 951 Kerr LJ held 'Our courts should hesitate long' before reaching the conclusion that the answer to a question of EC law was so obvious as to leave no room for reasonable doubt. This view seems now to prevail over Lord Denning's (much criticised) approach in *Bulmer* v *Bollinger* [1974] All ER 1226: 'The point of EC law must be conclusive of the case; if there has been a previous ruling on the point by the ECJ or if the English court considers the point is reasonably clear and free from doubt, there is no need to make a reference.' A set of guidelines on the need to make Article 177 references has been laid down by MacPherson J in *R* v *Treasury, ex parte Daily Mail* [1987] 2 CMLR 1. However, it would be unfortunate if lower national courts declined to decide Community law questions themselves save as in clear cases.

In the light of the above, the discretionary power of the lower courts to make references should not be curtailed. Otherwise, important questions may be left unresolved and the rights of individuals completely unprotected. The risk of procedural blockages for the functioning of the Common Market would also be a matter of serious concern.

It would also be unacceptable that references by lower courts should be made subject to the consent of a higher court. In many cases it will be clear from the outset that an ECJ ruling will be required and interposing a higher court will simply cause unnecessary delay and expense. There may however be certain areas (employment, taxation, social security), where the lower court (or tribunal) may refrain from making the reference and leave the matter to the first appellate court that is concerned only with issues of law. In those areas the appellate court would be better placed to make a reference to the ECJ.

Editorial Comments (1991) 28 CML Rev 241

Use of the preliminary procedure

. . .

Preliminary rulings are authentic interpretation of Community law and therefore, in principle, important for all Member States. They must be decided by the (full) Court of Justice. When the Court of First Instance was created, it was especially charged with the cases which require fact finding. Preliminary rulings may not be delegated to the Court of First Instance (Article 168A EEC). Possibilities for speeding up matters by delegating preliminary rulings to a chamber of the Court are limited, as any such delegation may be vetoed by any Member State. An effort to shorten the period of time needed will have to be made by the Court of Justice itself. We may just hope that the establishment of the Court of First Instance and a more extensive reference to chambers by the Court of Justice will provide for the time needed to decide preliminary rulings faster. But even if maximum attention is given to them, preliminary rulings necessarily take a considerable amount of time. Because of their importance, the Member States, the Commission and the parties must have an opportunity to send in their comments in writing and – in order to be able to comment each other – also orally. Often, written comments need to be translated. In addition, preliminary rulings are costly for the parties concerned. It is true that the parties are not obliged to make use of their right to submit statements of case or written observations under Article 20 of the Statute of the Court or to plead during the oral hearing, but in practice they always do. Lawyers probably fear that if ever they were to renounce this right and subsequently lose their case they might also lose their client.

One may dispute whether a preliminary ruling on any question of Community law is always necessary. Some questions are so unique or so unimportant that one might submit that even a court against whose decisions there is no judicial remedy under national law should not necessarily request a preliminary ruling. This holds in particular for some issues concerning the interpretation of the common external tariff. The classification of a product under the external tariff is a question of interpretation of the tariff-regulations and therefore subject to the preliminary procedure. But, sometimes the differences between the possible solutions is minimal, sometimes the product is so specialized that further imports of the same product are unlikely. In a conference in the Hague, organized by the Asser Instituut in 1985, Professor Weiler proposed what he called a 'green light procedure'. This would allow the national courts to state their own view of the correct interpretation and to forward that to the Court of Justice. If the Advocate General and the Judge Rapporteur agree with that interpretation and neither the Commission, nor any Member State raises objection then this interpretation would stand. To some extent one could compare this with the opposition procedure in competition law. When exemption is asked for an agreement and no reply received in six months the agreement may be considered exempted.

The 'green light procedure' would mean a kind of controlled application of the theory of *acte clair* in the broad sense of the expression – as often used in French law – viz. under the circumstances of the case, the act is clear enough for the domestic court to be able to decide by itself. Perhaps, one could go even further by accepting a more frequent use of *acte clair* with only *post facto* control. So far, the Commission has been reluctant to use Article 169 with respect to decisions of the national judiciary. On a few occasions where they should have requested preliminary rulings, supreme courts have failed to do so. In reply to parliamentary questions the Commission indicated that it will not act under Article 169 as long as such failures can be seen as incidents. . ..

An action under Article 169 EEC may lead to the undesirable result that a Member State will be required under Article 171 to take measures against its judiciary. The independence of the judiciary being of essential importance also for the application of Community law, it seems justified that the Commission will take this chance only in extreme cases.

Should one permit a wider use of *acte clair* by national courts without the Commission applying Article 169 if mistakes are made, then the risk will grow of divergent interpretations of particular rules of Community law. To prevent this one could perhaps attribute a further task to the Advocates General of the Court. In 1975 a Dutch committee, charged with writing a report on European Union suggested that an Advocate General of the Court of Justice should be empowered to raise preliminary questions before the Court of Justice whenever a national court of last instance has failed to do so. Even if it is impossible to apply the ruling then given to the case in which the question arose, the authentic interpretation would then be available to future cases. A follow-up of this suggestion was not considered necessary as refusals to request preliminary rulings are rare. Should one, however, drastically expand the possibility for specialized courts to apply the theory of *acte clair*, then the suggestion of allowing one or more Advocates

General to raise the question before the Court of Justice for the sake of future cases could be useful.

Any development as suggested above requires loyal cooperation of the national judiciaries. When the Communities were established one was not at all sure of such cooperation. That is why many authors were afraid of any application of *acte clair*. Now, especially since the *Nicolo* Case of the French *Conseil d'Etat*, developments have shown that the national judiciaries loyally cooperate in the development of Community law. In many respects it is no longer a strange or foreign legal system for them. Most supreme courts, and especially those which are frequently faced with questions of Community law, are perfectly able to identify the important legal questions which they should subject to the preliminary procedure notwithstanding delay and costs. There would be little harm in allowing them to interpret the unimportant questions themselves, thus obtaining the greater benefit for the litigants of saving time and costs.

Seen from the point of view of Community law none of the above-mentioned suggestions would be an improvement. The question rather is whether the mature Community legal order can make sacrifices for the sake of the litigating citizens.

COMMISSIONERS OF CUSTOMS AND EXCISE v SpA SAMEX [1983] 1 All ER 1042, Queen's Bench Division

The UK issued Samex with an import licence for textiles shipped on or before 31 December 1979. The goods were imported in January 1980 and were seized by Customs. Samex argued that both the time limit on the licence and the seizure were contrary to Community law.

It was held that a reference to the Court of Justice under Article 177 should be made.

BINGHAM J (at pp. 1054c–1056h): That, therefore, being the background, so far as the law, the facts and the submissions of the parties are concerned, I turn to consider whether in all the circumstances it is proper for the questions which counsel for the defendant has raised to be referred to the Court of Justice under Art. 177 of the Treaty. Article 177 reads:

> The Court of Justice shall have jurisdiction to give preliminary rulings concerning: (a) the interpretation of this Treaty; (b) the validity and interpretation of acts of the institutions of the Community; (c) the interpretation of the statutes of bodies established by an act of the Council, where those statutes so provide.
>
> Where such a question is raised before any court or tribunal of a Member State, that court or tribunal may, if it considers that a decision on the question is necessary to enable it to give judgment, request the Court of Justice to give a ruling thereon.
>
> Where any such question is raised in a case pending before a court or tribunal of a Member State, against whose decisions there is no judicial remedy under national law, that court or tribunal shall bring the matter before the Court of Justice.

From the language of the article it is, I think, clear that, so far as the court of first instance is concerned, there are two questions to be answered: first, whether a decision on the question of Community law is necessary to enable it to give judgment, and, if it is so necessary, whether the court should in the exercise of its discretion order that a reference be made.

The guidelines as to the proper approach on both those questions were given by the Court of Appeal in *H P Bulmer Ltd v J Bollinger SA* [1974] 2 All ER 1226 at 1234ff, [1974] Ch 401 at 422ff. Lord Denning MR draws attention to four points relevant to the question whether a decision is necessary. The first of those is that the point must be conclusive. On the facts of this case, as I understand it, the answer to be given by the Court of Justice will be conclusive in this sense, that if the answers are adverse to the defendant that will admittedly be the end of its case. If the answers are given favourably to the defendant, then depending on what those answers are and which of them are favourable, there may be some short issues or a short issue to be tried, but there is, I think, no doubt that the answer which the Court of Justice will give will be substantially, if not quite totally, determinative of this litigation.

The second point raised with reference to the necessity of a decision is previous ruling. Lord Denning MR says ([1974] 2 All ER 1226 at 1235, [1974] Ch 401 at 422):

In some cases, however, it may be found that the same point – or substantially the same point – has already been decided by the European Court in a previous case. In that event it is not necessary for the English court to decide it. It can follow the previous decision without troubling the European Court.

That, no doubt true in some cases, does not, I think, apply in this case, since it is not suggested that there is any previous ruling either on this regulation or on any analogous regulation which yields a clear answer to the present litigation.

Third, Lord Denning MR lists acte claire and says ([1974] 2 All ER 1226 at 1235, [1974] Ch 401 at 423):

> In other cases the English court may consider the point is reasonably clear and free from doubt. In that event there is no need to interpret the treaty but only to apply it, and that is the task of the English court.

It certainly is of course the task of the English court to apply it, but it must apply the treaty properly interpreted. As I have indicated, I myself feel that the first three questions raised should certainly, if it rested with me, be answered in favour of the commissioners, but I do not regard the matter as so free from doubt as to render those points acte claire, and I certainly do not regard the fourth point on the principle of proportionality as either reasonably clear or reasonably free from doubt.

Point four: Lord Denning MR says, 'Decide the facts first'. That, with respect, is an injunction of obvious merit. The present case is one in which the essential facts are agreed and on the very minor areas of disagreement or non-agreement the facts can without doubt be settled in a form which will enable the relevant question to be answered.

I therefore turn to the guidelines which Lord Denning MR has indicated governing the exercise of discretion. He mentions, first, the time to get a ruling, second, the undesirability of overloading the Court of Justice, third, the need to formulate the question clearly, fourth, the difficulty and importance of the point. Under that head he says ([1974] 2 All ER 1226 at 1236, [1974] Ch 401 at 424):

> *Difficulty and importance.* Unless the point is really difficult and important, it would seem better for the English judge to decide it himself. For in so doing, much delay and expense will be saved. So far the English judges have not shirked their responsibilities. They have decided several points of interpretation on the treaty to the satisfaction, I hope, of the parties.

He refers, fifth, to expense, and sixth, to the wishes of the parties. Under that head he says ([1974] 2 All ER 1226 at 1236, [1974] Ch 401 at 425):

> If both parties want the point to be referred to the European Court, the English court should have regard to their wishes, but it should not give them undue weight. The English court should hesitate before making a reference against the wishes of one of the parties, seeing the expense and delay which it involves.

Lord Denning MR then goes on to discuss the principles of interpretation and draws attention to the different approach which is required in interpreting Community legislation as compared with our own domestic legislation.

In endeavouring to follow and respect these guidelines I find myself in some difficulty, because it was submitted by counsel on behalf of the defendant that the issues raised by his client should be resolved by the Court of Justice as the court best fitted to do so, and I find this a consideration which does give me some pause for thought. Sitting as a judge in a national court, asked to decide questions of Community law, I am very conscious of the advantages enjoyed by the Court of Justice. It has a panoramic view of the Community and its institutions, a detailed knowledge of the treaties and of much subordinate legislation made under them, and an intimate familiarity with the functioning of the Community market which no national judge denied the collective experience of the Court of Justice could hope to achieve. Where questions of administrative intention and practice arise the Court of Justice can receive submissions from the Community institutions, as also where relations between the Community and non-member states are in issue. Where the interests of member states are affected they can intervene to make their views known. That is a material consideration in this case since there is some slight evidence that the practice of different member states is divergent. Where comparison falls to made between Community texts in different languages, all texts being equally authentic, the multinational Court of Justice is equipped to carry out the task in a way which no national judge, whatever his linguistic skills, could rival. The interpretation of Community instruments involves very often not the process familiar to common lawyers of laboriously extracting the meaning from words used but the more creative process of supplying flesh to a spare and loosely constructed skeleton. The choice between alternative submissions may turn not on purely legal considerations, but on a broader view of what the orderly development of the Community requires. These are matters which the Court of Justice is very much better placed to assess and determine than a national court.

It does not follow from this that a reference should be made by a national court of first instance wherever a litigant raises a serious point of Community law and seeks a reference, or wherever he indicates an intention to appeal, even if he announces an intention to appeal, if necessary, to the highest court which is effectively bound to refer the question to the Court of Justice. For example, as *H P Bulmer Ltd* v *J Bollinger SA* points out, it can rarely be necessary to make a reference until the relevant facts have been found, and unless the points raised are substantially determinative of the action. Or the question raised may admit of only one possible answer, or it may be covered by Community authority precisely in point, although even here some slight caution is necessary since the Court of Justice is not strictly bound by its own decisions. These considerations relate to whether a decision is necessary. Other considerations may affect the exercise of discretion. Sometimes no doubt it may appear that the question is raised mischievously, not in the bona fide hope of success but in order to obstruct or delay an almost inevitable adverse judgment, denying the other party his remedy meanwhile. In my judgment none of these contra-indications obtains here. While I think the defendant unlikely to succeed, I do not regard its arguments as hopeless and they are of potential importance. I have been referred to no authority precisely in point and, so far as I know, Regulation 3059/78 has never been considered by the Court of Justice. The defendant is at present denied the possession or use of the yarn but is paying and will continue to pay for its storage, at least unless some other arrangement is made for disposal of the goods. It has already given security for the commissioners' costs under para 10(2) of Sch 3 to the Customs and Excise Management Act 1979, and has expressed willingness to increase that security. If a reference produces a ruling unfavourable to it, it will almost certainly be ordered to pay the costs incurred by the commissioners as a result of it. It has nothing to hope from delay, save the hope of success. The reference to the Court of Justice would be unlikely to take longer than appeals have normally taken to reach the Court of Appeal, at least until recently, and unlikely to cost much more. If, at the Court of Appeal stage, a reference were held to be necessary, the delay and expense would be roughly doubled. I discount the indication of counsel for the defendant that if denied a reference in this court his client would probably, according to his present instructions, appeal to the Court of Appeal and seek a reference there, but in all the circumstances this does appear to me to be an appropriate case in which questions of potentially great importance in the operation of the Community's system for regulating imports to member states should be reviewed.

I shall accordingly order a reference under Article 177 of the EEC Treaty. The precise form of that reference is something that I think will have to be the subject of discussion hereafter.

6.4 Mandatory References

6.4.1 COURT OF JUSTICE GUIDELINES

CILFIT AND LANIFICIO DI GAVARDO SPA v *MINISTRY OF HEALTH* (Case 283/81)
[1982] ECR 3415, Court of Justice

A number of textile firms complained that an Italian levy on wool was contrary to Community law. The Italian government claimed that a reference was unnecessary because the meaning of the Community law in question was clear. The Italian court made a reference to the Court of Justice on the obligations of a court from whose decisions there was no judicial remedy.

It was held that a court whose decision was final was not obliged to refer the matter to the Court of Justice if any one of three conditions was fulfilled.

7.   That obligation to refer a matter to the Court of Justice is based on co-operation, established with a view to ensuring the proper application and uniform interpretation of Community law in all the Member States, between national courts, in their capacity as courts responsible for the application of Community law, and the Court of Justice. More particularly, the third paragraph of Article 177 seeks to prevent the occurrence within the Community of divergences in judicial decisions on questions of Community law. The scope of that obligation must therefore be assessed, in view of those objectives, by reference to the powers of the national courts, on the one hand, and those of the Court of Justice, on the other, where such a question of interpretation is raised within the meaning of Article 177.

8.   In this connection, it is necessary to define the meaning for the purposes of Community law of the expression 'where any such question is raised' in order to determine the circumstances in which a national court or tribunal against whose decisions there is no judicial remedy under national law is obliged to bring a matter before the Court of Justice.

9.   In this regard, it must in the first place be pointed out that Article 177 does not constitute a means of redress available to the parties to a case pending before a national court or tribunal. Therefore the mere fact that a party contends that the dispute gives rise to a question concerning the interpretation of Community law does not mean that the court or tribunal concerned is compelled to consider that a question has been raised within the meaning of Article 177. On the other hand, a national court or tribunal may, in an appropriate case, refer a matter to the Court of Justice of its own motion.

10.   Secondly, it follows from the relationship between the second and third paragraphs of Article 177 that the courts or tribunals referred to in the third paragraph have the same discretion as any other national court or tribunal to ascertain whether a decision on a question of Community law is necessary to enable them to give judgment. Accordingly, those courts or tribunals are not obliged to refer to the Court of Justice a question concerning the interpretation of Community law raised before them if that question is not relevant, that is to say, if the answer to that question, regardless of what it may be, can in no way affect the outcome of the case.

11.   If, however, those courts or tribunals consider that recourse to Community law is necessary to enable them to decide a case, Article 177 imposes an obligation on them to refer to the Court of Justice any question of interpretation which may arise.

12.   The question submitted by the Corte di Cassazione seeks to ascertain whether, in certain circumstances, the obligation laid down by the third paragraph of Article 177 might none the less be subject to certain restrictions.

13.   It must be remembered in this connection that in its judgment of 27 March 1963 in Joined Cases 28 to 30/62 (*Da Costa* v *Nederlandse Belastingadministratie* [1963] ECR 31) the Court ruled that: 'Although the third paragraph of Article 177 unreservedly requires courts or tribunals of a Member State against whose decisions there is no judicial remedy under national law . . . to refer to the Court every question of interpretation raised before them, the authority of an interpretation under Article 177 already given by the Court may deprive the obligation of its purpose and thus empty it of its substance. Such is the case especially when the question raised is materially identical with a question which has already been the subject of a preliminary ruling in a similar case'.

14.   The same effect, as regards the limits set to the obligation laid down by the third paragraph of Article 177, may be produced where previous decisions of the Court have already dealt with the point of law in question, irrespective of the nature of the proceedings which led to those decisions, even though the questions at issue are not strictly identical.

15.   However, it must not be forgotten that in all such circumstances national courts and tribunals, including those referred to in the third paragraph of Article 177, remain entirely at liberty to bring a matter before the Court of Justice if they consider it appropriate to do so.

16.   Finally, the correct application of Community law may be so obvious as to leave no scope for any reasonable doubt as to the manner in which the question raised is to be resolved. Before it comes to the conclusion that such is the case, the national court or tribunal must be convinced that the matter is equally obvious to the courts of the other Member States and to the Court of Justice. Only if those conditions are satisfied may the national court or tribunal refrain from submitting the question to the Court of Justice and take upon itself the responsibility for resolving it.

17.   However, the existence of such a possibility must be assessed on the basis of the characteristic features of Community law and the particular difficulties to which its interpretation gives rise.

18.   To begin with, it must be borne in mind that Community legislation is drafted in several languages and that the different language versions are all equally authentic. An interpretation of a provision of Community law thus involves a comparison of the different language versions.

19.   It must also be borne in mind, even where the different language versions are entirely in accord with one another, that Community law uses terminology which is peculiar to it. Furthermore, it must be emphasized that legal concepts do not necessarily have the same meaning in Community law and in the law of the various Member States.

20.   Finally, every provision of Community law must be placed in its context and interpreted in the light of the provisions of Community law as a whole, regard being had to the objectives thereof and to its state of evolution at the date on which the provision in question is to be applied.

21.   In the light of all those considerations, the answer to the question submitted by the Corte Suprema di Cassazione must be that the third paragraph of Article 177 of the EEC Treaty is to be interpreted as meaning that a court or tribunal against whose decisions there is no judicial remedy under national law is required, where a question of Community law is raised before it, to comply with its obligation to bring the matter before the Court of Justice, unless it has established that the question raised is irrelevant or that the Community provision in question has already been interpreted by the Court or that the correct application of Community law is so obvious as to leave no scope for any reasonable doubt. The existence of such a possibility must be assessed in the light of the specific characteristics of Community law, the particular difficulties to which its interpretation gives rise and the risk of divergences in judicial decisions within the Community.

The Role and Future of the European Court of Justice, **The British Institute
of International and Comparative Law, 1996**

(c)   Encouraging national courts to decide more questions of Community law without references to the ECJ

. . .

(ii)   courts of last instance
If the discretion of lower national courts is to be retained, the question arises as to the duty of the highest national courts to make references. These contribute significantly to the number of preliminary references, making up about one-quarter of all references (see Annex V).

The main obstacle to encouraging national courts of last instance to resolve more EC cases is the restrictive nature of *acte clair* as it was formulated in *CILFIT* v *Ministry of Health* (Case 283/81) [1982] ECR 3415.

A final court in a Member State is under no obligation to refer to the ECJ even where a question of Community law is relevant if the correct application of Community law is 'so obvious as to leave no scope for reasonable doubt as to the manner in which the question raised is to be resolved' (para 16).

Before the national court reaches that conclusion, it must be convinced that the matter would be equally obvious to the courts of the other Member States and to the ECJ. In that respect it must take account of the characteristic features of Community law and the particular difficulties to which its interpretation gives rise and it must compare the different versions of the text in the various Community languages:

. . . every provision of Community law must be placed in its context and interpreted in the light of the provisions of Community law as a whole, regard being had to the objectives thereof and to its state of evolution at the date on which the provision in question is to be applied (para. 20).

In the *Factortame* case ([1989] 2 CMLR 355) Hodgson J referred to the *CILFIT* test as '. . . intimidating to an English judge . . .'. Compliance with these requirements for *acte clair* is virtually impossible. In practice this test is completely unworkable.

Moreover, the ECJ further limited the scope of application of the doctrine of *acte clair* in *Foto-Frost* v *Hauptzollamt Lübeck-Ost* (Case 314/85) [1987] ECR 4199 to cases where the question of Community law raised before the national court is one of interpretation, not the validity of an act of a Community institution.

In 1982, when *CILFIT* was decided, not all of the supreme courts of the Member States recognised the primacy of Community law. It was, therefore, probably appropriate not to extend the cases in which they could have decided Community law questions themselves and to apply the *acte clair* doctrine restrictively. Has not the time come when they should also be given a similar power of appreciation to that exercised by the lower courts?

The dangers of such a course are evident. Supreme courts might well choose not to refer cases which might be prejudicial to perceived national interests, or might lead to an extension of Community competence, etc. Cases where national courts have refused to refer a question of Community law on grounds which did not meet the *CILFIT* criteria have been highly criticised. For example, in *Re Sandhu, The Times,* 10 May 1985 the House of Lords refused to make a reference on the basis that the point had been decided by the ECJ in a previous ruling (*Diatta* v *Land Berlin* (Case 267/83) [1985] ECR 567) and the minority thought *acte clair* applied. But that decision was subject to much academic criticism.

In this context, it is undesirable — as a general rule — to curtail the duty of the national courts of last instance to refer Community law questions. The present system is considered beneficial to the achievement of a uniform Community legal system. Yet it is for consideration whether the *acte clair* test laid down in *CILFIT* should not be viewed as a set of guidelines rather than as a set of rules. But that could lead to extensive divergence in the national courts' approach to the issue in practice. On the one hand, a national court may feel placed under significant constraints so that a refusal to refer would take place only when matters really were unequivocally clear. On the other hand, the *CILFIT* test may be seen as a flexible tool which can be manipulated by national courts to justify a refusal to refer where they have formed a view as to how the points of Community law at issue *should* be resolved. In order to ensure legal certainty, the ECJ should be prepared to review the *CILFIT* ruling if and when it gets the opportunity.

6.4.2 CASELAW OF THE UK COURTS

MAGNAVISION v *GENERAL OPTICAL COUNCIL (No. 2)* [1987] 2 CMLR 262, Queen's Bench Division

For the facts, see *Magnavision* v *General Optical Council No. 2* at **6.2** above.

WATKINS LJ: [3]   When the appeal was argued before us, an application was made by the appellants for an order of reference by this Court to the European Court. We heard argument upon that application, at the conclusion of which we determined, having given the matter very careful thought, that we were not obliged to make such a reference, seeing that we were content with the construction we placed in our judgments upon the relevant legislation. Our view of the intendment and meaning of that legislation was clear and, I should add, for my part remains so.

. . .

[5]   In addition to the argument we heard as to whether or not it was appropriate to refer a question to the European Court, we heard a great deal of most interesting argument, with copious reference to case law, upon the issues arising out of the

provisions of **Articles 30** and **36** of the Treaty. Our conclusion was, as our judgments show, that we were satisfied that the Justices had reached a right conclusion upon a clear and proper construction of the relevant legislation.

. . .

[13]   He says further that the European Court itself has, in recent times, made it clear that it expects courts of final decision in member states to make a reference when a litigant has no other means of redress for a decision which has gone against him. In that connection, he made reference to a case I shall call, for short, *CILFIT* (Case 283/81) [1982] ECR 3415]. I do not propose to make any further reference to that case other than to observe, in agreement with the submission made by Mr Jacobs with regard to it, that if anything, it supports the proposition that when a court of final decision in a member state has come to a decision as a consequence of being clear in its mind as to the construction to be put upon relevant legislation, then it is under no obligation at all to make a reference to the European Court.

R v HENN AND DARBY [1980] 2 All ER 166, House of Lords

Importers of pornographic material argued that UK restrictions on such imports were in contravention of Article 30 of the Treaty of Rome. The Court of Appeal refused to make a reference to the Court of Justice on the ground that the application of Community law was clear.

It was held that a reference should be made because the application of Community law was not clear.

LORD DIPLOCK (at p. 197e-g): My Lords, in the light of this established case law of the European court, it appeared to me to be so free from any doubt that an absolute prohibition of importation of goods of a particular description from other member states fell within Art. 30 that I should not have been disposed to regard the instant case as involving any matter of interpretation of that Article that was open to question. But the strong inclination expressed by the Court of Appeal to adopt the contrary view shows that there is involved a question of interpretation on which judicial minds can differ. It serves as a timely warning to English judges not to be too ready to hold that because the meaning of the English text (which is one of six of equal authority) seems plain to them no question of interpretation can be involved. It was for this reason that your Lordships thought it proper to submit to the European court for a preliminary ruling the question as to the interpretation of Art. 30 which is set out hereafter; it was not through any doubts on your Lordships' part as to the answer that would be received.

R v SECRETARY OF STATE FOR TRANSPORT, EX PARTE FACTORTAME LTD [1989] 3 CMLR 1, House of Lords

For the facts, see **9.1.2.2** above.

LORD BRIDGE:
[39]   In the light of the course which I propose that your Lordships should take, it would serve no useful purpose for me to attempt an analysis of the voluminous Community case law to which the main arguments have been directed. It is significant to note, however, that Community law embodies a principle which appears closely analogous to the principle of English law that delegated legislation must be presumed to be valid unless and until declared invalid. In *Granaria BV v Hoofdproduktschap voor Akkerbouwprodukten* (Case 101/78) [1979] ECR 623 the validity of a regulation made by the Council of the EEC was challenged in proceedings before the court of a member state. In answering questions referred to it under **Article 177** of the Treaty of Rome, the ECJ held that every regulation which is brought into force in accordance with the Treaty must be presumed to be valid and must be treated as fully effective so long as a competent court has not made a finding that it is invalid. On the other hand, in *Firma Foto-Frost v Hauptzollamt Lübeck-Ost* (Case 314/85) [1988] 3 CMLR 57 at 80 the ECJ said in giving judgment, again on a reference under **Article 177**:

It should be added that the rule that national courts may not themselves declare Community acts invalid may have to be qualified in certain circumstances in the case of proceedings relating to an application for interim measures; however, that case is not referred to in the national court's question.

[40] In the light of these two authorities and in application of the principles laid down by the ECJ in *Srl Cilfit* v *Ministry of Health* (Case 283/81) [1982] ECR 3415, I do not think that it is open to your Lordships' House to decide one way or the other whether, in relation to the grant of interim protection in the circumstances of the instant case, Community law overrides English law and either empowers or obliges an English court to make an interim order protecting the putative rights claimed by the applicants. It follows, I think, that your Lordships are obliged under **Article 177** of the Treaty to seek a preliminary ruling from the ECJ.

R v SECRETARY OF STATE FOR THE ENVIRONMENT, EX PARTE RSPB
[1995] JPL 842

The RSPB challenged the decision of the Secretary of State for the Environment to exclude an area known as Lappel Bank from a designated Special Protection Area for birds ('SPA'), on the ground that the Birds Directive did not permit economic considerations to be taken into account in the particular circumstances of the case.

It was held by the House of Lords that a reference to the Court of Justice should be made.

LORD JAUNCEY OF TULLICHETTLE (at p. 844 and 845): By letter of March 16, 1993 [the Secretary of State] informed English Nature that he was minded to exclude the 26 hectares of Lappel Bank from the Medway Estuary SPA and on December 15, 1993 he announced his final decision in the following terms:

. . .

> I have concluded that the need not to inhibit the commercial viability of the port, and the contribution that expansion into this area will play, outweighs its nature conservation value, I must stress that my decision is an exceptional one taken to help to secure the economic future of Sheerness and the Isle of Sheppey.

The question is whether in reaching that conclusion he was entitled in the terms of the Birds Directive to have regard to economic considerations. The Divisional Court held that he was so entitled as did the majority of the Court of Appeal. In the latter court, Hirst and Steyn LJJ considered that the matter was *acte claire* and that a reference to the ECJ was unnecessary, whereas Hoffmann LJ considered that the Secretary of State was not entitled to have regard to economic considerations and that the matter was *acte claire* the other way.

. . .

My lords, faced with competing arguments of substance and with support for each of those arguments in conflicting judgments of two members of the Court of Appeal. I do not consider that your Lordships have any alternative but to refer the matter to the ECJ, under Article 177 of the Treaty, for the ruling.

6.5 Misuse of Article 177

6.5.1 NO GENUINE DISPUTE

FOGLIA v NOVELLO (No. 1) (Case 104/79) [1980] ECR 745, Court of Justice

A contract of sale provided that the buyer (Novello) would not be liable for any unlawfully levied taxes. The contract between the seller (Foglia) and the shipper provided that the seller was similarly not liable. France levied a tax on the goods, which the seller paid and which the buyer refused to reimburse on the ground that it was contrary to Community law. The parties alleged, before an Italian court, that the duty was illegal, and a reference to the Court of Justice was made.

It was held that a reference under Article 177 would not be accepted.

9.   In their written observations submitted to the Court of Justice the two parties to the main action have provided an essentially identical description of the tax discrimination which is a feature of the French legislation concerning the taxation of liqueur wines; the two parties consider that that legislation is incompatible with Community law. In the course of the oral procedure before the Court Foglia stated that he was participating in the procedure before the Court in view of the interest of his undertaking as such and as an undertaking belonging to a certain category of Italian traders in the outcome of the legal issues involved in the dispute.

10.   It thus appears that the parties to the main action are concerned to obtain a ruling that the French tax system is invalid for liqueur wines by the expedient of proceedings before an Italian court between two private individuals who are in agreement as to the result to be attained and who have inserted a clause in their contract in order to induce the Italian court to give a ruling on the point. The artificial nature of this expedient is underlined by the fact that Danzas did not exercise its rights under French law to institute proceedings over the consumption tax although it undoubtedly had an interest in doing so in view of the clause in the contract by which it was also bound and moreover of the fact that Foglia paid without protest that undertaking's bill which included a sum paid in respect of that tax.

11.   The duty of the Court of Justice under Article 177 of the EEC Treaty is to supply all courts in the Community with the information on the interpretation of Community law which is necessary to enable them to settle genuine disputes which are brought before them. A situation in which the Court was obliged by the expedient of arrangements like those described above to give rulings would jeopardize the whole system of legal remedies available to private individuals to enable them to protect themselves against provisions which are contrary to the Treaty.

12.   This means that the questions asked by the national court, having regard to the circumstances of this case, do not fall within the framework of the duties of the Court of Justice under Article 177 of the Treaty.

13.   The Court of Justice accordingly has no jurisdiction to give a ruling on the questions asked by the national court.

6.5.2   HYPOTHETICAL QUESTIONS

FOGLIA v *NOVELLO* (No. 2) (Case 244/80) [1981] ECR 3045, Court of Justice

(For the facts, see the previous case *Foglia* v *Novello* (No. 1).) The Italian court repeated its request for a preliminary ruling.

It was held that a reference under Article 177 would not be accepted.

8.   The order making the reference shows that the judgment of the Court of Justice was challenged by the defendant in the main action who considered that in making such an appraisal the Court had intervened in the discretion reserved to the Italian court. She considered that such an application of Article 177 by the Court gave rise at national level to a question of a constitutional nature. In the alternative she submitted a question concerning the interpretation of Article 177 of the EEC Treaty and further requested that the French Republic should be joined in the proceedings.

9.   When these claims were submitted to him the Pretore considered that it was necessary to refer the matter again to the Court of Justice and to submit to it certain questions on the interpretation of Article 177 of the Treaty in order to obtain a clearer and more precise appraisal of the scope and meaning of the judgment of 11 March 1980.

. . .

12.   In his first question the Pretore requested clarification of the limits of the power of appraisal reserved by the Treaty to the national court on the one hand and the Court of Justice on the other with regard to the wording of references for a preliminary ruling and of the appraisal of the circumstances of fact and of law in the main action, in particular where the national court is requested to give a declaratory judgment.

. . .

14.   With regard to the first question it should be recalled, as the Court has had occasion to emphasize in very varied contexts, that Article 177 is based on co-operation which entails a division of duties between the national courts and the Court of Justice in

the interest of the proper application and uniform interpretation of Community law throughout all the Member States.

15.   With this in view it is for the national court – by reason of the fact that it is seized of the substance of the dispute and that it must bear the reponsibility for the decision to be taken – to assess, having regard to the facts of the case, the need to obtain a preliminary ruling to enable it to give judgment.

16.   In exercising that power of appraisal the national court, in collaboration with the Court of Justice, fulfils a duty entrusted to them both of ensuring that in the interpretation and application of the Treaty the law is observed. Accordingly the problems which may be entailed in the exercise of its power of appraisal by the national court and the relations which it maintains within the framework of Article 177 with the Court of Justice are governed exclusively by the provisions of Community law.

17.   In order that the Court of Justice may perform its task in accordance with the Treaty it is essential for national courts to explain, when the reasons do not emerge beyond any doubt from the file, why they consider that a reply to their questions is necessary to enable them to give judgment.

18.   It must in fact be emphasized that the duty assigned to the Court by Article 177 is not that of delivering advisory opinions on general or hypothetical questions but of assisting in the administration of justice in the Member States. It accordingly does not have jurisdiction to reply to questions of interpretation which are submitted to it within the framework of procedural devices arranged by the parties in order to induce the Court to give its views on certain problems of Community law which do not correspond to an objective requirement inherent in the resolution of a dispute. A declaration by the Court that it has no jurisdiction in such circumstances does not in any way trespass upon the prerogatives of the national court but makes it possible to prevent the application of the procedure under Article 177 for purposes other than those appropriate for it.

19.   Furthermore, it should be pointed out that, whilst the Court of Justice must be able to place as much reliance as possible upon the assessment by the national court of the extent to which the questions submitted are essential, it must be in a position to make any assessment inherent in the performance of its own duties in particular in order to check, as all courts must, whether it has jurisdiction. Thus the Court, taking into account the repercussions of its decisions in this matter, must have regard, in exercising the jurisdiction conferred upon it by Article 177, not only to the interests of the parties to the proceedings but also to those of the Community and of the Member States. Accordingly it cannot, without disregarding the duties assigned to it, remain indifferent to the assessments made by the courts of the Member States in the exceptional cases in which such assessments may affect the proper working of the procedure laid down by Article 177.

20.   Whilst the spirit of co-operation which must govern the performance of the duties assigned by Article 177 to the national courts on the one hand and the Court of Justice on the other requires the latter to have regard to the national court's proper responsibilities, it implies at the same time that the national court, in the use which it makes of the facilities provided by Article 177, should have regard to the proper function of the Court of Justice in this field.

21.   The reply to the first question must accordingly be that whilst, according to the intended role of Article 177, an assessment of the need to obtain an answer to the questions of interpretation raised, regard being had to the circumstances of fact and of law involved in the main action, is a matter for the national court it is nevertheless for the Court of Justice, in order to confirm its own jurisdiction, to examine, where necessary, the conditions in which the case has been referred to it by the national court.

. . .

25.   In the fourth question the Pretore has asked whether the protection provided for individuals by the procedure under Article 177 is different, or indeed diminished, when such a question is raised in proceedings between individuals as opposed to proceedings between an individual and the administration.

26.   In answer to the question thus raised it must be emphasized that all individuals whose rights are infringed by measures adopted by a Member State which are contrary to Community law must have the opportunity to seek the protection of a court possessed of jurisdiction and that such a court, for its part, must be free to obtain information as to the scope of the relevant provisions of Community law by means of a procedure under Article

177. In principle the degree of protection afforded by the courts therefore must not differ according to whether such a question is raised in proceedings between individuals or in an action to which the State whose legislation is challenged is a party in one form or another.

27.   Nevertheless, as the Court has stated in its reply set our above to the first question it is for the Court of Justice to appraise the conditions in which a case is referred to it by a national court in order to confirm that it has jurisdiction. In that connection the question whether the proceedings are between individuals or are directed against the State whose legislation is called in question is not in all circumstances irrelevant.

28.   On the one hand it must be pointed out that the court before which, in the course of proceedings between individuals, an issue concerning the compatibility with Community law of legislation of another Member State is brought is not necessarily in a position to provide for such individuals effective protection in relation to such legislation.

29.   On the other hand, regard being had to the independence generally ensured for the parties by the legal systems of the Member States in the field of contract, the possibility arises that the conduct of the parties may be such as to make it impossible for the State concerned to arrange for an appropriate defence of its interests by causing the question of the invalidity of its legislation to be decided by a court of another Member State. Accordingly, in such procedural situations it is impossible to exclude the risk that the procedure under Article 177 may be diverted by the parties from the purposes for which it was laid down by the Treaty.

30.   The foregoing considerations as a whole show that the Court of Justice for its part must display special vigilance when, in the course of proceedings between individuals, a question is referred to it with a view to permitting the national court to decide whether the legislation of another Member State is in accordance with Community law.

31.   The reply to the fourth question must accordingly be that in the case of preliminary questions intended to permit the national court to determine whether provisions laid down by law or regulation in another Member State are in accordance with Community law the degree of legal protection may not differ according to whether such questions are raised in proceedings between individuals or in an action to which the State whose legislation is called in question is a party, but that in the first case the Court of Justice must take special care to ensure that the procedure under Article 177 is not employed for purposes which were not intended by the Treaty.

MEILICKE v *ADV/ORGA* (Case C-83/91) [1992] ECR I-4871, Court of Justice

21.   In view of the circumstances in which the Landgericht submitted its questions, it is necessary to rehearse and clarify a number of principles concerning the jurisdiction of the Court under Article 177 of the Treaty.

22.   It has consistently been held (see, in the first place, Case 16/65 *Schwarze* v *Einfuhr-und Vorratsstelle für Getreide und Futtermittel* [1965] ECR 877 and, most recently, Case C-147/91 *Criminal proceedings against Ferrer Laderer* [1992] ECR I-4097, paragraph 6) that the procedure provided for by Article 177 is an instrument for cooperation between the Court of Justice and the national courts.

23.   It is also settled law (see, in the first place, Case 83/78 *Pigs Marketing Board* v *Redmond* [1978] ECR 2347, paragraph 25, and, most recently, Case C-186/90 *Durighello* v *INPS* [1991] ECR I-5773, paragraph 8), that, in the context of such cooperation, the national court, which alone has direct knowledge of the facts of the case, is in the best position to assess, having regard to the particular features of the case, whether a preliminary ruling is necessary to enable it to give judgment.

24.   Consequently, since the questions submitted by the national court concern the interpretation of a provision of Community law, the Court is, in principle, bound to give a ruling (see Case C-231/89 *Gmurzynska-Bischer* v *Oberfinanzdirektion Köln* [1990] ECR I-4003, paragraph 20).

25.   Nevertheless, in Case 244/80 *Foglia* v *Novello* [1981] ECR 3045, paragraph 21, the Court considered that, in order to determine whether it has jurisdiction, it is a matter for the Court of Justice to examine the conditions in which the case has been referred to it by the national court. The spirit of cooperation which must prevail in the preliminary-ruling procedure requires the national court to have regard to the function entrusted to the Court of Justice, which is to assist in the administration of justice in the Member States and not to deliver advisory opinions on general or hypothetical questions (*Foglia*

v *Novello*, cited above, paragraphs 18 and 20, and Case 149/82 *Robards·*v *Insurance Officer* [1983] ECR 171, paragraph 19).

26.   The Court has already made it clear that the need to provide an interpretation of Community law which will be of use to the national court makes it essential to define the legal context in which the interpretation requested should be placed and that, in that respect, it may be convenient, in certain circumstances, for the facts of the case to be established and for questions of purely national law to be settled at the time the reference is made to the Court, so as to enable the latter to take cognizance of all the features of fact and of law which may be relevant to the interpretation of Community law which it is called upon to give (Joined Cases 36 and 71/80 *Irish Creamery Milk, Suppliers Association* v *Ireland* [1981] ECR 735, paragraph 6). Without such information, the Court may find it impossible to give a useful interpretation (see Case 52/76 *Benedetti* v *Munari* [1977] ECR 163, paragraphs 20, 21 and 22, and Joined Cases 205 to 215/82 *Deutsche Milchkontor* v *Germany* [1983] ECR 2633, paragraph 36).

27.   In the light of those considerations, it must first be observed that the specific context of the dispute which gave rise to the reference for a preliminary ruling is defined by paragraphs 131 and 132 of the Aktiengesetz. Those articles concern the right of shareholders to receive information from the management.

28.   The questions submitted do not relate directly to that right but essentially raise the problem of the compatibility with the Second Directive of the doctrine of disguised contributions in kind, as embodied in particular in the judgment of the Bundesgerichtshof of 15 January 1990, cited above. The national court considers that an answer to those questions is needed in order to enable it to adjudicate on the request for information made by Mr Meilicke. It states that the request would have to be rejected if it was found that the doctrine of disguised contributions in kind, as set out in the German case-law, was incompatible with the Second Directive.

29.   However, It is apparent from the documents before the Court that it has not been established that the conditions for the application of that doctrine have been satisfied in the main proceedings. Both in the proceedings before the national court and in its written observations to the Court of Justice, ADV/ORGA has rejected the view that the German case-law applies to the transactions entered into between it and Commerzbank. The national court's own reference to the issue is inconclusive, in that it states that Commerzbank's contribution may be contrary to the case-law in question.

30.   It follows that the problem of the compatibility of the doctrine of contributions in kind with the Second Directive is a hypothetical one.

31.   Moreover, the hypothetical nature of the problem on which the Court is requested to give a ruling is confirmed by the fact that the documents forwarded by the national court do not identify the matters of fact and of law which might make it possible to define the context in which ADV/ORGA's increase of capital took place and to establish the links between the contribution made by Commerzbank and the doctrine of disguised contributions in kind as set out in the German caselaw. The preliminary questions are specifically concerned with the compatibility of that doctrine with the Second Directive and therefore raise numerous problems, the answers to which largely depend on the circumstances in which the capital was increased.

32.   The Court is thus being asked to give a ruling on a hypothetical problem, without having before it the matters of fact or law necessary to give a useful answer to the questions submitted to it.

33.   Accordingly, the Court would be exceeding the limits of the function entrusted to it if it decided to answer the questions submitted to it.

34.   It follows that it is not appropriate to answer the questions submitted by the Landgericht Hannover.

DIAS LOURENÇO (MANUAL JOSÉ) v DIRECTOR DA ALFÂNDEGA DO PORTO
(Case C-343/90) [1992] ECR I-4675, Court of Justice

The relevance of the national court's questions

. . .

14.   The Court has consistently held (see, in the first place, Case 16/65 *Schwarze* v *Einfuhr-und Vorratsstelle Getreide* [1965] ECR 877 and, most recently, Case C-147/91

Criminal proceedings against Ferrer Laderer [1992] ECR I-4097, paragraph 6) that the procedure provided for in Article 177 of the Treaty is an instrument for cooperation between the Court of Justice and the national courts.

15.   It is also settled law (see, in the first place, Case 83/78 *Pigs Marketing Board* v *Redmond* [1978] ECR 2347, paragraph 25, and, most recently, Case C-186/90 *Durighello* v *INPS* [1991] ECR I-5773, paragraph 8), that in the context of that cooperation, the national court, which alone has direct knowledge of the facts of the case, is in the best position to assess, having regard to the particular features of the case, whether a preliminary ruling is necessary to enable it to give judgment.

16.   Consequently,, since the questions submitted by the national court concern the interpretation of a provision of Community law, the Court is, in principle, bound to give a ruling (see Case C-231/89 *Gmurzynska-Bischer* v *Oberfinanzdirektion Köln* [1990] ECR I-4003, paragraph 20).

17.   Nevertheless, in Case 244/80 *Foglia* v *Novello* [1981] ECR 3045, paragraph 21, the Court considered that, in order to determine whether it has jurisdiction, it is a matter for the Court of Justice to examine the conditions in which the case has been referred to it by the national court. The spirit of cooperation which must prevail in the preliminary ruling procedure requires the national court to have regard to the function entrusted to the Court of Justice, which is to assist in the administration of justice in the Member States and not to deliver advisory opinions on general or hypothetical questions (*Foglia* v *Novello*, cited above, paragraphs 18 and 20, and Case 149/82 *Robards* v *Insurance Officer* [1983] ECR 171, paragraph 19).

18.   In view of that task, the Court considers that it cannot give a preliminary ruling on a question raised in a national court where, *inter alia*, the interpretation requested relates to measures not yet adopted by the Community institutions (see Case 93/78 *Mattheus* v *Doego* [1978] ECR 2203, paragraph 8), the procedure before the court making the reference for a preliminary ruling has already been terminated (see Case 338/85 *Pardini* v *Ministero del commercio con l'estero* [1988] ECR 2041, paragraph 11) or the interpretation of Community law or the examination of the validity of a rule of Community law sought by the national court bears no relation to the actual nature of the case or to the subject-matter of the main action (Case 126/80 *Salonia* v *Poidomani and Giglio* [1981] ECR 1563, paragraph 6, and, most recently, *Durighello*, cited above, paragraph 9).

19.   It should also be borne in mind that, in order to enable the Court to provide a useful interpretation of Community law, it is appropriate that, before making the reference to the Court, the national court should establish the facts of the case and settle the questions of purely national law (see Joined Cases 36 and 71/80 *Irish Creamery Milk Suppliers Association* v *Ireland* [1981] ECR 735, paragraph 6). By the same token, it is essential for the national court to explain the reasons why it considers that a reply to its questions is necessary to enable it to give judgment (see, in the first place, *Foglia* v *Novello*, cited above, paragraph 17, and, most recently, Joined Cases 98, 162 and 258/85 *Bertini* v *Regione Lazio* [1986] ECR 1885, paragraph 6).

20.   With this information in its possession, the Court is in a position to ascertain whether the interpretation of Community law which is sought is related to the actual nature and subject-matter of the main proceedings. If it should appear that the question raised is manifestly irrelevant for the purposes of deciding the case, the Court must declare that there is no need to proceed to judgment.

21.   It is in the light of those guidelines that the objections alleging the absence of a connection between the questions referred to the Court for a preliminary ruling in the instant case and the actual dispute on which the national court is called upon to give judgment should be considered.

22.   Three matters should be taken into consideration in this regard. In the first place, it appears from the documents provided by the national court itself and from a document annexed to the observations of the public prosecutor that the vehicle whose conversion gave rise to the proceedings was new, having been manufactured and purchased in 1989, and had a cubic capacity of 1 360 cc. Secondly, as regards national law, the Portuguese Government informed the Court at the hearing that, since the separation panel in question had been replaced shortly after it was found to have been removed, motor-vehicle tax is not due and all the national court has to do is to determine the amount of

any fine payable, the legal basis for which is to be found in other legal provisions and not in the Decree-Law. Thirdly, the national court expresses its doubts about the compatibility with Community law of certain provisions of the Decree-Law, but has omitted to inform the Court how those provisions are to be applied in the context of the proceedings before it.

23. In the light of those considerations, it is necessary to start by considering the national court's first, third, fourth, fifth, sixth and seventh questions.

The question concerning the different tax system for imported second-hand vehicles and second-hand vehicles registered in Portugal

24. In its first question, the national court asks whether the first paragraph of Article 95 prohibits a Member State from imposing a motor-vehicle tax on second-hand vehicles imported from other Member States when it is not charged on second-hand vehicles which were new when they were imported or were originally assembled or manufactured in Portugal.

25. It is sufficient to recall in that connection that the motor vehicle which gave rise to the main proceedings was new when it was imported and purchased.

. . .

The question concerning the different period for the payment of the motor-vehicle tax depending on whether the vehicle was imported or of domestic manufacture

29. In its fourth question, the national court asks whether the second paragraph of Article 95 of the Treaty prohibits a Member State from laying down different periods for the payment of a motor-vehicle tax and different methods for collecting that tax depending on whether the vehicle was imported or manufactured in that Member State.

30. That question relates to Article 4 of the Decree-Law, which provides, in the case of vehicles intended for domestic sale which are assembled in Portugal or imported already assembled, that the tax is to be paid in accordance with the general rules on customs debt and deferred payment of import duties. Article 4 further provides that, in the case of motor vehicles manufactured in the country using national components or components treated as such or of vehicles which have been converted within the meaning of Article 1(2), an application for assessment and payment of the tax is to be made to the relevant customs directorate on the basis of the motor-vehicle tax form.

31. The national court infers from this that in the case of imported vehicles, motor-vehicle tax has, in principle, to be paid within ten days of the notification of the amount due pursuant to Article 8 of Council Regulation (EEC) No. 1854/89 of 14 June 1984 on the entry in the accounts and terms of payment of the amounts of the import duties or export duties resulting from a customs debt (OJ 1989 L 186, p. 1). It states that, in contrast, there is no period for payment for vehicles manufactured in Portugal.

32. As the United Kingdom rightly points out, this question is not germane to the determination of the dispute in the main proceedings: the vehicle in question was imported free of motor-vehicle tax in accordance with the national legislation. As a result, the importer did not suffer discrimination at the time when the vehicle was imported. . . .

The question concerning the restriction of the period during which foreign-registered vehicles intended to be definitively imported may circulate

33. In its fifth question, the national court asks whether the second paragraph of Article 95 prohibits a Member State from restricting the circulation of imported vehicles to 48 hours from their entry into Portugal where vehicles assembled or manufactured in Portugal are not subject to any restriction.

34. According to the order for reference, that question relates to Article 5(1) of the Decree-Law. Under that provision foreign-registered motor vehicles intended for definitive importation whose owners are resident or have their registered office in the national territory may circulate only for a period of 48 hours following their entry into Portugal.

35. However, as the national court's order itself states, the vehicle at issue in this case was registered for the first time in Portugal. It was hence never subject to the restrictions on circulation laid down by Article 5(1) of the Decree-Law.

The question concerning the differing customs formalities for imported vehicles and vehicles assembled in Portugal

36.   In its sixth question, the national court asks whether Article 95 debars a Member State from imposing time-limits for carrying out certain customs formalities relating to the importation of vehicles whereas vehicles of national manufacture are exempt therefrom.

37.   That question relates to Article 5(2) of the Decree-Law, which provides that the documents relating to the definitive importation of foreign-registered vehicles must be submitted to the customs within 60 days of their entry into Portugal.

38.   It should be observed that any discrimination entailed by Article 5(2) of the Decree-Law affects only vehicles which have already been registered abroad. However, as has already been pointed out, the proceedings pending before the national court relate to a vehicle which was registered for the first time in Portugal.

The question concerning the exemption for 'vintage' motor vehicles

39.   In its seventh question, the national court asks whether Article 95 prohibits a Member State from exempting the importation of 'vintage' motor vehicles from a tax when other vehicles do not qualify for such exemption.

40.   That question relates to Article 9 of the Decree-Law, which authorizes the importation free of motor-vehicle tax of motor vehicles manufactured no later than 1950, provided that they are of interest from the point of view of the national cultural heritage.

41.   Suffice it to say that the motor vehicle in question in this case was manufactured in 1989.

42.   In view of the foregoing considerations, there is no need to reply to the first, third, fourth, fifth, sixth and seventh questions since they are manifestly unrelated to the actual nature of the main proceedings.

EAU DE COLOGNE & PARFÜMERIE-FABRIK v *PROVIDE SRL* (Case C–150/88) [1989] ECR 3891, Court of Justice

Provide, an Italian company, ordered cosmetics from Eau de Cologne, a German company. The packing complied with Community law, but did not comply with Italian law and so Provide refused to accept or pay for the goods since they could not be marketed in Italy. Eau de Cologne sued Provide in the German courts. The German court made a reference to the Court of Justice on whether the Italian law was compatible with Community law. The Italian government alleged that the reference was inadmissible.

It was held that a reference would be accepted.

Jurisdiction of the Court

11.   The Italian Government notes that the preliminary questions arose in the context of a dispute between individuals, the genuineness of which is open to doubt, and that they are intended to permit a court in one Member State to determine whether the rules of another Member State are compatible with Community law. Referring to the Court's judgment of 16 December 1981 in Case 244/80 *Foglia* v *Novello* [1981] ECR 3045, the Italian Government therefore expresses its doubts as to the propriety of the request for a preliminary ruling. It further maintains that the Court has no jurisdiction under Article 177 to rule on the compatibility of national legislation with Community law.

12.   Those objections must be dismissed. First, the documents before the Court do not allow any doubt as to the genuineness of the dispute in the main proceedings or, therefore, the propriety of the request for a preliminary ruling. Secondly, the Court has consistently held (see, in particular, its judgment of 9 October 1984 in Joined Cases 91 and 127/83 *Heineken Brouwerijen BV* v *Inspecteurs der Vennootschapsbelasting, Amsterdam and Utrecht* [1984] ECR 3435) that, when ruling on questions intended to permit the national court to determine whether national provisions are in accordance with Community law, the Court may provide the criteria for the interpretation of Community law which will enable the national court to solve the legal problem with which it is faced. The same is true when it is to be determined whether the provisions of a Member State other than that of the court requesting the ruling are compatible with Community law.

VINAL v *ORBAT* (Case 46/80) [1981] ECR 77, Court of Justice

An importer, Vinal, contracted to supply goods to Orbat. The Italian authorities imposed an import duty on the goods which Vinal paid and which Orbat refused to reimburse on the ground that it was illegal. Both parties were based in Italy. A preliminary reference was opposed by the Italian government on the grounds that there was no real dispute and that the parties simply wished to impeach the duty so as to avoid paying it. The Italian court made a reference to the Court of Justice.

It was held that the Court of Justice had jurisdiction, but on the facts the duty was not illegal.

The jurisdiction of the Court

5. The Italian Government has put in issue the admissibility of the request for a preliminary ruling submitted by the Pretura, Casteggio. It raises the question whether the action brought before the national court is not really a fictitious dispute and whether the procedure under Article 177 has not been employed in this case to impeach the Italian State in the absence of any actual dispute giving rise to questions of Community law as between the parties. In these circumstances the Italian Government asks whether the situation should not be compared to that which formed the subject-matter of the judgment of the Court of 11 March 1980 in Case 104/79 *Foglia* v *Novello* [1980] ECR 745 in which the Court held that it had no jurisdiction to give a ruling on the questions put by the national court.

6. In view of that contention, which the Italian Government set out in its written observations, the Court requested the parties to supply it with additional information.

7. Having studied the replies given to those questions the Court considers that in this case it is possible to set aside the doubts expressed by the Italian Government and to broach the substance of the case.

G. Bebr, 'The Possible Implications of *Foglia* v *Novello II* (1982) 19 CML Rev 421

2. Powers of the Court in a reference procedure

This is the most controversial point raised by the notion of a fictitous litigation because it affects the relation of the referring national court to the Court of Justice. The Court must obviously have the power to ascertain whether it has jurisdiction to render a preliminary ruling under Article 177 of the EEC Treaty. Thus it has to verify whether the reference was made by a national court within the meaning of Article 177 and whether it concerns the interpretation of Community law or the review of validity of a Community act. The question becomes, however, delicate if the Court verifies the existence of a real, genuine or merely fictitious litigation, a verification which obviously implies a wide review of the findings of the referring court. Such a review does not merely concern the relevancy of questions raised for the outcome of the litigation. It reaches much further as it concerns the very nature and existence of a litigation and its real purpose. *Foglia* v *Novello II* modifies the unlimited, exclusive power of the referring court to appraise the relevancy of questions raised for settling the dispute.

At the beginning of its caselaw the Court resolutely rejected any such review. Thus in *Van Gend & Loos*, it stated that 'in order to confer jurisdiction on the Court . . . it is necessary only that the question raised should clearly be concerned with the interpretation of the Treaty. The considerations which may have led a national court or tribunal to its choice of questions as well as the relevance which it attributes to such questions in the context of a case before it are *excluded* from review by the Court of Justice'. In *Salgoil* the Court was less categoric and inclined to exercise such a review within a strict limit that is only then when the provisions to be interpreted were obviously raised by error. The scope of this review appears very modest and limited indeed as compared with the one which seems necessary for judging a litigation to be fictitious. Moreover, the purpose reaches much further. In fact the Court appears to have introduced this notion having two objectives in mind. First, to avoid giving an academic, advisory opinion; secondly, to prevent the reference procedure from being employed by an arranged litigation between parties against a Member State. It may well be that the latter is the primary reason for developing the notion of a fictitious litigation.

There are two considerations of the Court which seem to suggest that it may use judicial restraint when exercising such a review. First, the Court stated in *Foglia* v *Novello II* that it would engage in such a review in exceptional circumstances only. The opinion of Advocate-General Reischl, interpreting the conditions for such a review rather strictly, points in the same direction. Thus in *Vinal* v *Orbat* observing that 'since there is no unequivocal and clear evidence that, as in the *Foglia* case, a friendly suit has been pursued in order to charge a Member State with a failure to fulfil its obligations under the Treaty – and only in such cases should jurisdiction be exceptionally declined –' he proposed that the Court should recognize its jurisdiction and admit the reference. This view seems indirectly confirmed by a ruling of the third chamber of the Court, rendered shortly before the first *Foglia* case:

> . . . it is not for this Court to pronounce on the expediency of the request for a preliminary ruling . . . it is for the national court which is alone in having a direct knowledge of the facts of the case and of the arguments put forward by the parties, and which will have to give judgment in the case, to appreciate, with full knowledge of the matter before it, the relevance of the question of law raised by the dispute before it and the necessity for a preliminary ruling so as to enable it to give judgment.

And the Court, deciding in a plenary session, after *Foglia* v *Novello II*, still maintained:

> . . . a request from a national court may be rejected only if it is quite obvious that the interpretation of Community law sought by that court bears no relation to the actual nature of the case or to the subject-matter of the main action.

Secondly, the Court requires that a reference by a national court be supported by reason. This is a justified requirement, unfortunately missing in Article 177. It is sound for two reasons. Such a reasoning supporting a reference could, in the first place, spare the Court from exercising a rather delicate review which could irritate the national court. Moreover, it may oblige the referring national courts to formulate their questions properly and with greater precision. After all, it could preclude the unfortunate and deplorable practice of some courts which, instead of drafting a reference themselves, simply adopted the suggestions as made by one of the parties to the main litigation.

6.6 Issues of Validity

FOTO-FROST v *HAUPTZOLLAMT LÜBECK-OST* (Case 314/85) [1987] ECR 4199, Court of Justice

A Community levy was payable on imports of binoculars into Germany by Frost. The levy was subject to a waiver in certain circumstances, but the Commission ruled that in this instance, the waiver could not apply. Frost challenged the Commission's Decision before a German court which made a reference to the Court of Justice.

It was held that no national court could declare a Community act invalid, although it could make a declaration of validity.

11. In its first question the Finanzgericht asks whether it itself is competent to declare invalid a Commission decision such as the decision of 6 May 1983. It casts doubt on the validity of that decision on the ground that all the requirements laid down by Article 5(2) of Regulation No. 1697/79 for taking no action for the post-clearance recovery of duty seem to be fulfilled in this case. However, it considers that in view of the division of jurisdiction between the Court of Justice and the national courts set out in Article 177 of the EEC Treaty only the Court of Justice is competent to declare invalid acts of the Community institutions.

12. Article 177 confers on the Court jurisdiction to give preliminary rulings on the interpretation of the Treaty and of acts of the Community institutions and on the validity of such acts. The second paragraph of that article provides that national courts may refer such questions to the Court and the third paragraph of that article puts them under an obligation to do so where there is no judicial remedy under national law against their decisions.

13. In enabling national courts, against those decisions where there is a judicial remedy under national law, to refer to the Court for a preliminary ruling questions on interpretation or validity, Article 177 did not settle the question whether those courts themselves may declare that acts of Community institutions are invalid.

14. Those courts may consider the validity of a Community act and, if they consider that the grounds put forward before them by the parties in support of invalidity are unfounded, they may reject them, concluding that the measure is completely valid. By taking that action they are not calling into question the existence of the Community measure.

15. On the other hand, those courts do not have the power to declare acts of the Community institutions invalid. As the Court emphasized in the judgment of 13 May 1981 in Case 66/80 *International Chemical Corporation* v *Amministrazione delle Finanze* [1981] ECR 1191, the main purpose of the powers accorded to the Court by Article 177 is to ensure that Community law is applied uniformly by national courts. That requirement of uniformity is particularly imperative when the validity of a Community act is in question. Divergences between courts in the Member States as to the validity of Community acts would be liable to place in jeopardy the very unity of the Community legal order and detract from the fundamental requirement of legal certainty.

16. The same conclusion is dictated by consideration of the necessary coherence of the system of judicial protection established by the Treaty. In that regard it must be observed that requests for preliminary rulings, like actions for annulment, constitute means for reviewing the legality of acts of the Community institutions. As the Court pointed out in its judgment of 23 April 1986 in Case 294/83 *Parti Ecologiste 'les Verts'* v *European Parliament* [1986] ECR 1339, 'in Articles 173 and 184, on the one hand, and in Article 177, on the other, the Treaty established a complete system of legal remedies and procedures designed to permit the Court of Justice to review the legality of measures adopted by the institutions'.

17. Since Article 173 gives the Court exclusive jurisdiction to declare void an act of a Community institution, the coherence of the system requires that where the validity of a Community act is challenged before a national court the power to declare the act invalid must also be reserved to the Court of Justice.

18. It must also be emphasized that the Court of Justice is in the best position to decide on the validity of Community acts. Under Article 20 of the Protocol on the Statute of the Court of Justice of the EEC, Community institutions whose acts are challenged are entitled to participate in the proceedings in order to defend the validity of the acts in question. Furthermore, under the second paragraph of Article 21 of that Protocol the Court may require the Member States and institutions which are not participating in the proceedings to supply all information which it considers necessary for the purposes of the case before it.

19. It should be added that the rule that national courts may not themselves declare Community acts invalid may have to be qualified in certain circumstances in the case of proceedings relating to an application for interim measures; however, that case is not referred to in the national court's question.

20. The answer to the first question must therefore be that the national courts have no jurisdiction themselves to declare that acts of Community institutions are invalid.

6.7 The Effect of a Ruling

DEFRENNE v *SABENA* (Case 43/75) [1976] 2 ECR 455, Court of Justice

For the facts and judgment in this case, see **5.1.1**

The temporal effect of this judgment

[69] The Governments of Ireland and the United Kingdom have drawn the Court's attention to the possible economic consequences of attributing direct effect to the provisions of Article 119, on the ground that such a decision might, in many branches of economic life, result in the introduction of claims dating back to the time at which such effect came into existence.

[70]   In view of the large number of people concerned such claims, which undertakings could not have foreseen, might seriously affect the financial situation of such undertakings and even drive some of them to bankruptcy.

[71]   Although the practical consequences of any judicial decision must be carefully taken into account, it would be impossible to go so far as to diminish the objectivity of the law and compromise its future application on the ground of the possible repercussions which might result, as regards the past, from such a judicial decision.

[72]   However, in the light of the conduct of several of the Member States and the views adopted by the Commission and repeatedly brought to the notice of the circles concerned, it is appropriate to take exceptionally into account the fact that, over a prolonged period, the parties concerned have been led to continue with practices which were contrary to Article 119, although not yet prohibited under their national law.

[73]   The fact that, in spite of the warnings given, the Commission did not initiate proceedings under Article 169 against the Member States concerned on grounds of failure to fulfil an obligation was likely to consolidate the incorrect impression as to the effects of Article 119.

[74]   In these circumstances, it is appropriate to hold that, as the general level at which pay would have been fixed cannot be known, important considerations of legal certainty affecting all the interests involved, both public and private, make it impossible in principle to reopen the question as regards the past.

[75]   Therefore, the direct effect of Article 119 cannot be relied on in order to support claims concerning pay periods prior to the date of this judgment, except as regards those workers who have already brought legal proceedings or made an equivalent claim.

6.8   Conclusion

A. Barav, 'Some Aspects of the Preliminary Rulings Procedure in EEC Law' (1977) 2 EL Rev 3

Introduction

As a means of collaboration between domestic courts and tribunals and the European Court, the preliminary rulings procedure reflects in two ways the distribution of power between the Community and the Member States. First, the application of Community law is left for domestic courts and tribunals, while the European Court may only exercise the powers expressly conferred upon it by the Treaty. The magnitude of the power attributed to national courts and tribunals could have adversely affected the necessary unity which is the very essence of the Community legal order. Secondly, the principle of division of power is at the very core of the economy of the preliminary rulings procedure where it appears under two distinct forms. On the one hand, the jurisdiction of the European Court is confined, respectively, within the limits of interpretation of Community law and assessment of its validity. In other terms, the Court may not take cognisance of a case in its entirety but may deal with one of its aspects only, namely that which is specifically concerned with Community law, and here too, not in its totality since it may not actually apply this law. On the other hand, Article 177 makes a distinction between courts and tribunals deciding in the last instance and those whose decisions may be appealed against. Only courts and tribunals of the first category are under the obligation to refer questions on interpretation and on validity to the European Court. Those belonging to the second group may do so if they consider that a preliminary ruling is necessary to enable them to give judgment. In other words, the dissociation of competence established under the Treaty automatically applies only in the first case. Conversely, in the second hypothesis, domestic courts and tribunals are entitled to exercise the plenitude of their judicial power, *i.e.* interpret Community law, apply it and decide on its validity, without seeking the assistance of the European Court. It is therefore easy to comprehend the extent to which the procedure of preliminary rulings is conditioned by a division of power which, paradoxically, it contributes to determine.

Another characteristic feature of this procedure is that it is merely a step in an action pending before national courts or tribunals. Here, beyond the normative relations existing between the legal orders of the Community and of the Member States, are established procedural links between the European Court and national courts and tribunals. Article 177 thus provides for an organic check-point between the judicial authorities of the Member States and of the Community. Significantly these relations are not established on a hierarchical basis which would have implied the subordination of national courts and tribunals to the European Court. Rather, they rest upon a mode of collaboration in the pursuit of common goals. But the absence of an organic hierarchy does not affect the incontestable supremacy of Community law. If national courts and tribunals are not subordinate to the European Court in the way which they are to their domestic supreme courts, they are nevertheless bound by the normative hierarchy existing between Community law and national law. Through this somewhat intermediary device is introduced a pyramidal element into the collaborative relations between the European Court and courts and tribunals of the Member States, the consequences of which are apparent particularly when the binding force of decisions rendered by the Court in the framework of Article 177 is considered.

Thus under different aspects the analysis of the procedure of preliminary rulings is a striking indicator of the intrinsic characteristics of the Community legal order, its structure and its objectives.

6.9 End of Chapter Assessment Question

Discuss, with examples from case law, the obligations of national courts under Article 177.

6.10 End of Chapter Assessment Outline Answer

A reference under Article 177 is obligatory from a court against whose decisions there is no judicial remedy but merely discretionary from other courts if the point is necessary to the resolution of the case.

The Court of Justice has laid down few guidelines for the exercise of the discretion by the national court, although it has ruled that a reference is not precluded by either a previous Court of Justice decision on the point (*Da Costa*) or by national rules of precedent (*Rheinmühlen*); that it may be appropriate to defer a reference until the factual and legal issues have been resolved (*Irish Creamery Milk Suppliers Association*); and that the point need not be conclusive, but merely relevant (*Dzodzi*).

By contrast, in the UK, the Court of Appeal laid down a comprehensive and extremely restrictive set of guidelines in *Bulmer* v *Bollinger*, which appear to be designed to discourage the making of references. A reference may be made only if the point is necessary to the resolution of the case, and the point will be necessary only if it is conclusive of the case, there have been no previous rulings, the measure is unclear and the facts of the case have been resolved. Even when a point complies with these conditions, so that a reference **may** be made, the court should take into account the difficulty and importance of the point, the danger of overloading the Court of Justice, the expense and delay involved and the wishes of the parties, when exercising its discretion.

In the case of *Commissioners of Customs and Excise* v *Samex*, Bingham J referred to these guidelines but also outlined the advantages of a reference. He pointed out that the Court of Justice was able to take an overview of the Community and its legal system, was able to compare the meanings of the measure in all the Community languages and was used to taking the necessary creative and purposive approach to interpretation which Community measures required.

As mentioned above, a reference under Article 177 is obligatory from a court against whose decisions there is no judicial remedy under national law. However, the Court of Justice, in *CILFIT*, ruled that this obligation was not absolute and that in some circumstances, a reference might be discretionary. This would be so if either the question is not relevant, or there has been a previous Court of Justice ruling, or the doctrine of *acte clair* applies, that is to say, the application of the measure is clear and free from doubt. In this case, the question is clearly relevant, and assuming that there has been no previous ruling, the requirement to refer turns on the application of the doctrine of *acte clair*. The Court of Justice gave further guidelines in *CILFIT* regarding *acte clair*. A court should consider whether the measure was clear in all its authentic language texts, whether legal concepts referred to had equivalent meanings in the law of the Community and of all Member States, and the current status of Community law.

English case law reflects an inconsistent approach to the use of the doctrine of *acte clair*. In *Henn & Darby*, *Factortame I* and *RSPB, the CILFIT* guidelines were effectively followed, while in *Magnavision* and *Freight Transport Association*, the courts simply asserted that the measure was clear and refused to refer. In *Henn and Darby* and *RSPB*, the House of Lords recognised that a measure was not truly *acte clair* if the Court of Appeal and the House of Lords, or different judges in the Court of Appeal had concluded that the measure was clear but had reached different conclusions as to its clear meaning. However, in *Freight Transport Association*, the House of Lords ignored similar judicial disagreement and refused to make a decision on the ground of *acte clair*. On the English authorities it is therefore uncertain whether the refusal by the House of Lords to refer in the present case is consistent with Article 177 or not.

CHAPTER SEVEN

CHALLENGING COMMUNITY ACTS

7.1 Article 173

THE TREATY OF ROME

Article 173.
The Court of Justice shall review the legality of acts adopted jointly by the European Parliament and the Council, of acts of the Council, of the Commission and of the ECB, other than recommendations and opinions, and of acts of the European Parliament intended to produce legal effects *vis-à-vis* third parties.

It shall for this purpose have jurisdiction in actions brought by a Member State, the Council or the Commission on grounds of lack of competence, infringement of an essential procedural requirement, infringement of this Treaty or of any rule of law relating to its application, or misuse of powers.

The Court shall have jurisdiction under the same conditions in actions brought by the European Parliament and by the ECB for the purpose of protecting their prerogatives.

Any natural or legal person may, under the same conditions, institute proceedings against a decision addressed to that person or against a decision which, although in the form of a regulation or a decision addressed to another person, is of direct and individual concern to the former.

The proceedings provided for in this Article shall be instituted within two months of the publication of the measure, or of its notification to the plaintiff, or, in the absence thereof, of the day on which it came to the knowledge of the latter, as the case may be.

7.1.1 ACTS WHICH MAY BE CHALLENGED

IBM CORPORATION v COMMISSION (Case 60/81) [1981] ECR 2639, Court of Justice

IBM challenged under Article 173 both a Commission decision to initiate proceedings against it under Community competition law, and a statement of objections to its anti-competitive behaviour which was provided with the notification of this decision.

It was held that neither of these acts could be challenged under Article 173.

8. According to Article 173 of the Treaty proceedings may be brought for a declaration that acts of the Council and the Commission other than recommendations or opinions are void. That remedy is available in order to ensure, as required by Article 164, that in the interpretation and application of the Treaty the law is observed, and it would be inconsistent with that objective to interpret restrictively the conditions under which the action is admissible by limiting its scope merely to the categories of measures referred to in Article 189.

9. In order to ascertain whether the measures in question are acts within the meaning of Article 173 it is necessary, therefore, to look to their substance. According to the consistent case law of the Court any measure the legal effects of which are binding on,

and capable of affecting the interests of, the applicant by bringing about a distinct change in his legal position is an act or decision which may be the subject of an action under Article 173 for a declaration that it is void. However, the form in which such acts or decisions are cast is, in principle, immaterial as regards the question whether they are open to challenge under that article.

. . .

20.   An application for a declaration that the initiation of a procedure and a statement of objections are void might make it necessary for the Court to arrive at a decision on questions on which the Commission has not yet had an opportunity to state its position and would as a result anticipate the arguments on the substance of the case, confusing different procedural stages both administrative and judicial. It would thus be incompatible with the system of the division of powers between the Commission and the Court and of the remedies laid down by the Treaty, as well as the requirements of the sound administration of justice and the proper course of the administrative procedure to be followed in the Commission.

21.   It follows from the foregoing that neither the initiation of a procedure nor a statement of objections may be considered, on the basis of their nature and the legal effects they produce, as being decisions within the meaning of Article 173 of the EEC Treaty which may be challenged in an action for a declaration that they are void. In the context of the administrative procedure as laid down by Regulations No. 17 and No. 99/63, they are procedural measures adopted preparatory to the decision which represents their culmination.

7.1.2   LOCUS STANDI

7.1.2.1   The intermediate category of applicants

PARLIAMENT v COUNCIL (CHERNOBYL) (Case C–70/88) [1990] ECR I–2041, Court of Justice

A Regulation concerning radioactivity in foodstuffs was adopted on the basis of a public health provision in the Euratom Treaty which specified that the consultation procedure should be used in adopting legislation. The Parliament argued that the measure should properly have been based on the internal market provisions of the Treaty of Rome, which at that time specified the use of the cooperation procedure. It brought an action under Article 146 of the Euratom Treaty and Article 173 of the Treaty, arguing that its prerogatives had been infringed, since under the consultation procedure it had less input than under the cooperation procedure.

It was held that the Parliament had locus standi to bring an action under Article 173 in order to protect its prerogatives. The proceedings would be continued with regard to the substance of the case.

13.   First of all, in the first paragraph of Article 173 or Article 146, the Parliament is not included among the institutions which, like the Member States, can bring an action for annulment against any measure of another institution.

14.   Furthermore, since the Parliament is not a legal person it cannot bring an action before the Court under the second paragraph of the articles in question, the scheme of which would, in any event, be inappropriate to an action for annulment brought by the Parliament.

15.   In the judgment in Case 302/87, after having stated the reasons why the Parliament did not have capacity to bring an action under Article 173 of the EEC Treaty, the Court pointed out that various legal remedies were available to ensure that the Parliament's prerogatives were defended. As was observed in that judgment, not only does the Parliament have the right to bring an action for failure to act, but the Treaties provide means for submitting for review by the Court acts of the Council or the Commission adopted in disregard of the Parliament's prerogatives.

16.   However, the circumstances and arguments adduced in the present case show that the various legal remedies provided for both in the Euratom Treaty and in the EEC Treaty, however effective and diverse they may be, may prove to be ineffective or uncertain.

17. First, an action for failure to act cannot be used to challenge the legal basis of a measure which has already been adopted.

18. Secondly, the submission of a reference for a preliminary ruling on the validity of such an act or the bringing of an action by Member States or individuals for the annulment of the act are mere contingencies, and the Parliament cannot be sure that they will materialize.

19. Finally, while the Commission is required to ensure that the Parliament's prerogatives are respected, that duty cannot go so far as to oblige it to adopt the Parliament's position and bring an action for annulment which the Commission itself considers unfounded.

20. It follows from the foregoing that the existence of those various legal remedies is not sufficient to guarantee, with certainty and in all circumstances, that a measure adopted by the Council or the Commission in disregard of the Parliament's prerogatives will be reviewed.

21. Those prerogatives are one of the elements of the institutional balance created by the Treaties. The Treaties set up a system for distributing powers among the different Community institutions, assigning to each institution its own role in the institutional structure of the Community and the accomplishment of the tasks entrusted to the Community.

22. Observance of the institutional balance means that each of the institutions must exercise its powers with due regard for the powers of the other institutions. It also requires that it should be possible to penalize any breach of that rule which may occur.

23. The Court, which under the Treaties has the task of ensuring that in the interpretation and application of the Treaties the law is observed, must therefore be able to maintain the institutional balance and, consequently, review the observance of the Parliament's prerogatives when called upon to do so by the Parliament, by means of a legal remedy which is suited to the purpose which the Parliament seeks to achieve.

24. In carrying out that task the Court cannot, of course, include the Parliament among the institutions which may bring an action under Article 173 of the EEC Treaty or Article 146 of the Euratom Treaty without being required to demonstrate an interest in bringing an action.

25. However, it is the Court's duty to ensure that the provisions of the Treaties concerning the institutional balance are fully applied and to see to it that the Parliament's prerogatives, like those of the other institutions, cannot be breached without it having available a legal remedy, among those laid down in the Treaties, which may be exercised in a certain and effective manner.

26. The absence in the Treaties of any provision giving the Parliament the right to bring an action for annulment may constitute a procedural gap, but it cannot prevail over the fundamental interest in the maintenance and observance of the institutional balance laid down in the Treaties establishing the European Communities.

27. Consequently, an action for annulment brought by the Parliament against an act of the Council or the Commission is admissible provided that the action seeks only to safeguard its prerogatives and that it is founded only on submissions alleging their infringement. Provided that condition is met, the Parliament's action for annulment is subject to the rules laid down in the Treaties for actions for annulment brought by the other institutions.

28. In accordance with the Treaties, the Parliament's prerogatives include participation in the drafting of legislative measures, in particular participation in the co-operation procedure laid down in the EEC Treaty.

29. In the present case, the Parliament claims that the contested regulation is based on Article 31 of the Euratom Treaty, which provides only that the Parliament is to be consulted, whereas it ought to have been based on Article 100a of the EEC Treaty, which requires implementation of the procedure for co-operation with the Parliament.

30. The Parliament infers from that that the Council's choice of legal basis for the contested regulation led to a breach of its prerogatives by denying it the possibility, which the co-operation procedure offers, of participating in the drafting of the measure more closely and actively than it could in the consultation procedure.

31. Since the Parliament claims that its prerogatives were breached as a result of the choice of legal basis for the contested measure, it follows from all the foregoing that the

present action is admissible. The Council's objection of inadmissibility must therefore be dismissed and the proceedings must be continued with regard to the substance of the case.

COMMISSION v COUNCIL (GENERALISED TARIFF PREFERENCES)
(Case 45/86) [1987] ECR 1493, Court of Justice

Certain Regulations were challenged under Article 173 for failure to identify their legislative bases.

It was held that the Regulations would be annulled.

5. Article 190 of the Treaty provides that: 'Regulations, directives and decisions of the Council and of the Commission shall state the reasons on which they are based'. According to the case law of the Court (in particular the judgment of 7 July 1981 in Case 158/80 *REWE-Handelsgesellschaft Nord GmbH v Hauptzollamt Kiel* [1981] ECR 1805), in order to satisfy that requirement to state reasons, Community measures must include a statement of the facts and law which led the institution in question to adopt them, so as to make possible review by the Court and so that the Member States and the nationals concerned may have knowledge of the conditions under which the Community institutions have applied the Treaty.

6. It is therefore necessary to consider whether the contested regulations satisfy those requirements.

7. In that connection the Council contends that, although the indication of the legal basis is not precise, the recitals in the preamble to the regulations, taken as a whole, provide sufficient alternative information as to the aims pursued by the Council, that is to say both commercial aims and aims of development-aid policy.

8. However, those indications are not sufficient to identify the legal basis by virtue of which the Council acted. Although the recitals in the preambles to the regulations do refer to improving access for developing countries to the markets of the preference-giving countries, they merely state that adaptations to the Community system of generalized preferences have proved to be necessary in the light of experience in the first 15 years. Moreover, according to information given the Court by the Council itself, the wording 'Having regard to the Treaty' was adopted as a result of differences of opinion about the choice of the appropriate legal basis. Consequently, the wording chosen was designed precisely to leave the legal basis of the regulations in question vague.

9. Admittedly, failure to refer to a precise provision of the Treaty need not necessarily constitute an infringement of essential procedural requirements when the legal basis for the measure may be determined from other parts of the measure. However, such explicit reference is indispensable where, in its absence, the parties concerned and the Court are left uncertain as to the precise legal basis.

COMMISSION v COUNCIL (TITANIUM DIOXIDE) (Case C–300/89)
[1991] ECR 2867, Court of Justice

The facts of the case (brought under Article 173) and the decision of the Court of Justice appear in the extract below.

4. Taking the view that Directive 89/428/EEC lacked a valid legal basis, in that it was based on Article 130s but should have been based on Article 100a, the Commission brought the present action for annulment.

5. By order of 21 February 1990, the Parliament was granted leave to intervene in support of the applicant.

6. Reference is made to the Report for the Hearing for a fuller account of the facts of the case, the course of the procedure and the pleas and arguments of the parties, which are mentioned or discussed hereinafter only in so far as is necessary for the reasoning of the Court.

7. The Commission, supported by the Parliament, claims that the directive, although contributing to environmental protection, has as its 'main purpose' or 'centre of gravity'

the improvement of conditions of competition in the titanium dioxide industry. It is therefore a measure concerning the establishment and functioning of the internal market, within the meaning of Article 100a, and should therefore have been based on the latter enabling provision.

8. The Commission states that the very text of Articles 100a and 130s shows that the requirements of environmental protection form an integral part of the harmonizing action to be taken on the basis of Article 100a. It follows, according to the Commission, that Article 100a, which relates to the establishment and functioning of the internal market, constitutes a *lex specialis* in relation to Article 130s, the latter article not being intrinsically directed towards the attainment of that objective.

9. The Council, for its part, contends that Article 130s is the correct legal basis for Directive 89/428/EEC. Whilst conceding that that directive is intended also to harmonize conditions of competition in the industrial sector concerned and thus to foster the establishment and functioning of the internal market, it considers that the 'centre of gravity' of the contested measure is the elimination of the pollution caused by waste from the titanium dioxide manufacturing process. That objective is one of those referred to in Article 130r, which are pursued by means of measures adopted under Article 130s.

10. It must first be observed that in the context of the organization of the powers of the Community the choice of the legal basis for a measure may not depend simply on an institution's conviction as to the objective pursued but must be based on objective factors which are amenable to judicial review (see the judgment in Case 45/86 *Commission v Council* [1987] ECR 1493, paragraph 11). Those factors include in particular the aim and content of the measure.

11. As regards the aim pursued, Article 1 of Directive 89/428/EEC indicates that it is intended, on the one hand, to harmonize the programmes for the reduction and ultimate elimination of pollution caused by waste from existing establishments in the titanium dioxide industry and, on the other, to improve the conditions of competition in that industry. It thus pursues the twofold aim of environmental protection and improvement of the conditions of competition.

12. As regards its content, Directive 89/428/EEC prohibits, or, according to strict standards, requires reduction of the discharge of waste from existing establishments in the titanium dioxide industry and lays down time-limits for the implementation of the various provisions. By thus imposing obligations concerning the treatment of waste from the titanium dioxide production process, the directive conduces, at the same time, to the reduction of pollution and to the establishment of greater uniformity of production conditions and therefore of conditions of competition, since the national rules on the treatment of waste which the directive seeks to harmonize have an impact on production costs in the titanium dioxide industry.

13. It follows that, according to its aim and content, as they appear from its actual wording, the directive is concerned, indissociably, with both the protection of the environment and the elimination of disparities in conditions of competition.

14. Article 130s of the Treaty provides that the Council is to decide what action is to be taken by the Community concerning the environment. Article 100a(1), for its part, is concerned with the adoption by the Council of measures for the approximation of the provisions laid down by law, regulation or administrative action in Member States which have as their object the establishment and functioning of the internal market. According to the second paragraph of Article 8a of the EEC Treaty, that market is to comprise 'an area without internal frontiers in which the free movement of goods, persons, services and capital is ensured'. By virtue of Articles 2 and 3 of the Treaty, a precondition for such a market is the existence of conditions of competition which are not distorted.

15. In order to give effect to the fundamental freedoms mentioned in Article 8a, harmonizing measures are necessary to deal with disparities between the laws of the Member States in areas where such disparities are liable to create or maintain distorted conditions of competition. For that reason, Article 100a empowers the Community to adopt measures for the approximation of the provisions laid down by law, regulation or administrative action in Member States and lays down the procedure to be followed for that purpose.

16. It follows that, in view of its aim and content, the directive at issue displays the features both of action relating to the environment with which Article 130s of the Treaty

is concerned and of a harmonizing measure which has as its object the establishment and functioning of the internal market, within the meaning of Article 100a of the Treaty.

17.   As the Court held in Case 165/87 *Commission* v *Council* [1988] ECR 5545, paragraph 11, where an institution's power is based on two provisions of the Treaty, it is bound to adopt the relevant measures on the basis of the two relevant provisions. However, that ruling is not applicable to the present case.

18.   One of the enabling provisions at issue, Article 100a, requires recourse to the co-operation procedure provided for in Article 149(2) of the Treaty, whereas the other, Article 130s, requires the Council to act unanimously after merely consulting the European Parliament. As a result, use of both provisions as a joint legal basis would divest the co-operation procedure of its very substance.

19.   Under the co-operation procedure, the Council acts by a qualified majority where it intends accepting the amendments to its common position proposed by the Parliament and included by the Commission in its re-examined proposal, whereas it must secure unanimity if it intends taking a decision after its common position has been rejected by the Parliament or if it intends modifying the Commission's re-examined proposal. That essential element of the co-operation procedure would be undermined if, as a result of simultaneous reference to Articles 100a and 130s, the Council were required, in any event, to act unanimously.

20.   The very purpose of the co-operation procedure, which is to increase the involvement of the European Parliament in the legislative process of the Community, would thus be jeopardized. As the Court stated in its judgments in Case 138/79 *Roquette Frères* v *Council* [1980] ECR 3333 and Case 139/79 *Maizena* v *Council* [1980] ECR 3393, paragraph 34, that participation reflects a fundamental democratic principle that the peoples should take part in the exercise of power through the intermediary of a representative assembly.

21.   It follows that in the present case recourse to the dual legal basis of Articles 100a and 130s is excluded and that it is necessary to determine which of those two provisions is the appropriate legal basis.

22.   It must be observed in the first place that, pursuant to the second sentence of Article 130r(2) of the Treaty, 'environmental protection requirements shall be a component of the Community's other policies'. That principle implies that a Community measure cannot be covered by Article 130s merely because it also pursues objectives of environmental protection.

23.   Secondly, as the Court held in its judgments in Cases 91/79 and 92/79 *Commission* v *Italy* [1980] ECR 1099 (paragraph 8), and 1115 (paragraph 8), provisions which are made necessary by considerations relating to the environment and health may be a burden upon the undertakings to which they apply and, if there is no harmonization of national provisions on the matter, competition may be appreciably distorted. It follows that action intended to approximate national rules concerning production conditions in a given industrial sector with the aim of eliminating distortions of competition in that sector is conducive to the attainment of the internal market and thus falls within the scope of Article 100a, a provision which is particularly appropriate to the attainment of the internal market.

24.   Finally, it must be observed that Article 100a(3) requires the Commission, in its proposals for measures for the approximation of the laws of the Member States which have as their object the establishment and functioning of the internal market, to take as a base a high level of protection in matters of environmental protection. That provision thus expressly indicates that the objectives of environmental protection referred to in Article 130r may be effectively pursued by means of harmonizing measures adopted on the basis of Article 100a.

25.   In view of all the foregoing considerations, the contested measure should have been based on Article 100a of the EEC Treaty and must therefore be annulled.

7.1.3   DIRECT CONCERN

UNICME AND OTHERS v *COUNCIL* (Case 123/77) [1978] ECR 845, Court of Justice

A Regulation stated that imports of Japanese motorcyles into Italy were subject to the issue of an import licence from the Italian authorities.

It was held that the importers of such motorcycles did not have *locus standi* to challenge the Regulation.

7.   It is unnecessary to consider whether the contested measure may be regarded as a regulation and it is sufficient to establish whether it is in fact of direct and individual concern to the applicants.

8.   Regulation No. 1692/77 establishes for a limited period a system covering the importation into Italy of motor-cycles specified therein and originating in Japan.

9.   That system consists in introducing a requirement to produce an import authorization issued by the Italian authorities, and for the year 1977 such authorizations were not to be issued for more than 18,000 items.

10.   The system would only affect the interests of the importers in the event of the necessary authorizations being refused them.

11.   Consequently Regulation No. 1692/77 would only be of concern to the applicants if, pursuant to that measure, they were refused an import authorization.

12.   In that case they will be able to raise the matter before the national court having jurisdiction, if necessary raising before that court their questions concerning the validity of the regulation, which the court will, if it thinks fit be able to deal with by means of the procedure under Article 177 of the Treaty.

13.   In the present case the condition laid down in Article 173, to the effect that the contested measure must be of direct and individual concern to the applicants, is not fulfilled.

14.   The applicants claim that, taken together, they represent all the importers affected by the import system introduced for motor-cycles originating in Japan.

15.   They state that even before Regulation No. 1692/77 was adopted it could have been established that they were the only persons concerned and that they were all concerned.

16.   The possibility of determining more or less precisely the number or even the identity of the persons to whom a measure applies by no means implies that it must be regarded as being of individual concern to them.

17.   In the present case the fact that all the applicants might possibly be refused an import authorization pursuant to Regulation No. 1692/77 does not provide a sufficient basis for regarding the regulation as being of individual concern to them in the same way as if a decision had been addressed to them.

18.   On the contrary the regulation will not produce effects in individual cases until it is implemented by the Italian authorities.

19.   Consequently, the second condition laid down by Article 173 likewise remains unfulfilled.

20.   Since the conditions laid down by Article 173 have not been fulfilled the application must accordingly be dismissed as inadmissible.

BOCK v COMMISSION (Case 62/70) [1971] ECR 897, Court of Justice

The German authorities notified Bock that they would refuse his application for a licence to import Chinese mushrooms as soon as they were authorised by the Commission so to do. A Decision was issued giving this authorisation. Bock challenged the Decision under Article 173.

It was held that Bock had locus standi to challenge the Decision. The Decision was annulled insofar as it applied to importers with licence applications pending at the time the Decision came into force.

6.   (2)   The defendant contends that in any event an authorization granted to the Federal Republic is not of direct concern to the applicant since the Federal Republic remained free to make use of it.

7.   The appropriate German authorities had nevertheless already informed the applicant that they would reject its application as soon as the Commission had granted them the requisite authorization. They had requested that authorization with particular reference to the applications already before them at that time.

8.   It follows therefore that the matter was of direct concern to the applicant.

PIRAIKI-PATRAIKI v COMMISSION (Case 11/82) [1985] ECR 207, Court of Justice

A Commission Decision authorised France to impose quotas on imports of yarn from Greece. The Greek importers sought to challenge this Decision under Article 173.

It was held that Greek importers with prior contracts had locus standi to challenge the Decision. The Decision would be annulled insofar as it applied to contracts entered into before the date of its notification and to be performed during the period of its application.

5.   It is common ground that in this case the contested decision is not addressed to the applicants. It is therefore necessary, without going into the legal nature of the decision, to consider whether the decision is nevertheless of direct and individual concern to the applicants.

6.   With regard to the question of direct concern, the Commission and the Government of the French Republic argue that the applicants are not directly affected by the decision at issue since that decision merely authorizes the French Republic to institute a quota system on imports of cotton yarn from Greece, and thus leaves the Member State which requested the authorization free to make use of it or not. The decision therefore does not itself establish a system limiting imports but, in order to have practical effect, requires implementing measures on the part of the French authorities.

7.   It is true that without implementing measures adopted at the national level the Commission decision could not have affected the applicants. In this case, however, that fact does not in itself prevent the decision from being of direct concern to the applicants if other factors justify the conclusion that they have a direct interest in bringing the action.

8.   In that respect it should be pointed out that, as the Commission itself admitted during the written procedure, even before being authorized to do so by the Commission the French Republic applied a very restrictive system of licences for imports of cotton yarn of Greek origin. It should moreover be observed that the request for protective measures not only came from the French authorities but sought to obtain the Commission's authorization for a system of import quotas more strict than that which was finally granted.

9.   In those circumstances the possibility that the French Republic might decide not to make use of the authorization granted to it by the Commission decision was entirely theoretical, since there could be no doubt as to the intention of the French authorities to apply the decision.

10.   It must therefore be accepted that the decision at issue was of direct concern to the applicants.

7.1.4   INDIVIDUAL CONCERN

PLAUMANN & CO. v COMMISSION (Case 25/62) [1963] ECR 95, Court of Justice

The Commission issued a Decision refusing permission to the German government to reduce the duty on imports of clementines. Plaumann, an importer, challenged the Decision under Article 173.

It was held that Plaumann had no *locus standi* to challenge the Decision.

I — On the application for annulment
Admissibility
Under the second paragraph of Article 173 of the Treaty private individuals may institute proceedings for annulment against decisions which, although addressed to another person, are of direct and individual concern to them, but in the present case the defendant denies that the contested decision is of direct and individual concern to the applicant.

It is appropriate in the first place to examine whether the second requirement of admissibility is fulfilled because, if the applicant is not individually concerned by the decision, it becomes unneccessary to enquire whether he is directly concerned.

Persons other than those to whom a decision is addressed may only claim to be individually concerned if that decision affects them by reason of certain attributes which are peculiar to them or by reason of circumstances in which they are differentiated from all other persons and by virtue of these factors distinguishes them individually just as in the case of the person addressed. In the present case the applicant is affected by the disputed Decision as an importer of clementines, that is to say, by reason of a commercial activity which may at any time be practised by any person and is not therefore such as to distinguish the applicant in relation to the contested Decision as in the case of the addressee.

For these reasons the present action for annulment must be declared inadmissible.

7.1.4.1 The 'closed class' test

SPIJKER KWASTEN BV v *COMMISSION* (Case 231/82) [1983] ECR 259, Court of Justice

Spijker Kwasten, a Dutch importer of Chinese brushes, applied for an import licence which the Dutch authorities stated that they would refuse if they were authorised to do so. A Decision authorised them to ban such imports for a period of six months. Spijker Kwasten sought the annulment of the Decision under Article 173.

It was held that Spijker Kwasten had no locus standi to challenge the Decision.

5. The Commission objects that the contested decision is addressed to the Benelux States alone and that it is neither of direct nor of individual concern to the applicant within the meaning of the second paragraph of Article 173 of the Treaty.

6. On the other hand the applicant contends in support of the admissibility of the action that the said decision is of direct and individual concern to it with regard to its legal position since it is the only trader-importer established in the Benelux States which regularly imports into the Netherlands brushes originating in the People's Republic of China and since, moreover, the contested decision was adopted on account of the importation with which the present case is concerned.

7. Under the second paragraph of Article 173 of the Treaty the admissibility of an action for a declaration that a decision is void brought by a natural or legal person to whom the decision was not addressed is subject to the requirements that the decision must be of direct and individual concern to the applicant. In this case since Spijker Kwasten BV is not one of the persons to whom the contested decision was addressed it is necessary to consider whether the decision is of direct or individual concern to it.

8. The Court has already stated in its judgment of 15 July 1963 in Case 25/62 *Plaumann* [1963] ECR 95 that persons other than those to whom a decision is addressed may claim to be individually concerned by that decision only if it affects them by reason of certain attributes which are peculiar to them or by reason of circumstances in which they are differentiated from all other persons and if by virtue of those factors it distinguishes them individually just as in the case of the person addressed.

9. That is not the case in the present proceedings. The contested decision concerns the applicant merely by virtue of its objective capacity as an importer of the goods in question in the same manner as any other trader who is, of might be in the future, in the same situation. In fact the purpose of the decision is to authorize the Benelux States not to apply Community treatment for a fixed period to all imports of brushes originating in the People's Republic of China and in free circulation in another Member State. With regard to the importers of such products it is therefore a measure of general application covering situations which are determined objectively and it entails legal effects for categories of persons envisaged in a general and abstract manner. Thus the contested decision is not of individual concern to the applicant.

10. That conclusion is not invalidated by the fact that the applicant, according to its statement which was not disputed by the Commission, is the only trader-importer established in the Benelux States regularly importing into the Netherlands brushes originating in the People's Republic of China and that it was one of its imports which led to the adoption of the contested decision. As the Court stated in its judgment of 6 October 1982 in Case 307/81 *Alusuisse* [1982] ECR 3463, a measure does not cease to be a regulation because it is possible to determine the number or even the identity of the

persons to whom it applies at any given time as long as it is established that such application takes effect by virtue of an objective legal or factual situation defined by the measure in relation to its purpose.

INTERNATIONAL FRUIT COMPANY AND OTHERS v COMMISSION (Cases 41–4/70) [1971] ECR 411, Court of Justice

Under a Regulation, only 80% of applications for a licence to import apples in a particular week were granted, and a number of disappointed applicants challenged the Regulation under Article 173.

It was held that the applicants had locus standi to challenge the Regulation but, on the facts, it was not illegal and would not be annulled.

Admissibility

2.   The defendant submits that no decision was addressed to the applicants, and that the refusal to grant them import licences emanates from the PGF and is in reality an administrative measure governed by national law.

3.   It states that the only 'decisions' of the Commission concerning the grant of import licences were contained in Regulation No. 565/70 and the subsequent amending regulations.

4.   These 'decisions' were of general application and in the nature of regulations, and the defendant submits that they could not therefore be of individual concern to the applicants within the meaning of the second paragraph of Article 173.

5.   By Regulation No. 459/70, adopted on the basis of Regulations Nos. 2513/69 and 2514/69 of the Council, protective measures were taken with the object of limiting the import of dessert apples from third countries into the Community in the period from 1 April 1970 to 30 June 1970.

6.   This regulation provides for a system of import licences, which are granted to the extent to which the state of the Community market allows.

7.   Under this system and in accordance with Article 2(1) of Regulation No. 459/70, 'at the end of each week . . . the Member States shall communicate to the Commission the quantities for which import licences have been requested during the preceding week, stating the months to which they relate'.

8.   The following paragraph of the same article provides that the Commission, on the basis *inter alia* of these communications, 'shall assess the situation and decide on the issue of the licences'.

9.   On the basis of the latter provision, the Commission subsequently stipulated in Article 1 of Regulation No. 565/70 of 25 March 1970 that 'applications for import licences lodged up to 20 March 1970 shall be treated in accordance with the provisions of Article 1 of Regulation No. 459/70, within the quantity limit shown in the application and up to 80% of a reference quantity'.

10.   The criteria for fixing this reference quantity were stated in greater detail, and amended, by Article 2 of Regulation No. 686/70 of 15 April 1970.

11.   By various regulations published in the period between 2 April 1970 and 20 July 1970, the expiry date of 20 March 1970 specified in Article 1 of Regulation No. 565/70 was repeatedly postponed.

12.   By these postponements the said measures were periodically extended and made applicable to applications for import licences submitted within each period.

13.   By virtue of Article 1 of Regulation No. 983/70 of 28 May 1970, this system was applied in the period in which the applications for licences were submitted by the applicants.

14.   Hence, the issue of admissibility in the present cases must be determined in the light of the lastmentioned regulation.

15.   For this purpose, it is necessary to consider whether the provisions of that regulation – in so far as they make the system established by Article 1 of Regulation No. 565/70 applicable – are of direct and individual concern to the applicants within the meaning of the second paragraph of Article 173 of the Treaty.

16.   It is indisputable that Regulation No. 983/70 was adopted with a view on the one hand to the state of the market and on the other to the quantities of dessert apples for

which applications for import licences had been made in the week ending on 22 May 1970.

17. It follows that when the said regulation was adopted, the number of applications which could be affected by it was fixed.

18. No new application could be added.

19. To what extent, in percentage terms, the applications could be granted, depended on the total quantity in respect of which applications had been submitted.

20. Accordingly, by providing that the system introduced by Article 1 of Regulation No. 565/70 should be maintained for the relevant period, the Commission decided, even though it took account only of the quantities requested, on the subsequent fate of each application which had been lodged.

21. Consequently, Article 1 of Regulation No. 983/70 is not a provision of general application within the meaning of the second paragraph of Article 189 of the Treaty, but must be regarded as a conglomeration of individual decisions taken by the Commission under the guise of a regulation pursuant to Article 2(2) of Regulation No. 459/70, each of which decisions affects the legal position of each author of an application for a licence.

ROQUETTE FRÈRES v COUNCIL (Case 138/79) [1978] ECR 3333, Court of Justice

A Regulation imposed quotas on isoglucose production and listed the producers to which these quotas applied. It was passed without Parliamentary consultation as required by the Treaty. A producer challenged the validity of the Regulation under Article 173.

It was held that the producer had locus standi to challenge the Regulation and it would be annulled.

Admissibility of the application

13. In the Council's view the application is inadmissible for it is directed against a regulation and the conditions provided for in the second paragraph of Article 173 of the Treaty are not satisfied. The contested measure is claimed not to constitute a decision in the form of a regulation and not to be of direct and individual concern to the applicant. The applicant maintains on the other hand that the contested regulation is a set of individual decisions one of which is taken in respect of the applicant and is of direct and individual concern to it.

14. Article 9(1), (2) and (3) of Regulation No. 1111/77 as amended by Article 3 of Regulation No. 1293/79 provides:

1. A basic quota shall be allotted to each isoglucose producing undertaking established in the Community, for the period referred to in Article 8(1).

Without prejudice to implementation of paragraph (3), the basic quota of each such undertaking shall be equal to twice its production as determined, under this regulation, during the period 1 November 1978 to 30 April 1979.

2. To each undertaking having a basic quota, there shall also be allotted a maximum quota equal to its basic quota multiplied by a coefficient. This coefficient shall be that fixed by virtue of the second subparagraph of Article 25(2) of Regulation (EEC) No. 3330/74 for the period 1 July 1979 to 30 June 1980.

3. The basic quota referred to in paragraph (1) shall, if necessary, be corrected so that the maximum quota determined in accordance with paragraph (2):
–does not exceed 85 %,
–is not less than 65 %
of the technical production capacity per annum of the undertaking in question.

15. Article 9(4) provides that the basic quotas established pursuant to paragraphs (1) and (3) are fixed for each undertaking as set out in Annex II. That annex, which is an integral part of Article 9, provides that the applicant's basic quota is 15,887 tonnes.

16. It follows that Article 9(4) of Regulation No. 1111/77 (as amended by Article 3 of Regulation No. 1293/79) in conjunction with Annex II, itself applies the criteria laid down in Article 9(1) to (3) to each of the undertakings in question who are the addressees and thus directly and individually concerned. Regulation No. 1293/79 therefore is a

measure against which the undertakings concerned manufacturing isoglucose may bring proceedings for a declaration that it is void pursuant to the second paragraph of Article 173 of the Treaty.

7.1.4.2   The 'factual' test

TOEPFER AND GETREIDE-IMPORT GESELLSCHAFT v COMMISSION (Cases 106 & 107/63) [1965] ECR 405, Court of Justice

For one day only, 1 October, a zero levy was imposed on maize imports into Germany. (A Commission Decision of 10 October raised the levy with effect from 2 October.) A Commission Decision of 4 October authorised Germany to refuse applications for import licences made between 1 and 4 October. A German maize importer, Toepfer, challenged this Decision under Article 173.

It was held that those importers which had applied for a licence on the day of the zero levy had locus standi. The Decision would be annulled.

Admissibility of the applications (at pp. 410–11)
As the contested decision was not addressed to the applicants the defendant argues that it was not of direct and individual concern to them within the meaning of Article 173 of the Treaty; it only concerns the applicants through the effect of the protective measure in question, and thus indirectly.

The defendant further argues that, since the protective measure was drawn up in general terms applicable to all importers in a position to ask for an import licence during the period between 1 and 4 October 1963, neither this measure nor the decision which upheld it is of individual concern to the applicants.
. . .
The expression 'of . . . individual concern' (at pp. 411–12)
It is clear from the fact that on 1 October 1963 the Commission took a decision fixing new free-at-frontier prices for maize imported into the Federal Republic as from 2 October, that the danger which the protective measures retained by the Commission were to guard against no longer existed as from this latter date.

Therefore the only persons concerned by the said measures were importers who had applied for an import licence during the course of the day of 1 October 1963. The number and identity of these importers had already become fixed and ascertainable before 4 October, when the contested decision was made. The Commission was in a position to know that its decision affected the interests and the position of the said importers alone.

The factual situation thus created differentiates the said importers, including the applicants, from all other persons and distinguishes them individually just as in the case of the person addressed.

Therefore the objection of inadmissibility which has been raised is unfounded and the applications are admissible.

BOCK v COMMISSION (Case 62/70) [1971] ECR 897, Court of Justice

For the facts, see **7.1.3** above.

9.   (3)   The defendant claims that the contested decision is not of individual concern to the applicant but covers in the abstract all traders wishing to import the products in question into Germany while the decision is in force.

10.   However, the applicant had challenged the decision only to the extent to which it also covers imports for which applications for import licences were already pending at the date of its entry into force. The number and identity of importers concerned in this way was already fixed and ascertainable before that date. The defendant was in a position to know that the contested provision in its decision would affect the interests and situation of those importers alone. The factual situation thus created differentiates the latter from all other persons and distinguishes them individually just as in the case of the person addressed.

11.   The objection of inadmissibility must therefore be dismissed.

PIRAIKI-PATRAIKI AND OTHERS v COMMISSION (Case 11/82) [1985] ECR 207,
Court of Justice

For the facts, see **7.1.3** above.

11.   With regard to the question whether the applicants are also individually concerned, it should first be pointed out, as the Court stated in its judgment of 15 July 1963 (Case 25/62, *Plaumann*, [1963] ECR 95), that 'persons other than those to whom a decision is addressed may only claim to be individually concerned if that decision affects them by reason of certain attributes which are peculiar to them or by reason of circumstances in which they are differentiated from all other persons and by virtue of these factors distinguishes them individually just as in the case of the person addressed'.

12.   The applicants argue that they fulfil the conditions set out above since they are the main Greek undertakings which produce and export cotton yarn to France. They argue that they therefore belong to a class of traders individually identifiable on the basis of criteria having to do with the product in question, the business activities carried on and the length of time during which they have been carried on. In that regard the applicants emphasize that the production and export to France of cotton yarn of Greek origin requires an industrial and commercial organization which cannot be established from one day to the next, and certainly not during the short period of application of the decision in question.

13.   That proposition cannot be accepted. It must first be pointed out that the applicants are affected by the decision at issue only in their capacity as exporters to France of cotton yarn of Greek origin. The decision is not intended to limit the production of those products in any way, nor does it have such a result.

14.   As for the exportation of those products to France, that is clearly a commercial activity which can be carried on at any time by any undertaking whatever. It follows that the decision at issue concerns the applicants in the same way as any other trader actually or potentially finding himself in the same position. The mere fact that the applicants export goods to France is not therefore sufficient to establish that they are individually concerned by the contested decision.

15.   The applicants argue however that their situation may be distinguished from that of any other exporter to France of cotton yarn of Greek origin inasmuch as they had entered into a series of contracts of sale with French customers, to be performed during the period of application of the decision and covering quantities of cotton yarn in excess of the quotas authorized by the Commission. The applicants state that those contracts could not be carried out because of the quota system applied by the French authorities. They take the view that in those circumstances their individual interests were affected by the decision in question.

16.   According to the applicants the Commission was in a position, and even under an obligation, to identify the traders who, like the applicants, were individually concerned by its decision. In failing to obtain information in that regard it did not comply with the conditions of application of Article 130 of the Act of Accession, since in the applicants' view that provision obliges the Commission, before making a decision, to ascertain which traders, in this case Greek traders, would be individually concerned by the protective measures authorized.

17.   It should first be observed that if that argument were held to be well founded, it would only avail those applicants who could show that before the date of the contested decision they had entered into contracts with French customers for the delivery of cotton yarn from Greece during the period of application of that decision.

18.   Since neither Vomvyx PV Svolopoulos and Chr. Koutroubis AE nor Unicot Hellas AE provided evidence in that respect, the application must be declared inadmissible in so far as they are concerned.

19.   With regard to the other applicants, it must be held that the fact, before the adoption of the decision at issue, they had entered into contracts which were to be carried out during the months to which the decision applied constitutes a circumstance which distinguishes them from any other person concerned by the decision, in so far as the execution of their contracts was wholly or partly prevented by the adoption of the decision.

20. The Commission, however, challenges the assertion that that circumstance is sufficient in itself for the applicants to be regarded as individually concerned. It argues that in any event when it adopted the decision it was unaware of the number of contracts already entered into for the period covered by that decision and that, in contrast to the cases considered in previous decisions of the Court, it had no way of obtaining information in that regard, since the contracts in question were governed by private law and there was no obligation to declare them to Community or national authorities.

21. In that respect it must be observed that the reply to be given to the question whether and to what extent the Commission was aware, or could have made itself aware, which Greek exporters had entered into contracts covering the period of application of the contested decision depends on the interpretation given to Article 130 of the Act of Accession, and in particular on the question whether the Commission, before authorizing a protective measure under that provision, is obliged to make appropriate enquiries as to the economic effects of the decision to be taken and the undertakings which would be affected by it. Since arguments related to that problem were raised in support of the assertion that the decision at issue is unlawful, the admissibility of the application from that point of view must be considered in conjunction with the substance of the case.

22. The applicants argue first that in the adoption of the contested decision the conditions laid down in Article 130 of the Act of Accession were not met. In that regard the applicants make three distinct submissions. In the first place they maintain that the product covered by the decision at issue does not constitute a 'sector of the economy' as envisaged by Article 130. In their second submission they argue that the sectoral or regional difficulties referred to in that article did not exist in this case. In their third submission they assert that the content of the decision in question was not restricted to the measures strictly necessary, contrary to Article 130 (3).

23. Taking into account what has already been said with regard to the admissibility of the action, this last submission should be considered first.

24. It should be borne in mind in this regard that under Article 130(1) of the Act of Accession a Member State may apply for authorization to take protective measures with regard to the Hellenic Republic 'if . . . difficulties arise which are serious and liable to persist in any sector of the economy or which could bring about serious deterioration in the economic situation of a given area'.

25. Article 130 (3) provides that:

the measures authorized under paragraph (2) may involve derogations from the rules of the EEC Treaty and of this Act to such an extent and for such periods as are strictly necessary in order to attain the objectives referred to in paragraph (1). Priority shall be given to such measures as will least disturb the functioning of the common market.

26. That requirement may be explained by the fact that a provision permitting the authorisation of protective measures with regard to a Member State which derogate, even temporarily and in respect of certain products only, from the rules relating to the free movement of goods must, like any provision of that nature, be interpreted strictly.

27. The applicants argue that the decision at issue has a serious impact on the Greek traders concerned, even though there is not the slightest indication in the statement of the reasons on which that decision is based that the Commission took into account the very serious effects which its decision would have for those traders.

28. It must be observed that in order to ascertain whether the measure whose authorization is being considered meets the conditions laid down in Article 130(3) the Commission must also take into account the situation in the Member State with regard to which the protective measure is requested. In particular, in so far as the circumstances of the case permit, the Commission must inquire into the negative effects which its decision might have on the economy of that Member State as well as on the undertakings concerned. In that connection it must also consider, in so far as is possible, the contracts which those undertakings, relying on the continuation of free trade within the Community, have already entered into and whose execution will be wholly or partially prevented by the decision authorizing the protective measure.

29. In that regard the Commission objects that it would be impossible for it, during the brief period within which it must act, to make itself aware of the exact number of contracts meeting that description.

30. That argument cannot be accepted in the light of the circumstances of this case. Before adopting the contested decision the Commission had sufficient time to obtain the necessary information. As the Commission admitted at the hearing, moreover, it had arranged a meeting with representatives of the Greek Government and of the trade interests concerned, which even included certain of the applicants.

31. In those circumstances it must be concluded that the Commission was in a position to obtain sufficiently exact information on the contracts already entered into which were to be performed during the period of application of the decision at issue. It follows that the undertakings which were party to contracts meeting that description must be considered as individually concerned for the purpose of the admissibility of this action, as members of a limited class of traders identified or identifiable by the Commission and by reason of those contracts particularly affected by the decision at issue.

32. The objection of inadmissibility raised by the Commission and supported by the Government of the French Republic must be dismissed, except as regards the two applicants referred to above in paragraph 18.

CODONIU SA v *COUNCIL* (Case C-309/89)
[1995] 2 CMLR 561

Cordoniu, a Spanish producer of quality sparkling wine, applied under Article 173 for the annulment of a Regulation which restricted the use of the term 'crémant' to quality sparkling wine originating in France and Luxembourg.

It was held by the Court of Justice that Cordoniu had locus standi and the Regulation would be annulled.

Admissibility

[14] In support of its objection of inadmissibility the Council states that it did not adopt the contested provision on the basis of the circumstances peculiar to certain producers but on the basis of a choice of wine-marketing policy in relation to a particular product. The contested provision reserves the use of the term *'crémant'* to quality sparkling wines manufactured under specific conditions in certain Member States. It thus constitutes a measure applicable to an objectively determined situation which has legal effects in respect of categories of persons considered in a general and abstract manner.

[15] According to the Council, Codorniu is concerned by the contested provision only in its capacity as a producer of quality sparkling wine psr using the term *'crémant'*, like any other producer in an identical situation. Even if when that provision was adopted the number or identity of producers of sparkling wines using the term *'crémant'* could theoretically be determined, the measure in question remains essentially a regulation inasmuch as it applies on the basis of an objective situation of law or fact defined by the measure in relation to its objective.

[16] Codorniu alleges that the contested provision is in reality a decision adopted in the guise of a regulation. It has no general scope but affects a well-determined class of producers which cannot be altered. Such producers are those who on 1 September 1989 traditionally designated their sparkling wines with the term *'crémant'*. For that class the contested provision has no general scope. Furthermore, the direct result of the contested provision will be to prevent Codorniu from using the term *'Gran Crémant'* which will involve a loss of 38 per cent of its turnover. The effect of that damage is to distinguish it, within the meaning of the second paragraph of **Article 173** of the Treaty, from any other trader. Codorniu alleges that the Court has already recognised the admissibility of an action for annulment brought by a natural or legal person against a regulation in such circumstances.

[17] Under the second paragraph of **Article 173** of the Treaty the institution of proceedings by a natural or legal person for a declaration that a regulation is void is subject to the condition that the provisions of the regulation at issue in the proceedings constitute in reality a decision of direct and individual concern to that person.

[18]   As the Court has already held, the general applicability, and thus the legislative nature, of a measure is not called into question by the fact that it is possible to determine more or less exactly the number or even the identity of the persons to whom it applies at any given time, as long as it is established that it applies to them by virtue of an objective legal or factual situation defined by the measure in question in relation to its purpose.

[19]   Although it is true that according to the criteria in the second paragraph of **Article 173** of the Treaty the contested provision is, by nature and by virtue of its sphere of application, of a legislative nature in that it applies to the traders concerned in general, that does not prevent it from being of individual concern to some of them.

[20]   Natural nor legal persons may claim that a contested provision is of individual concern to them only if it affects them by reason of certain attributes which are peculiar to them or by reason of circumstances in which they are differentiated from all other persons.

[21]   Codorniu registered the graphic trade mark 'Gran Crémant de Codorniu' in Spain in 1924 and traditionally used that mark both before and after registration. By reserving the right to use the term 'crémant' to French and Luxembourg producers, the contested provision prevents Codorniu from using its graphic trade mark.

[22]   It follows that Codorniu has established the existence of a situation which from the point of view of the contested provision differentiates it from all other traders.

[23]   It follows that the objection of inadmissibility put forward by the Council must be dismissed.

SOFRIMPORT SARL v COMMISSION (Case C–152/88) [1990] ECR I–2477, Court of Justice

Sofrimport had shipped apples from Chile prior to the issue of a Regulation which suspended import licences for Chilean apples. Sofrimport was then unable to obtain an import licence and applied for annulment of the Regulation under Article 173 and damages under Article 215.

It was held that Sofrimport had locus standi to challenge the Regulation and it would be annulled insofar as it applied to goods in transit.

The application for annulment

Admissibility

8.   With regard to the admissibility of the application for annulment, it must be determined whether the contested measures are of direct and individual concern to the applicant within the meaning of the second paragraph of Article 173 of the Treaty.

9.   The applicant is directly concerned by the contested measures because Regulation No. 962/88 requires the national authorities to reject pending applications for import licences and thus leaves them no discretion.

10.   With regard to the question whether the applicant is individually concerned, it must be determined whether the contested measures affect it by reason of certain attributes which are peculiar to it or by reason of circumstances in which it is differentiated from all other persons (see the judgment of 14 July 1983 in Case 231/82 *Spijker* v *Commission* [1983] ECR 259, paragraph 8).

11.   It should be observed first of all that the applicant is in the position referred to in Article 3(3) of Council Regulation (EEC) No. 2707/72 of 19 December 1972 laying down the conditions for applying protective measures for fruit and vegetables (Official Journal, English Special Edition 1972 (28 to 30 December), p. 3) which requires the Commission, in adopting such measures, to take account of the special position of products in transit to the Community. Only importers of Chilean apples whose goods were in transit when Regulation No. 962/88 was adopted are in that position. Those importers thus constitute a restricted group which is sufficiently well defined in relation to any other importer of Chilean apples and cannot be extended after the suspensory measures in question take effect.

12.   Secondly, since Article 3 of Regulation No. 2707/72 gives specific protection to those importers, they must therefore be able to enforce observance of that protection and bring legal proceedings for that purpose.

13. Importers whose goods were in transit when the contested regulations came into force must therefore be considered to be individually concerned by those regulations in so far as they concern those goods. The application for annulment is therefore admissible only in so far as it challenges the application of protective measures to products in transit.

UNIFRUIT HELLAS v EC COMMISSION (Case T-489/93) [1996] 1 CMLR 267, Court of First Instance

[21] It is also settled case law that the fact that it is possible to determine more or less exactly the number or even the identity of the persons to whom a measure applies at any given time is not sufficient to call into question the legislative nature of the measure, as long as it is established that it applies to them by virtue of an objective legal or factual situation defined by the measure in question in relation to its purpose. In order for a measure of general application adopted by a Community institution to be of individual concern to traders, it must affect their legal position because of a factual situation which differentiates them from all other persons and distinguishes them individually in the same way as a person to whom it is addressed.

[22] In the present case, the applicant seeks the annulment of Regulation 846/93 introducing a countervailing charge on apples originating in Chile and of a number of subsequent regulations modifying the amount of that charge.

[23] The Court considers that those regulations, which impose a countervailing charge on apples originating in Chile, are not directed specifically at the applicant. They concern the applicant only in its objective capacity as an importer of Chilean apples in the same way as any other trader in an identical situation.

[24] The applicant, referring to the judgment in *Sofrimport*, cited above, maintains that it is sufficiently distinguished individually by the fact that its goods were already in transit to the Community at the time when the contested regulations introduced the countervailing charge but that argument cannot be accepted. In the *Sofrimport* case, the applicant sought, *inter alia*, the annulment of Commission Regulation 962/88 suspending the issue of import licences for dessert apples originating in Chile and of Commission Regulation 984/88 amending Regulation 962/88. The Court of Justice held that the applicant was in the position referred to in Article 3(3) of Regulation 2707/72 which requires the Commission, in adopting such protective measures, to take account of the special position of products in transit to the Community. Importers whose goods were in transit to the Community when the measure was adopted thus constituted, in the Court's view, a closed and restricted group which was sufficiently well defined in relation to any other importer of Chilean apples. The Court also considered that because the said Article 3(3) gave specific protection to those importers, they must be able to enforce observance of that protection and bring legal proceedings for that purpose. It therefore held the action for annulment to be admissible in so far as it challenged the application of protective measures to products in transit to the Community.

[25] In the present case, the Court considers that those importers whose goods were in transit to the Community at the time when Regulation 846/93 introducing the countervailing charge was adopted also constituted a closed group of persons identifiable at that moment. However, in accordance with the case law cited in paragraph [21] above, that circumstance is not in itself sufficient for the regulation in question to be of individual concern to traders. If the present claim for annulment is to be declared admissible, the criteria established in the *Sofrimport* case mean, in addition, that the rules on the introduction of countervailing charges must require the Commission to take account of the special position of products in transit to the Community.

[26] The Court notes that, unlike Article 3(3) of Regulation 2707/72 with regard to protective measures, neither Article 25(1) of Regulation 1035/72, which provides for the introduction of a countervailing charge when certain conditions are fulfilled, nor any other provision relating to countervailing charges requires the Commission to take account of the special position of products in transit to the Community when it adopts a regulation introducing a countervailing charge.

[27] The Court further considers that the fact that the apples purchased by the applicant were the subject of the surveillance measures provided for in Regulation

384/93 is also not such as to distinguish the applicant individually from any other importer of apples. In that regard, it should be borne in mind that the purpose of the measures introduced by Regulation 384/93, the legality of which is not contested in the present case, was the surveillance of all imports of apples into the Community, regardless of their origin, and that those measures thus affected the applicant in the same way as any other importer of apples. In those circumstances, the applicant cannot argue that, by reason of the application of the surveillance measures provided for in Regulation 384/93, its legal position is affected by the regulations introducing and amending the countervailing charge in the same way as a person to whom an individual decision is addressed.

[28] Thus, even on the assumption that it were proven that the applicant's goods were in transit to the Community at the time when Regulation 846/93 was adopted, the applicant would still not be individually concerned by that regulation or by the other regulations amending it, adopted subsequently.

[29] In those circumstances, without there being any need to enquire whether the applicant is directly concerned by the contested regulations, the application must be dismissed as inadmissible in so far as it seeks the annulment of Regulations 846/93, 915/93, 1396/93 and 1467/93.

7.1.4.3 The 'theoretical' test

KSH NV v *COUNCIL AND COMMISSION* **(Case 101/76) [1977] ECR 797,**
Court of Justice

One of only three or four isoglucose producers in the Community challenged, under Article 173, a Regulation which provided for the reduction, and eventual abolition, of subsidies on isoglucose production.

It was held that the producer had no locus standi to challenge the Regulation.

5.   Article 173 of the EEC Treaty empowers a natural or a legal person to contest a decision addressed to that person or a decision which, although in the form of a regulation or a decision addressed to another person, is of direct and individual concern to the former.

6.   The objective of this provision is in particular to prevent the Community institutions from being in a position, merely by choosing the form of a regulation, to exclude an application by an individual against a decision which concerns him directly and individually.

7.   The choice of form cannot change the nature of the measure.

8.   In order to make a decision as to the admissibility of the application it is therefore necessary to examine whether the contested measures are regulations or decisions within the meaning of Article 173 of the Treaty.

9.   By virtue of the second paragraph of Article 189 of the Treaty the criterion for distinguishing between a regulation and a decision is whether the measure at issue is of general application or not.

10.   The nature of the contested measures must therefore be studied and in particular the legal effects which it is intended to or does actually produce.

. . .

20.   A regulation which provides for the reduction of a production refund for a whole marketing year with regard to a certain product processed from cereals and rice and for its complete abolition from the following marketing year is by its nature a measure of general application within the meaning of Article 189 of the Treaty.

21.   It in fact applies to objectively determined situations and produces legal effects with regard to categories of persons regarded generally and in the abstract.

22.   It only affects the applicant by virtue of its capacity as a producer of glucose having a high fructose content without any other specification.

23.   Moreover, the nature of a measure as a regulation is not called in question by the possibility of determining more or less precisely the number or even the identity of the persons to whom it applies at a given moment as long as it is established that it is applied by virtue of an objective legal or factual situation defined by the measure in relation to the objective of the latter.

24.   Moreover, the fact that a legal provision may have different actual effects for the various persons to whom it applies is not inconsistent with its nature as a regulation when that situation is objectively defined.

25.   To refuse to acknowledge that rules on production refunds amounted to a regulation only because they concerned a specific product and to take the view that such rules affected the manufacturers of that product by virtue of circumstances which differentiated them from all other persons would enlarge the concept of a decision to such an extent as to jeopardize the system of the Treaty which only permits an application for annulment to be brought by any person against an individual decision which affects him as the person to whom it is addressed or against a measure which affects him as in the case of such a person.

26.   For the same reasons it is necessary to sustain the objection raised by the Commission.

27.   It follows that the application must be dismissed as inadmissible.

CALPAK SPA AND SOCIETÀ EMILIANA LAVORAZIONE FRUTTA SPA v COMMISSION (Cases 789–790/79) [1980] ECR 1949, Court of Justice

A Regulation made an alteration to the calculation of subsidies on processed pears, which was to the disadvantage of the Italian producers, but not to the French producers. The Italian producers challenged the Regulation under Article 173.

It was held that the Italian producers had no locus standi to challenge the Regulation.

6.   The Commission's main contention is that as the disputed provisions were adopted in the form of regulations their annulment may only be sought if their content shows them to be, in fact, decisions. But in the Commission's view the provisions in question, which lay down rules of general application, are truly in the nature of regulations within the meaning of Article 189 of the Treaty. By selecting the 1978/79 marketing year as the reference period the Commission's intention was to limit and stabilize production at a level as low as that of that year. It is said to be possible, but certainly not indefensible that such a restriction has a greater incidence upon marginal producers such as the applicants than, for example, upon co-operatives, but that does not mean that the applicants are individually concerned within the meaning of the second paragraph of Article 173, which hypothesis the Commission denies in any case.

7.   The second paragraph of Article 173 empowers individuals to contest, *inter alia*, any decision which, although in the form of a regulation, is of direct and individual concern to them. The objective of that provision is in particular to prevent the Community institutions from being in a position, merely by choosing the form of a regulation, to exclude an application by an individual against a decision which concerns him directly and individually; it therefore stipulates that the choice of form cannot change the nature of the measure.

8.   By virtue of the second paragraph of Article 189 of the Treaty the criterion for distinguishing between a regulation and a decision is whether the measure at issue is of general application or not.

As the amendment to Regulation No. 1530/78 made by Article 1(3) of Regulation No. 1732/79 concerning the information to be submitted in support of the application for aid is merely the natural consequence of the limitation imposed by Article 1 of Regulation No. 1731/79, consideration need only be given to the nature of the latter provision.

9.   A provision which limits the granting of production aid for all producers in respect of a particular product to a uniform percentage of the quantity produced by them during a uniform preceding period is by nature a measure of general application within the meaning of Article 189 of the Treaty. In fact the measure applies to objectively determined situations and produces legal effects with regard to categories of persons described in a generalized and abstract manner. The nature of the measure as a regulation is not called in question by the mere fact that it is possible to determine the number or even the identity of the producers to be granted the aid which is limited thereby.

10.   Nor is the fact that the choice of reference period is particularly important for the applicants, whose production is subject to considerable variation from one marketing

year to another as a result of their own programme of production, sufficient to entitle them to an individual remedy. Moreover, the applicants have not established the existence of circumstances such as to justify describing that choice – the conformity of which with the Council's regulations, and especially with the basic regulation, is only relevant to the substantive issues of the case – as a decision adopted specifically in relation to them and, as such, entitling them to institute proceedings under the second paragraph of Article 173.

11.   It follows that the objection raised by the Commission must be accepted as regards the applications for the annulment of the provisions in the two regulations in question.

Nanette A.E.M. Neuwahl, 'Article 173 Paragraph 4 EC: Past, Present and Possible Future'
(1996) 21 El Rev 17

. . .

The exit of the cumulative test

For individuals to have standing when challenging a Regulation, the fourth paragraph of Article 173 lays down a three-fold test: the Regulation must in truth be a decision, and there must be direct and individual concern.

The criterion for the distinction between true Regulations and Decisions in terms of Article 173 was derived by the Court of Justice from Article 189. It is to be found in the general 'application' or otherwise of the measure in question: Regulations are essentially legislative in nature and apply to categories of persons viewed abstractly and in their entirety,' whereas Decisions are characterised by the limited number of persons to whom they are addressed. On this account, whereas a Decision binds a specific set or class of people, a Regulation is potentially binding on everyone.

The test for deciding *direct concern* is somewhat similar to that of direct applicability. A measure is of direct concern if it is the 'direct cause of an effect' on the applicant. The measure must not depend on the exercise of any discretionary power by a third party, unless such power is bound to be exercised in a particular way. In particular, a Community act is not of direct concern to the applicant if it leaves any (real) discretion to the Member States. If it does, any challenges should be directed at acts which the national authorities may take in the exercise of their discretion.

The concept of *individual concern* is far more complicated. In *Plaumann* v *Commission* (Case 25/62) [1963] ECR 95 the Court of Justice gave what has come to be the classic definition of individual concern:

> Persons other than those to whom a decision is addressed may only claim to be individually concerned if that decision affects them by reason of certain attributes which are peculiar to them or by reason of circumstances in which they are differen-tiated from all other persons and *by virtue of these factors distinguishes them individually just as in the case of the person addressed.*

In terms of the *Plaumann* test somebody cannot claim to be individually concerned by a measure when he belongs to a general group of traders similarly affected by and defined in abstract terms in the measure which is being challenged. He must be distinguished in some form or other just as an addressee. Further particulars as to how the condition is applied by the Court of Justice will be given below.

Anyone dealing from time to time with questions of *locus standi* may find that the question whether a Regulation is in substance a Decision and the question whether there is individual concern can often be established only by reference to the same set of criteria. A good example is the *CAM* case (*CAM SA* v *Commission* (Case 100/74) [1975] ECR 1393), where the Court of Justice held an action admissible upon establishing that it was of direct and individual concern. The applicant had entered into private law contracts before the contested decision was taken. Although this is not apparent from the text of the measure, the Commission was aware of this and was in fact deciding their particular situation. One could view the act of the Commission in substance as a Decision, but this question was not addressed separately by the Court.

Several commentators have therefore voiced criticism against the wording of Article 173 which in its fourth paragraph requires a cumulative test. If one is not to dismiss the paragraph as gobbledegook, one is to assume that at least in some cases a cumulative test makes sense, for example, a provision in a Regulation can mention company X by name and be a decision concerning him, but it must not be of individual concern to company Y or Z. Indeed, for the first company the tests for *locus standi* may be fulfilled because the Community was obviously deciding on its situation, but one of the other companies may be able to satisfy the *Plaumann* test in connection with the same Community act by reference to different criteria.

A cumulative test does not, however, exactly facilitate access to judicial review for most private applicants. The reasons why at several instances the Court of Justice has insisted that the cumulative test was to be applied would appear to be of a different nature. It is this. If the element of 'Decision' were not required, then any Regulation could be challenged by individuals, and the authors of the Treaty did not mean this to occur. If there was no requirement of 'individual concern', then anybody could challenge the measure in question without having to show an interest in doing so. Although there may well exist legal systems where legal protection is that generous, in the Treaty of Rome a more restrictive system has been provided for. In particular the possibility that an individual could be directly and individually concerned by a measure which was truly normative in character was not foreseen. This question was to be tackled by the Court of Justice in *Codorniu* (see below).

Well before that case, however, the Court of Justice has abandoned the cumulative test in particular cases. This happened in particular in cases involving anti-dumping measures and the like, where a cumulative test runs into difficulties of a fundamental character. For those less familiar with the issue, it is recalled that dumping is the situation where goods are being imported into the Community at a price below that of the same goods in their home market. If it occurs, companies producing similar goods in the Community may see their market position threatened. If they become aware, say, that Japanese CD players are imported more cheaply into the Community than what they would cost in Japan, they may complain to the Commission by virtue of the so-called 'Basic Regulation' in order to solicit an investigation of the matter. The Commission can take action after collecting information from traders and governments inside and outside the Community with a view to comparing the price of the product paid (or payable) for export in the third country concerned with a so-called 'normal value' of the like product. This is normally a laborious procedure as it may involve evaluating thousands of invoices on a transaction-by-transaction basis or using weighted averages. In the end, if dumping is found, if it causes injury and if it is in the interest of the Community to do so, the Commission will issue a Regulation levying a so-called 'provisional anti-dumping duty' on all imports of such goods from the country concerned. The actual amounts are not payable until definitive duties are imposed by Council Regulations, but the importers must provide some form of security for the imports pending the decision by the Council. The purpose of both provisional and definitive measures is to protect the Community industry producing the like product, commonly an open category of persons.

For purposes of *locus standi* it is important to note that anti-dumping Regulations in principle apply to categories of persons objectively determined. They do not apply to someone specific, although the names of certain companies sometimes appear in their text, notably when an exception is created for those foreign firms that undertake to refrain from dumping, or when a higher duty is imposed on certain imports. Apart from this, anti-dumping measures are general legislative acts aiming at action to be taken in respect to all prospective importers of the product concerned.

Now, anti-dumping measures have presented the Court of Justice with the following dilemma. If one were to admit that anti-dumping measures are in substance Decisions, or bundles of Decisions, then they are being adopted in the wrong form. However, because they are (in principle) acts of general application, concerning as they do indiscriminately *all* imports of the product from the country concerned, the Basic Regulation provides that anti-dumping measures must be adopted by Regulation.

Nevertheless, maintaining that anti-dumping measures are always Regulations has its own difficulties, because then – on the terms of Article 173 – individuals other than those who happen to be mentioned in such an act do not have standing. This would be severe in particular to a complainant and other individuals (i.e. exporting companies) who participated in the procedure leading up to the decision. Obviously, persons who have been given a right to complain or to be heard under the Basic Regulation may be deprived of the effective enjoyment of this right if they cannot challenge the (non-)action by the Commission before a court at least for the purpose of the defence of the rights so granted. As we shall see, the Court of Justice recognises this in its case law regarding individual concern.

In these circumstances it must have been tempting for the Court of Justice to say that an anti-dumping measure would be a Decision as regards all those who were named in the Regulation or who had participated in the proceedings leading up to it. However, apart from the fact that that would have gone further than required for the protection of individuals who had an indirect remedy it might not have gone far enough in another respect, as it would have entailed an artificial distinction between foreign companies, prejudicing the position of those foreign firms who had not participated in the proceedings (see further below). In addition, such a sophisticated distinction between Regulations and Decisions does not fit well in the system of the Treaty, where a Regulation is a Regulation and a Decision a Decision.

Therefore, instead of enhancing uncertainty by blurring the distinction between Decisions and Regulations, the Court of Justice has decided with regard to anti-dumping measures to skip the question of the true nature of the act and focus on individual concern. Of course if (a provision of) a Regulation mentions a specific individual by name, e.g., in case of an individual exception to an anti-dumping regime, one can still regard the part of the Regulation concerned as the equivalent of a decision. Similarly, where (a provision of) a Community measure 'targets' one or more specific individuals such as in *CAM*, one may still conceive the provisions concerned as (a bundle of) decisions with regard to them. An exhaustive treatment would then, in the alternative, plead direct and individual concern.

In the meantime, the latest development of the law involving a case unrelated to anti-dumping or similar measures seems to suggest that the Court of Justice is no longer attaching great importance to the requirement that a Regulation must in substance be a Decision. Considering the following quote from *Codorniu v Council* (Case C-309/89) [1994] ECR I-1853 it is difficult to imagine that the Court would look behind the label of a Regulation when considering the *locus standi* of individuals, as the emphasis is squarely on *how* an individual is affected:

> Although it is true that according to the criteria in the second paragraph of Article 173 of the Treaty the contested provision is, by nature and by virtue of its sphere of application, of a legislative nature in that it applies to the traders concerned in general, that does not prevent it from being of individual concern to some of them.

In spite of the text of Article 173 Regulations are now created in the same way as Decisions addressed to third parties. The requirement of individual concern seems to be the overriding criterion for ascertaining *locus standi*; but we shall see that it is also a very difficult condition for individuals to fulfil. Arguably, it is already difficult to establish individual concern in the case of Decisions addressed to other persons (in particular, Member States), but it is certainly at least as difficult in the case of Regulations.

In view of this difficulty it may well be that a distinction between Decisions and Regulations remains relevant, at least under the present wording of Article 173: if an individual is able to establish that a provision of a Regulation is in fact a decision regarding him or an act addressed to him, he need not satisfy the test of (direct and) individual concern. Should he, however, not succeed, he must go through the other procedural requirements as well. In so far as this may amount to double work, it is clear that a rationalisation of *locus standi* would be a relief to private applicants and their lawyers.

Nevertheless, after *Codorniu* the test for *locus standi* of individuals appears to have become an alternative rather than a cumulative one. Given moreover the well-known fact that the Court of Justice has generally been active before in widening the category of Community acts which could be challenged, the fourth paragraph of Article 173 can now be read as granting *locus standi* to individuals in actions against 'any Community measure having legal effect addressed to him *or* by which he is directly and individually concerned'. This is a satisfying development from the point of view of the judicial protection of individuals against infringements of Community law regarding them. . . .

7.1.5 GROUNDS

ROQUETTE FRÈRES v *COUNCIL* (Case 138/79) [1978] ECR 3333, Court of Justice

For the facts, see 7.1.4.2 above.

On 25 June 1979 the Council without obtaining the opinion requested adopted the regulation proposed by the Commission which thus became Regulation No. 1293/79 amending Regulation No. 1111/77. The third reference in the preamble to Regulation No. 1293/79 refers to consultation of the Parliament. The Council nevertheless took account of the absence of an opinion from the Parliament by observing in the third recital in the preamble to the regulation that 'the European Parliament which was consulted on 19 March 1979 on the Commission proposal did not deliver its opinion at its May part-session; whereas it had referred the matter to the Assembly for its opinion'.

Infringement of essential procedural requirements
32.   The applicant and the Parliament in its intervention maintain that since Regulation No. 1111/77 as amended was adopted by the Council without regard to the consultation procedure provided for in the second paragraph of Article 43 of the Treaty it must be treated as void for infringement of essential procedural requirements.
33.   The consultation provided for in the third subparagraph of Article 43(2), as in other similar provisions of the Treaty, is the means which allows the Parliament to play an actual part in the legislative process of the Community. Such power represents an essential factor in the institutional balance intended by the Treaty. Although limited, it reflects at Community level the fundamental democratic principle that the peoples should take part in the exercise of power through the intermediary of a representative assembly. Due consultation of the Parliament in the cases provided for by the Treaty therefore constitutes an essential formality disregard of which means that the measure concerned is void.
34.   In that respect it is pertinent to point out that observance of that requirement implies that the Parliament has expressed it opinion. It is impossible to take the view that the requirement is satisfied by the Council's simply asking for the opinion. The Council is, therefore, wrong to include in the references in the preamble to Regulation No. 1293/79 a statement to the effect that the Parliament has been consulted.
35.   The Council has not denied that consultation of the Parliament was in the nature of an essential procedural requirement. It maintains however that in the circumstances of the present case the Parliament, by its own conduct, made observance of that requirement impossible and that it is therefore not proper to rely on the infringement thereof.
36.   Without prejudice to the questions of principle raised by that argument of the Council it suffices to observe that in the present case on 25 June 1979 when the Council adopted Regulation No. 1293/79 amending Regulation No. 1111/77 without the opinion of the Assembly the Council had not exhausted all the possibilities of obtaining the preliminary opinion of the Parliament. In the first place the Council did not request the application of the emergency procedure provided for by the internal regulation of the Parliament although in other sectors and as regards other draft regulations it availed itself of that power at the same time. Further the Council could have made use of the possibility it had under Article 139 of the Treaty to ask for an extraordinary session of the Assembly especially as the Bureau of the Parliament on 1 March and 10 May 1979 drew its attention to that possibility.
37.   It follows that in the absence of the opinion of the Parliament required by Article 43 of the Treaty Regulation No. 1293/79 amending Council Regulation No. 1111/77 must be declared void without prejudice to the Council's power following the present judgment to take all appropriate measures pursuant to the first paragraph of Article 176 of the Treaty.

7.2   The Plea of Illegality

THE TREATY OF ROME

Article 184.
Notwithstanding the expiry of the period laid down in the fifth paragraph of Article 173, any party may, in proceedings in which a regulation adopted jointly by the European Parliament and the Council, or a regulation of the Council, of the Commission, or of the ECB is at issue, plead the grounds specified in the second paragraph of Article 173 in order to invoke before the Court of Justice the inapplicability of that regulation.

7.3   Article 175

THE TREATY OF ROME

Article 175.
Should the European Parliament, the Council or the Commission, in infringement of this Treaty, fail to act, the Member States and the other institutions of the Community may bring an action before the Court of Justice to have the infringement established.

The action shall be admissible only if the institution concerned has first been called upon to act. If, within two months of being so called upon, the institution concerned has not defined its position, the action may be brought within a further period of two months.

Any natural or legal person may, under the conditions laid down in the preceding paragraphs, complain to the Court of Justice that an institution of the Community has failed to address to that person any act other than a recommendation or an opinion.

The Court of Justice shall have jurisdiction, under the same conditions, in actions or proceedings brought by the ECB in the areas falling within the latter's field of competence and in actions or proceedings brought against the latter.

7.3.1   MEANING OF 'FAIL TO ACT'

ALFONS LÜTTICKE GMBH AND OTHERS v COMMISSION (Case 48/65) [1966] ECR 19, Court of Justice

Lütticke made a formal application requiring the Commission to take infringement proceedings against Germany under Article 169 in respect of a German tax on imports of dried milk which the applicants alleged was contrary to Community law. The Commission disagreed and refused to take such proceedings. Lütticke then sought to challenge this refusal under Article 175.

It was held that the Commission had not 'failed to act' within the meaning of Article 175.

In their alternative conclusions the applicants complain of failure to act under Article 175.
The defendant claims that the alternative application is also inadmissible.
Under the terms of the second paragraph of Article 175, proceedings for failure to act may only be brought if at the end of a period of two months from being called upon to act the institution has not defined its position.
It is established that the Commission has defined its position and has notified this position to the applicants within the prescribed period.
The plea of inadmissibility is therefore well founded.

7.3.2   LOCUS STANDI

LORD BETHELL v COMMISSION (Case 246/81) [1982] ECR 2277, Court of Justice

Lord Bethell notified the Commission of alleged anti-competitive practices by European airlines and requested an inquiry and a Decision on the matter. When the Commission failed to take such action, Lord Bethell challenged this failure under Article 175.

It was held that Lord Bethell had no locus standi to challenge the Commission's alleged failure to act.

12.   According to the third paragraph of Article 175, any natural or legal person may, under the conditions laid down in that article, complain to the Court that an institution of the Community 'has failed to address to that person any act other than a recommendation or an opinion'.

13.   It appears from the provisions quoted that the applicant, for his application to be admissible, must be in a position to establish either that he is the addressee of a measure of the Commission having specific legal effects with regard to him, which is, as such, capable of being declared void, or that the Commission, having been duly called upon to act in pursuance of the second paragraph of Article 175, has failed to adopt in relation to him a measure which he was legally entitled to claim by virtue of the rules of Community law.

14.   In reply to a question from the Court the applicant stated that the measure to which he believed himself to be entitled was 'a response, an adequate answer to his complaint saying either that the Commission was going to act upon it or saying that it was not and, if not, giving reasons'. Alternatively the applicant took the view that the letter addressed to him on 17 July 1981 by the Director-General for Competition was to be described as an act against which proceedings may be instituted under the second paragraph of Article 173.

15.   The principal question to be resolved in this case is whether the Commission had, under the rules of Community law, the right and the duty to adopt in respect of the applicant a decision in the sense of the request made by the applicant to the Commission in his letter of 13 May 1981. It is apparent from the content of that letter and from the explanations given during the proceedings that the applicant is asking the Commission to undertake an investigation with regard to the airlines in the matter of the fixing of air fares with a view to a possible application to them of the provisions of the Treaty with regard to competition.

16.   It is clear therefore that the applicant is asking the Commission, not to take a decision in respect of him, but to open an inquiry with regard to third parties and to take decisions in respect of them. No doubt the applicant, in his double capacity as a user of the airlines and a leading member of an organization of users of air passenger services, has an indirect interest, as other users may have, in such proceedings and their possible outcome, but he is nevertheless not in the precise legal position of the actual addressee of a decision which may be declared void under the second paragraph of Article 173 or in that of the potential addressee of a legal measure which the Commission has a duty to adopt with regard to him, as is the position under the third paragraph of Article 175.

17.   It follows that the application is admissible from the point of view of both Article 175 and Article 173.

7.4   Relationship between Article 173 and Article 175

ERIDANIA AND OTHERS v COMMISSION (Joined Cases 10 & 18/68) [1969] ECR 459, Court of Justice

A number of sugar producers asked the Commission to annul a Decision granting aid to certain of their competitors. The Commission refused to do this and the producers then made both an Article 173 and an Article 175 application to the Court of Justice. (The Court joined the two cases.)

It was held that neither application should succeed.

Admissibility of Application 10/68

. . .

11.   It appears from these facts that such EAGGF aid as that granted by the contested decisions has no influence upon the distribution of quotas except to the extent to which the criteria adopted by the governments allow it.

Consequently this aid has no direct effect on the said distribution.

12.   The applicants have further alleged that the contested decisions, and in particular that concerning the Castiglion Fiorentino sugar refinery, influenced the distribution of the basic quantity by the Italian Government, by reason of the fact that they made the payment of aid subject to an undertaking from the said Government to allocate to the recipients a basic quota corresponding to their increased capacity.

13.   Nevertheless, the condition mentioned cannot be regarded as having determined the content of the criteria for distribution adopted by the Italian Government.

On the contrary, the Commission could not grant EAGGF aid without being previously assured of the conformity of these decisions with the distribution policy which the Italian Government intended to adopt in accordance with the regulations on the common organization of the market in sugar.

14.   The circumstances relied upon by the applicants do not, therefore, establish that the contested decisions were of direct and individual concern to them.

Consequently, and without its being necessary to consider the other submissions of inadmissibility, Application 10/68 must be held to be inadmissible.

Admissibility of Application 18/68

15.   This application concerns the annulment of the implied decision of rejection resulting from the silence maintained by the Commission in respect of the request addressed to it by the applicants seeking the annulment or revocation of the three disputed decisions for illegality or otherwise because they are inappropriate.

16.   The action provided for in Article 175 is intended to establish an illegal omission as appears from that article, which refers to a failure to act 'in infringement of this Treaty' and from Article 176 which refers to a failure to act declared to be 'contrary to this Treaty'.

Without stating under which provision of Community law the Commission was required to annul or revoke the said decisions, the applicants have confined themselves to alleging that those decisions were adopted in infringement of the Treaty and that this fact alone would thus suffice to make the Commission's failure to act subject to the provisions of Article 175.

17.   The Treaty provides, however, particularly in Article 173, other methods of recourse by which an allegedly illegal Community measure may be disputed and if necessary annulled on the application of a duly qualified party.

To admit, as the applicants wish to do, that the parties concerned could ask the institution from which the measure came to revoke it and, in the event of the Commission's failing to act, refer such failure to the Court as an illegal omission to deal with the matter would amount to providing them with a method of recourse parallel to that of Article 173, which would not be subject to the conditions laid down by the Treaty.

18.   This application does not therefore satisfy the requirements of Article 175 of the Treaty and must thus be held to be inadmissible.

7.5 End of Chapter Assessment Question

The Community operates a system of production licences, administered by the Member States, in respect of soft toys, in order to avoid the development of a soft toy mountain. The Council has recently issued a Regulation, which has immediate effect, prohibiting the grant of import licences in respect of cuddly penguins.

The two Community producers of cuddly penguins wish to challenge the Regulation.

Do they have *locus standi* to do so?

7.6 End of Chapter Assessment Outline Answer

Article 173 provides that as non-privileged applicants, individuals and companies may challenge only certain Community acts, and then only in certain circumstances. The producers in this case may challenge the Regulation only if they can show firstly that they are directly and individually concerned by it, and secondly that it is not a genuine Regulation but is really a disguised Decision.

In order to show direct concern, the producers must show that the act (the Regulation) had an effect on them (prohibited from producing goods) without any intervening action. Such intervening action has typically been in the form of a Member State's discretion in implementing the measure. For example, in the case of *UNICME*, the Court of Justice ruled that a Regulation subjecting imports of Japanese motorcycles into Italy to the grant of an import licence by the Italian authorities did not directly affect the applicant importers, since it was for the Italian authorities to grant or refuse licences. In contrast, in *Bock*, the German Government had already notified Bock that it would implement a Community Decision refusing him an import licence, if such a Decision were issued. The Court of Justice ruled that the Decision had direct effect on Bock, because the Court had already used its discretion.

In the present case it would appear that the Regulation does not leave any discretion to the Member States and that therefore the two producers are directly affected.

In order to show individual concern there are a number of possible tests. If the producers can show that all potential applicants in respect of the measure can be identified at the time it was passed, this will be sufficient to comply with the 'closed class' test. In *Plaumann*, the Court of Justice specified that the measure must affect the applicants as a result of certain attributes or circumstances which distinguished them from all others so as to identify them personally, just as if the measure had been addressed to them. In that case, a measure which affected clementine importers generally was held not to individually affect a particular clementine importer, since anyone could become involved in such a business. In the present case, it may be that the position is similar, since any producer of soft toy penguins would be affected, and the two producers are not sufficiently distinguished merely by being in that business.

The two producers could argue that the measure should be annulled insofar as it applies to existing producers, since they are distinguished by a 'factual' test. In the case of *Bock*, the measure was annulled insofar as it applied to those who had already applied for import licences. Similarly, in *Sofrimport*, the Court of Justice accepted that a Regulation suspending import licences could be annulled insofar as it applied to producers with goods in transit. In this case, the measure could be annulled insofar as it applies to existing producers. However, in *Unifruit Hellas*, on similar facts, the Court ruled that there was no individual concern because the Regulation there did not expressly require account to be taken of such producers.

On occasion the Court of Justice has imposed a third test, requiring that the wording as well as the effect of a Regulation, be specific. In *KSH*, the Court of Justice refused to classify a Regulation which applied to three or four companies only as a Decision, on the ground that its wording referred to a general category of persons, even though its practical application was more specific. If the Regulation simply applies to 'importers of cuddly penguins', it is unlikely that it will fulfil this test and therefore the producers will not be able to challenge it.

CHAPTER EIGHT

THE LIABILITY OF THE COMMUNITY

8.1 Introduction

W. van Gerven, 'Taking Article 215 EC Treaty Seriously', *New Directions in European Public Law*, Hart Publishing

THE REFERENCE TO ARTICLE 215 IS TOO LIMITED IN SCOPE

Let us first explore the scope of the ECJ's reference to 'Article 215 case law' in *Brasserie* (Joined Cases C–46 & 48/93 [1996] ECR I–1029), as it was made in connection with breaches of Community law by a national legislature. In its judgment, the Court distinguishes three points: (1) the existence of the principle of state liability (paragraphs 16 ff.); (2) the conditions for such liability to arise (paragraphs 37 ff.); and (3) the conditions under, and the extent to which the remedy of reparation is to be put into effect (paragraphs 67 ff. and paragraphs 81 ff.). The role assigned to Article 215 is different for each of these three points.

As for the *principle* itself, the reference is, and can only be, of an exemplary nature since Article 215 deals with breaches by Community institutions, and not with breaches emanating from national authorities. To find liability in a situation of legislative wrong by a Member State the ECJ explains that it must:

> rule on such a question in accordance with generally accepted methods of interpretation, in particular by reference to the fundamental principles of the Community legal system and, where necessary, general principles common to the legal systems of the Member States (paragraph 27).

The Court elicits that ruling as follows. First it states that Article 215 'is simply an expression of [a] general principle familiar to the legal systems of the Member States' (paragraph 29), whereby it refers undoubtedly to the liability of national public authorities *in general* to make good damage caused by an unlawful act or omission. Then it goes on to say, turning its attention to the *specific* situation of *legislative* wrong, that the principle of state liability holds good for any breach 'whatever be the organ of the State whose act or omission was responsible for the breach' (paragraph 32). The problem with the latter statement is that the Court could indeed draw inspiration from Article 215 to acknowledge the principle of state liability on behalf of all organs, including the legislature – since Article 215 applies to all Community institutions, that is including the Council and the Parliament – *but* that it could not draw inspiration from Article 215 in so far as it refers to general common principles – because it is generally not in accordance with the general principles common to the laws of the Member States to recognise liability for wrongs committed by the legislature proper. Therefore, to justify the extension of the principle of state liability to legislative wrongs proper, the Court had, on the one hand, to play down the role of general common principles of which the Court states, as recalled above, that they will only be used 'where necessary', and, on the other hand, to find other grounds of justification, namely 'the fundamental requirement of the Community legal order that Community law be uniformly applied' (paragraph 33), *and* the rules of international law which view a State 'as a single entity, irrespective of whether the breach . . . is attributable to the legislature, the judiciary or the executive' (paragraph 34).

As for the *conditions for state liability to arise*, particularly in a situation of legislative wrong, the ECJ felt more at ease in referring to Article 215 stating boldly that all breaches of Community law should be treated equally regardless, 'in the absence of particular justification', of whether a national authority or a Community authority is responsible for the breach (paragraph 42). To bolster that position the Court emphasises that it draws inspiration from general common principles not only in the area of Article 215 liability but also in other areas of Community law, by which it means in this connection the area of state liability (paragraph 41). For indeed, once it is accepted that the liability of Community institutions under Article 215 and the liability of Member States under *Francovich/Brasserie* are to be founded on the same general common principles, the conditions for such liability to arise must be the same under both regimes, at least in principle, that is 'in the absence of particular justification'.

Having said that, the ECJ enunciates three conditions to be met for Community law to confer a right to reparation:

the rule of law infringed must be intended to confer rights on individuals; the breach must be sufficiently serious; and there must be a *direct* causal link between the breach . . . and the damage sustained by the injured parties (paragraph 51, emphasis added).

Those conditions, the Court adds,

correspond in substance to those defined by the Court in relation to Article 215 in its case law on liability of the Community for damage caused to individuals by unlawful legislative measures adopted by its institutions (paragraph 53).

It is not the place here to go further into the substance of these conditions. A few remarks may suffice. Seen from the perspective of national laws, and from the Court's Article 215 case law itself, it is remarkable that the Court does not, at least not explicitly, name damage or injury as a condition for liability to arise, in addition to breach and causation – even though the condition of damage is a condition under the Court's Article 215 case law in accordance with the laws of the Member States. It is also interesting to note that the Court, in spite of its intention to interpret the liability conditions in the light of Article 215, does not follow that up when it deals with causation, without giving any 'particular justification' for it. On the contrary, in paragraph 65 of the *Brasserie* judgment, it states that 'it is for the national courts to determine whether there is a direct causal link between the breach of the obligation borne by the State and the damage . . .', by which the Court probably means that it is also for national law to determine whether there is such a causal link. It is also noteworthy that the Court, in order to define the first two conditions (i.e. that of a rule intending to confer rights on individuals *and* that the breach must be sufficiently serious), takes account only of the *Schöppenstedt* part of its case law and makes no effort whatever to take account of its Article 215 case law as a whole. We will deal with that point further on.

As for the conditions and the extent of the *remedy of compensation*, which the ECJ acknowledges exists as soon as the three aforementioned conditions are fulfilled, the Court no longer refers, again without 'particular justification', to Article 215, although its case law under that Article allows much inspiration to be drawn from it. It simply says that it is for the domestic rules on liability to determine the conditions for reparation (paragraph 67) as well as to set the criteria for determining the extent of reparation (paragraph 83) subject, however, in both cases to the principle of equality of treatment between Community based and similar domestic claims and to the principle of minimal effectiveness, i.e. that reparation must not in practice be made impossible or excessively difficult.

To conclude this point, it appears from the foregoing that the reference in *Brasserie* to Article 215 as a source of inspiration to elaborate the principle of state liability and the conditions for such liability to arise and for the remedy of compensation to apply is, to use a British understatement, rather limited in scope. The reference is made only to help the ECJ to define two out of the three conditions mentioned (breach of a rule intending to protect individuals and sufficiently serious fault). It is not used by the Court to define the third condition (causation), nor is it used to define the notion of damage or to establish the conditions and the extent of the remedy of compensation. The result is that much room is left to the national courts to define the conditions further, which does not help to ensure the uniform application of Community law throughout the Member States, a principle which the Court has repeatedly said is a fundamental requirement of Community law. It is our conviction that the ECJ should go further in making the conditions for state liability more uniform, at least if it wishes to protect individuals and enterprises in the different Member States alike or, in other words, if it wishes to maintain the uniformity of Community law also in its enforcement, provided however, as emphasised later on, that such uniformity must be the result of a genuine search for common general principles underlying the national legal systems. If the Court does not wish to use Article 215 any further than it has done so far, it must give a 'particular justification' for it, as it has itself emphasised in paragraph 42 of *Brasserie* (see above).

8.2   Contractual Liability

THE TREATY OF ROME

Article 215
The contractual liability of the Community shall be governed by the law applicable to the contract in question.

. . .

8.3   Non-contractual Liability

Article 215

. . .

In the case of non-contractual liability, the Community shall, in accordance with the general principles common to the laws of the Member States, make good any damage caused by its institutions or by its servants in the performance of their duties.

The preceding paragraph shall apply under the same conditions to damage caused by the ECB or by its servants in the performance of their duties.

The personal liability of its servants towards the Community shall be governed by the provisions laid down in their Staff Regulations or in the Conditions of Employment applicable to them.

THE TREATY OF ROME

Article 178.
The Court of Justice shall have jurisdiction in disputes relating to compensation for damage provided for in the second paragraph of Article 215.

8.3.1   GENERAL PRINCIPLES

ALFONS LÜTTICKE v *COMMISSION* (Case 4/69) [1971] ECR 325, Court of Justice

Lütticke alleged that a German levy on its imports was contrary to Community law, and requested the Commission to bring proceedings against the German government. The Commission refused to do this and Lütticke brought an Article 215 action to recover damages caused by the Commission's inaction.

It was held that damages could not be awarded because the Commission's conduct had not been illegal.

10.   By virtue of the second paragraph of Article 215 and the general principles to which this provision refers, the liability of the Community presupposes the existence of a set of circumstances comprising actual damage, a causal link between the damage claimed and the conduct alleged against the institution, and the illegality of such conduct.

8.3.1.1   Actual damage

GAEC v *COUNCIL AND COMMISSION* (Case 253/84) [1987] ECR 123, Court of Justice

A Decision provided subsidies to German farmers. French farmers brought an Article 215 action claiming damages for losses caused to them by competition from subsidised German agricultural products.
   It was held that damages would not be awarded.

9.   With a view to considering whether the action is well founded it is appropriate to recall the conditions in which the Community may be held to be liable under the second paragraph of Article 215 of the EEC Treaty. The Court has consistently held (judgment of 2 July 1974 in Case 153/73 *Holtz & Willemsen GmbH* v *Council and Commission* [1974] ECR 675; and judgment of 4 March 1980 in Case 49/79 *Richard Pool* v *Council* [1980] ECR 569) that Community liability depends on the coincidence of a set of conditions as regards the unlawfulness of the acts alleged against the institution, the fact of damage, and the existence of a direct link in the chain of causality between the wrongful act and the damage complained of.
   10.   It is in the light of those criteria that the merits of the case must be assessed. It must be observed that the applicant has sought mainly to show that Council Decision 84/361 was unlawful and has developed a number of arguments in that connection, whereas as regards the fact of the damage and the existence of a causal link between that decision and the damage complained of, its allegations are imprecise. The first point to be considered, therefore, is whether the applicant has made out the fact of the damage for which it is seeking compensation and, if so, whether there is a causal link between the decision and that damage.
   11.   The preliminary observation may be made that GAEC maintains that the damage for which compensation is sought arose because the aid granted to German farmers by virtue of Decision 84/361 enabled those farmers to reduce their prices and hence to increase very substantially their exports to France of beef and veal, milk and poultry, triggering a fall in prices on the French market.
   12.   As regards the fact of the damage, although GAEC provisionally set an estimate of FF 60,000 on the damage which it allegedly suffered in respect of all of its products up to the date on which the application was brought, it has since provided no particulars of its losses on sales of milk and poultry, even though the Court asked it to provide figures, at least for the second half of 1984, for the damage suffered by it as a result of the discrimination caused by the contested aid.
   13.   In those circumstances it must be held that, as far as milk and poultry are concerned, GAEC has not proved that it has suffered damage.

Contributory negligence

ADAMS v COMMISSION (Case 145/83) [1985] ECR 3539, Court of Justice

Adams supplied the Commission with confidential information concerning breaches of Community competition law by his employer, Hoffman-La Roche. In the course of proceedings, the Commission gave papers to Hoffman-La Roche which enabled it to identify Adams as the source of the leak, and then failed to warn Adams that Hoffman-La Roche was planning to prosecute him. When Adams returned to Switzerland, he was arrested and convicted of industrial espionage. Adams sought damages under Article 215.

It was held that damages would be awarded to Adams but would be reduced.

34. As regards the existence of a duty of confidentiality it must be pointed out that Article 214 of the EEC Treaty lays down an obligation, in particular for the members and the servants of the institutions of the Community 'not to disclose information of the kind covered by the obligation of professional secrecy, in particular information about undertakings, their business relations or their cost components'. Although that provision primarily refers to information gathered from undertakings, the expression 'in particular' shows that the principle in question is a general one which applies also to information supplied by natural persons, if that information is 'of the kind' that is confidential. That is particularly so in the case of information supplied on a purely voluntary basis but accompanied by a request for confidentiality in order to protect the informant's anonymity. An institution which accepts such information is bound to comply with such a condition.

35. As regards the case before the Court, it is quite clear from the applicant's letter of 25 February 1973 that he requested the Commission not to reveal his identity. It cannot therefore be denied that the Commission was bound by a duty of confidentiality towards the applicant in that respect. In fact the parties disagree not so much as to the existence of such a duty but as to whether the Commission was bound by a duty of confidentiality after the applicant had left his employment with Roche.

36. In that respect it must be pointed out that the applicant did not qualify his request by indicating a period upon the expiry of which the Commission would be released from its duty of confidentiality regarding the identity of its informant. No such indication can be inferred from the fact that the applicant was prepared to appear before any court after he had left Roche. The giving of evidence before a court implies that the witness has been duly summoned, that he is under a duty to answer the questions put to him, and is, in return, entitled to all the guarantees provided by a judicial procedure. The applicant's offer to confirm the accuracy of his information under such conditions cannot therefore be interpreted as a general statement releasing the Commission from its duty of confidentiality. Nor can any such intention be inferred from the applicant's subsequent conduct.

37. It must therefore be stated that the Commission was under a duty to keep the applicant's identity secret even after he had left his employer.

38. Of the events mentioned by the applicant, the only occasion on which the Commission directly revealed the identity of its informant was the telephone conversation between Mr Schlieder and Dr Alder at the beginning of February 1975. However, that conversation took place after the applicant had caused an anonymous letter to be sent to the Commission informing it of his detention and seeking its help. It is difficult to see how the Commission could have acted on that request without confirming, at least by implication, that the applicant was indeed its informant. Moreover, it transpired subsequently that at that time the applicant had already admitted to the Swiss police that he had given information, at least orally, to the Commission and it is clear from the decisions of the Swiss courts that the confirmation of the fact by Mr Schlieder did not have a decisive bearing on the applicant's conviction. The disclosure of the applicant's identity at that time and in those circumstances cannot be regarded as constituting a breach of the duty of confidentiality which could give rise to the Commission's liability *vis-à-vis* the applicant.

39. On the other hand, it is clear that the handing over of the edited photocopies to members of the staff of the Roche subsidiaries enabled Roche to identify the applicant as the main suspect in the complaint which it lodged with the Swiss Public Prosecutor's Office. It was therefore that handing over of the documents which led to the applicant's arrest and which in addition supplied the police and the Swiss courts with substantial evidence against him.

40. It appears from the documents before the Court that the Commission was fully aware of the risk that the handing over to Roche of the photocopies supplied by the applicant might reveal the informant's identity to the company. For that reason the Commission officials first attempted to obtain other copies of the documents in question from the Roche subsidiaries in Paris and Brussels. When that attempt failed, the Commission prepared new copies of the documents which it considered were the least

likely to lead to the discovery of the applicant's identity and it took care to remove from those copies any indication which it considered might reveal the source of the documents. However, since it was not familiar with Roche's practices regarding the distribution of the documents in question within the company, the Commission could not be sure that those precautions were sufficient to eliminate all risk of the applicant's being identified by means of the copies handed over to Roche. The Commission was therefore, in any event, imprudent in handing over those copies to Roche without having consulted the applicant.

41.   It is not however necessary to decide whether, in view of the situation at the time and in particular of the information in the Commission's possession, the handing over of the documents is sufficient to give rise to the Commission's liability regarding the consequences of the applicant's being identified as the informant. Although the Commission was not necessarily aware, when those documents were handed over, of the gravity of the risk to which it was exposing the applicant, Dr Alder's visit on 8 November 1974, on the other hand, provided it with all the necessary information in that respect. Following that visit the Commission knew that Roche was determined to discover how the Commission had come into possession of the documents in question and that it was preparing to lay a complaint against the informant under Article 273 of the Swiss Penal Code, the contents of which Dr Alder even took care to explain. The Commission also knew that there was a possibility of obtaining from Roche, in return for the disclosure of the informant's identity, an undertaking not to take action against him. It could not however pursue that possibility without the applicant's consent.

42.   In those circumstances it was not at all sufficient for the Commission merely to take the view that it was unlikely that the applicant would be identified, that he was probably never going to return to Switzerland and that, in any event, the Swiss authorities did not intend to institute criminal proceedings against him. On the contrary, the Commission was under a duty to take every possible step to warn the applicant, thereby enabling him to make his own arrangements in the light of the information given by Dr Alder, and to consult him as to the approach to be adopted in relation to Dr Alder's proposals.

43.   Although the appplicant had not left any precise address making it possible for the Commission to contact him easily, in his letter of 25 February 1973 he had already indicated his intention of setting up his own meat business in Italy, near Rome. Even in the absence of other indications, that information would have enabled the Commission to make inquiries with a view to discovering where the applicant was staying. It is common ground that the Commission did not even attempt to find the applicant although it allowed almost one month to elapse before communicating to Dr Alder its final refusal to discuss the origin of the documents in its possession, a refusal which was followed by the lodging of Roche's complaint at the Swiss Public Prosecutor's Office.

44.   It must therefore be concluded that, by failing to make all reasonable efforts to pass on to the applicant the information which was available to it following Dr Alder's visit of 8 November 1974, even though the communication of that information might have prevented, or at least limited, the damage which was likely to result from the discovery of the applicant's identity by means of the documents which it had handed over to Roche, the Commission has incurred liability towards the applicant in respect of that damage.

. . .

Damages

53.   It must therefore be concluded that in principle the Community is bound to make good the damage resulting from the discovery of the applicant's identity by means of the documents handed over to Roche by the Commission. It must however be recognised that the extent of the Commission's liability is diminished by reason of the applicant's own negligence. The applicant failed to inform the Commission that it was possible to infer his identity as the informant from the documents themselves, although he was in the best position to appreciate and to avert that risk. Nor did he ask the Commission to keep him informed of the progress of the investigation of Roche, and in particular of any use that might be made of the documents for that purpose. Lastly, he went back to Switzerland without attempting to make any inquiries in that respect, although he must

have been aware of the risks to which his conduct towards his former employer had exposed him with regard to Swiss legislation.

54. Consequently, the applicant himself contributed significantly to the damage which he suffered. In assessing the conduct of the Commission on the one hand and that of the applicant on the other, the Court considers it equitable to apportion responsibility for that damage equally between the two parties.

55. It follows from all the foregoing considerations that the Commission must be ordered to compensate the applicant to the extent of one half of the damage suffered by him as a result of the fact that he was identified as the source of information regarding Roche's anti-competitive practices. For the rest, however the application must be dismissed. The amount of the damages is to be determined by agreement between the parties or, failing such agreement, by the Court.

Duty to mitigate any loss

MULDER AND OTHERS v COUNCIL AND COMMISSION
(Joined Cases C–104/89 & C–37/90) [1992] ECR I-3061, Court of Justice

A Regulation allocated milk quotas to producers on the basis of the previous year's production. A number of producers, such as Mulder, had not produced any milk in the previous year as a result of a Community agreement to reduce over-production, and so a second Regulation was introduced which provided quotas for these producers, but at a lower rate than for other producers. The producers then claimed damages under Article 215.

It was held that reduced damages would be awarded in respect of the first Regulation, but no damages at all would be awarded in the respect of the second Regulation.

26. As regards the extent of the damage which the Community should make good, in the absence of particular circumstances warranting a different assessment, account should be taken of the loss of earnings consisting in the difference between, on the one hand, the income which the applicants would have obtained in the normal course of events from the milk deliveries which they would have made if, during the period between 1 April 1984 (the date of entry into force of Regulation No. 857/84) and 29 March 1989 (the date of entry into force of Regulation No. 764/89), they had obtained the reference quantities to which they were entitled and, on the other hand, the income which they actually obtained from milk deliveries made during that period in the absence of any reference quantity, plus any income which they obtained, or could have obtained, during that period from any replacement activities.
. . .

32. The basis which should be taken for calculating the income which the applicants would have received in the normal course of events if they had made milk deliveries corresponding to the reference quantities to which they were entitled is the profitability of a farm representative of the type of farm run by each of the applicants, it being understood that account can be taken in that regard of the reduced profitability generally shown by such a farm during the period when milk production is started up.

33. As regards income from any replacement activities which is to be deducted from the hypothetical income referred to above, it must be noted that that income must be taken to include not only that which the applicants actually obtained from replacement activities, but also that income which they could have obtained had they reasonably engaged in such activities. This conclusion must be reached in the light of a general principle common to the legal systems of the Member States to the effect that the injured party must show reasonable diligence in limiting the extent of his loss or risk having to bear the damage himself. Any operating losses incurred by the applicants in carrying out such a replacement activity cannot be attributed to the Community, since the origin of such losses does not lie in the effects of the Community rules.

34. It follows that the amount of compensation payable by the Community should correspond to the damage which it caused. The defendant institutions' contention that the amount of the compensation should be calculated on the basis of the amount of the non-marketing premium paid to each of the applicants must therefore be rejected. It must

be noted in this regard that that premium constitutes the *quid pro quo* for the non-marketing undertaking and has no connection with the damage which the applicants suffered owing to the application of the rules on the additional levy, which were adopted at a later date.

8.3.1.2   Wrongful acts

General legislative measures

ZUCKERFABRIK SCHÖPPENSTEDT v COUNCIL (Case 5/71) [1971] ECR 975, Court of Justice

German sugar producers alleged that a Regulation imposing minimum and maximum prices for raw sugar was discriminatory as between different producers and that damages should therefore be awarded under Article 215.

It was held that damages would not be awarded.

11.   In the present case the non-contractual liability of the Community presupposes at the very least the unlawful nature of the act alleged to be the cause of the damage. Where legislative action involving measures of economic policy is concerned, the Community does not incur noncontractual liability for damage suffered by individuals as a consequence of that action, by virtue of the provisions contained in Article 215, second paragraph, of the Treaty, unless a sufficiently flagrant violation of a superior rule of law for the protection of the individual has occurred. For that reason the Court, in the present case, must first consider whether such a violation has occurred.

12.   Regulation No. 769/68 was adopted pursuant to Article 37(1) of Regulation No. 1009/67 which requires the Council to adopt provisions concerning the measures needed to offset the difference between national sugar prices and prices valid from 1 July 1968, and it authorizes the Member State in which the price of white sugar is higher than the target price to grant compensation for such quantities of white sugar and raw sugar which are in free circulation in its territory at 0.00 hours on 1 July 1968. The applicant points out that as regards Member States with a low price this regulation provides for the payment of dues on sugar stocks only if the previous prices were less than the intervention price valid from 1 July 1968 and concludes from this that by adopting different criteria for the right to compensation of sugar producers in a Member State with high prices, the regulation infringes the provision of the last subparagraph of Article 40(3) of the Treaty according to which any common price policy shall be based on common criteria and uniform methods of calculation.

13.   The difference referred to does not constitute discrimination because it is the result of a new system of common organization of the market in sugar which does not recognise a single fixed price but has a maximum and minimum price and lays down a framework of prices within which the level of actual prices depends on the development of the market. Thus it is not possible to challenge the justification of transitional rules which proceeded on the basis that where the previous prices were already within the framework set up they must be governed by market forces and which therefore required the payment of dues only in cases where the previous prices were still too low to come within the new framework of prices and authorized compensation only in cases where the previous prices were too high to come within the said framework.

14.   In addition, having regard to the special features of the system established with effect from 1 July 1968, the Council by adopting Regulation No. 769/68 satisfied the requirements of Article 37 of Regulation No. 1009/67.

15.   It is also necessary to dismiss the applicant's claim that Regulation No. 769/68 infringed the provisions of Article 40 of the Treaty because the method of calculating the compensation and dues for the raw sugar stocks was derived from that adopted for white sugar, which could, according to the applicant, result in the unequal treatment of the producers of raw sugar. Although, relying on hypothetical cases, the applicant stated that the calculation methods selected did not necessarily lead to uniform results with regard to producers of raw sugar, it was not proved that this could have been the case on 1 July 1968.

16.   The applicant's action founded upon the Council's liability does not therefore satisfy the first condition mentioned above and must be dismissed.

BAYERISCHE HNL VERMEHRUNGSBETREIBE GMBH & CO. KG AND OTHERS v COUNCIL AND COMMISSION ('SECOND SKIMMED MILK POWDER') (Cases 83 & 94/76, 4, 15 & 40/77) [1978] ECR 1209, Court of Justice

A Regulation provided for the compulsory purchase of skimmed milk powder for use in animal feedstuffs. In rulings under Article 177, the Court of Justice had held this Regulation be void for discrimination and lack of proportionality. Poultry producers then claimed damages against the Community under Article 215 for the increased price of animal feed.

It was held that the Community was not liable because there had been no sufficiently flagrant breach of a superior rule of law for the protection of the individual.

4.   The finding that a legislative measure such as the regulation in question is null and void is however insufficient by itself for the Community to incur non-contractual liability for damage caused to individuals under the second paragraph of Article 215 of the EEC Treaty. The Court of Justice has consistently stated that the Community does not incur liability on account of a legislative measure which involves choices of economic policy unless a sufficiently serious breach of a superior rule of law for the protection of the individual has occurred.

5.   In the present case there is no doubt that the prohibition on discrimination laid down in the second subparagraph of the third paragraph of Article 40 of the Treaty and infringed by Regulation No. 563/76 is in fact designed for the protection of the individual, and that it is impossible to disregard the importance of this prohibition in the system of the Treaty. To determine what conditions must be present in addition to such breach for the Community to incur liability in accordance with the criterion laid down in the case law of the Court of Justice it is necessary to take into consideration the principles in the legal systems of the Member States governing the liability of public authorities for damage caused to individuals by legislative measures. Although these principles vary considerably from one Member State to another, it is however possible to state that the public authorities can only exceptionally and in special circumstances incur liability for legislative measures which are the result of choices of economic policy. This restrictive view is explained by the consideration that the legislative authority, even where the validity of its measures is subject to judicial review, cannot always be hindered in making its decisions by the prospect of applications for damages whenever it has occasion to adopt legislative measures in the public interest which may adversely affect the interests of individuals.

6.   It follows from these considerations that individuals may be required, in the sectors coming within the economic policy of the Community, to accept within reasonable limits certain harmful effects on their economic interests as a result of a legislative measure without being able to obtain compensation from public funds even if that measure has been declared null and void. In a legislative field such as the one in question, in which one of the chief features is the exercise of a wide discretion essential for the implementation of the Common Agricultural Policy, the Community does not therefore incur liability unless the institution concerned has manifestly and gravely disregarded the limits on the exercise of its powers.

7.   This is not so in the case of a measure of economic policy such as that in the present case, in view of its special features. In this connexion it is necessary to observe first that this measure affected very wide categories of traders, in other words all buyers of compound feeding-stuffs containing protein, so that its effects on individual undertakings were considerably lessened. Moreover, the effects of the regulation on the price of feeding-stuffs as a factor in the production costs of those buyers were only limited since that price rose by little more than 2%. This price increase was particularly small in comparison with the price increases resulting, during the period of application of the regulation, from the variations in the world market prices of feeding-stuffs containing protein, which were three or four times higher than the increase resulting from the obligation to purchase skimmed-milk powder introduced by the regulation. The effects

of the regulation on the profit-earning capacity of the undertakings did not ultimately exceed the bounds of the economic risks inherent in the activities of the agricultural sectors concerned.

8. In these circumstances the fact that the regulation is null and void is insufficient for the Community to incur liability under the second paragraph of Article 215 of the Treaty. The application must therefore be dismissed as unfounded.

DUMORTIER FRÈRES SA AND OTHERS v COUNCIL (Cases 64 and 113/76) [1979] ECR 3091, Court of Justice

A Regulation abolished production refunds for maize gritz but not for maize starch, which was a competing product. Both products were used in brewing and in baking, and were in direct competition. The maize gritz producers sought damages under Article 215.

It was held that damages would be awarded, but only for certain losses.

10. In the circumstances of these cases, the Court is led to the conclusion that there was on the part of the Council such a grave and manifest disregard of the limits on the exercise of its discretionary powers in matters of the Common Agricultural Policy. In this regard the Court notes the following findings in particular.

11. In the first place it is necessary to take into consideration that the principle of equality, embodied in particular in the second subparagraph of Article 40(3) of the EEC Treaty, which prohibits any discrimination in the common organisation of the agricultural markets, occupies a particularly important place among the rules of Community law intended to protect the interests of the individual. Secondly, the disregard of that principle in this case affected a limited and clearly defined group of commercial operators. It seems, in fact, that the applicants in these cases and in the related Cases 241/78 and others *Deutsche Getreideverwertung und Rheinische Kraftfutterwerk GmbH and Others v Council and Commission* [1979] ECR 3017 comprise the entire maize gritz industry of the Community. Further, the damage alleged by the applicants goes beyond the bounds of economic risks inherent in the activities in the sector concerned. Finally, equality of treatment with the producers of maize starch, which had been observed from the beginning of the common organization of the market in cereals, was ended by the Council in 1975 without sufficient justification.

12. The Council's disregard of the limits imposed upon its discretionary power is rendered all the more manifest by the fact that, as the Court pointed out in its judgment of 19 October 1977, the Council has not acted upon a proposal made by the Commission in June 1975 to re-introduce the funds for maize gritz on the ground that the absence of such refunds could foreseeably upset the balance between the breweries' raw materials costs in maize gritz and maize starch.

13. For those reasons the Court arrives at the conclusion that the Community incurs liability for the abolition of the refunds for maize gritz under Regulation No. 665/75 of the Council.

MULDER AND OTHERS v COUNCIL AND COMMISSION (Joined Cases C-104/89 & C-37/90) [1992] ECR I-3061, Court of Justice

For the facts, see **8.3.1.1** above.

12. The second paragraph of Article 215 of the Treaty provides that, in the case of non-contractual liability, the Community, in accordance with the general principles common to the laws of the Member States, is to make good any damage caused by its institutions in the performance of their duties. The scope of that provision has been specified in the sense that the Community does not incur liability on account of a legislative measure involving choices of economic policy unless a sufficiently serious breach of a superior rule of law for the protection of the individual has occurred (see, in particular, the judgment in Joined Cases 83 and 94/76, 4, 15 and 40/77 *HNL v Council and Commission* [1978] ECR 1209, paragraphs 4, 5 and 6). More specifically, in a legislative field such as the one in question, which is characterized by the exercise of a wide discretion essential for the implementation of the Common Agricultural Policy, the Community cannot incur liability unless the institution concerned has manifestly and

gravely disregarded the limits on the exercise of its powers (see in particular the judgment in *HNL* v *Commission and Council*, paragraph 6).

13.   The Court has also consistently held that, in order for the Community to incur non-contractual liability, the damage alleged must go beyond the bounds of the normal economic risks inherent in the activities in the sector concerned.

. . .

14.   Those conditions are fulfilled in the case of Regulation No. 857/84 as supplement-ed by Regulation No. 1371/84.

. . .

18.   In contrast, contrary to the applicants' assertions, the Community cannot incur liability on account of the fact that Regulation No. 764/89 introduced the 60% rule.

19.   Admittedly, that rule also infringes the legitimate expectation of the producers concerned with regard to the limited nature of their non-marketing or conversion undertaking, as the Court held in the judgments in *Spagl* and *Pastätter*, cited above. However, the breach of the principle of the protection of legitimate expectations which was held to exist cannot be described as being sufficiently serious within the meaning of the case-law on the non-contractual liability of the Community.

20.   In that regard, it must be borne in mind first that, unlike the 1984 rules, which made it impossible for the producers concerned to market milk, the 60% rule enabled those traders to resume their activities as milk producers. Consequently, in the amending regulation, Regulation No. 764/89, the Council did not fail to take the situation of the producers concerned into account.

21.   Secondly, it must be observed that, by adopting Regulation No. 764/89 following the judgments of 28 April 1988 in *Mulder* and *von Deetzen*, cited above, the Community legislature made an economic policy choice with regard to the manner in which it was necessary to implement the principles set out in those judgments. That was based, on the one hand, on the 'overriding necessity of not jeopardizing the fragile stability that currently obtains in the milk products sector' (fifth recital in the preamble to Regulation No. 764/89) and, on the other, on the need to strike a balance between the interests of the producers concerned and the interests of the other producers subject to the scheme. The Council made that choice in such a way as to maintain the level of other producers' reference quantities unchanged while increasing the Community reserve by 600,000 tonnes, or 60% of aggregate foreseeable applications for the allocation of special reference quantities, which, in its view, was the highest quantity compatible with the aims of the scheme. Accordingly, the Council took account of a higher public interest, without gravely and manifestly disregarding the limits of its discretionary power in this area.

22.   In the light of the foregoing, it must therefore be held that the Community is bound to make good the damage suffered by the applicants as a result of the application of Regulation No. 857/84, as supplemented by Regulation No. 1371/84, cited above, but not the damage resulting from the application of Regulation No. 764/89, cited above.

AMYLUM NV AND TUNNEL REFINERIES LIMITED v *COUNCIL AND COMMISSION* (Joined Cases 116 & 124/77) [1979] ECR 3479, Court of Justice

KONINKLIJKE SCHOLTEN HONIG NV v *COUNCIL AND COMMISSION* (Case 43/77) [1979] ECR 3583, Court of Justice

A Regulation imposing a production levy on isoglucose had been ruled invalid by the Court in an Article 177 reference. There were only three or four isoglucose producers in the Community and the effect of the levies had been severe that one producer had been forced to close down its isoglucose business altogether. The producers, therefore, brought an action for damages under Article 215.

(Apart from the recital of the facts and the numbering of the paragraphs, the two judgments are identical.)

It was held that damages would not be awarded.

12.   Since the Court has already established in its judgment of 25 October 1978 that the imposition of an isoglucose production levy of five units of account per 100 kg. of

dry matter was incompatible with the principle of equality, the first question which arises in these cases is whether that illegality is such as to involve the Community in liability under the second paragraph of Article 215 of the Treaty.

13. A finding that a legal situation resulting from legislative measures by the Community is illegal is insufficient by itself to involve it in liability. The Court has already stated this in its judgment of 25 May 1978 in Joined Cases 83/76 and Others, *Bayerische HNL & Others* v *Council and Commission* ([1978] ECR 1209). In this connection the Court referred to its consistent case law in accordance with which the Community does not incur liability on account of a legislative measure which involves choices of economic policy unless a sufficiently serious breach of a superior rule of law for the protection of the individual has occurred. Having regard to the principles in the legal systems of the Member States, governing the liability of public authorities for damage caused to individuals by legislative measures, the Court has stated that in the context of Community legislation in which one of the chief features is the exercise of a wide discretion essential for the implementation of the Common Agricultural Policy, the liability of the Community can arise only exceptionally in cases in which the institution concerned has manifestly and gravely disregarded the limits on the exercise of its powers.

14. This is confirmed in particular by the fact that, even though an action for damages under Articles 178 and 215 of the Treaty constitutes an independent action, it must nevertheless be assessed having regard to the whole of the system of legal protection of individuals set up by the Treaty. If an individual takes the view that he is injured by a Community legislative measure which he regards as illegal he has the opportunity, when the implementation of the measure is entrusted to national authorities, to contest the validity of the measure, at the time of its implementation, before a national court in an action against the national authority. Such a court may, or even must, in pursuance of Article 177, refer to the Court of Justice a question on the validity of the Community measure in question. The existence of such an action is by itself of such a nature as to ensure the efficient protection of the individuals concerned.

15. These considerations are of importance where, as in these cases, the Court, within the framework of a reference for a preliminary ruling, has declared a production levy to be illegal and where the competent institution, following that finding, has abolished the levy concerned with retroactive effect.

16. It is appropriate to enquire in the light of these considerations whether, in the circumstances of these cases, there has been, on the part of the Council and the Commission, a grave and manifest disregard of the limits which they are required to observe in exercising their discretion within the framework of the Common Agriculture Policy.

17. In this respect it must be recalled that the Court did not declare invalid any isoglucose production levy but only the method of calculation adopted and the fact that the levy applied to the whole of the isoglucose production. Having regard to the fact that the production of isoglucose was playing a part in increasing sugar surpluses it was permissible for the Council to impose restrictive measures on such production.

18. Although, in its judgment of 25 October 1978, giving a preliminary ruling within the framework of a consideration of the validity of Regulation 1111/77, the Court found that the charges borne in pursuance of that regulation by isoglucose producers by way of production levy were manifestly unequal as compared with those imposed on sugar producers, it does not follow that, for the purposes of an assessment of the illegality of the measure in connexion with Article 215 of the Treaty, the Council has manifestly and gravely disregarded the limits on the exercise of its discretion.

19. In fact, even though the fixing of the isoglucose production levy at five units of account per 100 kg. of dry matter was vitiated by errors, it must nevertheless be pointed out that, having regard to the fact that an appropriate levy was fully justified, these were not errors of such gravity that it may be said that the conduct of the defendant institutions in this respect was verging on the arbitrary and was thus of such a kind as to involve the Community in non-contractual liability.

20. It must also be recalled that Regulation 1111/77 was adopted in particular to deal with an emergency situation characterised by growing surpluses of sugar and in circumstances which, in accordance with the principles set out in Article 39 of the Treaty

permitted a certain preference in favour of sugar beet, Community production of which was in surplus, whilst Community production of maize was to a considerable extent in deficit.

21. It follows from these considerations that the Council and the Commission did not disregard the limits which they were required to observe in the exercise of their discretion in the context of the Common Agriculture Policy in such a serious manner as to incur the non-contractual liability of the Community.

22. The application must be dismissed as unfounded.

ROQUETTE FRÈRES SA v *COMMISSION* (Case 20/88) [1989] ECR 1553, Court of Justice

A Regulation which provided for compensation to be given or levies imposed on agriculture imports and exports, in order to iron out the effects of exchange rate fluctuations had been declared invalid in earlier proceedings. Roquette Frères claimed damages under Article 215 in respect of payments which it had had to make under the invalid Regulation.

It was held that although the Regulation was invalid, damages would not be awarded.

(d) The damage arising through loss of profit

21. The applicant refers in the second place to the real damage which it allegedly suffered in the form of a considerable loss of profit. It maintains that the effects of a difference between the rate of monetary compensatory amounts actually applied and the lawful rate are always twofold since when one trader pays too much another trader receives too much. Moreover, since the price of the goods subject to the monetary compensatory amounts is unregulated, the applicant was unable to pass on to its purchasers the adverse incidence of those amounts; it was therefore compelled to align its prices with those of its competitors, in particular with those of companies established in Member States with strong currencies.

22. The amount advanced in this respect, calculated on the basis of the exchange rates ruling on the day of the hearing, represents about 52% of the total claim of ECU 10 million. However, it must be pointed out that the applicant has given no indication of the manner in which that amount was calculated and that, both in its pleadings and at the hearing, it merely repeated that the rate of the monetary compensatory amounts not only placed certain undertakings at a disadvantage but, by the same token, also placed other undertakings at an advantage.

23. The Court has consistently held that the Community's non-contractual liability cannot be incurred through the adoption of a legislative measure involving a choice of economic policy unless a sufficiently flagrant violation of a superior rule of law for the protection of the individual has occurred. In a legislative context characterized by a wide margin of discretion, which is essential for the implementation of the common agricultural policy, such liability can therefore be incurred only if the institution concerned has manifestly and gravely disregarded the limits on the exercise of its powers (judgment of 25 May 1978 in Joined Cases 83 and 94/76, 4, 15, and 40/77 *Bayerische HNL* v *Commission* [1978] ECR 1209).

24. It is therefore necessary to consider the nature of the rule which, according to the judgment in Case 145/79, was infringed by the fixing of the monetary compensatory amounts applicable to starch products. It is contained, for the most part, in Article 2(2) of Regulation No. 974/71 of the Council of 12 May 1971 on certain measures of conjunctural policy to be taken in agriculture following the temporary widening of the margins of fluctuation for the currencies of certain Member States (Official Journal, English Special Edition 1971 (I), p. 257), the basic regulation concerning monetary compensatory amounts. Under that provision, the monetary compensatory amounts applicable to products processed from maize or wheat must be equal to the incidence, on the product concerned, of the application of the compensatory amount to the price of the basic product.

25. The Court has admitted that the calculation of that incidence raised difficult technical and economic problems regarding products whose manufacturing process and composition might vary in different regions of the Community. However, it took the

view that the Commission, in fixing the monetary compensatory amounts applicable to starch products, had made errors of calculation resulting in the fixing of amounts much higher than those corresponding to the incidence of the amounts applicable to the basic products and that it had thus exceeded the limits of its discretion. Those errors related in particular to the supply price of the maize and wheat used for the production of starch, the total of the amounts applicable to all the by-products obtained from the same quantity of maize or wheat in a specified manufacturing process, and the alignment of the amounts applicable to potato starch with those applicable to maize starch.

26.   It is apparent from the foregoing considerations that the fixing of the contested monetary compensatory amounts resulted from a technical error which, even if it led *de facto* to unequal treatment for certain producers established in countries with weak currencies, cannot be considered to constitute a serious breach of a superior rule of law for the protection of the individual or a manifest and grave disregard by the Commission of the limits of its discretion.

27.   Since the conditions for the Community to incur non-contractual liability under the second paragraph of Article 215 of the Treaty for unlawful legislative action are not satisfied, the action must be dismissed in its entirety.

SOFRIMPORT v *COMMISSION* (Case C–152/88) [1990] ECR I–2477, Court of Justice

For the facts, see **7.1.4.2** above.

26.   It should be observed first that the purpose of the first subparagraph of Article 3(3) of Regulation No. 2707/72 is to protect traders who import goods covered by that regulation into the Community from the unfavourable consequences of protective measures which might be adopted by the Community institutions. That provision thus gives rise to a legitimate expectation the disregard of which constitutes a breach of that superior rule of law.

27.   Secondly, it must be held that by failing completely to take account of the position of traders such as Sofrimport, without invoking any overriding public interest, the Commission committed a sufficiently serious breach of Article 3(3) of Regulation No. 2707/72.

28.   Thirdly, the damage alleged by Sofrimport goes beyond the limits of the economic risks inherent in the business in issue inasmuch as the purpose of that provision is precisely to limit those risks with regard to goods in transit.

29.   Consequently, the Community must make good the damage caused to Sofrimport by the adoption of the contested regulations.

CNTA SA v *COMMISSION* (Case 74/74) [1975] ECR 533, Court of Justice

A Regulation abolished, without warning, compensation for the effect of exchange rate fluctuations on trade in colza and rape seeds. One of the traders affected by the abolition claimed damages under Article 215.

It was held that damages would be awarded.

39.   The conditions governing the application and abolition of the system of compensatory amounts in a specific sector do not take into account the individual situations of traders and do not guarantee to them a continuous application of the system.

40.   It follows that the system of compensatory amounts cannot be considered to be tantamount to a guarantee for traders against the risks of alteration of exchange rates.

41.   Nevertheless the application of the compensatory amounts in practice avoids the exchange risk, so that a trader, even a prudent one, might be induced to omit to cover himself against such risk.

42.   In these circumstances, a trader may legitimately expect that for transactions irrevocably undertaken by him because he has obtained, subject to a deposit, export licences fixing the amount of the refund in advance, no unforeseeable alteration will occur which could have the effect of causing him inevitable loss, by re-exposing him to the exchange risk.

43.   The Community is therefore liable if, in the absence of an overriding matter of public interest, the Commission abolished with immediate effect and without warning

the application of compensatory amounts in a specific sector without adopting transitional measures which would at least permit traders either to avoid the loss which would have been suffered in the performance of export contracts, the existence and irrevocability of which are established by the advance fixing of the refunds, or to be compensated for such loss.

44.   In the absence of an overriding matter of public interest, the Commission has violated a superior rule of law, thus rendering the Community liable, by failing to include in Regulation No. 189/72 transitional measures for the protection of the confidence which a trader might legitimately have had in the Community rules.

A. Durdan, 'Restitution or Damages: National Court or European Court?' (1976) 1 EL Rev 431

Apart from the rare case of a flagrant infringement of the empowering Regulation or of a rule contained in the Treaty there is one other 'superior rule' inherent in the Community legal order the infringement of which has been found capable of giving rise to liability on the part of the Community institutions: the so-called principle by which the legitimate expectations of individuals merits protection.

The doctrine of 'legitimate expectations' is somewhat similar to the idea of an equitable estoppel save that it can be both a sword and a shield. If a trader enters into a transaction in legitimate reliance on a representation by the Community as to its future conduct, then the Community is obliged either to provide transitional provisions or to indemnify the trader if it later adopts a different course of conduct to the detriment of the trader. The representation can be express or implied. There has hitherto been only one case of an express representation, the case of *Continentale France.*

The institutions have in subsequent cases argued that there must always be something in the nature of a promise or a misleading statement intended to be relied upon. It is now, however, clear that there can be an implied representation.

The *locus classicus* is *CNTA* v *Commission* (Case 74/74) [1975] ECR 533 where the applicant claimed that it was induced by the existence of the monetary compensatory amount scheme to purchase Community oil seed in the expectation of receiving a compensatory amount on export to a third country. If the scheme had not existed it would have bought on the world market. The scheme was abolished without warning in mid-season. On an application for damages the Court held that the Community was liable if, in the absence of an overriding public interest, it abolished with immediate effect and without warning the application of compensatory amounts in a specific sector without adopting transitional measures which would at least permit traders to avoid a loss which would have been suffered in the performance of export contracts, the existence and irrevocability of which are established by the advance fixing.

Subsequent cases have shown that a high standard of prudence is expected from traders. There need not be express notice that a particular pecuniary advantage is to be abolished. It is sufficient if the reasonably prudent trader could have foreseen the abolition.

KAMPFFMEYER AND OTHERS v COMMISSION (Joined Cases 5, 7 & 13–24/66) [1967] ECR 245, Court of Justice

The facts were the same as those in *Alfred Toepfer* v *Commission* (see **7.1.4.2**). The applicants sought damages under Article 215.

It was held that damages were awarded, subject to a reduction in respect of certain claims. Final judgment as to any Community liability in damages was not given.

(At pp. 262–3) With regard to the argument that the rule of law which is infringed is not intended to protect the interests of the applicants, the said Article 22, together with the other provisions of Regulation No. 19, is directed, according to the wording of the fourth recital in the preamble to the regulation, to ensuring appropriate support for agricultural markets during the transitional period on the one hand, and to allowing the progressive establishment of a single market by making possible the development of the free movement of goods on the other. Furthermore, the interests of the producers in the

Member States and of free trade between these States are expressly mentioned in the preamble to the said regulation. It appears in particular from Article 18 that the exercise of freedom of trade between States is subject only to the general requirements laid down by its own provisions and those of subsequent regulations. Article 22 constitutes an exception to these general rules and consequently an infringement of that article must be regarded as an infringement of those rules and of the interests which they are intended to protect. The fact that these interests are of a general nature does not prevent their including the interests of individual undertakings such as the applicants which as cereal importers are parties engaged in intra-Community trade. Although the application of the rules of law in question is not in general capable of being of direct and individual concern to the said undertakings, that does not prevent the possibility that the protection of their interests may be – as in the present case it is in fact – intended by those rules of law. The defendant's argument that the rule of law contained in Article 22 of Regulation No. 19 is not directed towards the protection of the interests of the applicants cannot therefore be accepted.

Administrative Acts

CATO v *COMMISSION* (Case C–55/90) [1992] ECR I-2533, Court of Justice

Cato failed to qualify for compensation in respect of a decommissioned fishing vessel, under the terms of a UK scheme which had been set up pursuant to a Directive. Cato applied for damages under Article 215 on the basis that the UK scheme was contrary to the Directive and that the Commission had therefore acted wrongfully in approving it.

It was held that the scheme did not contravene the Directive, and therefore the approval of it could not be wrongful.

21.   In this connection it is to be noted, first, that the object of the Directive is to encourage temporary or permanent reduction of production capacity in the fisheries sector. In order to attain that objective, the Directive authorises Member States to introduce a system of financial aid for measures reducing such capacity and provides for financial contributions by the Community to the aid thus granted under the conditions set out in the Directive.

22.   It follows that the Directive leaves it to Member States to choose whether or not to introduce such an aid scheme and to determine its form and details, provided that the latter are not at variance with the objectives of the Directive.

23.   Secondly, it is to be noted that the power of verification conferred on the Commission by Articles 7 and 8 of the Directive is intended solely to determine whether the schemes proposed by Member States satisfy the conditions for financial contributions from the Community, having regard to their compliance with the Directive and bearing in mind other structural measures already existing or envisaged for the fisheries sector.

24.   In that context, the fact that a national scheme requires the persons concerned to establish that the vessel will in future be used for purposes other than fishing is not at variance with the objectives of the Directive. Since the aim of the Directive, as mentioned above, is to encourage reduction of production capacity by means of scrapping, the definitive transfer of the vessel to a third country or its assignment to purposes other than fishing, the above requirement of proof cannot be regarded as constituting an obstacle to the attainment of the objective set.

25.   Admittedly, Mr Cato argues that the United Kingdom Scheme imposes an impossible evidential burden on him since no one can prove that a vessel intended to be used for other purposes will not, prior to its destruction, be used once again in the unforeseeable future for fishing within Community waters.

26.   Such a requirement in this connection would, it is clear, amount to a prohibition of a reduction in production capacity of the fishing fleet by methods other than the scrapping of the vessel or its definitive transfer to a third country, whereas Article 5(1) of the Directive also envisages its assignment to purposes other than fishing in Community waters. Mr Cato, however, has been unable to refer to any specific provision in the United Kingdom Scheme in support of his view and there is nothing in that scheme to suggest that it allows the national authorities to impose on an applicant for the grant such an impossible condition.

27.   As the judgment of the Court of Appeal of 15 June 1989, cited above, makes clear, the United Kingdom Minister has no discretion as to the grant of aid once the conditions

laid down have been satisfied. The Minister therefore, contrary to the view taken by Mr Cato, has no discretion such as would constitute an obstacle to the attainment of the Directive's objectives.

28.   The fact that the actual conduct of the United Kingdom authorities in the course of events may not be entirely free of blame cannot, no matter how regrettable, be attributed to the Commission in the exercise of its power of prior verification.

29.   It follows from all the foregoing that the Commission, in approving the United Kingdom Scheme by way of Decision 84/17, did not act unlawfully in such a way as to entail liability on the part of the Community.

8.3.1.3   Acts by Community Servants

SAYAG AND ANOTHER v LEDUC AND OTHERS (Case 9/69) [1969] [ECR] 329, Court of Justice

Leduc was injured in a road accident caused by a Euratom official, Sayag, who was driving his private car in performance of his official duties. The Belgian court referred to the Court of Justice (under Article 150 of the Euratom Treaty) the question of whether the Community was liable for Sayag's actions, under Article 188 of the Euratom Treaty (a parallel provision to Article 215).

It was held that Euratom was not liable, because the wrongful act by its servant had not been committed 'in the performance of his duties'.

7.   By referring at one and the same time to damage caused by the institutions and to that caused by the servants of the Community, Article 188 indicates that the Community is only liable for those acts of its servants which, by virtue of an internal and direct relationship, are the necessary extension of the tasks entrusted to the institutions.

8.   In the light of the special nature of this legal system, it would not therefore be lawful to extend it to categories of acts other than those referred to above.

9.   A servant's use of his private car for transport during the performance of his duties does not satisfy the conditions set out above.

10.   A reference to a servant's private car in a travel order does not bring the driving of such car within the performance of his duties, but is basically intended to enable any necessary reimbursement of the travel expenses involved in the use of this means of transport to be made in accordance with the standards laid down for this purpose.

11.   Only in the case of *force majeure* or in exceptional circumstances of such overriding importance that without the servant's using private means of transport the Commuity would have been unable to carry out the tasks entrusted to it, could such use be considered to form part of the servant's performance of his duties, within the meaning of the second paragraph of Article 188 of the Treaty.

12.   It follows from the above that the driving of a private car by a servant cannot in principle constitute the performance of his duties within the meaning of the second paragraph of Article 188 of the EAEC Treaty.

8.3.1.4   Causation

GAEC v COUNCIL AND COMMISSION (Case 253/84) [1987] ECR 123, Court of Justice

For the facts, see **8.3.1.1** above.

14.   As regards sales of beef and veal, GAEC, in answer to a question put by the Court, estimated its losses in the second half of 1984 at FF 10,894, on the basis of its profit and loss account and balance sheet for 1984.

15.   The Council and the Government of the Federal Republic of Germany, which has intervened in support of the defendants' conclusions, contend that the low level of beef and veal prices on the French market during the period in question was due to factors other than the aid granted to German farmers. In particular, it was attributable to the increased supply of cows for slaughter following the implementation, as from 1 April 1984, of a super-levy introduced with a view to encouraging the dairy sector to reduce output.

16. It must be observed in the first place that, contrary to the statements made by GAEC, only part of the second half of 1984 was marked by an increase in imports into France of German beef and veal. It is clear from uncontested statistics produced by the Government of the Federal Republic of Germany as an annex to its intervention that it was only in July and August 1984 that there was a discernible increase in German exports to France of beef and veal as compared with the corresponding period of 1983, whereas in subsequent months such exports were running at a lower level than in the corresponding period of 1983.

17. Furthermore, it must be emphasized that increases, and, on occasion, even higher increases in imports of German beef and veal had already been recorded in the early months of 1984, even prior to the adoption of Decision 84/361.

18. It is also clear from the statistics on beef and veal price trends produced by the parties at the Court's request that prices had already begun to decline on the French market in the closing months of 1983 and continued to fall during the first half of 1984, that is to say well before the entry into force of Decision 84/361.

19. Accordingly, it must be held that GAEC has not succeeded in showing that the decline in beef and veal prices in France was the direct consequence of the aforesaid decision.

20. In so far as GAEC, relying on the Court's judgment of 2 June 1976 in Joined Cases 56 to 60/74 *Kampffmeyer v Commission and Council* [1976] ECR 711, asks the Court to declare that the Community is liable in respect of damage which, although it is not yet in existence, is nevertheless 'imminent damage foreseeable with sufficient certainty', it must be observed that GAEC has not adduced any evidence in support of that claim other than the evidence put forward to support its view that there was a causal link between Decision 84/361 and the damage alleged to have been suffered by it. There is therefore even less reason for considering GAEC to have shown that the decision in question was, as the judgment cited above requires, the 'certain cause' of imminent and foreseeable damage.

21. It follows from the foregoing that GAEC has not been able to prove that the conditions of the fact of damage and the existence of a causal link between the contested act and the alleged damage are fulfilled in this case. That is sufficient ground for dismissing the action without it being necessary for the Court to pronounce on the lawfulness of the Council decision of 30 June 1984.

DUMORTIER FRÈRES SA AND OTHERS v COUNCIL (Cases 64 & 113/76) [1979] ECR 3091, Court of Justice

For the facts, see **8.3.1.2** above.

14. This said, it is necessary to go on to examine the damage resulting from the discrimination to which the gritz producers were subjected. The origin of the damage complained of by the applicants lies in the abolition by the Council of the refunds which would have been paid to the gritz producers if equality of treatment with the producers of maize starch had been observed. Hence, the amount of those refunds must provide a yardstick for the assessment of the damage suffered.

15. The Council objected to that method of calculating the damage on the ground that the gritz producers eliminated the damage by passing on the loss resulting from the abolition of the refunds in their selling prices. In principle, in the context of an action for damages, such an objection may not be dismissed as unfounded. In fact, it must be admitted that if the loss from the abolition of the refunds has actually been passed on in the prices the damage may not be measured by reference to the refunds not paid. In that case the price increase would take the place of the refunds, thus compensating the producer.

16. For their part, the applicants dispute that the loss was passed on in the way alleged by the Council, except for a brief initial period during the 1975/1976 marketing year. They state that, faced with the competition from the starch producers benefiting from refunds, they chose, as a matter of commercial policy, to sell gritz at a loss in order to retain their markets, rather than raise the prices at the risk of losing those markets. The price increases referred to by the Council are, in the applicants' submission, due to the rise in the threshold price of maize and to the increase in production costs.

17. The parties have put forward statistics and other data in support of their respective submissions. Those data do not permit the conclusion advanced by the Council to be accepted. The conclusion which emerges is rather that during the period in dispute the prices of gritz and starch developed along similar lines without reflecting the absence of refunds for gritz. The only exception concerns the period covering the last months of 1975 and the beginning of 1976, during which the prices of gritz were increased by amounts corresponding to the unpaid refunds. However, the applicants have explained that those increases were accepted by the breweries provisonally on condition that a clause was inserted in the contracts of sale guaranteeing the buyer the benefit, retroactively in the appropriate case, of any new refund granted by the Community.

18. It follows that the loss for which the applicants must be compensated has to be calculated on the basis of its being equivalent to the refunds which would have been paid to them if, during the period from 1 August 1975 to 19 October 1977 the use of maize for the manufacture of gritz used by the brewing industry had conferred a right to the same refunds as the use of maize for the manufacture of starch; an exception will have to be made for the quantities of maize used for the manufacture of gritz which was sold at prices increased by the amount of the unpaid refunds under contracts guaranteeing the buyer the benefit of any re-introduction of the refunds.

19. Some of the applicants have also submitted claims for compensation for certain additional items of damage which they claim to have suffered.

20. In the case of the two maize processors established in the north of France, the further damage lies particularly in a substantial fall in their sales to breweries. Although it is beyond dispute that the figures submitted by the applicants clearly show such a fall, that fact can hardly be ascribed to the absence of refunds. In fact, as has already been said, the applicants have insisted on the fact that the selling prices of gritz were not increased on account of the abolition of the refunds. On the contrary, as the Court recognized when examining the development of the prices, the gritz producers chose to sell at a loss in order to retain their markets, and not to increase their prices at the risk of losing those markets. Thus the inequality which existed between gritz and starch as regards the granting of refunds was not reflected in the selling prices. If in spite of that commercial policy the gritz producers' sales fell, the reason for this must be sought in something other than the inequality caused by the abolition of the refunds.

21. In the case of certain other applicants the further damage alleged is of a different nature. Two undertakings were forced to close their factories and a third had to commence insolvency proceedings. The Council argued that the origin of the difficulties experienced by those undertakings is to be found in the circumstances peculiar to each of them, such as the obsolescence of their plant and managerial or financial problem. The data supplied by the parties on that question in the course of the proceedings are not such as to establish the true causes of the further damage alleged. However, it is sufficient to state that even if it were assumed that the abolition of the refunds exacerbated the difficulties encountered by those applicants, those difficulties would not be a sufficiently direct consequence of the unlawful conduct of the Council to render the Community liable to make good the damage. In the field of non-contractual liability of public authorities for legislative measures, the principles common to the laws of the Member States to which the second paragraph of Article 215 of the EEC Treaty refers cannot be relied on to deduce an obligation to make good every harmful consequence, even a remote one, of unlawful legislation.

22. It follows that the claims for compensation for the further damage alleged cannot be upheld.

KAMPFFMEYER AND OTHERS v COMMISSION (Joined Cases 5, 7 & 13–24/66) [1967]
ECR 245, Court of Justice

For the facts, see **8.3.1.2** above.

(At pp. 263–4 and 265–6) Since the liability of the Community has been recognised in principle, it is necessary to establish the facts of the alleged injury to which that liability relates.

In this connexion, it is necessary to distinguish three categories of injury. In the first place, after the refusal of the grant of import licences on 3 October 1963, certain applicants made the imports in question during the month of January, paying the German authorities the levy required for the quantities of maize purchased on 1 October in anticipation of the issue of the licences applied for. In the second place, certain applicants purchased quantities of maize on the French market on 1 October, and repudiated the contracts of purchase after the said refusal to grant licences. In the third place, after the said refusal to grant licences, certain applicants did not carry out the proposed importation, so that it was, as far as they were concerned, a transaction the performance of which had not begun, but one which had merely given rise to the lodging of applications for licences.

As to the first category, as the applicants purchased the maize in anticipation of importation subject to a zero levy, their injury was caused by the necessity to import subject to the payment of a levy. However, the refusal to grant the import licences subject to a zero levy in respect of this transaction had no legal basis, as the decision of the Commission of 3 October had been annulled by the above-mentioned judgment of 1 July 1965 and, furthermore, as, according to the documents provided by the applicants, the German protective measure had been declared illegal by the German courts for reasons based on German law. Consequently the charging of the levy, made in the name of and for the benefit of the Treasury of the Federal Republic of Germany, is thus shown to be contrary to both Community law and German law. In these circumstances, the question arises whether the damage alleged would be made good by the repayment of the sums improperly paid by way of levy.

During the oral procedure, the existence in the present case of the right to such repayment was put in doubt by the applicants. The Court cannot, however, rely on such a statement to accept the conclusive nature of the alleged damage. It is proper, therefore, to ask the applicants concerned to prove that they have exhausted all methods of recourse both administrative and judicial under the relevant national law to obtain reimbursement of the sums improperly paid by way of levy. Only after production of such evidence would there be reason to consider whether any injury exists which the Community should make good.

The applicants in Cases 5/66, 7/66, 14/66, 15/66, 16/66, 19/66 and 21/66 must be regarded as belonging to the first category mentioned above, as they purchased on 1 October quantities of maize in anticipation of the issue of the licences applied for and imported these quantities into the Federal Republic of Germany either during the month of January 1964 or on prior or subsequent dates sufficiently close to that month to justify the supposition that an importation during that month would have been possible. It is thus appropriate to ask the above-mentioned applicants to produce the evidence indicated above.

It should, however, be stated at this stage that only the imports of maize purchased in reliance on the announcement of the issue of licences subject to a zero levy may be taken into account for the fixing of the damage for which the Community may be liable. It is appropriate therefore to ask the above-mentioned applicants to produce evidence that the quantities of maize imported in or near the month of January 1964, to which they refer, were purchased by contracts made on 1 October.

. . .

As to the second category mentioned above, as certain applicants repudiated some of the contracts of purchase concluded on 1 October 1963 in anticipation of the issue of the import licences applied for, they allege that they have suffered injury because of both the expense which they have had to bear in repudiating the said contracts as well as the loss of profit which they have suffered in respect of the quantities of maize purchased but not imported in consequence of the protective measure.

The penalties paid for the repudiation of the concluded contracts of purchase are the direct consequence, on the one hand, of the confidence of the applicants concerned in the proper application of Regulation No. 19 and, on the other hand, of the unforeseen factor constituted by the protective measure which was retained by the decision of the Commission of 3 October 1963. In purchasing the quantities of maize in question on 1 October 1963, the applicants concerned legitimately relied upon the system of levies in force in order to enter into contractual obligations in respect of imports into the Federal

Republic. They thus have the right to be reimbursed for the whole of the injury suffered through payment of penalties, unless the amount of such penalties was higher than necessary.

The applicants in Cases 5/66, 13/66, 15/66 and 21/66 must thus be allowed to show that the repudiated contracts of purchase were made on 1 October 1963, the right to produce evidence that they acted in knowledge of the withdrawal which took place at 2.15 p.m. being reserved to the defendant.

The alleged injury in respect of the loss of profit is based on facts of an essentially speculative nature. In fact, it should be said first of all that the hasty lodging of an abnormally large number of applications for import licences on 1 October provides an indication that the persons concerned know that the decisions in force on 1 October 1963 offered unusual advantages. Furthermore, as the applicants for licences knew the French market and the actual level of prices ruling there, they were able to perceive the error committed by the Commission in the decision of 27 September 1963, fixing the free-at-frontier prices. Thus the applicants may be regarded as having been aware of the abnormal speculative nature of the transaction involved in their purchase of maize. By cancelling the transactions concerned, they avoided any commercial risk to themselves inherent in importation into the Federal Republic. Consequently it is not justifiable to acknowledge their right to recover the whole profit that they would have been able to obtain if the transaction which had been started had been performed. Taking this into account, the injury resulting from loss of profit for which the Community must be regarded as being liable cannot equitably be evaluated at a sum exceeding 10% of that which the applicants would have paid by way of levy, if they had carried out the purchases made but cancelled.

8.3.2   THE REQUIREMENT OF FAULT

BIOVILAC N.V. v *EEC* (Case 59/83) [1984] ECR 4057, Court of Justice

Biovilac, a producer of piglet feedstuffs, claimed that it had been particularly harmed by the cheap sale of Community skimmed milk powder which was a competing feedstuff for piglets. Biovilac claimed damages under Article 215 on the alternative grounds of an unlawful act, or a lawful act which had resulted in a special sacrifice by it, the latter being a concept which gave rise to liability under both French and German law, even in the absence of fault.

It was held that damages would not be awarded.

Liability in the absence of illegality
27.   To support its alternative claim the applicant relies on the German law concept of 'Sonderopfer' [special sacrifice] and the French law concept of 'rupture de l'égalité devant les charges publiques' [unequal discharge of public burdens]; it contends that, even in the absence of any illegality, the Community is nevertheless liable, under the second paragraph of Article 215 of the EEC Treaty, to make good any loss of property which an individual suffers in consequence of general measures which are lawful in themselves if he is particularly affected and harmed by them, namely if he is affected in a different way and much more seriously than all other traders and producers.

28.   In this regard it need only be observed that the Court has held in a consistent line of decisions that an action for damages brought under Article 215 of the Treaty for unlawful legislative action cannot succeed unless the damage alleged by the applicant exceeds the limits of the economic risks inherent in operating in the sector concerned. That principle would have to be applied *a fortiori* if the concept of liability without fault were accepted in Community law. In this case those limits were not exceeded since the applicant ought to have anticipated when marketing its products in 1978 and 1980 that Regulations Nos. 368/77 and 443/77, which were suspended only temporarily and which originally did not contain any mechanism for preventing skimmed milk powder sold under them from being used for feeding piglets, which is not the case now, would be brought back into force if the circumstances which existed at the time of their adoption were later to re-occur. When it was established in 1974 the applicant also ought to have anticipated, or at any rate could have anticipated, that special measures would

be adopted under the second subparagraph of Article 7(2) of Regulation No. 804/68 in order to dispose of skimmed milk powder which could not be marketed on normal terms during a milk year.

29. The foreseeability of the risks inherent in the market conditions at the time when the applicant began to manufacture and market those products excludes the possibility of any recompense for the loss of competitiveness which it has suffered. Those risks form part of the economic risks inherent in the activities of an industrial and commercial undertaking in this sector, as does the increase in energy costs which, on the plaintiff's evidence, is one of the main causes of the considerable increase in the price of its products in the space of four years.

30. It follows from the foregoing considerations that the alternative claim must also be dismissed.

8.3.3   THE RELATIONSHIP BETWEEN ARTICLE 215 AND OTHER ACTIONS

KROHN & CO. IMPORT-EXPORT (GMBH AND CO. KG) v *COMMISSION*
(Case 175/84) [1986] ECR 753, Court of Justice

The Commission authorised the German authorities to refuse to grant an import licence to Krohn in respect of Thai manioc. Krohn brought an action for damages under Article 215 while its action in the German courts was pending and after it had become time barred from bringing an Article 173 action (see **Chapter 7**).

The Court of Justice held, as a preliminary matter, that an action for damages under Article 215 was admissible (and stated that the case should proceed to a consideration of the substance).

The third argument against admissibility

30. The Commission notes that Krohn failed to bring an action under the second paragraph of Article 173 of the Treaty to obtain the annulment of its telex instructions to the Bundesanstalt on 23 November and 21 December 1982. Those individual decisions have thus become definitive with regard to Krohn. According to a decision of the Court (judgment of 15 July 1963 in Case 25/62 *Plaumann* v *Commission* [1963] ECR 95), an application for compensation cannot be brought if it would nullify the legal effects of an individual decision which has become definitive.

31. Krohn argues that only the Bundesanstalt's decision was notified to it and that at the time nothing indicated that the Commission had adopted an actual decision directly concerning it. In any event, the admissibility of its application cannot be conditional on its having previously brought an action for the annulment of the Commission's decision.

32. As the Court has pointed out above, the action provided for by Article 178 and the second paragraph of Article 215 of the Treaty was introduced as an autonomous form of action with a particular purpose to fulfil. It differs from an action for annulment in particular in that its purpose is not to set aside a specific measure but to repair the damage caused by an institution. It follows that the existence of an individual decision which has become definitive cannot act as a bar to the admissibility of such an action.

33. The decision cited by the Commission relates solely to the exceptional case where an application for compensation is brought for payment of an amount precisely equal to the duty which the applicant was required to pay under an individual decision, so that the application seeks in fact the withdrawal of that individual decision. At all events, such considerations are foreign to this case.

34. It follows that the third argument against admissibility must also be rejected.

ALFONS LÜTTICKE v *COMMISSION* (Case 4/69) [1971] ECR 325, Court of Justice

For the facts, see **8.3.1** above.

5. Secondly, the defendant contests the admissibility of the action by reason of the fact that, although introduced on the basis of Article 178 and the second paragraph of Article 215, it seeks in reality to establish a failure to act on the part of the Commission and to constrain it indirectly to initiate against the Federal Republic of Germany the

procedure under the second paragraph of Article 97 and, possibly, that under Article 169. It is claimed that this manner of proceeding has the effect of distorting the conditions to which Article 175 has subjected actions for failure to act.

6. The action for damages provided for by Article 178 and the second paragraph of Article 215 was established by the Treaty as an independent form of action with a particular purpose to fulfil within the system of actions and subject to conditions for its use, conceived with a view to its specific purpose. It would be contrary to the independent nature of this action as well as to the efficacy of the general system of forms of action created by the Treaty to regard as a ground of inadmissibility the fact that, in certain circumstances, an action for damages might lead to a result similar to that of an action for failure to act under Article 175.

7. This objection of inadmissibility must therefore be dismissed.

8.3.4 CONCURRENT LIABILITY

KAMPFFMEYER v *COMMISSION* (Joined Cases 5, 7 & 13–24/66) [1967] ECR 245, Court of Justice

For the facts, see **8.3.1.2** above.

(At pp. 266–7) However, with regard to any injury suffered by the applicants belonging to the first and second categories above-mentioned, those applicants have informed the Court that the injury alleged is the subject of two actions for damages, one against the Federal Republic of Germany before a German court and the other against the Community before the Court of Justice. It is necessary to avoid the applicants' being insufficiently or excessively compensated for the same damage by the different assessment of two different courts applying different rules of law. Before determining the damage for which the Community should be held liable, it is necessary for the national court to have the opportunity to give judgment on any liability on the part of the Federal Republic of Germany. This being the case, final judgment cannot be given before the applicants have produced the decision of the national court on this matter, which may be done independently of the evidence asked of the applicants in the first category to the effect that they have exhausted all methods of recourse for the recovery of the amounts improperly paid by way of levy. Furthermore, if it were established that such recovery was possible, this fact might have consequences bearing upon the calculation of the damages concerning the second category. However, the decisive nature of the said evidence required does not prevent the applicants from producing the other evidence previously indicated in the meantime.

KROHN & CO. IMPORT-EXPORT (GmbH and Co. KG) v *COMMISSION* (Case 175/84) [1986] ECR 753, Court of Justice

For the facts, see above.

The second argument against admissibility

24. The Commission submits that according to the decisions of the Court, an application for compensation under Article 178 and the second paragraph of Article 215 of the Treaty is admissible only if the applicant has exhausted the procedure enabling him to seek the annulment of the national authority's decision by the national courts. In this case, however, Krohn has brought an action before the Verwaltungsgericht Frankfurt am Main for the annulment of the Bundesanstalt's refusal of the import licences and for an order requiring them to be issued, and that case has not reached final judgment. The applicant's rights of action under national law have therefore not been exhausted.

25. Krohn argues that the application for compensation provided for by the second paragraph of Article 215 of the Treaty is in no way dependant on rights of action under national law. Furthemore, in this case an action for annulment would not have enabled it to achieve its desired objective which was to repair the damage caused to it by the refusal of the import licences.

26. According to an established body of decisions of the Court, the application for compensation provided for by Article 178 and the second paragraph of Article 215 of the

Treaty was introduced as an autonomous form of action with a particular purpose to fulfil within the system of actions and subject to conditions on its use dictated by its specific nature.

27.   Nonetheless, it is true that such actions must be examined in the light of the whole system of legal protection for the individual established by the Treaty and that the admissibility of such an action may in certain cases be dependent on the exhaustion of national rights of action available to obtain the annulment of a national authority's decision. In order for that to be the case, however, it is necessary that those national rights of action should provide an effective means of protection for the individual concerned and be capable of resulting in compensation for the damage alleged.

28.   That is not the case here. There is nothing to suggest that the annulment of the Bundesanstalt's decision and the issue, after a lapse of several years, of the import licences claimed in 1982 would compensate Krohn for the damage suffered by it at that time; such an annulment would therefore not remove the need for the applicant, if it is to obtain compensation, to bring an action before the Court under Article 178 and the second paragraph of Article 215 of the Treaty.

29.   In those circumstances, the admissibility of this action cannot be made dependent on the exhaustion of the national rights of action available against the Bundesanstalt's decision, and the second argument against admissibilty must also be rejected.

8.4   End of Chapter Assessment Question

Discuss the development by the Court of Justice of the 'general principles' referred to in Article 215.

8.5   End of Chapter Assessment Outline Answer

Article 215 provides that the Community is liable, in accordance with the general principles common to the Member States, to make good any damage caused by its institutions or servants. In *Alfons Lütticke* v *Commission*, the Court of Justice stated that these general principles required an applicant to show a wrongful act by the Community, damage to itself and a causal link between the two.

The Court of Justice will require applicants to prove their damage (*GAEC* v *Council and Commission*), and to mitigate their loss. In *Mulder*, the Court of Justice reduced the damages awarded by the amount that the producers could reasonably have earned had they undertaken reasonable alternative activities.

It is for the applicants to prove causation; the Court of Justice will not make an assumption from the existence of a wrongful act and damage. In *Dumortier Frères*, the abolition of subsidies did not lead to increased prices, and therefore could not be proved to have caused the drop in sales. The Court of Justice also ruled that factory closures and bankruptcy were not sufficiently direct consequences of the abolition of subsidies.

Where the allegedly wrongful act is a general legislative measure, the applicants must prove that it fulfils the *Second Skimmed Milk Powder* test. There must be a sufficiently serious breach of a superior rule of law which is for the protection of individuals. In the *Second Skimmed Milk Powder* case, the Court of Justice stated that there would be a sufficiently serious breach only where the Community had manifestly and gravely disregarded the limits on the exercise of its powers. In that case, the Court of Justice considered that the wide category of those affected, and the limited price rises which had resulted, indicated that the effect of the measure did not go beyond the inherent economic risks of that business. However, in the *Isoglucose* cases, which involved an affected category of only three or four companies, and damage so serious that one producer went out of business, the Court of Justice rejected the claim that the Community had manifestly and gravely disregarded the limits on its powers, and ruled that only if its conduct was 'verging on the arbitrary', would the Community incur liability.

Superior rules of law include most Treaty Articles and the general principles of law such as non-discrimination. It is generally easy to prove that these rules of law are for the protection of individuals. For example, in the *Second Skimmed Milk Powder* case, the Court of Justice stated that the rule against discrimination was for the protection of individuals and was so important to the system of legal protection established by the Treaty of Rome that it amounted to a superior rule.

CHAPTER NINE

FREE MOVEMENT OF GOODS

9.1 Overview of the Community Free Movement Provisions

9.1.1 THE CUSTOMS UNION

THE TREATY OF ROME

Article 9

1.   The Community shall be based upon a customs union which shall cover all trade in goods and which shall involve the prohibition between Member States of customs duties on imports and exports and of all charges having equivalent effect, and the adoption of a common customs tariff in their relations with third countries.

2.   The provisions of Chapter 1, Section 1, and of Chapter 2 of this Title shall apply to products originating in Member States and to products coming from third countries which are in free circulation in Member States.

Article 10

1.   Products coming from a third country shall be considered to be in free circulation in a Member State if the import formalities have been complied with and any customs duties or charges having equivalent effect which are payable have been levied in that Member State, and if they have not benefited from a total or partial drawback of such duties or charges.

9.1.2 APPLICATION OF THE PRINCIPLE OF FREE MOVEMENT OF GOODS

SOCIAAL FONDS VOOR DE DIAMANTARBEIDERS v *CHOUGOL DIAMOND CO.* (Cases 2 & 3/69) [1969] ECR 211, Court of Justice

A Belgian law imposed a levy on imported diamonds, the proceeds of which were paid into a social security fund for workers in the Belgian diamond industry. The charge was not protectionist, for Belgium did not produce diamonds. (Article 177 reference.)

[5/6]   According to Article 9, the Community shall be based upon a customs union founded upon the prohibition between Member States of customs duties and of 'all charges having equivalent effect', and the adoption of a common customs tariff in their relations with third countries. Article 12 prohibits the introduction of 'new customs duties on imports . . . or any charges having equivalent effect'.

[7/10]   The position of these articles at the beginning of that Part of the Treaty reserved for the 'Foundations of the Community', Article 9 being the first provision appearing at the very beginning of the Title dealing with the 'Free movement of goods' and Article 12 heading the section on the 'Elimination of customs duties between Member States', is sufficient to show the fundamental role of the prohibitions laid down therein. The importance of these prohibitions is such that, in order to prevent their circumvention by means of various customs and fiscal measures, the Treaty was intended to prevent any possible failure in their implementation. Article 17 therefore specifies that the prohibitions in Article 9 shall also apply to customs duties of a fiscal nature. Article 95, which appears both in that Part of the Treaty which deals with the 'Policy of the

Community' and in the Chapter on 'Tax provisions', is intended to fill in any breaches which a fiscal measure might open in the prohibitions laid down, by prohibiting the imposition on imported products of internal taxation in excess of that imposed on domestic products.

[11/14]   In prohibiting the imposition of customs duties, the Treaty does not distinguish between goods according to whether or not they enter into competition with the products of the importing country. Thus, the purpose of the abolition of customs barriers is not merely to eliminate their protective nature, as the Treaty sought on the contrary to give general scope and effect to the rule on the elimination of customs duties and charges having equivalent effect in order to ensure the free movement of goods. It follows from the system as a whole and from the general and absolute nature of the prohibition of any customs duty applicable to goods moving between Member States that customs duties are prohibited independently of any consideration of the purpose for which they were introduced and the destination of the revenue obtained therefrom. The justification for this prohibition is based on the fact that any pecuniary charge — however small — imposed on goods by reason of the fact that they cross a frontier constitutes an obstacle to the movement of such goods.

[15/18]   The extension of the prohibition of customs duties to charges having equivalent effect is intended to supplement the prohibition against obstacles to trade created by such duties by increasing its efficiency. The use of these two complementary concepts thus tends, in trade between Member States, to avoid the imposition of any pecuniary charge on goods circulating within the Community by virtue of the fact that they cross a national frontier. Thus, in order to ascribe to a charge an effect equivalent to a customs duty, it is important to consider this effect in the light of the objectives of the Treaty, in the Parts, Titles and Chapters in which Articles 9 and 12 are to be found, particularly in relation to the free movement of goods. Consequently, any pecuniary charge, however small and whatever its designation and mode of application, which is imposed unilaterally on domestic or foreign goods by reason of the fact that they cross a frontier, and which is not a customs duty in the strict sense, constitutes a charge having equivalent effect within the meaning of Articles 9 and 12 of the Treaty, even if it is not imposed for the benefit of the State, is not discriminatory or protective in effect or if the product on which the charge is imposed is not in competition with any domestic product.

9.1.3   OUTLINE OF THE TREATY ARTICLES PROVIDING FOR THE FREE MOVEMENT OF GOODS

THE TREATY OF ROME

Article 3
For the purposes set out in Article 2, the activities of the Community shall include, as provided in this Treaty and in accordance with the timetable set out therein:

(a)   the elimination, as between Member States, of customs duties and quantitative restrictions on the import and export of goods, and of all other measures having equivalent effect. . . .

Article 7a
The Community shall adopt measures with the aim of progressively establishing the internal market over a period expiring on 31 December 1992. . . .

The internal market shall comprise an area without internal frontiers in which the free movement of goods, persons, services and capital is ensured in accordance with the provisions of this Treaty.

9.2   Article 12: the Prohibition of New Customs Duties and Charges having Equivalent Effect

THE TREATY OF ROME

Article 12
Member States shall refrain from introducing between themselves any new customs duties on imports or exports or any charges having equivalent effect, and from increasing those which they already apply in their trade with each other.

9.2.1   DIRECT EFFECT OF ARTICLE 12

VAN GEND EN LOOS v *NEDERLANDSE ADMINISTRATIE DER BELASTINGEN*
(Case 26/62) [1963] ECR 1, Court of Justice

The Netherlands Government had increased the level of duty imposed on imports of ureaformaldehyde. Could van Gend, an importer, rely on Article 12 of the Treaty to challenge this increase? (Article 177 reference.)

The first question of the Tariefcommissie is whether Article 12 of the Treaty has direct application in national law in the sense that nationals of Member States may on the basis of this Article lay claim to rights which the national court must protect.

To ascertain whether the provisions of an international treaty extend so far in their effects it is necessary to consider the spirit, the general scheme and the wording of those provisions.

. . .

With regard to the general scheme of the Treaty as it relates to customs duties and charges having equivalent effect it must be emphasized that Article 9, which bases the Community upon a customs union, includes as an essential provision the prohibition of these customs duties and charges. This provision is found at the beginning of the part of the Treaty which defines the 'Foundations of the Community'. It is applied and explained by Article 12.

The wording of Article 12 contains a clear and unconditional prohibition which is not a positive but a negative obligation. This obligation, moreover, is not qualified by any reservation on the part of states which would make its implementation conditional upon a positive legislative measure enacted under national law. The very nature of this prohibition makes it ideally adapted to produce direct effects in the legal relationship between Member States and their subjects.

. . . according to the spirit, the general scheme and the wording of the Treaty, Article 12 must be interpreted as producing direct effects and creating individual rights which national courts must protect.

9.2.2   MEANING OF 'CUSTOMS DUTIES' AND 'CHARGES HAVING EQUIVALENT EFFECT'

COMMISSION v *LUXEMBOURG AND BELGIUM (GINGERBREAD)* **(Cases 2 & 3/62)
[1962] ECR 425, Court of Justice**

It was claimed by the Luxembourg and Belgian Governments that a charge on imported gingerbread was necessary to compensate for the high domestic tax on rye, one of the ingredients of gingerbread. The charge had been increased since the entering into force of the Treaty of Rome. In enforcement proceedings, the Commission relied partly on Article 12 of the Treaty. (Article 169 proceedings.)

The concept of 'a charge having equivalent effect' to a customs duty, far from being an exception to the general rule prohibiting customs duties, is on the contrary necessarily complementary to it and enables that prohibition to be made effective.

This expression, invariably linked to that of 'customs duties' is evidence of a general intention to prohibit not only measures which obviously take the form of the classic customs duty but also all those which, presented under other names or introduced by the indirect means of other procedures, would lead to the same discriminatory or protective results as customs duties.

In order to see whether a charge has an equivalent effect to a customs duty, it is important to consider this effect in connexion with the objectives of the Treaty, notably in that Part, Title and Chapter containing Articles 9 and 12, that is in relation to the free movement of goods, and still more generally the objectives of Article 3 which are aimed at preventing the distortion of competition.

It is, therefore, of little importance to know whether all the effects of customs duties are present at the same time, or whether it is merely a question of one only, or again whether side by side with these effects other principal or ancillary objectives were intended, since the charge jeopardizes the objectives of the Treaty and is the result not of a Community procedure but of a unilateral decision.

It follows from all these factors that a charge having equivalent effect within the meaning of Articles 9 and 12, whatever it is called and whatever its mode of application, may be regarded as a duty imposed unilaterally either at the time of importation or subsequently, and which, if imposed specifically upon a product imported from a Member State to the exclusion of a similar domestic product, has, by altering its price, the same effect upon the free movement of products as a customs duty.

. . .

The defendants have in effect asserted that the charge in dispute was intended to 'equate the price of the foreign product with the price of the Belgian product' (Statement of Defence, p. 19). They have even expressed doubt whether it is 'compatible with the general scheme of the Treaty that within the Common Market the producers of one country may acquire raw materials at a cheaper price than the producers of another Member State' (Rejoinder, p. 29).

This argument ignores the principle according to which the activities of the Community shall include the institution of a system ensuring that competition in the Common Market is not distorted (Article 3(f)).

To accept the argument of the defendants would lead, therefore, to an absurd situation which would be the exact opposite of that intended by the Treaty.

. . . it must be concluded that the 'special import duty' on gingerbread, increased and extended in Belgium and Luxembourg after the Treaty entered into force, contains all the elements of a charge having equivalent effect to a customs duty referred to in Articles 9 and 12.

It must therefore be declared and adjudged that the decisions to increase or extend this duty, taken after 1 January 1958, constituted infringements of the Treaty.

COMMISSION v ITALY (STATISTICAL LEVY) (Case 24/68)
[1969] ECR 193, Court of Justice

The Italian Government maintained that a charge imposed on all imports and exports did not constitute a charge having equivalent effect to a customs duty because it comprised the consideration for services rendered. The levy was used to fund a statistical service which, it was claimed, was of benefit to importers and exporters. (Article 169 proceedings.)

[6]   In prohibiting the imposition of customs duties, the Treaty does not distinguish between goods according to whether or not they enter into competition with the products of the importing country.

Thus, the purpose of the abolition of customs barriers is not merely to eliminate their protective nature, as the Treaty sought on the contrary to give general scope and effect to the rule on the elimination of customs duties and charges having equivalent effect, in order to ensure the free movement of goods.

[7]   It follows from the system as a whole and from the general and absolute nature of the prohibition of any customs duty applicable to goods moving between Member States that customs duties are prohibited independently of any consideration of the purpose for which they were introduced and the destination of the revenue obtained therefrom.

The justification for this prohibition is based on the fact that any pecuniary charge, however small, imposed on goods by reason of the fact that they cross a frontier constitutes an obstacle to the movement of such goods.

[8]   The extension of the prohibition of customs duties to charges having equivalent effect is intended to supplement the prohibition against obstacles to trade created by such duties by increasing its efficiency.

The use of these two complementary concepts thus tends, in trade between Member States, to avoid the imposition of any pecuniary charge on goods circulating within the Community by virtue of the fact that they cross a national frontier.

[9]   Thus, in order to ascribe to a charge an effect equivalent to a customs duty, it is important to consider this effect in the light of the objectives of the Treaty, in the Parts, Titles and Chapters in which Articles 9, 12, 13 and 16 are to be found, particularly in relation to the free movement of goods.

Consequently, any pecuniary charge, however small and whatever its designation and mode of application, which is imposed unilaterally on domestic or foreign goods by reason of the fact that they cross a frontier, and which is not a customs duty in the strict sense, constitutes a charge having equivalent effect within the meaning of Articles 9, 12, 13 and 16 of the Treaty, even if it is not imposed for the benefit of the State, is not discriminatory or protective in effect and if the product on which the charge is imposed is not in competition with any domestic product.

[10]   It follows from all the provisions referred to and from their relationship with the other provisions of the Treaty that the prohibition of new customs duties or charges having equivalent effect, linked to the principle of the free movement of goods, constitutes a fundamental rule which, without prejudice to the other provisions of the Treaty, does not permit of any exceptions.

. . .

Although it is not impossible that in certain circumstances a specific service actually rendered may form the consideration for a possible proportional payment for the service in question, this may only apply in specific cases which cannot lead to the circumvention of the provisions of Articles 9, 12, 13 and 16 of the Treaty.

. . .

[15]   The Italian Government . . . maintains that the disputed charge constitutes the consideration for a service rendered and as such cannot be designated as a charge having equivalent effect.

According to the Italian Government the object of the statistics in question is to determine precisely the actual movements of goods and, consequently, changes the state of the market. It claims that the exactness of the information thus supplied affords importers a better competitive position in the Italian market whilst exporters enjoy a similar advantage abroad and that the special advantages which dealers obtain from the survey justifies their paying for this public service and moreover demonstrates that the disputed charge is in the nature of a *quid pro quo*.

[16]   The statistical information in question is beneficial to the economy as a whole and *inter alia* to the relevant administrative authorities.

Even if the competitive position of importers and exporters were to be particularly improved as a result, the statistics still constitute an advantage so general, and so difficult to assess, that the disputed charge cannot be regarded as the consideration for a specific benefit actually conferred.

9.2.3   CHARGES FOR SERVICES RENDERED

COMMISSION v *BELGIUM (CUSTOMS WAREHOUSES)* (Case 132/82)
[1983] ECR 1649, Court of Justice

Community rules enabled imported goods to be given customs clearance at public warehouses located in the interior of a Member State, rather then at the point of entry on to the territory. Belgium imposed storage charges upon goods deposited at such warehouses to await customs formalities. Charges were also imposed on imported goods which were simply presented at the warehouses for customs clearance. (Article 169 proceedings.)

[8]   It is appropriate to recall, in the first place, that according to the established case-law of the Court, any pecuniary charge, however small and whatever its designation and mode of application, which is imposed unilaterally on the goods by reason of the fact that they cross a frontier and which is not a customs duty in the strict sense, constitutes a charge having equivalent effect within the meaning of Articles 9, 12, 13 and 16 of the Treaty, even if it is not levied by the State. The position is different only if the charge in question is the consideration for a service actually rendered to the importer and is of an amount commensurate with that service, when the charge concerned, as in this case, is payable exclusively on imported products.

[9]   The prohibition of charges having an effect equivalent to customs duties, laid down in provisions of the Treaty, is justified on the ground that pecuniary charges imposed by reason or on the occasion of the crossing of the frontier represent an obstacle to the free movement of goods.

[10]   It is in the light of those principles that the question whether the disputed storage charges may be classified as charges having an effect equivalent to customs duties must be assessed. It should therefore be noted, in the first place, that the placing of imported goods in temporary storage in the special stores of public warehouses clearly represents a service rendered to traders. A decision to deposit the goods there can indeed be taken only at the request of the trader concerned and then ensures their storage without payment of duties, until the trader has decided how they are to be dealt with. Moreover the Commission does not dispute that the placing of goods in temporary storage may legally give rise to the payment of charges commensurate with the service thus rendered.

[11]   However, it appears . . . that the storage charges are payable equally when the goods are presented at the public warehouse solely for the completion of customs formalities, even though they have been exempted from storage and the importer has not requested that they be put in temporary storage.

[12]   Admittedly the Belgian Government claims that even in that case a service is rendered to the importer. It is always open to the latter to avoid payment of the disputed charges by choosing to have his goods cleared through customs at the frontier, where such a procedure is free. Moreover, by using a public warehouse, the importer is enabled to have the goods declared through customs near the places for which his products are bound and he is therefore relieved of the necessity of himself either having at his own disposal premises suitable for their clearance or having recourse to private premises, the use of which is more expensive than that of the public warehouses. It is therefore legitimate, in the Belgian Government's view, to impose a charge commensurate with that service.

[13]   That argument cannot however be accepted. Whilst it is true that the use of a public warehouse in the interior of the country offers certain advantages to importers it seems clear first of all that such advantages are linked solely with the completion of customs formalities which, whatever the place, is always compulsory. It should moreover be noted that such advantages result from the scheme of Community transit introduced . . . not in the interests of individual traders but . . . in order to increase the fluidity of the movement of goods and to facilitate transport within the Community. There can therefore be no question of levying any charges for customs clearance facilities accorded in the interests of the common market.

[14]   It follows from the foregoing, that when payment of storage charges is demanded solely in connection with the completion of customs formalities, it cannot be regarded as the consideration for a service actually rendered to the importer.

[15]   Consequently, it must be declared that, by levying storage charges on goods which originate in a Member State or are in free circulation, and which are imported into Belgium, and presented merely for the completion of customs formalities at a special store, the Kingdom of Belgium has failed to fulfil its obligations under Articles 9 and 12 of the Treaty.

REWE-ZENTRALFINANZ v DIREKTOR DER LANDWIRTSCHAFTSKAMMER WESTFALEN-LIPPE (Case 39/73) [1973] ECR 1039, Court of Justice

The national court asked the Court of Justice whether a charge imposed by the German authorities for phyto-sanitary examinations of imported vegetable substances constituted a charge having equivalent effect to a customs duty under Article 13 of the Treaty (elimination of *existing* customs duties and charges having equivalent effect). (Article 177 reference.)

    . . .

[3]   The concept of charges having an effect equivalent to customs duties on imports is directed to any charge exacted at the time or because of import, which, specifically affecting an imported product to the exclusion of a similar domestic product, has the same restrictive effect on the free movement of goods as a customs duty.

    . . .

[4]   Although it is not ruled out that there may be certain circumstances in which a particular service rendered may possibly give rise to some consideration, which should not exceed either the value or the cost of the service they can only be special cases which cannot lead to the provisions of Article 13 of the Treaty being circumvented.

The activity of the administration of the State intended to maintain a phyto-sanitary system imposed in the general interest cannot be regarded as a service rendered to the importer such as to justify the imposition of a pecuniary charge.

[5]   Consequently, pecuniary charges, whatever their amount, imposed for reasons of phyto-sanitary examination of products when they cross the frontier, which are determined according to criteria of their own, which criteria are not comparable with those for determining the pecuniary charges attaching to similar domestic products, are deemed charges having an effect equivalent to customs duties.

COMMISSION v BELGIUM (HEALTH INSPECTION SERVICE) (Case 314/82) [1984] ECR 1543, Court of Justice

Under Belgian legislation, fees were charged for the inspection of imports of poultry-meat. The Belgian Government argued that the imposition of such fees did not constitute a breach of Articles 9 and 12 of the Treaty since the health checks were expressly permitted by Article 9 of Directive 71/118. (Article 169 proceedings.)

[1]   By an application lodged at the Court Registry on 10 December 1982, the Commission of the European Communities brought an action under Article 169 of the EEC Treaty for a declaration that by levying inspection charges for imports of fresh, dried, salted and smoked poultrymeat from other Member States, the Kingdom of Belgium has failed to fulfil its obligations under Articles 9 and 12 of the EEC Treaty.

. . .

[6]   . . . the Belgian Government has relied particularly on Article 9 of Directive 71/118 which allows a Member State to prohibit the marketing in its territory of fresh poultrymeat from another Member State if at the time of the health inspection carried out in the country of destination it is found that such meat is unfit for human consumption. The checks in this case are thus, it is claimed, provided for in the directive itself, in respect of which, according to the Court's case-law, a fee may therefore be charged.

. . .

[8]   As regards the argument based on Article 9 of Directive 71/118, it is sufficient to note that Article 9 of that directive in no way requires Member States to carry out such checks on imported meat but may at most be understood as permitting them. Since they are not checks carried out in application of Directive 71/118, that directive cannot be relied upon to justify the levying of an inspection charge in respect thereof.

COMMISSION v GERMANY (Case 18/87) [1988] ECR 5427, Court of Justice

Pursuant to Directive 81/389 on the protection of animals during international transit, a fee was charged in respect of veterinary inspections carried out on live animals on their importation into Germany. (Article 169 proceedings.)

[8]   Since the contested fee was charged in connection with inspections carried out pursuant to a Community provision, it should be noted that according to the case-law of the Court . . . such fees may not be classified as charges having an effect equivalent to a customs duty if the following conditions are satisfied:
(a)   they do not exceed the actual costs of the inspections in connection with which they are charged;
(b)   the inspections in question are obligatory and uniform for all the products concerned in the Community;
(c)   they are prescribed by Community law in the general interest of the Community;
(d)   they promote the free movement of goods, in particular by neutralizing obstacles which could arise from unilateral measures of inspection adopted in accordance with Article 36 of the Treaty.
[9]   In this instance these conditions are satisfied by the contested fee. In the first place it has not been contested that it does not exceed the real cost of the inspections in connection with which it is charged.

[10]   Moreover, all the Member States of transit and destination are required, under, *inter alia*, Article 2(1) of Directive 81/389/EEC, cited above, to carry out the veterinary inspections in question when the animals are brought into their territories, and therefore the inspections are obligatory and uniform for all the animals concerned in the Community.

[11]   Those inspections are prescribed by Directive 81/389/EEC, which establishes the measures necessary for the implementation of Council Directive 77/489/EEC of 18 July 1977 on the protection of animals during international transport, with a view to the protection of live animals, an objective which is pursued in the general interest of the Community and not a specific interest of individual States.

[12]   Finally, it appears from the preambles to the two abovementioned directives that they are intended to harmonize the laws of the Member States regarding the protection of animals in international transport in order to eliminate technical barriers resulting from disparities in the national laws . . . In addition, failing such harmonization, each Member State was entitled to maintain or introduce, under the conditions laid down in Article 36 of the Treaty, measures restricting trade which were justified on grounds of the protection of the health and life of animals. It follows that the standardization of the inspections in question is such as to promote the free movement of goods.

9.3   Article 95: Prohibition of Discriminatory Taxation

9.3.1   THE SCOPE OF ARTICLE 95

DENKAVIT v *FRANCE* (Case 132/78) [1979] ECR 1923, Court of Justice

This case concerned a charge imposed under French legislation on a consignment of lard imported from Germany. The Court of Justice distinguished between those charges constituting charges having equivalent effect and those falling within the scope of Article 95 of the Treaty. (Article 177 reference.)

[7]   As the Court has acknowledged several times, and in particular in its judgment of 25 January 1977 in Case 46/76, *WJG Bauhuis* v *The Netherlands State* [1977] ECR 5, any pecuniary charge, whatever its designation and mode of application, which is imposed unilaterally on goods by reason of the fact that they cross a frontier and which is not a customs duty in the strict sense, constitutes a charge having an equivalent effect within the meaning of Articles 9, 12, 13 and 16 of the Treaty. Such a charge however escapes that classification if it constitutes the consideration for a benefit provided in fact for the importer or exporter representing an amount proportionate to the said benefit. It also escapes that classification if it relates to a general system of internal dues applied systematically and in accordance with the same criteria to domestic products and imported products alike, in which case it does not come within the scope of Articles 9, 12, 13 and 16 but within that of Article 95 of the Treaty.

9.3.2   THE ARTICLE 95 PROHIBITION

THE TREATY OF ROME

Article 95
No Member State shall impose, directly or indirectly, on the products of other Member States any internal taxation of any kind in excess of that imposed directly or indirectly on similar domestic products.

Further, no Member State shall impose on the products of other Member States any internal taxation of such a nature as to afford indirect protection to other products.

Member States shall, not later than at the beginning of the second stage, repeal or amend any provisions existing when this Treaty enters into force which conflict with the preceding rules.

LÜTTICKE (ALFONS) GMBH v HAUPTZOLLAMT SAARLOUIS (Case 57/65)
[1966] ECR 205, Court of Justice

The payment of turnover equalisation tax was demanded on a consignment of powdered milk imported by Lütticke into Germany from Luxembourg. The domestic product was not subject to such a tax.

This directly discriminatory taxation was condemned by the Court of Justice. Holding Article 95(1) to be directly effective, the Court underlined the importance to the functioning of the common market of the prohibition against discrimination contained in this Article. (Article 177 reference.)

The first paragraph of Article 95 sets forth, as a general and permanent rule of Community law that Member States shall not impose on the products of other Member States any internal taxation in excess of that imposed on similar domestic products. Such a system, often adopted by the Treaty to ensure the equal treatment of nationals within the Community under national legal systems, constitutes in fiscal matters the indispensable foundation of the Common Market.

9.3.3 ARTICLE 95(1): THE PROHIBITION OF DISCRIMINATORY TAXATION OF SIMILAR PRODUCTS

MOLKEREI-ZENTRALE v HAUPTZOLLAMT PADERBORN (Case 28/67)
[1968] ECR 143, Court of Justice

The German Federal Finance Court put to the Court of Justice several questions concerning the interpretation of Article 95, including the meaning of 'internal taxation imposed indirectly on similar domestic products'. (Article 177 reference.)

The Bundesfinanzhof's fifth question seeks to obtain a ruling from the Court on what must be understood by 'internal taxation imposed . . . indirectly on similar domestic products' within the meaning of the first paragraph of Article 95 of the Treaty.

. . .

. . . it should be observed that the terms 'directly or indirectly' taking account of the general scheme of the said provision must be widely interpreted.
The first paragraph of Article 95 refers to all taxation which is actually and specifically imposed on the domestic product at all earlier stages of its manufacture and marketing or which corresponds to the stage at which the product is imported from other Member States it being nevertheless understood that the effect of this taxation diminishes in proportion as the previous stages of manufacture and of marketing become more remote and that this burden tends rapidly to become negligible. Consequently, when the Member States calculate the taxation imposed indirectly on domestic products they must observe the conditions and limitations emerging from these considerations.

COMMISSION v IRELAND (EXCISE PAYMENTS) (Case 55/79)
[1980] ECR 481, Court of Justice

Irish producers of spirits, beer and wine were granted deferment of payment of tax beyond the date on which the products were put on the market, whilst importers had to pay tax on importation of the products. (Article 169 proceedings.)

[2] The facts which gave rise to the action are not contested by Ireland. It is in, fact common ground that the legal provisions applicable in Ireland, in particular pursuant to the Imposition of Duties (No. 221) (Excise Duties) Order 1975, provide in favour of producers of spirits, beer and made wine for deferment of payment of between four and six weeks according to the product whereas, in the case of the same products from other Member States, the duty is payable either at the date of importation or of delivery from the customs warehouse.

[3] The Commission acknowledges that there is no discrimination as regards the rates of duty applicable. On the other hand, it considers that the fact that Irish products are

granted deferment of payment beyond the date on which the products are put on the market amounts to conferring on national producers a financial benefit in comparison with importers who are obliged to pay the duty on the actual date on which the products are released to the market. This results, according to the Commission, in a disadvantage to imported products in competition with the corresponding Irish national production.

. . .

[8] . . . it is necessary, for the purposes of the application of the prohibition on discrimination laid down in Article 95, to take into consideration the provisions relating to the basis of assessment and the detailed rules for levying the various duties in addition to the rate of tax. In fact the decisive criterion of comparison for the purposes of the application of Article 95 is the actual effect of each tax on national production on the one hand and on imported products on the other, since even where the rate of tax is equal the effect of that tax may vary according to the detailed rules for the basis of assessment and levying thereof applied to national production and imported products respectively.

[9] Such is the case with the difference in treatment applied to the alcoholic beverages referred to in the application according to whether those beverages produced in Ireland or imported from other Member States. Although the benefit reserved to national production in the form of facilities for deferred payment is small, the discrimination against products imported from other Member States is none the less obvious.

HUMBLOT v DIRECTEUR DES SERVICES FISCAUX (Case 112/84)
[1985] ECR 1367, Court of Justice

Mr Humblot sought a refund of the tax he had paid on his 36 CV car. The Tribunal de grande instance, Belfort, referred to the Court of Justice a question concerning the interpretation of Article 95. (Article 177 reference.)

[3] It appears from the documents before the Court that there are in France two different types of tax due annually on motor vehicles. First there is a differential tax to which cars rated at 16 CV [fiscal horsepower] or less are subject and secondly a special tax on vehicles rated at more than 16 CV. Whereas the amount of differential tax payable increases progressively and uniformly with the power rating for tax purposes, the special tax is levied at a single and considerably higher rate.

[4] In 1981 Mr Humblot became the owner of a car rated at 36 CV. Before he could put the vehicle on the road Mr Humblot had to pay the special tax, which, at that time, amounted to FF 5,000. After paying that sum Mr Humblot brought a complaint before the tax administration with a view to obtaining a refund of the difference between that sum and the highest rate of the differential tax (at the time FF 1,100).

. . .

[7] It appears from the documents in the case that the essence of the question is whether Article 95 prohibits the charging on cars exceeding a given power rating for tax purposes of a special fixed tax the amount of which is several times the highest amount of the progressive tax payable on cars of less than the said power rating for tax purposes, where the only cars subject to the special tax are imported, in particular from other Member States.

. . .

[12] It is appropriate in the first place to stress that as Community law stands at present the Member States are at liberty to subject products such as cars to a system of road tax which increases progressively in amount depending on an objective criterion, such as the power rating for tax purposes, which may be determined in various ways

[13] Such a system of domestic taxation is, however, compatible with Article 95 only in so far as it is free from any discriminatory or protective effect.

[14] That is not true of a system like the one at issue in the main proceedings. Under that system there are two distinct taxes: a differential tax which increases progressively and is charged on cars not exceeding a given power rating for tax purposes and a fixed tax on cars exceeding that rating which is almost five times as high as the highest rate of the differential tax. Although the system embodies no formal distinction based on the origin of products it manifestly exhibits discriminatory or protective features contrary to Article 95, since the power rating determining liability to the special tax has been fixed at a level such that only imported cars, in particular from other Member States, are

subject to the special tax whereas all cars of domestic manufacture are liable to the distinctly more advantageous differential tax.

[15]   In the absence of considerations relating to the amount of the special tax, consumers seeking comparable cars as regards such matters as size, comfort, actual power, maintenance costs, durability, fuel consumption and price would naturally choose from among cars above and below the critical power rating laid down by French law. However, liability to the special tax entails a much larger increase in taxation than passing from one category of car to another in a system of progressive taxation embodying balanced differentials like the system on which the differential tax is based. The resultant additional taxation is liable to cancel out the advantages which certain cars imported from other Member States might have in consumers' eyes over comparable cars of domestic manufacture, particularly since the special tax continues to be payable for several years. In that respect the special tax reduces the amount of competition to which cars of domestic manufacture are subject and hence is contrary to the principle of neutrality with which domestic taxation must comply.

[16]   In the light of the foregoing considerations the question raised by the national court for a preliminary ruling should be answered as follows: Article 95 of the EEC Treaty prohibits the charging on cars exceeding a given power rating for tax purposes of a special fixed tax the amount of which is several times the highest amount of the progressive tax payable on cars of less than the said power rating for tax purposes, where the only cars subject to the special tax are imported, in particular from other Member States.

COMMISSION v FRANCE (Case 196/85) [1987] ECR 1597, Court of Justice

Under the French General Tax Code, the duty payable on natural sweet wines was less than that imposed upon other kinds of liqueur and similar wines. The Commission claimed that this scheme of taxation infringed Article 95. (Article 169 proceedings.)

[2]   . . . According to the Commission, the scheme is discriminatory inasmuch as it makes entitlement to preferential taxation subject to conditions which are less favourable to products imported from other Member States than to comparable domestic (French) products.

. . .

[4]   The Commission asserts that discrimination contrary to Article 95 of the Treaty arises from the fact that French legislation confines the preferential tax scheme to those liqueur wines whose production is 'traditional and customary'. Although it ostensibly applies without distinction to domestic products and to imports from other Member States, that requirement can be fulfilled only by domestic products. Furthermore, the Commission claims that 'traditional and customary production' is not an objective criterion since it leaves the authorities a margin of discretion in its application.

[5]   The French Government denies the existence of any discrimination. It contends that the concept of 'traditional and customary production' has both a historical aspect, alluding to time-honoured products closely associated with a particular locality, whose long ancestry is part of their fame, and a technical meaning, referring to oenological rules and practices which codify fair and traditional practices. Moreover, the concept is also used in Community legislation on the common organization of the market in wine.

[6]   It should first be pointed out that, as the Court has consistently held . . . at its present stage of development Community law does not restrict the freedom of each Member State to lay down tax arrangements which differentiate between certain products, even products which are similar within the meaning of the first paragraph of Article 95, on the basis of objective criteria, such as the nature of the raw materials used or the production processes employed. Such differentiation is compatible with Community law if it pursues objectives of economic policy which are themselves compatible with the requirements of the Treaty and its secondary legislation, and if the detailed rules are such as to avoid any form of discrimination, direct or indirect, in regard to imports from other Member States or any form of protection of competing domestic products.

[7]   More specifically, the Court has held on several occasions that in the present state of Community law Article 95 of the EEC Treaty does not prohibit Member States, in the

pursuit of legitimate economic or social aims, from granting tax advantages, in the form of exemptions from or reduction of taxes, to certain types of spirits or to certain classes of producers, provided that such preferential systems are extended without discrimination to imported products conforming to the same conditions as preferred domestic products.

[8]   The above criteria are satisfied in this instance.

[9]   With regard to the aims pursued by the contested tax scheme, the French Government explained during the oral procedure that natural sweet wines are made in regions characterized by low rainfall and relatively poor soil, in which the difficulty of growing other crops means that the local economy depends heavily on their production. The French Government maintains that the tax advantage enjoyed by those wines thus tends to offset the more severe conditions under which they are produced, in order to sustain the output of quality products which are of particular economic importance for certain regions of the Community. Such economic policies must be regarded as compatible with the requirements of Community law.

[10]   Furthermore, with regard to the extension of the preferential scheme to imported products, it must be concluded that the criterion of 'traditional and customary production' applies without distinction to domestic and imported products. There is nothing in the evidence before the Court to suggest that the application of the scheme in fact gives preference to French wines at the expense of wines with the same characteristics from other Member States. In particular, it has not been demonstrated that because of physical factors or patterns of production the tax advantage in question operates solely, or even preponderantly, to the benefit of the French product. It should be added that national provisions which cover both domestic and imported products without distinction cannot be regarded as contrary to Community law merely because they might lend themselves to discriminatory application, unless it is proved that they are actually applied in that way.

[11]   Consequently, the objection based on the fact that the benefit of the preferential tax scheme is confined to liqueur wines whose production is 'traditional and customary' must be rejected.

CHEMIAL FARMACEUTICI SPA v DAF SPA (Case 140/79) [1981] ECR 1

In Italy, synthetic alcohol attracted a higher rate of taxation than alcohol produced by fermentation, despite the fact that the two products had identical uses. Italy produced very little synthetic alcohol. (Article 177 reference.)

[13]   . . . the different taxation of synthetic alcohol and of alcohol produced by fermentation in Italy is the result of an economic policy decision to favour the manufacture of alcohol from agricultural products and, correspondingly, to restrain the processing into alcohol of ethylene, a derivative of petroleum, in order to reserve that raw material for other more important economic uses. It accordingly constitutes a legitimate choice of economic policy to which effect is given by fiscal means. The implementation of that policy does not lead to any discrimination since although it results in discouraging imports of synthetic alcohol into Italy, it also has the consequence of hampering the development in Italy itself of production of alcohol from ethylene, that production being technically perfectly possible.

[14]   As the Court has stated on many occasions, particularly in the judgments cited by the Italian Government, in its present stage of development Community law does not restrict the freedom of each Member State to lay down tax arrangements which differentiate between certain products on the basis of objective criteria, such as the nature of the raw materials used or the production processes employed. Such differentiation is compatible with Community law if it pursues economic policy objectives which are themselves compatible with the requirements of the Treaty and its secondary law and if the detailed rules are such as to avoid any form of discrimination, direct or indirect, in regard to imports from other Member States or any form of protection of competing domestic products.

[15]   Differential taxation such as that which exists in Italy for denatured synthetic alcohol on the one hand and denatured alcohol obtained by fermentation on the other

satisfies these requirements. It appears in fact that that system of taxation pursues an objective of legitimate industrial policy in that it is such as to promote the distillation of agricultural products as against the manufacture of alcohol from petroleum derivatives. That choice does not conflict with the rules of Community law or the requirements of a policy decided within the framework of the Community.

[16]   The detailed provisions of the legislation at issue before the national court cannot be considered as discriminatory since, on the one hand, it is not disputed that imports from other Member States of alcohol obtained by fermentation qualify for the same tax treatment as Italian alcohol produced by fermentation and, on the other hand, although the rate of tax prescribed for synthetic alcohol results in restraining the importation of synthetic alcohol originating in other Member States, it has an equivalent economic effect in the national territory in that it also hampers the establishment of profitable production of the same product by Italian industry.

[17]   The reply to the questions submitted by the national court should therefore be that tax arrangements which impose heavier charges on denatured synthetic alcohol than on denatured alcohol obtained by fermentation on the basis of the raw materials and the manufacturing processes employed for the two products are not at variance with the first paragraph of Article 95 of the EEC Treaty if they are applied identically to the two categories of alcohol originating in other Member States.

[18]   Where, by reason of the taxation of synthetic alcohol, it has been impossible to develop profitable production of that type of alcohol on national territory, the application of such tax arrangements cannot be considered as constituting indirect protection of national production of alcohol obtained by fermentation within the meaning of the second paragraph of Article 95 on the sole ground that their consequence is that the product subject to the heavier taxation is in fact a product which is exclusively imported from other Member States of the Community.

JOHN WALKER v *MINISTERIET FOR SKATTER* (Case 243/84) [1986] ECR 875, Court of Justice

Under Dutch legislation, Scotch whisky was taxed at a higher rate than fruit wine of the liqueur type. John Walker, a Scotch whisky producer, claimed that this taxation system infringed Article 95. The Court of Justice was asked by the national court for an interpretation of the term 'similar . . . products' within the meaning of this Article. (Article 177 reference.)

[11]   . . . in order to determine whether products are similar it is necessary first to consider certain objective characteristics of both categories of beverages, such as their origin, the method of manufacture and their organoleptic properties, in particular taste and alcohol content, and secondly to consider whether or not both categories of beverages are capable of meeting the same needs from the point of view of consumers.

[12]   It should be noted that the two categories of beverages exhibit manifestly different characteristics. Fruit wine of the liqueur type is a fruit-based product obtained by natural fermentation, whereas Scotch whisky is a cereal-based product obtained by distillation. The organoleptic properties of the two products are also different . . . the fact that the same raw material, for example alcohol, is to be found in the two products is not sufficient reason to apply the prohibition contained in the first paragraph of Article 95. For the products to be regarded as similar that raw material must also be present in more or less equal proportions in both products. In that regard, it must be pointed out that the alcoholic strength of Scotch whisky is 40% by volume, whereas the alcoholic strength of fruit wine of the liqueur type, to which the Danish tax legislation applies, does not exceed 20% by volume.

[13]   The contention that Scotch whisky may be consumed in the same way as fruit wine of the liqueur type, as an aperitif diluted with water or with fruit juice, even if it were established, would not be sufficient to render Scotch whisky similar to fruit wine of the liqueur type, whose intrinsic characteristics are fundamentally different.

[14]   The answer to the first question must therefore be that the first paragraph of Article 95 of the EEC Treaty must be interpreted as meaning that products such as Scotch whisky and fruit wine of the liqueur type may not be regarded as similar products.

9.3.4   ARTICLE 95(2): PROHIBITION OF TAXATION AFFORDING INDIRECT PROTECTION TO OTHER PRODUCTS

COMMISSION v UNITED KINGDOM (EXCISE DUTIES ON WINE) (Case 170/78)
[1980] ECR 417, [1983] ECR 2265, Court of Justice

In the UK, wine was taxed at a higher rate than beer. Since the two products were clearly not similar within the terms of Article 95(1), the Commission relied on Article 95(2). It claimed that wine and beer were in competition and that the higher tax on wine gave indirect protection to beer producers in the UK. Initially, the Court of Justice declined to deliver a final judgment, asking the parties to come back with further information regarding consumer prices and annual consumption of the two products. The following extract is from the final judgment (Article 169 proceedings).

[7]   In its judgment of 27 February 1980, the Court emphasized that the second paragraph of Article 95 applied to the treatment for tax purposes of products which, without fulfilling the criterion of similarity laid down in the first paragraph of that article, were nevertheless in competition, either partially or potentially, with certain products of the importing country. It added that, in order to determine the existence of a competitive relationship within the meaning of the second paragraph of Article 95, it was necessary to consider not only the present state of the market but also possible developments regarding the free movement of goods within the Community and the further potential for the substitution of products for one another which might be revealed by intensification of trade, so as fully to develop the complementary features of the economies of the Member States in accordance with the objectives laid down by Article 2 of the Treaty.

[8]   As regards the question of competition between wine and beer, the Court considered that, to a certain extent at least, the two beverages in question were capable of meeting identical needs, so that it had to be acknowledged that there was a degree of substitution for one another. It pointed out that, for the purpose of measuring the possible degree of substitution, attention should not be confined to consumer habits in a Member State or in a given region. Those habits, which were essentially variable in time and space, could not be considered to be immutable; the tax policy of a Member State must not therefore crystallize given consumer habits so as to consolidate an advantage acquired by national industries concerned to respond to them.

[9]   The Court nonetheless recognized that, in view of the substantial differences between wine and beer, it was difficult to compare the manufacturing processes and the natural properties of those beverages, as the Government of the United Kingdom had rightly observed. For that reason, the Court requested the parties to provide additional information with a view to dispelling the doubts which existed concerning the nature of the competitive relationship between the two products.

. . .

[12]   . . . In view of the substantial differences in the quality and, therefore, in the price of wines, the decisive competitive relationship between beer, a popular and widely consumed beverage, and wine must be established by reference to those wines which are the most accessible to the public at large, that is to say, generally speaking, the lightest and cheapest varieties. Accordingly, that is the appropriate basis for making fiscal comparisons by reference to the alcoholic strength or to the price of the two beverages in question.

. . .

[26]   After considering the information provided by the parties, the Court has come to the conclusion that, if a comparison is made on the basis of those wines which are cheaper than the types of wine selected by the United Kingdom and of which several varieties are sold in significant quantities on the United Kingdom market, it becomes apparent that precisely those wines which, in view of their price, are most directly in competition with domestic beer production are subject to a considerably higher tax burden.

[27]   It is clear, therefore . . . that the United Kingdom's tax system has the effect of subjecting wine imported from other Member States to an additional tax burden so as to

afford protection to domestic beer production, inasmuch as beer production constitutes the most relevant reference criterion from the point of view of competition. Since such protection is most marked in the case of the most popular wines, the effect of the United Kingdom tax system is to stamp wine with the hallmarks of a luxury product which, in view of the tax burden which it bears, can scarcely constitute in the eyes of the consumer a genuine alternative to the typical domestically produced beverage.

[28]   It follows from the foregoing considerations that, by levying excise duty on still light wines made from fresh grapes at a higher rate, in relative terms, than on beer, the United Kingdom has failed to fulfil its obligations under the second paragraph of Article 95 of the EEC Treaty.

9.4   Articles 30–34: The Elimination of Quantitative Restrictions and all Measures having Equivalent Effect

THE TREATY OF ROME

Article 30
Quantitative restrictions on imports and all measures having equivalent effect shall, without prejudice to the following provisions, be prohibited between Member States.

Article 34
Quantitative restrictions on exports, and all measures having equivalent effect, shall be prohibited between Member States.

R v ROYAL PHARMACEUTICAL SOCIETY OF GREAT BRITAIN (Cases 266 & 267/87) [1989] ECR 1295, Court of Justice

The rules of the Royal Pharmaceutical Society of Great Britain prohibited pharmacists from substituting, except in an emergency, any other product for the product specifically named in prescriptions written by doctors, dentists and veterinary surgeons. In a statement issued on 12 July 1986, the Council of the Society drew attention to these rules and confirmed that they applied both to domestically produced and imported medicines. The Association of Pharmaceutical Importers and its members claimed that the statement and the Society's subsequent refusal to revoke it constituted an infringement of Article 30. (Article 177 reference.)

Three questions were referred to the Court of Justice by the English Court of Appeal:

(1)   Is a national rule of a Member State inconsistent with Article 30 of the EEC Treaty where it requires a pharmacist, in response to a prescription calling for a medicinal product by its trade mark or proprietary name, to dispense only a product bearing that trade mark or proprietary name where the effect of such a rule is to prevent the pharmacist from dispensing a therapeutically equivalent product licensed by the competent national authorities . . . and manufactured by the same company or group of companies or by a licensee of that company but bearing a trade mark or proprietary name applied to it in another Member State which differs from the trade mark or proprietary name appearing in the prescription?

(2)   In the event of the first question being answered in the affirmative, is such a national rule justifiable on grounds of protection of public health or the protection of industrial or commercial property?

(3)   In either event, was the statement of the Council of the Pharmaceutical Society of Great Britain published in the *Pharmaceutical Journal* on 12 July 1986 or its decision as set out in its letter of 12 August 1986 not to revoke that statement a 'measure' within the meaning of Article 30 of the EEC Treaty?

. . .

Third question
[13]   Before the question whether the measures at issue fall under the prohibition in Article 30 of the Treaty or whether they are justified under Article 36 of the Treaty is

considered, the point raised by the national court's third question, which is whether a measure adopted by a professional body such as the Pharmaceutical Society of Great Britain may come within the scope of the said articles, should be resolved.

[14]   According to the documents before the Court, that Society, which was incorporated by Royal Charter in 1843 and whose existence is also recognized in United Kingdom legislation, is the sole professional body for pharmacy. It maintains the register in which all pharmacists must be enrolled in order to carry on their business. As can be seen from the order for reference, it adopts rules of ethics applicable to pharmacists. Finally, United Kingdom legislation has established a disciplinary committee within the Society which may impose disciplinary sanctions on a pharmacist for professional misconduct; those sanctions may even involve his removal from the register. An appeal lies to the High Court from decisions of that committee.

[15]   It should be stated that measures adopted by a professional body on which national legislation has conferred powers of that nature may, if they are capable of affecting trade between Member States, constitute 'measures' within the meaning of Article 30 of the Treaty.

[16]   The reply to the third question should therefore be that measures adopted by a professional body, such as the Pharmaceutical Society of Great Britain, which lays down rules of ethics applicable to the members of the profession and has a committee upon which national legislation has conferred disciplinary powers that could involve removal from the register of persons authorized to exercise the profession, may constitute 'measures' within the meaning of Article 30 of the EEC Treaty.

. . .

The first two questions

[18]   . . . it is common ground between the parties to the main proceedings that the 50 or so products imported in parallel, which have brand names different from those of the equivalent products previously authorized in the United Kingdom, were marketed in that Member State in significant quantities for several years but their importation practically ceased during the summer of 1986, which is the time when the Pharmaceutical Society of Great Britain published its statement drawing attention to the ethical rule prohibiting pharmacists from substituting another product for a specifically named product even if the other product has identical therapeutic effect and confirming that that rule applied to imported products as well as to domestic products.

[19]   In those circumstances, and although the existence of a causal link is a matter of dispute between the parties, the Court cannot exclude the possibility that, in the particular circumstances of the case, the said rule is capable of hindering intra Community trade. For that reason, and without there being any need to decide whether a rule prohibiting a pharmacist from substituting another product with the same therapeutic effect for the medicinal product prescribed by the doctor treating the patient generally constitutes a measure having equivalent effect within the meaning of Article 30 of the Treaty, it is necessary to consider whether such a rule may be justified under Article 36 (second question).

[20]   In that regard, it should be noted that among the grounds of public interest set out in Article 36, only the protection of health could be relevant. A rule prohibiting a trader from substituting, even with the consumer's consent, another product for the brand ordered would go beyond what could be necessary for the protection of industrial and commercial property. . . .

[21]   On the other hand, the rules concerning the relationship between doctors and pharmacists and in particular those rules relating to the attending doctor's freedom to prescribe any product he chooses and to any possibility which the pharmacist may have to dispense a medicinal product other than that prescribed in the prescription are part of the national public health system. As long as those matters have not been regulated by Community legislation, it is for the Member States, within the limits laid down in Article 36, to decide on the degree to which they wish to protect human health and life and how that degree of protection is to be achieved.

[22]   There is no evidence in this case to justify a conclusion by the Court that a rule prohibiting pharmacists from substituting another medicinal product for one designated by name in the prescription, even if the other product has the same therapeutic effect,

goes beyond what is necessary to achieve the objective in view, which is to leave the entire responsibility for the treatment of the patient in the hands of the doctor treating him. In particular, the Court finds itself unable to discount the reasons, based on psychosomatic phenomena, for which, according to the observations submitted by the Pharmaceutical Society of Great Britain and by the governments of several Member States, a specific proprietary medicinal product might be prescribed rather than a generic product or any other proprietary medicinal product having the same therapeutic effect.

[23]   Furthermore, the arguments put forward by the Association of Pharmaceutical Importers do not disclose any evidence that the application of such a general rule to products imported from other Member States, in which they may be marketed lawfully, constitutes a means of arbitrary discrimination or a disguised restriction on trade between Member States within the meaning of the last sentence of Article 36.

[24]   The reply to the first two questions should therefore be that a national rule of a Member State requiring a pharmacist, in response to a prescription calling for a medicinal product by its trade mark or proprietary name, to dispense only a product bearing that trade mark or proprietary name may be justified under Article 36 of the Treaty on grounds of the protection of public health even where the effect of such a rule is to prevent the pharmacist from dispensing a therapeutically equivalent product licensed by the competent national authorities . . . and manufactured by the same company or group of companies or by a licensee of that company but bearing a trade mark or proprietary name applied to it in another Member State which differs from the trade mark or proprietary name appearing in the prescription.

9.4.1   QUANTITATIVE RESTRICTIONS ON IMPORTS: ARTICLE 30

R v HENN AND DARBY (Case 34/79) [1979] ECR 3795, Court of Justice

The defendants appealed against convictions under English customs legislation which prohibited the importation of indecent or obscene articles. The articles in question formed part of a consignment of obscene films and magazines which had arrived at Felixstowe from Rotterdam.

The appellants claimed that the prohibition constituted arbitrary discrimination under Article 36 of the Treaty because it resulted in the application to imported goods of rules which were stricter than those applied to goods of domestic origin. Whereas customs legislation applied to 'indecent and obscene' material, internal regulation under the Obscene Publications Acts 1959 and 1964 applied to a narrower class of material, namely that which tended to 'deprave or corrupt'. Moreover, the mere possession, for non-commercial purposes, of either kind of material was not a criminal offence in the UK.

The appellants further claimed that there was no consistent policy of public morality in the UK with respect to indecent or obscene articles. Different rules applied in England and Wales, Scotland, Northern Ireland and the Isle of Man.

The House of Lords referred a number of questions to the Court of Justice. (Article 177 reference.)

First question

[11]   The first question asks whether a law of a Member State which prohibits the import into that State of pornographic articles is a measure having equivalent effect to a quantitative restriction on imports within the meaning of Article 30 of the Treaty.

[12]   That article provides that 'quantitative restrictions on imports and all measures having equivalent effect' shall be prohibited between Member States. It is clear that this provision includes a prohibition on imports inasmuch as this is the most extreme form of restriction. The expression used in Article 30 must therefore be understood as being the equivalent of the expression 'prohibitions or restrictions on imports' occurring in Article 36.

[13]   The answer to the first question is therefore that a law such as that referred to in this case constitutes a quantitative restriction on imports within the meaning of Article 30 of the Treaty.

Second and third questions

[14] The second and third questions are framed in the following terms:

> 2. If the answer to Question 1 is in the affirmative, does the first sentence of Article 36 upon its true construction mean that a Member State may lawfully impose prohibitions on the importation of goods from another Member State which are of an indecent or obscene character as understood by the laws of that Member State?
>
> 3.   In particular:
>
> (i)   is the Member State entitled to maintain such prohibitions in order to prevent, to guard against or to reduce the likelihood of breaches of the domestic law of all constituent parts of the customs territory of the State?
>
> (ii)   is the Member State entitled to maintain such prohibitions having regard to the national standards and characteristics of that State as demonstrated by the domestic laws of the constituent parts of the customs territory of that State including the law imposing the prohibition, notwithstanding variations between the laws of the constituent parts?

It is convenient to consider these questions together.

[15] Under the terms of Article 36 of the Treaty the provisions relating to the free movement of goods within the Community are not to preclude prohibitions on imports which are justified *inter alia* 'on grounds of public morality'. In principle, it is for each Member State to determine in accordance with its own scale of values and in the form selected by it the requirements of public morality in its territory. In any event, it cannot be disputed that the statutory provisions applied by the United Kingdom in regard to the importation of articles having an indecent or obscene character come within the powers reserved to the Member States by the first sentence of Article 36.

[16] Each Member State is entitled to impose prohibitions on imports justified on grounds of public morality for the whole of its territory, as defined in Article 227 of the Treaty, whatever the structure of its constitution may be and however the powers of legislating in regard to the subject in question may be distributed. The fact that certain differences exist between the laws enforced in the different constituent parts of a Member State does not thereby prevent that State from applying a unitary concept in regard to prohibitions on imports imposed, on grounds of public morality, on trade with other Member States.

[17] The answer to the second and third questions must therefore be that the first sentence of Article 36 upon its true construction means that a Member State may, in principle, lawfully impose prohibitions on the importation from any other Member State of articles which are of an indecent or obscene character as understood by its domestic laws and that such prohibitions may lawfully be applied to the whole of its national territory even if, in regard to the field in question, variations exist between the laws in force in the different constituent parts of the Member State concerned.

Fourth, fifth and sixth questions

[These questions concerned the claim of arbitrary discrimination and disguised restriction on trade between Member States contrary to the requirements of Article 36]

. . .

[19] In these questions the House of Lords takes account of the appellants' submissions based upon certain differences between, on the one hand, the prohibition on importing the goods in question, which is absolute, and, on the other, the laws in force in the various constituent parts of the United Kingdom, which appear to be less strict in the sense that the mere possession of obscene articles for non-commercial purposes does not constitute a criminal offence anywhere in the United Kingdom and that, even if it is generally forbidden, trade in such articles is subject to certain exceptions, notably those in favour of articles having scientific, literary, artistic or educational interest. Having regard to those differences the question has been raised whether the prohibition on imports might not come within the second sentence of Article 36.

[20] According to the second sentence of Article 36 the restrictions on imports referred to in the first sentence may not 'constitute a means of arbitrary discrimination or a disguised restriction on trade between Member States'.

[21] In order to answer the questions which have been referred to the Court it is appropriate to have regard to the function of this provision, which is designed to prevent restrictions on trade based on the grounds mentioned in the first sentence of Article 36 from being diverted from their proper purpose and used in such a way as either to create discrimination in respect of goods originating in other Member States or indirectly to protect certain national products. That is not the purport of a prohibition, such as that in force in the United Kingdom, on the importation of articles which are of an indecent or obscene character. Whatever may be the differences between the laws on this subject in force in the different constituent parts of the United Kingdom, and notwithstanding the fact that they contain certain exceptions of limited scope, these laws, taken as a whole, have as their purpose the prohibition, or at least, the restraining, of the manufacture and marketing of publications or articles of an indecent or obscene character. In these circumstances it is permissible to conclude, on a comprehensive view, that there is no lawful trade in such goods in the United Kingdom. A prohibition on imports which may in certain respects be more strict than some of the laws applied within the United Kingdom cannot therefore be regarded as amounting to a measure designed to give indirect protection to some national product or aimed at creating arbitrary discrimination between goods of this type depending on whether they are produced within the national territory or another Member State.

[22] The answer . . . must therefore be that if a prohibition on the importation of goods is justifiable on grounds of public morality and if it is imposed with that purpose the enforcement of that prohibition cannot, in the absence within the Member State concerned of a lawful trade in the same goods, constitute a means of arbitrary discrimination or a disguised restriction on trade contrary to Article 36.

9.4.2 MEANING OF 'MEASURES HAVING EQUIVALENT EFFECT TO QUANTITATIVE RESTRICTIONS' ON IMPORTS: DIRECTIVE 70/50

COMMISSION DIRECTIVE 70/50/EEC OF 22 DECEMBER 1969 BASED ON THE PROVISIONS OF ARTICLE 33(7), ON THE ABOLITION OF MEASURES WHICH HAVE AN EFFECT EQUIVALENT TO QUANTITATIVE RESTRICTIONS ON IMPORTS AND ARE NOT COVERED BY OTHER PROVISIONS ADOPTED IN PURSUANCE OF THE EEC TREATY (1970) OJ (Special Edition) (I), p. 17

(Preamble omitted)

Article 1
The purpose of this Directive is to abolish the measures referred to in Articles 2 and 3, which were operative at the date of entry into force of the EEC Treaty.

Article 2
1. This Directive covers measures, other than those applicable equally to domestic or imported products, which hinder imports which could otherwise take place, including measures which make importation more difficult or costly than the disposal of domestic production.

2. In particular, it covers measures which make imports or the disposal, at any marketing stage, of imported products subject to a condition — other than a formality — which is required in respect of imported products only, or a condition differing from that required for domestic products and more difficult to satisfy. Equally, it covers, in particular, measures which favour domestic products or grant them a preference, other than an aid, to which conditions may or may not be attached.

3. The measures referred to must be taken to include those measures which:

(a) lay down, for imported products only, minimum or maximum prices below or above which imports are prohibited, reduced or made subject to conditions liable to hinder importation;

(b) lay down less favourable prices for imported products than for domestic products;

(c) fix profit margins or any other price components for imported products only or fix these differently for domestic products and for imported products, to the detriment of the latter;

(d)   preclude any increase in the price of the imported product corresponding to the supplementary costs and charges inherent in importation;

(e)   fix the prices of products solely on the basis of the cost price or the quality of domestic products at such a level as to create a hindrance to importation;

(f)   lower the value of an imported product, in particular by causing a reduction in its intrinsic value, or increase its costs;

(g)   make access of imported products to the domestic market conditional upon having an agent or representative in the territory of the importing Member State;

(h)   lay down conditions of payment in respect of imported products only, or subject imported products to conditions which are different from those laid down for domestic products and more difficult to satisfy;

(i)   require, for imports only, the giving of guarantees or making of payments on account;

(j)   subject imported products only to conditions, in respect, in particular of shape, size, weight, composition, presentation, identification or putting up, or subject imported products to conditions which are different from those for domestic products and more difficult to satisfy;

(k)   hinder the purchase by private individuals of imported products only, or encourage, require or give preference to the purchase of domestic products only;

(l)   totally or partially preclude the use of national facilities or equipment in respect of imported products only, or totally or partially confine the use of such facilities or equipment to domestic products only;

(m) prohibit or limit publicity in respect of imported products only, or totally or partially confine publicity to domestic products only;

(n)   prohibit, limit or require stocking in respect of imported products only; totally or partially confine the use of stocking facilities to domestic products only, or make the stocking of imported products subject to conditions which are different from those required for domestic products and more difficult to satisfy;

(o)   make importation subject to the granting of reciprocity by one or more Member States;

(p)   prescribe that imported products are to conform, totally or partially, to rules other than those of the importing country;

(q)   specify time limits for imported products which are insufficient or excessive in relation to the normal course of the various transactions to which these time limits apply;

(r)   subject imported products to controls, other than those inherent in the customs clearance procedure, to which domestic products are not subject or which are stricter in respect of imported products than they are in respect of domestic products, without this being necessary in order to ensure equivalent protection;

(s)   confine names which are not indicative of origin or source to domestic products only.

Article 3

This Directive also covers measures governing the marketing of products which deal, in particular, with shape, size, weight, composition, presentation, identification or putting up and which are equally applicable to domestic and imported products, where the restrictive effect of such measures on the free movement of goods exceeds the effects intrinsic to trade rules.

This is the case, in particular, where:

— the restrictive effects on the free movement of goods are out of proportion to their purpose;

— the same objective can be attained by other means which are less of a hindrance to trade.

(Remaining provisions omitted.)

WALTER RAU LEBENSMITTELWERKE v *DE SMEDT PVBA* (Case 261/81)
[1982] ECR 3961, Court of Justice

Belgian legislation prohibited the retailing of margarine which was not in cube shaped form or packed in cube shaped packaging. The Government maintained that this provision could not be classified as a measure having equivalent effect to a quantitative restriction and, even if it could be so classified, was necessary for the protection of the consumer in order to prevent confusion between margarine and butter. (Article 177 reference.)

[12] . . . it must be recalled, as the Court has repeatedly held . . . that in the absence of common rules relating to the marketing of the products concerned, obstacles to free movement within the Community resulting from disparities between the national laws must be accepted in so far as such rules, applicable to domestic and to imported products without distinction, may be recognized as being necessary in order to satisfy mandatory requirements relating *inter alia* to consumer protection. It is also necessary for such rules to be proportionate to the aim in view. If a Member State has a choice between various measures to attain the same objective it should choose the means which least restricts the free movement of goods.

[13] Although the requirement that a particular form of packaging must also be used for imported products is not an absolute barrier to the importation into the Member State concerned of products originating in other Member States, nevertheless it is of such a nature as to render the marketing of those products more difficult or more expensive either by barring them from certain channels of distribution or owing to the additional costs brought about by the necessity to package the products in question in special packs which comply with the requirements in force on the market of their destination.

[14] In this case the protective effect of the Belgian rules is moreover demonstrated by the fact, affirmed by the Commission and not disputed by the Belgian Government, that despite prices appreciably higher than those in some other Member States there is practically no margarine of foreign origin to be found on the Belgian market.

[15] Therefore it may not be claimed that the requirement of special packaging for the product is not an obstacle to marketing.

[16] Furthermore, the Belgian Government contends that the requirement of the cubic form is necessary for the protection of the consumer in order to prevent confusion between butter and margarine. It states that the cubic form used for the sale of margarine is 'rooted' in the habits of Belgian consumers and is therefore an effective safeguard in that respect.

[17] It cannot be reasonably denied that in principle legislation designed to prevent butter and margarine from being confused in the mind of the consumer is justified. However, the application by one Member State to margarine lawfully manufactured and marketed in another Member State of legislation which prescribes for that product a specific kind of packaging such as the cubic form to the exclusion of any other form of packaging considerably exceeds the requirements of the object in view. Consumers may in fact be protected just as effectively by other measures, for example by rules on labelling, which hinder the free movement of goods less.

9.4.3 MEANING OF 'MEASURES HAVING EQUIVALENT EFFECT TO QUANTITATIVE RESTRICTIONS' ON IMPORTS: THE *DASSONVILLE* FORMULA

PROCUREUR DU ROI v *DASSONVILLE* (Case 8/74) [1974] ECR 837, Court of Justice

Criminal proceedings were instituted in Belgium against traders who had imported Scotch whisky from France without being in possession of the certificate of origin required by a Belgian provision. The national court asked the Court of Justice whether the national provision constituted a measure having equivalent effect to a quantitative restriction within the meaning of Article 30. (Article 177 reference.)

[2] By the first question it is asked whether a national provision prohibiting the import of goods bearing a designation of origin where such goods are not accompanied by an official document issued by the government of the exporting country certifying their right to such designation constitutes a measure having an effect equivalent to a quantitative restriction within the meaning of Article 30 of the Treaty.

[3] This question was raised within the context of criminal proceedings instituted in Belgium against traders who duly acquired a consignment of Scotch whisky in free

circulation in France and imported it into Belgium without being in possession of a certificate of origin from the British customs authorities, thereby infringing Belgian rules.

[4] It emerges from the file and from the oral proceedings that a trader, wishing to import into Belgium Scotch whisky which is already in free circulation in France, can obtain such a certificate only with great difficulty, unlike the importer who imports directly from the producer country.

[5] All trading rules enacted by Member States which are capable of hindering, directly or indirectly, actually or potentially, intra-Community trade are to be considered as measures having an effect equivalent to quantitative restrictions.

[6] In the absence of a Community system guaranteeing for consumers the authenticity of a product's designation of origin, if a Member State takes measures to prevent unfair practices in this connexion, it is however subject to the condition that these measures should be reasonable and that the means of proof required should not act as a hindrance to trade between Member States and should, in consequence, be accessible to all Community nationals.

[7] Even without having to examine whether or not such measures are covered by Article 36, they must not, in any case, by virtue of the principle expressed in the second sentence of that Article, constitute a means of arbitrary discrimination or a disguised restriction on trade between Member States.

[8] That may be the case with formalities, required by a Member State for the purpose of proving the origin of a product, which only direct importers are really in a position to satisfy without facing serious difficulties.

[9] Consequently, the requirement by a Member State of a certificate of authenticity which is less easily obtainable by importers of an authentic product which has been put into free circulation in a regular manner in another Member State than by importers of the same product coming directly from the country of origin constitutes a measure having an effect equivalent to a quantitative restriction as prohibited by the Treaty.

9.4.4 EXAMPLES OF DISTINCTLY APPLICABLE MEASURES CAUGHT BY ARTICLE 30

REWE-ZENTRALFINANZ v LANDWIRTSCHAFTSKAMMER BONN (Case 4/75) [1975] ECR 843, Court of Justice

The national court referred to the Court of Justice certain questions on the interpretation of Articles 30 and 36 of the Treaty in the context of an action concerning phytosanitary inspections carried out on plant products, such as apples, imported into West Germany. The purpose of the inspections was to prevent the spread of a pest known as San Jose Scale. In particular, the national court asked whether such inspections were to be regarded as measures having equivalent effect to quantitative restrictions within the meaning of Article 30 and whether they constituted a 'means of arbitrary discrimination' within the meaning of Article 36 on the ground that similar domestic products were not subject to compulsory inspections before being distributed within Germany. (Article 177 reference.)

[3] Article 30 of the Treaty prohibits quantitative restrictions on imports and all measures having equivalent effect between Member States.

For the purposes of this prohibition it is enough for the measures in question to be capable of acting as a direct or indirect, real or potential hindrance to imports between Member States.

In accordance with Article 2(2) of Commission Directive No 70/50/EEC of 22 December 1969. . . . measures having equivalent effect are those which make imports subject to a condition which is required in respect of imported products only or a condition differing from that required for domestic products and more difficult to satisfy.

[4] It is clear from the questions put that the phytosanitary inspections in question only concern importations of plant products and that similar domestic products, such as apples, are not subject to comparable compulsory examinations for the purpose of distribution.

These inspections thus amount to a condition which is required in respect of imported products only, within the meaning of Article 2(2) of the abovementioned directive.

Moreover, as a result, in particular, of the delays inherent in the inspections and the additional transport costs which the importer may incur thereby, the inspections in question are likely to make importation more difficult or more costly.

[5] It follows that phytosanitary inspections at the frontier which plant products, such as apples, coming from another Member State are required to undergo, constitute measures having an effect equivalent to quantitative restrictions within the meaning of Article 30 of the Treaty, and are prohibited under that provision subject to the exceptions laid down by Community law.

[6] Under the first sentence of Article 36 of the Treaty, the provisions of Articles 30 to 34 are not to preclude restrictions on imports and, therefore, measures having equivalent effect, which are justified for reasons of protection of the health of plants.

. . .

[7] . . . a phytosanitary inspection carried out by a Member State on the importation of plant products constitutes, in principle, one of the restrictions on imports which are justified under the first sentence of Article 36 of the Treaty.

[8] However, the restrictions on imports referred to in the first sentence of Article 36 cannot be accepted under the second sentence of that article if they constitute a means of arbitrary discrimination.

The fact that plant products imported from another Member State are subject to a phytosanitary inspection although domestic products are not subject to an equivalent examination when they are despatched within the Member State might constitute arbitrary discrimination within the meaning of the abovementioned provision.

. . .

The different treatment of imported and domestic products, based on the need to prevent the spread of the harmful organism could not, however, be regarded as arbitrary discrimination if effective measures are taken in order to prevent the distribution of contaminated domestic products and if there is reason to believe, in particular on the basis of previous experience, that there is a risk of the harmful organism's spreading if no inspection is held on importation.

[9] The reply to the questions put must therefore be that a requirement to submit imports of plant products, such as apples, from another Member State to a phytosanitary inspection at the frontier in order to establish whether such products are carriers of certain organisms harmful to plants constitutes a measure having an effect equivalent to quantitative restrictions within the meaning of Article 30 of the Treaty and is prohibited under that provision, subject to the exceptions laid down in Article 36 of the Treaty.

COMMISSION v IRELAND ('BUY IRISH' CAMPAIGN) (Case 249/81)
[1982] ECR 4005, Court of Justice

The Irish Government introduced a three year programme to help promote Irish products with the aim of achieving 'a switch from imports to Irish products equivalent to 3% of total consumer spending'. The two main elements of the campaign were widespread advertising of Irish products and the use of the 'Guaranteed Irish' symbol. The Commission claimed that the campaign contravened Article 30. (Article 169 proceedings.)

[25] Whilst it may be true that the two elements of the programme which have continued in effect, namely the advertising campaign and the use of the 'Guaranteed Irish' symbol, have not had any significant success in winning over the Irish market to domestic products, it is not possible to overlook the fact that, regardless of their efficacity, those two activities form part of a government programme which is designed to achieve the substitution of domestic products for imported products and is liable to affect the volume of trade between Member States.

[26] The advertising campaign to encourage the sale and purchase of Irish products cannot be divorced from its origin as part of the government programme, or from its connection with the introduction of the 'Guaranteed Irish' symbol and with the organization of a special system for investigating complaints about products bearing that symbol. The establishment of the system for investigating complaints about Irish products provides adequate confirmation of the degree of organization surrounding the 'Buy Irish' campaign and of the discriminatory nature of the campaign.

[27]   In the circumstances the two activities in question amount to the establishment of a national practice, introduced by the Irish Government and prosecuted with its assistance, the potential effect of which on imports from other Member States is comparable to that resulting from government measures of a binding nature.

[28]   Such a practice cannot escape the prohibition laid down by Article 30 of the Treaty solely because it is not based on decisions which are binding upon undertakings. Even measures adopted by the government of a Member State which do not have binding effect may be capable of influencing the conduct of traders and consumers in that State and thus of frustrating the aims of the Community as set out in Article 2 and enlarged upon in Article 3 of the Treaty.

[29]   That is the case where, as in this instance, such a restrictive practice represents the implementation of a programme defined by the government which affects the national economy as a whole and which is intended to check the flow of trade between Member States by encouraging the purchase of domestic products, by means of an advertising campaign on a national scale and the organization of special procedures applicable solely to domestic products, and where those activities are attributable as a whole to the government and are pursued in an organized fashion throughout the national territory.

9.4.5   EXAMPLES OF INDISTINCTLY APPLICABLE MEASURES CAUGHT BY ARTICLE 30

COMMISSION v UNITED KINGDOM (ORIGIN MARKING OF GOODS)
(Case 207/83) [1985] ECR 1202, Court of Justice

Under English legislation, certain categories of goods – clothing and textiles, domestic electrical appliances, footwear and cutlery – could not be sold in the UK unless they were marked with or accompanied by an indication of origin. The UK Government argued that the rule, which applied indistinctly to imported and domestic products, was necessary to protect consumers who, it was claimed, associate the quality of certain goods with the countries where they are made. The Commission sought a declaration that the legislation breached Article 30. (Article 169 proceedings.)

[13]   The United Kingdom's defence is in substance limited to developing the two arguments which it has already put forward during the procedure prior to the application to the Court. First, it contends that the Order is a national measure which applies to imported and national products alike and the effect of which on trade between Member States is uncertain, if not non-existent. Secondly, it maintains that, in the case of the goods to which the Order applies, the requirements relating to indications of origin meet the requirements of consumer protection since consumers regard the origin of the goods which they buy as an indicator of their quality or true value.

[14]   Those two arguments must be examined in turn.

[15]   As regards the possible effect of the contested Order on trade, the United Kingdom points out that the requirements laid down in Article 2 of the Order concern the retail sale of all the goods covered by the Order, whether imported or not. Some of those goods, for example woollen knitwear and cutlery, are produced in the United Kingdom in substantial quantities.

[16]   It should first be observed, with regard to that argument, that in order to escape the obligations imposed on him by the legislation in question the retailer will tend, as the Commission has rightly pointed out, to ask his wholesalers to supply him with goods which are already origin-marked. That tendency has been confirmed by complaints received by the Commission. Thus, it emerges from the documents before the Court that the Groupement des industries françaises des appareils d'équipement ménager [French Domestic Appliance Manufacturers' Association] informed the Commission that French manufacturers of domestic appliances who wish to sell their products on the United Kingdom market have had to mark such products systematically in response to pressure brought to bear on them by their distributors. The effects of the contested provisions are therefore liable to spread to the wholesale trade and even to manufacturers.

[17]   Secondly, it has to be recognized that the purpose of indications of origin or origin-marking is to enable consumers to distinguish between domestic and imported

products and that this enables them to assert any prejudices which they may have against foreign products. As the Court has had occasion to emphasize in various contexts, the Treaty, by establishing a common market and progressively approximating the economic policies of the Member States seeks to unite national markets in a single market having the characteristics of a domestic market. Within such a market, the origin-marking requirement not only makes the marketing in a Member State of goods produced in other Member States in the sectors in question more difficult; it also has the effect of slowing down economic interpenetration in the Community by handicapping the sale of goods produced as the result of a division of labour between Member States.

[18] It follows from those considerations that the United Kingdom provisions in question are liable to have the effect of increasing the production costs of imported goods and making it more difficult to sell them on the United Kingdom market.

[19] The second argument advanced by the United Kingdom is in effect that the contested legislation, applicable without distinction to domestic and imported products, is necessary in order to satisfy imperative requirements relating to consumer protection. It states that a survey carried out amongst United Kingdom consumers has shown that they associate the quality of certain goods with the countries in which they are made. They like to know, for example, whether leather shoes have been made in Italy, woollen knitwear in the United Kingdom, fashion-wear in France and domestic electrical appliances in Germany.

[20] That argument must be rejected. The requirements relating to the indication of origin of goods are applicable without distinction to domestic and imported products only in form because, by their very nature, they are intended to enable the consumer to distinguish between those two categories of products, which may thus prompt him to give his preference to national products.

[21] It must also be observed that the fact that United Kingdom consumers associate a product's quality with its national origin does not appear to have been a consideration which prompted the United Kingdom Government when it suggested to the Commission that, as far as the Member States of the Community were concerned, it was prepared to accept the indication 'Made in the European Community'. Besides, if the national origin of goods brings certain qualities to the minds of consumers, it is in manufacturers' interests to indicate it themselves on the goods or on their packaging and it is not necessary to compel them to do so. In that case, the protection of consumers is sufficiently guaranteed by rules which enable the use of false indications of origin to be prohibited. Such rules are not called in question by the EEC Treaty.

[22] Those considerations lead to the conclusion that Article 2 of the Order constitutes a measure which makes the marketing of goods imported from other Member States more difficult than the marketing of domestically-produced goods and for which Community law does not recognize any ground of justification. That provision therefore falls within the prohibition laid down in Article 30 of the EEC Treaty.

[23] It must therefore be declared that, by prohibiting the retail sale of certain goods imported from other Member States unless they are marked with or accompanied by an indication of origin, the United Kingdom has failed to fulfil an obligation incumbent on it under Article 30 of the EEC Treaty.

9.4.6 *CASSIS DE DIJON:* THE TWO *CASSIS* PRINCIPLES

REWE-ZENTRAL AG v *BUNDESMONOPOLVERWALTING FÜR BRANNTWEIN*
(Case 120/78) [1979] ECR 649, Court of Justice

The applicant was refused authorisation to import a consignment of 'Cassis de Dijon' (blackcurrant liqueur) into Germany from France because the product did not meet German requirements. German legislation provided that the marketing of fruit liqueurs was conditional upon a minimum alcohol content of 25%, whereas the alcohol content of 'Cassis de Dijon', which was freely marketed in France, was between 15% and 20%. The applicant claimed (*inter alia*) that this requirement constituted a measure having equivalent effect to a quantitative restriction on imports contrary to Article 30. (Article 177 reference.)

[8]   In the absence of common rules relating to the production and marketing of alcohol . . . it is for the Member States to regulate all matters relating to the production and marketing of alcohol and alcoholic beverages on their own territory.

Obstacles to movement within the Community resulting from disparities between the national laws relating to the marketing of the products in question must be accepted in so far as those provisions may be recognized as being necessary in order to satisfy mandatory requirements relating in particular to the effectiveness of fiscal supervision, the protection of public health, the fairness of commercial transactions and the defence of the consumer.

[9]   The Government of the Federal Republic of Germany, intervening in the proceedings, put forward various arguments which, in its view, justify the application of provisions relating to the minimum alcohol content of alcoholic beverages, adducing considerations relating on the one hand to the protection of public health and on the other to the protection of the consumer against unfair commercial practices.

[10]   As regards the protection of public health the German Government states that the purpose of the fixing of minimum alcohol contents by national legislation is to avoid the proliferation of alcoholic beverages on the national market, in particular alcoholic beverages with a low alcohol content, since, in its view, such products may more easily induce a tolerance towards alcohol than more highly alcoholic beverages.

[11]   Such considerations are not decisive since the consumer can obtain on the market an extremely wide range of weakly or moderately alcoholic products and furthermore a large proportion of alcoholic beverages with a high alcohol content freely sold on the German market is generally consumed in a diluted form.

[12]   The German Government also claims that the fixing of a lower limit for the alcohol content of certain liqueurs is designed to protect the consumer against unfair practices on the part of producers and distributors of alcoholic beverages.

This argument is based on the consideration that the lowering of the alcohol content secures a competitive advantage in relation to beverages with a higher alcohol content, since alcohol constitutes by far the most expensive constituent of beverages by reason of the high rate of tax to which it is subject.

Furthermore, according to the German Government, to allow alcoholic products into free circulation wherever, as regards their alcohol content, they comply with the rules laid down in the country of production would have the effect of imposing as a common standard within the Community the lowest alcohol content permitted in any of the Member States, and even of rendering any requirements in this field inoperative since a lower limit of this nature is foreign to the rules of several Member States.

[13]   As the Commission rightly observed, the fixing of limits in relation to the alcohol content of beverages may lead to the standardization of products placed on the market and of their designations, in the interests of a greater transparency of commercial transactions and offers for sale to the public.

However, this line of argument cannot be taken so far as to regard the mandatory fixing of minimum alcohol contents as being an essential guarantee of the fairness of commercial transactions, since it is a simple matter to ensure that suitable information is conveyed to the purchaser by requiring the display of an indication of origin and of the alcohol content on the packaging of products.

[14]   It is clear from the foregoing that the requirements relating to the minimum alcohol content of alcoholic beverages do not serve a purpose which is in the general interest and such as to take precedence over the requirements of the free movement of goods, which constitutes one of the fundamental rules of the Community.

In practice, the principle effect of requirements of this nature is to promote alcoholic beverages having a high alcohol content by excluding from the national market products of other Member States which do not answer that description.

It therefore appears that the unilateral requirement imposed by the rules of a Member State of a minimum alcohol content for the purposes of the sale of alcoholic beverages constitutes an obstacle to trade which is incompatible with the provisions of Article 30 of the Treaty.

There is therefore no valid reason why, provided that they have been lawfully produced and marketed in one of the Member States, alcoholic beverages should not be introduced into any other Member State; the sale of such products may not be subject to a legal prohibition on the marketing of beverages with an alcohol content lower than the limit set by the national rules.

[15] Consequently, the first question should be answered to the effect that the concept of 'measures having an effect equivalent to quantitative restrictions on imports' contained in Article 30 of the Treaty is to be understood to mean that the fixing of a minimum alcohol content for alcoholic beverages intended for human consumption by the legislation of a Member State also falls within the prohibition laid down in that provision where the importation of alcoholic beverages lawfully produced and marketed in another Member State is concerned.

COMMISSION v IRELAND (RESTRICTIONS ON IMPORTATION OF SOUVENIRS) (Case 113/80) [1981] ECR 1625, Court of Justice

Irish legislation prohibited the importation and sale of items of jewellery of foreign origin depicting motifs suggesting that they were souvenirs of Ireland – such as shamrocks – unless they were marked with an indication of their country of origin or with the word 'foreign'. The Irish Government did not dispute that the relevant orders were an obstacle to the free movement of goods but sought to justify them on the grounds of consumer protection and the fairness of commercial transactions. The Commission claimed that the legislation infringed Article 30. (Article 169 proceedings.)

[8] In view of the fact that neither the protection of consumers nor the fairness of commercial transactions is included amongst the exceptions set out in Article 36, those grounds cannot be relied upon as such in connexion with that article.

[9] However, since the Irish Government describes its recourse to these concepts as 'the central issue in the case', it is necessary to study this argument in connexion with Article 30 and to consider whether it is possible, in reliance on those concepts, to say that the Irish orders are not measures having an effect equivalent to quantitative restrictions on imports within the meaning of that article, bearing in mind that, according to the established case-law of the Court, such measures include 'all trading rules enacted by Member States which are capable of hindering, directly or indirectly, actually or potentially, intra-Community trade' (judgment of 11 July 1974 in Case 8/74 *Dassonville* [1974] ECR 837).

[10] In this respect, the Court has repeatedly affirmed. . . . that 'in the absence of common rules relating to the production and marketing of the product in question it is for Member States to regulate all matters relating to its production, distribution and consumption on their own territory subject, however, to the condition that those rules do not present an obstacle . . . to intra-Community trade' and that 'it is only where national rules, which apply without discrimination to both domestic and imported products, may be justified as being necessary in order to satisfy imperative requirements relating in particular to . . . the fairness of commercial transactions and the defence of the consumer that they may constitute an exception to the requirements arising under Article 30'.

[11] The orders concerned in the present case are not measures which are applicable to domestic products and to imported products without distinction but rather a set of rules which apply only to imported products and are therefore discriminatory in nature, with the result that the measures in issue are not covered by the decisions cited above which relate exclusively to provisions that regulate in a uniform manner the marketing of domestic products and imported products.

COMMISSION v DENMARK (DISPOSABLE BEER CANS) (Case 302/86) [1988] ECR 4607, Court of Justice

Denmark introduced legislation which required all containers for beer and soft drinks to be re-usable and subject to a deposit-and-return system. The legislation also provided that all containers must be approved by the National Agency for the Protection of the Environment, which could refuse approval of new kinds of container. Approval would be refused if a container was not suitable for a system of return or if the return system to be set up did not ensure that a sufficient proportion of containers were re-used. These rules were subsequently modified to allow drinks producers to use non-approved containers for quantities not exceeding 3,000 hectolitres a year and for the sale of imported drinks introduced to test the market in Denmark, provided a deposit-and-return system was set up. The Commission argued that the legislation infringed Article 30. (Article 169 proceedings.)

[6] The first point which must be made in resolving this dispute is that, according to an established body of case-law of the Court. . . ., in the absence of common rules relating to the marketing of the products in question, obstacles to free movement within the Community resulting from disparities between the national laws must be accepted in so far as such rules, applicable to domestic and imported products without distinction, may be recognized as being necessary in order to satisfy mandatory requirements recognized by Community law. Such rules must also be proportionate to the aim in view. If a Member State has a choice between various measures for achieving the same aim, it should choose the means which least restricts the free movement of goods.

[7] In the present case the Danish Government contends that the mandatory collection system for containers of beer and soft drinks applied in Denmark is justified by a mandatory requirement related to the protection of the environment.

[8] The Court has already held . . . that the protection of the environment is 'one of the Community's essential objectives', which may as such justify certain limitations of the principle of the free movement of goods. That view is moreover confirmed by the Single European Act.

[9] In view of the foregoing, it must therefore be stated that the protection of the environment is a mandatory requirement which may limit the application of Article 30 of the Treaty.

[10] The Commission submits that the Danish rules are contrary to the principle of proportionality in so far as the aim of the protection of the environment may be achieved by means less restrictive of intra-Community trade.

[11] In that regard, it must be pointed out that in its aforementioned judgment of 7 February 1985 the Court stated that measures adopted to protect the environment must not 'go beyond the inevitable restrictions which are justified by the pursuit of the objective of environmental protection'.

[12] It is therefore necessary to examine whether all the restrictions which the contested rules impose on the free movement of goods are necessary to achieve the objectives pursued by those rules.

[13] First of all, as regards the obligation to establish a deposit-and-return system for empty containers, it must be observed that this requirement is an indispensable element of a system intended to ensure the re-use of containers and therefore appears necessary to achieve the aims pursued by the contested rules. That being so, the restrictions which it imposes on the free movement of goods cannot be regarded as disproportionate.

[14] Next, it is necessary to consider the requirement that producers and importers must use only containers approved by the National Agency for the Protection of the Environment.

[15] The Danish Government stated in the proceedings before the Court that the present deposit-and-return system would not work if the number of approved containers were to exceed 30 or so, since the retailers taking part in the system would not be prepared to accept too many types of bottles owing to the higher handling costs and the need for more storage space. For that reason the Agency has hitherto followed the practice of ensuring that fresh approvals are normally accompanied by the withdrawal of existing approvals.

[16] Even though there is some force in that argument, it must nevertheless be observed that under the system at present in force in Denmark the Danish authorities may refuse approval to a foreign producer even if he is prepared to ensure that returned containers are re-used.

[17] In those circumstances, a foreign producer who still wished to sell his products in Denmark would be obliged to manufacture or purchase containers of a type already approved, which would involve substantial additional costs for that producer and therefore make the importation of his products into Denmark very difficult.

[18] To overcome that obstacle the Danish Government altered its rules by the aforementioned Order No. 95 of 16 March 1984, which allows a producer to market up

to 3,000 hectolitres of beer and soft drinks a year in non-approved containers, provided that a deposit-and-return system is established.

[19]   The provision in Order No. 95 restricting the quantity of beer and soft drinks which may be marketed by a producer in non-approved containers to 3,000 hectolitres a year is challenged by the Commission on the ground that it is unnecessary to achieve the objectives pursued by the system.

[20]   It is undoubtedly true that the existing system for returning approved containers ensures a maximum rate of re-use and therefore a very considerable degree of protection of the environment since empty containers can be returned to any retailer of beverages. Non-approved containers, on the other hand, can be returned only to the retailer who sold the beverages, since it is impossible to set up such a comprehensive system for those containers as well.

[21]   Nevertheless, the system for returning non-approved containers is capable of protecting the environment and, as far as imports are concerned, affects only limited quantities of beverages compared with the quantity of beverages consumed in Denmark owing to the restrictive effect which the requirement that containers should be returnable has on imports. In those circumstances, a restriction of the quantity of products which may be marketed by importers is disproportionate to the objective pursued.

[22]   It must therefore be held that by restricting, by Order No. 95 of 16 March 1984, the quantity of beer and soft drinks which may be marketed by a single producer in non-approved containers to 3,000 hectolitres a year, the Kingdom of Denmark has failed, as regards imports of those products from other Member States, to fulfil its obligations under Article 30 of the EEC Treaty.

CRIMINAL PROCEEDINGS AGAINST KARL PRANTL (Case 16/83)
[1984] ECR 1299, Court of Justice

An Italian national, Karl Prantl, imported into Germany Italian red wine bottled in 'Bocksbeutel' bottles. Such bottles, of a characteristic bulbous shape, were traditional to certain regions of both Italy and Germany. German legislation restricted the use of the 'Bocksbeutel' in Germany to wine produced in those German regions. Prantl was charged in criminal proceedings in Germany with making improper use of the 'Bocksbeutel'.

On a reference from the national court concerning Article 30, the Court of Justice reiterated (*inter alia*) the principle of mutual recognition. (Article 177 reference.)

[25]   . . . it is true, as the Court has held many times, that in the absence of comprehensive Community legislation on the bottling of the products in question, obstacles to free trade within the Community owing to disparities between national rules must be accepted in so far as such rules, applicable to domestic and imported products alike, may be justified on the ground that it is necessary to satisfy mandatory requirements relating in particular to consumer protection and fair trading.

[26]   In principle, the justification for adopting legislation designed to prevent customers from confusing wines of different quality and origin cannot be denied. That concern is particularly worthy in the case of wines, for traditions and pecularities play an important role in this field. . . .

[27]   Where, however, it is a matter of determining whether the legislation of a Member State may, in order to protect an indirect designation of geographical origin in the interests of consumers, prohibit the marketing of wines imported in a certain type of bottle, it must be observed that in the system of the common market consumer protection and fair trading as regards the presentation of wines must be guaranteed with regard on all sides for the fair and traditional practices observed in the various Member States.

[28]   In this regard the arguments advanced before the Court have revealed that bottles which are identical in shape to the Bocksbeutel bottle or differ from it only in ways imperceptible to the consumer are traditionally used to market wines originating in certain regions of Italy. An exclusive right to use a certain type of bottle granted by national legislation in a Member State may not therefore be used as a bar to imports of wines originating in another Member State put up in bottles of the same or similar shape in accordance with a fair and traditional practice observed in that Member State.

9.4.7 EXTENSION OF THE MANDATORY REQUIREMENTS

OEBEL (Case 155/80) [1981] ECR 1993, Court of Justice

The German court referred certain questions to the Court of Justice concerning the conformity with Community law of national legislation prohibiting night working in bakeries and night deliveries of bakery products. In particular, did such prohibitions amount to measures having equivalent effect to quantitative restrictions?

The Court ruled that the prohibitions were compatible with Articles 30 and 34 because 'trade within the Community remains possible at all times' and it was consequently not necessary for the German Government to justify the legislation. However, the Court accepted that legitimate interests of economic and social policy, designed to improve the working conditions in a particular industry, could constitute a mandatory requirement. (Article 177 reference.)

[12] It cannot be disputed that the prohibition in the bread and confectionery industry on working before 4 a.m. in itself constitutes a legitimate element of economic and social policy, consistent with the objectives of public interest pursued by the Treaty. Indeed, this prohibition is designed to improve working conditions in a manifestly sensitive industry, in which the production process exhibits particular characteristics resulting from both the nature of the product and the habits of consumers.

[13] For these reasons, several Member States of the Community as well as a number of non-member States have introduced similar rules concerning nightwork in this industry. In this regard it is appropriate to mention Convention No. 20 of the International Labour Organization of 8 June 1925 concerning nightwork in bakeries which, subject to certain exceptions, prohibits the production of bread, pastries or similar products during the night.

[14] The accused maintains that the prohibition on the production of ordinary and fine baker's wares before 4 a.m. constitutes an export barrier prohibited by Article 34 of the Treaty. This is alleged to be the case particularly with regard to products which have to be delivered fresh in time for breakfast and which must therefore be produced during the night before the day on which they are offered for sale.

[15] . . . Article 34 concerns national measures which have as their specific object or effect the restriction of patterns of exports and thereby the establishment of a difference in treatment between the domestic trade of a Member State and its export trade, in such a way as to provide a particular advantage for national production or for the domestic market of the State in question.

[16] This is clearly not the case with rules such as those in issue, which are part of economic and social policy and apply by virtue of objective criteria to all the undertakings in a particular industry which are established within the national territory, without leading to any difference in treatment whatsoever on the ground of the nationality of traders and without distinguishing between the domestic trade of the State in question and the export trade.

CINÉTHÈQUE SA v *FÉDÉRATION NATIONALE DES CINÉMAS FRANÇAIS*
(Cases 60 & 61/84) [1985] ECR 2605, Court of Justice

Under French legislation, films could not be re-issued on video for sale or hire within a period of one year from cinema showing. Cinéthèque, which had offered for sale video recordings of a certain film within the stipulated period and whose recordings had been seized by the National Federation of French Cinemas, claimed that the legislation infringed the free movement provisions. (Article 177 reference.)

[20] It must be stated first that . . . the national legislation at issue in the main proceedings of these cases forms part of a body of provision applied in the majority of Member States, whether in the form of contractual, administrative or legislative provisions and of variable scope, but the purpose of which, in all cases, is to delay the distribution of films by means of video-cassettes during the first months following their release in the cinema in order to protect their exploitation in the cinema, which

protection is considered necessary in the interests of the profitability of cinematographic production, as against exploitation through video-cassettes. It must also be observed that, in principle, the Treaty leaves it to the Member States to determine the need for such a system, the form of such a system and any temporal restrictions which ought to be laid down.

[21]   In that connection it must be observed that such a system, if it applies without distinction to both video-cassettes manufactured in the national territory and to imported video-cassettes, does not have the purpose of regulating trade patterns; its effect is not to favour national production as against the production of other Member States, but to encourage cinematographic production as such.

[22]   Nevertheless, the application of such a system may create barriers to intra-Community trade in video-cassettes because of the disparities between the systems operated in the different Member States and between the conditions for the release of cinematographic works in the cinemas of those States. In those circumstances a prohibition of exploitation laid down by such a system is not compatible with the principle of the free movement of goods provided for in the Treaty unless any obstacle to intra-Community trade thereby created does not exceed that which is necessary in order to ensure the attainment of the objective in view and unless that objective is justified with regard to Community law.

[23]   It must be conceded that a national system which, in order to encourage the creation of cinematographic works irrespective of their origin, gives priority, for a limited initial period, to the distribution of such works through the cinema, is so justified.

TORFAEN BOROUGH COUNCIL v B & Q PLC (Case 145/88)
[1989] ECR 3851, Court of Justice

B & Q claimed that s. 47 of the Shops Act 1950, which (with certain exceptions) prohibited Sunday trading in the UK, was a measure having equivalent effect to a quantitative restriction on imports within the meaning of Article 30 and that it was not justified under Article 36 or by virtue of any 'mandatory requirement'. (Article 177 reference.)

[13]   . . . it is . . . necessary in a case such as this to consider first of all whether rules such as those at issue pursue an aim which is justified with regard to Community law. As far as that question is concerned, the Court has already stated in its judgment of 14 July 1981 in Case 155/80 *Oebel* [1981] ECR 1993 that national rules governing the hours of work, delivery and sale in the bread and confectionery industry constitute a legitimate part of economic and social policy, consistent with the objectives of public interest pursued by the Treaty.

[14]   The same consideration must apply as regards national rules governing the opening hours of retail premises. Such rules reflect certain political and economic choices in so far as their purpose is to ensure that working and non-working hours are so arranged as to accord with national or regional socio-cultural characteristics, and that, in the present state of Community law, is a matter for the Member States. Furthermore, such rules are not designed to govern the patterns of trade between Member States.

9.4.8 JUDICIAL DEVELOPMENTS ON INDISTINCTLY APPLICABLE MEASURES

CRIMINAL PROCEEDINGS AGAINST KECK AND MITHOUARD
(Cases C-267 & 268/91) [1993] ECR I-6097, Court of Justice

Mr Keck and Mr Mithouard were prosecuted for reselling products in an unaltered state at prices lower than their actual purchase price ('resale at a loss') contrary to French legislation. Keck and Mithouard raised Article 30 as a defence, claiming that the national provisions were incompatible with the Community principle of free movement of goods. Although the questions referred by the national court concerned specifically Articles 3 and 7 of the Treaty, the Court of Justice, in order to give 'a useful reply to the referring court', looked at the prohibition from the perspective of the free movement of goods. (Article 177 reference.)

[11]   By virtue of Article 30, quantitative restrictions on imports and all measures having equivalent effect are prohibited between Member States. The Court has consistently held that any measure which is capable of directly or indirectly, actually or potentially, hindering intra-Community trade constitutes a measure having equivalent effect to a quantitative restriction.

[12]   It is not the purpose of national legislation imposing a general prohibition on resale at a loss to regulate trade in goods between Member States.

[13]   Such legislation may, admittedly, restrict the volume of sales, and hence the volume of sales of products from other Member States, in so far as it deprives traders of a method of sales promotion. But the question remains whether such a possibility is sufficient to characterize the legislation in question as a measure having equivalent effect to a quantitative restriction on imports.

[14]   In view of the increasing tendency of traders to invoke Article 30 of the Treaty as a means of challenging any rules whose effect is to limit their commercial freedom even where such rules are not aimed at products from other Member States, the Court considers it necessary to re-examine and clarify its case-law on this matter.

[15]   In 'Cassis de Dijon' (Case 120/78 *Rewe-Zentral* v *Bundesmonopolverwaltung für Branntwein* [1979] ECR 649) it was held that, in the absence of harmonization of legislation, measures of equivalent effect prohibited by Article 30 include obstacles to the free movement of goods where they are the consequence of applying rules that lay down requirements to be met by such goods (such as requirements as to designation, form, size, weight, composition, presentation, labelling, packaging) to goods from other Member States where they are lawfully manufactured and marketed, even if those rules apply without distinction to all products unless their application can be justified by a public-interest objective taking precedence over the free movement of goods.

[16]   However, contrary to what has previously been decided, the application to products from other Member States of national provisions restricting or prohibiting certain selling arrangements is not such as to hinder directly or indirectly, actually or potentially, trade between Member States within the meaning of the *Dassonville* judgment (Case 8/74 [1974] ECR 837), provided that those provisions apply to all affected traders operating within the national territory and provided that they affect in the same manner, in law and in fact, the marketing of domestic products and of those from other Member States.

[17]   Where those conditions are fulfilled, the application of such rules to the sale of products from another Member State meeting the requirements laid down by that State is not by nature such as to prevent their access to the market or to impede access any more than it impedes the access of domestic products. Such rules therefore fall outside the scope of Article 30 of the Treaty.

STOKE-ON-TRENT COUNCIL v B & Q (Case 169/91) [1993] 1 CMLR 426, Court of Justice

B & Q were prosecuted for opening their shops on Sundays in contravention of the Shops Act 1950. The national court referred to the Court of Justice a number of questions on the interpretation of Article 30. In responding, the Court referred to two of its previous judgments concerning national rules prohibiting the employment of workers on Sundays *Union Départementale des Syndicats CGT de l'Aisne* v *Sidef Conforama* (Case C-312/89 [1991] ECR I-997, [1993] 3 CMLR 746 and *Marchandise* (Case C-332/89) [1991] ECR I-1027, [1993] 3 CMLR 746) and to its judgment in *Torfaen Borough Council* v *B & Q plc* Case 145/88. (Article 177 reference.)

[9]   In those three judgments the Court found that the various bodies of national legislation concerning the closing of shops on Sundays were not intended to regulate the flow of goods.

[10]   It is also apparent from those judgments that such legislation may indeed have adverse repercussions on the volume of sales of certain shops, but that it affects the sale of both domestic and imported products. The marketing of products from other member-States is not therefore made more difficult than the marketing of national products.

[11] Furthermore, in the abovementioned judgments the Court recognised that the legislation at issue pursued an aim which was justified under Community law. National rules restricting the opening of shops on Sundays reflected certain choices relating to particular national or regional socio-cultural characteristics. It was for the member-States to make those choices in compliance with the requirements of Community law, in particular the principle of proportionality.

[12] As far as that principle is concerned, the Court stated in its judgment in the *Torfaen Borough Council* case that such rules were not prohibited by Article 30 EEC where the restrictive effects on Community trade which might result from them did not exceed the effects intrinsic to such rules and that the question whether the effects of those rules actually remained within that limit was a question of fact to be determined by the national court.

[13] In its judgments in the *Conforama* and *Marchandise* cases, however, the Court found it necessary to make clear, with regard to similar rules, that the restrictive effects on trade which might result from them did not appear to be excessive in relation to the aim pursued.

[14] The Court considered that it had all the information necessary for it to rule on the question of the proportionality of such rules and that it had to do so in order to enable national courts to assess their compatibility with Community law in a uniform manner since such an assessment cannot be allowed to vary according to the findings of fact made by individual courts in particular cases.

[15] Appraising the proportionality of national rules which pursue a legitimate aim under Community law involves weighing the national interest in attaining that aim against the Community interest in ensuring the free movement of goods. In that regard, in order to verify that the restrictive effects on intra-Community trade of the rules at issue do not exceed what is necessary to achieve the aim in view, it must be considered whether those effects are direct, indirect or purely speculative and whether those effects do not impede the marketing of imported products more than the marketing of national products.

[16] It was on the basis of those considerations that in its judgments in the *Conforama* and *Marchandise* cases the Court ruled that the restrictive effects on trade of national rules prohibiting the employment of workers on Sundays in certain retailing activities were not excessive in relation to the aim pursued. For the same reasons, the Court must make the same finding with regard to national rules prohibiting shops from opening on Sundays.

[17] It must therefore be stated in reply to the first question that Article 30 EEC is to be interpreted as meaning that the prohibition which it lays down does not apply to national legislation prohibiting retailers from opening their premises on Sundays.

CRIMINAL PROCEEDINGS AGAINST TANKSTATION T'HEUKSKE VOF AND J.B.E. BOERMANS (Joined Cases C-401/92 & C-402/92) [1994] ECR I-2199, Court of Justice

Dutch legislation regulated the conditions under which and the times at which certain goods could be offered for sale, laying down maximum numbers of opening hours and periods of compulsory closure. A derogation from that legislation permitted the sale outside lawful opening hours by motorway petrol stations and shops associated with them of articles linked to journeys, such as petrol, snacks and tobacco. Further provisions related to the conditions of sale of tobacco by all other petrol stations outside lawful opening hours. Appealing against their convictions for breaches of the legislation in the national courts, Tankstation t'Heukske and Mr Boermans claimed that the national legislation concerning the compulsory closure of shops was contrary to Community law. In a reference to the Court of Justice, the Gerechtshof (Regional Court of Appeal) asked whether Article 30 of the Treaty precludes such legislation. (Article 177 reference.)

Article 30 of the Treaty

10. Under Article 30 of the Treaty quantitative restrictions on imports and all measures having equivalent effect are prohibited between the Member States.

11. The Court has consistently held that all measures which are capable of hindering, directly or indirectly, actually or potentially, intra-Community trade constitute measures

having an effect equivalent to quantitative restrictions (judgment in Case 8/74 *Procureur du Roi* v *Dassonville* [1974] ECR 837, paragraph 5).

12. However, the application to products from other Member States of national provisions restricting or prohibiting certain selling arrangements is not such as to hinder, directly or indirectly, actually or potentially, trade between Member States within the meaning of the *Dassonville* judgment, cited above, provided that those provisions apply to all relevant traders operating within the national territory and provided that they affect in the same manner, in law and in fact, the marketing of domestic products and of those from other Member States. Where those conditions are fulfilled, the application of such rules to the sale of products from another Member State meeting the requirements laid down by that State is not by nature such as to prevent their access to the market or to impede access any more than it impedes the access of domestic products. Such rules therefore fall outside the scope of Article 30 of the Treaty (see the judgment in Joined Cases C-267/91 and C-268/91 *Keck and Mithouard* [1993] ECR I-6097, paragraphs 16 and 17).

13. The conditions laid down in the judgment last cited are fulfilled in the case of rules such as those at issue in the main proceedings.

14. The rules in question relate to the times and places at which the goods in question may be sold to consumers. However, they apply to all relevant traders without distinguishing between the origin of the products in question and do not affect the marketing of products from other Member States in a manner different from that in which they affect domestic products.

15. Consequently, the reply to be given to the Gerechtshof is that Article 30 of the Treaty is to be interpreted as not applying to national rules concerning the closing of shops which apply to all traders operating within the national territory and which affect in the same manner, in law and in fact, the marketing of domestic products and of products from other Member States.

9.4.9 ARTICLE 30 AS A DEFENCE

See *Criminal proceedings against Keck and Mithouard* at **9.4.8** above.

9.5 Article 36: Derogation from Articles 30–34

9.5.1 THE ARTICLE 36 EXCEPTIONS

THE TREATY OF ROME

Article 36
The provisions of Articles 30 to 34 shall not preclude prohibitions or restrictions on imports, exports or goods in transit justified on grounds of public morality, public policy or public security; the protection of health and life of humans, animals or plants; the protection of national treasures possessing artistic, historic or archaeological value; or the protection of industrial and commercial property. Such prohibitions or restrictions shall not, however, constitute a means of arbitrary discrimination or a disguised restriction on trade between Member States.

9.5.2 PUBLIC MORALITY

CONEGATE LTD v *CUSTOMS AND EXCISE COMMISSIONERS* (Case 121/85)
[1986] ECR 1007, Court of Justice

A consignment of inflatable dolls of a sexual nature and other erotic articles imported from Germany by Conegate Ltd were seized by the UK customs authorities on the grounds that they were 'indecent or obscene' under English customs legislation. Subsequently, the Uxbridge Magistrates ordered the forfeiture of the goods. Conegate Ltd argued that the forfeiture infringed Article 30 and could not be justified on grounds of public morality under Article 36. The High Court referred to the Court of Justice questions concerning the meaning of the term 'lawful trade' (employed in the judgment in *Henn and Darby*, see **9.4.1**) and the application of Article 36. (Article 177 reference.)

[14] . . . it must be borne in mind that according to Article 36 of the EEC Treaty the provisions relating to the free movement of goods within the Community do not preclude prohibitions on imports justified 'on grounds of public morality'. . . in principle it is for each Member State to determine in accordance with its own scale of values and in the form selected by it the requirements of public morality in its territory.

[15] However, although Community law leaves the Member States free to make their own assessments of the indecent or obscene character of certain articles, it must be pointed out that the fact that goods cause offence cannot be regarded as sufficiently serious to justify restrictions on the free movement of goods where the Member State concerned does not adopt, with respect to the same goods manufactured or marketed within its territory, penal measures or other serious and effective measures intended to prevent the distribution of such goods in its territory.

[16] It follows that a Member State may not rely on grounds of public morality in order to prohibit the importation of goods from other Member States when its legislation contains no prohibition on the manufacture or marketing of the same goods on its territory.

[17] It is not for the Court, within the framework of the powers conferred upon it by Article 177 of the EEC Treaty, to consider whether, and to what extent, the United Kingdom legislation contains such a prohibition. However, the question whether or not such a prohibition exists in a State comprised of different constituent parts which have their own internal legislation, can be resolved only by taking into consideration all the relevant legislation. Although it is not necessary for the purposes of the application of the above-mentioned rule, that the manufacture and marketing of the products whose importation has been prohibited should be prohibited in the territory of all the constituent parts, it must at least be possible to conclude from the applicable rules, taken as a whole, that their purpose is, in substance, to prohibit the manufacture and marketing of those products.

[18] In this instance, in the actual wording of its first question the High Court took care to define the substance of the national legislation the compatibility of which with Community law is a question which it proposes to determine. Thus it refers to rules in the importing Member State under which the goods in question may be manufactured freely and marketed subject only to certain restrictions, which it set out explicitly, namely an absolute prohibition on the transmission of such goods by post, a restriction on their public display and, in certain areas of the Member State concerned, a system of licensing of premises for the sale of those goods to customers aged 18 years and over. Such restrictions cannot however be regarded as equivalent in substance to a prohibition on manufacture and marketing.

. . .

[20] . . . it must therefore be stated that a Member State may not rely on grounds of public morality within the meaning of Article 36 of the Treaty in order to prohibit the importation of certain goods on the grounds that they are indecent or obscene, where the same goods may be manufactured freely on its territory and marketed on its territory subject only to an absolute prohibition on their transmission by post, a restriction on their public display and, in certain regions, a system of licensing of premises for the sale of those goods to customers aged 18 and over.

[21] That conclusion does not preclude the authorities of the Member State concerned from applying to those goods, once imported, the same restrictions on marketing which are applied to similar products manufactured and marketed within the country.

9.5.3 PUBLIC SECURITY

CAMPUS OIL LTD v MINISTER FOR INDUSTRY AND ENERGY (Case 72/83)
[1983] ECR 2727, Court of Justice

Irish rules required importers of petroleum products to purchase a certain proportion of their requirements at fixed prices from a state-owned refinery. A number of importers claimed that the rules infringed Article 30. The national court asked whether the rules were in breach of Article 30 and, if so, whether they fell within the Article 36 exceptions. The Court of Justice held that the rules constituted measures having equivalent effect to quantitative restrictions and then considered the question of justification under Article 36. (Article 177 reference.)

[32]   . . . the purpose of Article 36 of the Treaty is not to reserve certain matters to the exclusive jurisdiction of the Member States; it merely allows national legislation to derogate from the principle of the free movement of goods to the extent to which this is and remains justified in order to achieve the objectives set out in the article.

[33]   It is in the light of those statements that it must be decided whether the concept of public security, on which the Irish Government places particular reliance and which is the only one relevant in this case, since the concept of public policy is not pertinent, covers reasons such as those referred to in the question raised by the national court.

[34]   It should be stated in this connection that petroleum products, because of their exceptional importance as an energy source in the modern economy, are of fundamental importance for a country's existence since not only its economy but above all its institutions, its essential public services and even the survival of its inhabitants depend upon them. An interruption of supplies of petroleum products, with the resultant dangers for the country's existence, could therefore seriously affect the public security that Article 36 allows States to protect.

[35]   It is true that, as the Court has held on a number of occasions, . . . Article 36 refers to matters of a non-economic nature. A Member State cannot be allowed to avoid the effects of measures provided for in the Treaty by pleading the economic difficulties caused by the elimination of barriers to intra-Community trade. However, in the light of the seriousness of the consequences that an interruption in supplies of petroleum products may have for a country's existence, the aim of ensuring a minimum supply of petroleum products at all times is to be regarded as transcending purely economic considerations and thus as capable of constituting an objective covered by the concept of public security.

[36]   It should be added that to come within the ambit of Article 36, the rules in question must be jusitified by objective circumstances corresponding to the needs of public security. Once that justification has been established, the fact that the rules are of such a nature as to make it possible to achieve, in addition to the objectives covered by the concept of public security, other objectives of an economic nature which the Member State may also seek to achieve, does not exclude the application of Article 36. . . .

[37]   . . . Article 36, as an exception to a fundamental principle of the Treaty, must be interpreted in such a way that its scope is not extended any further than is necessary for the protection of the interests which it is intended to secure and the measures taken pursuant to that article must not create obstacles to imports which are disproportionate to those objectives. Measures adopted on the basis of Article 36 can therefore be justified only if they are such as to serve the interest which that article protects and if they do not restrict intra-Community trade more than is absolutely necessary.

. . .

[42]   The plaintiffs in the main action and the Commission consider . . . that even if the operation of a refinery is justified in the interest of public security, it is not necessary in order to achieve that objective, and, in any event, it is disproportionate in relation to that objective, to oblige importers to satisfy a certain proportion of their requirements by purchase from the national refinery at a price fixed by the competent minister.

. . .

[44]   It must be pointed out in this connection that a Member State may have recourse to Article 36 to justify a measure having equivalent effect to a quantitative restriction on imports only if no other measure, less restrictive from the point of view of the free movement of goods, is capable of achieving the same objective.

[45]   In the present case, therefore, it is necessary to consider whether the obligation placed on importers of petroleum products to purchase at prices determined on the basis of the costs incurred by the refinery in question is necessary, albeit only temporarily, for the purpose of ensuring that enough of the refinery's production can be marketed so as to guarantee, in the interest of public security, a minimum supply of petroleum products to the State concerned in the event of a supply crisis.

[46]   That obligation could be necessary if the distributors that hold the major share of the market concerned refuse, as the Irish Government contends, to purchase supplies from the refinery in question. It is on the assumption that the refinery charges prices which are competitive on the market concerned that it must be determined whether the refinery's products could be freely marketed. If it is not possible by means of industrial and commercial measures to avoid any financial losses resulting from such prices, those losses must be borne by the Member State concerned, subject to the application of Articles 92 and 93 of the Treaty.

[47]   As regards, in the next place, the quantities of petroleum products which may, as the case may be, be covered by such a system of purchasing obligations, it should be stressed that they must in no case exceed the minimum supply requirements of the State concerned without which its public security, as defined above, and in particular the operation of its essential public services and the survival of its inhabitants, would be affected.

[48]   Furthermore, the quantities of petroleum products whose marketing can be ensured under such a system must not exceed the quantities which are necessary, so far as production is concerned, on the one hand, for technical reasons in order that the refinery may operate currently at a sufficient level of its production capacity to ensure that its plant will be available in the event of a crisis and, on the other hand, in order that it may continue to refine at all times the crude oil covered by the long-term contracts which the State concerned has entered into so that it may be assured of regular supplies.

[49]   The proportion of the total needs of importers of petroleum products that may be made subject to a purchasing obligation must not, therefore, exceed the proportion which the quantities set out above represent of the current total consumption of petroleum products in the Member State concerned.

9.5.4   PROTECTION OF HEALTH AND LIFE OF HUMANS, ANIMALS OR PLANTS

COMMISSION v *GERMANY (BEER PURITY LAWS)* (Case 178/84)
[1987] ECR 1227, Court of Justice

German legislation (including the Biersteuergesetz) required all beverages marketed in Germany under the designation 'Bier' to be produced only from certain ingredients and imposed an absolute ban on the marketing of beers containing additives. The Commission considered that these provisions contravened Article 30.
The Court of Justice first examined the national provisions relating to designation, which the German Government sought to justify on grounds of consumer protection. It claimed that the German consumer associated the designation 'Bier' with a drink manufactured from the ingredients listed in the Biersteuergesetz and would be misled if beer produced from other ingredients were marketed as 'Bier'. The Court ruled that the desired objective could be achieved by means which were less of a hindrance to trade, namely by affixing labels indicating the ingredients of the product. The Court then considered the ban on the use of all additives in beer. (Article 169 proceedings.)

[39]   . . . the German Government considers that in view of the dangers resulting from the utilization of additives whose long-term effects are not yet known and in particular of the risks resulting from the accumulation of additives in the organism and their interaction with other substances, such as alcohol, it is necessary to minimize the quantity of additives ingested. Since beer is a foodstuff of which large quantities are consumed in Germany, the German Government considers that it is particularly desirable to prohibit the use of any additive in its manufacture, especially in so far as the use of additives is not technologically necessary and can be avoided if only the ingredients laid down in the Biersteuergesetz are used. In those circumstances, the German rules on additives in beer are fully justified by the need to safeguard public health and do not infringe the principle of proportionality. . .

[48]   . . . the German Government, citing experts' reports, has referred to the risks inherent in the ingestion of additives in general. It maintains that it is important, for reasons of general preventive health protection, to minimize the quantity of additives ingested, and that it is particularly advisable to prohibit altogether their use in the

manufacture of beer, a foodstuff consumed in considerable quantities by the German population.

[49]   However, it appears from the tables of additives authorized for use in the various foodstuffs submitted by the German Government itself that some of the additives authorized in other Member States for use in the manufacture of beer are also authorized under the German rules, in particular the Regulation on Additives, for use in the manufacture of all, or virtually all, beverages. Mere reference to the potential risks of the ingestion of additives in general and to the fact that beer is a foodstuff consumed in large quantities does not suffice to justify the imposition of stricter rules in the case of beer.

[50]   As regards the need, and in particular the technological need, for additives, the German Government argues that there is no need for additives if beer is manufactured in accordance with the requirements of Article 9 of the Biersteuergesetz.

[51]   It must be emphasized that mere reference to the fact that beer can be manufactured without additives if it is made from only the raw materials prescribed in the Federal Republic of Germany does not suffice to preclude the possibility that some additives may meet a technological need. Such an interpretation of the concept of technological need, which results in favouring national production methods, constitutes a disguised means of restricting trade between Member States.

[52]   The concept of technological need must be assessed in the light of the raw materials utilized and bearing in mind the assessment made by the authorities of the Member State where the product was lawfully manufactured and marketed. Account must also be taken of the findings of international scientific research and in particular the work of the Community's Scientific Committee for Food, the Codex Alimentarius Committee of the FAO and the World Health Organization.

[53]   Consequently, in so far as the German rules on additives in beer entail a general ban on additives, their application to beers imported from other Member States is contrary to the requirements of Community law as laid down in the case-law of the Court, since that prohibition is contrary to the principle of proportionality and is therefore not covered by the exception provided for in Article 36 of the EEC Treaty.

9.5.5   NO ECONOMIC JUSTIFICATIONS UNDER ARTICLE 36

R v SECRETARY OF STATE FOR HOME DEPARTMENT, EX PARTE EVANS MEDICAL LTD AND MACFARLAN SMITH LTD (Case C-324/93) [1995] ECR I-563, Court of Justice

Under government policy aimed to prevent diamorphine being diverted to illicit trade, until 1992 Evans Medical and Macfarlan Smith had exclusive rights in the UK in relation to the importation, manufacture and processing of that drug. When Generics (UK) Ltd sought judicial review of the Secretary of State's refusal, in 1990, to grant the company a licence to import diamorphine, the Secretary of State acknowledged that the refusal of the licence was not justified and announced a review of his decision. In letters to Evans and Macfarlan he stated that he considered the policy on importation of the drug to be a hindrance to intra-Community trade and that reliability of supplies of the drug could be guaranteed by the introduction of a tendering scheme. Evans and Macfarlan brought proceedings against the Secretary of State in the High Court. One of the questions referred by the High Court to the Court of Justice concerned economic justifications for the restriction of trade between Member States. (Article 177 reference.)

Question 1(c)

34.   By this question the national court asks whether a Member State is entitled to refuse a licence for importation of narcotic drugs from another Member State on the ground that importation of such drugs from another Member State threatens the viability of the sole licensed manufacturer in the first State and jeopardizes reliability of supply of diamorphine for medical purposes.

35.   Article 36 of the Treaty allows a Member State to maintain or introduce measures prohibiting or restricting trade if those measures are justified on, *inter alia*, grounds of public morality, public policy, public security or the protection of health and life of humans, and provided that they do not constitute a means of arbitrary discrimination or a disguised restriction on intra-Community trade.

36. It is clear from the Court's case-law that Article 36 relates to measures of a non-economic nature (judgment in Case 238/82 *Duphar and Others* v *Netherlands* [1984] ECR 523). A measure which restricts intra-Community trade cannot therefore be justified by a Member State's wish to safeguard the survival of an undertaking.

37. On the other hand, the need to ensure that a country has reliable supplies for essential medical purposes may, under Article 36 of the Treaty, justify a barrier to intra-Community trade if that objective is one of protecting the health and life of humans.

38. It must, however, be borne in mind that the derogation provided for in Article 36 cannot apply to national rules or practices if the health and life of humans can be as effectively protected by measures less restrictive of intra-Community trade . . .

39. The answer to this question must therefore be that a national practice of refusing licences for importation of drugs from another Member State is not covered by the derogation provided for in Article 36 of the Treaty if it is based on the need to safeguard an undertaking's survival but that derogation may apply to it if protection of the health and life of humans requires a reliable supply of drugs for essential medical purposes to be safeguarded and that objective cannot be achieved as effectively by measures less restrictive of intra-Community trade.

9.6   End of Chapter Assessment Questions

1(a)   Explain the distinction between distinctly applicable measures and indistinctly applicable measures. Give one example of each, drawn from cases decided by the Court of Justice.

(b)   Why is this distinction important?

2   Consider the following (fictitious) measures and comment on their compatibility with Community provisions on the free movement of goods.

(a)   A recently introduced Italian tax on wine with an alcohol content exceeding 9%. Importers from other Member States are required to pay the tax at the date of importation. Domestic producers may defer payment until up to six weeks after the product has been put on the market.

(b)   A Belgian regulation requiring all imported (but not domestically produced) onions to undergo inspections. The Belgian Government claims that the measure is designed to control the spread of the onion beetle, which is a very destructive pest.

(c)   German legislation requiring vegetarian cheese to be packed in triangular boxes. The Government claims that the measure is aimed to protect the consumer.

(d)   English legislation which prohibits video shops and all other video retail outlets from opening between 9pm and 8am.

9.7   End of Chapter Assessment Outline Answers

(Unless otherwise stated, references in the following answers are to the Treaty of Rome.)

1(a)   In the context of Community provisions relating to the free movement of goods, both terms are applied to measures having equivalent effect to quantitative restrictions under Article 30. Distinctly applicable measures are those which do not apply equally to domestic and imported products. Indistinctly applicable measures are those which apply equally to imported and domestic products. Several examples could be given, including those below.

The introduction by the Irish Government of a 'Buy Irish' campaign in order to promote Irish products can be classified as a distinctly applicable measure (*Commission v Ireland ('Buy Irish' Campaign)*). By contrast, a UK requirement that certain goods offered for retail sale in the UK be marked with their country of origin was an indistinctly applicable measure (*Commission v United Kingdom (Origin Marking of Goods)*).

(b)   The importance of the distinction lies in the range of justifications available for measures falling within the respective classifications. Distinctly applicable measures which breach Article 30 can only be justified under Article 36. Moreover, they will not be lawful unless they come within the specific grounds listed in that Article. That list is exhaustive. Indistinctly applicable measures can be considered under the *Cassis* rule of reason. The list of 'mandatory requirements' in *Cassis* is not exhaustive and has been extended by the Court of Justice to allow justifications based, for instance, on the protection of the environment (*Commission v Denmark (Disposable Beer Cans)*), legitimate interests of social and economic policy (*Oebel*) and cultural activities (*Cinéthèque*).

2   All these measures concern the free movement of goods within the Community. Each suggested answer given below is incomplete without some *brief* remarks on the concept of the internal market and (if appropriate) the Court of Justice's very narrow interpretation of exceptions to the free movement provisions. In relation to measures having equivalent effect to quantitative restrictions, you should also point out that such

measures can only be justified under Article 36 and *Cassis* in the absence of Community harmonising legislation covering the interest concerned.

(a)   The first question to be decided is whether the 'tax' is a genuine tax (permissible if it complies with Article 95) or a customs duty (unlawful under Article 12). The Court of Justice has defined a tax as a charge relating to 'a general system of internal dues applied systematically and in accordance with the same criteria to domestic products and imported products alike'. The Italian tax is clearly a genuine tax within the scope of Article 95. Article 95(1) prohibits internal taxation of any kind on imports in excess of that imposed directly or indirectly on similar products. Here, the imported and domestic products are similar and the tax rate does not discriminate between them. However, there is discrimination arising from the rules relating to the collection of the tax. This amounts to unlawful discriminatory taxation under Article 95(1) (*Commission* v *Ireland (Excise Payments)*).

(b)   The first consideration is whether the Belgian regulation breaches Article 30, which prohibits two kinds of non-tariff barrier to trade, quantitative restrictions and measures having equivalent effect (MEQRs). The former, covering bans and quotas does not apply to these facts.

In deciding whether the measure is an MEQR, we should consider Directive 70/50 which, although it is a transitional provision which is no longer applicable, provides non-binding guidelines on the meaning of MEQRs. As a distinctly applicable measure (applying to imported onions but not to the domestic products) which delays import-ation and thereby hinders 'imports which could otherwise take place' and makes 'importation more difficult or costly than the disposal of the domestic product', the regulation comes within the scope of Article 2(1) of the Directive.

In *Procureur du Roi* v *Dassonville*, the Court of Justice gave its own definition of MEQRs, the *Dassonville* formula, which provides that 'all trading rules enacted by Member States which are capable of hindering, directly or indirectly, actually or potentially, intra-Community trade are to be considered as measures having an effect equivalent to quantitative restrictions.' This definition takes in the Belgian regulation, which is an actual hindrance to intra-Community trade.

The Belgian Government claims that the regulation is designed to control the onion beetle. As a distinctly applicable MEQR, the regulation cannot be justified under *Cassis* principles (see for instance *Commission* v *Ireland (Restrictions on Importation of Souvenirs)* but the Article 36 exception to the free movement provisions which relates to the protection of health and life of humans, animals or plants might apply.

In order to succeed in justifying the measure under this head, the Belgian Government must show that there is a real risk that the beetle will spread to domestically produced onions and that effective measures are taken to prevent the distribution of domestic onions affected by the pest. The regulation must also satisfy the proportionality test – it must be justified, or be no more than is necessary to achieve the desired aim. If these requirements are satisfied, the discriminatory treatment of imports and domestic onions will meet the 'negative' conditions set out in Article 36 and will not constitute 'arbitrary discrimination or a disguised restriction on trade between Member States'. In a similar case (*San Jose Scale*), the Court of Justice ruled that plant health inspections of imported apples was in principle justified under Article 36.

(c)   Your answer should begin by considering whether the German legislation breaches Article 30. Look at the first three paragraphs of the answer to 2(b) above for an outline. Note, however, that in this case the legislation is indistinctly applicable because it applies both to imported and domestically produced vegetarian cheese. You should make reference to Article 3 of Directive 70/50 and point out that whilst the measure is on its face non-discriminatory, it is likely to be discriminatory in its effect. Consequently, there appears to be a breach of Article 30.

The German Government seeks to justify the legislation on the grounds that it protects the consumer. This justification is not one of the specific exceptions to the free movement provisions set out in the Article 36 list and, since that list is non-exhaustive (*Commission* v *Ireland (Restrictions on Importation of Souvenirs)*, the measure can only be considered under *Cassis* principles. As it is an indistinctly applicable measure, this is possible. If the legislation is compatible with the *Cassis* principles, it will not breach Article 30.

The second *Cassis* principle, the principle of mutual recognition, gives rise to a presumption that where goods have been lawfully produced and marketed in one

Member State, there is no valid reason why they should not be introduced into another Member State. Because of the importance of the principle of freedom of movement of goods throughout the Community, this presumption is not easily displaced. However, under the first *Cassis* principle, known as the 'rule of reason', in the absence of Community rules governing the interest concerned the presumption may be displaced where national measures are 'necessary in order to satisfy mandatory requirements', including 'the effectiveness of fiscal supervision, the protection of public health, the fairness of commercial transactions and the defence of the consumer'. The German legislation falls within the fourth category.

However, the German Government must also show that the legislation is necessary (that is no more than is necessary) to satisfy the mandatory requirement, in other words it must be proportionate to that objective. In *Cassis*, the Court of Justice held that the German Government could have used other means to protect the consumer which were less of a hindrance to trade, such as a requirement that the spirits in question be labelled to indicate origin and alcohol content. Similarly, in the *Walter Rau* case, a Belgian requirement that all margarine for retail sale be cube-shaped or packed in cube-shaped containers went beyond what was necessary to protect the consumer. Labelling would have given sufficient protection and would have been less of an obstacle to the free movement of goods. On that basis, the German legislation cannot be justified under *Cassis* and contravenes Article 30.

(d)   Prior to the ruling in *Keck*, it would have been appropriate to draw on analogies with the English Sunday trading legislation, which was challenged by traders as being contrary to Article 30 but found by the Court of Justice to be justified under the *Cassis* rule of reason. However, such analogies would have been rather strained, since there is no indication of the arguments which the UK Government might advance in order to justify the restrictions relating to video shop opening hours.

However, in so far as restrictive legislation of this kind is concerned, the *Keck* judgment removes the need to strain for justifications. In *Keck*, the Court of Justice ruled that national measures restricting or prohibiting 'certain selling arrangements' and thereby affecting imports do not fall within the *Dassonville* formula 'provided that those provisions apply to all affected traders operating within the national territory and provided that they affect in the same manner, in law and in fact, the marketing of domestic products and of those from other Member States'. The English legislation on video shop opening hours seems to apply to all affected traders in the territory and has no greater effect on imported videos than on domestically produced videos. Consequently, it appears to fall outside the scope of Article 30 altogether.

CHAPTER TEN

FREE MOVEMENT OF PERSONS

10.1 Outline of the Legislation

THE TREATY OF ROME

Article 3
For the purposes set out in Article 2, the activities of the Community shall include, as provided in this Treaty and in accordance with the timetable set out therein:
. . .

    (c) an internal market characterised by the abolition, as between Member States, of obstacles to the free movement of goods, persons, services and capital
. . .

10.2 The Free Movement of Workers

10.2.1 OUTLINE OF THE LEGISLATION

THE TREATY OF ROME

Article 6
Within the scope of application of this Treaty and without prejudice to any special provisions contained therein, any discrimination on grounds of nationality shall be prohibited.
. . .

Article 48
  1. Freedom of movement for workers shall be secured within the Community by the end of the transitional period at the latest.

  2. Such freedom of movement shall entail the abolition of any discrimination based on nationality between workers of the Member States as regards employment, remuneration and other conditions of work and employment.

  3. It shall entail the right, subject to limitations justified on grounds of public policy, public security or public health:

    (a) to accept offers of employment actually made;

    (b) to move freely within the territory of Member States for this purpose;

    (c) to stay in a Member State for the purpose of employment in accordance with the provisions governing the employment of nationals of that State laid down by law, regulation or administrative action;

    (d) to remain in the territory of a Member State after having been employed in that State, subject to conditions which shall be embodied in implementing regulations to be drawn up by the Commission.

  4. The provisions of this Article shall not apply to employment in the public service.

MORSON AND JHANJAN v NETHERLANDS (Cases 35 and 36/82)
[1982] ECR 3723, Court of Justice

Two Surinamese nationals, Mrs Morson and Mrs Jhanjan wished to reside in the Netherlands with their daughter and son respectively, on whom they were dependent, but were refused rights of entry and residence. The children, who were Dutch nationals and worked in the Netherlands, had never been employed in another Member State. Seeking review of the decision refusing their application, the applicants invoked Articles 7 (now Article 6) and 48 of the Treaty and Article 10 of Regulation 1612/68. (Article 177 reference.)

Second question

[11]   In substance the second question seeks to ascertain whether, and if so in which circumstances, Community law prohibits a Member State from refusing to allow a relative, as referred to in Article 10 of Regulation No. 1612/68 . . . of a worker employed within that Member State's territory to enter or reside within its territory if the worker has the nationality of that State and the relative the nationality of a non-member country.

[12]   Article 48 of the Treaty provides that freedom of movement of workers within the Community is to entail the abolition of any discrimination based on nationality between workers of the Member States. Article 10 of Regulation No. 1612/68 of the Council of 15 October 1968 on freedom of movement for workers within the Community . . . provides that specified members of a worker's family, including dependent relatives in the ascending line, 'shall, irrespective of their nationality, have the right to install themselves with a worker who is a national of one Member State and who is employed in the territory of another Member State'.

[13]   Since that provision does not cover the position of dependent relatives of a worker who is a national of the Member State within whose territory he is employed, the answer to the preliminary question depends on whether it may be inferred from the context of the provisions and the place which they occupy in the Community legal system as a whole that they have a right of entry and residence.

[14]   In this regard the applicants in the main proceedings rely on the rule prohibiting discrimination on grounds of nationality which Article 7 of the Treaty enunciates in general terms and to which Article 48 gives more specific expression.

[15]   It is however clear that Article 7 and Article 48 may be invoked only where the case in question comes within the area to which Community law applies, which in this case is that concerned with freedom of movement of workers within the Community. Not only does that conclusion emerge from the wording of those articles, but it also accords with their purpose, which is to assist in the abolition of all obstacles to the establishment of a common market in which the nationals of the Member States may move freely within the territory of those states in order to pursue their economic activities.

[16]   It follows that the Treaty provisions on freedom of movement for workers and the rules adopted to implement them cannot be applied to cases which have no factor linking them with any of the situations governed by Community law.

[17]   Such is undoubtedly the case with workers who have never exercised the right to freedom of movement within the Community.

[18]   The answer to the second question submitted by the Hoge Raad must therefore be that Community law does not prohibit a Member State from refusing to allow a relative, as referred to in Article 10 of Regulation No. 1612/68 of the Council of 15 October 1968 on freedom of movement for workers within the Community, of a worker employed within the territory of that State who has never exercised the right to freedom of movement within the Community to enter or reside within its territory if that worker has the nationality of that State and the relative the nationality of a non-member country.

10.2.2   MEANING OF 'WORKER'

HOEKSTRA (NÉE UNGER) v BESTUUR DER BEDRIJFSVERENIGING VOOR DETAILHANDEL EN AMBACHTEN (Case 75/63) [1964] ECR 177, Court of Justice

Mrs Hoekstra was resident in the Netherlands. She had worked there but was not currently in employment. Her entitlement to certain insurance payments in respect of medical expenses incurred by her during a visit to her parents in Germany depended upon her status as a 'wage-earner or assimilated worker' under Council Regulation No. 3 on social security.

In response to questions referred by the Dutch social security court, the Court of Justice, first of all emphasising that 'worker' has a Community meaning, went on to elucidate the scope of the term under Article 48 of the Treaty. (Article 177 reference.)

A reference for a preliminary ruling under Article 177 of the EEC Treaty has been duly made to the Court by the Centrale Raad van Beroep.

1.   The question put by that court requests the Court of Justice to rule, in the first place, whether the concept of a 'wage-earner or assimilated worker' as used in Article 19(1) of Regulation No. 3 is defined by the legislation of each Member State or by Community law as having a supranational meaning.

. . .

The reply to the question put . . . depends essentially upon the scope, whether Community or otherwise, of the provisions of the Treaty from which the concept of 'wage-earner or assimilated worker' in so far as they affect the field of social security, was drawn by the said Regulation.

. . .

Articles 48 to 51 of the Treaty, by the very fact of establishing freedom of movement for 'workers', have given Community scope to this term.

If the definition of this term were a matter within the competence of national law, it would therefore be possible for each Member State to modify the meaning of the concept of 'migrant worker' and to eliminate at will the protection afforded by the Treaty to certain categories of person.

Moreover nothing in Articles 48 to 51 of the Treaty leads to the conclusion that these provisions have left the definition of the term 'worker' to national legislation.

On the contrary, the fact that Article 48(2) mentions certain elements of the concept of 'workers', such as employment and remuneration, shows that the Treaty attributes a Community meaning to that concept.

Articles 48 to 51 would therefore be deprived of all effect and the above-mentioned objectives of the Treaty would be frustrated if the meaning of such a term could be unilaterally fixed and modified by national law.

The concept of 'workers' in the said Articles does not therefore relate to national law, but to Community law.

. . .

2.   The Centrale Raad requests the Court, in the second part of its question, and in the event that the expression in dispute should be given a Community meaning, to give a ruling on what that meaning is, because a definition of the term is necessary when deciding whether the aforementioned Article 19(1) prevents the non-payment of sickness expenses to persons in a situation similar to that in this case.

It follows both from the Treaty and from Regulation No. 3, that the protected 'worker' is not exclusively one who is currently employed.

Article 48(3) of the Treaty also applies to persons likely 'to remain in the territory of a Member State after having been employed in that State . . .'.

Article 4 of Regulation No. 3 mentions wage-earners or assimilated workers who are 'or have been' subject to the legislation of one or more of the Member States.

The Treaty and Regulation No. 3 thus did not intend to restrict protection only to the worker in employment but tend logically to protect also the worker who, having left his job, is capable of taking another.

LEVIN v STAATSSECRETARIS VAN JUSTITIE (Case 53/81)
[1982] ECR 1035, Court of Justice

The Dutch authorities refused Mrs Levin (a British national and the wife of a national of a non-member country) a permit to reside in the Netherlands on the grounds that she was not engaged in a gainful occupation. She had subsequently taken up part-time work, earning less than the income considered in the Netherlands to be the minimum necessary for subsistence. She claimed that she and her husband had more than sufficient income to support themselves. The Netherlands Government maintained that the Article 48 rights applied only to persons whose income from employment reaches at least the subsistence level laid down by the host State or who work the number of hours considered normal for full-time employment in any particular sector.

Reiterating that the term 'worker' has a Community meaning, the Court of Justice rejected the Netherlands Government's contention, though it emphasised that the activity must be 'effective and genuine'. Moreover, provided the work is 'effective and genuine', an individual's motives in seeking employment in another Member State have no bearing on his or her status as a worker. (Article 177 reference.)

First and second questions

[6]   In its first and second questions, which should be considered together, the national court is essentially asking whether the provisions of Community law relating to freedom of movement for workers also cover a national of a Member State whose activity as an employed person in the territory of another Member State provides him with an income less than the minimum required for subsistence within the meaning of the legislation of the second Member State. In particular the court asks whether those provisions cover such a person where he either supplements his income from his activity as an employed person with other income so as to arrive at that minimum or is content with means of support which fall below it.

[7]   Under Article 48 of the Treaty freedom of movement for workers is to be secured within the Community. That freedom is to entail the abolition of any discrimination based on nationality between workers of the Member States as regards employment, remuneration and other conditions of work and is to include the right, subject to limitations justified on grounds of public policy, public security or public health, to accept offers of employment actually made, to move freely within the territory of Member States for this purpose, to stay in a Member State for the purpose of employment and to remain there after the termination of that employment.

. . .

[9]   Although the rights deriving from the principle of freedom of movement for workers and more particularly the right to enter and stay in the territory of a Member State are thus linked to the status of a worker or of a person pursuing an activity as an employed person or desirous of so doing, the terms 'worker' and 'activity as an employed person' are not expressly defined in any of the provisions on the subject. It is appropriate, therefore, in order to determine their meaning, to have recourse to the generally recognized principles of interpretation, beginning with the ordinary meaning to be attributed to those terms in their context and in the light of the objectives of the Treaty.

[10]   The Netherlands and Danish Governments have maintained that the provisions of Article 48 may only be relied upon by persons who receive a wage at least commensurate with the means of subsistence considered as necessary by the legislation of the Member State in which they work, or who work at least for the number of hours considered as usual in respect of full-time employment in the sector in question. In the absence of any provisions to that effect in Community legislation, it is suggested that it is necessary to have recourse to national criteria for the purpose of defining both the minimum wage and the minimum number of hours.

[11]   That argument cannot, however, be accepted. As the Court has already stated in its judgment of 19 March 1964 in *Hoekstra (née Unger)* (Case 75/63) [1964] ECR 1977 the terms 'worker' and 'activity as an employed person' may not be defined by reference to the national laws of the Member States but have a Community meaning. If that were not the case, the Community rules on freedom of movement for workers would be frustrated, as the meaning of those terms could be fixed and modified unilaterally, without any control by the Community institutions, by national laws which would thus be able to exclude at will certain categories of persons from the benefit of the Treaty.

[12]   Such would, in particular, be the case if the enjoyment of the rights conferred by the principle of freedom of movement for workers could be made subject to the criterion of what the legislation of the host State declares to be a minimum wage, so that the field

of application *ratione personae* of the Community rules on this subject might vary from one Member State to another. The meaning and the scope of the terms 'worker' and 'activity as an employed person' should thus be clarified in the light of the principles of the legal order of the Community.

[13]   In this respect it must be stressed that these concepts define the field of application of one of the fundamental freedoms guaranteed by the Treaty and, as such, may not be interpreted restrictively.

[14]   In conformity with this view the recitals in the preamble to Regulation (EEC) No. 1612/68 contain a general affirmation of the right of all workers in the Member States to pursue the activity of their choice within the Community, irrespective of whether they are permanent, seasonal or frontier workers or workers who pursue their activities for the purpose of providing services. Furthermore, although Article 4 of Directive 68/360/ EEC grants the right of residence to workers upon the mere production of the document on the basis of which they entered the territory and of a confirmation of engagement from the employer or a certificate of employment, it does not subject this right to any condition relating to the kind of employment or to the amount of income derived from it.

[15]   An interpretation which reflects the full scope of these concepts is also in conformity with the objectives of the Treaty which include, according to Articles 2 and 3, the abolition, as between Member States, of obstacles to freedom of movement for persons, with the purpose *inter alia* of promoting throughout the Community a harmonious development of economic activities and a raising of the standard of living. Since part-time employment, although it may provide an income lower than what is considered to be the minimum required for subsistence, constitutes for a large number of persons an effective means of improving their living conditions, the effectiveness of Community law would be impaired and the achievement of the objectives of the Treaty would be jeopardized if the enjoyment of rights conferred by the principle of freedom of movement for workers were reserved solely to persons engaged in full-time employment and earning, as a result, a wage at least equivalent to the guaranteed minimum wage in the sector under consideration.

[16]   It follows that the concepts of 'worker' and 'activity as an employed person' must be interpreted as meaning that the rules relating to freedom of movement for workers also concern persons who pursue or wish to pursue an activity as an employed person on a part-time basis only and who, by virtue of that fact obtain or would obtain only remuneration lower than the minimum guaranteed remuneration in the sector under consideration. In this regard no distinction may be made between those who wish to make do with their income from such an activity and those who supplement that income with other income, whether the latter is derived from property or from the employment of a member of their family who accompanies them.

[17]   It should however be stated that whilst part-time employment is not excluded from the field of application of the rules on freedom of movement for workers, those rules cover only the pursuit of effective and genuine activities, to the exclusion of activities on such a small scale as to be regarded as purely marginal and ancillary. It follows both from the statement of the principle of freedom of movement for workers and from the place occupied by the rules relating to that principle in the system of the Treaty as a whole that those rules guarantee only the free movement of persons who pursue or are desirous of pursuing an economic activity.

[18]   The answer to be given to the first and second questions must therefore be that the provisions of Community law relating to freedom of movement for workers also cover a national of a Member State who pursues, within the territory of another Member State, an activity as an employed person which yields an income lower than that which, in the latter State, is considered as the minimum required for subsistence, whether that person supplements the income from his activity as an employed person with other income so as to arrive at that minimum or is satisfied with means of support lower than the said minimum, provided that he pursues an activity as an employed person which is effective and genuine.

Third question

[19]   The third question essentially seeks to ascertain whether the right to enter and reside in the territory of a Member State may be denied to a worker whose main

objectives, pursued by means of his entry and residence, are different from that of the pursuit of an activity as an employed person as defined in the answer to the first and second questions.

[The judgment then refers to the various Community provisions dealing with freedom of movement for persons]

[21]   . . . the advantages which Community law confers in the name of that freedom may be relied upon only by persons who actually pursue or seriously wish to pursue activities as employed persons. They do not, however, mean that the enjoyment of this freedom may be made to depend upon the aims pursued by a national of a Member State in applying for entry upon and residence in the territory of another Member State, provided that he there pursues or wishes to pursue an activity which meets the criteria specified above, that is to say, an effective and genuine activity as an employed person.

[22]   Once this condition is satisfied, the motives which may have prompted the worker to seek employment in the Member State concerned are of no account and must not be taken into consideration.

[23]   The answer to be given to the third question put to the Court by the Raad van State must therefore be that the motives which may have prompted a worker of a Member State to seek employment in another Member State are of no account as regards his right to enter and reside in the territory of the latter State provided that he there pursues or wishes to pursue an effective and genuine activity.

LAWRIE-BLUM v *LAND BADEN-WÜRTTEMBERG* (Case 66/85)
[1986] ECR 2121, Court of Justice

Two questions were referred by the national court. Must a trainee teacher be regarded as a worker within the meaning of Article 48 of the Treaty? Are trainee teachers employees in the public service within the meaning of Article 48(4)? (Article 177 reference.)

[10]   The national court is essentially asking in the first place whether a trainee teacher undergoing a period of service as preparation for the teaching profession during which he enjoys civil service status and provides services by conducting classes for which he receives remuneration must be regarded as a worker within the meaning of Article 48 of the EEC Treaty and secondly whether such preparatory service must be regarded as employment in the public service within the meaning of Article 48(4) to which nationals of other Member States may be refused admission.
. . .

[16]   Since freedom of movement for workers constitutes one of the fundamental principles of the Community, the term 'worker' in Article 48 may not be interpreted differently according to the law of each Member State but has a Community meaning. Since it defines the scope of that fundamental freedom, the Community concept of a 'worker' must be interpreted broadly (judgment of 23 March 1982 in *Levin* v *Staatssec-retaris van Justitie* (Case 53/81) [1982] ECR 1035).

[17]   That concept must be defined in accordance with objective criteria which distinguish the employment relationship by reference to the rights and duties of the persons concerned. The essential feature of an employment relationship, however, is that for a certain period of time a person performs services for and under the direction of another person in return for which he receives remuneration.

[18]   In the present case it is clear that during the entire period of preparatory service the trainee teacher is under the direction and supervision of the school to which he is assigned. It is the school that determines the services to be performed by him and his working hours and it is the school's instructions that he must carry out and its rules that he must observe. During a substantial part of the preparatory service he is required to give lessons to the school's pupils and thus provides a service of some economic value to the school. The amounts which he receives may be regarded as remuneration for the services provided and for the duties involved in completing the period of preparatory

service. Consequently the three criteria for the existence of an employment relationship are fulfilled in this case.

. . .

[21] The fact that trainee teachers give lessons for only a few hours a week and are paid remuneration below the starting salary of a qualified teacher does not prevent them from being regarded as workers. In its judgment in *Levin*, cited above, the Court held that the expressions 'worker' and 'activity as an employed person' must be understood as including persons who because they are not employed full time, receive pay lower than that for full-time employment provided that the activities performed are effective and genuine. The latter requirement is not called into question in this case.

[22] Consequently the reply to the first part of the question must be that a trainee teacher who under the direction and supervision of the school authorities is undergoing a period of service in preparation for the teaching profession during which he provides services by giving lessons and receives remuneration must be regarded as a worker within the meaning of Article 48(1) of the EEC Treaty irrespective of the legal nature of the employment relationship.

On the meaning of 'employment in the public service' in Article 48(4)

[23] Mrs Lawrie-Blum points out that, according to case-law, a post is covered by the reservation in Article 48(4) only if it involves the exercise of powers conferred by public law and contributes to safeguarding the general interests of the State. The activities of a teacher and *a fortiori* of a trainee teacher do not, however, involve the exercise of powers conferred by public law.

. . .

[26] . . . access to certain posts may not be limited by reason of the fact that in a given Member State persons appointed to such posts have the status of civil servants. To make the application of Article 48(4) dependent on the legal nature of the relationship between the employee and the administration would enable the Member States to determine at will the posts covered by the exception laid down in that provision.

[27] As the Court has already stated in its judgment of 17 December 1980 in *Commission* v *Belgium* (Case 149/79) [1980] ECR 3881 and of 26 May 1982 in *Commission* v *Belgium* (Case 149/79) [1982] ECR 1845, 'employment in the public service' within the meaning of Article 48(4), which is excluded from the ambit of Article 48(1), (2) and (3), must be understood as meaning those posts which involve direct or indirect participation in the exercise of powers conferred by public law and in the discharge of functions whose purpose is to safeguard the general interests of the State or of other public authorities and which therefore require a special relationship of allegiance to the State on the part of persons occupying them and reciprocity of rights and duties which form the foundation of the bond of nationality. The posts excluded are confined to those which, having regard to the tasks and responsibilities involved, are apt to display the characteristics of the specific activities of the public service in the spheres described above.

[28] Those very strict conditions are not fulfilled in the case of a trainee teacher, even if he does in fact take the decisions described by the *Land Baden-Württemberg.*

[29] Consequently, the reply to the second part of the question must be that the period of preparatory service for the teaching profession cannot be regarded as employment in the public service within the meaning of Article 48(4) to which nationals of other Member States may be denied access.

KEMPF v *STAATSSECRETARIS VAN JUSTITIE* (Case 139/85)
[1986] ECR 1741, Court of Justice

Mr Kempf, a German national, was resident in the Netherlands where he worked as a part-time music teacher, giving twelve lessons per week. His income was supplemented by social security benefit. Kempf was refused a residence permit on the grounds that he was not a worker (and therefore not a 'favoured EEC citizen') because his income from employment did not meet his needs. The national court had found that Kempf's work was not on such a small scale as to be purely a marginal and ancillary activity. (Article 177 reference.)

[13] The Court has consistently held that freedom of movement for workers forms one of the foundations of the Community. The provisions laying down that fundamental freedom and, more particularly, the terms 'worker' and 'activity as an employed person' defining the sphere of application of those freedoms must be given a broad interpretation in that regard, whereas exceptions to and derogations from the principle of freedom of movement for workers must be interpreted strictly.

[14] It follows that the rules on this topic must be interpreted as meaning that a person in effective and genuine part-time employment cannot be excluded from their sphere of application merely because the remuneration he derives from it is below the level of the minimum means of subsistence and he seeks to supplement it by other lawful means of subsistence. In that regard it is irrelevant whether those supplementary means of subsistence are derived from property or from the employment of a member of his family, as was the case in *Levin*, or whether, as in this instance, they are obtained from financial assistance drawn from the public funds of the Member State in which he resides, provided that the effective and genuine nature of his work is established.

[15] That conclusion is, indeed, corroborated by the fact that, as the Court held most recently in *Levin*, the terms 'worker' and 'activity as an employed person' for the purposes of Community law may not be defined by reference to the national laws of the Member States but have a meaning specific to Community law. Their effect would be jeopardized if the enjoyment of rights conferred under the principle of freedom of movement for workers could be precluded by the fact that the person concerned has had recourse to benefits chargeable to public funds and created by the domestic legislation of the host State.

[16] For those reasons, it must be stated in answer to the question submitted for a preliminary ruling that where a national of a Member State pursues within the territory of another Member State by way of employment activities which may in themselves be regarded as effective and genuine work, the fact that he claims financial assistance payable out of the public funds of the latter Member State in order to supplement the income he receives from those activities does not exclude him from the provisions of Community law relating to freedom of movement for workers.

STEYMANN v *STAATSSECRETARIS VAN JUSTITIE* (Case 196/87)
[1988] ECR 6159, Court of Justice

Following a short period of employment as a plumber in the Netherlands, Mr Steymann, a German national, joined a Dutch religious community known as the Bhagwan Community. Here, he undertook plumbing work and general household duties and participated in the Community's commercial activities which included running a disco-theque, a bar and a launderette. His application for a residence permit was turned down on the grounds that he was not a 'favoured EEC national'. On a reference from the Council of State of the Netherlands, the Court of Justice was asked (*inter alia*) to what extent activities performed by members of a religious community may be regarded as economic activities bringing those persons within the scope of the Community free movement provisions. (Article 177 reference.)

[11] As regards the activities in question in this case, it appears from the documents before the Court that they consist of work carried out within and on behalf of the Bhagwan Community in connection with the Bhagwan Community's commercial activities. It appears that such work plays a relatively important role in the way of life of the Bhagwan Community and that only in special circumstances can the members of the community avoid taking part therein. In turn, the Bhagwan Community provides for the material needs of its members, including pocket-money, irrespective of the nature and the extent of the work which they do.

[12] In a case such as the one before the national court it is impossible to rule out *a priori* the possibility that work carried out by members of the community in question constitutes an economic activity . . . In so far as the work, which aims to ensure a measure of self-sufficiency for the Bhagwan Community, constitutes an essential part of participation in that community, the services which the latter provides to its members may be regarded as being an indirect quid pro quo for their work.

[13]   However, it must be observed, as the Court held in its judgment of 23 March 1982 in Case 53/81 (*Levin* v *Staatssecretaris van Justitie* [1982] ECR 1035), that the work must be genuine and effective and not such as to be regarded as purely marginal and ancillary. In this case the national court has held that the work was genuine and effective.

[14]   Accordingly, the answer given to the first question must be that . . . activities performed by members of a community based on religion or another form of philosophy as part of the commercial activities of that community constitute economic activities in so far as the services which the community provides to its members may be regarded as the indirect quid pro quo for genuine and effective work.

BETTRAY v *STAATSSECRETARIS VAN JUSTITIE* (Case 344/87)
[1989] ECR 1621, Court of Justice

The Netherlands authorities refused to grant Mr Bettray a residence permit on three occasions. Bettray had given as one of the reasons for his residence in the Netherlands 'a stay in a rehabilitation centre for drug addicts'. At the centre, under a scheme set up under the Dutch Social Employment Act, individuals were engaged in work for which they received payment but which was aimed to enable them eventually to take up ordinary employment or lead as normal a life as possible. The Court of Justice was asked by the Council of State of the Netherlands whether such persons were workers under Community law. (Article 177 reference.)

[9]   The question raised by the national court seeks essentially to ascertain whether Article 48(1) of the EEC Treaty must be interpreted as meaning that a national of a Member State employed in another Member State in the framework of a scheme such as that provided for in the Social Employment Law may be regarded on that ground alone as a worker for the purposes of Community law.

[10]   The Commission and the plaintiff in the main proceedings consider that the reply to the national court's question must be in the affirmative, having regard to the Court's case-law on the concept of worker, while the Netherlands Government argues that having regard to the special characteristics of the scheme set up by the Social Employment Law persons working under that scheme should not be regarded as workers for the purposes of Community law. It points in particular to the *sui generis* nature of the employment relationship under the Social Employment Law, the very low productivity of the persons employed, whose remuneration is financed largely by subsidies from public funds, and the pre-eminently social and non-economic nature of the scheme.

[11]   It should be pointed out first of all that according to now established case-law the term 'worker' in Article 48 of the Treaty has a Community meaning and, inasmuch as it defines the scope of one of the fundamental freedoms of the Community, must be interpreted broadly (see, in particular, the judgment of 3 July 1986 in *Lawrie-Blum* v *Land Baden-Württemberg* (Case 66/85) [1986] ECR 2121).

[12]   According to the same judgment, that concept must be defined in accordance with objective criteria which distinguish the employment relationship by reference to the rights and duties of the persons concerned, and the essential feature of an employment relationship is that for a certain period of time a person performs services for and under the direction of another person in return for which he receives remuneration.

[13]   It is clear both from the terms in which the principle of freedom of movement for workers is expressed and the place occupied by the provisions concerning that principle in the structure of the Treaty that those provisions guarantee freedom of movement only for persons pursuing or wishing to pursue an economic activity and that, consequently, they cover only the pursuit of an effective and genuine activity (see the judgment of 23 March 1982 in *Levin* v *Staatssecretaris van Justitie* (Case 53/81) [1982] ECR 1035).

[14]   It appears from the order for reference that persons employed under the scheme set up by the Social Employment Law perform services under the direction of another person in return for which they receive remuneration. The essential feature of an employment relationship is therefore present.

[15]   That conclusion is not altered by the fact that the productivity of persons employed in the scheme is low and that, consequently, their remuneration is largely provided by subsidies from public funds. Neither the level of productivity nor the origin of the funds from which the remuneration is paid can have any consequence in regard to whether or not the person is to be regarded as a worker.

[16]   Nor can the person cease to be regarded as a worker merely by virtue of the fact that the employment relationship under the Social Employment Law is of a *sui generis* nature in national law. As the Court has held (see, primarily, the judgment of 12 February 1974 in *Sotgiu* v *Deutsches Bundespost* (Case 152/73) [1974] ECR 153), the nature of the legal relationship between the employee and the employer is of no consequence in regard to the application of Article 48 of the Treaty.

[17]   However, work under the Social Employment Law cannot be regarded as an effective and genuine economic activity if it constitutes merely a means of rehabilitation or reintegration for the persons concerned and the purpose of the paid employment, which is adapted to the physical and mental possibilities of each person, is to enable those persons sooner or later to recover their capacity to take up ordinary employment or to lead as normal as possible a life.

[18]   It appears from the order for reference that the jobs in question are reserved for persons who, by reason of circumstances relating to their situation, are unable to take up employment under normal conditions and that the social employment ends once the local authority is informed by the employment office that the person concerned will be able within a short period to take up employment under normal conditions.

[19]   It also appears from the order for reference that persons employed under the Social Employment Law are not selected on the basis of their capacity to perform a certain activity; on the contrary, it is the activities which are chosen in the light of the capabilities of the persons who are going to perform them in order to maintain, re-establish or develop their capacity for work. Finally, the activities involved are pursued in the framework of undertakings or work associations created solely for that purpose by local authorities.

[20]   The reply to the national court's question must therefore be that Article 48(1) of the EEC Treaty is to be interpreted as meaning that a national of a Member State employed in another Member State under a scheme such as that established under the Social Employment Law, in which the activities carried out are merely a means of rehabilitation or reintegration, cannot on that basis alone be regarded as a worker for the purposes of Community law.

10.2.3   MEANING OF 'FAMILIES'

REGULATION (EEC) NO. 1612/68 OF THE COUNCIL OF 15 OCTOBER 1968 ON FREEDOM OF MOVEMENT FOR WORKERS WITHIN THE COMMUNITY AS AMENDED BY REGULATION 312/76 (1968) OJ (Special Edition) (II) 475

PART I   EMPLOYMENT AND WORKERS' FAMILIES
TITLE I   ELIGIBILITY FOR EMPLOYMENT

(Preamble omitted)

Article 1

1.   Any national of a Member State, shall, irrespective of his place of residence, have the right to take up an activity as an employed person, and to pursue such activity, within the territory of another Member State in accordance with the provisions laid down by law, regulation or administrative action governing the employment of nationals of that State.

2.   He shall, in particular, have the right to take up available employment in the territory of another Member State with the same priority as nationals of that State.

Article 2

Any national of a Member State and any employer pursuing an activity in the territory of a Member State may exchange their applications for and offers of employment, and may conclude and perform contracts of employment in accordance with the provisions in force laid down by law, regulation or administrative action, without any discrimination resulting therefrom.

Article 3

1.   Under this Regulation, provisions laid down by law, regulation or administrative action or administrative practices of a Member State shall not apply:

— where they limit application for and offers of employment, or the right of foreign nationals to take up and pursue employment or subject these to conditions not applicable in respect of their own nationals; or

— where, though applicable irrespective of nationality, their exclusive or principal aim or effect is to keep nationals of other Member States away from the employment offered.

This provision shall not apply to conditions relating to linguistic knowledge required by reason of the nature of the post to be filled.

2.   There shall be included in particular among the provisions or practices of a Member State referred to in the first subparagraph of paragraph 1 those which:

(a)   prescribe a special recruitment procedure for foreign nationals;

(b)   limit or restrict the advertising or vacancies in the press or through any other medium or subject it to conditions other than those applicable in respect of employers pursuing their activities in the territory of that Member State;

(c)   subject eligibility for employment to conditions of registration with employment offices or impede recruitment of individual workers, where persons who do not reside in the territory of that State are concerned.

Article 4

1.   Provisions laid down by law, regulation or administrative action of the Member States which restrict by number or percentage the employment of foreign nationals in any undertaking, branch of activity or region, or at a national level, shall not apply to nationals of the other Member States.

2.   When in a Member State the granting of any benefit to undertakings is subject to a minimum percentage of national workers being employed, nationals of the other Member States shall be counted as national workers, subject to the provisions of the Council Directive of 15 October 1963.

Article 5

A national of a Member State who seeks employment in the territory of another Member State shall receive the same assistance there as that afforded by the employment offices in that State to their own nationals seeking employment.

Article 6

1.   The engagement and recruitment of a national of one Member State for a post in another Member State shall not depend on medical, vocational or other criteria which are discriminatory on grounds of nationality by comparison with those applied to nationals of the other Member State who wish to pursue the same activity.

2.   Nevertheless, a national who holds an offer in his name from an employer in a Member State other than that of which he is a national may have to undergo a vocational test, if the employer expressly requests this when making his offer of employment.

TITLE II   EMPLOYMENT AND EQUALITY OF TREATMENT

Article 7

1.   A worker who is a national of a Member State may not, in the territory of another Member State, be treated differently from national workers by reason of his nationality in respect of any conditions of employment and work, in particular as regards remuneration, dismissal, and should he become unemployed, reinstatement or re-employment.

2.   He shall enjoy the same social and tax advantages as national workers.

3.   He shall also, by virtue of the same right and under the same conditions as national workers, have access to training in vocational schools and retraining centres.

4. Any clause of a collective or individual agreement or of any other collective regulation concerning eligibility for employment, employment, remuneration and other conditions of work or dismissal shall be null and void in so far as it lays down or authorises discriminatory conditions in respect of workers who are nationals of the other Member States.

Article 8

1. A worker who is a national of a Member State and who is employed in the territory of another Member State shall enjoy equality of treatment as regards membership of trade unions and the exercise of rights attaching thereto, including the right to vote and to be eligible for the administration or management posts of a trade union; he may be excluded from taking part in the management of bodies governed by public law and from holding an office governed by public law. Furthermore, he shall have the right of eligibility for workers' representative bodies in the undertaking. The provisions of this Article shall not affect laws or regulations in certain Member States which grant more extensive rights to workers coming from the other Member States.

2. This Article shall be reviewed by the Council on the basis of a proposal from the Commission which shall be submitted within not more than two years.

Article 9

1. A worker who is a national of a Member State and who is employed in the territory of another Member State shall enjoy all the rights and benefits accorded to national workers in matters of housing, including ownership of the housing he needs.

2. Such worker may, with the same right as nationals, put his name down on the housing lists in the region in which he is employed, where such lists exist; he shall enjoy the resultant benefits and priorities.

If his family has remained in the country whence he came, they shall be considered for this purpose as residing in the said region, where national workers benefit from a similar presumption.

TITLE III   WORKERS' FAMILIES

Article 10

1. The following shall, irrespective of their nationality, have the right to install themselves with a worker who is a national of one Member State and who is employed in the territory of another Member State:

(a) his spouse and their descendants who are under the age of 21 years or are dependants;

(b) dependent relatives in the ascending line of the worker and his spouse.

2. Member States shall facilitate the admission of any member of the family not coming within the provisions of paragraph 1 if dependent on the worker referred to above or living under his roof in the country whence he comes.

3. For the purposes of paragraphs 1 and 2, the worker must have available for his family housing considered as normal for national workers in the region where he is employed; this provision, however must not give rise to discrimination between national workers and workers from the other Member States.

Article 11

Where a national of a Member State is pursuing an activity as an employed or self-employed person in the territory of another Member State, his spouse and those of the children who are under the age of 21 years or dependent on him shall have the right to take up any activity as an employed person throughout the territory of that same State, even if they are not nationals of any Member State.

Article 12

The children of a national of a Member State who is or has been employed in the territory of another Member State shall be admitted to that State's general educational, apprenticeship and vocational training courses under the same conditions as the nationals of that State, if such children are residing in its territory.

Member States shall encourage all efforts to enable such children to attend these courses under the best possible conditions.
(Remaining provisions omitted.)

CENTRE PUBLIC D'AIDE SOCIALE DE COURCELLES v LEBON (Case 316/85)
[1987] ECR 2811, Court of Justice

The Public Social Welfare Centre at Courcelles discontinued payment of the 'minimex' (the minimum means of subsistence granted under Belgian law) to Mrs Lebon. She was a French national living in Belgium with her father, also of French nationality. The questions referred to the Court of Justice concerned (*inter alia*) the rights of descendants of migrant workers who have reached the age of 21, are no longer dependent on the worker and are not themselves workers to 'the same social and tax advantages as national workers' under Article 7(2) of Regulation 1612/68; the status of 'dependent member of a worker's family'; and the rights of a Community migrant job seeker under Article 7(2) of Regulation 1612/68. (Article 177 reference.)

[10] It must be pointed out that the principle of equal treatment is derived in the first place from Article 7 of the EEC Treaty, according to which 'within the scope of application of this Treaty, and without prejudice to any special provisions contained therein, any discrimination on grounds of nationality shall be prohibited'. As the Court emphasized in its judgment of 17 April 1986 in Case 59/85 (*Netherlands* v *Reed* [1985] ECR 1283 *et seq.*), that principle was applied specifically with regard to freedom of movement for workers within the Community in Article 48 of the EEC Treaty, a provision implemented by Regulation No. 1612/68 which provides in Article 7(2) that in the host State a worker who is a national of another Member State must 'enjoy the same social and tax advantages as national workers'.

[11] The equality of treatment enjoyed by workers who are nationals of Member States and are employed within the territory of another Member State in relation to workers who are nationals of that State, as regards the advantages which are granted to the members of a worker's family, contributes to the integration of migrant workers in the working environment of the host country in accordance with the objectives of the free movement of workers.

[12] However, the members of a worker's family, within the meaning of Article 10 of Regulation No. 1612/68, qualify only indirectly for the equal treatment accorded to the worker himself by Article 7 of Regulation No. 1612/68. Social benefits such as the income guaranteed to old people by the legislation of a Member State . . . or guaranteeing in general terms the minimum means of subsistence operate in favour of members of the worker's family only if such benefits may be regarded as a social advantage, within the meaning of Article 7(2) of Regulation No. 1612/68, for the worker himself.

[13] It follows that, where a worker who is a national of one Member State was employed within the territory of another Member State and exercised the right to remain there, his descendants who have reached the age of 21 and are no longer dependent on him may not rely on the right to equal treatment guaranteed by Community law in order to claim a social benefit provided for by the legislation of the host Member State and guaranteeing in general terms the minimum means of subsistence. In the circumstances, that benefit does not constitute for the worker a social advantage within the meaning of Article 7(2) of Regulation No. 1612/68, inasmuch as he is no longer supporting his descendant.

[14] The answer to the first question must therefore be that, where a worker who is a national of one Member State was employed within the territory of another Member State and remains there after obtaining a retirement pension, his descendants do not retain the right to equal treatment with regard to a social benefit provided for by the legislation of the host Member State and guaranteeing in general terms the minimum means of subsistence where they have reached the age of 21, are no longer dependent on him and do not have the status of workers.

. . .

[16] In its third question, the national court seeks essentially to ascertain whether the status of dependent member of a worker's family, to which Article 10 of Regulation No.

1612/68 refers, results from a factual situation, namely the provision of support by the worker, without there being any need to determine the reasons for recourse to the worker's support.

. . .

[20]   It must be pointed out, in the first place, that a claim for the grant of the minimex submitted by a member of a migrant worker's family who is dependent on the worker cannot affect the claimant's status as a dependent member of the worker's family. To decide otherwise would amount to accepting that the grant of the minimex could result in the claimant forfeiting the status of dependent member of the family and consequently justify either the withdrawal of the minimex itself or even the loss of the right of residence. Such a solution would in practice preclude a dependent member of a worker's family from claiming the minimex and would, for that reason, undermine the equal treatment accorded to the migrant worker. The status of dependent member of a worker's family should therefore be considered independently of the grant of the minimex.

[21]   It must be pointed out, secondly, that the status of dependent member of a worker's family does not presuppose the existence of a right to maintenance either. If that were the case, the composition of the family would depend on national legislation, which varies from one State to another, and that would lead to the application of Community law in a manner that is not uniform.

[22]   Article 10(1) and (2) of Regulation No. 1612/68 must be interpreted as meaning that the status of dependent member of a worker's family is the result of a factual situation. The person having that status is a member of the family who is supported by the worker and there is no need to determine the reasons for recourse to the worker's support or to raise the question whether the person concerned is able to support himself by taking up paid employment.

. . .

[24]   The answer to the third question must therefore be that the status of dependent member of a worker's family, to which Article 10(1) and (2) of Regulation No. 1612/68 refers, is the result of a factual situation, namely the provision of support by the worker, without there being any need to determine the reasons for recourse to the worker's support.

. . .

[25]   It is clear from the context that the fourth question seeks, in substance, to ascertain whether equal treatment with regard to social and tax advantages, which is laid down by Article 7(2) of Regulation No. 1612/68, also applies to persons who move in search of employment.

[26]   It must be pointed out that the right to equal treatment with regard to social and tax advantages applies only to workers. Those who move in search of employment qualify for equal treatment only as regards access to employment in accordance with Article 48 of the EEC Treaty and Articles 2 and 5 of Regulation No. 1612/68.

[27]   The answer to the fourth question must therefore be that the equal treatment with regard to social and tax advantages which is laid down by Article 7(2) of Regulation No. 1612/68 operates only for the benefit of workers and does not apply to nationals of Member States who move in search of employment.

10.2.3.1   Cohabitees

NETHERLANDS v REED (Case 59/85) [1985] ECR 1283, Court of Justice

Miss Reed, an unmarried British national, had lived in the Netherlands with her partner, Mr W, for five years. Mr W was a British migrant worker. Miss Reed had not been in employment since her arrival in the country and her application for a residence permit was turned down. Relying on Articles 7 and 48 of the Treaty and Article 10 of Regulation 1612/68, Miss Reed claimed that, as the companion of Mr W, she was entitled to a permit. Under Dutch policy concerning aliens, an alien in a stable relationship with a Dutch national could, under certain conditions, be permitted to reside in the Netherlands. Two main questions arose from these circumstances. Could Miss Reed be treated as a 'spouse' within the meaning of Article 10(1)(a) of Regulation 1612/68? Must Articles 7 and 48 of the Treaty be interpreted as meaning that a Member State which permits the unmarried companions of its nationals, who are not themselves nationals of that Member State, to reside in its territory cannot refuse to grant the same advantage to migrant workers who are nationals of other Member States? (Article 177 reference.)

[14]   Article 10(1) of Regulation No. 1612/68 provides that certain members of the 'family' of a worker, including his 'spouse', irrespective of their nationality, 'have the right to install themselves with a worker who is a national of one Member State and who is employed in the territory of another Member State'.

[15]   In the absence of any indication of a general social development which would justify a broad construction, and in the absence of any indication to the contrary in the Regulation, it must be held that the term 'spouse' in Article 10 of the Regulation refers to a marital relationship only.

[16]   The answer to the third question must therefore be that Article 10(1) of Regulation No. 1612/68 cannot be interpreted as meaning that the companion, in a stable relationship, of a worker who is a national of a Member State and is employed in the territory of another Member State must in certain circumstances be treated as his 'spouse' for the purposes of that provision.

. . .

[28]   . . . it must be recognized that the possibility for a migrant worker of obtaining permission for his unmarried companion to reside with him, where that companion is not a national of the host Member State, can assist his integration in the host State and thus contribute to the achievement of freedom of movement for workers. Consequently, that possibility must also be regarded as falling within the concept of a social advantage for the purposes of Article 7(2) of Regulation No. 1612/68.

[29]   It must therefore be concluded that the Member State which grants such an advantage to its own nationals cannot refuse to grant it to workers who are nationals of other Member States without being guilty of discrimination on grounds of nationality, contrary to Articles 7 and 48 of the Treaty.

[30]   The answer to the first and second questions must therefore be that Article 7 of the Treaty, in conjunction with Article 48 of the Treaty and Article 7(2) of Regulation No. 1612/68, must be interpreted as meaning that a Member State which permits the unmarried companions of its nationals, who are not themselves nationals of that Member State, to reside in its territory cannot refuse to grant the same advantage to migrant workers who are nationals of other Member States.

10.2.3.2 The effect of divorce and separation

DIATTA v LAND BERLIN (Case 267/83) [1985] ECR 567, Court of Justice

Mrs Diatta, a Senegalese national, was married to a French national who resided and worked in Berlin. After having lived with her husband for some time, she moved into separate accommodation, intending to seek a divorce. (Article 177 reference.)

[7]   The two questions referred to the Court by the Bundesverwaltungsgericht are intended to establish whether the members of a migrant worker's family, as defined in Article 10 of Regulation No. 1612/68, are necessarily required to live with him permanently in order to qualify for a right of residence under that provision, and whether Article 11 of that regulation establishes a right of residence independent of that provided for in Article 10.

. . .

[18]   In providing that a member of a migrant worker's family has the right to install himself with the worker, Article 10 of the regulation does not require that the member of the family in question must live permanently with the worker, but, as is clear from Article 10(3), only that the accommodation which the worker has available must be such as may be considered normal for the purpose of accommodating his family. A requirement that the family must live under the same roof permanently cannot be implied.

[19]   In addition such an interpretation corresponds to the spirit of Article 11 of the regulation, which gives the member of the family the right to take up any activity as an

employed person throughout the territory of the Member State concerned, even though that activity is exercised at a place some distance from the place where the migrant worker resides.

[20]   It must be added that the marital relationship cannot be regarded as dissolved so long as it has not been terminated by the competent authority. It is not dissolved merely because the spouses live separately, even where they intend to divorce at a later date.

[21]   As regards Article 11 of Regulation No. 1612/68, it is clear from the terms of that provision that it does not confer on the members of a migrant worker's family an independent right of residence, but solely a right to exercise any activity as employed persons throughout the territory of the State in question. Article 11 cannot therefore constitute the legal basis for a right of residence without reference to the conditions laid down in Article 10.

[22]   Consequently, in reply to the questions referred to the Court by the Bundesverwaltungsgericht, it must be stated that the members of a migrant worker's family, as defined in Article 10 of Regulation No. 1612/68, are not necessarily required to live permanently with him in order to qualify for a right of residence under that provision and Article 11 of the same regulation does not establish a right of residence independent of that provided for in Article 10.

10.2.4   THE RIGHTS OF WORKERS AND THEIR FAMILIES

10.2.4.1   Directive 68/360: rights of entry and residence

COUNCIL DIRECTIVE 68/360/EEC OF 15 OCTOBER 1968 ON THE ABOLITION OF RESTRICTIONS ON MOVEMENT AND RESIDENCE WITHIN THE COMMUNITY FOR WORKERS OF MEMBER STATES AND THEIR FAMILIES (1968) OJ (Special Edition) (II) 485

(Preamble omitted.)

Article 1
Member States shall, acting as provided in this Directive, abolish restrictions on the movement and residence of nationals of the said States and of members of their families to whom Regulation (EEC) No. 1612/68 applies.

Article 2
1.   Member States shall grant the nationals referred to in Article 1 the right to leave their territory in order to take up activities as employed persons and to pursue such activities in the territory of another Member State. Such right shall be exercised simply on production of a valid identity card or passport. Members of the family shall enjoy the same right as the national on whom they are dependent.

2.   Member States shall, acting in accordance with their laws, issue to such nationals, or renew, an identity card or passport, which shall state in particular the holder's nationality.

3.   The passport must be valid at least for all Member States and for countries through which the holder must pass when travelling between Member States. Where a passport is the only document on which the holder may lawfully leave the country, its period of validity shall be not less than five years.

4.   Member States may not demand from the nationals referred to in Article 1 any exit visa or any equivalent document.

Article 3
1.   Member States shall allow the persons referred to in Article 1 to enter their territory simply on production of a valid identity card or passport.

2.   No entry visa or equivalent document may be demanded save from members of the family who are not nationals of a Member State. Member States shall accord to such persons every facility for obtaining any necessary visas.

Article 4

1. Member States shall grant the right of residence in their territory to the persons referred to in Article 1 who are able to produce the documents listed in paragraph 3.

2. As proof of the right of residence, a document entitled 'Residence Permit for a National of a Member State of the EEC' shall be issued. This document must include a statement that it has been issued pursuant to Regulation (EEC) No. 1612/68 and to the measures taken by the Member States for the implementation of the present Directive. The text of such statement is given in the Annex to this Directive.

3. For the issue of a Residence Permit for a National of a Member State of the EEC, Member States may require only the production of the following documents;

— by the worker:

    (a)   the document with which he entered their territory;

    (b)   a confirmation of engagement from the employer or a certificate of employment;

— by the members of the worker's family:

    (c)   the document with which they entered the territory;

    (d)   a document issued by the competent authority of the State of origin or the State whence they came, proving their relationship;

    (e)   in the cases referred to in Article 10(1) and (2) of Regulation (EEC) No. 1612/68, a document issued by the competent authority of the State of origin or the State whence they came, testifying that they are dependent on the worker or that they live under his roof in such country.

4. A member of the family who is not a national of a Member State shall be issued with a residence document which shall have the same validity as that issued to the worker on whom he is dependent.

Article 5

Completion of the formalities for obtaining a residence permit shall not hinder the immediate beginning of employment under a contract concluded by the applicants.

Article 6

1. The residence permit:

    (a)   must be valid throughout the territory of the Member State which issued it;

    (b)   must be valid for at least five years from the date of issue and be automatically renewable.

2. Breaks in residence not exceeding six consecutive months and absence on military service shall not affect the validity of a residence permit.

3. Where a worker is employed for a period exceeding three months but not exceeding a year in the service of an employer in the host State or in the employ of a person providing services, the host Member State shall issue him a temporary residence permit, the validity of which may be limited to the expected period of the employment. Subject to the provisions of Article 8(1)(c), a temporary residence permit shall be issued also to a seasonal worker employed for a period of more than three months. The period of employment must be shown in the documents referred to in paragraph 4(3)(b).

Article 7

1. A valid residence permit may not be withdrawn from a worker solely on the grounds that he is no longer in employment, either because he is temporarily incapable of work as a result of illness or accident, or because he is involuntarily unemployed, this being duly confirmed by the competent employment office.

2. When the residence permit is renewed for the first time, the period of residence may be restricted, but not to less than twelve months, where the worker has been involuntarily unemployed in the Member State for more than twelve consecutive months.

Article 8

1. Member States shall, without issuing a residence permit, recognise the right of residence in their territory of:

    (a)   a worker pursuing an activity as an employed person, where the activity is not expected to last for more than three months. The document with which the person concerned entered the territory and a statement by the employer on the expected duration of the employment shall be sufficient to cover his stay; a statement by the employer shall not, however, be required in the case of workers coming within the provisions of the Council Directive of 25 February 1964 on the attainment of freedom of establishment and freedom to provide services in respect of the activities of intermediaries in commerce, industry and small craft industries;

(b) a worker who, while having his residence in the territory of a Member State to which he returns as a rule, each day or at least once a week, is employed in the territory of another Member State. The competent authority of the State where he is employed may issue such worker with a special permit valid for five years and automatically renewable;

(c) a seasonal worker who holds a contract of employment stamped by the competent authority of the Member State on whose territory he has come to pursue his activity.

2. In all cases referred to in paragraph 1, the competent authorities of the host Member State may require the worker to report his presence in the territory.

Article 9

1. The residence documents granted to nationals of a Member State of the EEC referred to in this Directive shall be issued and renewed free of charge or on payment of an amount not exceeding the dues and taxes charged for the issue of identity cards to nationals.

2. The visa referred to in Article 3(2) and the stamp referred to in Article 8(1)(c) shall be free of charge.

3. Member States shall take the necessary steps to simplify as much as possible the formalities and procedure for obtaining the documents mentioned in paragraph 1.

Article 10

Member States shall not derogate from the provisions of this Directive save on grounds of public policy, public security or public health.
(Remaining provisions omitted.)

PROCUREUR DU ROI v *ROYER* (Case 48/75) [1976] ECR 497, Court of Justice

It was perhaps not surprising that the Belgian authorities were unhappy about Mr Royer's presence in Belgium. In his country of origin, France, he had been convicted of procuring and prosecuted (though not convicted) for various armed robberies. The present case arose out of criminal proceedings against him in Belgium for illegal entry into and illegal residence in the country, where his wife, also a French national, ran a café and dance hall. Royer had been served with a notice of expulsion. The authorities gave as one of the reasons for his expulsion that he had not 'observed the conditions attached to the residence of aliens and he has no permit to establish himself in the Kingdom'.

The Belgian court referred a number of questions concerning the source of the right of a national of a Member State to enter into and reside in the territory of another Member State. In particular, the court asked, is this right conferred directly by the Treaty or does it depend upon the issue of a residence permit by the host Member State? Does the failure by a national of a Member State to comply with administrative formalities for the control of aliens in the host State justify expulsion?

In responding to these questions, the Court of Justice indicated (at paragraph 31(a) of the judgment) that the right of entry into a Member State includes the right to enter in search of work. (Article 177 reference.)

[Referring to the rights granted by Articles 48, 52 and 59 of the Treaty]

[23] These provisions, which may be construed as prohibiting Member States from setting up restrictions or obstacles to the entry into and residence in their territory of nationals of other Member States, have the effect of conferring rights directly on all

persons falling within the ambit of the above-mentioned articles, as later given closer articulation by regulations or directives implementing the Treaty.

[24]   This interpretation has been recognized by all the measures of secondary law adopted for the purpose of implementing the above-mentioned provisions of the Treaty.

[25]   Thus Article 1 of Regulation No. 1612/68 provides that any national of a Member State, shall, irrespective of his place of residence, have 'the right to take up activity as an employed person and to pursue such activity within the territory of another Member State' and Article 10 of the same regulation extends the 'right to install themselves' to the members of the family of such a national.

[26]   Article 4 of Directive No. 68/360 provides that 'Member States shall grant the right of residence in their territory' to the persons referred to and further states that as 'proof' of this right an individual residence permit shall be issued.

[27]   Further the preamble to Directive No. 73/148 states that freedom of establishment can be fully attained only 'if a right of permanent residence is granted to the persons who are to enjoy freedom of establishment' and that freedom to provide services entails that persons providing and receiving services should have 'the right of residence for the time during which the services are being provided'.

[28]   These provisions show that the legislative authorities of the Community were aware that, while not creating new rights in favour of persons protected by Community law, the regulation and directives concerned determined the scope and detailed rules for the exercise of rights conferred directly by the Treaty.

. . .

[31]   (a)   It follows from the foregoing that the right of nationals of a Member State to enter the territory of another Member State and reside there for the purposes intended by the Treaty – in particular to look for or pursue an occupation or activities as employed or self-employed persons, or to rejoin their spouse or family – is a right conferred directly by the Treaty, or, as the case may be, by the provisions adopted for its implementation.

[32]   It must therefore be concluded that this right is acquired independently of the issue of a residence permit by the competent authority of a Member State.

[33]   The grant of this permit is therefore to be regarded not as a measure giving rise to rights but as a measure by a Member State serving to prove the individual position of a national of another Member State with regard to provisions of Community law.

[34]   (b)   Article 4(1) and (2) of Directive No. 68/360 provides, without prejudice to Article 10 thereof that Member States shall 'grant' the right of residence in their territory to persons who are able to produce the documents listed in the directive and that 'proof' of the right of residence shall be constituted by issue of a special residence permit.

[35]   The above-mentioned provisions of the directive are intended to determine the practical details regulating the exercise of rights conferred directly by the Treaty.

[36]   It follows therefore, that the right of residence must be granted by the authorities of the Member States to any person falling within the categories set out in Article 1 of the directive and who is able to prove, by producing the documents specified in Article 4(3), that he falls within one of these categories.

[37]   The answer to the question put should therefore be that Article 4 of Directive No. 68/360 entails an obligation for Member States to issue a residence permit to any person who provides proof, by means of the appropriate documents, that he belongs to one of the categories set out in Article 1 of the directive.

[38]   (c)   The logical consequence of the foregoing is that the mere failure by a national of a Member State to complete the legal formalities concerning access, movement and residence of aliens does not justify a decision ordering expulsion.

R v *IMMIGRATION APPEAL TRIBUNAL, EX PARTE ANTONISSEN* (Case 292/89) [1991] ECR I-745, Court of Justice

Under UK Immigration Rules, a national of another Member State could be deported if after six months from admission to the UK he had not found employment. The question referred by the national court concerned the compatibility of a six month time limit with the Community free movement provisions. The question arose in the context of the expulsion from the UK of Mr Antonissen, who had been convicted in the UK of unlawful possession of cocaine and possession of that drug with intent to supply.

The Court of Justice held that unless the person concerned provides evidence that he is continuing to seek employment and has genuine chances of being engaged, a Member State may require such person to leave its territory if he has not found employment within six months. However, the Court did not specify a time limit. It also ruled that there was 'no necessary link' between the right of an individual who goes to another Member State in search of employment to unemployment benefit under Regulation 1408/71 (limited to a maximum period of three months) in the Member State of origin and the right to stay in the host State. (Article 177 reference.)

[8]　By means of the questions submitted to the Court for a preliminary ruling the national court essentially seeks to establish whether it is contrary to the provisions of Community law governing the free movement of workers for the legislation of a Member State to provide that a national of another Member State who entered the first State in order to seek employment may be required to leave the territory of that State (subject to appeal) if he has not found employment there after six months.

[9]　In that connection it has been argued that, according to the strict wording of Article 48 of the Treaty, Community nationals are given the right to move freely within the territory of the Member States for the purpose only of accepting offers of employment actually made (Article 48(3)(a) and (b)) whilst the right to stay the territory of a Member State is stated to be for the purpose of employment (Article 48(3)(c)).

[10]　Such an interpretation would exclude the right of a national of a Member State to move freely and to stay in the territory of the other Member States in order to seek employment there, and cannot be upheld.

[11]　Indeed, as the Court has consistently held, freedom of movement for workers forms one of the foundations of the Community and, consequently, the provisions laying down that freedom must be given a broad interpretation. . .

[12]　Moreover, a strict interpretation of Article 48(3) would jeopardize the actual chances that a national of a Member State who is seeking employment will find it in another Member State, and would, as a result, make that provision ineffective.

[13]　It follows that Article 48(3) must be interpreted as enumerating, in a non-exhaustive way, certain rights benefiting nationals of Member States in the context of the free movement of workers and that that freedom also entails the right for nationals of Member States to move freely within the territory of the other Member States and to stay there for the purposes of seeking employment.

[14]　Moreover, that interpretation of the Treaty corresponds to that of the Community legislature, as appears from the provisions adopted in order to implement the principle of free movement, in particular Articles 1 and 5 of Regulation No. 1612/68/EEC . . . on freedom of movement for workers within the Community . . . which presuppose that Community nationals are entitled to move in order to look for employment, and hence to stay, in another Member State.

[15]　It must therefore be ascertained whether the right, under Article 48 and the provisions of Regulation No. 1612/68 (cited above), to stay in a Member State for the purposes of seeking employment can be subjected to a temporal limitation.

[16]　In that regard, it must be pointed out in the first place that the effectiveness of Article 48 is secured in so far as Community legislation or, in its absence, the legislation of a Member State gives persons concerned a reasonable time in which to apprise themselves, in the territory of the Member State concerned, of offers of employment corresponding to their occupational qualifications and to take, where appropriate, the necessary steps in order to be engaged.

. . .

[19]　For their part, the United Kingdom and the Commission argue that, under Article 69(1) of Council Regulation No. 1408/71/EEC on the application of social security schemes to employed persons, to self-employed persons and to members of their families moving within the States . . . the Member States may limit to three months the period during which nationals from other Member States may stay in their territory in order to seek employment. According to the provision in question, an unemployed person who has acquired entitlement to benefits in a Member State and goes to another Member State to seek employment there retains entitlement to those benefits for a maximum period of three months.

[20] That argument cannot be upheld. As the Advocate General has rightly observed, there is no necessary link between the right to employment benefit in the Member State of origin and the right to stay in the host State.

[21] In the absence of a Community provision prescribing the period during which Community nationals seeking employment in a Member State may stay there, a period of six months, such as that laid down in the national legislation at issue in the main proceedings, does not appear in principle to be insufficient to enable the persons concerned to apprise themselves, in the host Member State, of offers of employment corresponding to their occupational qualifications and to take, where appropriate, the necessary steps in order to be engaged and, therefore, does not jeopardize the effectiveness of the principle of free movement. However, if after the expiry of that period the person concerned provides evidence that he is continuing to seek employment and that he has genuine chances of being engaged, he cannot be required to leave the territory of the host Member State.

[22] It must therefore be stated in reply to the questions submitted by the national court that it is not contrary to the provisions of Community law governing the free movement of workers for the legislation of a Member State to provide that a national of another Member State who entered the first State in order to seek employment may be required to leave the territory of that State (subject to appeal) if he has not found employment there after six months, unless the person concerned provides evidence that he is continuing to seek employment and that he has genuine chances of being engaged.

10.2.4.2 Directive 68/360: residence permits

CRIMINAL PROCEEDINGS AGAINST LYNNE WATSON AND ALESSANDRO BELMANN (Case 118/75) [1976] ECR 1185, Court of Justice

The questions referred by the Pretura, Milan, to the Court of Justice were raised in the context of criminal proceedings against a British national and an Italian national who had allegedly failed to comply with an Italian law requiring them to report to the Italian authorities the presence of the British national in Italy. The national court asked (*inter alia*) whether rules such as those contained in the Italian legislation breached Community free movement provisions. (Article 177 reference.)

[2] These questions have been raised within the context of criminal proceedings against, on the one hand, a British national who spent several months in Italy and, on the other, an Italian national who gave her accommodation.

[3] The said British national is alleged to have failed to discharge the obligation to report, within three days of her entry into the territory of the Italian Republic, to the police authorities of the place where she was staying 'in order to notify [her] presence and to make a declaration of residence'. This obligation is imposed by Italian legislation on all foreign nationals, with the exception of certain categories of employed workers from other Member States, and the penalties provided for in the event of a failure to discharge it are a maximum fine of Lit. 80,000 or a maximum of three months' detention and, in addition, possible deportation from the national territory, entailing a prohibition on re-entry without the permission of the Minister for the Interior.

[4] The Italian national is charged with having failed to inform the said authorities within twenty-four hours of the identity of the British national in question. This obligation is imposed by Italian legislation on 'any person who provides board and lodging, on whatever basis, to a foreign national or a stateless person, . . . or for any reason whatever takes such person into his employment', and failure to discharge it renders the person concerned liable to a maximum fine of Lit. 240,000 or a maximum of six months' detention.

[5] The questions referred to the Court ask essentially whether such rules are contrary to the provisions of Articles 7 and 48 to 66 of the Treaty, on the ground that they constitute discrimination based on nationality and a restriction on freedom of movement for persons within the Community.

. . .

[17] By creating the principle of freedom of movement for persons and by conferring on any person falling within its ambit the right of access to the territory of the Member

States, for the purposes intended by the Treaty, Community law has not excluded the power of Member States to adopt measures enabling the national authorities to have an exact knowledge of population movements affecting their territory.

[18]   Under the terms of Article 8(2) of Directive No. 68/360 and Article 4(2) of Directive No. 73/148, the competent authorities in the Member States may require nationals of the other Member States to report their presence to the authorities of the State concerned.

Such an obligation could not in itself be regarded as an infringement of the rules concerning freedom of movement for persons.

However, such an infringement might result from the legal formalities in question if the control procedures to which they refer were such as to restrict the freedom of movement required by the Treaty or to limit the right conferred by the Treaty on nationals of the Member States to enter and reside in the territory of any other Member State for the purposes intended by Community law.

[19]   In particular as regards the period within which the arrival of foreign nationals must be reported, the provisions of the Treaty are only infringed if the period fixed is unreasonable.

[20]   Among the penalties attaching to a failure to comply with the prescribed declaration and registration formalities, deportation, in relation to persons protected by Community law, is certainly incompatible with the provisions of the Treaty since, as the Court has already confirmed in other cases, such a measure negates the very right conferred and guaranteed by the Treaty.

[21]   As regards other penalties, such as fines and detention, whilst the national authorities are entitled to impose penalties in respect of a failure to comply with the terms of provisions requiring foreign nationals to notify their presence which are comparable to those attaching to infringements of provisions of equal importance by nationals, they are not justified in imposing a penalty so disproportionate to the gravity of the infringement that it becomes an obstacle to the free movement of persons.

[22]   In so far as national rules concerning the control of foreign nationals do not involve restrictions on freedom of movement for persons and on the right, conferred by the Treaty on persons protected by Community law, to enter and reside in the territory of the Member States, the application of such legislation, where it is based upon objective factors, cannot constitute 'discrimination on grounds of nationality', prohibited under Article 7 of the Treaty.

[23]   Provisions which require residents of the host State to inform the public authorities of the identity of foreign nationals for whom they provide accommodation, and which are for the most part connected with the internal order of the State, can only be called into question from the point of view of Community law if they place an indirect restriction on freedom of movement for persons.

MESSNER (Case C-265/88) [1989] ECR 4209, Court of Justice

The question referred in this case was more specific than that raised in *Watson and Belmann*. The Italian court asked whether it was lawful for Italy 'to impose on nationals of another Member State of the Community an obligation to make a formal declaration of residence within three days of entering Italian territory, failing which they are liable to a criminal penalty, in view of the fact that a feudal obligation of that kind, whose nature and purpose are manifestly oppressive and which is clearly inspired by xenophobia, cannot be justified on any specific ground of public policy, public security or public health'. (Article 177 reference.)

[5]   The question asked by the national court is, in essence, whether the fact that a Member State imposes on nationals of the other Member States, exercising their right to freedom of movement, the obligation to make a declaration of residence within three days of entering that State's territory, subject to a penal sanction for failure to comply, is compatible with the provisions of Community law on the free movement of persons.

[6]   In the judgment in *Watson and Belmann* (Case 118/75) [1976] ECR 1185, the Court has already held that by creating the principle of freedom of movement for persons and by conferring on any person falling within its ambit the right of access to the territory of

the Member States, for the purposes intended by the Treaty, Community law has not excluded the power of Member States to adopt measures enabling the national authorities to have an exact knowledge of population movements affecting their territory.

[7]   The Court pointed out that under Article 8(2) of Council Directive 68/360/EEC of 15 October 1968 on the abolition of restrictions on movement and residence within the Community for workers of Member States and their families. . . . and Article 4(2) of Council Directive 73/148/EEC. . . . on the abolition of restrictions on movement and residence within the Community for nationals of Member States with regard to establishment and the provision of services. . . ., the competent authorities in the Member States may require nationals of the other Member States to report their presence to the authorities of the State concerned.

[8]   The Court accordingly concluded that such an obligation could not in itself be regarded as an infringement of the rules concerning freedom of movement for persons. It pointed out, however, that such an infringement might result from legal formalities if those formalities were designed in such a way that they restricted the freedom of movement required by the Treaty or limited the right conferred on nationals of the Member States to enter and reside in the territory of any other Member State for the purposes intended by Community law (paragraph 18 of the judgment in *Watson and Belmann*, cited above).

[9]   It is evident from the judgment in *Watson and Belmann* that such is the case, in particular, when the time allowed for making the declaration of arrival by foreigners is not reasonable or when the penalties for failure to discharge that obligation are disproportionate to the gravity of the infringement.

[10]   It must be pointed out in that regard that the period of three days referred to in the preliminary question appears excessively restrictive in view of the need of those concerned to have sufficient time to travel from the frontier to their destination and to inquire there about the competent authority and the required administrative formalities.

[11]   The imposition of such a time-limit does not appear to be absolutely necessary in order to protect the host State's interest in obtaining exact knowledge of population movements affecting its territory. There is no reason to suppose that that interest would be compromised if a longer period were allowed. Moreover, that view is confirmed by the fact that the majority of the Member States of the Community imposing a similar obligation allow those concerned appreciably longer periods.

[12]   It follows that a time-limit of three days cannot be regarded as reasonable.

[13]   With regard to the penalties laid down for infringement of the legislation at issue, which consist of imprisonment or a fine, it must be pointed out that a fine cannot be allowed if the time-limit imposed for making the declaration of residence is not reasonable.

[14]   Moreover, it must be added that, as the Court has already held in its judgment of 3 July 1980 in *Regina* v *Pieck* (Case 157/79) [1980] ECR 2171, in relation to a failure to comply with the formalities required to establish the right of residence of a worker enjoying the protection of Community law, whilst the national authorities are entitled to make the failure to comply with such provisions subject to penalties comparable to those attaching to minor offences committed by their own nationals, they are not justified in imposing a penalty so disproportionate to the gravity of the infringement that it becomes an obstacle to the free movement of workers. This would be especially so if the penalty consisted of imprisonment.

[15]   The reply to the national court must therefore be that it is incompatible with the provisions of Community law on the free movement of persons for a Member State to impose on nationals of other Member States exercising their right to freedom of movement the obligation, subject to a penal sanction for failure to comply, to make a declaration of residence within three days of entering that State's territory.

R v PIECK (Case 157/79) [1980] ECR 2171, Court of Justice

Mr Pieck was residing and working in Cardiff. He had been granted limited leave to remain in the UK and had stayed on beyond the six month time limit. He did not hold a residence permit. On a reference from the Pontypridd Magistrates, the Court of Justice ruled on the compatibilty with Community law of penalties attached to non-compliance with formalities. (Article 177 reference.)

[18] Among the penalties attaching to a failure to comply with the formalities required as proof of the right of residence of a worker enjoying the protection of Community law, deportation is certainly incompatible with the provisions of the Treaty since, as the Court has already confirmed in other cases, such a measure negates the very right conferred and guaranteed by the Treaty.

[19] As regards other penalties such as fines and imprisonment, whilst the national authorities are entitled to impose penalties in respect of failure to comply with the terms of provisions relating to residence permits which are comparable to those attaching to minor offences by nationals, they are not justified in imposing a penalty so disproportionate to the gravity of the infringement that it becomes an obstacle to the free movement of persons. This would be especially so if that penalty included imprisonment.

[20] It follows that the failure on the part of a national of a Member State of the Community, to whom the rules on freedom of movement for workers apply, to obtain the special residence permit prescribed in Article 4 of Directive No. 68/360 may not be punished by a recommendation for deportation or by measures which go as far as imprisonment.

10.2.4.3   Regulation 1612/68: eligibility for employment (Articles 1–6)

GROENER v *MINISTER FOR EDUCATION* (Case 379/87) [1989] ECR 3967, Court of Justice

Irish rules made the appointment to permanent full-time posts as lecturers in public vocational education institutions conditional upon proof of adequate knowledge of the Irish language. Mrs Groener failed an Irish language test and was refused a full-time appointment as an art lecturer. She sought judicial review, maintaining that the rules were contrary to Article 48 and Regulation 1612/68.

One of the questions referred to the Court of Justice by the Dublin High Court was as follows: 'In considering the meaning of the phrase "the nature of the post to be filled" in Article 3 of Regulation (EEC) No. 1612/68 of the Council, is regard to be had to a policy of the Irish State that persons holding the post should have a competent knowledge of the Irish language, where such knowledge is not required to discharge the duties attached to the post?'. (Article 177 reference.)

[12] It should be borne in mind first of all that the second indent of Article 3(1) of Regulation No. 1612/68 provides that national provisions or administrative practices of a Member State are not to apply where, 'though applicable irrespective of nationality, their exclusive or principal aim or effect is to keep nationals of other Member States away from the employment offered'. The last subparagraph of Article 3(1) provides that that provision is not to 'apply to conditions relating to linguistic knowledge required by reason of the nature of the post to be filled'.

[13] It is apparent from the documents before the Court that the obligation to prove a knowledge of the Irish language imposed by the national provisions in question applies without distinction to Irish and other Community nationals, except as regards the exemptions which may be allowed for nationals of other Member States.

[14] Since the second indent of Article 3(1) is not applicable where linguistic requirements are justified by the nature of the post, it is appropriate to consider first the second question submitted by the national court, which is essentially whether the nature of a permanent full-time post of lecturer in art in public vocational education institutions is such as to justify the requirement of a knowledge of the Irish language.

[15] According to the documents before the Court, the teaching of art, like that of most other subjects taught in public vocational education schools, is conducted essentially or indeed exclusively in the English language. It follows that, as indicated by the terms of the second question submitted, knowledge of the Irish language is not required for the performance of the duties which teaching of the kind at issue specifically entails.

[16] However, that finding is not in itself sufficient to enable the national court to decide whether the linguistic requirement in question is justified 'by reason of the nature of the post to be filled', within the meaning of the last subparagraph of Article 3(1) of Regulation No. 1612/68.

[17] To apprehend the full scope of the second question, regard must be had to the special linguistic situation in Ireland, as it appears from the documents before the Court. By virtue of Article 8 of the 'Bunreacht na hEireann' (Irish Constitution):

(1) The Irish language as the national language is the first official language.
(2) The English language is recognized as a second official language.
(3) Provision may, however, be made by law for the exclusive use of either of the said languages for any one or more official purposes, either throughout the State or in any part thereof.

[18] As is apparent from the documents before the Court, although Irish is not spoken by the whole Irish population, the policy followed by Irish governments for many years has been designed not only to maintain but also to promote the use of Irish as a means of expressing national identity and culture. It is for that reason that Irish courses are compulsory for children receiving primary education and optional for those receiving secondary education. The obligation imposed on lecturers in public vocational education schools to have a certain knowledge of the Irish language is one of the measures adopted by the Irish Government in furtherance of that policy.

[19] The EEC Treaty does not prohibit the adoption of a policy for the protection and promotion of a language of a Member State which is both the national language and the first official language. However, the implementation of such a policy must not encroach upon a fundamental freedom such as that of the free movement of workers. Therefore, the requirements deriving from measures intended to implement such a policy must not in any circumstances be disproportionate in relation to the aim pursued and the manner in which they are applied must not bring about discrimination against nationals of other Member States.

[20] The importance of education for the implementation of such a policy must be recognized. Teachers have an essential role to play, not only through the teaching which they provide but also by their participation in the daily life of the school and the privileged relationship which they have with their pupils. In those circumstances, it is not unreasonable to require them to have some knowledge of the first national language.

[21] It follows that the requirement imposed on teachers to have an adequate knowledge of such a language must, provided that the level of knowledge required is not disproportionate in relation to the objective pursued, be regarded as a condition corresponding to the knowledge required by reason of the nature of the post to be filled within the meaning of the last subparagraph of Article 3(1) of Regulation No. 1612/68.

. . .

[24] Accordingly, the reply to the second question must be that a permanent full-time post of lecturer in public vocational education institutions is a post of such a nature as to justify the requirement of linguistic knowledge, within the meaning of the last subparagraph of Article 3(1) of Regulation No. 1612/68 of the Council, provided that the linguistic requirement in question is imposed as part of a policy for the promotion of the national language which is, at the same time, the first official language and provided that that requirement is applied in a proportionate and non-discriminatory manner.

10.2.4.4 Regulation 1612/68: employment and equality of treatment (Articles 7–9)

MARSMAN v *ROSSKAMP* **(Case 44/72) [1972] ECR 1243, Court of Justice**

German legislation excluded non-national workers resident outside Germany from special protection in the event of loss of earning capacity resulting from industrial accident. Under the legislation, such protection was available to all German nationals, irrespective of their place of residence, but only to those non-nationals who lived in Germany. On a reference from the Arbeitsgericht Rheine, the Court of Justice was asked whether the prohibition on discrimination referred to in Article 48 of the Treaty and Article 7 of Regulation 1612/68 concerned the special protection which the legislation of a Member State accords to specific categories of workers for reasons of a social nature. (Article 177 reference.)

[3]   It is clear from the file that the main action concerns whether a worker of Dutch nationality employed in a German undertaking who suffers an industrial accident in the Federal Republic of Germany resulting in a loss of earning capacity of more than 50% enjoys the special protection against dismissal introduced by Paragraph 14 of the Schwerbeschädigtengesetz of 16 June 1963 when he fulfils the conditions to which the grant of such protection is subject except that he does not live in the Federal Republic of Germany and the latter condition is required only of foreign workers and not of those of German nationality. The question referred by the national court therefore asks whether the prohibition on discrimination referred to in Article 48 of the Treaty and in Article 7 of Regulation No. 1612/68 also concerns the special protection against dismissal which the legislature of a Member State only grants, on specific social grounds, to certain fixed categories of workers.

[4]   Article 48 of the Treaty prescribes the abolition of any discrimination based on nationality between workers as regards employment, remuneration and other conditions of work and employment in order to ensure freedom of movement for workers which is essential to the Common Market. This provision is subject only to the conditions which are laid down restrictively in Article 48(3) and relate to public policy, public security or public health. The Community rules on social security are based on the principle that the law of each Member State must give the nationals of other Member States employed on its territory all the advantages which it grants its own nationals. It follows that the prohibition on discrimination set out in Article 48 also concerns the special protection which the legislation of a Member State accords to specific categories of workers for reasons of a social nature.

[5]   When Article 7 of Regulation No. 1612/68 specifically mentioned dismissal amongst the conditions of work and employment which workers of other Member States must enjoy on an equal footing with national workers, it merely ensured the proper implementation of Article 48. It follows that this provision also refers to the special conditions, in particular regarding dismissal, which may be enjoyed in a Member State by specific categories of national workers.

SOTGIU v *DEUTSCHE BUNDESPOST* (Case 152/73) [1974] ECR 153, Court of Justice

Increases in the separation allowances paid by the German Federal Post Office to those of its employees working away from their place of residence were higher for employees resident in Germany at the time of their recruitment. Mr Sotgiu, an Italian national employed by the Federal Post Office, brought an action against his employer, claiming that its policy was discriminatory. The questions referred by the national court concerned (*inter alia*) the public service exception to the free movement provisions contained in Article 48(4) of the Treaty and the indirectly discriminatory treatment of non-national workers. (Article 177 reference.)

On the first question
[2]   The first question asks whether, having regard to the exception provided for in Article 48(4) of the EEC Treaty, workers employed in the public service of a member State – in this case the postal service – by virtue of a contract of employment under private law, may be excluded from the rule of non-discrimination set out in Article 7(1) and (4) of Regulation No. 1612/68.

   . . .

[4]   Taking account of the fundamental nature, in the scheme of the Treaty, of the principles of freedom of movement and equality of treatment of workers within the Community, the exceptions made by Article 48(4) cannot have a scope going beyond the aim in view of which this derogation was included.

   The interests which this derogation allows Member States to protect are satisfied by the opportunity of restricting admission of foreign nationals to certain activities in the public service.

   On the other hand this provision cannot justify discriminatory measures with regard to remuneration or other conditions of employment against workers once they have been admitted to the public service.

The very fact that they have been admitted shows indeed that those interests which justify the exceptions to the principle of non-discrimination permitted by Article 48(4) are not at issue.

. . .

On the third question

[10] The third question asks whether Article 7(1) and (4) of Regulation No. 1612/68 is to be interpreted as containing a prohibition not only against treating a worker differently because he is a national of another Member State of the EEC, but also against treating him differently because he is resident in another Member State.

[11] The rules regarding equality of treatment, both in the Treaty and in Article 7 of Regulation No. 1612/68, forbid not only overt discrimination by reason of nationality but also all covert forms of discrimination which, by the application of other criteria of differentiation, lead in fact to the same result.

This interpretation, which is necessary to ensure the effective working of one of the fundamental principles of the Community, is explictly recognized by the fifth recital of the preamble to Regulation No. 1612/68 which requires that equality of treatment of workers shall be ensured 'in fact and in law'.

It may therefore be that criteria such as place of origin or residence of a worker may, according to circumstances, be tantamount, as regards their practical effect, to discrimination on the grounds of nationality, such as is prohibited by the Treaty and the Regulation.

[12] However, this would not be the case with a separation allowance the conditions of allotment and rules for the payment of which took account of objective differences which the situation of workers may involve according to whether their residence, at the time of their taking up a given post, is within the territory of the State in question or abroad.

In this respect the fact that, for workers whose home is within the territory of the State concerned, payment of the separation allowance is only temporary and is not bound up with any obligation to transfer the residence to the place of employment, whilst the same allowance is paid for an indefinite period and is not bound up with any such obligation in the case of workers whose residence is abroad, whatever their nationality, may be a valid reason for differentiating between the amounts paid.

In any case it is not possible to state that there is discrimination contrary to the Treaty and the Regulation, if it is apparent from a comparison between the two schemes of allowances taken as a whole that those workers who retain their residence abroad are not placed at a disadvantage by comparison with those whose residence is established within the territory of the State concerned.

[13] The reply to the question put should be that the taking into consideration as a criterion for the grant of a separation allowance of the fact that a worker has his residence in the territory of another Member State may, according to the circumstances, constitute discrimination forbidden by Article 7(1) and (4) of Regulation No. 1612/68.

This is not the case however if the scheme relating to such an allowance takes account of objective differences in the situations of workers according to whether their residence at the time when they take up their employment is within the territory of the State concerned or abroad.

CRISTINI v *SNCF* (Case 32/75) [1975] ECR 1085, Court of Justice

The special fare reduction card offered by the SNCF (French Railways) to large families was issued only to French nationals or to foreigners whose state of origin had entered into a reciprocal arrangement with France. Italy and France had not entered into such an arrangement. The widow of an Italian worker, herself an Italian national, who had four infant children, was refused the card on grounds of her nationality. The Paris Cour d'Appel asked the Court of Justice for a ruling on whether the fare reduction card constituted a 'social advantage' under Article 7(2) of Regulation 1612/68. (Article 177 reference.)

[4] The French Law of 29 October 1921, as amended by the Law of 24 December 1940 and the Decree of 3 November 1961, provides that in families of three or more children

under the age of eighteen years the father, the mother and each child shall, at the request of the head of the family, receive an identity card entitling them to certain reductions in the fares of the SNCF.

[5] Article 20 of the Code français de la famille et de l'aide sociale (French Family and Social Security Code). . . . provides that for the purpose of assisting families in bringing up their children, they shall be granted certain allowances and benefits, which are listed, albeit not exhaustively, and include, apart from family benefits provided for by the social security legislation and tax reductions or exemptions, reductions in the railway fares prescribed by the Law concerned in the present case.

    . . .

[7] Article 7(1) of Regulation (EEC) No. 1612/68. . . . provides that a worker who is a national of a Member State may not, in the territory of the other Member States, be treated differently from national workers by reason of his nationality in respect of any conditions of employment and work.

[8] Under paragraph (2) of that article he is to enjoy 'the same social and tax advantages as national workers'.

[9] Under paragraph (3) of that article he must also, 'by virtue of the same right and under the same conditions as national workers, have access to training in vocational schools and retraining centres'.

[10] The respondent in the main action has argued that the advantages thus prescribed are exclusively those attaching to the status of worker since they are connected with the contract of employment itself.

[11] Although it is true that certain provisions in this article refer to relationships deriving from the contract of employment, there are others, such as those concerning reinstatement and re-employment should a worker become unemployed, which have nothing to do with such relationships and even imply the termination of a previous employment.

[12] In these circumstances the reference to 'social advantages' in Article 7(2) cannot be interpreted restrictively.

[13] It therefore follows that, in view of the equality of treatment which the provision seeks to achieve, the substantive area of application must be delineated so as to include all social and tax advantages, whether or not attached to the contract of employment, such as reductions in fares for large families.

[14] It then becomes necessary to examine whether such an advantage must be granted to the widow and children after the death of the migrant worker when the national law provides that, at the request of the head of the family, each member of the family shall be issued with an identity card entitling him or her to the reduction.

[15] If the widow and infant children of a national of the Member State in question are entitled to such cards provided that the request had been made by the father before his death, the same must apply where the deceased father was a migrant worker and a national of another Member State.

[16] It would be contrary to the purpose and the spirit of the Community rules on freedom of movement for workers to deprive the survivors of such a benefit following the death of the worker whilst granting the same benefit to the survivors of a national.

    . . .

[19] Accordingly the answer to the question should be that Article 7(2) of Regulation (EEC) No. 1612/68. . . . must be interpreted as meaning that the social advantages referred to by that provision include fares reduction cards issued by a national railway authority to large families and that this applies, even if the said advantage is only sought after the worker's death, to the benefit of his family remaining in the same Member State.

10.2.4.5   Regulation 1612/68: workers' families (Articles 10–12)

GÜL v REGIERUNGS PRÄSIDENT DÜSSELDORF (Case 131/85)
[1986] ECR 1573, Court of Justice

Emir Gül, a doctor of Cypriot nationality, his British wife and their family were resident in Germany where he practised medicine. His wife worked as a hairdresser. The Regierungspräsident had refused to renew his authorisation to practise medicine in

Germany and claimed that Article 11 of Regulation 1612/68 did not grant to the spouse of a migrant Community worker the right to take up a particular occupation. The Court of Justice disagreed, though it emphasised that the individual concerned must hold the necessary qualifications and observe any rules governing the pursuit of that occupation. (Article 177 reference.)

[11]   Under Article 11 of Regulation No. 1612/68, the interpretation of which is requested, where a national of a Member State is pursuing an activity as an employed or self-employed person in the territory of another Member State, his spouse and those of the children who are under the age of 21 years or dependent on him are entitled to take up any activity as an employed person throughout the territory of that same State, even if they are not nationals of any Member State.

[12]   According to the Regierungspräsident, that provision must be interpreted as meaning that the right to take up employment granted to the spouse of a migrant worker does not include the right to pursue a particular occupation, such as the medical profession, access to which is governed by special legal provisions.

[13]   For Mr Gül and the Commission, on the other hand, it is clear from the very wording of Article 11 of Regulation No. 1612/68 that the right of the spouse, whatever his nationality, to take up employment covers any activity as an employed person; the spouse must therefore be subject to the same rules regarding access to and pursuit of the occupation as nationals of the host Member State.

[14]   The latter argument must be upheld. First of all, Article 11 does not exclude any type of employment from its area of application; furthermore, that provision must be interpreted in the light of the objective of Regulation No. 1612/68, which is to ensure freedom of movement for workers within the Community. As the preamble to the regulation states, freedom of movement is a fundamental right 'of workers and their families' (third recital) and it requires that obstacles to the mobility of workers should be eliminated, in particular as regards 'the worker's right to be joined by his family' and 'the conditions for the integration of that family into the host country' (fifth recital).

[15]   In order to pursue an occupation, such as the medical profession, the access to and pursuit of which are governed by special rules, the spouse of a migrant worker who is a national of a non-member country must meet two requirements: he must show that he has the qualifications and diplomas necessary for the pursuit of that occupation in accordance with the legislation of the host Member State and must observe the specific rules governing the pursuit of that occupation; those requirements must be the same as those imposed by the host Member State on its own nationals. It appears from the documents before the Court that Mr Gül meets both these requirements.

COMMISSION v *GERMANY* (Case 249/86) [1989] ECR 1263, Court of Justice

German legislation concerning the residence of Community nationals provided that 'a residence permit granted to members of the family of workers shall be extended on demand for a period of at least five years if the conditions for the issue thereof continue to be fulfilled'. The Commission had received complaints that Germany had refused in some cases to renew the residence permits of migrant workers' families and had threatened to expel them because their housing no longer met prevailing housing standards in the regions where the workers were employed. The Commission considered that the national legislation was incompatible with Article 48 of the Treaty and Article 10(3) of Regulation 1612/68. (Article 169 proceedings.)

[8]   It should first of all be pointed out that Regulation No. 1612/68. . . . defines more precisely the principle of freedom of movement for workers as formulated in Articles 48 and 49 of the EEC Treaty. Consequently, that regulation must be interpreted in the light of those provisions of the Treaty, which call for the adoption of the measures required to bring about, by progressive stages, freedom of movement for workers.

[9]   Furthermore, as the Court held in its judgment of 8 April 1976 in *Royer* (Case 48/75) [1976] ECR 497, the right of nationals of a Member State to enter the territory of another Member State and reside there for the purposes intended by the Treaty – in particular to look for or pursue an occupation or activities as employed or self-employed

persons, or to rejoin their spouse or family – is a right conferred directly by the Treaty or, as the case may be, by the provisions adopted for its implementation, and that right is acquired independently of the issue of a residence permit by the competent authority of a Member State.

[10]   Regulation No. 1612/68 must also be interpreted in the light of the requirement of respect for family life set out in Article 8 of the Convention for the Protection of Human Rights and Fundamental Freedoms. That requirement is one of the fundamental rights which, according to the Court's settled case-law, restated in the preamble to the Single European Act, are recognized by Community law.

[11]   Finally, Article 10(3) of Regulation No. 1612/68 must be interpreted in the context of the overall structure and purpose of that regulation. It is apparent from the provisions of the regulation, taken as a whole, that in order to facilitate the movement of members of workers' families the Council took into account, first, the importance for the worker, from a human point of view, of having his entire family with him and, secondly, the importance, from all points of view, of the integration of the worker and his family into the host Member State without any difference in treatment in relation to nationals of that State.

[12]   It follows from the foregoing that Article 10(3) must be interpreted as meaning that the requirement to have available housing considered as normal applies solely as a condition under which each member of the worker's family is permitted to come to live with him and that once the family has been brought together, the position of the migrant worker cannot be different in regard to housing requirements from that of a worker who is a national of the Member State concerned.

[13]   Consequently, if the housing regarded as normal at the time of the arrival of members of the migrant worker's family no longer fulfils that requirement as a result of a new event, such as the birth or arrival at the age of majority of a child, the measures which may be adopted in regard to members of the worker's family cannot be different from those required in regard to nationals of that Member State and cannot lead to discrimination between those nationals and nationals of other Member States.

[14]   A different solution would be compatible with the objectives which Article 10(3) of Regulation No. 1612/68 seeks to achieve only if the migrant worker had obtained suitable housing solely in order to obtain the right to have members of his family living with him and had left that housing once he had obtained such authorization.

[15]   The German legislation is therefore incompatible with the obligations arising under Community law in so far as it provides for non-renewal of a residence permit or a reduction *a posteriori* of the period of validity of a residence permit for a member of the family of a migrant worker by virtue of the fact that the family's housing can no longer be regarded as suitable according to the criteria applied in that regard in the place of residence, whereas sanctions of comparable severity are not provided for in regard to German nationals.

CASAGRANDE v *LANDESHAUPTSTADT MÜNCHEN* (Case 9/74)
[1974] ECR 773, Court of Justice

A grant available in Germany to secondary school pupils was refused to the child of a migrant Italian worker attending school in Munich on the grounds that a Bavarian law on educational grants referred only to German nationals, stateless persons and aliens granted asylum. The national court sought from the Court of Justice an interpretation of Article 12 of Regulation 1612/68. (Article 177 reference.)

[5]   Under Article 12 'the children of a national of a Member State who is or has been employed in the territory of another Member State shall be admitted to that State's general educational, appenticeship and vocational training courses under the same conditions as the nationals of that State, if such children are residing in its territory', and Member States are required to encourage 'all efforts to enable such children to attend these courses under the best possible conditions'.

[6]   According to the fifth recital of the Regulation, the latter was issued, *inter alia*, for the reason that 'the right of freedom of movement, in order that it may be exercised, by objective standards, in freedom and dignity, requires . . . that obstacles to the mobility

of workers shall be eliminated, in particular as regards the worker's right to be joined by his family and the conditions for the integration of that family into the host country'.

[7] Such integration presupposes that, in the case of the child of a foreign worker who wishes to have secondary education, this child can take advantage of benefits provided by the laws of the host country relating to educational grants, under the same conditions as nationals who are in a similar position.

[8] It follows from the provision in the second paragraph of Article 12, according to which Member States are to encourage all efforts to enable such children to attend the courses under the best possible conditions, that the article is intended to encourage special efforts, to ensure that the children may take advantage on an equal footing of the education and training facilities available.

[9] It must be concluded that in providing that the children in question shall be admitted to educational courses 'under the same conditions as the nationals' of the host State, Article 12 refers not only to rules relating to admission, but also to general measures intended to facilitate educational attendance.

10.2.4.6 Article 48(4): exclusion of employment in the public service

COMMISSION v BELGIUM (PUBLIC EMPLOYEES) (Case 149/79)
[1980] ECR 3881

Only Belgian nationals could apply for certain posts on the Belgian railways and in the City of Brussels and the Commune of Auderghem. The Commission took the view that this policy was incompatible with Article 48 of the Treaty and Regulation 1612/68 since the posts in question were not covered by Article 48(4). (Article 169 proceedings.)

[2] In its reasoned opinion and application to the Court the Commission referred generally to 'various vacancies' advertised by the Société Nationale des Chemins de Fer Belges [Belgian National Railway Company] and the Société Nationale des Chemins de Fer Vicinaux [National Local Railway Company] concerning posts for unskilled workers, and to vacancies advertised 'during recent years' by the City of Brussels and the Commune of Auderghem and the Commission gave only a brief indication of the posts involved. Through information requested by the Court. . . . it became possible to establish an exact list of the posts in issue.

[3] From that information and that list it emerges that the vacancies referred to concern posts for trainee locomotive drivers, loaders, plate-layers, shunters and signallers with the national railways and unskilled workers with the local railways as well as posts for hospital nurses, children's nurses, night-watchmen, plumbers, carpenters, electricians, garden hands, architects, and supervisors with the City of Brussels and the Commune of Auderghem.
. . .

[9] Article 48(4) of the Treaty provides that 'the provisions of this article shall not apply to employment in the public service'.

[10] That provision removes from the ambit of Article 48(1) to (3) a series of posts which involve direct or indirect participation in the exercise of powers conferred by public law and duties designed to safeguard the general interests of the State or of other public authorities. Such posts in fact presume on the part of those occupying them the existence of a special relationship of allegiance to the State and reciprocity of rights and duties which form the foundation of the bond of nationality.

[11] The scope of the derogation made by Article 48(4) to the principles of freedom of movement and equality of treatment laid down in the first three paragraphs of the article should therefore be determined on the basis of the aim pursued by that article. However, determining the sphere of application of Article 48(4) raises special difficulties since in the various Member States authorities acting under powers conferred by public law have assumed responsibilities of an economic and social nature or are involved in activities which are not identifiable with the functions which are typical of the public service yet which by their nature still come under the sphere of application of the Treaty. In these circumstances the effect of extending the exception contained in Article 48(4) to posts which, whilst coming under the State or other organizations governed by public law, still do not involve any association with tasks belonging to the public service

properly so called, would be to remove a considerable number of posts from the ambit of the principles set out in the Treaty and to create inequalities between Member States according to the different ways in which the State and certain sectors of economic life are organized.

[12]   Consequently it is appropriate to examine whether the posts covered by the action may be associated with the concept of public service within the meaning of Article 48(4), which requires uniform interpretation and application throughout the Community. It must be acknowledged that the application of the distinguishing criteria indicated above gives rise to problems of appraisal and demarcation in specific cases. It follows from the foregoing that such a classification depends on whether or not the posts in question are typical of the specific activities of the public service in so far as the exercise of powers conferred by public law and responsibility for safeguarding the general interests of the State are vested in it.

[13]   Where, in the case of posts which, although offered by public authorities, are not within the sphere to which Article 48(4) applies, a worker from another Member State is, like a national worker, required to satisfy all other conditions of recruitment, in particular concerning the competence and vocational training required, the provisions of the first three paragraphs of Article 48 and Regulation No. 1612/68 do not allow him to be debarred from those posts simply on the grounds of his nationality.

10.2.5   THE RIGHT OF MEMBER STATES TO RESTRICT ENTRY AND RESIDENCE

10.2.5.1   The scope of Article 48(3)

RUTILI v *MINISTRE DE L'INTERIEUR* (Case 36/75) [1975] ECR 1219, Court of Justice

The residence permit granted by the French authorities to Mr Rutili, an Italian national, was subject to a prohibition on his residence in four French *départements*, including the one in which he and his family were habitually resident. It was alleged that by reason of his political and trade union activities, he was 'likely to disturb public policy'. The questions referred to the Court of Justice by the national court concerned the scope of Article 48(3). (Article 177 reference.)

[22]   The second question asks what is the precise meaning to be attributed to the word 'justified' in the phrase 'subject to limitations justified on grounds of public policy' in Article 48(3) of the Treaty.

. . .

[26]   By virtue of the reservation contained in Article 48(3), Member States continue to be, in principle, free to determine the requirements of public policy in the light of their national needs.

[27]   Nevertheless, the concept of public policy must, in the Community context and where, in particular, it is used as a justification for derogating from the fundamental principles of equality of treatment and freedom of movement for workers, be interpreted strictly, so that its scope cannot be determined unilaterally by each Member State without being subject to control by the institutions of the Community.

[28]   Accordingly, restrictions cannot be imposed on the right of a national of any Member State to enter the territory of another Member State, to stay there and to move within it unless his presence or conduct constitutes a genuine and sufficiently serious threat to public policy.

. . .

[40]   The questions put by the Tribunal administratif were raised in connexion with a measure prohibiting residence in a limited part of the national territory.

[41]   In reply to a question from the Court, the Government of the French Republic stated that such measures may be taken in the case of its own nationals either, in the case of certain criminal convictions, as an additional penalty, or following the declaration of a state of emergency.

[42]   The provisions enabling certain areas of the national territory to be prohibited to foreign nationals are, however, based on legislative instruments specifically concerning them.

. . .

[46]   Right of entry into the territory of Member States and the right to stay there and to move freely within it is defined in the Treaty by reference to the whole territory of these States and not by reference to its internal subdivisions.

[47]   The reservation contained in Article 48(3) concerning the protection of public policy has the same scope as the rights the exercise of which may, under that paragraph, be subject to limitations.

[48]   It follows that prohibitions on residence under the reservation inserted to this effect in Article 48(3) may be imposed only in respect of the whole of the national territory.

[49]   On the other hand, in the case of partial prohibitions on residence, limited to certain areas of the territory, persons covered by Community law must, under Article 7 of the Treaty and within the field of application of that provision, be treated on a footing of equality with the nationals of the Member State concerned.

[50]   It follows that a Member State cannot, in the case of a national of another Member State covered by the provisions of the Treaty, impose prohibitions on residence which are territorially limited except in circumstances where such prohibitions may be imposed on its own nationals.

10.2.5.2   The scope of Directive 64/221

COUNCIL DIRECTIVE 64/221/EEC OF 25 FEBRUARY 1964 ON THE CO-ORDINATION OF SPECIAL MEASURES CONCERNING THE MOVEMENT AND RESIDENCE OF FOREIGN NATIONALS WHICH ARE JUSTIFIED ON GROUNDS OF PUBLIC POLICY, PUBLIC SECURITY OR PUBLIC HEALTH (1963–64) OJ (Special Edition) 117

(Preamble omitted)

Article 1

1.   The provisions of this Directive shall apply to any national of a Member State who resides in or travels to another Member State of the Community, either in order to pursue an activity as an employed or self-employed person, or as a recipient of services.

2.   These provisions shall apply also to the spouse and to members of the family who come within the provisions of the regulations and directives adopted in this field in pursuance of the Treaty.

Article 2

1.   This Directive relates to all measures concerning entry into their territory, issue or renewal of residence permits, or expulsion from their territory, taken by Member States on grounds of public policy, public security or public health.

2.   Such grounds shall not be invoked to service economic ends.

Article 3

1.   Measures taken on grounds of public policy or of public security shall be based exclusively on the personal conduct of the individual concerned.

2.   Previous criminal convictions shall not in themselves constitute grounds for the taking of such measures.

3.   Expiry of the identity card or passport used by the person concerned to enter the host country and to obtain a residence permit shall not justify expulsion from the territory.

4.   The State which issued the identity card or passport shall allow the holder of such document to re-enter its territory without any formality even if the document is no longer valid or the nationality of the holder is in dispute.

Article 4

1.   The only diseases or disabilities justifying refusal of entry into a territory or refusal to issue a first residence permit shall be those listed in the Annex to this Directive.

2.   Diseases or disabilities occurring after a first residence permit has been issued shall not justify refusal to renew the residence permit or expulsion from the territory.

3.   Member States shall not introduce new provisions or practices which are more restrictive than those in force at the date of notification of this Directive.

Article 5

1.   A decision to grant or to refuse a first residence permit shall be taken as soon as possible and in any event not later than six months from the date of application for the permit.

The person concerned shall be allowed to remain temporarily in the territory pending a decision either to grant or to refuse a residence permit.

2.   The host country may, in cases where this is considered essential, request the Member State of origin of the applicant, and if need be other Member States, to provide information concerning any previous police record. Such enquiries shall not be made as a matter of routine. The Member State consulted shall give its reply within two months.

Article 6

The person concerned shall be informed of the grounds of public policy, public security, or public health upon which the decision taken in his case is based, unless this is contrary to the interests of the security of the State involved.

Article 7

The person concerned shall be officially notified of any decision to refuse the issue or renewal of a residence permit or to expel him from the territory. The period allowed for leaving the territory shall be stated in this notification. Save in cases of urgency, this period shall be not less than fifteen days if the person concerned has not yet been granted a residence permit and not less than one month in all other cases.

Article 8

The person concerned shall have the same legal remedies in respect of any decision concerning entry, or refusing the issue or renewal of a residence permit, or ordering expulsion from the territory, as are available to nationals of the State concerned in respect of acts of the administration.

Article 9

1.   Where there is no right of appeal to a court of law, or where such appeal may be only in respect of the legal validity of the decision, or where the appeal cannot have suspensory effect, a decision refusing renewal of a residence permit or ordering the expulsion of the holder of a residence permit from the territory shall not be taken by the administrative authority, save in cases of urgency, until an opinion has been obtained from a competent authority of the host country before which the person concerned enjoys such rights of defence and of assistance or representation as the domestic law of that country provides for.

This authority shall not be the same as that empowered to take the decision refusing renewal of the residence permit or ordering expulsion.

2.   Any decision refusing the issue of a first residence permit or ordering expulsion of the person concerned before the issue of the permit shall, where that person so requests, be referred for consideration to the authority whose prior opinion is required under paragraph I. The person concerned shall then be entitled to submit his defence in person, except where this would be contrary to the interests of national security.

. . .

ANNEX

A.   *Diseases which might endanger public health:*

1.   Diseases subject to quarantine listed in International Health Regulation No. 2 of the World Health Organisation of 25 May 1951;

2.   Tuberculosis of the respiratory system in an active state or showing a tendency to develop;

3.   Syphilis;

4.   Other infectious diseases or contagious parasitic diseases if they are the subject of provisions for the protection of nationals of the host country.

B. *Diseases and disabilities which might threaten public policy or public security:*
   1. Drug addiction;
   2. Profound mental disturbance; manifest conditions of psychotic disturbance with agitation, delirium, hallucinations or confusion.

R v BOUCHEREAU (Case 30/77) [1977] ECR 1999, Court of Justice

Following Mr Bouchereau's second conviction for drugs offences, the Marlborough Street Magistrates were considering recommending his deportation from the UK. The Court of Justice was asked to clarify the scope of the public policy ground of limitation to the Community free movement provisions. (Article 177 reference.)

The first question
[6] The first question asks 'whether a recommendation for deportation made by a national court of a Member State to the executive authority of that State (such recommendation being persuasive but not binding on the executive authority) constitutes a "measure" within the meaning of Article 3(1) and (2) of Directive No. 64/221/EEC'.
. . .
[21] For the purposes of the directive, a 'measure' is any action which affects the right of persons coming within the field of application of Article 48 to enter and reside freely in the Member States under the same conditions as the nationals of the host State.
. . .

The second question
[25] The second question asks 'whether the wording of Article 3(2) of Directive No. 64/221/EEC, namely that previous criminal convictions shall not "in themselves" constitute grounds for the taking of measures based on public policy or public security means that previous criminal convictions are solely relevant in so far as they manifest a present or future propensity to act in a manner contrary to public policy or public security; alternatively, the meaning to be attached to the expression "in themselves" in Article 3(2) of Directive No. 64/221/EEC'.
[26] According to the terms of the order referring the case to the Court, that question seeks to discover whether, as the defendant maintained before the national court, 'previous criminal convictions are solely relevant in so far as they manifest a present or future intention to act in a manner contrary to public policy or public security' or, on the other hand, whether, as Counsel for the prosecution sought to argue, although 'the court cannot make a recommendation for deportation on grounds of public policy based on the fact alone of a previous conviction' it 'is entitled to take into account the past conduct of the defendant which resulted in the previous conviction'.
[27] The terms of Article 3(2) of the directive, which states that 'previous criminal convictions shall not in themselves constitute grounds for the taking of such measures' must be understood as requiring the national authorities to carry out a specific appraisal from the point of view of the interests inherent in protecting the requirements of public policy, which does not necessarily coincide with the appraisals which formed the basis of the criminal conviction.
[28] The existence of a previous criminal conviction can, therefore, only be taken into account in so far as the circumstances which gave rise to that conviction are evidence of personal conduct constituting a present threat to the requirements of public policy.
[29] Although, in general, a finding that such a threat exists implies the existence in the individual concerned of a propensity to act in the same way in the future, it is possible that past conduct alone may constitute such a threat to the requirements of public policy.
[30] It is for the authorities and, where appropriate, for the national courts, to consider that question in each individual case in the light of the particular legal position of persons subject to Community law and of the fundamental nature of the principle of the free movement of persons.

The third question
[31] The third question asks whether the words 'public policy' in Article 48(3) are to be interpreted as including reasons of state even where no breach of the public peace or

order is threatened or in a narrower sense in which is incorporated the concept of some threatened breach of the public peace, order or security, or in some other wider sense.

[32]   Apart from the various questions of terminology, this question seeks to obtain a definition of the interpretation to be given to the concept of 'public policy' referred to in Article 48.

[33]   In its judgment of 4 December 1974 (*Van Duyn* v *Home Office* (Case 41/74) [1974] ECR 1337, at p. 1350) the Court emphasized that the concept of public policy in the context of the Community and where, in particular, it is used as a justification for derogating from the fundamental principle of freedom of movement for workers, must be interpreted strictly, so that its scope cannot be determined unilaterally by each Member State without being subject to control by the institutions of the Community.

[34]   Nevertheless, it is stated in the same judgment that the particular circumstances justifying recourse to the concept of public policy may vary from one country to another and from one period to another and it is therefore necessary in this matter to allow the competent national authorities an area of discretion within the limits imposed by the Treaty and the provisions adopted for its implementation.

[35]   In so far as it may justify certain restrictions on the free movement of persons subject to Community law, recourse by a national authority to the concept of public policy presupposes, in any event, the existence, in addition to the perturbation of the social order which any infringement of the law involves, of a genuine and sufficiently serious threat to the requirements of public policy affecting one of the fundamental interests of society.

10.2.5.3   Limitation on grounds of public policy

VAN DUYN v *HOME OFFICE* (Case 41/74) [1974] ECR 1337, Court of Justice

Ms van Duyn, a Dutch national, was refused leave to enter the UK to take up a post as secretary with the 'Church of Scientology', an organisation considered by the UK Government to be 'socially harmful'. Van Duyn sought a declaration that she had the right, under Article 48 of the Treaty, to enter and remain in the UK. She maintained that the public policy exception in Directive 64/221 did not apply, since the justification for the refusal of entry was not based upon her personal conduct but on the UK Government's general policy of refusing work permits to all foreign nationals wishing to take up employment with the Church. (Article 177 reference.)

[16]   By the third question the Court is asked to rule whether Article 48 of the Treaty and Article 3 of Directive No. 64/221 must, be interpreted as meaning that

a Member State, in the performance of its duty to base a measure taken on grounds of public policy exclusively on the personal conduct of the individual concerned is entitled to take into account as matters of personal conduct:
(a) the fact that the individual is or has been associated with some body or organization the activities of which the Member State considers contrary to the public good but which are not unlawful in that State;
(b) the fact that the individual intends to take employment in the Member State with such a body or organization it being the case that no restrictions are placed upon nationals of the Member State who wish to take similar employment with such a body or organization.

[17]   It is necessary, first, to consider whether association with a body or an organization can in itself constitute personal conduct within the meaning of Article 3 of Directive No. 64/221. Although a person's past association cannot in general justify a decision refusing him the right to move freely within the Community, it is nevertheless the case that present association, which reflects participation in the activities of the body or of the organization as well as identification with its aims and its designs, may be considered a voluntary act of the person concerned and, consequently, as part of his personal conduct within the meaning of the provision cited.

[18]   This third question further raises the problem of what importance must be attributed to the fact that the activities of the organization in question, which are

considered by the Member State as contrary to the public good are not however prohibited by national law. It should be emphasized that the concept of public policy in the context of the Community and where, in particular, it is used as a justification for derogating from the fundamental principle of freedom of movement for workers, must be interpreted strictly, so that its scope cannot be determined unilaterally by each Member State without being subject to control by the institutions of the Community. Nevertheless, the particular circumstances justifying recourse to the concept of public policy may vary from one country to another and from one period to another, and it is therefore necessary in this matter to allow the competent national authorities an area of discretion within the limits imposed by the Treaty.

[19]   It follows from the above that where the competent authorities of a Member State have clearly defined their standpoint as regards the activities of a particular organization and where, considering it to be socially harmful, they have taken administrative measures to counteract these activities, the Member State cannot be required, before it can rely on the concept of public policy, to make such activities unlawful, if recourse to such a measure is not thought appropriate in the circumstances.

[20]   The question raises finally the problem of whether a Member State is entitled, on grounds of public policy, to prevent a national of another Member State from taking gainful employment within its territory with a body or organization, it being the case that no similar restriction is placed upon its own nationals.

[21]   In this connexion, the Treaty, while enshrining the principle of freedom of movement for workers without any discrimination on grounds of nationality, admits, in Article 48(3), limitations justified on grounds of public policy, public security or public health to the rights deriving from this principle. Under the terms of the provision cited above, the right to accept offers of employment actually made, the right to move freely within the territory of Member States for this purpose, and the right to stay in a Member State for the purpose of employment are, among others all subject to such limitations. Consequently, the effect of such limitations, when they apply, is that leave to enter the territory of a Member State and the right to reside there may be refused to a national of another Member State.

[22]   Furthermore, it is a principle of international law, which the EEC Treaty cannot be assumed to disregard in the relations between Member States, that a State is precluded from refusing its own nationals the right of entry or residence.

[23]   It follows that a Member State, for reasons of public policy, can, where it deems necessary, refuse a national of another Member State the benefit of the principle of freedom of movement for workers in a case where such a national proposes to take up a particular offer of employment even though the Member State does not place a similar restriction upon its own nationals.

[24]   Accordingly, the reply to the third question must be that Article 48 of the EEC Treaty and Article 3(1) of Directive No. 64/221 are to be interpreted as meaning that a Member State, in imposing restrictions justified on grounds of public policy, is entitled to take into account, as a matter of personal conduct of the individual concerned, the fact that the individual is associated with some body or organization the activities of which the Member State considers socially harmful but which are not unlawful in that State, despite the fact that no restriction is placed upon nationals of the said Member State who wish to take similar employment with these same bodies or organizations.

BONSIGNORE v OBERSTADTDIREKTOR OF THE CITY OF COLOGNE (Case 67/74)
[1975] ECR 297, Court of Justice

The German authorities ordered the deportation of Mr Bonsignore, an Italian national, following his conviction for unlawful possession of a firearm and causing death by negligence. He had been fined for the first offence but no punishment was imposed for the second offence, which involved the accidental killing of his brother through careless handling of the firearm. The national court considered that the only possible justification for the deportation would be 'reasons of a general preventive nature', based on 'the deterrent effect which the deportation of an alien found in illegal possession of a firearm would have in immigrant circles having regard to the resurgence of violence in the large urban centres'. The national court asked the Court of Justice whether 'reasons of a general preventive nature' justified expulsion, in particular where it was clear that the individual concerned would not commit further offences. (Article 177 reference.)

[5]   According to Article 3(1) and (2) of Directive No 64/221, 'Measures taken on grounds of public policy or of public security shall be based exclusively on the personal conduct of the individual concerned' and 'Previous criminal convictions shall not in themselves constitute grounds for the taking of such measures'.

These provisions must be interpreted in the light of the objectives of the directive which seeks in particular to coordinate the measures justified on grounds of public policy and for the maintenance of public security envisaged by Articles 48 and 56 of the Treaty, in order to reconcile the application of these measures with the basic principle of the free movement of persons within the Community and the elimination of all discrimination, in the application of the Treaty, between the nationals of the State in question and those of the other Member States.

[6]   With this in view, Article 3 of the directive provides that measures adopted on grounds of public policy and for the maintenance of public security against the nationals of Member States of the Community cannot be justified on grounds extraneous to the individual case, as is shown in particular by the requirement set out in paragraph (1) that 'only' the 'personal conduct' of those affected by the measures is to be regarded as determinative.

As departures from the rules concerning the free movement of persons constitute exceptions which must be strictly construed, the concept of 'personal conduct' expresses the requirement that a deportation order may only be made for breaches of the peace and public security which might be committed by the individual affected.

[7]   The reply to the questions referred should therefore be that Article 3(1) and (2) of Directive No. 64/221 prevents the deportation of a national of a Member State if such deportation is ordered for the purpose of deterring other aliens, that is, if it is based, in the words of the national court, on reasons of a 'general preventive nature'.

ADOUI AND CORNUAILLE v *BELGIAN STATE* (Joined Cases 115 and 116/81) [1982] ECR 1665, Court of Justice

Ms Adoui and Ms Cornuaille were French nationals whose applications for residence permits had been turned down by the Belgian authorities on the ground that their conduct was considered to be contrary to public policy because they worked as waitresses in a bar which was suspect from the point of view of morals. (Article 177 reference.)

[5]   Questions 1 to 9, 11 and 12 are essentially concerned with the question whether a Member State may, by virtue of the reservations contained in Articles 48 and 56 of the EEC Treaty, expel from its territory a national of another Member State or deny him access to that territory by reason of activities which, when attributable to the former State's own nationals, do not give rise to repressive measures.

[6]   Those questions are motivated by the fact that prostitution as such is not prohibited by Belgian legislation, although the Law does prohibit certain incidental activities, which are particularly harmful from the social point of view, such as the exploitation of prostitution by third parties and various forms of incitement to debauchery.

[7]   The reservations contained in Articles 48 and 56 of the EEC Treaty permit Member States to adopt, with respect to the nationals of other Member States and on the grounds specified in those provisions, in particular grounds justified by the requirements of public policy, measures which they cannot apply to their own nationals, inasmuch as they have no authority to expel the latter from the national territory or to deny them access thereto. Although that difference of treatment, which bears upon the nature of the measures available, must therefore be allowed, it must nevertheless be stressed that, in a Member State, the authority empowered to adopt such measures must not base the exercise of its powers on assessments of certain conduct which would have the effect of applying an arbitrary distinction to the detriment of nationals of other Member States.

[8]   It should be noted in that regard that reliance by a national authority upon the concept of public policy presupposes, as the Court held in its judgment of 27 October

1977 in *Bouchereau* (Case 30/77) [1977] ECR 1999, the existence of 'a genuine and sufficiently serious threat affecting one of the fundamental interests of society'. Although Community law does not impose upon the Member States a uniform scale of values as regards the assessment of conduct which may be considered as contrary to public policy, it should nevertheless be stated that conduct may not be considered as being of a sufficiently serious nature to justify restrictions on the admission to or residence within the territory of a Member State of a national of another Member State in a case where the former Member State does not adopt, with respect to the same conduct on the part of its own nationals repressive measures or other genuine and effective measures intended to combat such conduct.

[9]   The answer to Questions 1 to 9, 11 and 12 should therefore be that a Member State may not, by virtue of the reservation relating to public policy contained in Articles 48 and 56 of the Treaty, expel a national of another Member State from its territory or refuse him access to its territory by reason of conduct which, when attributable to the former State's own nationals, does not give rise to repressive measures or other genuine and effective measures intended to combat such conduct.

10.2.5.4   Previous criminal convictions

See *R* v *Bouchereau* (Case 30/77) [1977] ECR 1999 at **10.2.5.2** above

10.3   Freedom of Movement for the Self-employed

10.3.1   RIGHT OF ESTABLISHMENT AND TO PROVIDE SERVICES

THE TREATY OF ROME

Article 52
Within the framework of the provisions set out below, restrictions on the freedom of establishment of nationals of a Member State in the territory of another Member State shall be abolished by progressive stages in the course of the transitional period. Such progressive abolition shall also apply to restrictions on the setting up of agencies, branches or subsidiaries by nationals of any Member State established in the territory of any Member State.

  Freedom of establishment shall include the right to take up and pursue activities as self-employed persons and to set up and manage undertakings, in particular companies or firms within the meaning of the second paragraph of Article 58, under the conditions laid down for its own nationals by the law of the country where such establishment is effected, subject to the provisions of the Chapter relating to capital.

Article 59
Within the framework of the provisions set out below, restrictions on freedom to provide services within the Community shall be progressively abolished during the transitional period in respect of nationals of Member States who are established in a State of the Community other than that of the person for whom the services are intended.

  The Council may, acting by a qualified majority on a proposal from the Commission, extend the provisions of the Chapter to nationals of a third country who provide services and who are established within the Community.

Article 60
Services shall be considered to be 'services' within the meaning of this Treaty where they are normally provided for remuneration, in so far as they are not governed by the provisions relating to freedom of movement for goods, capital and persons.

  'Services' shall in particular include:
    (a)   activities of an industrial character;
    (b)   activities of a commercial character;
    (c)   activities of craftsmen;
    (d)   activities of the professions.

Without prejudice to the provisions of the Chapter relating to the right of establishment, the person providing a service may, in order to do so, temporarily pursue his activity in the State where the service is provided, under the same conditions as are imposed by the State on its own nationals.

10.3.2 DIRECT EFFECT OF ARTICLES 52 AND 59

REYNERS v *BELGIUM* (Case 2/74) [1974] ECR 631, Court of Justice

Mr Reyners, a Dutch national, did not satisfy the nationality requirement of the Belgian *Code Judiciaire* relating to entry to the profession of advocate in Belgium. He was therefore excluded from that profession although he held the necessary academic qualifications. Two questions were raised by the Conseil d'État in an Article 177 reference. The Court of Justice was asked whether Article 52 was directly effective, despite the absence of directives as prescribed by Articles 54 and 57 of the Treaty. The second question concerned the interpretation of Article 55 of the Treaty. (Article 177 reference.)

[26]   In laying down that freedom of establishment shall be attained at the end of the transitional period, Article 52 thus imposes an obligation to attain a precise result, the fulfilment of which had to be made easier by, but not made dependent on, the implementation of a programme of progressive measures.

[27]   The fact that this progression has not been adhered to leaves the obligation itself intact beyond the end of the period provided for its fulfilment.

[28]   This interpretation is in accordance with Article 8(7) of the Treaty, according to which the expiry of the transitional period shall constitute the latest date by which all the rules laid down must enter into force and all the measures required for establishing the common market must be implemented.

[29]   It is not possible to invoke against such an effect the fact that the Council has failed to issue the directives provided for by Articles 54 and 57 or the fact that certain of the directives actually issued have not fully attained the objective of non-discrimination required by Article 52.

[30]   After the expiry of the transitional period the directives provided for by the Chapter on the right of establishment have become superfluous with regard to implementing the rule on nationality, since this is henceforth sanctioned by the Treaty itself with direct effect.

[31]   These directives have however not lost all interest since they preserve an important scope in the field of measures intended to make easier the effective exercise of the right of freedom of establishment.

[32]   It is right therefore to reply to the question raised that, since the end of the transitional period, Article 52 of the Treaty is a directly applicable provision despite the absence, in a particular sphere, of the directives prescribed by Articles 54(2) and 57(1) of the Treaty.

. . .

[33]   The Conseil d'État has also requested a definition of what is meant in the first paragraph of Article 55 by 'activities which in that State are connected, even occasionally, with the exercise of official authority'.

[34]   More precisely, the question is whether, within a profession such as that of *avocat*, only those activities inherent in this profession which are connected with the exercise of official authority are excepted from the application of the Chapter on the right of establishment, or whether the whole of this profession is excepted by reason of the fact that it comprises activities connected with the exercise of this authority.

. . .

[44]   The first paragraph of Article 55 must enable Member States to exclude non-nationals from taking up functions involving the exercise of official authority which are connected with one of the activities of self-employed persons provided for in Article 52.

[45]   This need is fully satisfied when the exclusion of nationals is limited to those activities which, taken on their own, constitute a direct and specific connexion with the exercise of official authority.

[46] An extension of the exception allowed by Article 55 to a whole profession would be possible only in cases where such activities were linked with that profession in such a way that freedom of establishment would result in imposing on the Member State concerned the obligation to allow the exercise, even occasionally, by non-nationals of functions appertaining to official authority.

[47] This extension is on the other hand not possible when, within the framework of an independent profession, the activities connected with the exercise of official authority are separable from the professional activity in question taken as a whole.

VAN BINSBERGEN v BESTUUR VAN DE BEDRIJFSVERENIGING VOOR DE METAALNIJVERHEID (Case 33/74) [1974] ECR 1299, Court of Justice

A Dutch national who was qualified as an advocate in Holland was informed that, having moved his residence to Belgium, he could no longer represent a client in Holland because Dutch law provided that only persons established in Holland had rights of audience before certain tribunals.

The Court of Justice held that a residence requirement would be compatible with Articles 59 and 60 of the Treaty if it were objectively justified by the need to ensure observance of professional rules of conduct. Such rules, relating for instance to professional ethics and organisation are not incompatible with the Treaty provided they are non-discriminatory, objectively justified and proportionate. The Court further held that the first paragraph of Article 59 and the third paragraph of Article 60 have direct effect. (Article 177 reference.)

[9] The question put by the national court therefore seeks to determine whether the requirement that legal representatives be permanently established within the territory of the State where the service is to be provided can be reconciled with the prohibition, under Articles 59 and 60, on all restrictions on freedom to provide services within the Community.

[10] The restrictions to be abolished pursuant to Articles 59 and 60 include all requirements imposed on the person providing the service by reason in particular of his nationality or of the fact that he does not habitually reside in the State where the service is provided, which do not apply to persons established within the national territory or which may prevent or otherwise obstruct the activities of the person providing the service.

[11] In particular a requirement that the person providing the service must be habitually resident within the territory of the State where the service is to be provided may, according to the circumstances, have the result of depriving Article 59 of all useful effect, in view of the fact that the precise object of that Article is to abolish restrictions on freedom to provide services imposed on persons who are not established in the State where the service is to be provided.

[12] However, taking into account the particular nature of the services to be provided, specific requirements imposed on the person providing the service cannot be considered incompatible with the Treaty where they have as their purpose the application of professional rules justified by the general good – in particular rules relating to organization, qualifications, professional ethics, supervision and liability – which are binding upon any person established in the State in which the service is provided, where the person providing the service would escape from the ambit of those rules by being established in another Member State.

[13] Likewise, a Member State cannot be denied the right to take measures to prevent the exercise by a person providing services whose activity is entirely or principally directed towards its territory of the freedom guaranteed by Article 59 for the purpose of avoiding the professional rules of conduct which would be applicable to him if he were established within that State; such a situation may be subject to judicial control under the provisions of the chapter relating to the right of establishment and not of that on the provision of services.

[14] In accordance with these principles, the requirement that persons whose functions are to assist the administration of justice must be permanently established for professional purposes within the jurisdiction of certain courts or tribunals cannot be considered incompatible with the provisions of Articles 59 and 60, where such require-

ment is objectively justified by the need to ensure observance of professional rules of conduct connected, in particular, with the administration of justice and with respect for professional ethics.

[15]   That cannot, however, be the case when the provision of certain services in a Member State is not subject to any sort of qualification or professional regulation and when the requirement of habitual residence is fixed by reference to the territory of the State in question.

[16]   In relation to a professional activity the exercise of which is similarly unrestricted within the territory of a particular Member State, the requirement of residence within that State constitutes a restriction which is incompatible with Articles 59 and 60 of the Treaty if the administration of justice can satisfactorily be ensured by measures which are less restrictive, such as the choosing of an address for service.

[17]   It must therefore be stated in reply to the question put to the Court that the first paragraph of Article 59 and the third paragraph of Article 60 of the EEC Treaty must be interpreted as meaning that the national law of a Member State cannot, by imposing a requirement as to habitual residence within that State, deny persons established in another Member State the right to provide services, where the provision of services is not subject to any special condition under the national law applicable. . . .

[18]   The court is also asked whether the first paragraph of Article 59 and the third paragraph of Article 60 of the EEC Treaty are directly applicable and create individual rights which national courts must protect.
. . .

[26]   . . . as regards at least the specific requirement of nationality or of residence, Articles 59 and 60 impose a well-defined obligation, the fulfilment of which by the Member States cannot be delayed or jeopardized by the absence of powers which were to be adopted in pursuance of powers conferred under Articles 63 and 66.

[27]   Accordingly, the reply should be that the first paragraph of Article 59 and the third paragraph of Article 60 have direct effect and may therefore be relied on before national courts, at least in so far as they seek to abolish any discrimination against a person providing a service by reason of his nationality or of the fact that he resides in a Member State other than that in which the service is provided.

10.3.3   RECOGNITION OF QUALIFICATIONS

THIEFFRY v CONSEIL DE L'ORDRE DES AVOCATS À LA COUR DE PARIS
(Case 71/76) [1977] ECR 765, Court of Justice

Mr Thieffry, a Belgian advocate, applied for admission to the Paris Bar. His application was rejected on the ground that he did not hold the necessary French qualifications and despite the fact that his Belgian qualifications were officially recognised in France as equivalent.

The Court of Justice held, on a reference from the Paris Cour d'Appel, that in circumstances such as these it is incompatible with Article 52 of the Treaty to restrict admission to a profession to those individuals holding a national diploma. (Article 177 reference.)

[18]   Since the practical enjoyment of freedom of establishment can . . . in certain circumstances depend upon national practice or legislation, it is incumbent upon the competent public authorities – including legally recognized professional bodies – to ensure that such practice or legislation is applied in accordance with the objective defined by the provisions of the Treaty relating to freedom of establishment.

[19]   In particular, there is an unjustified restriction on that freedom where, in a Member State, admission to a particular profession is refused to a person covered by the Treaty who holds a diploma which has been recognized as an equivalent qualification by the competent authority of the country of establishment and who furthermore has fulfilled the specific conditions regarding professional training in force in that country, solely by reason of the fact that the person concerned does not possess the national diploma corresponding to the diploma which he holds and which has been recognized as an equivalent qualification.

VLASSOPOULOU v *MINISTERIUM FÜR JUSTIZ* (Case 340/89)
[1991] ECR I-2357, Court of Justice

A Greek national who was a member of the Athens Bar was refused permission to practise as a lawyer in certain local and regional courts in Germany on the grounds that she did not possess the necessary German qualifications. (Article 177 reference.)

[9] . . . it must be stated first of all that in the absence of harmonization of the conditions of access to a particular occupation the Member States are entitled to lay down the knowledge and qualifications needed in order to pursue it and to require the production of a diploma certifying that the holder has the relevant knowledge and qualifications.

. . .

[15] It must be stated in this regard that, even if applied without any discrimination on the basis of nationality, national requirements concerning qualifications may have the effect of hindering nationals of the other Member States in the exercise of their right of establishment guaranteed to them by Article 52 of the EEC Treaty. That could be the case if the national rules in question took no account of the knowledge and qualifications already acquired by the person concerned in another Member State.

[16] Consequently, a Member State which receives a request to admit a person to a profession to which access, under national law, depends upon the possession of a diploma or a professional qualification must take into consideration the diplomas, certificates and other evidence of qualifications which the person concerned has acquired in order to exercise the same profession in another Member State by making a comparison between the specialized knowledge and abilities certified by those diplomas and the knowledge and qualifications required by the national rules.

. . .

[19] If that comparative examination of diplomas results in the finding that the knowledge and qualifications certified by the foreign diploma correspond to those required by the national provisions, the Member State must recognize that diploma as fulfilling the requirements laid down by its national provisions. If, on the other hand, the comparison reveals that the knowledge and qualifications certified by the foreign diploma and those required by the national provisions correspond only partially, the host Member State is entitled to require the person concerned to show that he has acquired the knowledge and qualifications which are lacking.

[20] In this regard, the competent national authorities must assess whether the knowledge acquired in the host Member State, either during a course of study or by way of practical experience, is sufficient in order to prove possession of the knowledge which is lacking.

[21] If completion of a period of preparation or training for entry into the profession is required by the rules applying in the host Member State, those national authorities must determine whether professional experience acquired in the Member State of origin or in the host Member State may be regarded as satisfying that requirement in full or in part.

. . .

[23] Consequently, the answer to the question submitted by the Bundesgerichtshof must be that Article 52 of the EEC Treaty must be interpreted as requiring the national authorities of a Member State to which an application for admission to the profession of lawyer is made by a Community subject who is already admitted to practise as a lawyer in his country of origin and who practises as a legal adviser in the first-mentioned Member State to examine to what extent the knowledge and qualifications attested by the diploma obtained by the person concerned in his country of origin correspond to those required by the rules of the host State; if those diplomas correspond only partially, the national authorities in question are entitled to require the person concerned to prove that he has acquired the knowledge and qualifications which are lacking.

10.3.4 RULES OF PROFESSIONAL CONDUCT

See *Van Binsbergen* v *Bestuur van de Bedrijfsvereniging voor de Metaalnijverheid* (Case 33/74) [1974] ECR 1299 at **10.3.2** above.

MANFRED SÄGER v *DENNEMEYER & CO. LTD* (Case C-76/90) [1991] ECR I-4221,
Court of Justice

Under German legislation, only persons holding the necessary licence were permitted to
provide legal services. Such licences were available to persons holding certain professional qualifications, including patent agents, but were not issued to persons who, like
Dennemeyer, only offered patent renewal services. Säger, a German patent agent,
challenged Dennemeyer's right to provide patent renewal services in Germany. The
German court asked the Court of Justice whether, under Article 59 of the Treaty, a British
company may be required by German legislation to obtain a licence in order to provide
patent renewal services, when such activities may be carried out without licence in many
of the Member States. (Article 177 reference.)

16. . . . it should first be pointed out that national legislation, such as that described
by the national court, is clearly intended to protect the recipients of the services in
question against the harm which they could suffer as a result of legal advice given to
them by persons who did not possess the necessary professional or personal qualifications.

17. It should next be stated that the public interest in the protection of the recipients
of the services in question against such harm justifies a restriction of the freedom to
provide services. However, such a provision goes beyond what is necessary to protect
that interest if it makes the pursuit, by way of business, of an activity such as that at
issue, subject to the possession by the persons providing the service of a professional
qualification which is quite specific and disproportionate to the needs of the recipients.

18. As the Advocate General has pointed out in paragraph 33 of his Opinion, a
person providing a service such as that referred to in the present case does not advise
his clients, who are themselves often patent agents or undertakings who employ
qualified patent experts. He confines himself to alerting them when renewal fees have to
be paid in order to prevent a patent from lapsing and requesting them to state whether
they wish to renew the patent and to paying the corresponding fees on their behalf if
they so desire. Those tasks, which are carried out without its being necessary for the
provider of the service to travel, are essentially of a straightforward nature and do not
call for specific professional aptitudes, as is indicated by the high level of computerization which, in the present case, appears to have been attained by the defendant in the
main proceedings.

19. It should be added that, as the Commission has rightly pointed out, the risk for
a holder of a patent of the failure by a company entrusted with monitoring German
patents to fulfil its obligations is very limited. Two months after the date for renewal, the
German patent office sends an official reminder to the holder of the patent pointing out
that, failing payment of the fee, increased by a surcharge of 10%, his patent will expire
four months after the sending of the reminder (Paragraph 17(3) of the Patentgesetz).

20. It must therefore be stated that neither the nature of a service such as that at issue
nor the consequences of a default on the part of the person providing the service justifies
reserving the provision of that service to persons possessing a specific professional
qualification, such as lawyers or patent agents. Such a restriction must be regarded as
disproportionate to the objective pursued.

10.3.5 OTHER KINDS OF RESTRICTION ON THE FREEDOM TO PROVIDE SERVICES

HM CUSTOMS AND EXCISE v *GERHART SCHINDLER AND JÖRG SCHINDLER*
(Case C-275/92) [1994] ECR I-1039, Court of Justice

Envelopes dispatched from Germany to the UK by Gerhart and Jörg Schindler contained
invitations to participate in a lottery organised in Germany. They were confiscated by
the United Kingdom Commissioners of Customs and Excise at Dover on the ground that
they were imported in breach of national revenue legislation prohibiting the importation
of materials which contravened lotteries legislation. On a reference from the High Court,

the Court of Justice held that lottery activities constitute services within the meaning of Article 60 of the Treaty and thus fall within the scope of Article 59. The Court next considered whether national legislation prohibiting (with exceptions) the holding of lotteries restricts the freedom to provide services and , if so, whether such restriction may be justified on grounds of social policy and the prevention of fraud. (Article 177 reference.)

39.   The essence of the national court's fifth question is whether national legislation which, like the United Kingdom Legislation on lotteries, prohibits, subject to specified exceptions, the holding of lotteries in a Member State constitutes an obstacle to the freedom to provide services.

. . .

42.   According to the case-law of the Court (see the judgment in Case C-76/90 *Säger* v *Dennemeyer* [1991] ECR I-421, at paragraph 12) national legislation may fall within the ambit of Article 59 of the Treaty, even if it is applicable without distinction, when it is liable to prohibit or otherwise impede the activities of a provider of services established in another Member State where he lawfully provides similar services.

43.   It is sufficient to note that this is the case with national legislation such as the United Kingdom legislation on lotteries which wholly precludes lottery operators from other Member States from promoting their lotteries and selling their tickets, whether directly or through independent agents, in the Member State which enacted that legislation.

44.   Accordingly, the reply to the fifth question should be that national legislation which, like the United Kingdom legislation on lotteries, prohibits, subject to specified exceptions, the holding of lotteries in a Member State is an obstacle to the freedom to provide services.

. . .

46.   The national court's sixth question raises the issue whether the Treaty provisions relating to the freedom to provide services preclude legislation such as the United Kingdom lotteries legislation, where there are concerns of social policy and of the prevention of fraud to justify it.

. . .

60.   First of all, it is not possible to disregard the moral, religious or cultural aspects of lotteries, like other types of gambling, in all the Member States. The general tendency of the Member States is to restrict, or even prohibit, the practice of gambling and to prevent it from being a source of private profit. Secondly, lotteries involve a high risk of crime or fraud, given the size of the amounts which can be staked and of the winnings which they can hold out to the players, particularly when they are operated on a large scale. Thirdly, they are an incitement to spend which may have damaging individual and social consequences. A final ground which is not without relevance, although it cannot in itself be regarded as an objective justification, is that lotteries may make a significant contribution to the financing of benevolent or public interest activities such as social works, charitable works, sport or culture.

61.   Those particular factors justify national authorities having a sufficient degree of latitude to determine what is required to protect the players and, more generally, in the light of the specific social and cultural features of each Member State, to maintain order in society, as regards the manner in which lotteries are operated, the size of the stakes, and the allocation of the profits they yield. In those circumstances, it is for them to assess not only whether it is necessary to restrict the activities of lotteries but also whether they should be prohibited, provided that those restrictions are not discriminatory.

62.   When a Member State prohibits in its territory the operation of large-scale lotteries and in particular the advertising and distribution of tickets for that type of lottery, the prohibition on the importation of materials intended to enable nationals of that Member State to participate in such lotteries organized in another Member State cannot be regarded as a measure involving an unjustified interference with the freedom to provide services. Such a prohibition on import is a necessary part of the protection which that Member State seeks to secure in its territory in relation to lotteries.

63.   Accordingly, the reply to be given to the sixth question must be that the Treaty provisions relating to freedom to provide services do not preclude legislation such as the

United Kingdom lotteries legislation, in view of the concerns of social policy and of the prevention of fraud which justify it.

10.3.6   ARTICLE 55: ACTIVITIES CONCERNED WITH THE EXERCISE OF OFFICIAL AUTHORITY

THE TREATY OF ROME

Article 55
The provisions of this Chapter shall not apply, so far as any given Member State is concerned, to activities which in that State are connected, even occasionally with the exercise of official authority.

The Council may, acting by a qualified majority on a proposal from the Commission, rule that the provisions of this Chapter shall not apply to certain activities.

10.3.7   FREEDOM TO RECEIVE SERVICES

COWAN v *LE TRÉSOR PUBLIC* (Case 186/87) [1989] ECR 195, Court of Justice

Mr Cowan, a British national, was violently attacked at the exit of a metro station whilst on a short visit to Paris. The French Treasury refused him compensation. He challenged this decision, relying on Article 7 of the Treaty. (Article 177 reference.)

[1]   By order of 5 June 1987, which was received at the Court on 16 June 1987, the Commission d'indemnisation des victimes d'infraction attached to the tribunal de grande instance, Paris, referred to the Court for a preliminary ruling under Article 177 of the EEC Treaty a question on the interpretation of the prohibition of discrimination laid down in Article 7 of the Treaty, in order to be able to assess whether a provision of the French Code de procédure pénale (Code of Criminal Procedure) was compatible with Community law.

[2]   That question arose in a dispute between the French Trésor public (Treasury) and a British citizen, Ian William Cowan, concerning compensation for injury resulting from a violent assault suffered by him at the exit of a metro station during a brief stay in Paris.

[3]   Since his assailants could not be identified Mr Cowan applied to the Commission d'indemnisation des victimes d'infraction attached to the tribunal de grande instance, Paris, for compensation under Article 706-3 of the code de procédure pénale. That provision allows compensation to be obtained from the State *inter alia* when the victim of an assault which has caused physical injury with consequences of a certain severity is unable to obtain effective and adequate compensation for the harm from any other source.

[4]   Before the Commission d'indemnisation the Law Officer of the Treasury submitted that Mr Cowan did not satisfy the conditions for obtaining the abovementioned compensation provided for in Article 706-15 of the code de procedure pénale. That article provides that only the following persons may receive the compensation in question:

Persons who are of French nationality or foreign nationals who prove:

(i)   that they are nationals of a State which has concluded a reciprocal agreement with France for the application of the said provisions and that they satisfy the conditions laid down in the agreement; or

(ii)   that they are holders of a residence permit.

. . .

[14]   Under Article 7 of the Treaty the prohibition of discrimination applies 'within the scope of application of this Treaty' and 'without prejudice to any special provisions contained therein'. This latter expression refers particularly to other provisions of the Treaty in which the application of the general principle set out in that article is given concrete form in respect of specific situations. Examples of that are the provisions concerning free movement of workers, the right of establishment and the freedom to provide services.

. . .

[16] At the hearing the French Government submitted that as Community law now stands a recipient of services may not rely on the prohibition of discrimination to the extent that the national law at issue does not create any barrier to freedom of movement. A provision such as that at issue in the main proceedings, it says, imposes no restrictions in that respect. Furthermore, it concerns a right which is a manifestation of the principle of national solidarity. Such a right presupposes a closer bond with the State than that of a recipient of services, and for that reason it may be restricted to persons who are either nationals of that State or foreign nationals resident on the territory of that State.

[17] That reasoning cannot be accepted. When Community law guarantees a natural person the freedom to go to another Member State the protection of that person from harm in the Member State in question, on the same basis as that of nationals and persons residing there, is a corollary of that freedom of movement. It follows that the prohibition of discrimination is applicable to recipients of services within the meaning of the Treaty as regards protection against the risk of assault and the right to obtain financial compensation provided for by national law when that risk materializes. The fact that the compensation at issue is financed by the Public Treasury cannot alter the rules regarding the protection of the rights guaranteed by the Treaty.

10.4 Access to Education

10.4.1 RIGHTS OF WORKERS

LAIR v *UNIVERSITÄT HANNOVER* (Case 39/86) [1988] ECR 3161, Court of Justice

Under German legislation, only those persons (including German nationals and certain categories of foreigners) who had resided and been engaged in regular occupational activity in Germany for a total period of five years were eligible for financial assistance with training, including university study. The University of Hanover refused Ms Lair, a French national, a maintenance and training grant on the grounds that she did not satisfy this condition. Lair had resided in Germany for more than five years, during which she had gone through periods of unemployment and retraining as well as employment. She was currently pursuing a course of study in Romance and Germanic languages at the University. It was not disputed that this course led to a professional qualification. Lair claimed that the refusal of the grant constituted a breach of Article 7 of the Treaty.

In this context, the Court of Justice gave a ruling on the interpretation of Article 7 of the Treaty and Article 7 of Regulation 1612/68. (Article 177 reference.)

Interpretation of Article 7 of the EEC Treaty (the second question)

[11] This question seeks in essence to determine whether the first paragraph of Article 7 of the EEC Treaty applies to grants for maintenance and training made by a Member State to its nationals for the purpose of university studies.

[12] It should be pointed out first of all that in its judgment of 13 February 1985 in *Gravier* v *City of Liège* (Case 293/83) [1985] ECR 593, at p. 593, the Court held that unequal treatment based on nationality is to be regarded as discrimination prohibited by Article 7 of the Treaty if it falls within the scope of the Treaty and that conditions for access to vocational training do fall within its scope. In its judgment of 2 February 1988 in *Blaizot* v *University of Liège* (Case 24/86) [1988] ECR 379, the Court further ruled that, in general, university studies fulfil the conditions required in order to be regarded as vocational training for the purposes of the EEC Treaty.

[13] On the other hand, the Court did not have occasion to express a view in those judgments as to whether a national of another Member State is entitled, when undertaking such studies, to assistance given by a Member State to its own nationals.

[14] It is only to the extent to which assistance of that kind is intended to cover registration and other fees, in particular tuition fees, charged for access to education that by virtue of the judgment in *Gravier* it falls, as relating to conditions of access to vocational training, within the scope of the EEC Treaty and that, consequently, the prohibition of discrimination on grounds of nationality laid down by Article 7 of the EEC Treaty is applicable.

[15] Subject to that reservation, it must be stated that at the present stage of development of Community law assistance given to students for maintenance and for training falls in principle outside the scope of the EEC Treaty for the purposes of Article 7. It is, on the one hand, a matter of educational policy, which is not as such included in the spheres entrusted to the Community institutions (see *Gravier*) and, on the other, a matter of social policy, which falls within the competence of the Member States in so far as it is not covered by specific provisions of the EEC Treaty. . . .

[16] The answer to the second question must therefore be that at the present stage of development of Community law the first paragraph of Article 7 of the EEC Treaty applies to assistance for maintenance and training given by a Member State to its nationals for the purposes of university studies only in so far as such assistance is intended to cover registration and other fees, in particular tuition fees, charged for access to education.

[In response to the first question, the Court of Justice considered (*inter alia*) whether maintenance grants constitute a social advantage within the meaning of Article 7(2) of Regulation 1612/68]

The concept of social advantage

[18] In order to define the concept of social advantage within the meaning of Article 7(2) of Regulation No. 1612/68, it must first be recalled that the aim of that regulation is to enable the objectives laid down in Articles 48 and 49 of the EEC Treaty in the field of freedom of movement for workers to be achieved. That freedom forms part of the freedom of movement for persons referred to in Article 3(c) of the EEC Treaty and the fundamental freedoms guaranteed by the Treaty.

[19] A worker who is a national of a Member State and who has exercised that fundamental freedom is, under Article 7(2) of Regulation No. 1612/68, to enjoy 'the same social . . . advantages as national workers' in the host Member State.

[20] In addition to the specific right mentioned in Article 7(1) of that regulation not to be treated differently from national workers in respect of any conditions of employment and work, in particular as regards reinstatement or re-employment, 'social advantages' include all other advantages by means of which the migrant worker is guaranteed, in the words of the third recital in the preamble to the regulation, the possibility of improving his living and working conditions and promoting his social advancement.

[21] In that connection the Court has ruled that it follows from Regulation 1612/68 as a whole and from the objective pursued that the advantages which that regulation extends to workers who are nationals of other Member States are all those which, whether or not linked to a contract of employment, are generally granted to national workers primarily because of their status as workers or by virtue of the mere fact of their residence on the national territory and whose extension to workers who are nationals of other Member States therefore seems likely to facilitate the mobility of such workers within the Community . . .

[22] It follows that a worker who is a national of another Member State and has exercised his right as such to freedom of movement is entitled in the same way as national workers to all the advantages available to such workers for improving their professional qualifications and promoting their social advancement.

[23] It must now be considered whether or not a grant such as that at issue in the present case is covered by the concept of social advantage as interpreted above. It should be pointed out that such assistance, awarded for the student's maintenance and training, is particularly appropriate from a worker's point of view for improving his professional qualifications and promoting his social advancement. Moreover, the grant and the repayment of the benefits received are linked in national law to the beneficiary's means, and are thus dependent on social criteria.

[24] It follows that such a grant constitutes a social advantage within the meaning of Article 7(2) of Regulation No. 1612/68.

[25] It was argued before the Court that the application of Article 7(2) of Regulation No. 1612/68 was precluded by Article 7(3) of the same regulation by virtue of the specific content of the latter, which provides that a worker who is a national of a Member State 'shall also, by virtue of the same right and under the same conditions as national workers, have access to training in vocational schools and retraining centres'.

[26] In that regard, it should be noted that in order for an educational institution to be regarded as a vocational school for the purposes of that provision the fact that some vocational training is provided is not sufficient. The concept of a vocational school is a more limited one and refers exclusively to institutions which provide only instruction either alternating with or closely linked to an occupational activity, particularly during apprenticeship. That is not true of universities.

[27] However, while it is true that Article 7(3) of the regulation provides for a specific social advantage, that does not mean that a grant awarded for maintenance and training with a view to the pursuit of studies in an institution which does not fall within the concept of a vocational school under that provision cannot be held to be a social advantage within the meaning of Article 7(2).

[28] The answer to the first branch of the first question must therefore be that a grant awarded for maintenance and training with a view to the pursuit of university studies leading to a professional qualification constitutes a social advantage within the meaning of Article 7(2) of Regulation No. 1612/68.

The concept of worker

[29] In this connection, the three Member States which have submitted observations argue that a person loses the status of worker, on which the social advantages depend, when, in the host State, he gives up either his previous occupational activity or, if unemployed, his search for employment in order to pursue full-time studies. The Commission disagrees with that view.

[30] It should be noted first of all that neither Article 7(2) of Regulation No. 1612/68 nor Articles 48 or 49 of the EEC Treaty provides an express answer to the question whether a migrant worker who has interrupted his occupational activity in the host State in order to pursue university studies leading to a professional qualification is to be regarded as having retained his status as a migrant worker for the purposes of Article 7 of the regulation.

[31] Although the wording of those provisions does not provide an express answer to that question, there is nevertheless a basis in Community law for the view that the rights guaranteed to migrant workers do not necessarily depend on the actual or continuing existence of an employment relationship.

[32] With regard to nationals of another Member State who have not yet taken up employment in the host State, it should first be noted that Article 48(3)(a) and (b) guarantees such persons the right to accept offers of employment actually made and to move freely within the territory of the Member States for that purpose. Those provisions were implemented by Part I, Title I of Regulation No. 1612/68.

[33] Persons who have previously pursued in the host Member State an effective and genuine activity as an employed person as defined by the Court . . . but who are no longer employed are nevertheless considered to be workers under certain provisions of Community law.

[34] First, under Article 48(3)(d) of the EEC Treaty, persons who remain in the territory of a Member State after having been employed in that State are regarded as workers. Regulation (EEC) No. 1251/70 . . . on the right of workers to remain in the territory of a Member State after having been employed in that State . . . which implemented that provision of the Treaty, gives workers whose occupational activity has terminated and their families the right, under certain conditions, to remain permanently in the territory of a Member State. Secondly, Council Directive 68/360/EEC . . . on the abolition of restrictions on movement and residence within the Community for workers of Member States and their families . . . prohibits Member States in certain circumstances from withdrawing a residence permit from a worker solely on the ground that he is no longer in employment. Thirdly, and lastly, under Article 7(1) of Regulation No. 1612/68 a migrant worker who has become unemployed may not be treated differently from national workers in the same position as regards reinstatement or re-employment.

[35] Furthermore, Article 7(3) of Regulation No. 1612/68 guarantees migrant workers access, by virtue of the same right and under the same conditions as national workers, to training in vocational schools and retraining centres. That right to specific training, guaranteed by Community legislation, does not depend on the continued existence of an employment relationship.

[36]   It is therefore clear that migrant workers are guaranteed certain rights linked to the status of worker even when they are no longer in an employment relationship.

[37]   In the field of grants for university education, such a link between the status of worker and a grant awarded for maintenance and training with a view to the pursuit of university studies does, however, presuppose some continuity between the previous occupational activity and the course of study; there must be a relationship between the purpose of the studies and the previous occupational activity. Such continuity may not, however, be required where a migrant has involuntarily become unemployed and is obliged by conditions on the job market to undertake occupational retraining in another field of activity.

[38]   Such a conception of freedom of movement for migrant workers corresponds, moreover, to current developments in careers. Continuous careers are less common than was formerly the case. Occupational activities are therefore occasionally interrupted by periods of training or retraining.

[39]   The answer to the second part of the first question should therefore be that a national of another Member State who has undertaken university studies in the host State leading to a professional qualification, after having engaged in occupational activity in that State, must be regarded as having retained his status as a worker and is entitled as such to the benefit of Article 7(2) of Regulation No. 1612/68, provided that there is a link between the previous occupational activity and the studies in question.

10.4.2   RIGHTS OF WORKERS' CHILDREN

See *Casagrande* v *Landeshauptstadt München* (Case 9/74) [1974] ECR 773 at **10.2.4.5** above.

10.4.3   RIGHTS OF NON-WORKERS

GRAVIER v *CITY OF LIÈGE* (Case 293/83) [1985] ECR 593, Court of Justice

Françoise Gravier, a French national, was studying strip cartoon art at the Académie Royale des Beaux-Arts in Liège. She refused to pay an enrolment fee for the course, the 'minerval', which was levied under Belgian law on certain foreign students. Gravier claimed that the imposition of the fee constituted discrimination on grounds of nationality contrary to Article 7 of the Treaty and infringed her right of free movement as a recipient of services under Article 59 of the Treaty. (Article 177 reference.)

[14]   . . . it is clear from the content of the Belgian legislation and from the practice followed in relation to the fee, as summarized above, that the cost of higher art education is not borne by students of Belgian nationality, whereas foreign students must bear part of that cost. The inequality of treatment is therefore based on nationality, and that finding is not affected by the mere fact that there are certain exceptions to the distinction made between Belgian and foreign students, some based on nationality, such as the special situation of Luxembourg students, and some on other criteria such as the residence in Belgium of parents who pay taxes in that country.

[15]   Such unequal treatment based on nationality must be regarded as discrimination prohibited by Article 7 of the Treaty if it falls within the scope of the Treaty.

. . .

[19]   . . . although educational organization and policy are not as such included in the spheres which the Treaty has entrusted to the Community institutions, access to and participation in courses of instruction and apprenticeship, in particular vocational training, are not unconnected with Community law.

. . .

[21]   . . . Article 128 of the Treaty provides that the Council is to lay down general principles for implementing a common vocational training policy capable of contributing to the harmonious development both of the national economies and of the common market. The first principle established in Council Decision No. 63/266/EEC . . . laying down those general principles . . . states that 'the general principles must enable every person to receive adequate training, with due regard for freedom of choice of occupation, place of training and place of work'.

[22] The particular attention which the Community institutions have given to problems of access to vocational training and its improvement throughout the Community may be seen, moreover, in the 'general guidelines' which the Council laid down in 1971 for drawing up a Community programme on vocational training . . ..

[23] The common vocational training policy referred to in Article 128 of the Treaty is thus gradually being established. It constitutes, moreover, an indispensible element of the activities of the Community, whose objectives include *inter alia* the free movement of persons, the mobility of labour and the improvement of the living standards of workers.

[24] Access to vocational training is in particular likely to promote free movement of persons throughout the Community, by enabling them to obtain a qualification in the Member State where they intend to work and by enabling them to complete their training and develop their particular talents in the Member State whose vocational training programmes include the special subject desired.

[25] It follows from all the foregoing that the conditions of access to vocational training fall within the scope of the Treaty.

[26] The answer to the first question must therefore be that the imposition on students who are nationals of other Member States, of a charge, a registration fee or the so-called 'minerval' as a condition of access to vocational training, where the same fee is not imposed on students who are nationals of the host Member State, constitutes discrimination on grounds of nationality contrary to Article 7 of the Treaty.

[27] In its second question the national court wishes to know what criteria must be used in deciding whether courses in strip cartoon art constitute vocational training.

[28] According to Decision No. 63/266/EEC, referred to above, the general principles for implementing a common vocational training policy cover 'the training of young persons and adults who might be or already are employed in posts up to supervisory level'. Such a common policy must 'enable every person to acquire the technical knowledge and skill necessary to pursue a given occupation and to reach the highest possible level of training, whilst encouraging, particularly as regards young persons, intellectual and physical advancement, civic education and physical development'.

[29] The general guidelines laid down by the Council in 1971, referred to above, state that 'in view of the constantly changing needs of the economy the aim' of vocational training 'should be to offer everyone the opportunity of basic and advanced training and a continuity of in-service training designed, from a general and vocational point of view, to enable the individual to develop his personality and to take up a career'.

[30] It follows from those statements that any form of education which prepares for a qualification for a particular profession, trade or employment or which provides the necessary training and skills for such a profession, trade or employment is vocational training, whatever the age and the level of training of the pupils or students, and even if the training programme includes an element of general education.

[31] The answer to the second question must consequently be that the term 'vocational training' includes courses in strip cartoon art provided by an institution of higher Article education where that institution prepares students for a qualification for a particular profession, trade or employment or provides them with the skills necessary for such a profession, trade or employment.

10.5   Citizenship of the European Union

THE TREATY OF ROME

Article 8

1.   Citizenship of the Union is hereby established.

Every person holding the nationality of a Member State shall be a citizen of the Union.

2.   Citizens of the Union shall enjoy the rights conferred by this Treaty and shall be subject to the duties imposed thereby.

Article 8a

1.   Every citizen of the Union shall have the right to move and reside freely within the territory of the Member States, subject to the limitations and conditions laid down in this Treaty and by the measures adopted to give it effect.

10.6   End of Chapter Assessment Questions

1.   George, a British national, has taken up employment in Paris as a journalist with a French magazine, working 12 hours per week. He is joined by his wife Sue and daughter Anne (aged 23), also British nationals. George and his family apply for residence permits but these are refused by the French authorities. George is told that because he is a part-time worker whose earnings are insufficient to support himself and his family financially, neither he nor his family are entitled to remain in France. Advise George, Sue and Anne.

2.   Marcel, a French national, has been offered employment in London. He is refused entry to the UK on grounds of public policy. Two years ago, Marcel was convicted by a French court of unlawful possession and supply of a controlled drug. Advise Marcel.

10.7   End of Chapter Assessment Outline Answers

Your answers to Questions (1) and (2) should begin by making *brief* comments on the importance of the principle of the free movement of persons and refer to Article 3(c) of the Treaty. In answering Question (2), you should point out that the Court of Justice has given very narrow scope to the limitations to the right of free movement.

(Unless otherwise stated, references in the following answers are to the Treaty of Rome.)

QUESTION 1

Article 48 of the Treaty grants the right of free movement within the Community to workers of the Member States, entailing the right, *inter alia*, to stay in a Member State in order to work there (Article 48(3)(c)). George, as a national of a Member State, can benefit from this right if he is a worker. Although there is no Treaty definition of 'worker', the Court of Justice has held that the term has a Community meaning and may not be defined by reference to national laws (*Hoekstra, Levin*). The Court has indicated that the essential characteristics of a worker are that he or she performs services for another during a certain period of time, under the direction of another and for remuneration (*Lawrie-Blum*). The term 'worker' includes a person whose income from employment does not provide sufficient means of support, provided the work is 'effective and genuine' (*Levin*), even if the worker needs to supplement that income by drawing state benefit (*Kempf*). Although he only works part-time, George is engaged in an economic activity which is 'effective and genuine' and clearly falls within the Community definition of 'worker'.

   Directive 68/360 requires Member States to grant the right of residence to Community migrant workers and their families and, on the production of certain documents – their documents of entry, evidence of employment (for the worker) and evidence of their relationship with the worker (for family members) (Article 4(3)) – to issue them with residence permits (Article 4(2)). As a worker, George is entitled to a residence permit.

   The right of family members, irrespective of their nationality, to install themselves with the worker in another Member State is conferred by Regulation 1612/68 (Article 10(1)), which defines family members as (*inter alia*) the worker's spouse and their descendants who are under the age of 21 or are dependants (Article 10(1)(a)). As George's wife, Sue is a member of his family. However, Anne is over the age of 21 and does not fall within the scope of Article 10(1)(a) unless she is dependent upon him. The Court of Justice has ruled that the status of dependant results from a factual situation in which the worker is actually providing support and not from any factors giving rise to a need for support (*Lebon*). Assuming that Anne is a dependant, under Article 4(2) of Directive 68/360 both Sue and Anne, as members of George's family, are entitled to residence permits. These must be valid for a period of at least five years from the date of issue and be automatically renewable.

If Anne is not dependent on George, she is not a member of his family within the definition contained in Regulation 1612/68 and has no right, derived from George's worker status, to remain in France. However, she should be advised that, as she is a national of a Member State, she can acquire the right to remain in France by becoming a worker herself. Part-time work will be sufficient for this purpose (*Levin, Kempf*). Alternatively, she will be entitled to remain (though not to have a residence permit) for a limited period of time if she is looking for work. The Court of Justice has not set a specific time limit to a job seeker's right to stay but held in *Antonissen* that the UK could deport a Community migrant who had not found employment after six months. The Court indicated that this period should be extended if the individual concerned was making genuine efforts to find work and had a real chance of being employed.

Under Article 8 of Directive 64/221, George, Sue and Anne must be granted the same legal remedies in respect of the decision not to issue residence permits as are available to French nationals in respect of acts of the administration. In particular, they have the right of appeal or review of the decision before a competent authority different from the authority which first refused the issue of the residence permits and are entitled to submit their defence in person (Article 9(2)).

QUESTION 2

The first part of your answer should set out Marcel's right of free movement as a worker under Article 48 of the Treaty, as substantiated by Directive 68/360.

You should then discuss the UK's right to restrict entry on grounds of public policy under Article 48(3) and Articles 1–4 of Directive 64/221. The main issue is Marcel's previous criminal conviction, which does not *in itself* constitute grounds for refusing entry on grounds of public policy (Article 3(2) of Directive 64/221). Article 3(1) of the Directive provides that measures taken on grounds of public policy shall be based exclusively on the personal conduct of the individual concerned. Thus, in *Bonsignore*, the Court of Justice held that a Member State has no right to deport an individual simply for the purpose of deterring others from similar behaviour.

The Court of Justice has ruled that a previous criminal conviction can be taken into account as evidence of personal conduct which is contrary to the requirements of public policy only if the circumstances giving rise to that conviction are evidence of personal conduct 'constituting a present threat to the requirements of public policy' and if the individual concerned shows a propensity to behave in the same way in the future. Moreover, the threat to public policy must be such as 'to affect one of the fundamental interests of society' (*Bouchereau*). Marcel might try to argue that his past conduct and previous conviction (now two years old) do not constitute a present threat to public policy and that he has no propensity to similar behaviour in the future because he no longer has any involvement with controlled drugs. If that were the case, the UK's refusal to allow him entry would be unjustified.

You might then point out that if Marcel is addicted to drugs, the UK's action is justified. Drug addiction is listed in section B of the Annex to Directive 64/221 as one of the disabilities justifying refusal of entry into a Member State (Article 4(1) of the Directive).

Under Article 8 of Directive 64/221, Marcel is entitled to the same legal remedies in respect of the refusal to allow him entry as are available to UK nationals in respect of acts of the administration.

CHAPTER ELEVEN

COMPETITION LAW: ARTICLE 85

11.1   Outline of the Community Competition Rules

THE TREATY OF ROME

Article 3
For the purposes set out in Article 2, the activities of the Community shall include, as provided in this Treaty and in accordance with the timetable set out therein:
. . .

(g)   a system ensuring that competition in the internal market is not distorted . . .

11.2   The Framework of Article 85

11.2.1   OUTLINE OF ARTICLE 85(1), (2) and (3)

THE TREATY OF ROME

Article 85
1.   The following shall be prohibited as incompatible with the common market: all agreements between undertakings, decisions by associations of undertakings and concerted practices which may affect trade between Member States and which have as their object or effect the prevention, restriction or distortion of competition within the common market, and in particular those which:

(a)   directly or indirectly fix purchase or selling prices or any other trading conditions;

(b)   limit or control production, markets, technical development, or investment;

(c)   share markets or sources of supply;

(d)   apply dissimilar conditions to equivalent transactions with other trading parties, thereby placing them at a competitive disadvantage;

(e)   make the conclusion of contracts subject to acceptance by the other parties of supplementary obligations which, by their nature or according to commercial usage, have no connection with the subject of such contracts.

2.   Any agreements or decisions prohibited pursuant to this Article shall be automatically void.

3.   The provisions of paragraph 1 may, however, be declared inapplicable in the case of:

– any agreement or category of agreements between undertakings;
– any decision or category of decisions by associations of undertakings;
– any concerted practice or category of concerted practices;

which contributes to improving the production or distribution of goods or to promoting technical or economic progress, while allowing consumers a fair share of the resulting benefit, and which does not;

(a)   impose on the undertakings concerned restrictions which are not indispensable to the attainment of these objectives;

(b) afford such undertakings the possibility of eliminating competition in respect of a substantial part of the products in question.

11.2.2   ARTICLE 85(2)

SOCIÉTÉ TECHNIQUE MINIÈRE v *MASCHINENBAU ULM GMBH* (Case 56/65) [1966] ECR 235, Court of Justice

Maschinenbau Ulm (MU), a German company which produced heavy earth-moving equipment, entered into an agreement with Société Technique Minière (STM) for the supply of 37 grading machines. Under the contract, STM was given the exclusive right to sell such machines in France, MU agreeing not to supply to any other distributor in the territory, nor to sell there itself. The agreement did not prevent parallel imports and exports: other French distributors were able to obtain supplies from outside France and STM could sell the machines outside the territory. The agreement entailed a high degree of commercial risk for STM because the machinery was specialised and very expensive. A dispute arose between the parties and STM claimed that the contract was invalid under Article 85(1). (Article 177 reference.)

. . . The prohibition of such an agreement depends on one question alone, namely whether, taking into account the circumstances of the case, the agreement, objectively considered, contains the elements constituting the said prohibition as set out in Article 85(1).

The necessity for an agreement 'between undertakings'
In order to fall within this prohibition, an agreement must have been made between undertakings. Article 85(1) makes no distinction as to whether the parties are at the same level in the economy (so-called 'horizontal' agreements), or at different levels (so-called 'vertical' agreements). Therefore an agreement containing a clause 'granting an exclusive right of sale' may fulfil this condition.

The effects on trade between Member States
The agreement must also be one which 'may affect trade between Member States'.
This provision, clarified by the introductory words of Article 85 which refers to agreements in so far as they are 'incompatible with the Common Market', is directed to determining the field of application of the prohibition by laying down the condition that it may be assumed that there is a possibility that the realization of a single market between Member States might be impeded. It is in fact to the extent that the agreement may affect trade between Member States that the interference with competition caused by that agreement is caught by the prohibitions in Community law found in Article 85, whilst in the converse case it escapes those prohibitions. For this requirement to be fulfilled it must be possible to foresee with a sufficient degree of probability on the basis of a set of objective factors of law or of fact that the agreement in question may have an influence, direct or indirect, actual or potential, on the pattern of trade between Member States. Therefore, in order to determine whether an agreement which contains a clause 'granting an exclusive right of sale' comes within the field of application of Article 85, it is necessary to consider in particular whether it is capable of bringing about a partitioning of the market in certain products between Member States and thus rendering more difficult the interpenetration of trade which the Treaty is intended to create.

The effects of the agreement on competition
Finally, for the agreement at issue to be caught by the prohibition contained in Article 85(1) it must have as its 'object or effect the prevention, restriction or distortion of competition within the Common Market'.
The fact that these are not cumulative but alternative requirements, indicated by the conjunction 'or', leads first to the need to consider the precise purpose of the agreement, in the economic context in which it is to be applied. This interference with competition referred to in Article 85(1) must result from all or some of the clauses of the agreement itself. Where, however, an analysis of the said clauses does not reveal the effect on

competition to be sufficiently deleterious, the consequences of the agreement should then be considered and for it to be caught by the prohibition it is then necessary to find that those factors are present which show that competition has in fact been prevented or restricted or distorted to an appreciable extent.

The competition in question must be understood within the actual context in which it would occur in the absence of the agreement in dispute. In particular it may be doubted whether there is an interference with competition if the said agreement seems really necessary for the penetration of a new area by an undertaking. Therefore, in order to decide whether an agreement containing a clause 'granting an exclusive right of sale' is to be considered as prohibited by reason of its object or of its effect, it is appropriate to take into account in particular the nature and quantity, limited or otherwise, of the products covered by the agreement, the position and importance of the grantor and the concessionnaire on the market for the products concerned, the isolated nature of the disputed agreement or, alternatively, its position in a series of agreements, the severity of the clauses intended to protect the exclusive dealership or, alternatively, the opportunities allowed for other commercial competitors in the same products by way of parallel re-exportation and importation.

The second question relating to the interpretation of Article 85(2)

Article 85(2) provides that 'Any agreements or decisions prohibited pursuant to this Article shall be automatically void'.

This provision, which is intended to ensure compliance with the Treaty, can only be interpreted with reference to its purpose in Community law, and it must be limited to this context. The automatic nullity in question only applies to those parts of the agreement affected by the prohibition, or to the agreement as a whole if it appears that those parts are not severable from the agreement itself. Consequently any other contractual provisions which are not affected by the prohibition, and which therefore do not involve the application of the Treaty, fall outside Community law.

11.3   The Article 85(1) Prohibition

11.3.1   AGREEMENTS, DECISIONS AND CONCERTED PRACTICES

IAZ INTERNATIONAL BELGIUM NV v COMMISSION
(Cases 96–102, 104, 105, 108 and 110/82)
[1983] ECR 3369, Court of Justice

A Belgian water suppliers' trade association recommended its members not to connect washing machines and dishwashers to the mains water supply system unless they carried a conformity label issued by the Belgian manufacturers' trade association indicating that they satisfied certain standards laid down by national legislation. The system was operated in such a way as to discriminate against machines produced in other Member States. The applicants sought annulment of a Commission Decision finding a breach of Article 85(1), contending (*inter alia*) that a non-binding recommendation fell outside the scope of that provision. (Article 173 proceedings.)

[20]   . . . Article 85(1) of the Treaty applies also to associations of undertakings in so far as their own activities or those of the undertakings affiliated to them are calculated to produce the results which it aims to suppress. . . . a recommendation, even if it has no binding effect, cannot escape Article 85(1) where compliance with the recommendation by the undertakings to which it is addressed has an appreciable influence on competition in the market in question.

IMPERIAL CHEMICAL INDUSTRIES LTD v COMMISSION (DYESTUFFS)
(Case 48/69) [1972] ECR 619, Court of Justice

The Commission issued a Decision finding that three general and uniform increases in the prices of aniline dyes imposed in the Community by a number of undertakings between 1964 and 1967 were the result of concerted practices and infringed Article 85(1). One of those undertakings, ICI, sought annulment of that Decision.

Relying on evidence of advance price announcements and informal contact between the undertakings which had enabled them to introduce uniform increases almost simultaneously, the Court of Justice dismissed the application. (Article 173 proceedings.)

[51]   The applicant complains that the Commission has not proved the existence of concerted practices within the meaning of Article 85(1) of the EEC Treaty in relation to any of the three increases mentioned in the contested decision.

[52]   That decision states that *prima facie* evidence that the increase of 1964, 1965 and 1967 took place as the result of concerted action is to be found in the facts that the rates introduced for each increase by the different producers in each country were the same, that with very rare exceptions the same dyestuffs were involved, and that the increases were put into effect over only a very short period, if not actually on the same date.

[53]   It is contended that these increases cannot be explained simply by the oligopolistic character of the structure of the market.

[54]   It is said to be unrealistic to suppose that without previous concertation the principal producers supplying the Common Market could have increased their prices on several occasions by identical percentages at practically the same moment for one and the same important range of products including speciality products for which there are few, if any, substitutes, and that they should have done so in a number of countries where conditions on the dyestuffs market are different.

[55]   The Commission has argued before the Court that the interested parties need not necessarily have drawn up a common plan with a view to adopting a certain course of behaviour for it to be said that there has been concertation.

[56]   It is argued that it is enough that they should previously have informed each other of the attitude which they intended to adopt so that each could regulate his conduct safe in the knowledge that his competitors would act in the same way.

[57]   The applicant argues that the contested decision is based on an inadequate analysis of the market in the products in question and on an erroneous understanding of the concept of a concerted practice, which is wrongly identified by the decision with the conscious parallelism of members of an oligopoly, whereas such conduct is due to independent decisions adopted by each undertaking, determined by objective business needs, and in particular by the need to increase the unsatisfactorily low rate of profit on the production of dyestuffs.

[58]   It is argued that in fact the prices of the products in question displayed a constant tendency to fall because of lively competition between producers which is typical of the market in those products, not only as regards the quality of the products and technical assistance to customers, but also as regards prices, particularly the large reductions granted individually to the principal purchasers.

[59]   The fact that the rates of increase were identical was the result, it is said, of the existence of the 'price-leadership' of one undertaking.

. . .

The concept of a concerted practice

[64]   Article 85 draws a distinction between the concept of 'concerted practices' and that of 'agreements between undertakings' or of 'decisions by associations of undertakings'; the object is to bring within the prohibition of that article a form of coordination between undertakings which, without having reached the stage where an agreement properly so-called has been concluded, knowingly substitutes practical cooperation between them for the risks of competition.

[65]   By its very nature, then, a concerted practice does not have all the elements of a contract but may *inter alia* arise out of coordination which becomes apparent from the behaviour of the participants.

[66]   Although parallel behaviour may not by itself be identified with a concerted practice, it may however amount to strong evidence of such a practice if it leads to conditions of competition which do not correspond to the normal conditions of the market, having regard to the nature of the products, the size and number of the undertakings, and the volume of the said market.

[67] This is especially the case if the parallel conduct is such as to enable those concerned to attempt to stabilize prices at a level different from that to which competition would have led, and to consolidate established positions to the detriment of effective freedom of movement of the products in the Common Market and of the freedom of consumers to choose their suppliers.

. . .

[118] Although every producer is free to change his prices, taking into account in so doing the present or foreseeable conduct of his competitors, nevertheless it is contrary to the rules on competition contained in the Treaty for a producer to cooperate with his competitors, in any way whatsoever, in order to determine a coordinated course of action relating to a price increase and to ensure its success by prior elimination of all uncertainty as to each other's conduct regarding the essential elements of that action, such as the amount, subject-matter, date and place of the increases.

AHLSTRÖM & ORS v COMMISSION (WOODPULP)
(Cases C-89, 104, 114, 116, 117, 125–129/85) [1993] 4 CMLR 407, Court of Justice

Certain wood pulp producers and associations of wood pulp producers contested a Commission Decision finding that they had infringed Article 85(1) through concertation on prices for their products by means of a system of quarterly price announcements. (Article 173 proceedings.)

[The Commission argued that the system of quarterly price announcements in itself constituted an infringement of Article 85 of the Treaty.]

[60] First, the Commission considers that that system was deliberately introduced by the pulp producers in order to enable them to ascertain the prices that would be charged by their competitors in the following quarters. The disclosure of prices to third parties, especially to the press and agents working for several producers, well before their application at the beginning of a new quarter gave the other producers sufficient time to announce their own, corresponding, new prices before that quarter and to apply them from the commencement of that quarter.

[61] Secondly, the Commission considers that the implementation of that mechanism had the effect of making the market artificially transparent by enabling producers to obtain a rapid and accurate picture of the prices quoted by their competitors.

[62] In deciding on that point, it must be borne in mind that Article 85(1) EEC prohibits all agreements between undertakings, decisions by associations of undertakings and concerted practices which may affect trade between member-States and which have as their object or effect the prevention, restriction or distortion of competition within the Common Market.

[63] According to the Court's judgment in *Suiker Unie* (Cases 40–48, 50, 54-56, 111, 113–114/73) [1975] ECR 1663), a concerted practice refers to a form of co-ordination between undertakings which, without having been taken to the stage where an agreement properly so-called has been concluded, knowingly substitutes for the risks of competition practical co-operation between them. In the same judgment, the Court added that the criteria of co-ordination and co-operation must be understood in the light of the concept inherent in the provisions of the Treaty relating to competition that each economic operator must determine independently the policy which he intends to adopt on the Common Market.

[64] In this case, the communications arise from the price announcements made to users. They constitute in themselves market behaviour which does not lessen each undertaking's uncertainty as to the future attitude of its competitors. At the time when each undertaking engages in such behaviour, it cannot be sure of the future conduct of the others.

[65] Accordingly, the system of quarterly price announcements on the pulp market is not to be regarded as constituting in itself an infringement of Article 85(1) EEC.

. . .

[126] . . . it must be stated that, in this case, concertation is not the only plausible explanation for the parallel conduct. To begin with, the system of price announcements

may be regarded as constituting a rational response to the fact that the pulp market constituted a long-term market and to the need felt by both buyers and sellers to limit commercial risks. Further, the similarity in the dates of price announcements may be regarded as a direct result of the high degree of market transparency, which does not have to be described as artificial. Finally, the parallelism of prices and the price trends may be satisfactorily explained by the oligopolistic tendencies of the market and by the specific circumstances prevailing in certain periods. Accordingly, the parallel conduct established by the Commission does not constitute evidence of concertation.

[127] In the absence of a firm, precise and consistent body of evidence, it must be held that concertation regarding announced prices has not been established by the Commission.

COOPERATIEVE VERENIGING 'SUIKER UNIE' UA v COMMISSION
(Cases 40–48, 50, 54–56, 111, 113–114/73) [1975] ECR 1663, Court of Justice

The applicant sugar producers claimed that they had not taken part in concerted practices aimed at protecting the Dutch market. They argued that a concerted practice entails the existence of a plan. (Article 173 proceedings.)

[173] The criteria of coordination and cooperation laid down by the case-law of the Court, which in no way require the working out of an actual plan, must be understood in the light of the concept inherent in the provisions of the Treaty relating to competition that each economic operator must determine independently the policy which he intends to adopt on the common market including the choice of the persons and undertakings to which he makes offers or sells.

[174] Although it is correct to say that this requirement of independence does not deprive economic operators of the right to adapt themselves intelligently to the existing and anticipated conduct of their competitors, it does however strictly preclude any direct or indirect contact between such operators, the object or effect whereof is either to influence the conduct on the market of an actual or potential competitor or to disclose to such a competitor the course of conduct which they themselves have decided to adopt or contemplate adopting on the market.

11.3.2   VERTICAL AND HORIZONTAL AGREEMENTS

ÉTABLISSEMENTS CONSTEN SA v COMMISSION (Cases 56 & 58/64)
[1966] ECR 299, Court of Justice

Under a dealership agreement between Consten and Grundig, Consten had the exclusive right to sell Grundig's electronic products in France. As a result of prohibitions on exports and parallel imports, Consten had absolute territorial protection: Consten undertook not to sell the goods outside the contract territory and enjoyed the benefit of similar undertakings given to Grundig by distributors in other Member States. Consten was able to enforce its exclusive rights in France by means of the GINT trade mark which Grundig had assigned to it.

When another French company, UNEF, began to sell Grundig products (which it had acquired in Germany) in France more cheaply than Consten, Consten brought proceedings for infringement of its trade mark. Following an application by UNEF alleging that the Consten-Grundig agreement breached Article 85(1), the Commission issued a Decision finding an infringement. Consten sought annulment of that Decision.

The Court of Justice held that if it were possible to sever the offending clauses of an agreement, the provision in Article 85(2) rendering prohibited agreements void applied only to those clauses. In relation to this agreement, the only clauses which were prohibited under Article 85 were those giving absolute territorial protection. Since the Commission Decision indicated that the infringement lay in the agreement as a whole, that Decision must be annulled in so far as it declared void all the clauses of the agreement. (Article 173 proceedings.)

The applicants submit that the prohibition in Article 85(1) applies only to so-called horizontal agreements. The Italian Government submits furthermore that sole distributorship contracts do not constitute 'agreements between undertakings' within the meaning of that provision, since the parties are not on a footing of equality. With regard to these contracts, freedom of competition may only be protected by virtue of Article 86 of the Treaty.

Neither the wording of Article 85 nor that of Article 86 gives any ground for holding that distinct areas of application are to be assigned to each of the two Articles according to the level in the economy at which the contracting parties operate. Article 85 refers in a general way to all agreements which distort competition within the Common Market and does not lay down any distinction between those agreements based on whether they are made between competitors operating at the same level in the economic process or between non-competing persons operating at different levels. In principle, no distinction can be made where the Treaty does not make any distinction.

Furthermore, the possible application of Article 85 to a sole distributorship contract cannot be excluded merely because the grantor and the concessionaire are not competitors *inter se* and not on a footing of equality. Competition may be distorted within the meaning of Article 85(1) not only by agreements which limit it as between the parties, but also by agreements which prevent or restrict the competition which might take place between one of them and third parties. For this purpose, it is irrelevant whether the parties to the agreement are or are not on a footing of equality as regards their position and function in the economy. This applies all the more, since, by such an agreement, the parties might seek, by preventing or limiting the competition of third parties in respect of the products, to create or guarantee for their benefit an unjustified advantage at the expense of the consumer or user, contrary to the general aims of Article 85.

. . .

The applicants and the German Government maintain that the Commission has relied on a mistaken interpretation of the concept of an agreement which may affect trade between Member States and has not shown that such trade would have been greater without the agreement in dispute.

The defendant replies that this requirement in Article 85(1) is fulfilled once trade between Member States develops, as a result of the agreement, differently from the way in which it would have done without the restriction resulting from the agreement, and once the influence of the agreement on market conditions reaches a certain degree. Such is the case here, according to the defendant, particularly in view of the impediments resulting within the Common Market from the disputed agreement as regards the exporting and importing of Grundig products to and from France.

The concept of an agreement 'which may affect trade between Member States' is intended to define, in the law governing cartels, the boundary between the areas respectively covered by Community law and national law. It is only to the extent to which the agreement may affect trade between Member States that the deterioration in competition caused by the agreement falls under the prohibition of Community law contained in Article 85; otherwise it escapes the prohibition.

In this connexion, what is particularly important is whether the agreement is capable of constituting a threat, either direct or indirect, actual or potential, to freedom of trade between Member States in a manner which might harm the attainment of the objectives of a single market between States. Thus the fact that an agreement encourages an increase, even a large one, in the volume of trade between States is not sufficient to exclude the possibility that the agreement may 'affect' such trade in the abovementioned manner. In the present case, the contract between Grundig and Consten, on the one hand by preventing undertakings other than Consten from importing Grundig products into France, and on the other hand by prohibiting Consten from re-exporting those products to other countries of the Common Market, indisputably affects trade between Member States. These limitations on the freedom of trade, as well as those which might ensue for third parties from the registration in France by Consten of the GINT trade mark, which Grundig places on all its products, are enough to satisfy the requirement in question.

. . . The infringement which was found to exist by the contested decision results from the absolute territorial protection created by the said contract in favour of Consten on the basis of French law. The applicants thus wished to eliminate any possibility of competition at the wholesale level in Grundig products in the territory specified in the contract essentially by two methods.

First, Grundig undertook not to deliver even indirectly to third parties products intended for the area covered by the contract. The restrictive nature of that undertaking is obvious if it is considered in the light of the prohibition on exporting which was imposed not only on Consten but also on all the other sole concessionnaires of Grundig, as well as the German wholesalers. Secondly, the registration in France by Consten of the GINT trade mark, which Grundig affixes to all its products, is intended to increase the protection inherent in the disputed agreement, against the risk of parallel imports into France of Grundig products, by adding the protection deriving from the law on industrial property rights. Thus no third party could import Grundig products from other Member States of the Community for resale in France without running serious risks.

The defendant properly took into account the whole distribution system thus set up by Grundig. In order to arrive at a true representation of the contractual position the contract must be placed in the economic and legal context in the light of which it was concluded by the parties. Such a procedure is not to be regarded as an unwarrantable interference in legal transactions or circumstances which were not the subject of the proceedings before the Commission.

The situation as ascertained above results in the isolation of the French market and makes it possible to charge for the products in question prices which are sheltered from all effective competition. In addition, the more producers succeed in their efforts to render their own makes of product individually distinct in the eyes of the consumer, the more the effectiveness of competition between producers tends to diminish. Because of the considerable impact of distribution costs on the aggregate cost price, it seems important that competition between dealers should also be stimulated. The efforts of the dealer are stimulated by competition between distributors of products of the same make. Since the agreement thus aims at isolating the French market for Grundig products and maintaining artificially, for products of a very well-known brand, separate national markets within the Community, it is therefore such as to distort competition in the Common Market.

It was therefore proper for the contested decision to hold that the agreement constitutes an infringement of Article 85(1).

. . .

The applicant Grundig and the German Government complain that the Commission did not exclude from the prohibition, in the operative part of the contested decision, those clauses of the contract in respect of which there was found no effect capable of restricting competition, and that it thereby failed to define the infringement.

It is apparent from the statement of the reasons for the contested decision, as well as from Article 3 thereof, that the infringement declared to exist by Article 1 of the operative part is not to be found in the undertaking by Grundig not to make direct deliveries in France except to Consten. That infringement arises from the clauses which, added to this grant of exclusive rights, are intended to impede, relying upon national law, parallel imports of Grundig products into France by establishing absolute territorial protection in favour of the sole concessionnaire.

The provision in Article 85(2) that agreements prohibited pursuant to Article 85 shall be automatically void applies only to those parts of the agreement which are subject to the prohibition, or to the agreement as a whole if those parts do not appear to be severable from the agreement itself. The Commission should, therefore, either have confined itself in the operative part of the contested decision to declaring that an infringement lay in those parts only of the agreement which came within the prohibition, or else it should have set out in the preamble to the decision the reasons why those parts did not appear to it to be severable from the whole agreement.

It follows, however, from Article 1 of the decision that the infringement was found to lie in the agreement as a whole, although the Commission did not adequately state the reasons why it was necessary to render the whole of the agreement void when it is not established that all the clauses infringed the provisions of Article 85(1). The state of affairs found to be incompatible with Article 85(1) stems from certain specific clauses of the contract of 1 April 1957 concerning absolute territorial protection and from the additional agreement on the GINT trade mark rather than from the combined operation of all the clauses of the agreement, that is to say, from the aggregate of its effects.

Article 1 of the contested decision must therefore be annulled in so far as it renders void, without any valid reason, all the clauses of the agreement by virtue of Article 85(2).

11.3.3 'WHICH MAY AFFECT TRADE BETWEEN MEMBER STATES'

WINDSURFING INTERNATIONAL INC v COMMISSION (Case 193/83)
[1986] ECR 611, Court of Justice

Windsurfing International sought annulment of a Commission Decision holding that a number of the restrictions in its agreements with certain Community undertakings licensing them to sell its patented windsurfing rigs infringed Article 85(1). The company argued (*inter alia*) that each individual restrictive clause did not have an appreciable effect on inter-state trade. (Article 173 proceedings.)

[95]   Windsurfing International further argues that even though certain clauses in the licensing agreements may have been of such a nature as to restrict competition, they could not have had any appreciable effect on trade between Member States.

[96]   That argument must be rejected. Article 85(1) of the Treaty does not require that each individual clause in an agreement should be capable of affecting intra-Community trade. Community law on competition applies to agreements between undertakings which may affect trade between Member States; only if the agreement as a whole is capable of affecting trade is it necessary to examine which are the clauses of the agreement which have as their object or effect a restriction or distortion of competition.

[97]   In a case such as the present one, in which there is no doubt as to the significance of the agreements at issue for trade between Member States, it is therefore unnecessary to examine whether each clause restricting competition, taken in isolation, may affect intra-Community trade.

VACUUM INTERRUPTERS LTD, RE [1977] 1 CMLR D67 (Commission Decision 77/160)

Although both parties to a joint venture agreement for the development of vacuum interrupters, Associated Electrical Industries Ltd and Reyrolle Parsons Ltd, operated within the UK, the Commission found that the agreement was capable of affecting trade between Member States. (Commission Decision.)

[17]   Both Associated Electrical Industries Ltd and Reyrolle Parsons Ltd are major manufacturers of switchgear apparatus in the United Kingdom. It is reasonable to assume that if a market were to develop in the other Member States of the EEC for the vacuum interrupter and if both Associated Electrical Industries Ltd and/or their associated companies and Reyrolle Parsons Ltd had developed and manufactured the vacuum type interrupter independently of each other, each should have been able to obtain a market for it in the other Member States, where they would have been in direct competition not only with each other but also with such other undertakings as might manufacture this type of interrupter. There could have developed an export trade between each of these undertakings in the United Kingdom and customers in other Member States in which each would have been in competition with the other and with local manufacturers. Exports from the United Kingdom to other Member States are now likely to start earlier and form a different pattern, thus affecting the flow of trade from the United Kingdom to other Member States. Further, both Associated Electrical Industries Ltd and Reyrolle Parsons Ltd have as customers in the United Kingdom the Central Electricity Generating Board and other area boards and most of the large industrial undertakings which take electricity from high voltage lines. The fact that two companies, each with an important market position in heavy electrical equipment in the United Kingdom, have combined their activity in the field of vacuum interrupters in a joint subsidiary must reduce the possibility that another manufacturer or other manufacturers of electrical equipment from other Member States of the EEC would be able to enter the United Kingdom for the purpose of manufacturing and selling or selling only the

vacuum interrupter in competition with Vacuum Interrupters Ltd. It might well have been easier for such manufacturers to build up a market for the vacuum interrupter in the United Kingdom if they were not to be in competition with one economically and technically strong competitor but with two competitors, each separately economically and technically weaker.

PRONUPTIA DE PARIS GMBH v *PRONUPTIA DE PARIS IRMGARD SCHILLGALIS* (Case 161/84) [1986] ECR 353, Court of Justice

A distribution franchise agreement between Pronuptia de Paris GmbH (the franchisor) and Mrs Schillgalis (the franchisee) relating to the retail sale of wedding dresses and other clothes worn at weddings, contained many restrictive clauses. A dispute between the parties concerning the payment of royalties came before the national court, which referred to the Court of Justice certain questions on the application of Article 85 to franchise agreements. (Article 177 reference.)

[15] In a system of distribution franchises of that kind an undertaking which has established itself as a distributor on a given market and thus developed certain business methods grants independent traders, for a fee, the right to establish themselves in other markets using its business name and the business methods which have made it successful. Rather than a method of distribution, it is a way for an undertaking to derive financial benefit from its expertise without investing its own capital. Moreover, the system gives traders who do not have the necessary experience access to methods which they could not have learned without considerable effort and allows them to benefit from the reputation of the franchisor's business name. Franchise agreements for the distribution of goods differ in that regard from dealerships or contracts which incorporate approved retailers into a selective distribution system, which do not involve the use of a single business name, the application of uniform business methods or the payment of royalties in return for the benefits granted. Such a system, which allows the franchisor to profit from his success, does not in itself interfere with competition. In order for the system to work two conditions must be met.

[16] First, the franchisor must be able to communicate his know-how to the franchisees and provide them with the necessary assistance in order to enable them to apply his methods, without running the risk that that know-how and assistance might benefit competitors, even indirectly. It follows that provisions which are essential in order to avoid that risk do not constitute restrictions on competition for the purposes of Article 85(1). That is also true of a clause prohibiting the franchisee, during the period of validity of the contract and for a reasonable period after its expiry, from opening a shop of the same or a similar nature in an area where he may compete with a member of the network. The same may be said of the franchisee's obligation not to transfer his shop to another party without the prior approval of the franchisor; that provision is intended to prevent competitors from indirectly benefiting from the know-how and assistance provided.

[17] Secondly, the franchisor must be able to take the measures necessary for maintaining the identity and reputation of the network bearing his business name or symbol. It follows that provisions which establish the means of control necessary for that purpose do not constitute restrictions on competition for the purposes of Article 85(1).

[18] The same is true of the franchisee's obligation to apply the business methods developed by the franchisor and to use the know-how provided.

[19] That is also the case with regard to the franchisee's obligation to sell the goods covered by the contract only in premises laid out and decorated according to the franchisor's instructions, which is intended to ensure uniform presentation in conformity with certain requirements. The same requirements apply to the location of the shop, the choice of which is also likely to affect the network's reputation. It is thus understandable that the franchisee cannot transfer his shop to another location without the franchisor's approval.

[20] The prohibition of the assignment by the franchisee of his rights and obligations under the contract without the franchisor's approval protects the latter's right freely to choose the franchisees, on whose business qualifications the establishment and maintenance of the network's reputation depend.

[21] By means of the control exerted by the franchisor on the selection of goods offered by the franchisee, the public is able to obtain goods of the same quality from each franchisee. It may in certain cases – for instance, the distribution of fashion articles – be impractical to lay down objective quality specifications. Because of the large number of franchisees it may also be too expensive to ensure that such specifications are observed. In such circumstances a provision requiring the franchisee to sell only products supplied by the franchisor or by suppliers selected by him may be considered necessary for the protection of the network's reputation. Such a provision may not however have the effect of preventing the franchisee from obtaining those products from other franchisees.

[22] Finally, since advertising helps to define the image of the network's name or symbol in the eyes of the public, a provision requiring the franchisee to obtain the franchisor's approval for all advertising is also essential for the maintenance of the network's identity, so long as that provision concerns only the nature of the advertising.

[23] It must be emphasized on the other hand that, far from being necessary for the protection of the know-how provided or the maintenance of the network's identity and reputation, certain provisions restrict competition between the members of the network. That is true of provisions which share markets between the franchisor and franchisees or between franchisees or prevent franchisees from engaging in price competition with each other.

[24] In that regard, the attention of the national court should be drawn to the provision which obliges the franchisee to sell goods covered by the contract only in the premises specified therein. That provision prohibits the franchisee from opening a second shop. Its real effect becomes clear if it is examined in conjunction with the franchisor's undertaking to ensure that the franchisee has the exclusive use of his business name or symbol in a given territory. In order to comply with that undertaking the franchisor must not only refrain from establishing himself within that territory but also require other franchisees to give an undertaking not to open a second shop outside their own territory. A combination of provisions of that kind results in a sharing of markets between the franchisor and the franchisees or between franchisees and thus restricts competition within the network. As is clear from the judgment of 13 July 1966 (*Consten and Grundig* v *Commission* (Joined Cases 56 and 58/64) [1966] ECR 299), a restriction of that kind constitutes a limitation of competition for the purposes of Article 85(1) if it concerns a business name or symbol which is already well-known. It is of course possible that a prospective franchisee would not take the risk of becoming part of the chain, investing his own money, paying a relatively high entry fee and undertaking to pay a substantial annual royalty, unless he could hope, thanks to a degree of protection against competition on the part of the franchisor and other franchisees, that his business would be profitable. That consideration, however, is relevant only to an examination of the agreement in the light of the conditions laid down in Article 85(3).

[25] Although provisions which impair the franchisee's freedom to determine his own prices are restrictive of competition, that is not the case where the franchisor simply provides franchisees with price guidelines, so long as there is no concerted practice between the franchisor and the franchisees or between the franchisees themselves for the actual application of such prices. It is for the national court to determine whether that is indeed the case.

[26] Finally, it must be added that franchise agreements for the distribution of goods which contain provisions sharing markets between the franchisor and the franchisees or between the franchisees themselves are in any event liable to affect trade between Member States, even if they are entered into by undertakings established in the same Member State, in so far as they prevent franchisees from establishing themselves in another Member State.

[27] In view of the foregoing, the answer to the first question must be that:

(1) The compatibility of franchise agreements for the distribution of goods with Article 85(1) depends on the provisions contained therein and on their economic context.

(2) Provisions which are strictly necessary in order to ensure that the know-how and assistance provided by the franchisor do not benefit competitors do not constitute restrictions of competition for the purposes of Article 85(1).

(3) Provisions which establish the control strictly necessary for maintaining the identity and reputation of the network identified by the common name or symbol do not constitute restrictions of competition for the purposes of Article 85(1).

(4)   Provisions which share markets between the franchisor and the franchisees or between franchisees constitute restrictions of competition for the purposes of Article 85(1).

(5)   The fact that the franchisor makes price recommendations to the franchisee does not constitute a restriction of competition, so long as there is no concerted practice between the franchisor and the franchisees or between the franchisees themselves for the actual application of such prices.

(6)   Franchise agreements for the distribution of goods which contain provisions sharing markets between the franchisor and the franchisees or between franchisees are capable of affecting trade between Member States.

BRASSERIE DE HAECHT SA v WILKIN (No. 1) (Case 23/67)
[1967] ECR 407, Court of Justice

Under three standard form loan agreements between the brewery Brasserie de Haecht and Mr and Mrs Wilkin relating in part to the purchase of furniture for the café run by the couple, the borrowers agreed, for so long as the debt was not paid off and for a further period of two years, to obtain all their supplies of beer and soft drinks exclusively from the brewery. Discovering that Mr and Mrs Wilkin had not complied with the exclusive purchasing obligation, the brewery began an action for the repayment of the loan. The couple argued that the agreements breached Article 85.

The national court asked the Court of Justice whether the examination of the effects of the agreements in question must be limited to consideration of these agreements in isolation or whether the simultaneous existence of a large number of contracts of the same type between a small number of Belgian breweries and a large number of liquor licensees must be taken into account. (Article 177 reference.)

The prohibition in Article 85(1) of the Treaty rests on three factors essential for a reply to the question referred. After stating the limits within which the prohibition is to apply, Article 85(1) mentions agreements, decisions and practices. By referring in the same sentence to agreements between undertakings, decisions by associations of undertakings and concerted practices, which may involve many parties, Article 85(1) implies that the constituent elements of those agreements, decisions and practices may be considered together as a whole.

Furthermore, by basing its application to agreements, decisions or practices not only on their subject-matter but also on their effects in relation to competition, Article 85(1) implies that regard must be had to such effects in the context in which they occur, that is to say, in the economic and legal context of such agreements, decisions or practices and where they might combine with others to have a cumulative effect on competition. In fact, it would be pointless to consider an agreement, decision or practice by reason of its effects if those effects were to be taken distinct from the market in which they are seen to operate and could only be examined apart from the body of effects, whether convergent or not, surrounding their implementation. Thus in order to examine whether it is caught by Article 85(1) an agreement cannot be examined in isolation from the above context, that is, from the factual or legal circumstances causing it to prevent, restrict or distort competition. The existence of similar contracts may be taken into consideration for this objective to the extent to which the general body of contracts of this type is capable of restricting the freedom of trade.

Lastly, it is only to the extent to which agreements, decisions or practices are capable of affecting trade between Member States that the alteration of competition comes under Community prohibitions. In order to satisfy this condition, it must be possible for the agreement, decision or practice, when viewed in the light of a combination of the objective, factual or legal circumstances, to appear to be capable of having some influence, direct or indirect, on trade between Member States, of being conducive to a partitioning of the market and of hampering the economic interpenetration sought by the Treaty. When this point is considered the agreement, decision or practice cannot therefore be isolated from all the others of which it is one.

The existence of similar contracts is a circumstance which, together with others, is capable of being a factor in the economic and legal context within which the contract must be judged. Accordingly, whilst such a situation must be taken into account it should not be considered as decisive by itself, but merely as one among others in judging whether trade between Member States is capable of being affected through any alteration in competition.

11.3.4 AN APPRECIABLE EFFECT ON INTER-STATE TRADE: THE *DE MINIMIS* PRINCIPLE

VOLK v *ÉTABLISSEMENTS VERVAECKE SPRL* (Case 5/69)
[1969] ECR 295, Court of Justice

The exclusive distribution agreement between Volk, a small-scale manufacturer of washing machines and Vervaecke, a Dutch distributor, sought to establish absolute territorial protection for Vervaecke. A contractual dispute arose between the parties. The national court asked the Court of Justice whether the manufacturer's share of the market (less than 1% in this case) should be taken into account in order to decide whether the disputed contract fell within the Article 85(1) prohibition. (Article 177 reference.)

[5/7] If an agreement is to be capable of affecting trade between Member States it must be possible to foresee with a sufficient degree of probability on the basis of a set of objective factors of law or of fact that the agreement in question may have an influence, direct or indirect, actual or potential, on the pattern of trade between Member States in such a way that it might hinder the attainment of the objectives of a single market between States. Moreover the prohibition in Article 85(1) is applicable only if the agreement in question also has as its object or effect the prevention, restriction or distortion of competition within the Common Market. Those conditions must be understood by reference to the actual circumstances of the agreement. Consequently an agreement falls outside the prohibition in Article 85 when it has only an insignificant effect on the markets, taking into account the weak position which the persons concerned have on the market of the product in question. Thus an exclusive dealing agreement, even with absolute territorial protection, may, having regard to the weak position of the persons concerned on the market in the products in question in the area covered by the absolute protection, escape the prohibition laid down in Article 85(1).

11.3.5 OBJECT OR EFFECT

See *Société Technique Minière* v *Maschinenbau Ulm GmbH* (Cases 56/65) [1966] ECR 235 at **11.2.2** above.

11.3.6 RESTRICTIVE AGREEMENTS WHICH FALL OUTSIDE ARTICLE 85(1)

11.3.6.1 Restrictions which protect a party taking high commercial risks

See *Société Technique Minière* v *Maschinenbau Ulm GmbH* (Cases 56/65) [1966] ECR 235 at **11.2.2**.

11.3.6.2 Restrictions which are necessary to the performance of a particular type of agreement

REMIA BV v *COMMISSION* (Case 42/84) [1985] ECR 2545, Court of Justice

The Court of Justice upheld a Commission Decision that non-competition clauses taken on the sale of two businesses under which the vendor undertook not to compete in the purchasers' markets for periods of five and ten years infringed Article 85(1) and were not eligible for exemption under Article 85(3) because the time periods were excessive. However, the Court indicated that covenants of this kind fall outside the scope of Article 85(1) if they are necessary to the transfer of the business. (Article 173 proceedings.)

[18] In order to determine whether or not such clauses come within the prohibition in Article 85(1), it is necessary to examine what would be the state of competition if those clauses did not exist.

[19] If that were the case, and should the vendor and the purchaser remain competitors after the transfer, it is clear that the agreement for the transfer of the undertaking could not be given effect. The vendor, with his particularly detailed knowledge of the transferred undertaking, would still be in a position to win back his former customers immediately after the transfer and thereby drive the undertaking out of business. Against that background non-competition clauses incorporated in an agreement for the transfer of an undertaking in principle have the merit of ensuring that the transfer has the effect intended. By virtue of that very fact they contribute to the promotion of competition because they lead to an increase in the number of undertakings in the market in question.

[20] Nevertheless, in order to have that beneficial effect on competition, such clauses must be necessary to the transfer of the undertaking concerned and their duration and scope must be strictly limited to that purpose. . . .

11.3.6.3 Restrictions ensuring quality: selective distribution

METRO-SB-GROSSMÄRKTE GMBH & CO. KG v *COMMISSION (No. 1)* (Case 26/76)
[1977] ECR 1875, Court of Justice

SABA manufactured electronic equipment. This was distributed, under a selective distribution system, only to wholesalers approved by SABA. Metro, a wholesaler which had been refused supplies of SABA products, sought annulment of a Commission Decision granting negative clearance to certain aspects of the SABA system. (Article 173 proceedings.)

[20] The requirement contained in Articles 3 and 85 of the EEC Treaty that competition shall not be distorted implies the existence on the market of workable competition, that is to say the degree of competition necessary to ensure the observance of the basic requirements and the attainment of the objectives of the Treaty, in particular the creation of a single market achieving conditions similar to those of a domestic market.

In accordance with this requirement the nature and intensiveness of competition may vary to an extent dictated by the products or services in question and the economic structure of the relevant market sectors.

In the sector covering the production of high quality and technically advanced consumer durables, where a relatively small number of large- and medium-scale producers offer a varied range of items which, or so consumers may consider, are readily interchangeable, the structure of the market does not preclude the existence of a variety of channels of distribution adapted to the peculiar characteristics of the various producers and to the requirements of the various categories of consumers.

On this view the Commission was justified in recognizing that selective distribution systems constituted, together with others, an aspect of competition which accords with Article 85(1), provided that resellers are chosen on the basis of objective criteria of a qualitative nature relating to the technical qualifications of the reseller and his staff and the suitability of his trading premises and that such conditions are laid down uniformly for all potential resellers and are not applied in a discriminatory fashion.

. . .

[The Court considered the obligations imposed upon wholesalers by SABA, including the obligation upon non-specialist wholesalers to set up a special department for electronic equipment, the requirement to achieve a turnover comparable with a specialist wholesaler and to sign agreements containing obligations relating to purchases and the holding of stocks.]

[37] The obligation upon non-specialist wholesalers to open a special department for electronic equipment for the domestic leisure market is designed to guarantee the sale of the products concerned under appropriate conditions and accordingly does not constitute a restriction on competition within the meaning of Article 85(1).

On the other hand, the requirement to achieve a turnover comparable to that of a specialist wholesaler exceeds the strict requirements of the qualitative criteria inherent in a selective distribution system and it must accordingly be appraised in the light of Article 85(3).

[38]   Nevertheless, that obligation is linked in the present case to the obligation, repeated in the cooperation agreements, to achieve an adequate turnover, so that it must be considered in conjunction with the said agreements. . . .

[39]   The obligations . . . to sign cooperation agreements under which the wholesaler undertakes to achieve a turnover which SABA considers to be adequate and which involve six-monthly supply contracts and obligations relating to stocks, exceed both the normal obligations involved in running a wholesale business and the requirements of a selective distribution system based on qualitative criteria.

Those obligations bind appointed distributors closely to SABA and may entail the exclusion of undertakings which, although they fulfil the qualitative conditions for appointment, cannot or will not undertake such obligations, which thus indirectly bring about a limitation in the number and establishment of outlets.

Accordingly, they can be exempted from the prohibition contained in Article 85(1) only if the conditions contained in Article 85(3) are fulfilled.

L'ORÉAL NV v *DE NIEUWE AMCK PVBA* (Case 31/80) [1980] ECR 3775, Court of Justice

A selective distribution system for the sale of certain perfumery products imposed obligations on the distributor to hold minimum stocks and to guarantee a minimum turnover. It was claimed that the system infringed Community competition rules. (Article 177 reference.)

[15]   As the Court observed in its judgment of 25 October 1977 (*Metro* v *Commission* (Case 26/76) [1977] ECR 1875), selective distribution systems constitute an aspect of competition which accords with Article 85(1) provided that re-sellers are chosen on the basis of objective criteria of a qualitative nature relating to the technical qualifications of the re-seller and his staff and the suitability of his trading premises and that such conditions are laid down uniformly for all potential re-sellers and are not applied in a discriminatory fashion.

[16]   In order to determine the exact nature of such 'qualitative' criteria for the selection of re-sellers, it is also necessary to consider whether the characteristics of the product in question necessitate a selective distribution system in order to preserve its quality and ensure its proper use, and whether those objectives are not already satisfied by national rules governing admission to the re-sale trade or the conditions of sale of the product in question. Finally, inquiry should be made as to whether the criteria laid down do not go beyond what is necessary. In that regard it should be recalled that in Case 26/76, *Metro* v *Commission* cited above, the Court considered that the obligation to participate in the setting up of a distribution system, commitments relating to the achievement of turnovers and obligations relating to minimum supply and to stocks exceeded the requirements of a selective distribution system based on qualitative requirements.

[17]   When admission to a selective distribution network is made subject to conditions which go beyond simple objective selection of a qualitative nature and, in particular, when it is based on quantitative criteria, the distribution system falls in principle within the prohibition in Article 85(1), provided that, as the Court observed in its judgment of 30 June 1966 (*Société Technique Minière* v *Maschinenbau Ulm GmbH* (Case 56/65) [1966] ECR 235), the agreement fulfils certain conditions depending less on its legal nature than on its effects first on 'trade between Member States' and secondly on 'competition'.

. . .

[21]   Consequently . . . the agreements laying down a selective distribution system based on criteria for admission, which go beyond a mere objective selection of a qualitative nature, exhibit features making them incompatible with Article 85(1) where such agreements, either individually or together with other, may, in the economic and legal context in which they occur and on the basis of a set of objective factors of law or of fact, affect trade between Member States and have either as their object or effect the prevention, restriction or distortion of competition. It is for the Commission alone,

subject to review by the Court, to grant an exemption in respect of such agreements pursuant to Article 85(3).

11.3.7   EXAMPLES OF PROHIBITED AGREEMENTS: ARTICLE 85(1)(a)–(e)

11.3.7.1   Price fixing (Article 85(1)(a))

HENNESSY/HENKELL AGREEMENT, Re [1981] 1 CMLR 601
(Commission Decision 80/1333)

An exclusive distribution agreement for the sale of Hennessy cognac in Germany contained a number of restrictive clauses, including a clause (clause 6) fixing the minimum and maximum resale prices to be charged by the distributor, Henkell. The agreement was notified to the Commission. (Commission Decision.)

[Finding that the resale prices clause infringed Article 85(1), the Commission went on to consider exemption under Article 85(3).]

[26]   . . . a duly notified exclusive dealership agreement may be exempted after undergoing individual examination provided it satisfies the conditions laid down in Article 85(3). The latter specify that it must contribute to improving the distribution of products while allowing consumers a fair share of the resulting benefit, and it must not impose on the undertakings concerned restrictions which are not indispensable to the attainment of these objectives nor afford such undertakings the possibility of eliminating competition in respect of a substantial part of the products in question.

[27]   As the Commission has stated . . . in the present state of trade exclusive dealing agreements relating to international trade lead in general to an improvement in distribution. The fact that a producer maintains contacts with only one dealer in a country makes it easier to overcome sales difficulties resulting from linguistic, legal and other differences. In the case under consideration it can be conceded that the exclusive dealership agreement in question would, for the reasons outlined above, help improve the distribution of Hennessy products on the German market. In particular, Henkell, as the sole distributor of those products in the Federal Republic, would enjoy a certain measure of security which would encourage it to invest so as to ensure their wider distribution.

[28]   For such improvement to be effective, however, the exclusive dealer would have to be able to fix resale prices freely on the basis of the cost price of the products purchased from the manufacturer and by adapting his profit margin to the sales policy determined by him on the basis of the conditions obtaining on the market. This requirement is essential if Hennessy products are to penetrate the German market better, and to combat competition from other brands.

[29]   Such is not the case here, since Hennessy is enabled to over-see Henkell's prices. Under clause 6 of the agreement, 'Hennessy's consent is necessary when Henkell wishes to fix its resale prices above cost price plus 17 per cent or below cost price plus 12 per cent'. Henkell may, nevertheless, apply prices differing from those in its price-list, but only temporarily and provided Hennessy is notified as quickly as possible. Above all, such prices may not under any circumstances fall below the 'cost price' which includes a commission of 18 per cent paid by Hennessy to Henkell, whereas Henkell should be free to reduce this rebate and charge lower prices if it considered that necessary. . . .

[30]   Nor can it be concluded that a fair share of the benefits which could result from exclusive distribution is being set aside for consumers. An improvement in distribution should be accompanied, particularly, by a reduction in sales prices to consumers, whereas under clause 6 of the agreement Henkell is not free to take a decision on this, and it is clear from the manner in which the agreement has been applied that Hennessy has prevailed upon Henkell to fix higher prices than those which ought to have ensued from the agreement.

. . .

[32]   . . . the restriction of the concessionaire's freedom to fix his resale prices, contained in clause 6, cannot be regarded as indispensable to the attainment of the objectives of the agreement even if the products in question are considered, as Hennessy

considers them, to be luxury products. Hennessy stated in its letter of 3 November 1978 that the purpose of clause 6 of the agreement is to ensure that its products 'which are regarded as luxury products do not become subject to cut-price selling which would lead to business anarchy'. The Commission has already stated, however when considering selective distribution arrangements in the luxury perfumes industry, that 'the luxury character of a product could not in itself be regarded as an adequate ground for exemption under Article 85(3)'. Hennessy has also put the following argument . . . 'We consider that the relative freedom which we give to Henkell, to fix the prices of its products within limits which seem reasonable to us, is the counterpart of the exclusivity of sale which we guarantee to our distributor.'

But in the context of an exclusive concession contract, surveillance by the manufacturer of its distributor's resale prices cannot be considered indispensable to the attainment of any beneficial purpose, referred to at 27 above, which may exist. Moreover, the 'relative freedom' pleaded by Hennessy does not exist, since the latter was able to force Henkell to fix its prices outside the limits provided for in the contract.

[33] Hennessy maintained moreover . . . that 'to authorise a distributor to apply resale prices determined by him alone, where the market in question was that of a brand name and not of a distributor, might jeopardise the brand name and the product'. This argument is undermined, however, by the behaviour of Hennessy itself, which has not imposed such stringent clauses on other distributors of the same brands in the Common Market, or has agreed to abolish them at the Commission's request. . . .

11.3.7.2   Fixing other trading conditions (Article 85(1)(a))

See *Établissements Consten SA* v *Commission* (Cases 56 & 58/64) [1966] ECR 299 at **11.3.2**; *L'Oréal NV* v *De Nieuwe Amck PvbA* (Case 31/80) [1980] ECR 3775 at **11.3.6.3**; and *Pronuptia de Paris GmbH* v *Pronuptia de Paris Irmgard Schillgalis* (Case 161/84) [1986] ECR 353 at **11.3.3** above.

11.3.7.3   Other agreements likely to breach Article 85(1) (Article 85(1)(b)–(e))

ACEC/BERLIET, Re [1968] CMLR D35 (Commission Decision 68/319)

The agreement between ACEC and Berliet provided for technical cooperation and joint research on the development of a bus equipped with electric transmission. There were a number of restrictive clauses, including clauses controlling production and markets. Berliet was to develop the bus and ACEC the transmission system. ACEC undertook to deliver its transmission system only to Berliet in France and to only one manufacturer in each of the Member States. Berliet would buy transmission systems only from ACEC, though it was not subject to any territorial or other restrictions on the marketing of the bus.

Following notification of the agreement, the Commission found that it infringed Article 85(1). However, exemption was granted under Article 85(3), subject to the condition that the parties report the progress of the agreement after three years. (Commission Decision.)

[12]   The agreement aims at permitting the manufacture of the products in question in large runs. It provides for co-operation which takes the form, in particular, of specialisation and division of labour both in research and in manufacture. Thereby, each of the partners may devote itself entirely to the tasks for which it is most fitted, i.e., ACEC to research on electrical constructions and their manufacture, Berliet to research on vehicles and their manufacture using the results of the studies made by ACEC.

[13]   The agreement aims at perfecting, particularly by joint research, a new bus the features of which involve several advantages, *inter alia*: a simplification of the mechanical construction, better work from the internal combustion engine and an improvement in the conditions of exploitation, and a greater comfort for passengers. Consequently, the notified agreement contributes to improving production and promoting technical progress.

. . .

[15]   2.   An appreciation of the share of the benefit which reaches consumers can be based only on probabilities when it is a matter of agreements which have not yet

produced their effects. However, there is a sufficient probability that the hoped for results will be obtained more rapidly as a result of the joint research and that the consumers, particularly those exploiting bus companies, will benefit from them because a new product with interesting characteristics will be made available to them and because it is not likely that inequitable sales prices or other contractual conditions will be imposed upon them. Indeed it must be presumed that at the beginning great efforts will be necessary to introduce the new product to the consumers and that competition with buses equipped with traditional transmissions will prevent the exploitation of the agreement to the detriment of the users.

[16]   Even on the hypothesis that the buses with electric transmission turned out to be extremely superior to the other buses, the fact that ACEC will be able to conclude contracts with other bus manufacturers in the Common Market and outside it – which would very probably be the case – and that no restriction on competition between the bus manufacturers using the ACEC systems is provided for, would constitute a corrective element against any tendencies to exclude the consumers from a fair share of the benefit. Consequently it may be allowed that the condition in Article 85(3) whereby consumers must be allowed a fair share of the benefit resulting from the agreement is met in the present case.

. . .

[18]   3.   ACEC's undertaking to deliver in France its transmission only to Berliet and to co-operate only with the latter is aimed at not dispersing its efforts of creation and execution and at directing them towards perfecting and manufacturing a single range of vehicles. Furthermore, the undertaking has the effect of giving a certain protection to Berliet. If a manufacturer of buses did not have such a possibility of amortising its investments, it is to be feared that it would not bear the burden of the development of the new product with the high costs involved, so that the product would be in danger of not being perfected.

[19]   The reverse exclusivity prohibiting Berliet from purchasing electric trans- missions from other than ACEC is at the moment theoretical, since ACEC is the only producer of transmissions of this type. But as soon as a comparable system is on the market the exclusivity will constitute for ACEC a justified protection which should allow it to amortise its investments for the adaptation of its transmissions to the Berliet vehicles.

[20]   It could not reasonably be expected that one of the parties should take the trouble to develop a new technique in collaboration with another partner and then allow the latter to go on to exploit the result of the work with an outsider. Consequently, the undertakings of reciprocal exclusivity are indispensable to the obtaining of the favour- able results of the agreement.

[21]   ACEC's obligation to Berliet to deliver its transmission, within the Common Market, apart from Berliet and the Belgian users, only to one single manufacturer in each of the other member-countries, is aimed at concentrating production of buses with electric transmissions in the hands of a limited number of manufacturers, without restricting the possibility which each of those manufacturers has of selling in the whole of the Common Market.

[22]   The attainment of runs of some size is a necessary condition for reaching a profitable production. It seems probable that during the period of launching the demand will not be very strong. It may therefore be allowed that if during that period production had been dispersed among a large number of manufacturers, none of them would have succeeded in producing a run of any size, which could compromise the economic success of the new product. Consequently, the limitation of the number of purchasers of electric transmissions, crystallised by ACEC's obligation to deliver its products in the member- countries other than France and Belgium to only one manufacturer per country, is at present indispensable to the obtaining of the favourable effects of the agreement.

[23]   Consequently, the agreement does not impose on the undertakings in question restrictions which are not indispensable to the obtaining of the objectives of improvement of production and promotion of technical progress.

[24]   4.   The buses with electric transmission will be competing with the buses equipped with mechanical transmissions offered by other manufacturers. Furthermore, the agreement provides that, in the Common Market and outside, not only Berliet but

also several manufacturers will manufacture buses with electric transmission. No restriction is provided for, in particular no territorial restriction, as regards the distribution of the vehicles whatever their origin.

[25] It can be anticipated that the agreement will not be able to give the undertakings concerned the possibility of eliminating competition in a substantial part of the products in question.

[26] Consequently the conditions of application of Article 85(3) are fulfilled.

TRANSOCEAN MARINE PAINT ASSOCIATION, RE [1967] CMLR D9
(Commission Decision 67/454)

Several European and non-European manufacturers of marine paint created the Transocean Marine Paint Association with the aim of collaborating in the manufacture and worldwide marketing of their product. The paints were to be manufactured under a single formula determined by the Association and marketed in the same form. Each member remained free to fix its own prices. The same trade mark was to be used, though members were at liberty to add their own mark. Each member was granted a marketing territory corresponding to the country in which it was established. Sales into other members' territory could only be made with the prior agreement of the member concerned and on payment of a commission. The parties notified the agreement, requesting negative clearance or exemption. The Commission found that the agreement infringed Article 85(1) but granted exemption under Article 85(3). (Commission Decision.)

[22] 1. The agreement contributes to improving the distribution of the products. In fact, it allows the members to rationalise and intensify the sale of the marine paints manufactured by them to a common standard and presented under a common trade mark. The institution of granted territories in each of which the member there established is primarily responsible for the sale of these paint guarantees, through a judicious geographical distribution of the members and the good knowledge of the market, that the Transocean paints are offered and stored in a regular manner and in sufficient quantities in a large number of countries and ports and that each member is in a position without difficulty to make deliveries outside its own granted territory, either by itself exporting or through the intermediary of other members. The members of the association are, therefore in a position also to give a service to purchasers who wish to be able to obtain the marine paints which they use of an identical quality at any time and in any place at which they may have need of them. Were it not for this agreement, the members would be obliged to create their own distribution networks in a large number of countries, which would involve investments and risks which are excessive for undertakings of a medium size (the need to establish branches or to set up agencies, to maintain depots and an after-sales service). Thanks to the association and the co-ordination of the various individual sales network of its members, the latter are able, although being medium undertakings, to enter more actively into competition with the big marine paint manufacturers already represented in all the major countries, which results in an increase in the supply of the products and an improvement in the sales structure in the marine paint sector. The agreement thus involves perceptible objective advantages for the distribution of the products as compared with the situation which would obtain if it had not been concluded.

[23] 2. The consumers obtain a fair share of the resultant benefit, i.e., the advantages which flow from the agreement and which have been set out above. The agreement leads to an increase and an enlargement of the supply of marine paints. The consumers may, as in the past, purchase the products manufactured individually by the members of the association without being obliged to apply to the members of the association established in their country, since no absolute territorial protection has been agreed. Those consumers which decide to use Transocean paints thenceforth avoid the necessity to carry on the ship itself the paint required for its maintenance; they may obtain without difficulty or delay paint of an identical quality in the numerous depots maintained by the members of the association, while avoiding the loss of useful space in their ships. The purchasers of Transocean paint have the possibility of applying to the local member of the association, for example, when they wish to obtain technical advice and have the

work of painting supervised. They may, however, also apply to members established in other countries when their conditions (price, delivery date, etc.) seem to them more favourable. The ability to purchase from other members usefully corrects the artificial differences which may exist between the prices asked by the members and, when joined to the price competition to which the members are exposed from their competitors, contributes to guaranteeing to the consumers a fair share in the benefits of the agreement.

[24] 3. In its present form, the agreement contains no restriction which is not indispensable for obtaining the above mentioned objectives.

(a) As regards the special Transocean paints, the measures laid down for the concentration of production and sales efforts on the various granted territories are necessary to create as wide and as complete a distribution network as possible, a network which, itself, is a pre-condition for the successful launching of the Transocean products and for an active promotion of the new Transocean marks. Given their relatively modest positions on the market, such a launching requires particularly intensive efforts from the members. In the Common Market, the most important members manufacture only about . . . per cent. of the production of their countries in marine paints, and all are exposed to a lively competition from producers which are often much bigger. The members must, therefore, during the launching period, make particular efforts to draw the attention of purchasers to the new Transocean paints, of an identical quality and available in all the granted territories and, being producers which hitherto were unknown outside a limited area, to create a reputation as against their competitors which already have available a world sales network. Although the association was created in 1959, that launching period must be regarded as not yet ended. This is explained especially by the frequent changes which have occurred in the composition of the association and appears in practice in the fact that the proportion of Transocean paints sold by the members still represents at the present moment only . . . per cent. of their total paint production.

[25] In these particular circumstances, the best means of leading the members to promote intensively the sale of Transocean paints in their granted territory consists in imposing upon them the obligation to concentrate their main efforts on that territory so as to ensure that there is there a sufficient and regular supply for their customers, while being able to count on other members not carrying on in that territory such a large activity that it puts in question their own interest in promoting the sales.

[26] At present, intensive action by all the members on their respective territories could not be obtained if they were free to manufacture or have manufactured Transocean paints on the granted territory of other members. This intensive action could further be compromised for lack of a clause relating to commissions, which encourages each member which has received an order which is to be executed in the territory granted to another member to transmit it to the latter, and thereby contributes to giving to the members, for the territory for which they are responsible, a privileged position which is necessary if they are to have an interest in exerting an intensive sales effort there. This clause does not, however, exclude the possibility of Transocean paints being imported into the granted territory of each member on payment of a relatively small compensation, which does not have a prohibitive effect, and this encourages the member responsible for that territory to intensify its sales efforts there.

[27] This possibility of trade between Member States in Transocean paints, organised in this way by the clause relating to commissions, is not affected by the situation created by the agreement with regard to the right to the trade marks. The present case is characterised by the fact that one and the same mark is used simultaneously in different States by several producers to designate identical products, and this is done by virtue of an agreement which, in order to guarantee unreservedly the interchangeability of the products and to avoid the consumer being led into error, ensures that the products in question are qualitatively identical. In these circumstances, the members established in the Common Market cannot enforce the rights flowing from the marks registered in their favour on their granted territory in order to hinder the imports from other Member States of the Transocean products manufactured by other members. In fact, as the Court of Justice of the European Communities has indicated in *Consten & Grundig* v *EEC Commission*, the fundamental principle of the Community system of competition is opposed to the abusive exercise of the national trade mark rights to frustrate the effectiveness of the Community law on restrictive agreements.

[28]   In the light of these various circumstances, it can justly be admitted that the restrictions on competition in Transocean paints do not go beyond what is necessary to attain the objectives of the agreement.

. . .

[31]   During the launching period, the objectives of the agreement could not be attained without imposing upon the members the obligation to export their own brands to the granted territory of other members only after prior agreement of the latter and on payment of a relatively small compensation. The ability to refuse such authorisation where the envisaged export would clash with the interests of the association gives to the members the guarantee that none of them should, during the period of launching the Transocean paints, be able to pour exclusively or principally its products under its own trade marks on the granted territory of other members to the prejudice of the extension of the sales of the Transocean paints and, consequently, to the prejudice of the common interest of all the members. Furthermore, as a result of this restriction on the liberty to export, those members which receive orders to be executed on the territory granted to another member are encouraged to transmit them to that member, which leads them in practice to offer in preference to their customers Transocean paints, also available at the same quality in the country where the delivery is to take place, and thus to contribute to the promotion of the sales of these paints.

[32]   There is no factor indicating that the above-mentioned provisions lead, by the manner in which they are applied, to a restriction of the economic liberty of the members which goes beyond what is indispensable for attaining the objectives of the agreement.

. . .

[34]   4.   The agreement does not give to those concerned any possibility of eliminating competition in a substantial part of the products in question. According to the data available to the Commission, the share in the market of the Common Market members of the association is only about . . . per cent. and those members are subjected to a lively competition within the Common Market from other manufacturers of marine paint and in particular from the big international groups offering these paints in the Common Market, groups which are in no way hindered from access to that market by the agreement. Thus the last condition for the application of Article 85(3) is met.

11.4   Article 85(3): Individual Exemption

11.4.1   ECONOMIC BENEFIT: IMPROVING PRODUCTION OR DISTRIBUTION OR PROMOTING TECHNICAL OR ECONOMIC PROGRESS

See *ACEC/Berliet, Re* [1968] CMLR D35 (Commission Decision 68/319) at **11.3.7.3** and *Transocean Marine Paint Association, Re* [1967] CMLR D9 (Commission Decision 67/454) at **11.3.7.3** above.

11.4.2   ALLOWING CONSUMERS A FAIR SHARE OF THE RESULTING BENEFIT

See *ACEC/Berliet, Re* [1968] CMLR D35 (Commission Decision 68/319) at **11.3.7.3** and *Transocean Marine Paint Association, Re* [1967] CMLR D9 (Commission Decision 67/454) at **11.3.7.3** above.

11.4.3   RESTRICTIONS WHICH ARE NOT INDISPENSABLE

See *Établissements Consten SA* v *Commission* (Cases 56 & 58/64) [1966] ECR 299 at **11.3.2** above.

11.5 End of Chapter Assessment Questions

1   Samcad (UK) plc (Samcad) manufactures the 'Focus', a highly technically advanced home computer, which it markets through retail outlets in the UK, France and Denmark. The 'Focus' is supplied only to retailers who enter into a standard form contract with Samcad requiring them to:

(a)   ensure that all their sales staff are fully trained in the use of the 'Focus';

(b)   ensure that areas of their sales premises in which the 'Focus' is displayed have facilities enabling staff to give simple demonstrations of the use of the computer to customers.

Advise Samcad on the compatibilty of its standard agreement with Article 85.

2   How would your answer to Question 1 differ if Samcad's standard agreement also required retailers to:

(a)   hold minimum stocks of the 'Focus' computer;

(b)   charge prices fixed by Samcad?

In view of your conclusions, advise Samcad on any action it should take.

11.6 End of Chapter Assessment Outline Answers

(Unless otherwise stated, references in the following answers are to the Treaty of Rome.)

QUESTION 1

The aim of Community competition law is to ensure that the operation of the internal market, efficiency in production and distribution and the interests of consumers and small and medium-sized undertakings are not threatened by restrictive practices or by the anti-competitive behaviour of powerful undertakings. Article 85 of the Treaty is concerned with restrictive agreements.

Article 85(1) prohibits all agreements between undertakings, decisions by associations of undertakings and concerted practices which may affect trade between Member States and which have as their object or effect the prevention, restriction or distortion of competition within the common market. Article 85(1) is not infringed unless all these elements are present.

Since the term 'undertaking' includes any natural or legal persons engaged in commercial activity in the provision of goods or services, both Samcad and the retailers are undertakings for the purposes of Article 85(1). The standard form contract is clearly an agreement.

There is an effect on trade between Member States wherever it is 'possible to foresee with a sufficient degree of probability on the basis of a set of objective factors of law or of fact that the agreement in question may have an influence, direct or indirect, actual or potential, on the pattern of trade between Member States' (*Société Technique Minière*). *Any* effect, whether it be an increase or a decrease in trade is sufficient (*Établissements Consten SA v Commission*). The agreement between Samcad and each retailer may be looked at as part of the network of agreements operating in the UK, France and Denmark, which as a whole has an effect on the pattern of trade between Member States (*Brasserie de Haecht*).

The effect on inter-state trade must be *appreciable*. The Commission's 1997 Notice on Agreements of Minor Importance indicates that if the parties' share of the market for the relevant goods or services does not exceed certain thresholds, an agreement is *de minimis* and Article 85(1) will not normally apply. Without information on these matters, it is appropriate to proceed on the assumption that the Samcad agreement is not *de minimis*.

Article 85(1) refers to agreements which have as their object or effect the prevention, restriction or distortion of competition within the common market. An anti-competitive object is sufficient (*Société Technique Minière*) but if an agreement is not designed to prevent, restrict or distort competition, it will be necessary to make an economic analysis of its effects on competition.

There are certain kinds of agreement which, although they contain restrictions, are deemed not to have an anti-competitive object or effect. These include selective distribution agreements falling within the *Metro* doctrine.

The *Metro* doctrine applies to goods whose particular characteristics justify restrictions on the type of outlets dealing with them, such as technically advanced products (cars, cameras) or products carrying a certain brand image (perfumes, luxury cosmetics) but not to products which are commonplace or lacking in technical sophistication (*Ideal/ Standard Agreement*). Such restrictions must be no more than is necessary to protect the quality or brand image of the product. As a highly technically advanced product, the 'Focus' does have characteristics which justify restrictions.

The Samcad agreement will fall within the *Metro* doctrine and thus escape the scope of Article 85(1) if 'resellers are chosen on the basis of objective criteria of a qualitative nature relating to the technical qualifications of the reseller and his staff and the suitability of his trading premises and that such conditions are laid down uniformly for all potential resellers and are not applied in a discriminatory fashion'. The conditions in the Samcad agreement are qualitative in nature, relating to staff qualifications and to the suitability of the trading premises, and are no more than is necessary to protect the quality of the product. If these conditions are applied uniformly and without discrimination to all retail outlets selling the 'Focus', the Samcad agreement does not breach Article 85(1).

QUESTION 2

Since neither of these additional clauses falls within the *Metro* doctrine, the agreement is now brought within the scope of Article 85(1). It is therefore necessary to consider the possibility of exemption under Article 85(3). There is no block exemption applying to selective distribution. The agreement must be notified to the Commission if individual exemption is to be sought.

Samcad should be advised that agreements fixing prices, referred to specifically in Article 85(1)(a), are regarded as having obvious anti-competitive effects and that the grant of an exemption is extremely unlikely. The Commission would not, for instance, be impressed by the argument that fixed prices are necessary to protect the 'Focus' computer's brand image (*Hennessy/Henkell*).

The minimum stocks clause is quantitative. Although it falls outside the *Metro* doctrine, it may be eligible for individual exemption if it is necessary to the agreement as a whole (*L'Oréal*).

Article 85(2) provides that agreements prohibited under Article 85 shall be automatically void. The Commission has the power to fine parties to prohibited agreements. Samcad should therefore be advised to remove the price fixing clause from its agreement and to consider also removing the minimum stocks clause. If Samcad takes the view that the minimum stocks clause is indispensable, the company should consider notifying the agreement to the Commission with a view to individual exemption.

CHAPTER TWELVE

COMPETITION LAW: ARTICLE 86

12.1 The Article 86 Prohibition

THE TREATY OF ROME

Article 86

Any abuse by one or more undertakings of a dominant position within the common market or in a substantial part of it shall be prohibited as incompatible with the common market in so far as it may affect trade between Member States.

Such abuse may, in particular, consist in:

(a) directly or indirectly imposing unfair purchase or selling prices or other unfair trading conditions;

(b) limiting production, markets or technical development to the prejudice of consumers;

(c) applying dissimilar conditions to equivalent transactions with other trading parties, thereby placing them at a competitive disadvantage;

(d) making the conclusion of contracts subject to acceptance by the other parties of supplementary obligations which, by their nature or according to commercial usage, have no connection with the subject of such contracts.

12.2 Dominant Position

UNITED BRANDS CO. v *COMMISSION* (Case 27/76)
[1978] ECR 207, Court of Justice

United Brands Company of New York and United Brands Continental BV (referred to collectively in the Court's judgment as UBC) sought annulment of the Commission Decision referred to in the judgment. (Article 173 proceedings.)

[3] Article 1 of the decision declares that UBC has infringed Article 86 of the Treaty establishing the European Economic Community:

(a) by requiring its distributor/ripeners in the Belgo-Luxembourg Economic Union, Denmark, Germany, Ireland and the Netherlands to refrain from reselling its bananas while still green;

(b) by, in respect of its sales of Chiquita bananas, charging other trading parties, namely distributor/ripeners other than the Scipio Group in the Member States referred to above, dissimilar prices for equivalent transactions;

(c) by imposing unfair prices for the sale of Chiquita bananas on its customers in the Belgo-Luxembourg Economic Union, Denmark, the Netherlands and Germany (other than the Scipio Group);

(d) by refusing from 10 October 1973 to 11 February 1975 to supply Chiquita bananas to Th. Olesen A/S, Valby, Copenhagen, Denmark.

[UBC put forward the following submissions in support of its application.]

(1)   It challenges the analysis made by the Commission of the relevant market, and also of the product market and the geographic market;

(2)   It denies that it is in a dominant position on the relevant market within the meaning of Article 86 of the Treaty;

(3)   It considers that the clause relating to the conditions of sale of green bananas is justified by the need to safeguard the quality of the product sold to the consumer;

(4)   It intends to show that the refusal to continue to supply the Danish firm Th. Olesen was justified;

(5)   It takes the view that it has not charged discriminatory prices;

(6)   It takes the view that it has not charged unfair prices;

(7)   It complains that the administrative procedure was irregular;

(8)   It disputes the imposition of the fine and, in the alternative, asks the Court to reduce it.

Chapter 1 – The existence of a dominant position
Section 1 – The relevant market

[10]   In order to determine whether UBC has a dominant position on the banana market it is necessary to define this market both from the standpoint of the product and from the geographic point of view.

[11]   The opportunities for competition under Article 86 of the Treaty must be considered having regard to the particular features of the product in question and with reference to a clearly defined geographic area in which it is marketed and where the conditions of competition are sufficiently homogeneous for the effect of the economic power of the undertaking concerned to be able to be evaluated.

Paragraph 1. The Product Market

[12]   As far as the product market is concerned it is first of all necessary to ascertain whether, as the applicant maintains, bananas are an integral part of the fresh fruit market, because they are reasonably interchangeable by consumers with other kinds of fresh fruit such as apples, oranges, grapes, peaches, strawberries, etc. or whether the relevant market consists solely of the banana market which includes both branded bananas and unlabelled bananas and is a market sufficiently homogeneous and distinct from the market of other fresh fruit.

[13]   The applicant submits in support of its argument that bananas compete with other fresh fruit in the same shops, on the same shelves, at prices which can be compared, satisfying the same needs: consumption as a dessert or between meals.

[14]   The statistics produced show that consumer expenditure on the purchase of bananas is at its lowest between June and December when there is a plentiful supply of domestic fresh fruit on the market.

[15]   Studies carried out by the Food and Agriculture Organization (FAO) (especially in 1975) confirm that banana prices are relatively weak during the summer months and that the price of apples for example has a statistically appreciable impact on the consumption of bananas in the Federal Republic of Germany.

[16]   Again according to these studies some easing of prices is noticeable at the end of the year during the 'orange season'.

[17]   The seasonal peak periods when there is a plentiful supply of other fresh fruit exert an influence not only on the prices but also on the volume of sales of bananas and consequently on the volume of imports thereof.

[18]   The applicant concludes from these findings that bananas and other fresh fruit form only one market and that UBC's operations should have been examined in this context for the purpose of any application of Article 86 of the Treaty.

[19]   The Commission maintains that there is a demand for bananas which is distinct from the demand for other fresh fruit especially as the banana is a very important part of the diet of certain sections of the community.

[20]   The specific qualities of the banana influence customer preference and induce him not to readily accept other fruits as a substitute.

[21]   The Commission draws the conclusion from the studies quoted by the applicant that the influence of the prices and availabilities of other types of fruit on the prices and availabilities of bananas on the relevant market is very ineffective and that these effects

are too brief and too spasmodic for such other fruit to be regarded as forming part of the same market as bananas or as a substitute therefor.

[22] For the banana to be regarded as forming a market which is sufficiently differentiated from other fruit markets it must be possible for it to be singled out by such special features distinguishing it from other fruits that it is only to a limited extent interchangeable with them and is only exposed to their competition in a way that is hardly perceptible.

. . .

[27] Since the banana is a fruit which is always available in sufficient quantities the question whether it can be replaced by other fruits must be determined over the whole of the year for the purpose of ascertaining the degree of competition between it and other fresh fruit.

[28] The studies of the banana market on the Court's file show that on the latter market there is no significant long term cross-elasticity any more than – as has been mentioned – there is any seasonal substitutability in general between the banana and all the seasonal fruits, as this only exists between the banana and two fruits (peaches and table grapes) in one of the countries (West Germany) of the relevant geographic market.

[29] As far as concerns the two fruits available throughout the year (oranges and apples) the first are not interchangeable and in the case of the second there is only a relative degree of substitutability.

[30] This small degree of substitutability is accounted for by the specific features of the banana and all the factors which influence consumer choice.

[31] The banana has certain characteristics, appearance, taste, softness, seedlessness, easy handling, a constant level of production which enable it to satisfy the constant needs of an important section of the population consisting of the very young, the old and the sick.

[32] As far as prices are concerned two FAO studies show that the banana is only affected by the prices – falling prices – of other fruits (and only of peaches and table grapes) during the summer months and mainly in July and then by an amount not exceeding 20%.

[33] Although it cannot be denied that during these months and some weeks at the end of the year this product is exposed to competition from other fruits the flexible way in which the volume of imports and their marketing on the relevant geographic market is adjusted means that the conditions of competition are extremely limited and that its price adapts without any serious difficulties to this situation where supplies of fruit are plentiful.

[34] It follows from all these considerations that a very large number of consumers having a constant need for bananas are not noticeably or even appreciably enticed away from the consumption of this product by the arrival of other fresh fruit on the market and that even the personal peak periods only affect it for a limited period of time and to a very limited extent from the point of view of substitutability.

[35] Consequently the banana market is a market which is sufficiently distinct from the other fresh fruit markets.

Paragraph 2. The geographic market

[36] The Commission has taken the Federal Republic of Germany, Denmark, Ireland, the Netherlands and the BLEU as the geographic market and it is in respect of this market that it is necessary to consider whether UBC has the power to hinder effective competition.

[37] It takes the view that the economic conditions in this part of the Community allow importer/distributors of bananas to market their products there in the ordinary course without there being any significant economic barriers for UBC to overcome compared with other importer/distributors.

[38] The other Member States of the Community (France, Italy, the United Kingdom) must however be excluded from this geographic definition of the market notwithstanding the significant presence of UBC in these States, because of the special circumstances relating to import arrangements and trading conditions and the fact that bananas of various types and origin are sold there.

. . .

[44]   The conditions for the application of Article 86 to an undertaking in a dominant position presuppose the clear delimitation of the substantial part of the Common Market in which it may be able to engage in abuses which hinder effective competition and this is an area where the objective conditions of competition applying to the product in question must be the same for all traders.

[45]   The Community has not established a common organization of the agricultural market in bananas.

[46]   Consequently import arrangements vary considerably from one Member State to another and reflect a specific commercial policy peculiar to the States concerned.

[The judgment then details the different importing policies and arrangements in France, the UK and Italy.]

. . .

[51]   The effect of the national organization of these three markets is that the applicant's bananas do not compete on equal terms with the other bananas sold in these States which benefit from a preferential system and the Commission was right to exclude these three national markets from the geographic market under consideration.

[52]   On the other hand the six other States are markets which are completely free, although the applicable tariff provisions and transport costs are of necessity different but not discriminatory, and in which the conditions of competition are the same for all.

[53]   From the standpoint of being able to engage in free competition these six States form an area which is sufficiently homogeneous to be considered in its entirety.

. . .

[57]   It follows from all these considerations that the geographic market as determined by the Commission which constitutes a substantial part of the common market must be regarded as the relevant market for the purpose of determining whether the applicant may be in a dominant position.

. . .

Section 2 – UBC's position on the relevant market

[63]   Article 86 is an application of the general objective of the activities of the Community laid down by Article 3(f) of the Treaty: the institution of a system ensuring that competition in the common market is not distorted.

[64]   This article prohibits any abuse by an undertaking of a dominant position in a substantial part of the common market in so far as it may affect trade between Member States.

[65]   The dominant position referred to in this article relates to a position of economic strength enjoyed by an undertaking which enables it to prevent effective competition being maintained on the relevant market by giving it the power to behave to an appreciable extent independently of its competitors, customers and ultimately of its consumers.

[66]   In general a dominant position derives from a combination of several factors which, taken separately, are not necessarily determinative.

[67]   In order to find out whether UBC is an undertaking in a dominant position on the relevant market it is necessary first of all to examine its structure and then the situation on the said market as far as competition is concerned.

[68]   In doing so it may be advisable to take account if need be of the facts put forward as acts amounting to abuses without necessarily having to acknowledge that they are abuses.

Paragraph 1. The structure of UBC

[69]   It is advisable to examine in turn UBC's resources for and methods of producing, packaging, transporting, selling and displaying its product.

[70]   UBC is an undertaking vertically integrated to a high degree.

[71]   This integration is evident at each of the stages from the plantation to the loading on wagons or lorries in the ports of delivery and after those stages, as far as ripening and sale prices are concerned, UBC even extends its control to ripener/distributors and wholesalers by setting up a complete network of agents.

[72]   At the production stage UBC owns large plantations in Central and South America.

. . .

[78]   At the stage of packaging and presentation on its premises UBC has at its disposal factories, manpower, plant and material which enable it to handle the goods independently.

[79]   The bananas are carried from the place of production to the port of shipment by its own means of transport including railways.

[80]   At the carriage by sea stage it has been acknowledged that UBC is the only undertaking of its kind which is capable of carrying two thirds of its exports by means of its own banana fleet.

. . .

[82]   In the field of technical knowledge and as a result of continual research UBC keeps on improving the productivity and yield of its plantations by improving the draining system, making good soil deficiencies and combating effectively plant disease.

[83]   It has perfected new ripening methods in which its technicians instruct the distributor/ripeners of the Chiquita banana.

[84]   That is another factor to be borne in mind when considering UBC's position since competing firms cannot develop research at a comparable level and are in this respect at a disadvantage compared with the applicant.

. . .

[88]   Since 1967 UBC has based its general policy in the relevant market on the quality of its Chiquita brand banana.

. . .

[91]   UBC has made this product distinctive by large-scale repeated advertising and promotion campaigns which have induced the consumer to show a preference for it in spite of the difference between the price of labelled and unlabelled bananas (in the region of 30 to 40%) and also of Chiquita bananas and those which have been labelled with another brand name (in the region of 7 to 10%).

. . .

[93]   It has thus attained a privileged position by making Chiquita the premier banana brand name on the relevant market with the result that the distributor cannot afford not to offer it to the consumer.

[94]   At the selling stage this distinguishing factor – justified by the unchanging quality of the banana bearing this label – ensures that it has regular customers and consolidates its economic strength.

. . .

Paragraph 2. The situation with regard to competition

. . .

[107]   A trader can only be in a dominant position on the market for a product if he has succeeded in winning a large part of this market.

[108]   Without going into a discussion about percentages, which when fixed are bound to be to some extent approximations, it can be considered to be an established fact that UBC's share of the relevant market is always more than 40% and nearly 45%.

[109]   This percentage does not however permit the conclusion that UBC automatically controls the market.

[110]   It must be determined having regard to the strength and number of the competitors.

[111]   It is necessary first of all to establish that on the whole of the relevant market the said percentage represents *grosso modo* a share several times greater than that of its competitor Castle and Cooke which is the best placed of all the competitors, the others coming far behind.

[112]   This fact together with the others to which attention has already been drawn may be regarded as a factor which affords evidence of UBC's preponderant strength.

. . .

[125]   However UBC takes into account the losses which its banana division made from 1971 to 1976 – whereas during this period its competitors made profits – for the purpose of inferring that, since dominance is in essence the power to fix prices, making losses is inconsistent with the existence of a dominant position.

[126]   An undertaking's economic strength is not measured by its profitability; a reduced profit margin or even losses for a time are not incompatible with a dominant

position, just as large profits may be compatible with a situation where there is effective competition.

[127]   The fact that UBC's profitability is for a time moderate or non-existent must be considered in the light of the whole of its operations.

[128]   The finding that, whatever losses UBC may make, the customers continue to buy more goods from UBC which is the dearest vendor, is more significant and this fact is a particular feature of the dominant position and its verification is determinative in this case.

[129]   The cumulative effect of all the advantages enjoyed by UBC thus ensures that is has a dominant position on the relevant market.

Chapter II – Abuse of this dominant position
Section 1 Conduct vis-à-vis the ripeners
Paragraph 1. The clause prohibiting the resale of bananas while still green

[The Court held that the clause at issue forbidding the sale of green bananas infringed Article 86 of the Treaty.]

Paragraph 2. The refusal to continue supplies to Olesen

[163]   The Commission is of the opinion that UBC has infringed Article 86 of the Treaty by refusing to continue supplies of Chiquita bananas to Olesen from 10 October 1973 to 11 February 1975.

[164]   According to a telex message of 11 October 1973 from UBC to Olesen these supplies were discontinued because the ripener/distributor took part in an advertising campaign mounted during October 1973 in Denmark for Dole bananas.

. . .

[182]   . . . it is advisable to assert positively from the outset that an undertaking in a dominant position for the purpose of marketing a product – which cashes in on the reputation of a brand name known to and valued by the consumers – cannot stop supplying a long standing customer who abides by regular commercial practice, if the orders placed by that customer are in no way out of the ordinary.

[183]   Such conduct is inconsistent with the objectives laid down in Article 3(f) of the Treaty, which are set out in detail in Article 86, especially in paragraphs (b) and (e), since the refusal to sell would limit markets to the prejudice of consumers and would amount to discrimination which might in the end eliminate a trading party from the relevant market.

[184]   It is therefore necessary to ascertain whether the discontinuance of supplies by UBC in October 1973 was justified.

[185]   The reason given is in the applicant's letter of 11 October 1973 in which it upbraided Olesen in no uncertain manner for having participated in an advertising campaign for one of its competitors.

[186]   Later on UBC added to this reason a number of complaints, for example, that Olesen was the exclusive representative of its main competitor on the Danish market.

[187]   This was not a new situation since it goes back to 1969 and was not in any case inconsistent with fair trade practices.

[188]   Finally UBC has not put forward any relevant argument to justify the refusal of supplies.

[189]   Although it is true, as the applicant points out, that the fact that an undertaking is in a dominant position cannot disentitle it from protecting its own commercial interests if they are attacked, and that such an undertaking must be conceded the right to take such reasonable steps as it deems appropriate to protect its said interests, such behaviour cannot be countenanced if its actual purpose is to strengthen this dominant position and abuse it.

[190]   Even if the possibility of a counter-attack is acceptable that attack must still be proportionate to the threat taking into account the economic strength of the undertakings confronting each other.

[191]   The sanction consisting of a refusal to supply by an undertaking in a dominant position was in excess of what might, if such a situation were to arise, reasonably be contemplated as a sanction for conduct similar to that for which UBC blamed Olesen.

[192]   In fact UBC could not be unaware of the fact that by acting in this way it would discourage its other ripener/distributors from supporting the advertising of other brand

names and that the deterrent effect of the sanction imposed upon one of them would make its position of strength on the relevant market that much more effective.

[193]   Such a course of conduct amounts therefore to a serious interference with the independence of small and medium sized firms in their commercial relations with the undertaking in a dominant position and this independence implies the right to give preference to competitors' goods.

. . .

Section 2 – The Pricing Practice
Paragraph 1. Discriminatory prices
[204]   All the bananas marketed by UBC under the brand name 'Chiquita' on the relevant market have the same geographic origin, belong to the same variety (Cavendish Valery) and are of almost the same quality.

[205]   They are unloaded in two ports, Rotterdam and Bremerhaven, where unloading costs only differ by a few cents in the dollar per box of 20 kilogrammes, and are resold, except to Scipio and in Ireland, subject to the same conditions of sale and terms of payment after they have been loaded on the buyers' wagons or lorries, the price of a box amounting on average to between 3 and 4 dollars and going up to 5 dollars in 1974.

[206]   The costs of carriage from the unloading ports to the ripening installations and the amount of any duty payable under the Common Customs Tariff are borne by the purchaser except in Ireland.

[207]   This being so all those customers going to Rotterdam and Bremerhaven to obtain their supplies might be expected to find that UBC offers them all the same selling price for 'Chiquita' bananas.

[208]   The Commission blames the applicant for charging each week for the sale of its branded bananas – without objective justification – a selling price which differs appreciably according to the Member State where its customers are established.

. . .

[225]   In fact the bananas sold by UBC are all freighted in the same ships, are unloaded at the same cost in Rotterdam or Bremerhaven and the price differences relate to substantially similar quantities of bananas of the same variety, which have been brought to the same degree of ripening, are of similar quality and sold under the same 'Chiquita' brand name under the same conditions of sale and payment for loading on to the purchaser's own means of transport and the latter have to pay customs duties, taxes and transport costs from these ports.

. . .

[232]   These discriminatory prices, which varied according to the circumstances of the Member States, were just so many obstacles to the free movement of goods and their effect was intensified by the clause forbidding the resale of bananas while still green and by reducing the deliveries of the quantities ordered.

[233]   A rigid partitioning of national markets was thus created at price levels, which were artificially different, placing certain distributor/ripeners at a competitive disadvantage, since compared with what it should have been competition had thereby been distorted.

[234]   Consequently the policy of differing prices enabling UBC to apply dissimilar conditions to equivalent transactions with other trading parties, thereby placing them at a competitive disadvantage, was an abuse of a dominant position.

Paragraph 2. Unfair prices
[235]   The Commission is of the opinion that UBC has also abused its dominant position by charging its customers in Germany (other than the Scipio group), Denmark, the Netherlands and the BLEU unfair prices, which in the circumstances it considers are 'excessive in relation to the economic value of the product supplied'.

. . .

[248]   The imposition by an undertaking in a dominant position directly or indirectly of unfair purchase or selling prices is an abuse to which exception can be taken under Article 86 of the Treaty.

[249]   It is advisable therefore to ascertain whether the dominant undertaking has made use of the opportunities arising out of its dominant position in such a way as to

reap trading benefits which it would not have reaped if there had been normal and sufficiently effective competition.

[250]   In this case charging a price which is excessive because it has no reasonable relation to the economic value of the product supplied would be such an abuse.

[251]   This excess could, *inter alia,* be determined objectively if it were possible for it to be calculated by making a comparison between the selling price of the product in question and its cost of production, which should disclose the amount of the profit margin; however the Commission has not done this since it has not analysed UBC's costs structure.

. . .

[267]   . . . the Commission has not adduced adequate legal proof of the facts and evaluations which formed the foundation of its finding that UBC had infringed Article 86 of the Treaty by directly and indirectly imposing unfair selling prices for bananas.

[268]   Article 1(c) of the decision must therefore be annulled.

[UBC's submission relating to administrative procedure was dismissed. The Court reduced the fine imposed on UBC from ECU 1 million to ECU 850,000.]

12.2.1   PRODUCT SUBSTITUTION

EUROPEMBALLAGE CORP. AND CONTINENTAL CAN CO. INC. v *COMMISSION* (Case 6/72) [1973] ECR 215, Court of Justice

The applicants sought annulment of a Commission Decision finding that Continental Can Company had infringed Article 86 of the Treaty by acquiring, through its subsidiary Europemballage Corporation, an 80% share of Thomassen & Drijver-Verbliva NV. Continental Can was a very powerful packaging company which had a large share in Schmalbach-Lubeca-Werke AG (SLW), a German packaging company. The deal increased even further Continental Can's market power in Europe. The applicants maintained that Article 86 had no application to mergers.

The Court of Justice disagreed, holding that the strengthening of the position of an undertaking may be an abuse and prohibited under Article 86. However, the Court considered that the Commission's economic analysis of the relevant product market was inadequate. It consequently annulled the Decision. (Article 173 proceedings.)

[32]   For the appraisal of SLW's dominant position and the consequences of the disputed merger, the definition of the relevant market is of essential significance, for the possibilities of competition can only be judged in relation to those characteristics of the products in question by virtue of which those products are particularly apt to satisfy an inelastic need and are only to a limited extent interchangeable with other products.

[33]   In this context recitals Nos 5 to 7 of the second part of the decision deal in turn with a 'market for light containers for canned meat products', a 'market for light containers for canned seafood', and a 'market for metal closures for the food packing industry, other than crown corks', all allegedly dominated by SLW and in which the disputed merger threatens to eliminate competition. The decision does not, however, give any details of how these three markets differ from each other, and must therefore be considered separately. Similarly, nothing is said about how these three markets differ from the general market for light metal containers, namely the market for metal containers for fruit and vegetables, condensed milk, olive oil, fruit juices and chemico-technical products. In order to be regarded as constituting a distinct market, the products in question must be individualized, not only by the mere fact that they are used for packing certain products, but by particular characteristics of production which make them specifically suitable for this purpose. Consequently, a dominant position on the market for light metal containers for meat and fish cannot be decisive, as long as it has not been proved that competitors from other sectors of the market for light metal containers are not in a position to enter this market, by a simple adaptation, with sufficient strength to create a serious counterweight.

[34]   Besides, there are in the decision itself indications which make one doubt whether the three markets are to be considered separately from other markets for light metal containers, indications which rather lead one to conclude that they are parts of a larger market. . . .

[35]   Since there are in the decision no data on the particular characteristics of metal containers for meat and fish and metal closures (other than crown corks) designed for the food packing industry, whereby these goods constitute separate markets which could be dominated by the manufacturer holding the highest share of this market, it is for this reason characterized by an uncertainty which has an effect on the other statements from which the decision infers the absence of real or potential competition in the market in question.

12.2.2   SIGNIFICANCE OF THE RELEVANT PRODUCT MARKET

ISTITUTO CHEMIOTERAPICO ITALIANO SPA AND COMMERCIAL SOLVENTS CORPORATION v COMMISSION (Cases 6 & 7/73) [1974] ECR 223, Court of Justice

The Commission had found that Commercial Solvents Corporation (CSC) and its subsidiary Istituto Chemioterapico Italiano of Milan (Istituto) had infringed Article 86 by refusing supplies of the raw material aminobutanol, used in the manufacture of an anti-tuberculosis drug called ethambutol, to Laboratorio Chimico Farmaceutico Giorgio Zoja (Zoja). Istituto and CSC sought annulment of the Decision. They disputed the Commission's definition of the relevant product market and contended that the refusal to supply did not constitute an abuse. (Article 173 proceedings.)

(a)   Dominant position
[9]   The applicants dispute the findings in the Decision in question according to which the CSC-Istituto group 'has a dominant position in the Common Market for the raw material necessary for the manufacture of ethambutol', on the basis that it has 'a world monopoly in the production and sale of nitropropane and aminobutanol'.

[10]   For this purpose they rely on documents which, they claim, establish that aminobutanol is produced by at least one other Italian company from butanone, that a third Italian company manufactures ethambutol from other raw material, that a French company produced nitropropane independently and that another undertaking has brought thiophenol on to the market, a product which is said to be used in Eastern Europe to produce ethambutol.

[11]   Finally CSC produced a statement by an expert according to which there is at least one practical method of producing nitropropane other than the method used by CSC and at least three other processes for producing aminobutanol without using nitropropane.

[12]   During the course of the administrative proceedings the applicants adduced some of these particulars in support of a request that before taking a decision the Commission should obtain an expert's report to verify the alleged monopoly of CSC as regards the production of raw material for the manufacture of ethambutol. The Commission rejected this request, since it considered that the particulars relied on, even if they were established, would not affect the substance of its Notice of Objections. In the present proceedings the applicants renewed their request for an expert's report on the point at issue.

[13]   The Commission replied, without being seriously challenged, that the production of nitropropane by the French company is at present only in an experimental stage and that the researches of this company have been developed only subsequently to the events in dispute. The information as to the possibility of manufacturing ethambutol by using thiophenol is too vague and uncertain to be seriously considered. The statement of the expert produced by CSC takes account only of wellknown processes which have not proved themselves capable of adaptation to use on an industrial scale and at prices enabling them to be marketed. The production by the two Italian companies mentioned is on a modest scale and intended for their own needs, so that the processes used do not lend themselves to substantial and competitive marketing.

[14]   The Commission has produced an expert's opinion from Zoja according to which the production of aminobutanol based on butonone on a substantial industrial scale would be possible only at considerable expense and at some risk, which is disputed by the applicants who rely on two experts, according to whom such production would not present any difficulties or cause excessive costs.

[15] This dispute is of no great practical importance since it relates mainly to processes of an experimental nature, which have not been tested on an industrial scale and which have resulted in only a modest production. The question is not whether Zoja, by adapting its installations and its manufacturing processes, would have been able to continue its production of ethambutol based on other raw materials, but whether CSC had a dominant position in the market in raw material for the manufacture of ethambutol. It is only the presence on the market of a raw material which could be substituted without difficulty for nitropropane or aminobutanol for the manufacture of ethambutol which could invalidate the argument that CSC has a dominant position within the meaning of Article 86. On the other hand reference to possible alternative processes of an experimental nature or which are practised on a small scale is not sufficient to refute the grounds of the Decision in dispute.

[16] It is not disputed that the large manufacturers of ethambutol on the world market, that is to say CSC itself, Istituto, American Cyanamid and Zoja use raw material manufactured by CSC. Compared with the manufacture and sale of ethambutol by these undertakings, those of the few other manufacturers are of minor importance. The Commission was therefore entitled to conclude 'that in the present conditions of economic competition it is not possible to have recourse on an industrial scale to methods of manufacture of ethambutol based on the use of different raw materials'.

[17] It was justified therefore in refusing the request for an expert's report.

[18] For the same reasons the request made during the course of the present proceedings must be rejected, since the fact that CSC had a dominant position on the world market in the production and sale of the raw material in question has been sufficiently established in law.

(b) The market to be considered

[19] The applicants rely on the sixth recital of Section II-C of the Decision in dispute for the conclusion that the Commission considers the relevant market for determining the dominant position to be that of ethambutol. Such a market, they say, does not exist since ethambutol is only a part of a larger market in anti-tuberculosis drugs, where it is in competition with other drugs which are to a large extent interchangeable. Since a market in ethambutol does not exist, it is impossible to establish a separate market in the raw material for the manufacture of this product.

[20] The Commission replies that it has taken into account the dominant position in the Common Market in the raw material necessary for the production of ethambutol.

[21] Both in Section II-B and in the part of Section II-C of the Decision which precedes the finding that the conduct of the applicants 'therefore constitutes an abuse of a dominant position within the meaning of Article 86' (II-C, fourth recital), the Decision deals only with the market in raw materials for the manufacture of ethambutol. In taking the view that 'the conduct in question limits the market in raw material as well as the production of ethambutol and thus constitutes one of the abuses expressly prohibited by the said Article' the Decision in dispute considers the market in ethambutol only for the purpose of determining the effects of the conduct referred to. Although such an examination may enable the effects of the alleged infringement to be better appreciated, it is nevertheless irrelevant as regards the determination of the relevant market to be considered for the purpose of a finding that a dominant position exists.

[22] Contrary to the arguments of the applicants it is in fact possible to distinguish the market in raw material necessary for the manufacture of a product from the market on which the product is sold. An abuse of a dominant position on the market in raw materials may thus have effects restricting competition in the market on which the derivatives of the raw material are sold and these effects must be taken into account in considering the effects of an infringement, even if the market for the derivative does not constitute a self-contained market. The arguments of the applicants in this respect and in consequence their request that an expert's report on this subject be ordered are irrelevant and must be rejected.

(c) Abuse of the dominant position

[23] The applicants state that they ought not to be held responsible for stopping supplies of aminobutanol to Zoja for this was due to the fact that in the spring of 1970 Zoja itself informed Istituto that it was cancelling the purchase of large quantities of

aminobutanol which had been provided for in a contract then in force between Istituto and Zoja. When at the end of 1970 Zoja again contacted Istituto to obtain this product, the latter was obliged to reply, after consulting CSC, that in the meantime CSC had changed its commercial policy and that the product was no longer available. The change of policy by CSC was, they claim, inspired by a legitimate consideration of the advantage that would accrue to it of expanding its production to include the manufacture of finished products and not limiting itself to that of raw material or intermediate products. In pursuance of this policy it decided to improve its product and no longer to supply aminobutanol save in respect of commitments already entered into by its distributors.

[24] It appears from the documents and from the hearing that the suppliers of raw material are limited, as regards the EEC, to Istituto, which, as stated in the claim by CSC, started in 1968 to develop its own specialities based on ethambutol, and in November 1969 obtained the approval of the Italian government necessary for the manufacture and in 1970 started manufacturing its own specialities. When Zoja sought to obtain further supplies of aminobutanol, it received a negative reply. CSC had decided to limit, if not completely to cease, the supply of nitropropane and aminobutanol to certain parties in order to facilitate its own access to the market for the derivatives.

[25] However, an undertaking being in a dominant position as regards the production of raw material and therefore able to control the supply to manufacturers of derivatives, cannot, just because it decides to start manufacturing these derivatives (in competition with its former customers) act in such a way as to eliminate their competition which in the case in question, would amount to eliminating one of the principal manufacturers of ethambutol in the Common Market. Since such conduct is contrary to the objectives expressed in Article 3(f) of the Treaty and set out in greater detail in Articles 85 and 86, it follows that an undertaking which has a dominant position in the market in raw materials and which, with the object of reserving such raw material for manufacturing its own derivatives, refuses to supply a customer, which is itself a manufacturer of these derivatives, and therefore risks eliminating all competition on the part of this customer, is abusing its dominant position within the meaning of Article 86. In this context it does not matter that the undertaking ceased to supply in the spring of 1970 because of the cancellation of the purchases by Zoja, because it appears from the applicants' own statement that, when the supplies provided for in the contract had been completed, the sale of aminobutanol would have stopped in any case.

. . .

(d) The effects on trade between Member States
[32] . . . By prohibiting the abuse of a dominant position within the market in so far as it may affect trade between Member States, Article 86 . . . covers abuse which may directly prejudice consumers as well as abuse which indirectly prejudices them by impairing the effective competitive structure as envisaged by Article 3(f) of the Treaty.

[33] The Community authorities must therefore consider all the consequences of the conduct complained of for the competitive structure in the Common Market without distinguishing between production intended for sale within the market and that intended for export. When an undertaking in a dominant position within the Common Market abuses its position in such a way that a competitor in the Common Market is likely to be eliminated, it does not matter whether the conduct relates to the latter's exports or its trade within the Common Market, once it has been established that this elimination will have repercussions on the competitive structure within the Common Market.

HUGIN KASSAREGISTER AB v COMMISSION (Case 22/78) [1979] ECR 1869, Court of Justice

A Swedish company, Hugin Kassaregister AB, and its British subsidiary, Hugin Cash Registers Ltd (referred to jointly in the judgment as 'Hugin'), sought annulment of a Commission Decision finding that they had infringed Article 86 by refusing to supply spare parts for Hugin cash registers to Liptons Cash Registers and Business Equipment Ltd, a British company. (Article 173 proceedings.)

Hugin's position on the market

. . .

[5]   . . . it is necessary, first, to determine the relevant market. In this respect account must be taken of the fact that the conduct alleged against Hugin consists in the refusal to supply spare parts to Liptons and, generally, to any independent undertaking outside its distribution network. The question is, therefore, whether the supply of spare parts constitutes a specific market or whether it forms part of a wider market. To answer that question it is necessary to determine the category of clients who require such parts.

[6]   In this respect it is established, on the one hand, that cash registers are of such a technical nature that the user cannot fit the spare parts into the machine but requires the services of a specialized technician and, on the other, that the value of the spare parts is of little significance in relation to the cost of maintenance and repairs. That being the case, users of cash registers do not operate on the market as purchasers of spare parts, however they have their machines maintained and repaired. Whether they avail themselves of Hugin's after-sales service or whether they rely on independent undertakings engaged in maintenance and repair work, their spare part requirements are not manifested directly and independently on the market. While there certainly exists amongst users a market for maintenance and repairs which is distinct from the market in new cash registers, it is essentially a market for the provision of services and not for the sale of a product such as spare parts, the refusal to supply which forms the subject-matter of the Commission's decision.

[7]   On the other hand, there exists a separate market for Hugin spare parts at another level, namely that of independent undertakings which specialize in the maintenance and repair of cash registers, in the reconditioning of used machines and in the sale of used machines and the renting out of machines. The role of those undertakings on the market is that of businesses which require spare parts for their various activities. They need such parts in order to provide services for cash register users in the form of maintenance and repairs and for the reconditioning of used machines intended for re-sale or renting out. Finally, they require spare parts for the maintenance and repair of new or used machines belonging to them which are rented out to their clients. It is, moreover, established that there is a specific demand for Hugin spare parts, since those parts are not interchangeable with spare parts for cash registers of other makes.

[8]   Consequently the market thus constituted by Hugin spare parts required by independent undertakings must be regarded as the relevant market for the purposes of the application of Article 86 of the facts of the case. It is in fact the market on which the alleged abuse was committed.

[9]   It is necessary to examine next whether Hugin occupies a dominant position on that market. In this respect Hugin admits that it has a monopoly in new spare parts. For commercial reasons any competing production of spare parts which could be used in Hugin cash registers is not conceivable in practice. Hugin argues nevertheless that another source of supply does exist, namely the purchase and dismantling of used machines. The value of that source of supply is disputed by the parties. Although the file appears to show that the practice of dismantling used machines is current in the cash register sector it cannot be regarded as constituting a sufficient alternative source of supply. Indeed the figures relating to Liptons' turnover during the years when Hugin refused to sell spare parts to it show that Liptons' business in the selling, renting out and repairing of Hugin machines diminished considerably, not only when expressed in absolute terms but even more so in real terms, taking inflation into account.

[10]   On the market for its own spare parts, therefore, Hugin is in a position which enables it to determine its conduct without taking account of competing sources of supply. There is therefore nothing to invalidate the conclusion that it occupies, on that market, a dominant position within the meaning of Article 86.

Hugin's conduct on the market

[11]   The Commission takes the view that Hugin abused its dominant position by refusing to supply spare parts to Liptons and, generally, to any independent undertaking outside its own distribution network. That practice, which results from Hugin's policy of restricting the maintenance and repair of Hugin cash registers to its own technical departments, is said to constitute an abuse in that its effect is to prevent users of Hugin

machines from choosing freely the undertaking which is to service and repair those machines and in that it has the effect of excluding any competition, and in particular a substantial competitor, in the sector of the servicing, maintenance, repair, renting out and reconditioning of Hugin machines.

[12]   Hugin alleges that those statements are unfounded. In its view the practice in question did not substantially restrict competition and has not eliminated Liptons from the market or threatened its existence. That practice is, moreover, objectively justified by legitimate considerations relating to the commercial policy adopted by Hugin, which entails providing maintenance and repair services of the highest quality.

[13]   More particularly, Hugin states that it seeks to reserve maintenance and repair services to itself not as profitable operations in themselves but in order to maintain the good reputation for reliability of its cash registers in the face of competition from other makes which, it alleges, is evidenced by the fact that it maintains those services at a loss. Hugin explains, furthermore, that it is not engaged in the market in used cash registers or that of renting out cash registers and that it offered to supply Liptons with the spare parts it needed to recondition used machines. Nevertheless, in accordance with its commercial policy, Hugin wishes to reserve to its own technical departments the maintenance and repair of all Hugin cash registers, even those sold second-hand or rented out by independent undertakings.

[The Court found that there was no infringement of Article 86 because Hugin's restrictive practices had no effect on inter-state trade.]

GENERAL MOTORS CONTINENTAL NV v COMMISSION (Case 26/75)
[1975] ECR 1367, Court of Justice

As the sole authorised agent of the manufacturer of Opel cars in Belgium, General Motors had the sole right under Belgian legislation to issue the approval certificates required for the import of second-hand Opel vehicles into Belgium. General Motors sought annulment of a Commission Decision finding that the company had infringed Article 86 by charging an excessive amount for the issue of certificates and the necessary inspections in respect of five imported Opel vehicles. (Article 173 proceedings.)

The dominant position

. . .

[7]   The approval procedure in the context of which the impositions in question were made is, by nature, a duty governed by public law which is so delegated by the Belgian State that, for each make of motor car the performance of this duty is reserved exclusively to the manufacturer or its sole authorized agent, appointed by the public authority.

[8]   However, although it entrusted this task of inspection to private undertakings the State took no measures to fix or limit the charge imposed for the service rendered.

[9]   This legal monopoly, combined with the freedom of the manufacturer or sole authorized agent to fix the price for its service, leads to the creation of a dominant position within the meaning of Article 86 as, for any given make, the approval procedure can only be carried out in Belgium by the manufacturer or officially appointed authorized agent under conditions fixed unilaterally by that party.

[10]   It thus emerges that the submission which the applicant bases on the fact that it held no dominant position must be rejected.

The abuse

[11]   It is possible that the holder of the exclusive position referred to above may abuse the market by fixing a price – for a service which it is alone in a position to provide – which is to the detriment of any person acquiring a motor vehicle imported from another Member State and subject to the approval procedure.

[12]   Such an abuse might lie, *inter alia*, in the imposition of a price which is excessive in relation to the economic value of the service provided, and which has the effect of curbing parallel imports by neutralizing the possibly more favourable level of prices applying in other sales areas in the Community, or by leading to unfair trade in the sense of Article 86(2)(a).

. . .

[20] This conduct on the part of the applicant, the truth of which is not contested by the Commission, cannot be regarded as an 'abuse' within the meaning of Article 86.

[21] The applicant has given an adequate explanation of the circumstances in which, in order to meet a new responsibility transferred from the State testing-stations to the manufacturers or authorized agents of the different makes of motor car in Belgium, it applied, for an initial period, to European cars a rate which was normally applied to vehicles imported from America.

[22] The absence of any abuse is also shown by the fact that very soon afterwards the applicant brought its rates into line with the real economic cost of the operation, that it bore the consequences of doing so by reimbursing those persons who had made complaints to it and that it did so before any intervention on the part of the Commission.

[23] Although the decision in question may be explained by the Commission's wish to react energetically against any tendency to abuse what is clearly a dominant position, its intervention was unjustified in the actual temporal and factual circumstances in which it took place.

[24] In these circumstances the contested decision must be annulled but the parties must bear their own costs.

12.2.3   THE RELEVANT GEOGRAPHIC MARKET

HILTI AG v *COMMISSION* **(Case T-30/89) [1991] ECR II-1439, Court of First Instance**

Hilti manufactured nail guns and also cartridge strips, cartridges and nails for use with its nail guns. Profix Distribution Ltd (previously Eurofix) and Bauco (UK) Ltd produced nails compatible with Hilti tools. Following complaints by Eurofix and Bauco alleging breaches of Article 86 by Hilti, the Commission instigated investigations and in a final Decision found that Hilti had infringed Article 86. Hilti sought annulment of that Decision. Profix and Bauco obtained leave to intervene in the proceedings. (Article 173 proceedings.)

[The decision of the Court of First Instance dismissing Hilti's application in its entirety was upheld on appeal to the Court of Justice (Case C-53/92P [1994] ECR I-667, [1994] 4 CMLR 614).]

[16] With regard to Hilti's behaviour the Commission states that:

– Hilti pursued a policy of supplying cartridge strips to certain end users or distributors (such as plant-hire companies) only when such cartridge strips were purchased with the necessary complement of nails ('tying' of cartridge strips and nails).

– It also attempted to block the sale of competitors' nails by a policy of reducing discounts for orders of cartridges without nails. The reduction of discounts was – again according to the Commission – based substantially on the fact that the customer was purchasing nails from Hilti's competitors.

– Hilti exerted pressure on independent distributors, notably in the Netherlands, not to fulfil certain export orders, notably to the United Kingdom.

– It had a policy of not supplying cartridges to independent nail manufacturers, in particular the interveners.

– It sought to delay or frustrate the grant of patent licences, which were available in the United Kingdom from 1984 onwards in the form of licences of right and were requested by the interveners, by trying to fix the royalty so high as to amount to a refusal.

– Hilti admitted to a policy of refusing to supply cartridge strips, even to longstanding customers, where it thought that the cartridge strips ordered might be sold on to independent nail manufacturers.

– It acknowledged that it refused to honour the guarantees on its tools when non-Hilti nails were used.

– Lastly, Hilti applied selective or discriminatory policies directed against the businesses of both competitors and competitors' customers – normally (the Commission claims) in the form of selective price cuts or other advantageous terms.

. . .

[The relevant geographic market]

[81] The documents before the Court show that there are large price differences for Hilti products between the Member States and that transport costs for nails are low.

Those two factors make parallel trading highly likely between the national markets of the Community. It must therefore be concluded that the Commission was right in taking the view that the relevant geographic market in this case is the Community as a whole. The applicant's argument on this point must therefore be rejected.

. . .

[Factors indicating dominance]

[89]   The Commission has proved that Hilti holds a market share of around 70% to 80% in the relevant market for nails. That figure was supplied to the Commission by Hilti following a request by the Commission for information pursuant to Article 11 of Regulation No. 17. As the Commission has rightly emphasized, Hilti was therefore obliged to supply information which, to the best of its knowledge, was as accurate as possible. Hilti's subsequent assertion that the figures were unsound is not corroborated by any evidence or by any examples showing them to be unreliable. Moreover, Hilti has supplied no other figures to substantiate its assertion. This argument of the applicant must therefore be rejected.

[90]   The Court of Justice has held . . . that the dominant position referred to in Article 86 of the Treaty relates to a position of economic strength enjoyed by an undertaking which enables it to prevent effective competition being maintained on the relevant market by giving it the power to behave to an appreciable extent independently of its competitors, customers and ultimately of its consumers; the existence of a dominant position may derive from a combination of several factors which, taken separately, are not necessarily determinative but among which a highly important one is the existence of very large market shares.

[91]   With particular reference to market shares, the Court of Justice has held . . . that very large shares are in themselves, and save in exceptional circumstances, evidence of a dominant position.

[92]   In this case it is established that Hilti holds a share of between 70% and 80% in the relevant market. Such a share is, in itself, a clear indication of the existence of a dominant position in the relevant market. . . .

[93]   Furthermore, as regards the other factors noted by the Commission as helping to maintain and reinforce Hilti's position in the market, it must be pointed out that the very fact that Hilti holds a patent and, in the United Kingdom, invokes copyright protection in relation to the cartridge strips designed for use in its own tools strengthens its position in the markets for Hilti-compatible consumables. Hilti's strong position in those markets was enhanced by the patents which it held at the time on certain elements of its DX 450 nail gun. It should be added that, as the Commission rightly contended, it is highly improbable in practice that a non-dominant supplier will act as Hilti did, since effective competition will normally ensure that the adverse consequences of such behaviour outweigh any benefits.

[94]   On the basis of all those considerations, the Court holds that the Commission was entitled to take the view that Hilti held a dominant position in the market in nails for the nail guns which it manufactures.

RTE v COMMISSION (Case T-69/89) [1991] ECR II-485, Court of First Instance
BBC v COMMISSION (Case T-70/89) [1991] ECR II-535, Court of First Instance
ITP LTD v COMMISSION (Case T-76/89) [1991] ECR II-575, Court of First Instance

RTE, BBC and ITP reserved the exclusive right in Ireland and Northern Ireland to publish weekly programme schedules for their own channels in their own magazines. The companies allowed newspapers and periodicals, under licence but free of charge, to publish daily listings of the programmes. When *Magill TV Guide* published weekly listings, the companies obtained an interim injunction in Ireland restraining Magill from further publication of weekly listings. It was held that the programme schedules were protected under the Copyright Act 1963 and that Magill had breached that copyright.

Magill complained to the Commission, alleging that RTE, BBC and ITP abused their dominant position by refusing to grant licences for the publication of their respective weekly listings. The Commission issued a Decision finding infringements of Article 86. Concurrent actions were brought by the three applicant broadcasting companies seeking annulment of the Commission Decision.

The applications were dismissed by the Court of First Instance. These rulings were upheld on appeal to the Court of Justice (Joined Cases C-241 & 242/91P, *RTE and ITP* v *Commission* [1995] ECR I-743). The three judgments of the Court of First Instance are set out in similar terms. Consequently, extracts are reproduced only from *RTE* v *Commission* (Case T-69/89). (Article 173 proceedings.)

– The existence of a dominant position

[63]   With regard to the applicant's position on the relevant market, the Court notes that RTE enjoyed, as a consequence of its copyright in its programme listings, the exclusive right to reproduce and market those listings. It was thus able, at the material time, to secure a monopoly over the publication of its weekly listings in the *RTE Guide*, a magazine specializing in its own programmes. Consequently, the applicant clearly held at that time a dominant position both on the market represented by its weekly listings and on the market for the magazines in which they were published in Ireland and Northern Ireland. Third parties such as Magill who wished to publish a general television magazine were in a position of economic dependence on the applicant, which was thus in a position to hinder the emergence of any effective competition on the market for information on its weekly programmes . . .

– The extent of the relevant geographical market

[64]   As regards the size of the relevant geographical market, the Court finds that the geographical market represented by Ireland and Northern Ireland, that is to say by the territory of one Member State and a part of that of another Member State, is undeniably a substantial part of the common market, without it being necessary to take into consideration the share of the Community market in television magazines represented by Ireland and Northern Ireland . . .

. . .

– The existence of an abuse

[73]   In the present case, it must be noted that the applicant, by reserving the exclusive right to publish its weekly television programme listings, was preventing the emergence on the market of a new product, namely a general television magazine likely to compete with its own magazine, the *RTE Guide*. The applicant was thus using its copyright in the programme listings which it produced as part of its broadcasting activity in order to secure a monopoly in the derivative market of weekly television guides. It appears significant, in that connection, that the applicant also authorized, free of charge, the publication of its daily listings and of highlights of its weekly programmes in the press in both Ireland and the United Kingdom. Moreover, it authorized the publication of its weekly listings in other Member States, without charging royalties.

Conduct of that type – characterized by preventing the production and marketing of a new product, for which there is potential consumer demand, on the ancillary market of television magazines and thereby excluding all competition from that market solely in order to secure the applicant's monopoly – clearly goes beyond what is necessary to fulfil the essential function of the copyright as permitted in Community law. The applicant's refusal to authorize third parties to publish its weekly listings was, in this case, arbitrary in so far as it was not justified either by the specific needs of the broadcasting sector, with which the present case is not concerned, or by those peculiar to the activity of publishing television magazines. It was thus possible for the applicant to adapt to the conditions of a television magazine market which was open to competition in order to ensure the commercial viability of its weekly publication, the *RTE Guide*. The applicant's conduct cannot, therefore, be covered in Community law by the protection conferred by its copyright in the programme listings.

NEDERLANDSCHE BANDEN-INDUSTRIE MICHELIN NV v COMMISSION
(Case 322/81) [1983] ECR 3461, Court of Justice

Michelin NV, a company incorporated in the Netherlands, brought an action for a declaration that a Commission Decision finding that it had acted in breach of Article 86 was void. (Article 173 proceedings.)

[3]   In Article 1 of the Decision in question the Commission declared that during the period between 1975 and 1980 Michelin NV infringed Article 86 of the EEC Treaty on the market in new replacement tyres for lorries, buses and similar vehicles by:

(a)   tying tyre dealers in the Netherlands to itself through the granting of selective discounts on an individual basis conditional upon sales 'targets' and discount percentages, which were not clearly confirmed in writing, and by applying to them dissimilar conditions in respect of equivalent transactions; and

(b)   granting an extra annual bonus in 1977 on purchases of tyres for lorries, buses and the like and on purchases of car tyres, which was conditional upon attainment of a 'target' in respect of car tyre purchases.

. . .

(1)   The substantial part of the common market at issue

[23]   The applicant's first submission under this head challenges the Commission's finding that the substantial part of the common market on which it holds a dominant position is the Netherlands. Michelin NV maintains that this geographical definition of the market is too narrow. It is contradicted by the fact that the Commission itself based its decision on factors concerning the Michelin group as a whole, such as its technological lead and financial strength which, in the applicant's view, relate to a much wider market or even the world market. The activities of Michelin NV's main competitors are world-wide too.

[24]   The Commission maintains that this objection concerns less the definition of the market than the criteria used to establish the existence of a dominant position. Since tyre manufacturers have on the whole chosen to sell their products on the various national markets through the intermediary of national subsidiaries, the competition faced by Michelin NV is on the Netherlands market.

[25]   The point to be made in this regard is that the Commission addressed its decision not to the Michelin group as a whole but only to its Netherlands subsidiary whose activities are concentrated on the Netherlands market. It has not been disputed that Michelin NV's main competitors also carry on their activities in the Netherlands through Netherlands subsidiaries of their respective groups.

[26]   The Commission's allegation concerns Michelin NV's conduct towards tyre dealers and more particularly its discount policy. In this regard the commercial policy of the various subsidiaries of the groups competing at the European or even the world level is generally adapted to the specific conditions existing on each market. In practice dealers established in the Netherlands obtain their supplies only from suppliers operating in the Netherlands. The Commission was therefore right to take the view that the competition facing Michelin NV is mainly on the Netherlands market and that it is at that level that the objective conditions of competition are alike for traders.

[27]   This finding is not related to the question whether in such circumstances factors relating to the position of the Michelin group and its competitors as a whole and to a much wider market may enter into consideration in the adoption of a decision as to whether a dominant position exists on the relevant product market.

[28]   Hence the relevant substantial part of the common market in this case is the Netherlands and it is at the level of the Netherlands market that Michelin NV's position must be assessed.

. . .

(b)   The application of Article 86 to a system of target discounts

[70]   As regards the application of Article 86 to a system of discounts conditional upon the attainment of sales targets, such as described above, it must be stated first of all that in prohibiting any abuse of a dominant position on the market in so far as it may affect trade between Member States Article 86 covers practices which are likely to affect the structure of a market where, as a direct result of the presence of the undertaking in question, competition has already been weakened and which, through recourse to methods different from those governing normal competition in products or services based on traders' performance, have the effect of hindering the maintenance or development of the level of competition still existing on the market.

[71]   In the case more particularly of the grant by an undertaking in a dominant position of discounts to its customers the Court has held . . . that in contrast to a quantity

discount, which is linked solely to the volume of purchases from the manufacturer concerned, a loyalty rebate, which by offering customers financial advantages tends to prevent them from obtaining their supplies from competing manufacturers, amounts to an abuse within the meaning of Article 86 of the Treaty.

[72]   As regards the system at issue in this case, which is characterized by the use of sales targets, it must be observed that this system does not amount to a mere quantity discount linked solely to the volume of goods purchased since the progressive scale of the previous year's turnover indicates only the limits within which the system applies. Michelin NV has moreover itself pointed out that the majority of dealers who bought more than 3,000 tyres a year were in any case in the group receiving the highest rebates. On the other hand the system in question did not require dealers to enter into any exclusive dealing agreements or to obtain a specific proportion of their supplies from Michelin NV, and that this point distinguishes it from loyalty rebates of the type which the Court had to consider in its judgment of 13 February 1979 in *Hoffmann-La Roche*.

[73]   In deciding whether Michelin NV abused its dominant position in applying its discount system it is therefore necessary to consider all the circumstances, particularly the criteria and rules for the grant of the discount, and to investigate whether, in providing an advantage not based on any economic service justifying it, the discount tends to remove or restrict the buyer's freedom to choose his sources of supply, to bar competitors from access to the market, to apply dissimilar conditions to equivalent transactions with other trading parties or to strengthen the dominant position by distorting competition.

[74]   It is in the light of those considerations that the submissions put forward by the applicant in answer to the two objections raised in the contested decision to the discount system in general, namely that Michelin NV bound tyre dealers in the Netherlands to itself and that it applied to them dissimilar conditions in respect of equivalent transactions, must be examined.

[After examining all the circumstances, the Court held that Michelin had abused its dominant position in the market for new replacement tyres for heavy vehicles by binding dealers in the Netherlands to itself by means of its discounting system. However, on the facts, Michelin had not infringed Article 86 by applying to its dealers dissimilar conditions in respect of equivalent transactions.]

12.2.4   THE RELEVANT TEMPORAL MARKET

See *United Brands Co.* v *Commission* (Case 27/76) [1978] ECR 207 at **12.2** above.

12.2.5   ASSESSING DOMINANCE

12.2.5.1   Market share

HOFFMANN-LA ROCHE & CO. AG v *COMMISSION* (Case 85/76)
[1979] ECR 461, Court of Justice

A Commission Decision found that Roche had a dominant position in the markets in a number of vitamins and had abused that position by concluding agreements with customers obliging them or inducing them, by means of fidelity discounts, to buy all or most of their requirements of vitamins exclusively or in preference from Roche. The company sought annulment of the Decision. (Article 173 proceedings.)

[On the assessment of dominance:]
[41]   . . . although the importance of the market shares may vary from one market to another the view may legitimately be taken that very large shares are in themselves, and save in exceptional circumstances, evidence of the existence of a dominant position.

An undertaking which has a very large market share and holds it for some time, by means of the volume of production and the scale of the supply which it stands for – without those having much smaller market shares being able to meet rapidly the demand from those who would like to break away from the undertaking which has the largest market share – is by virtue of that share in a position of strength which makes it an unavoidable trading partner and which, already because of this secures for it, at the very least during relatively long periods, that freedom of action which is the special feature of a dominant position.

. . .

[48] . . . the relationship between the market shares of the undertaking concerned and of its competitors, especially those of the next largest, the technological lead of an undertaking over its competitors, the existence of a highly developed sales network and the absence of potential competition are relevant factors, the first because it enables the competitive strength of the undertaking in question to be assessed, the second and third because they represent in themselves technical and commercial advantages and the fourth because it is the consequence of the existence of obstacles preventing new competitors from having access to the market.

. . .

[On abuse:]

[89] An undertaking which is in a dominant position on a market and ties purchasers – even if it does so at their request – by an obligation or promise on their part to obtain all or most of their requirements exclusively from the said undertaking abuses its dominant position within the meaning of Article 86 of the Treaty, whether the obligation in question is stipulated without further qualification or whether it is undertaken in consideration of the grant of a rebate.

The same applies if the said undertaking, without tying the purchasers by a formal obligation, applies, either under the terms of agreements concluded with these purchasers or unilaterally, a system of fidelity rebates, that is to say discounts conditional on the customer's obtaining all or most of its requirements – whether the quantity of its purchases be large or small – from the undertaking in a dominant position.

[90] Obligations of this kind to obtain supplies exclusively from a particular undertaking, whether or not they are in consideration of rebates or of the granting of fidelity rebates intended to give the purchaser an incentive to obtain his supplies exclusively from the undertaking in a dominant position, are incompatible with the objective of undistorted competition within the Common Market, because – unless there are exceptional circumstances which may make an agreement between undertakings in the context of Article 85 and in particular of paragraph (3) of that article, permissible – they are not based on an economic transaction which justifies this burden or benefit but are designed to deprive the purchaser of or restrict his possible choices of sources of supply and to deny other producers access to the market.

The fidelity rebate, unlike quantity rebates exclusively linked with the volume of purchases from the producer concerned, is designed through the grant of a financial advantage to prevent customers from obtaining their supplies from competing producers.

Furthermore the effect of fidelity rebates is to apply dissimilar conditions to equivalent transactions with other trading parties in that two purchasers pay a different price for the same quantity of the same product depending on whether they obtain their supplies exclusively from the undertaking in a dominant position or have several sources of supply.

Finally these practices by an undertaking in a dominant position and especially on an expanding market tend to consolidate this position by means of a form of competition which is not based on the transactions effected and is therefore distorted.

. . .

[102] All the contracts in question except five . . . contain a clause, called the English clause, under which the customer, if he obtains from competitors offers at prices which are more favourable than those under the contracts at issue may ask Roche to adjust its prices to the said offers; if Roche does not comply with this request, the customer, in derogation from his undertaking to obtain his requirements exclusively from Roche, is entitled to get his supplies from the said competitor without for that reason losing the benefit of the fidelity rebates provided for in the contracts in respect of the other purchases already effected or still to be effected by him from Roche.

[103] In the applicant's view this clause destroys the restrictive effect on competition both of the exclusivity agreements and of the fidelity rebates.

. . .

[107] . . . even in the most favourable circumstances, the English clause does not in fact remedy to a great extent the distortion of competition caused by the clauses obliging purchasers to obtain their requirements exclusively from Roche and by the fidelity

rebates on a market where an undertaking in a dominant position is operating and where for this reason the structure of competition has already been weakened.

In fact the English clause under which Roche's customers are obliged to inform it of more favourable offers made by competitors together with the particulars above mentioned – so that it will be easy for Roche to identify the competitor – owing to its very nature, places at the disposal of the applicant information about market conditions and also about the alternatives open to, and the actions of, its competitors which is of great value for the carrying out of its market strategy.

The fact that an undertaking in a dominant position requires its customers or obtains their agreement under contract to notify it of its competitor's offers, whilst the said customers may have an obvious commercial interest in not disclosing them, is of such a kind as to aggravate the exploitation of the dominant position in an abusive way.

Finally by virtue of the machinery of the English clause it is for Roche itself to decide whether, by adjusting its prices or not, it will permit competition.

[108]   It is able in this way, owing to the information which its own customers supply, to vary its market strategy in so far as it affects them and its competitors.

It follows from all these factors that the Commission's view that the English clauses incorporated in the contracts at issue were not of such a kind as to take them out of the category of abuse of a dominant position has been arrived at by means of a proper construction and application of Article 86 of the Treaty.

12.2.5.2   Duration of market position

See *Hoffmann-La Roche & Co. AG* v *Commission* (Case 85/76) [1979] ECR 461 at **12.2.5.1** above.

12.2.5.3   Financial and technical resources

See *United Brands Co.* v *Commission* (Case 27/76) [1978] ECR 207 at **12.2** above.

12.2.5.4   Vertical integration

See *United Brands Co.* v *Commission* (Case 27/76) [1978] ECR 207 at **12.2** and *Hoffmann-La Roche & Co. AG* v *Commission* (Case 85/76) [1979] ECR 461 at **12.2.5.1** above.

12.2.5.5   Conduct

See *United Brands Co.* v *Commission* (Case 27/76) [1978] ECR 207 at **12.2** above.

12.2.5.6   Barriers to entry

RTE, BBC, ITP v *Commission* (Cases T-69, 70, 76/89) [1991] ECR II-485, 535, 575 at **12.2.3** and *Hilti AG* v *Commission* (Case T-30/89) [1991] ECR II-1439 at **12.2.3**.

12.3   Abuse of a Dominant Position

12.3.1   UNFAIR PRICES

See *United Brands Co.* v *Commission* (Case 27/76) [1978] ECR 207 at **12.2** and *General Motors Continental NV* v *Commission* (Case 26/75) [1975] ECR 1367 at **12.2.2** above.

12.3.2   PRICE DISCRIMINATION

United Brands Co. v *Commission* (Case 27/76) [1978] ECR 207 at **12.2** above.

12.3.3   DISCOUNTS

Hoffmann-La Roche & Co. AG v *Commission* (Case 85/76) [1979] ECR 461 at **12.2.5.1**; *Nederlandsche Banden-Industrie Michelin NV* v *Commission* (Case 322/81) [1983] ECR 3461 at **12.2.3**; and *Hilti AG* v *Commission* (Case T-30/89) [1991] ECR II-1439 at **12.2.3** above.

12.3.4   PREDATORY PRICING

AKZO CHEMIE v *COMMISSION* (Case C-62/86) [1991] ECR I-3359, Court of Justice

AKZO produced organic peroxides, which are chemicals used in the plastics industry. It also produced compounds based on benzoyl peroxide (an organic peroxide), a chemical used for bleaching flour. The company had a much higher turnover in the plastics sector than the flour additives sector. Until 1979, Engineering and Chemical Supplies Ltd (ECS) produced organic peroxides only for the flour additives market. In that year it decided to extend its activities to the plastics market. In response, AKZO reduced its prices in the flour additives sector. AKZO brought an action before the Court of Justice for the annulment of a Commission Decision finding that the company acted in breach of Article 86. (Article 173 proceedings.)

[69]   It should be observed that . . . the concept of abuse is an objective concept relating to the behaviour of an undertaking in a dominant position which is such as to influence the structure of a market where, as a result of the very presence of the undertaking in question, the degree of competition is weakened and through recourse to methods which, different from those which condition normal competition in products or services on the basis of the transactions of commercial operators, has the effect of hindering the maintenance of the degree of competition still existing in the market or the growth of that competition.

[70]   It follows that Article 86 prohibits a dominant undertaking from eliminating a competitor and thereby strengthening its position by using methods other than those which come within the scope of competition on the basis of quality. From that point of view, however, not all competition by means of price can be regarded as legitimate.

[71]   Prices below average variable costs (that is to say, those which vary depending on the quantities produced) by means of which a dominant undertaking seeks to eliminate a competitor must be regarded as abusive. A dominant undertaking has no interest in applying such prices except that of eliminating competitors so as to enable it subsequently to raise its prices by taking advantage of its monopolistic position, since each sale generates a loss, namely the total amount of the fixed costs (that is to say, those which remain constant regardless of the quantities produced) and, at least, part of the variable costs relating to the unit produced.

[72]   Moreover, prices below average total costs, that is to say, fixed costs plus variable costs, but above average variable costs, must be regarded as abusive if they are determined as part of a plan for eliminating a competitor. Such prices can drive from the market undertakings which are perhaps as efficient as the dominant undertaking but which, because of their smaller financial resources, are incapable of withstanding the competition waged against them.

12.3.5   TIE-INS

See *Hoffmann-La Roche & Co. AG* v *Commission* (Case 85/76) [1979] ECR 461 at **12.2.5.1** and *Hilti AG* v *Commission* (Case T-30/89) [1991] ECR II-1439 at **12.2.3** above.

12.3.6   REFUSAL TO SUPPLY

See *Istituto Chemioterapico Italiano SpA and Commercial Solvents Corporation* v *Commission* (Cases 6 & 7/73) [1974] ECR 223 at **12.2.2**; *Hugin Kassaregister AB* v *Commission* (Case 22/78) [1979] ECR 1869 at **12.2.2**; *United Brands Co.* v *Commission* (Case 27/76) [1978] ECR 207 at **12.2** and *RTE, BBC, ITP* v *Commission* (Cases T-69, 70, 76/89) [1991] ECR II-485, 535, 575 at **12.2.3** above.

12.3.7   IMPORT AND EXPORT BANS

See *Hilti AG* v *Commission* (Case T-30/89) [1991] ECR II-1439 at **12.2.3** above.

12.3.8   MERGERS

Europemballage Corp. and Continental Can Co. Inc. v *Commission* (Case 6/72) [1973] ECR 215 at **12.2.1** above.

12.4   Effect on Trade Between Member States

See *Istituto Chemioterapico Italiano SpA and Commercial Solvents Corporation* v *Commission* (Cases 6 & 7/73) [1974] ECR 223 at **12.2.2** and *Hugin Kassaregister AB* v *Commission* (Case 22/78) [1979] ECR 1869 at **12.2.2**.

12.5   Application of Article 86 to Collective Dominance

See *Europemballage Corp. and Continental Can Co. Inc.* v *Commission* (Case 6/72) [1973] ECR 215 at **12.2.1** and *Istituto Chemioterapico Italiano SpA and Commercial Solvents Corporation* v *Commission* (Cases 6 & 7/73) [1974] ECR 223 at **12.2.2** above.

12.6   End of Chapter Assessment Question

Happy Boy plc (Happy Boy) is a UK manufacturer of pet food. The company's share of the European Community pet food market is negligible. Happy Boy's most successful product is its dog food, 'Bing', which it has supplied for many years to wholesalers throughout the Community. The company's massive financial investment in extensive advertising and research and development has paid off. Bing has become so popular that it is now a leading brand in many Member States and Happy Boy has increased its share of the Community dog food market to 45%. The company's nearest rivals in this market hold, respectively, 6%, 4% and 2% market shares.

Waggles (UK) Ltd (Waggles) has produced dog food for the domestic market since the early 1970s. Last year, the company announced its intention to start exporting to the continent of Europe. Waggles has just learned that Happy Boy is now offering Bing to new and existing customers at considerably reduced prices and is negotiating further discounts with individual wholesalers based upon agreed sales targets for the coming year. It has also emerged that the French wholesaler Ani-Domestique SA (AD) (an established customer of Happy Boy), which agreed to distribute Waggles' promotional literature to its own customers, has been informed by Happy Boy that as from the end of the month, no further orders from AD for Happy Boy's products will be met.

Advise Waggles.

12.7   End of Chapter Assessment Outline Answer

(Unless otherwise stated, references are to the Treaty of Rome.)

In view of Happy Boy's market position, it appears that there may be an infringement of Article 86 of the Treaty. Happy Boy, as a company engaged in commercial activity, is an 'undertaking' within the meaning of this Article. In order to show that a breach has occurred, Waggles must establish the three elements of Article 86 – that Happy Boy is in a dominant position within the common market or a substantial part of it, that the company has abused that position and that the abuse is capable of affecting trade between Member States.

In *United Brands*, the Court of Justice defined dominance as 'a position of economic strength enjoyed by an undertaking which enables it to hinder the maintenance of effective competition on the relevant market by allowing it to behave to an appreciable extent independently of its competitors and customers and ultimately of its consumers'.

Thus, Happy Boy's dominant position (if any) will be assessed in relation to the relevant market, both the relevant product market (RPM) and the relevant geographic market. There does not appear to be a seasonal or temporal market for the company's products. It is in Happy Boy's interest to define the relevant market as widely as possible. If it is established, for instance, that the relevant market is the Community pet food market, Happy Boy will not be in a dominant position because its market share is 'negligible'. Conversely, a narrowly drawn market, for instance the Community dog food market, will assist Waggles' case. In *United Brands* the company maintained that the RPM was fresh fruit, whereas the Commission argued, successfully, that the RPM was the much narrower banana market.

The two product markets to which the question refers, namely the pet food market and the dog food market should be considered. Without further information, a discussion of other possibilities (for instance the market in food for dogs and cats) would be inconclusive. The RPM is determined by looking at product substitution or interchangeability. In *United Brands*, the Court of Justice found only a small degree of substitutability between bananas and other fresh fruit because of the banana's special characteristics. Consequently, there was little cross-elasticity of demand. If there is high cross-elasticity of demand between dog food and other pet food, these products are likely to be in the same product market. Similarly, the market will be widened if there is cross-elasticity of supply.

So far as cross-elasticity of demand is concerned, the test is whether the consumer (people or animals?!) would be prepared to accept other kinds of pet food as substitutes for dog food. The characteristics of the product, its price and intended use should be considered. The term 'pet food' presumably covers such products as cat food, fish food, rabbit food and so on. Even if the price of these products is comparable to that of dog food, it would be difficult to argue that their characteristics and intended use are sufficiently similar to place them in the same market.

On the supply side, *Continental Can* established that cross-elasticity of supply is a potentially important feature of product substitution. Here, the test is whether potential competitors could easily switch their processes to the production of the product in question. Without further information, it is impossible to make a full assessment of cross-elasticity of supply in relation to Happy Boy's product. In the absence of detailed information, it is submitted that the RPM is dog food and that, since Happy Boy supplies Bing throughout the Community, the whole of the Community is the relevant geographic market. This is clearly a geographic market 'within the common market or a substantial part of it'.

We now turn to dominance within the relevant market. A very important indicator of economic strength is the size of an undertaking's market share. Although Happy Boy's share of the dog food market stands at less than 50%, the structure of the market (in which its nearest rivals hold only 6%, 4% and 2% shares) suggests a dominant position. The Court of Justice found United Brands to be dominant in the banana market where the company's share was between 40% and 45% and was several times greater than the share of its rivals.

The other factor indicating Happy Boy's dominance of the dog food market is its financial resources which, as was the case with United Brands, has enabled it to invest in extensive advertising of Bing. Advertising is a very powerful marketing strategy because it can have the effect of reducing cross-elasticity of demand. The company is also able to erect technological barriers to entry through its financial investment in research and development.

It is not known how long Happy Boy has held this market position, but we do know that the company has been supplying Bing throughout the Member States for a number of years and that its market share has been increasing. This could indicate an entrenchment of market power (*Hoffmann-La Roche*). An additional factor is Happy Boy's conduct. The fact that the company is able to cut its prices and to act independently of its competitors and customers by refusing supplies may be an indicator of dominance (*United Brands*).

No breach of Article 86 has occurred unless Happy Boy has abused a dominant position. Three kinds of potentially abusive behaviour can be identified: considerably reduced prices for its dog food, the further negotiated discounts based upon sales targets and the refusal to supply. The concern is that Happy Boy may be indulging in these practices in order to keep Waggles out of the dog food market in the continent of Europe.

Happy Boy's price reductions amount to predatory pricing if they cannot be characterised as 'normal' price competition. Predatory pricing is an anti-competitive abuse. Both the Court of Justice and the Commission have taken the view that 'normal' price competition becomes predatory pricing when its intention is to eliminate competitors from the market (*AKZO Chemie*). As well as looking for evidence of intention, it will also be necessary to determine whether prices have been cut to near cost or below cost. This may indeed be the case, as Bing is being offered at 'considerably' reduced prices. If Bing is being sold at a minimal profit or at a loss, Happy Boy will find it difficult to argue convincingly that it is not indulging in predatory pricing.

Discounting does not constitute an abuse if it is linked solely to the volume of purchases and is applied to all customers without discrimination. In *Michelin*, the Court of Justice distinguished quantity discounting and target discounting and held that the latter was abusive to the extent that it tied customers to purchasing supplies from the company. The system of target discounting reduced competition in the market for new replacement tyres for heavy vehicles by putting pressure on dealers to reach the agreed sales target. If Happy Boy's discounting system is not linked solely to volume of purchases, it will amount to an abuse. Moreover, as negotiations are being conducted separately with individual wholesalers, Happy Boy's discounting arrangements may amount to the application of 'dissimilar conditions to equivalent transactions with other trading parties, thereby placing them at a competitive disadvantage' (Article 86(c)) or to the imposition of unfair prices (Article 86(a)).

Happy Boy is to cease supplying its products to AD. Cases such as *Commercial Solvents* and *Hugin* establish that a refusal to supply with anti-competitive intent constitutes an abuse. In *United Brands,* the refusal to supply was a retaliatory action by the dominant undertaking against a wholesaler which had taken part in an advertising campaign for one of United Brands' competitors. This was condemned by the Court of Justice as an abuse. Similarly, Happy Boy's action appears to be retaliatory abusive behaviour.

The last of the three elements of Article 86, an effect on trade between Member States, is typically the most easily established. Happy Boy supplies its products, both pet food generally and more specifically Bing, throughout the Community. The company's abusive behaviour is clearly capable of affecting trade between Member States.

Waggles should be advised that, on the facts supplied, Happy Boy has infringed Article 86 by abusing a dominant position in the relevant market. Unlike the situation with restrictive agreements under Article 85, there is no possibility of exemption under Article 86. Article 86 is directly effective and may be relied upon by Waggles in the national court, which must apply the same remedies as are available for similar breaches of national law. Alternatively, as a party with a legitimate interest, Waggles may apply to the Commission for an investigation of the alleged infringement. Should an infringement be established, the Commission has the power to impose substantial fines.

CHAPTER THIRTEEN

COMPETITION LAW: ARTICLES 85 AND 86: ENFORCEMENT AND PROCEDURE

13.1 Overview of the Powers and Duties of the Commission: Regulation 17/62

THE TREATY OF ROME

Article 89
1. Without prejudice to Article 88, the Commission shall, as soon as it takes up its duties, ensure the application of the principles laid down in Articles 85 and 86. On application by a Member State or on its own initiative, and in cooperation with the competent authorities in the Member States, who shall give it their assistance, the Commission shall investigate cases of suspected infringement of these principles. If it finds that there has been an infringement, it shall propose appropriate measures to bring it to an end.

2. If the infringement is not brought to an end, the Commission shall record such infringement of the principles in a reasoned decision. The Commission may publish its decision and authorise Member States to take the measures, the conditions and details of which it shall determine, needed to remedy the situation.

EXTRACTS FROM REGULATION (EEC) NO. 17/62, FIRST REGULATION IMPLEMENTING ARTICLES 85 AND 86 OF THE TREATY
(1959–62) OJ (Special Edition), 87

[Preamble omitted.]

Article 1   Basic provision
Without prejudice to Articles 6, 7 and 23 of this Regulation, agreements, decisions and concerted practices of the kind described in Article 85(1) of the Treaty and the abuse of a dominant position in the market, within the meaning of Article 86 of the Treaty, shall be prohibited, no prior decision to that effect being required.

Article 2   Negative clearance
Upon application by the undertakings or associations of undertakings concerned, the Commission may certify that, on the basis of the facts in its possession, there are no grounds under Article 85(1) or Article 86 of the Treaty for action on its part in respect of an agreement, decision or practice.

Article 3   Termination of infringements
1. Where the Commission, upon application or upon its own initiative, finds that there is infringement of Article 85 or Article 86 of the Treaty, it may by decision require

the undertakings or associations of undertakings concerned to bring such infringement to an end.

2.   Those entitled to make application are:

(a)   Member States;

(b)   natural or legal persons who claim a legitimate interest.

3.   Without prejudice to the other provisions of this Regulation, the Commission may, before taking a decision under paragraph 1, address to the undertakings or associations of undertakings concerned recommendations for termination of the infringement.

Article 4   Notification of new agreements, decisions and practices

1.   Agreements, decisions and concerted practices of the kind described in Article 85(1) of the Treaty which come into existence after the entry into force of this Regulation and in respect of which the parties seek application of Article 85(3) must be notified to the Commission. Until they have been notified, no decision in application of Article 85(3) may be taken.

. . .

Article 6   Decisions pursuant to Article 85(3)

1.   Whenever the Commission takes a decision pursuant to Article 85(3) of the Treaty, it shall specify therein the date from which the decision shall take effect. Such date shall not be earlier than the date of notification.

. . .

Article 8   Duration and revocation of decisions under Article 85(3)

1.   A decision in application of Article 85(3) of the Treaty shall be issued for a specified period and conditions and obligations may be attached thereto.

2.   A decision may on application be renewed if the requirements of Article 85(3) of the Treaty continue to be satisfied.

3.   The Commission may revoke or amend its decision or prohibit specified acts by the parties:

(a)   where there has been a change in any of the facts which were basic to the making of the decision;

(b)   where the parties commit a breach of any obligation attached to the decision;

(c)   where the decision is based on incorrect information or was induced by deceit;

(d)   where the parties abuse the exemption from the provisions of Article 85(1) of the Treaty granted to them by the decision.

In cases to which subparagraphs (b), (c) or (d) apply, the decision may be revoked with retroactive effect.

Article 9   Powers

1.   Subject to review of its decision by the Court of Justice, the Commission shall have sole power to declare Article 85(1) inapplicable pursuant to Article 85(3) of the Treaty.

2.   The Commission shall have power to apply Article 85(1) and Article 86 of the Treaty. . . .

3.   As long as the Commission has not initiated any procedure under Articles 2, 3 or 6, the authorities of the Member States shall remain competent to apply Article 85(1) and Article 86 in accordance with Article 88 of the Treaty . . .

Article 10   Liaison with the authorities of the Member States

1.   The Commission shall forthwith transmit to the competent authorities of the Member States a copy of the applications and notifications together with copies of the most important documents lodged with the Commission for the purpose of establishing the existence of infringements of Articles 85 or 86 of the Treaty or of obtaining negative clearance or a decision in application of Article 85(3).

2.   The Commission shall carry out the procedure set out in paragraph 1 in close and constant liaison with the competent authorities of the Member States; such authorities shall have the right to express their views upon the procedure.

. . .

Article 11   Requests for information

1.   In carrying out the duties assigned to it by Article 89 and by provisions adopted under Article 87 of the Treaty, the Commission may obtain all necessary information from the Governments and competent authorities of the Member States and from undertakings and associations of undertakings.

2.   When sending a request for information to an undertaking or association of undertakings, the Commission shall at the same time forward a copy of the request to the competent authority of the Member State in whose territory the seat of the undertaking or association of undertakings is situated.

3.   In its request the Commission shall state the legal basis and the purpose of the request and also the penalties provided for in Article 15(1)(b) for supplying incorrect information.

4.   The owners of the undertakings or their representatives and, in the case of legal persons, companies or firms, or of associations having no legal personality, the persons authorised to represent them by law or by their constitution shall supply the information requested.

5.   Where an undertaking or association of undertakings does not supply the information requested within the time limit fixed by the Commission, or supplies incomplete information, the Commission shall by decision require the information to be supplied. The decision shall specify what information is required, fix an appropriate time limit within which it is to be supplied and indicate the penalties provided for in Article 15(1)(b) and Article 16(1)(c) and the right to have the decision reviewed by the Court of Justice.

6.   The Commission shall at the same time forward a copy of its decision to the competent authority of the Member State in whose territory the seat of the undertaking or association of undertakings is situated.

Article 12   Inquiry into sectors of the economy

1.   If in any sector of the economy the trend of trade between Member States, price movements, inflexibility of prices or other circumstances suggest that in the economic sector concerned competition is being restricted or distorted within the common market, the Commission may decide to conduct a general inquiry into that economic sector and in the course thereof may request undertakings in the sector concerned to supply the information necessary for giving effect to the principles formulated in Articles 85 and 86 of the Treaty and for carrying out the duties entrusted to the Commission.

. . .

3.   When making inquiries pursuant to paragraph 2, the Commission shall also request undertakings or groups of undertakings whose size suggests that they occupy a dominant position within the common market or a substantial part thereof to supply to the Commission such particulars of the structure of the undertakings and of their behaviour as are requisite to an appraisal of their position in the light of Article 86 of the Treaty.

. . .

Article 13   Investigations by the authorities of the Member States

1.   At the request of the Commission, the competent authorities of the Member States shall undertake the investigations which the Commission considers to be necessary under Article 14(1), or which it has ordered by decision pursuant to Article 14(3). The officials of the competent authorities of the Member States responsible for conducting these investigations shall exercise their powers upon production of an authorisation in writing issued by the competent authority of the Member State in whose territory the investigation is to be made. Such authorisation shall specify the subject matter and purpose of the investigation.

2.   If so requested by the Commission or by the competent authority of the Member State in whose territory the investigation is to be made, the officials of the Commission may assist the officials of such authorities in carrying out their duties.

Article 14   Investigating powers of the Commission

1.   In carrying out the duties assigned to it by Article 89 and by provisions adopted under Article 87 of the Treaty, the Commission may undertake all necessary investiga-

tions into undertakings and associations of undertakings. To this end the officials authorised by the Commission are empowered:

(a)   to examine the books and other business records;

(b)   to take copies of or extracts from the books and business records;

(c)   to ask for oral explanations on the spot;

(d)   to enter any premises, land and means of transport of undertakings.

2.   The officials of the Commission authorised for the purpose of these investigations shall exercise their powers upon production of an authorisation in writing specifying the subject matter and purpose of the investigation and the penalties provided for in Article 15(1)(c) in cases where production of the required books or other business records is incomplete. In good time before the investigation, the Commission shall inform the competent authority of the Member State in whose territory the same is to be made of the investigation and of the identity of the authorised officials.

3.   Undertakings and associations of undertakings shall submit to investigations ordered by decision of the Commission. The decision shall specify the subject matter and purpose of the investigation, appoint the date on which it is to begin and indicate the penalties provided for in Article 15(1)(c) and Article 16(1)(d) and the right to have the decision reviewed by the Court of Justice.

4.   The Commission shall take decisions referred to in paragraph 3 after consultation with the competent authority of the Member State in whose territory the investigation is to be made.

5.   Officials of the competent authority of the Member State in whose territory the investigation is to be made may, at the request of such authority or of the Commission, assist the officials of the Commission in carrying out their duties.

6.   Where an undertaking opposes an investigation ordered pursuant to this Article, the Member State concerned shall afford the necessary assistance to the officials authorised by the Commission to enable them to make their investigation. . . .

Article 15   Fines

1.   The Commission may by decision impose on undertakings or associations of undertakings fines of from 100 to 5,000 units of account where, intentionally or negligently:

(a)   they supply incorrect or misleading information in an application pursuant to Article 2 or in a notification pursuant to Articles 4 or 5; or

(b)   they supply incorrect information in response to a request made pursuant to Article 11(3) or (5) or to Article 12, or do not supply information within the time limit fixed by a decision taken under Article 11(5); or

(c)   they produce the required books or other business records in incomplete form during investigations under Article 13 or 14, or refuse to submit to an investigation ordered by decision issued in implementation of Article 14(3).

2.   The Commission may by decision impose on undertakings or associations of undertakings fines of from 1,000 to 1,000,000 units of account, or a sum in excess thereof but not exceeding 10% of the turnover in the preceding business year of each of the undertakings participating in the infringement where, either intentionally or negligently:

(a)   they infringe Article 85(1) or Article 86 of the Treaty; or

(b)   they commit a breach of any obligation imposed pursuant to Article 8(1).

In fixing the amount of the fine, regard shall be had both to the gravity and to the duration of the infringement.

3.   Article 10(3) to (6) shall apply.

4.   Decisions taken pursuant to paragraphs 1 and 2 shall not be of a criminal law nature.

5.   The fines provided for in paragraph 2(a) shall not be imposed in respect of acts taking place:

(a)   after notification to the Commission and before its decision in application of Article 85(3) of the Treaty, provided they fall within the limits of the activity described in the notification;

. . .

6.   Paragraph 5 shall not have effect where the Commission has informed the undertakings concerned that after preliminary examination it is of opinion that Article 85(1) of the Treaty applies and that application of Article 85(3) is not justified.

Article 16   Periodic penalty payments

1.   The Commission may by decision impose on undertakings or associations of undertakings periodic penalty payments of from 50 to 1,000 units of account per day, calculated from the date appointed by the decision, in order to compel them:

(a)   to put an end to an infringement of Article 85 or 86 of the Treaty, in accordance with a decision taken pursuant to Article 3 of this Regulation;

(b)   to refrain from any act prohibited under Article 8(3);

(c)   to supply complete and correct information which it has requested by decision taken pursuant to Article 11(5);

(d)   to submit to an investigation which it has ordered by decision taken pursuant to Article 14(3).

2.   Where the undertakings or associations of undertakings have satisfied the obligation which it was the purpose of the periodic penalty payment to enforce, the Commission may fix the total amount of the periodic penalty payment at a lower figure than that which would arise under the original decision.

. . .

Article 17   Review by the Court of Justice

The Court of Justice shall have unlimited jurisdiction within the meaning of Article 172 of the Treaty to review decisions whereby the Commission has fixed a fine or periodic penalty payment; it may cancel, reduce or increase the fine or periodic penalty payment imposed.

. . .

Article 19   Hearing of the parties and of third persons

1.   Before taking decisions as provided for in Articles 2, 3, 6, 7, 8, 15 and 16, the Commission shall give the undertakings or associations of undertakings concerned the opportunity of being heard on the matters to which the Commission has taken objection.

2.   If the Commission or the competent authorities of the Member State consider it necessary, they may also hear other natural or legal persons. Applications to be heard on the part of such persons shall, where they show a sufficient interest, be granted.

3.   Where the Commission intends to give negative clearance pursuant to Article 2 or take a decision in application of Article 85(3) of the Treaty, it shall publish a summary of the relevant application or notification and invite all interested third parties to submit their observations within a time limit which it shall fix being not less than one month. Publication shall have regard to the legitimate interest of undertakings in the protection of their business secrets.

Article 20   Professional secrecy

1.   Information acquired as a result of the application of Articles 11, 12, 13 and 14 shall be used only for the purpose of the relevant request or investigation.

2.   Without prejudice to the provisions of Articles 19 and 21, the Commission and the competent authorities of the Member States, their officials and other servants shall not disclose information acquired by them as a result of the application of this Regulation and of the kind covered by the obligation of professional secrecy.

3.   The provisions of paragraphs 1 and 2 shall not prevent publication of general information or surveys which do not contain information relating to particular undertakings or associations of undertakings.

Article 21   Publication of decisions

1.   The Commission shall publish the decisions which it takes pursuant to Articles 2, 3, 6, 7 and 8.

2.   The publication shall state the names of the parties and the main content of the decisions; it shall have regard to the legitimate interest of undertakings in the protection of their business secrets.

(Remaining provisions omitted.)

13.2   Negative Clearance and Exemption

13.2.1   RIGHTS OF THE PARTIES AND OF THIRD PARTIES

13.2.1.1   Access to the Commission's file

HERCULES CHEMICALS NV v COMMISSION (Case T-7/89) [1991] ECR II-1711,
Court of First Instance

A Commission Decision fined fifteen producers of polypropylene for infringing Article 85(1). One of the producers, Hercules, sought annulment of the Decision in so far as it pertained to that company. One ground of challenge related to the rights of the defence and, in particular, the Commission's refusal to disclose to Hercules certain documents which the company had requested from it. (Article 173 proceedings.)

[51]   The Court observes that regard for the rights of the defence requires that an applicant must have been put in a position to express, as it sees fit, its views on all the objections raised against it by the Commission in the statement of objections addressed to it and on the evidence which is to be used to support those objections and is mentioned by the Commission in the statement of objections or annexed to it . . .

[52]   However, regard for the rights of the defence does not require that an undertaking involved in a procedure pursuant to Article 85(1) of the EEC Treaty must be able to comment on all the documents forming part of the Commission's file since there are no provisions requiring the Commission to divulge the contents of its files to the parties concerned . . .

[53]   It must be observed, however, that in establishing a procedure for providing access to the file in competition cases, the Commission imposed on itself rules exceeding the requirements laid down by the Court of Justice. According to those rules, which are explained in the Twelfth Report on Competition Policy (pages 40 and 41), the Commission

. . . permits the undertakings involved in a procedure to inspect the file on the case.

. . . Undertakings are informed of the contents of the Commission's file by means of an annex to the statement of objections or to the letter rejecting a complaint, listing all the documents in the file and indicating documents or parts thereof to which they may have access.

They are invited to come and consult these documents on the Commission's premises. If an undertaking wishes to examine only a few of them the Commission may forward copies.

However, the Commission regards the documents listed below as confidential and accordingly inaccessible to the undertaking concerned:

(i)   documents or parts thereof containing other undertakings' business secrets;

(ii)   internal Commission documents, such as notes, drafts or other working papers;

(iii)   any other confidential information, such as documents enabling complainants to be identified where they wish to remain anonymous, and information disclosed to the Commission subject to an obligation of confidentiality.

The Commission may not depart from rules which it has thus imposed on itself . . .

[54]   It follows that the Commission has an obligation to make available to the undertakings involved in Article 85(1) proceedings all documents, whether in their favour or otherwise, which it has obtained during the course of the investigation, save where the business secrets of other undertakings, the internal documents of the Commission or other confidential information are involved.

13.3   The Commission's Investigative Powers

13.3.1   ARTICLE 14(3): COMPULSORY INVESTIGATIONS

NATIONAL PANASONIC (UK) LTD v *COMMISSION* (Case 136/79)
[1980] ECR 2033, Court of Justice

Suspecting that National Panasonic acted in breach of Article 85(1), the Commission decided to carry out an investigation pursuant to Article 14(3) of Regulation 17 and adopted a Decision to that effect. Two officials authorised by the Commission, together with an official of the Office of Fair Trading, arrived at Panasonic's offices, handed the Decision to the directors of the company and proceeded with the investigation without waiting for Panasonic's lawyers to arrive. The applicant maintained that the Commission's action infringed fundamental rights, in particular Article 8 of the European Convention for the Protection of Human Rights and Fundamental Freedoms. (Article 173 proceedings.)

[17]   The applicant . . . claims that by failing previously to communicate to it beforehand the decision ordering an investigation in question, the Commission has in this instance infringed fundamental rights of the applicant . . . The applicant relies in particular on Article 8 of the European Convention for the Protection of Human Rights and Fundamental Freedoms of 4 November 1950 whereby 'everyone has the right to respect for his private and family life, his home and his correspondence'. It considers that those guarantees must be provided *mutatis mutandis* also to legal persons.

[18]   . . . fundamental rights form an integral part of the general principles of law, the observance of which the Court of Justice ensures, in accordance with constitutional traditions common to the Member States and with international treaties on which the Member States have collaborated or of which they are signatories.

[19]   In this respect it is necessary to point out that Article 8(2) of the European Convention, in so far as it applies to legal persons, whilst stating the principle that public authorities should not interfere with the exercise of the rights referred to in Article 8(1), acknowledges that such interference is permissible to the extent to which it 'is in accordance with the law and is necessary in a democratic society in the interests of national security, public safety or the economic well-being of the country, for the prevention of disorder or crime, for the protection of health or morals, or for the protection of the rights and freedom of others'.

[20]   In this instance, as follows from the seventh and eighth recitals of the preamble to Regulation No. 17, the aim of the powers given to the Commission by Article 14 of that regulation is to enable it to carry out its duty under the EEC Treaty of ensuring that the rules on competition are applied in the common market. The function of these rules is, as follows from the fourth recital of the preamble to the Treaty, Article 3(f) and Articles 85 and 86, to prevent competition from being distorted to the detriment of the public interest, individual undertakings and consumers. The exercise of the powers given to the Commission by Regulation No. 17 contributes to the maintenance of the system of competition intended by the Treaty which undertakings are absolutely bound to comply with. In these circumstances, it does not therefore appear that Regulation No. 17, by giving the Commission the powers to carry out investigations without previous notification, infringes the right invoked by the applicant.

HOECHST AG v *COMMISSION* (Joined Cases 46/87 and 227/88)
[1989] ECR 2859, Court of Justice

Hoechst refused to submit to an Article 14(3) investigation on the grounds that it constituted an unlawful search. The Commission subsequently obtained a search warrant from the national authorities and proceeded with its search of Hoechst's premises. By Decision, the Commission imposed periodic penalties on the company for its refusal to comply with the Decision ordering the investigation.

Contesting the Commission Decision issued pursuant to Article 14(3), the applicant company claimed (*inter alia*) that the Commission exceeded its powers of investigation.

The Court of Justice rejected this submission, though it held that, in carrying out compulsory investigations, the Commission is required to respect the relevant procedural guarantees laid down by national law. However, notwithstanding those procedural rights, the applicant was not released from liability to fines with respect to its initial refusal to cooperate with the Commission's investigations. (Article 173 proceedings.)

[Procedural safeguards]

[10]   The applicant considers that the contested decision is unlawful inasmuch as it permitted the Commission's officials to take steps which the applicant describes as a search, which are not provided for under Article 14 of Regulation No. 17 and which infringe fundamental rights recognized by Community law. It adds that if that provision is to be interpreted as empowering the Commission to carry out searches, it is unlawful on the ground that it is incompatible with fundamental rights, for the protection of which it is necessary that searches should be carried out only on the basis of a judicial warrant issued in advance.

. . .

[26]   Both the purpose of Regulation No. 17 and the list of powers conferred on the Commission's officials by Article 14 . . . show that the scope of investigations may be very wide. In that regard, the right to enter any premises, land and means of transport of undertakings is of particular importance inasmuch as it is intended to permit the Commission to obtain evidence of infringements of the competition rules in the places in which such evidence is normally to be found, that is to say, on the business premises of undertakings.

[27]   That right of access would serve no useful purpose if the Commission's officials could do no more than ask for documents or files which they could identify precisely in advance. On the contrary, such a right implies the power to search for various items of information which are not already known or fully identified. Without such a power, it would be impossible for the Commission to obtain the information necessary to carry out the investigation if the undertakings concerned refused to cooperate or adopted an obstructive attitude.

[28]   Although Article 14 of Regulation No. 17 thus confers wide powers of investigation on the Commission, the exercise of those powers is subject to conditions serving to ensure that the rights of the undertakings concerned are respected.

[29]   In that regard, it should be noted first that the Commission is required to specify the subject-matter and purpose of the investigation. That obligation is a fundamental requirement not merely in order to show that the investigation to be carried out on the premises of the undertakings concerned is justified but also to enable those undertakings to assess the scope of their duty to cooperate while at the same time safeguarding the rights of the defence.

[30]   It should also be pointed out that the conditions for the exercise of the Commission's investigative powers vary according to the procedure which the Commission has chosen, the attitude of the undertakings concerned and the intervention of the national authorities.

[31]   Article 14 of Regulation No. 17 deals in the first place with investigations carried out with the cooperation of the undertakings concerned, either voluntarily, where there is a written authorization, or by virtue of an obligation arising under a decision ordering an investigation. In the latter case, which is the situation here, the Commission's officials have, *inter alia*, the power to have shown to them the documents they request, to enter such premises as they choose, and to have shown to them the contents of any piece of furniture which they indicate. On the other hand, they may not obtain access to premises or furniture by force or oblige the staff of the undertaking to give them such access, or carry out searches without the permission of the management of the undertaking.

[32]   The situation is completely different if the undertakings concerned oppose the Commission's investigation. In that case, the Commission's officials may, on the basis of Article 14(6) and without the cooperation of the undertakings, search for any information necessary for the investigation with the assistance of the national authorities, which are required to afford them the assistance necessary for the performance of their duties. Although such assistance is required only if the undertaking expresses its opposition, it may also be requested as a precautionary measure, in order to overcome any opposition on the part of the undertaking.

[33]   It follows from Article 14(6) that it is for each Member State to determine the conditions under which the national authorities will afford assistance to the Commission's officials. In that regard, the Member States are required to ensure that the Commission's action is effective, while respecting the general principles set out above. It follows that, within those limits, the appropriate procedural rules designed to ensure respect for undertakings' rights are those laid down by national law.

[34]   Consequently, if the Commission intends, with the assistance of the national authorities, to carry out an investigation other than with the cooperation of the undertakings concerned, it is required to respect the relevant procedural guarantees laid down by national law.

. . .

[Imposition and amount of the periodic penalty payment]

[62]   . . . the applicant considers that the definitive amount is disproportionate, because the applicant acted solely on the basis of the higher interests of ensuring a lawful and constitutional investigation procedure.

[63]   It should be noted in that regard that the applicant did not merely oppose specific measures, which, in its view, went beyond the powers of the Commission's officials; it refused to cooperate in any way in the implementation of the decision addressed to it ordering the investigation.

[64]   Such conduct is incompatible with the obligation imposed upon all persons subject to Community law to acknowledge that measures adopted by the institutions are fully effective so long as they have not been declared invalid by the Court and to recognize their enforceability unless the Court has decided to suspend the operation of the said measures . . . and cannot be justified on the basis of superior legal interests.

[65]   It follows from all the matters considered by the Court that there are no grounds for reducing the amount of the periodic penalty payment. That claim must therefore be rejected.

13.4   The Commission's Duty of Confidentiality

13.4.1   BUSINESS SECRETS

THE TREATY OF ROME

Article 214
The members of the institutions of the Community, the members of committees, and the officials and other servants of the Community shall be required, even after their duties have ceased, not to disclose information of the kind covered by the obligation of professional secrecy, in particular information about undertakings, their business relations or their cost components.

AKZO CHEMIE BV v COMMISSION (Case 53/85) [1986] ECR 1965, Court of Justice

Engineering and Chemical Supplies (ECS) made a complaint to the Commission alleging an infringement of Article 86 by AKZO (for the substantive issues see *AKZO Chemie* v *Commission* (Case C-62/86) at **12.3.4** above). AKZO sought annulment of the Commission's Decision, adopted in connection with this complaint, to communicate documents of a confidential nature to ECS. (Article 173 proceedings.)

[28]   . . . Article 19(3) which provides for the publication of notices prior to the granting of negative clearance or exemptions, and Article 21 which provides for the publication of certain decisions, both require the Commission to have regard to the legitimate interest of undertakings in the protection of their business secrets. Business secrets are thus afforded very special protection. Although they deal with particular situations, those provisions must be regarded as the expression of a general principle which applies during the course of the administrative procedure. It follows that a third party who has submitted a complaint may not in any circumstances be given access to

documents containing business secrets. Any other solution would lead to the unacceptable consequence that an undertaking might be inspired to lodge a complaint with the Commission solely in order to gain access to its competitors' business secrets.

[29]   It is undoubtedly for the Commission to assess whether or not a particular document contains business secrets. After giving an undertaking an opportunity to state its views, the Commission is required to adopt a decision in that connection which contains an adequate statement of the reasons on which it is based and which must be notified to the undertaking concerned. Having regard to the extremely serious damage which could result from improper communication of documents to a competitor, the Commission must, before implementing its decision, give the undertaking an opportunity to bring an action before the Court with a view to having the assessments made reviewed by it and to preventing disclosure of the documents in question.

13.4.2   STANLEY ADAMS' CASE

ADAMS v *COMMISSION* (Case 145/83) [1985] ECR 3539, Court of Justice

Mr Stanley Adams, a senior executive with Hoffmann-La Roche in Switzerland, passed information about the company's activities to the Commission. He subsequently left the company. Following investigations, Hoffmann-La Roche was found to have acted in breach of Article 86 and a heavy fine was imposed. Although Adams had asked for his identity as informant to be kept secret, the Commission disclosed information and documents which allowed the company to discover his identity. Adams left Switzerland. When he returned he was arrested by Swiss police on charges of economic espionage and held in prison in solitary confinement. During this time his wife committed suicide. On conviction by a Swiss criminal court, Adams was given a one year suspended sentence.

In an action brought under Article 215, Adams succeeded in his claim for compensation from the Commission for the damage which he had suffered, though the damages were reduced to one half because of the applicant's own negligence. (Article 215 proceedings.)

[34]   As regards the existence of a duty of confidentiality it must be pointed out that Article 214 of the EEC Treaty lays down an obligation, in particular for the members and the servants of the institutions of the Community 'not to disclose information of the kind covered by the obligation of professional secrecy, in particular information about undertakings, their business relations or their cost components'. Although that provision primarily refers to information gathered from undertakings, the expression 'in particular' shows that the principle in question is a general one which applies also to information supplied by natural persons, if that information is 'of the kind' that is confidential. That is particularly so in the case of information supplied on a purely voluntary basis but accompanied by a request for confidentiality in order to protect the informant's anonymity. An institution which accepts such information is bound to comply with such a condition.

. . . .

[53]   . . . the Community is bound to make good the damage resulting from the discovery of the applicant's identity by means of the documents handed over to Roche by the Commission. It must however be recognized that the extent of the Commission's liability is diminished by reason of the applicant's own negligence. The applicant failed to inform the Commission that it was possible to infer his identity as the informant from the documents themselves, although he was in the best position to appreciate and to avert that risk. Nor did he ask the Commission to keep him informed of the progress of the investigation of Roche, and in particular of any use that might be made of the documents for that purpose. Lastly, he went back to Switzerland without attempting to make any inquiries in that respect, although he must have been aware of the risks to which his conduct towards his former employer had exposed him with regard to Swiss legislation.

[54]   Consequently, the applicant himself contributed significantly to the damage which he suffered. In assessing the conduct of the Commission on the one hand and that

of the applicant on the other, the Court considers it equitable to apportion responsibility for that damage equally between the two parties.

It follows from all the foregoing considerations that the Commission must be ordered to compensate the applicant to the extent of one half of the damage suffered by him as a result of the fact that he was identified as the source of information regarding Roche's anti-competitive practices.

13.5 Privilege

AUSTRALIAN MINING & SMELTING EUROPE LTD v COMMISSION
(Case 155/79) [1982] ECR 1575, Court of Justice

A Commission Decision addressed to AM & S Europe required the company to produce for examination by Commission officials documents for which the company claimed legal privilege. AM & S sought annulment of that Decision. (Article 173 proceedings.)

[2]   The application is based on the submission that in all the Member States written communications between lawyer and client are protected by virtue of a principle common to all those States, although the scope of that protection and the means of securing it vary from one country to another. According to the applicant, it follows from that principle which, in its view, also applies 'within possible limits' in Community law, that the Commission may not when undertaking an investigation pursuant to Article 14(3) of Regulation No. 17 . . . claim production, at least in their entirety, of written communications between lawyer and client if the undertaking claims protection and takes 'reasonable steps to satisfy the Commission that the protection is properly claimed' on the ground that the documents in question are in fact covered by legal privilege.

. . .

(a)   The interpretation of Article 14 of Regulation No. 17

[15]   The purpose of Regulation No. 17 of the Council which was adopted pursuant to the first subparagraph of Article 87(1) of the Treaty, is, according to paragraph (2)(a) and (b) of that article, 'to ensure compliance with the prohibitions laid down in Article 85(1) and in Article 86' of the Treaty and 'to lay down detailed rules for the application of Article 85(3)'. The regulation is thus intended to ensure that the aim stated in Article 3(f) of the Treaty is achieved. To that end it confers on the Commission wide powers of investigation and of obtaining information by providing in the eighth recital in its preamble that the Commission must be empowered, throughout the Common Market, to require such information to be supplied and to undertake such investigations 'as are necessary' to bring to light infringements of Articles 85 and 86 of the Treaty.

[16]   In Articles 11 and 14 of the regulation, therefore, it is provided that the Commission may obtain 'information' and undertake the 'necessary' investigations, for the purpose of proceedings in respect of infringements of the rules governing competition. Article 14(1) in particular empowers the Commission to require production of business records, that is to say, documents concerning the market activities of the undertaking, in particular as regards compliance with those rules. Written communications between lawyer and client fall, in so far as they have a bearing on such activities, within the category of documents referred to in Articles 11 and 14.

[17]   Furthermore, since the documents which the Commission may demand are, as Article 14(1) confirms, those whose disclosure it considers 'necessary' in order that it may bring to light an infringement of the Treaty rules on competition, it is in principle for the Commission itself, and not the undertaking concerned or a third party, whether an expert or an arbitrator, to decide whether or not a document must be produced to it.

(b)   Applicability of the protection of confidentiality in Community law

[18]   However, the above rules do not exclude the possibility of recognizing, subject to certain conditions, that certain business records are of a confidential nature. Community law, which derives from not only the economic but also the legal interpenetration of the Member States, must take into account the principles and concepts common to the laws of those States concerning the observance of confidentiality, in particular, as regards certain communications between lawyer and client. That confidentiality serves the

requirements, the importance of which is recognized in all of the Member States, that any person must be able, without constraint, to consult a lawyer whose profession entails the giving of independent legal advice to all those in need of it.

. . .

[21]   . . . there are to be found in the national laws of the Member States common criteria inasmuch as those laws protect, in similar circumstances, the confidentiality of written communications between lawyer and client provided that, on the one hand, such communications are made for the purposes and in the interests of the client's rights of defence and, on the other hand, they emanate from independent lawyers, that is to say, lawyers who are not bound to the client by a relationship of employment.

[22]   Viewed in that context Regulation No. 17 must be interpreted as protecting, in its turn, the confidentiality of written communications between lawyer and client subject to those two conditions, and thus incorporating such elements of that protection as are common to the laws of the Member States.

[23]   As far as the first of those two conditions is concerned, in Regulation No. 17 itself, in particular in the eleventh recital in its preamble and in the provisions contained in Article 19, care is taken to ensure that the rights of the defence may be exercised to the full, and the protection of the confidentiality of written communications between lawyer and client is an essential corollary to those rights. In those circumstances, such protection must, if it is to be effective, be recognized as covering all written communications exchanged after the initiation of the administrative procedure under Regulation No. 17 which may lead to a decision on the application of Articles 85 and 86 of the Treaty or to a decision imposing a pecuniary sanction on the undertaking. It must also be possible to extend it to earlier written communications which have a relationship to the subject-matter of that procedure.

[24]   As regards the second condition, it should be stated that the requirement as to the position and status as an independent lawyer, which must be fulfilled by the legal adviser from whom the written communications which may be protected emanate, is based on a conception of the lawyer's role as collaborating in the administration of justice by the courts and as being required to provide, in full independence, and in the overriding interests of that cause, such legal assistance as the client needs. The counterpart of that protection lies in the rules of professional ethics and discipline which are laid down and enforced in the general interest by institutions endowed with the requisite powers for that purpose. Such a conception reflects the legal traditions common to the Member States and is also to be found in the legal order of the Community . . .

[25]   Having regard to the principles of the Treaty concerning freedom of establishment and the freedom to provide services the protection thus afforded by Community law, in particular in the context of Regulation No. 17, to written communications between lawyer and client must apply without distinction to any lawyer entitled to practise his profession in one of the Member States, regardless of the Member State in which the client lives.

[26]   Such protection may not be extended beyond those limits, which are determined by the scope of the common rules on the exercise of the legal profession as laid down in Council Directive 77/249/EEC . . . which is based in its turn on the mutual recognition by all the Member States of the national legal concepts of each of them on this subject.

13.6   Self-incrimination

ORKEM v COMMISSION **(Case 374/87) [1989] ECR 3283, Court of Justice**

The Commission adopted a Decision pursuant to its powers under Article 11(5) of Regulation 17/62 requiring Orkem to reply to certain questions concerning alleged breaches of Article 85(1). In an application for annulment of the Decision, the company maintained that the Commission sought to compel the applicant to give evidence against itself and in so doing breached the rights of the defence. (Article 173 proceedings.)

Breach of the rights of the defence

[18]   The applicant claims, essentially, that the Commission used the contested decision to compel it to incriminate itself by confessing to an infringement of the

competition rules and to inform against other undertakings. By doing so, the Commission has, in its view, infringed the general principle that no one may be compelled to give evidence against himself, which forms part of Community law in so far as it is a principle upheld by the laws of the Member States, by the European Convention for the Protection of Human Rights and Fundamental Freedoms of 4 November 1950 (hereinafter referred to as 'the European Convention') and by the International Covenant on Civil and Political Rights of 19 December 1966 . . . hereinafter referred to as 'the International Covenant'. It has thus, in the applicant's view, infringed the rights of the defence.

. . .

[26]   In the course of the preliminary investigation procedure, Regulation No. 17 expressly accords only certain guarantees to the undertaking under investigation. Thus, a decision requiring information to be supplied may be taken only after a prior request has proved unsuccessful. Similarly, a decision fixing the definitive amount of a fine or penalty payment, in a case where the undertaking concerned fails to supply the information required by the decision, may be adopted only after the undertaking in question has been given an opportunity to make its views known.

[27]   On the other hand, Regulation No. 17 does not give an undertaking under investigation any right to evade the investigation on the ground that the results thereof might provide evidence of an infringement by it of the competition rules. On the contrary, it imposes on the undertaking an obligation to cooperate actively, which implies that it must make available to the Commission all information relating to the subject-matter of the investigation.

[28]   In the absence of any right to remain silent expressly embodied in Regulation No. 17, it is appropriate to consider whether and to what extent the general principles of Community law, of which fundamental rights form an integral part and in the light of which all Community legislation must be interpreted, require, as the applicant claims, recognition of the right not to supply information capable of being used in order to establish, against the person supplying it, the existence of an infringement of the competition rules.

[29]   In general, the laws of the Member States grant the right not to give evidence against oneself only to a natural person charged with an offence in criminal proceedings. A comparative analysis of national law does not therefore indicate the existence of such a principle, common to the laws of the Member States, which may be relied upon by legal persons in relation to infringements in the economic sphere, in particular infringements of competition law.

[30]   As far as Article 6 of the European Convention is concerned, although it may be relied upon by an undertaking subject to an investigation relating to competition law, it must be observed that neither the wording of that article nor the decisions of the European Court of Human Rights indicate that it upholds the right not to give evidence against oneself.

[31]   Article 14 of the International Covenant, which upholds, in addition to the presumption of innocence, the right (in paragraph 3(g)) not to give evidence against oneself or to confess guilt, relates only to persons accused of a criminal offence in court proceedings and thus has no bearing on investigations in the field of competition law.

[32]   It is necessary, however, to consider whether certain limitations on the Commission's powers of investigation are implied by the need to safeguard the rights of the defence which the Court has held to be a fundamental principle of the Community legal order . . .

[33]   In that connection, the Court observed recently, in its judgment of 21 September 1989 in *Hoechst* v *Commission* (Joined Cases 46/87 & 227/88) [1989] ECR 2859 paragraph 15, that whilst it is true that the rights of the defence must be observed in administrative procedures which may lead to the imposition of penalties, it is necessary to prevent those rights from being irremediably impaired during preliminary inquiry procedures which may be decisive in providing evidence of the unlawful nature of conduct engaged in by undertakings and for which they may be liable. Consequently, although certain rights of the defence relate only to contentious proceedings which follow the delivery of the statement of objections, other rights must be respected even during the preliminary inquiry.

[34]   Accordingly, whilst the Commission is entitled, in order to preserve the useful effect of Article 11(2) and (5) of Regulation No. 17, to compel an undertaking to provide

all necessary information concerning such facts as may be known to it and to disclose to it, if necessary, such documents relating thereto as are in its possession, even if the latter may be used to establish, against it or another undertaking, the existence of anti-competitive conduct, it may not, by means of a decision calling for information, undermine the rights of defence of the undertaking concerned.

[35] Thus, the Commission may not compel an undertaking to provide it with answers which might involve an admission on its part of the existence of an infringement which it is incumbent upon the Commission to prove.

13.7 Interim Measures

CAMERA CARE v *COMMISSION* (Case 792/79R) [1980] 1 CMLR 334, Court of Justice

Hasselblad, a manufacturer, refused to supply Camera Care, a repairer and retailer, with its camera equipment. Camera Care asked the Commission to make an interim decision ordering Hasselblad to resume supplies. The Commission declined to do this, taking the view that there was no legal basis in Community law for such a procedure. Camera Care asked the Court of Justice to annul this decision. (Article 173 proceedings.)

Power of the Commission to adopt interim measures
[12] The hesitation shown by the Commission stems from the fact that Regulation 17 does not expressly confer upon the Commission, after receiving applications under Article 3 of the regulation or when proceeding on its own initiative under the same provision, the power to adopt interim measures pending the time when it is in a position to adjudicate upon the substance of the case.

[13] It is recalled that Article 3(1) of the regulation provides that: 'Where the Commission, upon application or upon its own initiative, finds that there is infringement of Article 85 or Article 86 of the Treaty, it may by decision require the undertakings . . . concerned to bring such an infringement to an end.' Paragraph (3) of the same Article adds that the Commission, before taking a decision under paragraph (1), may 'address to the undertakings . . . concerned recommendations for termination of the infringement.'

[14] It is obvious that in certain circumstances there may be a need to adopt interim protective measures when the practice of certain undertakings in competition matters has the effect of injuring the interests of some member-States, causing damage to other undertakings, or of unacceptably jeopardising the Community's competition policy. In such circumstances it is important to ensure that, whilst enquiries are being carried out no irreparable damage is caused such as could not be remedied by any decision which the Commission might take at the conclusion of the administrative procedure.

[15] Although it is true that, from the point of view of both the efficacy of competition law and the protection of the legitimate interests of the member-States or undertakings concerned, the adoption of protective measures may seem to be necessary in certain circumstances, the provisions of Regulation 17 must nevertheless be examined to see whether they can accommodate this legal requirement.

[16] It is as well to observe on this point that Article 3 of the regulation entitles the Commission to take two types of action in order to bring to an end any infringements that it finds: first, the Commission may take 'decisions' which, according to Article 189 of the Treaty, are binding upon those to whom they are addressed and which, according to Articles 15 and 16 of Regulation 17, may be accompanied by fines and periodic penalty payments; secondly, before taking a binding decision, the Commission is always entitled under Article 3(3) to address to the undertakings concerned 'recommendations for termination of the infringement.' The object of this last provision is to enable the Commission to inform the undertakings concerned of its assessment of the situation with regard to Community law in order to persuade them to comply with its point of view without immediately resorting to legal enforcement. It cannot, however, be construed as a limitation upon the practical ways in which the power to take a decision, which is the core of Article 3, may be exercised.

[17] As regards the right to take decisions conferred upon the Commission by Article 3(1), it is essential that it should be exercised in the most efficacious manner best suited to the circumstances of each given situation. To this end the possibility cannot be

excluded that the exercise of the right to take decisions conferred upon the Commission should be linked in successive stages so that a decision finding that there is an infringement may be preceded by any preliminary measures which may appear necessary at any given moment.

[18]   From this point of view the Commission must also be able, within the bounds of its supervisory task conferred upon it in competition matters by the Treaty and Regulation 17, to take protective measures to the extent to which they might appear indispensable in order to avoid the exercise of the power to make decisions given by Article 3 from becoming ineffectual or even illusory because of the action of certain undertakings. The powers which the Commission holds under Article 3(1) of Regulation 17 therefore include the power to take interim measures which are indispensable for the effective exercise of its functions and, in particular, for ensuring the effectiveness of any decisions requiring undertakings to bring to an end infringements which it has found to exist.

[19]   However, the Commission could not take such measures without having regard to the legitimate interests of the undertaking concerned by them. For this reason it is essential that interim measures be taken only in cases proved to be urgent in order to avoid a situation likely to cause serious and irreparable damage to the party seeking their adoption, or which is intolerable for the public interest. A further requirement is that these measures be of a temporary and conservatory nature and restricted to what is required in the given situation. When adopting them the Commission is bound to maintain the essential safeguards guaranteed to the parties concerned by Regulation 17, in particular by Article 19. Finally, the decisions must be made in such a form that an action may be brought upon them before the Court of Justice by any party who considers he has been injured.

13.8   The Role of the National Courts

13.8.1   COMFORT LETTERS IN THE NATIONAL COURTS

LANCÔME v *ETOS* (Case 99/79) [1980] ECR 2511, Court of Justice

Lancôme set up a selective distribution system for the sale of its perfumery and beauty products. Following a dispute as to the compatibility of its sales organisation with Article 85(1), Lancôme amended the relevant agreements. In this connection, the company subsequently received a letter from the Directorate General for Competition of the Commission giving 'soft' clearance to the agreements. The Court of Justice was asked by the national court to rule on the legal nature of letters of this kind. (Article 177 reference.)

[4]   . . .
The letter concludes in these terms:

I have the honour to inform you that in these circumstances, in view of the small share in the market in perfumery, beauty products and toiletries held by your company in each of the countries of the Common Market and in view of the fairly large number of competing undertakings of comparable size on that market and because the financial links between your company and the Oréal group do not seem in this case likely to influence the volume of your turnover for the products in question, the Commission considers that there is no longer any need, on the basis of the facts known to it, for it to take actions in respect of the above-mentioned agreements under the provisions of Article 85(1) of the Treaty of Rome. The file on this case may therefore be closed.

. . .

The legal nature of the letters in question

[7]   Article 87(1) of the Treaty authorized the Council to adopt any appropriate regulations or directives to give effect to the principles set out in Articles 85 and 86. In accordance with that authorization the Council has adopted regulations, in particular

Regulation No. 17 of 6 February 1962 . . . which gave the Commission power to adopt various categories of regulation, decision and recommendation.

[8]   The instruments thus placed at the Commission's disposal for the accomplishment of its task include decisions granting negative clearance and decisions applying Article 85(3). So far as decisions granting negative clearance are concerned, Article 2 of Regulation No. 17 of the Council provides that, upon application by the undertakings concerned, the Commission may certify that, on the basis of the facts in its possession, there are no grounds under Article 85(1) or Article 86 of the Treaty for action on its part in respect of an agreement, decision or practice. So far as decisions applying Article 85(3) are concerned, Article 6 *et seq.* of Regulation No. 17 provide that the Commission may adopt decisions declaring the provisions of Article 85(1) to be inapplicable to a given agreement provided that the latter has been notified to it or notification has been dispensed with by virtue of Article 4(2) of the regulation.

[9]   Regulation No. 17 and the regulations issued in implementation thereof lay down the rules which must be followed by the Commission in adopting the aforementioned decisions. Where the Commission intends to give negative clearance pursuant to Article 2 or take a decision in application of Article 85(3) of the Treaty, it is bound, in particular, by virtue of Article 19(3) of Regulation No. 17 to publish a summary of the relevant application or notification and invite all interested third parties to submit their observations within a time-limit which it shall fix. Decisions granting negative clearance and exemption must be published as provided for by Article 21(1) of that regulation.

[10]   It is plain that a letter such as that which was sent to Lancôme by the Directorate-General for Competition, which was despatched without publication as laid down in Article 19(3) of Regulation No. 17 and which was not published pursuant to Article 21(1) of the regulation, constitutes neither a decision granting negative clearance nor a decision in application of Article 85(3) within the meaning of Articles 2 and 6 of Regulation No. 17. As is stressed by the Commission itself, it is merely an administrative letter informing the undertaking concerned of the Commission's opinion that there is no need for it to take action in respect of the contract in question under the provisions of Article 85(1) of the Treaty and that the file on the case may therefore be closed.

[11]   Such a letter, which is based only upon the facts in the Commission's possession, and which reflects the Commission's assessment and brings to an end the procedure of examination by the department of the Commission responsible for this, does not have the effect of preventing national courts before which the agreements in question are alleged to be incompatible with Article 85 from reaching a different finding as regards the agreements concerned on the basis of the information available to them. Whilst it does not bind the national courts, the opinion transmitted in such letters nevertheless constitutes a factor which the national courts may take into account in examining whether the agreements or conduct in question are in accordance with the provisions of Article 85.

13.9   End of Chapter Assessment Questions

1(a)   Explain the terms 'negative clearance' and 'exemption' as they are used in the context of Articles 85 and 86 of the Treaty.

(b)   Outline the powers of the Commission in relation to the grant of negative clearance and exemption and the powers of the national courts with respect to Articles 85 and 86.

2   Outline the powers of the Commission in the enforcement of Articles 85 and 86. How are the rights and interests of undertakings protected?

3   What general advice would you give to an undertaking on the advantages and disadvantages of notifying an agreement?

13.10   End of Chapter Assessment Outline Answers

QUESTION 1

(a)   Negative clearance is a declaration by the Commission that an agreement or practice does not infringe Community competition law because it falls outside the scope of Articles 85 and 86.

Individual exemption is granted by the Commission in respect of agreements which breach Article 85(1) but which satisfy certain conditions. Individual exemption is a declaration that the provisions of Article 85(1) are inapplicable. The block exemptions, adopted in the form of Regulations, give automatic exemption to certain categories of agreements. Exemption is not available in relation to Article 86.

(b)   Both the Commission and the national courts are empowered to apply Articles 85(1) and 86 and the block exemptions. The Commission alone has the power to grant individual exemption.

QUESTION 2

Unless otherwise stated, all references are to Regulation 17/62.

Under Regulation 17/62, the Commission is given substantial powers in relation to the enforcement of Articles 85 and 86 of the Treaty. It is empowered to grant negative clearance (Article 2) and exemption (Article 9) and, acting either on its own initiative or on application by Member States or by persons who can claim a legitimate interest, to investigate infringements. Where it finds that an infringement has occurred it may by decision order the termination of that infringement (Article 3) and impose fines and periodic penalty payments upon the undertakings concerned (Articles 15 and 16). The Court of Justice has held that the Commission may take interim measures which are necessary to ensure the effective exercise of its functions (*Camera Care*).

In pursuit of its investigations, the Commission has the power to request all necessary information from Member States, from the competent authorities of Member States and from undertakings and associations of undertakings (Article 11), to conduct inquiries into whole sectors of the economy (Article 12) and to require the competent authorities of the Member States to undertake such investigations as the Commission considers necessary (Article 13). The Commission is empowered to enter the premises, land and means of transport of undertakings, to examine and take copies of books and business records and to conduct oral examinations (Article 14) either in the course of voluntary (Article 14(2)) or compulsory (Article 14(3)) investigations. Fines and periodic penalty payments may be imposed by the Commission on any undertaking which fails to comply with requests for information, supplies incorrect or misleading information or refuses to submit to a compulsory investigation (Articles 15 and 16).

These extensive powers are granted by Regulation 17/62 in order that the Commission can effectively exercise its central role in the elimination of restrictive practices and abusive behaviour by dominant undertakings which threaten or distort competition within the common market. At the same time, the Regulation seeks to provide protection for the rights and interests of undertakings by laying down strict procedural requirements. In addition, the Commission is bound by a duty of confidentiality and its decisions are subject to judicial review.

Before a final decision is issued by the Commission, the undertakings concerned have a right to be heard on any matters to which the Commission has a taken objection (Article 19(1)). The Court of First Instance has ruled that they also have a right of access to the Commission's file (with the exception of internal documents and documents containing business secrets) (*Hercules*). Other parties who 'show a sufficient interest' may also be heard (Article 19(3)). If the Commission intends to grant negative clearance or exemption, interested third parties must be invited to submit their observations (Article 19(3)).

Commission officials carrying out investigations must produce written authorisation specifying the subject matter and purpose of the investigation and the penalties for production of incomplete books or records (Article 14(2)). Before conducting a compulsory investigation, the Commission is required to adopt a decision setting out the matters described above and also specifying the date for commencement of the investigation and indicating the penalties for non-compliance and the right to judicial review of the decision (Article 14(3)).

An undertaking is not entitled to be given prior warning of a compulsory investigation by the Commission (*National Panasonic*). Nevertheless, the Commission has no right of forcible entry and if an undertaking opposes such an investigation, its rights must be protected by the procedural guarantees laid down by national law. Member States are required to give all necessary assistance to Commission officials to enable them to carry out their investigations (Article 14(6)).

The Commission's duty of confidentiality with respect to the non-disclosure of business secrets to third parties arises from the Treaty (Article 214) from case law (*AKZO Chemie*) and from Regulation 17/62 (Articles 19(3) and 21(2)). In *Adams v Commission*, breach of the general duty of confidentiality resulted in a successful action for damages under Article 215 of the Treaty. Subject to certain exceptions, communications between an undertaking and its lawyers relating to Commission proceedings are covered by legal professional privilege (*AM & S v Commission*). An undertaking is entitled to refuse to answer questions if its responses would be self-incriminating (*Orkem*).

Commission decisions under the competition rules are subject to judicial review by the Court of First Instance under Article 173 of the Treaty and appeal lies on points of law to the Court of Justice. An action for failure to act may be brought under Article 175 of the Treaty if the Commission fails in its duty to consider complaints of infringements brought by persons claiming a legitimate interest, though the Commission is under no obligation to pursue a complaint to final decision.

QUESTION 3

Unless otherwise stated, all references are to Regulation 17/62.

As there is no duty of notification under Community law, the decision whether or not to notify an agreement which may be in breach of Article 85(1) of the Treaty is essentially a business decision, albeit a decision which should be taken in the light of legal advice on the possible advantages and disadvantages.

Notification gives immunity from fines from the date of notification up to the Commission's final decision (Article 15(5)(a)). This is a significant advantage, though it should be pointed out that the Commission may withdraw this immunity at any time if its preliminary investigations indicate that the agreement does breach Article 85(1) and will not be eligible for individual exemption under Article 85(3) (Article 15(6)).

Notification is clearly advantageous if the Commission responds by issuing a formal decision granting negative clearance or individual exemption. However, in the vast majority of cases the Commission, rather than proceeding to a final decision, will issue only a comfort letter. These 'administrative letters' are not binding and cannot be challenged in the Court of First Instance or the Court of Justice. National courts may rely on them, but are not obliged to do so. Thus, comfort letters do not provide certainty as to the enforceability of an agreement.

Notification may be used as a commercial strategy to display confidence in the enforceability of an agreement. It also provides the opportunity to advance one's own case before any challenges to an agreement's legality reach the Commission.

Set against these advantages are a number of significant disadvantages. The management time and legal costs involved in completing a notification are major disincentives, as is the delay to be expected before the Commission issues its response. Despite the safeguards, there may be fears about confidentiality and the disclosure of business secrets. Moreover, an investigation of an undertaking's affairs, conducted as a result of notification, may unearth information relating to other agreements or practices which breach the Community competition rules. Finally, the Commission's response to a notification may be to ask for amendments to an agreement. If the respective bargaining strengths of the parties have altered since their initial negotiations, it is open to a now more powerful party to insist upon more favourable terms before agreeing to any amendment.

Because of the disadvantages outlined above, the best general advice to undertakings is, wherever possible, to avoid any need for notification by drafting agreements which fall outside the scope of Article 85(1) altogether or which comply with the terms of one of the block exemptions.

CHAPTER FOURTEEN

SEX DISCRIMINATION LAW

14.1 Article 119: Equal Pay

14.1.1 ARTICLE 119

THE TREATY OF ROME

Article 119

Each Member State shall during the first stage ensure and subsequently maintain the application of the principle that men and women should receive equal pay for equal work.

For the purpose of this Article, 'pay' means the ordinary basic or minimum wage or salary and any other consideration, whether in cash or in kind, which the worker receives, directly or indirectly, in respect of his employment from his employer.

Equal pay without discrimination based on sex means:

(a) that pay for the same work at piece rates shall be calculated on the basis of the same unit of measurement;

(b) that pay for work at time rates shall be the same for the same job.

14.1.2 DIRECT EFFECT OF ARTICLE 119

DEFRENNE v SA BELGE DE NAVIGATION AÉRIENNE (SABENA) (No. 2) (Case 43/75) [1976] ECR 455, Court of Justice

The action between Ms Defrenne, an air hostess, and her employer, the airline SABENA, concerned a claim by Ms Defrenne for compensation on the ground that between February 1963 and February 1966 she had been paid at a lower rate than male cabin crew. It was not disputed that the work of an air hostess was identical to that of a cabin steward, nor that there had been pay discrimination. The questions before the Court of Justice concerned the direct effect of Article 119. (Article 177 reference.)

[4] The first question asks whether Article 119 of the Treaty introduces 'directly into the national law of each Member State of the European Community the principle that men and women should receive equal pay for equal work and does it therefore, independently of any national provision, entitle workers to institute proceedings before national courts in order to ensure its observance?'

[5] If the answer to this question is in the affirmative, the question further enquires as from what date this effect must be recognized.

[6] The reply to the final part of the first question will therefore be given with the reply to the second question.

[7] The question of the direct effect of Article 119 must be considered in the light of the nature of the principle of equal pay, the aim of this provision and its place in the scheme of the Treaty.

[8] Article 119 pursues a double aim.

[9] First, in the light of the different stages of the development of social legislation in the various Member States, the aim of Article 119 is to avoid a situation in which undertakings established in States which have actually implemented the principle of

equal pay suffer a competitive disadvantage in intra-Community competition as compared with undertakings established in States which have not yet eliminated discrimination against women workers as regards pay.

[10]   Secondly, this provision forms part of the social objectives of the Community, which is not merely an economic union, but is at the same time intended, by common action, to ensure social progress and seek the constant improvement of the living and working conditions of their peoples, as is emphasized by the Preamble to the Treaty.

. . .

[12]   This double aim, which is at once economic and social, shows that the principle of equal pay forms part of the foundations of the Community.

. . .

[40]   . . .the principle of equal pay contained in Article 119 may be relied upon before the national courts and that these courts have a duty to ensure the protection of the rights which this provision vests in individuals, in particular as regards those types of discrimination arising directly from legislative provisions or collective labour agreements, as well as in cases in which men and women receive unequal pay for equal work which is carried out in the same establishment or service whether private or public.

. . .

The temporal effect of this judgment

[69]   The Governments of Ireland and the United Kingdom have drawn the Court's attention to the possible economic consequences of attributing direct effect to the provisions of Article 119, on the ground that such a decision might, in many branches of economic life, result in the introduction of claims dating back to the time at which such effect came into existence.

[70]   In view of the large number of people concerned such claims, which undertakings could not have foreseen, might seriously affect the financial situation of such undertakings and even drive some of them to bankruptcy.

[71]   Although the practical consequences of any judicial decision must be carefully taken into account, it would be impossible to go so far as to diminish the objectivity of the law and compromise its future application on the ground of the possible repercussions which might result, as regards the past, from such a judicial decision.

[72]   However, in the light of the conduct of several of the Member States and the views adopted by the Commission and repeatedly brought to the notice of the circles concerned, it is appropriate to take exceptionally into account the fact that, over a prolonged period, the parties concerned have been led to continue with practices which were contrary to Article 119, although not yet prohibited under their national law.

[73]   The fact that, in spite of the warnings given, the Commission did not initiate proceedings under Article 169 against the Member States concerned on grounds of failure to fulfil an obligation was likely to consolidate the incorrect impression as to the effects of Article 119.

[74]   In these circumstances, it is appropriate to determine that, as the general level at which pay would have been fixed cannot be known, important considerations of legal certainty affecting all the interests involved, both public and private, make it impossible in principle to reopen the question as regards the past.

[75]   Therefore, the direct effect of Article 119 cannot be relied on in order to support claims concerning pay periods prior to the date of this judgment, except as regards those workers who have already brought legal proceedings or made an equivalent claim.

14.1.3   THE MEANING OF 'PAY'

WORRINGHAM v *LLOYDS BANK LTD* (Case 69/80) [1981] ECR 767, Court of Justice

The two retirement benefit schemes operated by Lloyds Bank did not discriminate between men and women in so far as the payment of benefits was concerned. However, the different rules of the respective schemes resulted in differentiation in other respects. The national court raised questions concerning the interpretation of 'pay' within the meaning of Article 119. (Article 177 reference.)

[5]   The unequal pay alleged in this case before the national court originates, according to the plaintiffs in the main action, in the provisions of these two retirement benefits schemes relating to the requirement to contribute applicable to staff who have not yet attained the age of 25. In fact, it is clear from the order making the reference that men under 25 years of age are required to contribute 5% of their salary to their scheme whereas women are not required to do so. In order to cover the contribution payable by the men, Lloyds adds an additional 5% to the gross salary paid to those workers which is then deducted and paid directly to the trustees of the retirement benefits scheme in question on behalf of those workers.

[6]   The order making the reference also shows that workers leaving their employment who consent to the transfer of their accrued rights to the State pension scheme receive a 'contributions equivalent premium' which entitles them to the refund, subject to deductions in respect of a part of the cost of the premium and in respect of income tax, of their past contributions to the scheme of which they were members with interest; that amount includes, in the case of men under the age of 25 the 5% contribution paid in their name by the employer.

[7]   Finally, as follows from the information provided by the national court, the amount of the salary in which the above-mentioned 5% contribution is included helps to determine the amount of certain benefits and social advantages such as redundancy payments, unemployment benefits and family allowances, as well as mortgage and credit facilities.

. . .

[14]   Under the second paragraph of Article 119 of the EEC Treaty, 'pay' means, for the purpose of that provision, 'the ordinary basic or minimum wage or salary and any other consideration, whether in cash or in kind, which the worker receives, directly or indirectly, in respect of his employment from his employer'.

[15]   Sums such as those in question which are included in the calculation of the gross salary payable to the employee and which directly determine the calculation of other advantages linked to the salary, such as redundancy payments, unemployment benefits, family allowances and credit facilities, form part of the worker's pay within the meaning of the second paragraph of Article 119 of the Treaty even if they are immediately deducted by the employer and paid to a pension fund on behalf of the employee. This applies *a fortiori* where those sums are refunded in certain circumstances and subject to certain deductions to the employee as being repayable to him if he ceases to belong to the contractual retirement benefits scheme under which they were deducted.

. . .

[17]   In view of all these facts it is therefore necessary to reply to Question 1(a) that a contribution to a retirement benefits scheme which is paid by the employer in the name of the employees by means of an addition to the gross salary and which helps to determine the amount of that salary is 'pay' within the meaning of the second paragraph of Article 119 of the EEC Treaty.

GARLAND v *BRITISH RAIL ENGINEERING LTD* (Case 12/81) [1982] ECR 359, Court of Justice

Following retirement, former female employees of British Rail Engineering Ltd (BRE) were no longer eligible for the special travel facilities granted during their employment for their spouses and dependent children. Retired male employees continued to receive these facilities. Mrs Garland, an employee of BRE, claimed that this constituted discrimination contrary to Article 119. BRE contended that the special facilities were not 'pay' within the meaning of Article 119 because they were not granted pursuant to a contractual obligation. (Article 177 reference.)

[5]   . . . in paragraph 6 of its judgment of 25 May 1971 in *Defrenne* (Case 80/70) [1971] ECR 445, at p. 451, the Court stated that the concept of pay contained in the second paragraph of Article 119 comprises any other consideration, whether in cash or in kind whether immediate or future, provided that the worker receives it albeit indirectly, in respect of his employment from his employer.

[6]   According to the order making the reference for a preliminary ruling, when male employees of the respondent undertaking retire from their employment on reaching

retirement age they continue to be granted special travel facilities for themselves their wives and their dependent children.

[7]   A feature of those facilities is that they are granted in kind by the employer to the retired male employee or his dependants directly or indirectly in respect of his employment.

[8]   Moreover, it appears from a letter sent by the British Railways Board to the trade unions on 4 December 1975 that the special travel facilities granted after retirement must be considered to be an extension of the facilities granted during the period of employment.

[9]   It follows from those considerations that rail travel facilities such as those referred to by the House of Lords fulfil the criteria enabling them to be treated as pay within the meaning of Article 119 of the EEC Treaty.

[10]   The argument that the facilities are not related to a contractual obligation is immaterial. The legal nature of the facilities is not important for the purposes of the application of Article 119 provided that they are granted in respect of the employment.

[11]   It follows that where an employer (although not bound to do so by contract) provides special travel facilities for former male employees to enjoy after their retirement this constitutes discrimination within the meaning of Article 119 against former female employees who do not receive the same facilities.

BILKA-KAUFHAUS GMBH v *WEBER VON HARTZ* (Case 170/84) [1986] ECR 1607, Court of Justice

Part-time employees of Bilka-Kaufhaus GmbH, a department store company, were excluded from the company's supplementary occupational pension scheme unless they had worked full-time for the company for at least 15 years over a total period of 20 years. Mrs Weber von Hartz, a part-time employee who did not satisfy this condition, claimed that the scheme infringed Article 119. She asserted that it disadvantaged female workers because, as a result of their family responsibilities, women were more likely than men to take part-time employment. (Article 177 reference.)

[16]   In its judgment of 25 May 1971 *Defrenne* v *Belgium* (Case 80/70) [1971] ECR 445, the Court examined the question whether a retirement pension paid under a statutory social security scheme constitutes consideration received by the worker indirectly from the employer in respect of his employment, within the meaning of the second paragraph of Article 119.

[17]   The Court replied in the negative, taking the view that, although pay within the meaning of Article 119 could in principle include social security benefits, it did not include social security schemes or benefits, in particular retirement pensions directly governed by legislation which do not involve any element of agreement within the undertaking or trade concerned and are compulsory for general categories of workers.

[18]   In that regard the Court pointed out that social security schemes guarantee workers the benefit of a statutory scheme to which workers, employers and in some cases the authorities contribute financially to an extent determined less by the employment relationship between the employer and the worker than by considerations of social policy, so that the employer's contribution cannot be regarded as a direct or indirect payment to the worker for the purposes of the second paragraph of Article 119.

[19]   The question therefore arises whether the conclusion reached by the Court in that judgment is also applicable to the case before the national court.

[20]   It should be noted that according to the documents before the Court the occupational pension scheme at issue in the main proceedings, although adopted in accordance with the provisions laid down by German legislation for such schemes, is based on an agreement between Bilka and the staff committee representing its employees and has the effect of supplementing the social benefits paid under national legislation of general application with benefits financed entirely by the employer.

[21]   The contractual rather than statutory nature of the scheme in question is confirmed by the fact that, as has been pointed out above, the scheme and the rules governing it are regarded as an integral part of the contracts of employment between Bilka and its employees.

[22]   It must therefore be concluded that the scheme does not constitute a social security scheme governed directly by statute and thus outside the scope of Article 119. Benefits paid to employees under the scheme therefore constitute consideration received by the worker from the employer in respect of his employment, as referred to in the second paragraph of Article 119.

[23]   The case before the national court therefore falls within the scope of Article 119.

[24]   In the first of its questions the national court asks whether a staff policy pursued by a department store company excluding part-time employees from an occupational pension scheme constitutes discrimination contrary to Article 119 where that exclusion affects a far greater number of women than men.

[25]   In order to reply to that question reference must be made to the judgment of 31 March 1981 (*Jenkins* v *Kingsgate* (Case 96/80) [1981] ECR 911).

[26]   In that judgment the Court considered the question whether the payment of a lower hourly rate for part-time work than for full-time work was compatible with Article 119.

[27]   Such a practice is comparable to that at issue before the national court in this case: Bilka does not pay different hourly rates to part-time and full-time workers, but it grants only full-time workers an occupational pension. Since, as was stated above, such a pension falls within the concept of pay for the purposes of the second paragraph of Article 119 it follows that, hour for hour, the total remuneration paid by Bilka to full-time workers is higher than that paid to part-time workers.

[28]   The conclusion reached by the Court in its judgment of 31 March 1981 is therefore equally valid in the context of this case.

[29]   If, therefore, it should be found that a much lower proportion of women than of men work full time, the exclusion of part-time workers from the occupational pension scheme would be contrary to Article 119 of the Treaty where, taking into account the difficulties encountered by women workers in working full-time, that measure could not be explained by factors which exclude any discrimination on grounds of sex.

[30]   However, if the undertaking is able to show that its pay practice may be explained by objectively justified factors unrelated to any discrimination on grounds of sex there is no breach of Article 119.

[31]   The answer to the first question referred by the national court must therefore be that Article 119 of the EEC Treaty is infringed by a department store company which excludes part-time employees from its occupational pension scheme, where that exclusion affects a far greater number of women than men, unless the undertaking shows that the exclusion is based on objectively justified factors unrelated to any discrimination on grounds of sex. . . .

[32]   In its second question the national court seeks in essence to know whether the reasons put forward by Bilka to explain its pay policy may be regarded as 'objectively justified economic grounds', as referred to in the judgment of 31 March 1981, where the interests of undertakings in the department store sector do not require such a policy.

[33]   In its observations Bilka argues that the exclusion of part-time workers from the occupational pension scheme is intended solely to discourage part-time work, since in general part-time workers refuse to work in the late afternoon and on Saturdays. In order to ensure the presence of an adequate workforce during those periods it was therefore necessary to make full-time work more attractive than part-time work, by making the occupational pension scheme open only to full-time workers. Bilka concludes that on the basis of the judgment of 31 March 1981 it cannot be accused of having infringed Article 119.

[34]   In reply to the reasons put forward to justify the exclusion of part-time workers Mrs Weber von Hartz points out that Bilka is in no way obliged to employ part-time workers and that if it decides to do so it may not subsequently restrict the pension rights of such workers, which are already reduced by reason of the fact that they work fewer hours.

[35]   According to the Commission, in order to establish that there has been no breach of Article 119 it is not sufficient to show that in adopting a pay practice which in fact discriminates against women workers the employer sought to achieve objectives other than discrimination against women. The Commission considers that in order to justify such a pay practice from the point of view of Article 119 the employer must, as the Court

held in its judgment of 31 March 1981, put forward objective economic grounds relating to the management of the undertaking. It is also necessary to ascertain whether the pay practice in question is necessary and in proportion to the objectives pursued by the employer.

[36]   It is for the national court, which has sole jurisdiction to make findings of fact, to determine whether and to what extent the grounds put forward by an employer to explain the adoption of a pay practice which applies independently of a worker's sex but in fact affects more women than men may be regarded as objectively justified economic grounds. If the national court finds that the measures chosen by Bilka correspond to a real need on the part of the undertaking, are appropriate with a view to achieving the objectives pursued and are necessary to that end, the fact that the measures affect a far greater number of women than men is not sufficient to show that they constitute an infringement of Article 119.

[37]   The answer . . . must therefore be that under Article 119 a department store company may justify the adoption of a pay policy excluding part-time workers, irrespective of their sex, from its occupational pension scheme on the ground that it seeks to employ as few part-time workers as possible, where it is found that the means chosen for achieving that objective correspond to a real need on the part of the undertaking, are appropriate with a view to achieving the objective in question and are necessary to that end.

RINNER-KÜHN v FWW SPEZIAL-GEBÄUDEREINIGUNG GMBH & CO. KG
(Case 171/88) [1989] ECR 2743, Court of Justice

German legislation allowed employers to exclude from entitlement to sick pay part-time workers who worked no more than 10 hours per week or 45 hours per month. Mrs Rinner-Kühn, a part-time worker, brought proceedings against her employer, FWW, in connection with its refusal to pay her for a period of eight hours when she was absent from work owing to illness. The national court made a reference to the Court of Justice for a preliminary ruling on a question of interpretation of Article 119. (Article 177 reference.)

[7]   As the national court correctly observes, the continued payment of wages to an employee in the event of illness falls within the concept of 'pay' within the meaning of Article 119 of the Treaty.

. . .

[10]   It appears from the documents before the Court that under the German legislative provision in question only those employees whose contract of employment provides for a normal period of work of more than 10 hours a week or 45 hours a month are entitled to the continued payment of wages by their employer in the event of illness. Since such payment falls within the concept of 'pay' within the meaning of the second paragraph of Article 119, the German legislative provision in question accordingly allows employers to maintain a distinction relating to total pay between two categories of employees: those who work the minimum number of weekly or monthly hours and those who, although performing the same type of work, do not work the minimum number of hours.

[11]   It is also clear from the order requesting a preliminary ruling that in percentage terms considerably less women than men work the minimum number of weekly or monthly hours required to entitle an employee to the continued payment of wages in the event of inability to work due to illness.

[12]   In such a situation, it must be concluded that a provision such as that in question results in discrimination against female workers in relation to male workers and must, in principle, be regarded as contrary to the aim of Article 119 of the Treaty. The position would be different only if the distinction between the two categories of employees were justified by objective factors unrelated to any discrimination on grounds of sex (see the judgment of 13 May 1986 in *Bilka-Kaufhaus GmbH* v *Karin Weber von Hartz* (Case 170/84) [1986] ECR 1607).

[13]   In the course of the procedure, the German Government stated, in response to the question put by the Court, that workers whose period of work amounted to less than

10 hours a week or 45 hours a month were not as integrated in, or as dependent on, the undertaking employing them as other workers.

[14]   It should, however, be stated that those considerations, in so far as they are only generalizations about certain categories of workers, do not enable criteria which are both objective and unrelated to any discrimination on grounds of sex to be identified. However, if the Member State can show that the means chosen meet a necessary aim of its social policy and that they are suitable and requisite for attaining that aim, the mere fact that the provision affects a much greater number of female workers than male workers cannot be regarded as constituting an infringement of Article 119.

[15]   It is for the national court, which has sole jurisdiction to assess the facts and interpret the national legislation, to determine whether and to what extent a legislative provision, which, though applying independently of the sex of the worker actually affects a greater number of women than men, is justified by reasons which are objective and unrelated to any discrimination on grounds of sex.

[16]   The reply to the question referred by the national court must therefore be that Article 119 of the EEC Treaty must be interpreted as precluding national legislation which permits employers to exclude employees whose normal working hours do not exceed 10 hours a week or 45 hours a month from the continued payment of wages in the event of illness, if that measure affects a far greater number of women than men, unless the Member State shows that the legislation concerned is justified by objective factors unrelated to any discrimination on grounds of sex.

BARBER v GUARDIAN ROYAL EXCHANGE ASSURANCE GROUP
(Case C-262/88) [1990] ECR I-1889, Court of Justice

Mr Barber was a member of the contracted-out occupational pension scheme established by his employer, Guardian Royal Exchange Assurance Group. Under the scheme, normal pensionable age was 62 for men and 57 for women. In the event of redundancy, members of the scheme were entitled to an immediate pension subject to having attained the age of 55 for men or 50 for women. Staff made redundant before reaching these ages received cash benefits calculated according to years of service and a deferred pension at the normal pensionable age.

Mr Barber was made redundant at 52. He received the cash benefits to which he was entitled under Guardian's scheme, the statutory redundancy payment and an *ex gratia* payment. However, in accordance with the terms of the pension scheme he would not be entitled to a retirement pension until he reached 62. It was not disputed that a woman in the same position would have received a package of benefits of greater value than those paid to Mr Barber. Mr Barber claimed that he was the victim of unlawful sex discrimination. His claim eventually came before the Court of Appeal. Following Mr Barber's death, proceedings were continued by his widow on behalf of his estate.

The Court of Appeal referred to the Court of Justice a number of questions concerning (*inter alia*) the interpretation of Article 119. (Article 177 reference.)

[The first question concerned benefits paid to a worker in connection with compulsory redundancy.]

[12] . . . the concept of pay, within the meaning of the second paragraph of Article 119, comprises any other consideration, whether in cash or in kind, whether immediate or future, provided that the worker receives it, albeit indirectly, in respect of his employment from his employer (see, in particular, the judgment of 9 February 1982 in *Garland* v *British Rail Engineering* (Case 12/81) [1982] ECR 359, paragraph 5). Accordingly, the fact that certain benefits are paid after the termination of the employment relationship does not prevent them from being in the nature of pay, within the meaning of Article 119 of the Treaty.

[13]   As regards, in particular, the compensation granted to a worker in connection with his redundancy, it must be stated that such compensation constitutes a form of pay to which the worker is entitled in respect of his employment, which is paid to him upon termination of the employment relationship, which makes it possible to facilitate his adjustment to the new circumstances resulting from the loss of his employment and

which provides him with a source of income during the period in which he is seeking new employment.

[14]   It follows that compensation granted to a worker in connection with his redundancy falls in principle within the concept of pay for the purposes of Article 119 of the Treaty.

[15]   At the hearing, the United Kingdom argued that the statutory redundancy payment fell outside the scope of Article 119 of the Treaty because it constituted a social security benefit and not a form of pay.

[16]   In that regard it must be pointed out that a redundancy payment made by the employer, such as that which is at issue, cannot cease to constitute a form of pay on the sole ground that, rather than deriving from the contract of employment, it is a statutory or *ex gratia* payment.

[17]   In the case of statutory redundancy payments it must be borne in mind that, as the Court held in its judgment of 8 April 1976 in *Defrenne* v *Sabena* (Case 43/75) [1976] ECR 455, paragraph 40, Article 119 of the Treaty also applies to discrimination arising directly from legislative provisions. This means that benefits provided for by law may come within the concept of pay for the purposes of that provision.

[18]   Although it is true that many advantages granted by an employer also reflect considerations of social policy, the fact that a benefit is in the nature of pay cannot be called in question where the worker is entitled to receive the benefit in question from his employer by reason of the existence of the employment relationship.

[19]   In the case of *ex gratia* payments by the employer, it is clear from the judgment of 9 February 1982 in *Garland* (Case 12/81), cited above paragraph 10, that Article 119 also applies to advantages which an employer grants to workers although he is not required to do so by contract.

[20]   Accordingly . . . the answer to the first question must be that the benefits paid by an employer to a worker in connection with the latter' s compulsory redundancy fall within the scope of the second paragraph of Article 119 whether they are paid under a contract of employment, by virtue of legislative provisions or on a voluntary basis.

[The second question concerned retirement pensions paid out under contracted-out private occupational schemes, in particular pensions awarded in connection with compulsory redundancy.]

[22]   It must be pointed out in that regard that, in its judgment of 25 May 1971 in *Defrenne* v *Belgium* (Case 80/70) [1971] ECR 445, paragraphs 7 and 8 the Court stated that consideration in the nature of social security benefits is not in principle alien to the concept of pay. However, the Court pointed out that this concept, as defined in Article 119, cannot encompass social security schemes or benefits in particular retirement pensions directly governed by legislation without any element of agreement within the undertaking or the occupational branch concerned, which are compulsorily applicable to general categories of workers.

[23]   The Court noted that those schemes afford the workers the benefit of a statutory scheme, to the financing of which workers, employers and possibly the public authorities contribute in a measure determined less by the employment relationship than by considerations of social policy.

[24]   In order to answer the second question, therefore, it is necessary to ascertain whether those considerations also apply to contracted-out private occupational schemes such as that referred to in this case.

[25]   In that regard it must be pointed out first of all that the schemes in question are the result either of an agreement between workers and employers or of a unilateral decision taken by the employer. They are wholly financed by the employer or by both the employer and the workers without any contribution being made by the public authorities in any circumstances. Accordingly, such schemes form part of the consideration offered to workers by the employer.

[26]   Secondly, such schemes are not compulsorily applicable to general categories of workers. On the contrary, they apply only to workers employed by certain undertakings, with the result that affiliation to those schemes derives of necessity from the employment relationship with a given employer. Furthermore, even if the schemes in question are

established in conformity with national legislation and consequently satisfy the conditions laid down by it for recognition of contracted-out schemes, they are governed by their own rules.

[27]   Thirdly, it must be pointed out that, even if the contributions paid to those schemes and the benefits which they provide are in part a substitute for those of the general statutory scheme, that fact cannot preclude the application of Article 119. It is apparent from the documents before the Court that occupational schemes such as that referred to in this case may grant to their members benefits greater than those which would be paid by the statutory scheme, with the result that their economic function is similar to that of the supplementary schemes which exist in certain Member States, where affiliation and contribution to the statutory scheme is compulsory and no derogation is allowed. In its judgment of 13 May 1986 in *Bilka-Kaufhaus* v *Weber von Hartz* (Case 170/84) [1986] ECR 1607, the Court held that the benefits awarded under a supplementary pension scheme fell within the concept of pay, within the meaning of Article 119.

[28]   It must therefore be concluded that, unlike the benefits awarded by national statutory social security schemes, a pension paid under a contracted-out scheme constitutes consideration paid by the employer to the worker in respect of his employment and consequently falls within the scope of Article 119 of the Treaty.

[29]   That interpretation of Article 119 is not affected by the fact that the private occupational scheme in question has been set up in the form of a trust and is administered by trustees who are technically independent of the employer, since Article 119 also applies to consideration received indirectly from the employer.

[30]   The answer to the second question submitted by the Court of Appeal must therefore be that a pension paid under a contracted-out private occupational scheme falls within the scope of Article 119 of the Treaty.

[The third question concerned different pensionable ages for men and women in contracted out occupational schemes. Do these breach Article 119 even if they are based on the difference in pensionable ages between men and women in national statutory schemes?]

[32]   . . . it is sufficient to point out that Article 119 prohibits any discrimination with regard to pay as between men and women, whatever the system which gives rise to such inequality. Accordingly, it is contrary to Article 119 to impose an age condition which differs according to sex in respect of pensions paid under a contracted-out scheme, even if the difference between the pensionable age for men and that for women is based on the one provided for by the national statutory scheme.

. . .

Effects of this judgment ratione temporis

[41]   As the Court acknowledged in its judgment of 8 April 1976 in *Defrenne* (Case 43/75), cited above, it may, by way of exception, taking account of the serious difficulties which its judgment may create as regards events in the past, be moved to restrict the possibility for all persons concerned of relying on the interpretation which the Court, in proceedings on a reference to it for a preliminary ruling, gives to a provision. A restriction of that kind may be permitted only by the Court in the actual judgment which gives the ruling on the interpretation requested.

[42]   With regard to this case, it must be pointed out that Article 7(1) of Council Directive 79/7/EEC of 19 December 1978 on the progressive implementation of the principle of equal treatment for men and women in matters of social security . . . authorized the Member States to defer the compulsory implementation of the principle of equal treatment with regard to the determination of pensionable age for the purposes of granting old-age pensions and the possible consequences thereof for other benefits That exception has been incorporated in Article 9(a) of Directive 86/378/EEC of 24 July 1986 on the implementation of the principle of equal treatment for men and women in occupational social security schemes . . . which may apply to contracted-out schemes such as the one at issue in this case.

[43]   In the light of those provisions, the Member States and the parties concerned were reasonably entitled to consider that Article 119 did not apply to pensions paid

under contracted-out schemes and that derogations from the principle of equality between men and women were still permitted in that sphere.

[44] In those circumstances, overriding considerations of legal certainty preclude legal situations which have exhausted all their effects in the past from being called in question where that might upset retroactively the financial balance of many contracted-out pension schemes. It is appropriate, however, to provide for an exception in favour of individuals who have taken action in good time in order to safeguard their right. Finally, it must be pointed out that no restriction on the effects of the aforesaid interpretation can be permitted as regards the acquisition of entitlement to a pension as from the date of this judgment.

[45] It must therefore be held that the direct effect of Article 119 of the Treaty may not be relied upon in order to claim entitlement to a pension with effect from a date prior to that of this judgment, except in the case of workers or those claiming under them who have before that date initiated legal proceedings or raised an equivalent claim under the applicable national law.

KOWALSKA v FREIE UND HANSESTADT HAMBURG (Case C-33/89)
[1990] ECR I-2591, Court of Justice

Workers employed full-time (at least 38 hours per week) in the public service in Germany were entitled to a severance grant on retirement. Mrs Kowalska was refused the grant because she was a part-time employee. Did the severance grant constitute 'pay' within the meaning of Article 119? (Article 177 reference.)

[9] As the Court has held, the concept of pay, within the meaning of the second paragraph of Article 119 of the EEC Treaty, comprises any other consideration whether in cash or kind, whether immediate or future, provided that the worker receives it, albeit indirectly, from his employer in respect of his employment (see most recently the judgment of 17 May 1990 in *Barber* v *Guardian Royal Exchange Assurance Group* (Case C-262/88) [1990] ECR I-1889, paragraph 12). Accordingly, the fact that certain benefits are paid after the termination of the employment relationship does not prevent them from being in the nature of pay, within the meaning of Article 119 of the Treaty.

[10] In particular, compensation granted to a worker on termination of the employment relationship is a form of deferred pay to which the worker is entitled by reason of his employment but which is paid to him on termination of the employment relationship with a view to enabling him to adjust to the new circumstances arising from such termination. . . .

[11] It follows that, in principle, compensation paid to a worker on termination of the employment relationship falls within the definition of pay contained in Article 119 of the Treaty.

VROEGE v NCIV INSTITUUT VOOR VOLKSHUISVESTING BV AND STICHTING
PENSIOENFONDS NCIV (Case C-57/93) [1994] ECR I-4541, Court of Justice

Under the rules of the occupational pension scheme established by Mrs Vroege's employer, only men and unmarried women employed on permanent contracts and working a minimum number of hours were eligible for membership. Since Mrs Vroege had never worked the required hours, she was excluded from the scheme.

The rules of the scheme were changed to extend its scope with effect from 1 January 1991. However, the new rules did not give Mrs Vroege the right to membership of the scheme in respect of periods of service prior to 1 January 1991. She claimed that the new rules were discriminatory and therefore incompatible with Article 119. The Court of Justice was asked (*inter alia*) whether the right to equal pay within the meaning of Article 119 includes the right to join an occupational pension scheme and whether the temporal limitation on the effect of *Barber* applies to discriminatory rules relating to access to and membership of occupational pension schemes. (Article 177 reference.)

[12] In its judgment of 13 May 1986 in *Bilka-Kaufhaus GmbH* v *Hartz* (Case 170/84) [1986] ECR 1607, the Court has already held that if a pension scheme, although adopted

in accordance with the provisions laid down by national legislation, is based on an agreement with the employees or their representatives and if the public authorities are not involved in its funding, such a scheme does not constitute a social security scheme governed directly by statute and thus falls outside the scope of Article 119, and that benefits paid to employees under the scheme constitute consideration received by the employees from the employer in respect of their employment, as referred to in the second paragraph of Article 119 (paragraphs 20 and 22).

. . .

[15]   It also follows from the *Bilka* judgment, cited above, that Article 119 covers not only entitlement to benefits paid by an occupational pension scheme but also the right to be a member of such a scheme.

. . .

[27]   . . . the limitation of the effects in time of the *Barber* judgment concerns only those kinds of discrimination which employers and pension schemes could reasonably have considered to be permissible owing to the transitional derogations for which Community law provided and which were capable of being applied to occupational pensions.

[28]   It must be concluded that, as far as the right to join an occupational scheme is concerned, there is no reason to suppose that the professional groups concerned could have been mistaken about the applicability of Article 119.

[29]   It has indeed been clear since the judgment in the *Bilka* case that a breach of the rule of equal treatment committed through not recognizing such a right is caught by Article 119.

[30]   Moreover, since the Court's judgment in the *Bilka* case included no limitation in time, the direct effect of Article 119 can be relied upon in order retroactively to claim equal treatment in relation to the right to join an occupational pension scheme and this may be done as from 8 April 1976, the date of the *Defrenne* judgment in which the Court held for the first time that Article 119 has direct effect.

14.1.4   PENSIONS AS PAY

DEFRENNE v *BELGIUM (No. 1)* (Case 80/70) [1971] ECR 445, Court of Justice

Belgian legislation concerning the provision of retirement pensions for civil aviation air crews excluded air hostesses from the pension scheme in question. Ms Defrenne, an air hostess employed by SABENA airlines, claimed that this exclusion infringed the principle of equality contained in Article 119 because the benefit of the pension constituted 'pay' within the meaning of that Article. (Article 177 reference.)

[5]   According to first paragraph of Article 119 of the EEC Treaty Member States are required to ensure the application of the principle that men and women should receive equal pay for equal work.

[6]   The provision in the second paragraph of the article extends the concept of pay to any other consideration, whether in cash or in kind, whether immediate or future, provided that the worker receives it, albeit indirectly, in respect of his employment from his employer.

[7]   Although consideration in the nature of social security benefits is not therefore in principle alien to the concept of pay, there cannot be brought within this concept, as defined in Article 119, social security schemes or benefits, in particular retirement pensions, directly governed by legislation without any element of agreement within the undertaking or the occupational branch concerned, which are obligatorily applicable to general categories of workers.

[8]   These schemes assure for the workers the benefit of a legal scheme, the financing of which workers, employers and possibly the public authorities contribute in a measure determined less by the employment relationship between the employer and the worker than by considerations of social policy.

[9]   Accordingly, the part due from the employers in the financing of such schemes does not constitute a direct or indirect payment to the worker.

[10]   Moreover the worker will normally receive the benefits legally prescribed not by reason of the employer's contribution but solely because the worker fulfils the legal conditions for the grant of benefits.

[11]   These are likewise characteristics of special schemes which, within the framework of the general system of social security established by legislation, relate in particular to certain categories of workers.

[12]   It must therefore be found that situations involving discrimination resulting from the application of such a system are not subject to the requirements of Article 119 of the Treaty.

[13]   It follows from the above that a retirement pension established within the framework of a social security scheme laid down by legislation does not constitute consideration which the worker receives indirectly in respect of his employment from his employer within the meaning of the second paragraph of Article 119.

COLOROLL PENSION TRUSTEES LTD v JAMES RICHARD RUSSELL
(Case C-200/91) [1994] ECR I-4397, Court of Justice

After the financial collapse of the Coloroll group of companies, the trustees of the companies' various pension funds had the task of winding up the pension schemes and disposing of their assets. In this connection, in a representative action before the High Court, the trustees sought directions concerning the exercise of their functions.

The High Court referred to the Court of Justice a number of questions on the interpretation of Article 119. The Court of Justice was asked (*inter alia*) whether Article 119 has direct effect in respect of claims brought against the trustees of a pension fund and whether it is compatible with Article 119 to provide benefits or payments under a scheme calculated by reference to actuarial considerations (including, in particular, actuarial assumptions as to life expectancy) which produce differing results as between men and women. (Article 177 reference.)

[May Article 119 be relied on not only against the employer but also against the trustees of an occupational pension fund?]

[20]   As regards the question whether Article 119 may be relied on against the trustees of an occupational pension scheme, the Court in the *Barber* judgment, after finding that pensions paid under such schemes fall within the scope of Article 119, held that this conclusion remains valid even where the scheme has been set up in the form of a trust and is administered by trustees who are formally independent of the employer, since Article 119 also applies to consideration received indirectly from the employer (paragraphs 28 and 29).

[21]   The employer cannot therefore avoid the obligations incumbent on him under Article 119 by setting up the occupational pension scheme in the legal form of a trust.

[22]   The trustees themselves, although not party to the employment relationship, are required to pay benefits which do not thereby lose their character of pay within the meaning of Article 119. They are therefore bound, in so doing, to do everything within the scope of their powers to ensure compliance with the principle of equal treatment.

[Is it compatible with Article 119 to provide benefits or payments under a scheme calculated by reference to actuarial considerations (including, in particular, actuarial assumptions as to life expectancy) which produce differing results as between men and women?]

[73]   The actuarial factors in question are essentially those linked to demographic assumptions. Since women live on average longer than men, their future pensions are more costly than those of men and require the employer to pay higher contributions.

[74]   As a result of such actuarial factors being taken into account, the sums to which male employees are entitled, in particular where part of the pension is converted into a capital sum or where acquired rights are transferred, are lower than those to which female employees are entitled.

[75]   In answering the question whether such differences are compatible with Article 119, the first question is whether transfer benefits and capital-sum benefits constitute pay within the meaning of that article.

[76]   In its judgment of 22 December 1993 in *Neath* v *Hugh Steeper Ltd* (Case C-152/91) [1993] ECR I-6935, the Court has already ruled that the use of actuarial factors differing according to sex in funded defined-benefit occupational pension schemes does not fall within the scope of Article 119 of the Treaty.

[77]   In arriving at that conclusion the Court first reiterated that the concept of pay, within the meaning of the second paragraph of Article 119, comprises any consideration, whether in cash or in kind, whether immediate or future, provided that the worker receives it, albeit indirectly, from his employer in respect of his employment (paragraph 28).

[78]   It then found that the assumption underlying that approach was that the employer commits himself, albeit unilaterally, to pay his employees defined benefits or to grant them specific advantages and that the employees in turn expect the employer to pay them those benefits or provide them with those advantages. Anything that is not a consequence of that commitment and does not therefore come within the corresponding expectations of the employees falls outside the concept of pay (paragraph 29).

[79]   In the context of defined-benefit occupational pension schemes, such as those in question in the *Neath* case and in the present case, the employer's commitment to his employees concerns the payment, at a given moment in time, of a periodic pension for which the determining criteria are already known at the time when the commitment is made and which constitutes pay within the meaning of Article 119. However, that commitment does not necessarily have to do with the funding arrangements chosen to secure the periodic payment of the pension, which thus remain outside the scope of Article 119 (paragraph 30).

14.1.5   LIMITATIONS ON THE *BARBER* JUDGMENT

PROTOCOL CONCERNING ARTICLE 119 OF THE TREATY ESTABLISHING THE EUROPEAN COMMUNITY

THE HIGH CONTRACTING PARTIES,
    HAVE AGREED UPON the following provision, which shall be annexed to the Treaty establishing the European Community:
    For the purposes of Article 119 of this Treaty, benefits under occupational social security schemes shall not be considered as remuneration if and in so far as they are attributable to periods of employment prior to 17 May 1990, except in the case of workers or those claiming under them who have before that date initiated legal proceedings or introduced an equivalent claim under the applicable national law.

FISSCHER v VOORHUIS HENGELO BV AND STICHTING BEDRIJFSPENSIOENFONDS VOOR DE DETAILHANDEL
(Case C-128/93) [1994] ECR I-4583, Court of Justice

Up to 31 December 1990 Mrs Fisscher was not able to join her employer's occupational pension scheme because the rules of the scheme excluded married women. From 1 January 1991, the scheme was extended to married women and Mrs Fisscher was able to become a member with effect from 1 January 1988. Asserting that the old rules were incompatible with Article 119, Mrs Fisscher claimed retroactive membership as from 1 January 1978, the date on which her employment with Voorhuis commenced.

    The Court of Justice reiterated that Article 119 covers the right to be a member of an occupational pension scheme and that the *Barber* limitation does not apply to such a right. However, the fact that a worker can claim retroactively the right to join an occupational pension scheme does not allow that worker to avoid paying back-dated contributions. (Article 177 reference.)

[34]   As far as the right to be a member of an occupational scheme is concerned, Article 119 requires that a worker should not suffer discrimination based on sex by being excluded from such a scheme.

[35]   This means that, where such discrimination has been suffered, equal treatment is to be achieved by placing the worker discriminated against in the same situation as that of workers of the other sex.

[36]   It follows that the worker cannot claim more favourable treatment, particularly in financial terms, than he would have had if he had been duly accepted as a member.

NEATH v HUGH STEEPER LTD (Case C-152/91) [1995] 2 CMLR 357, Court of Justice

Mr Neath was a member of his employer's contracted-out occupational pension scheme. When he was made redundant, he had a choice between two options available under the scheme. He could either have his acquired pension rights transferred to another pension scheme or receive a deferred pension at normal retirement age, with the further option to have part of that deferred pension paid as a capital sum.

Mr Neath discovered that, because of actuarial factors used in calculating employer contributions to the scheme, he would receive less under either of these options than a woman in the same circumstances. One of the questions referred to the Court of Justice by the Leeds Industrial Tribunal concerned the compatibility with Article 119 of the use in private occupational pension schemes of actuarial factors differing according to sex. (Article 177 reference.)

[19]   It appears that the occupational pension scheme of which Mr Neath was a member when he was made redundant is a defined-benefit/final-salary scheme which provides employees reaching retirement age with a defined pension corresponding to one-sixtieth of their final salary for each year of service.

[20]   The scheme is contributory, in the sense that it is funded not only by contributions from the employer but also by contributions from employees.

[21]   The employees' contributions correspond to a percentage, identical for men and women, of their salary.

[22]   The employer's contributions, however, which are calculated in the aggregate, vary over time, so as to cover the balance of the cost of the pensions promised. They are also higher for female employees than for male employees.

[23]   This variability and inequality are due to the use of actuarial factors in the mechanism for funding the scheme. The aim of an occupational retirement pension scheme being to provide for the future payment of periodic pensions, the scheme's financial resources, accrued through funding, must be adjusted to the pensions which, according to forecasts, will have to be paid. The assessments needed to give effect to this system are based on a number of objective factors, such as the return on the scheme's investments, the rate of increase in salaries and demographic assumptions, in particular those relating to the life expectancy of workers.

[24]   The fact that women live on average longer than men is one of the actuarial factors taken into account in determining how the scheme in question is to be funded. This is why the employer has to pay higher contributions for his female employees than for his male employees.

[25]   In the case of the transfer of acquired rights and in the case where part of a pension is converted into capital (the cases under consideration in the main proceedings), the fact that account is taken of different actuarial factors as just described has the result that male employees are entitled to sums lower than those to which female employees are entitled.

[26]   Essentially the national court wants to know whether such differences are compatible with Article 119 EEC. In order to reply to that question it must be determined whether transfer benefits and lump-sum options constitute pay within the meaning of that Article.

[27]   The Commission claims that this is indeed the case and that consequently any difference in treatment based on sex would be permissible only if it were objectively justified. Statistical data based on the life expectancy of the two sexes do not in its view constitute an objective justification because they reflect averages calculated on the basis of the entire male and female population whereas the right to equal treatment in the matter of pay is a right given to employees individually and not because they belong to a particular class.

[28]   It is, of course, settled law that the concept of pay within the meaning of the second paragraph of Article 119 comprises any consideration, whether in cash or in kind

whether immediate or future provided that the worker receives it, albeit indirectly in respect of his employment from his employer. The fact that certain benefits are paid after the end of the employment relationship does not prevent them from being pay within the meaning of Article 119. . . .

[29]   The assumption underlying this approach is that the employer commits himself, albeit unilaterally, to pay his employees defined benefits or to grant them specific advantages and that the employees in turn expect the employer to pay them those benefits or provide them with those advantages. Anything that is not a consequence of that commitment and does not therefore come within the corresponding expectations of the employees falls outside the concept of pay.

[30]   In the context of a defined-benefit occupational pension scheme such as that in question in the main proceedings, the employer's commitment to his employees concerns the payment, at a given moment in time, of a periodic pension for which the determining criteria are already known at the time when the commitment is made and which constitutes pay within the meaning of Article 119. However, that commitment does not necessarily have to do with the funding arrangements chosen to secure the periodic payment of the pension, which thus remain outside the scope of application of Article 119.

[31]   In contributory schemes, funding is provided through the contributions made by the employees and those made by the employers. The contributions made by the employees are an element of their pay since they are deduced directly from an employees's salary which by definition is pay. . . . The amount of those contributions must therefore be the same for all employees, male and female, which is indeed so in the present case. This is not so in the case of the employer's contributions which ensure the adequacy of the funds necessary to cover the cost of the pensions promised, so securing their payment in the future, that being the substance of the employer's commitment.

[32]   It follows that, unlike periodic payment of pensions, inequality of employers' contributions paid under funded defined-benefit schemes, which is due to the use of actuarial factors differing according to sex, is not struck by Article 119.

[33]   That conclusion necessarily extends to the specific aspects referred to in the question submitted, namely the conversion of part of the periodic pension into a capital sum and the transfer of pension rights, the value of which can be determined only by reference to the funding arrangements chosen.

14.2   Article 119 and Directive 75/117: Equal Work

14.2.1   'SAME WORK' AND 'WORK OF EQUAL VALUE'

MACARTHYS LTD v SMITH (Case 129/79) [1980] ECR 1275, Court of Justice

Mrs Smith was employed by Macarthys as a warehouse manager at a weekly salary of £50. Her male predecessor in the same job had been paid £60 per week. Mrs Smith claimed that she was the victim of discrimination. The case eventually came before the Court of Appeal, which decided to refer certain questions to the Court of Justice concerning the interpretation of Article 119. In particular, is the principle of equal pay for equal work, contained in Article 119, confined to situations in which men and women are contemporaneously doing equal work for an employer? (Article 177 reference.)

[9]   According to the first paragraph of Article 119 the Member States are obliged to ensure and maintain 'the application of the principle that men and women should receive equal pay for equal work'.

[10]   As the Court indicated in the *Defrenne* judgment of 8 April 1976, that provision applies directly and without the need for more detailed implementing measures on the part of the Community or the Member States, to all forms of direct and overt discrimination which may be identified solely with the aid of the criteria of equal work and equal pay referred to by the article in question. Among the forms of discrimination

which may be thus judicially identified, the Court mentioned in particular cases where men and women receive unequal pay for equal work carried out in the same establishment or service.

[11]   In such a situation the decisive test lies in establishing whether there is a difference in treatment between a man and a woman performing 'equal work' within the meaning of Article 119. The scope of that concept, which is entirely qualitative in character in that it is exclusively concerned with the nature of the services in question, may not be restricted by the introduction of a requirement of contemporaneity.

MURPHY v BORD TELECOM EIREANN (Case 157/86) [1988] ECR 673, Court of Justice

Mary Murphy and 28 other women employed by Bord Telecom Eireann to dismantle, clean and reassemble telephones and other equipment claimed that they were entitled to the same pay as a male stores labourer. It was established that the women's work was of higher value than the man's. The High Court of Ireland asked the Court of Justice whether the Community principle of equal pay for equal work extended to this situation. (Article 177 reference.)

[6]   . . . the first question essentially seeks to ascertain whether Article 119 of the EEC Treaty must be interpreted as covering a case where a worker who relies on that provision to obtain equal pay within the meaning thereof is engaged in work of higher value than that of the person with whom a comparison is to be made.

[7]   Under the first paragraph of Article 119 the Member States are to ensure and maintain 'the application of the principle that men and women should receive equal pay for equal work'. According to a consistent line of decisions beginning with the Court's judgment of 8 April 1976 in *Defrenne* v *SABENA* (Case 43/75) [1976] ECR 455, Article 119 is directly applicable in particular in cases where men and women receive unequal pay for equal work carried out in the same establishment or service, whether public or private.

[8]   Bord Telecom Eireann contends that the principle does not apply in the situation where a lower wage is paid for work of higher value. In support of its view it maintains that the term 'equal work' in Article 119 of the EEC Treaty cannot be understood as embracing unequal work and that the effect of a contrary interpretation would be that equal pay would have to be paid for work of different value.

[9]   It is true that Article 119 expressly requires the application of the principle of equality for men and women solely in the case of equal work or, according to a consistent line of decisions of the Court, in the case of work of equal value, and not in the case of work of unequal value. Nevertheless, if that principle forbids workers of one sex engaged in work of equal value to that of workers of the opposite sex to be paid a lower wage than the latter on grounds of sex, it *a fortiori* prohibits such a difference in pay where the lower-paid category of workers is engaged in work of higher value.

[10]   To adopt a contrary interpretation would be tantamount to rendering the principle of equal pay ineffective and nugatory. As the Irish Government rightly emphasized, in that case an employer would easily be able to circumvent the principle by assigning additional or more onerous duties to workers of a particular sex, who could then be paid a lower wage.

COUNCIL DIRECTIVE 75/117/EEC OF 10 FEBRUARY 1975 ON THE APPROXIMATION OF THE LAWS OF THE MEMBER STATES RELATING TO THE APPLICATION OF THE PRINCIPLE OF EQUAL PAY FOR MEN AND WOMEN OJ 1975 L 45/19

(Preamble omitted.)

Article 1
The principle of equal pay for men and women outlined in Article 119 of the Treaty, hereinafter called 'principle of equal pay', means, for the same work or for work to which equal value is attributed, the elimination of all discrimination on grounds of sex with regard to all aspects and conditions of remuneration.

In particular, where a job classification system is used for determining pay, it must be based on the same criteria for both men and women and so drawn up as to exclude any discrimination on grounds of sex.

Article 2
Member States shall introduce into their national legal systems such measures as are necessary to enable all employees who consider themselves wronged by failure to apply the principle of equal pay to pursue their claims by judicial process after possible recourse to other competent authorities.

Article 3
Member States shall abolish all discrimination between men and women arising from laws, regulations or administrative provisions which is contrary to the principle of equal pay.

Article 4
Member States shall take the necessary measures to ensure that provisions appearing in collective agreements, wage scales, wage agreements or individual contracts of employment which are contrary to the principle of equal pay shall be, or may be declared, null and void or may be amended.

Article 5
Member States shall take the necessary measures to protect employees against dismissal by the employer as a reaction to a complaint within the undertaking or to any legal proceedings aimed at enforcing compliance with the principle of equal pay.

Article 6
Member States shall, in accordance with their national circumstances and legal systems, take the measures necessary to ensure that the principle of equal pay is applied. They shall see that effective means are available to take care that this principle is observed.

Article 7
Member States shall take care that the provisions adopted pursuant to this Directive, together with the relevant provisions already in force, are brought to the attention of employees by all appropriate means, for example at their place of employment.
(Remaining provisions omitted.)

JENKINS v KINGSGATE (CLOTHING PRODUCTIONS) LTD (Case 96/80)
[1981] ECR 911, Court of Justice

Kingsgate, a women's clothing manufacturer, paid part-time workers at a rate which was 10% less than the rate paid to full-timers. All but one of the part-time workers employed by the company were female. Mrs Jenkins, a part-timer, claimed that this pay policy constituted discrimination on grounds of sex. The Employment Appeal Tribunal (EAT) asked the Court of Justice whether a difference in pay between part-timers and full-timers engaged in the same work amounted to discrimination contrary to Article 119 when the category of part-time workers is exclusively or predominantly comprised of women. The EAT also raised questions of interpretation concerning Article 1 of Directive 75/117. (Article 177 reference.)

[9] . . . the national court is principally concerned to know whether a difference in the level of pay for work carried out part-time and the same work carried out full-time may amount to discrimination of a kind prohibited by Article 119 of the Treaty when the category of part-time workers is exclusively or predominantly comprised of women.
[10]   The answer to the questions thus understood is that the purpose of Article 119 is to ensure the application of the principle of equal pay for men and women for the same work. The differences in pay prohibited by that provision are therefore exclusively those based on the difference of the sex of the workers. Consequently the fact that

part-time work is paid at an hourly rate lower than pay for full-time work does not amount *per se* to discrimination prohibited by Article 119 provided that the hourly rates are applied to workers belonging to either category without distinction based on sex.

[11]   If there is no such distinction, therefore, the fact that work paid at time rates is remunerated at an hourly rate which varies according to the number of hours worked per week does not offend against the principle of equal pay laid down in Article 119 of the Treaty in so far as the difference in pay between part-time work and full-time work is attributable to factors which are objectively justified and are in no way related to any discrimination based on sex.

[12]   Such may be the case, in particular, when by giving hourly rates of pay which are lower for part-time work than those for full-time work the employer is endeavouring, on economic grounds which may be objectively justified, to encourage full-time work irrespective of the sex of the worker.

[13]   By contrast, if it is established that a considerably smaller percentage of women than of men perform the minimum number of weekly working hours required in order to be able to claim the full-time hourly rate of pay, the inequality in pay will be contrary to Article 119 of the Treaty where, regard being had to the difficulties encountered by women in arranging to work that minimum number of hours per week, the pay policy of the undertaking in question cannot be explained by factors other than discrimination based on sex.

[14]   Where the hourly rate of pay differs according to whether the work is part-time or full-time it is for the national courts to decide in each individual case whether, regard being had to the facts of the case, its history and the employer's intention, a pay policy such as that which is at issue in the main proceedings although represented as a difference based on weekly working hours is or is not in reality discrimination based on the sex of the worker.

[15]   The reply . . . must therefore be that a difference in pay between full-time workers and part-time workers does not amount to discrimination prohibited by Article 119 of the Treaty unless it is in reality merely an indirect way of reducing the level of pay of part-time workers on the ground that that group of workers is composed exclusively or predominantly of women.

. . .

[19]   The national court also raises with regard to Article 1 of Council Directive 75/117/EEC of 10 February 1975 the same questions of interpretation as those examined above in relation to Article 119 of the Treaty.

[20]   As may be seen from the first recital in the preamble the primary objective of the above-mentioned directive is to implement the principle that men and women should receive equal pay which is 'contained in Article 119 of the Treaty'. For that purpose the fourth recital states that 'it is desirable to reinforce the basic laws by standards aimed at facilitating the practical application of the principle of equality'.

[21]   The provisions of Article 1 of that directive are confined in the first paragraph to restating the principle of equal pay set out in Article 119 of the Treaty and specify, in the second paragraph, the conditions for applying that principle where a job classification system is used for determining pay.

[22]   It follows, therefore, that Article 1 of Council Directive 75/117/EEC which is principally designed to facilitate the practical application of the principle of equal pay outlined in Article 119 of the Treaty in no way alters the content or scope of that principle as defined in the Treaty.

14.2.2   DIRECTIVE 75/117: WORK OF EQUAL VALUE

COMMISSION v UNITED KINGDOM (EQUAL PAY FOR EQUAL WORK)
(Case 61/81) [1982] ECR 2601, Court of Justice

The Commission claimed that UK legislation purportedly implementing Directive 75/117 was deficient. (Article 169 proceedings.)

[2]   The first article of the directive, which the Commission considers has not been applied by the United Kingdom, provides that:

The principle of equal pay for men and women outlined in Article 119 of the Treaty, hereinafter called 'principle of equal pay', means, for the same work or for work to which equal value is attributed, the elimination of all discrimination on grounds of sex with regard to all aspects and conditions of remuneration.

In particular, where a job classification system is used for determining pay, it must be based on the same criteria for both men and women and so drawn up as to exclude any discrimination on grounds of sex.

[3]   The reference to 'work to which equal value is attributed' is used in the United Kingdom in the Equal Pay Act 1970, as amended by the Sex Discrimination Act 1975. Section 1(5) of the Act provides that:

A woman is to be regarded as employed on work rated as equivalent with that of any men if, but only if, her job and their job have been given an equal value, in terms of the demand made on the worker under various headings (for instance effort, skill, decision), on a study undertaken with a view to evaluating in those terms the jobs to be done by all or any of the employees in an undertaking or group of undertakings, or would have been given an equal value but for the evaluation being made on a system setting different values for men and women on the same demand under any heading.

[4]   Comparison of those provisions reveals that the job classification system is, under the directive, merely one of several methods for determining pay for work to which equal value is attributed, whereas under the provision in the Equal Pay Act quoted above the introduction of such a system is the sole method of achieving such a result.

[5]   It is also noteworthy that, as the United Kingdom concedes, British legislation does not permit the introduction of a job classification system without the employer's consent. Workers in the United Kingdom are therefore unable to have their work rated as being of equal value with comparable work if their employer refuses to introduce a classification system.

[6]   The United Kingdom attempts to justify that state of affairs by pointing out that Article 1 of the directive says nothing about the right of an employee to insist on having pay determined by a job classification system. On that basis it concludes that the worker may not insist on a comparative evaluation of different work by the job classification method, the introduction of which is at the employer's discretion.

[7]   The United Kingdom's interpretation amounts to a denial of the very existence of a right to equal pay for work of equal value where no classification has been made. Such a position is not consonant with the general scheme and provisions of Directive 75/117. The recitals in the preamble to that directive indicate that its essential purpose is to implement the principle that men and women should receive equal pay contained in Article 119 of the Treaty and that it is primarily the responsibility of the Member States to ensure the application of this principle by means of appropriate laws, regulations and administrative provisions in such a way that all employees in the Community can be protected in these matters.

[8]   To achieve that end the principle is defined in the first paragraph of Article 1 so as to include under the term 'the same work', the case of 'work to which equal value is attributed', and the second paragraph emphasizes merely that where a job classification system is used for determining pay it is necessary to ensure that it is based on the same criteria for both men and women and so drawn up as to exclude any discrimination on grounds of sex.

[9]   It follows that where there is disagreement as to the application of that concept a worker must be entitled to claim before an appropriate authority that this work has the same value as other work and, if that is found to be the case, to have his rights under the Treaty and the directive acknowledged by a binding decision. Any method which excludes that option prevents the aims of the directive from being achieved.

. . .

[11]   In this instance, however, the United Kingdom has not adopted the necessary measures and there is at present no means whereby a worker who considers that this

post is of equal value to another may pursue his claims if the employer refuses to introduce a job classification system.

. . .

[14]   Accordingly, by failing to introduce into its national legal system in implementation of the provisions of Council Directive 75/117/EEC of 10 February 1975 such measures as are necessary to enable all employees who consider themselves wronged by failure to apply the principle of equal pay for men and women for work to which equal value is attributed and for which no system of job classification exists to obtain recognition of such equivalence, the United Kingdom has failed to fulfil its obligations under the Treaty.

RUMMLER v DATO-DRUCK GMBH (Case 237/85) [1986] ECR 2101, Court of Justice

A wage-rate agreement for employees in the German printing industry provided for wage groups determined according to the degree of knowledge, concentration, muscular demand or effort and responsibility required for different jobs. Gisela Rummler, an employee of Dato-Druck, was classified in Wage Group III. Her job required her to pack heavy parcels. This was heavy work for her and she considered that she ought to be classified in Wage Group IV. The German Labour Court asked the Court of Justice whether a job classification scheme based on the criteria of muscle demand or effort and the heaviness of the work was compatible with Directive 75/117. (Article 177 reference.)

[11]   . . . reference must first be made to the general rule laid down by the first paragraph of Article 1 of Directive 75/117, which provides for the elimination of all discrimination on grounds of sex with regard to all aspects and conditions of remuneration for the same work or for work to which equal value is attributed.

[12]   That general rule is applied in the second paragraph of Article 1, which provides that a job classification system 'must be based on the same criteria for both men and women and so drawn up as to exclude any discrimination on grounds of sex'.

[13]   It follows that the principle of equal pay requires essentially that the nature of the work to be carried out be considered objectively. Consequently, the same work or work to which equal value is attributed must be remunerated in the same manner whether it is carried out by a man or by a woman. Where a job classification system is used in determining remuneration, that system must be based on criteria which do not differ according to whether the work is carried out by a man or by a woman and must not be organized, as a whole, in such a manner that it has the practical effect of discriminating generally against workers of one sex.

[14]   Consequently, criteria corresponding to the duties performed meet the requirements of Article 1 of the directive where those duties by their nature require particular physical effort or are physically heavy. In differentiating rates of pay, it is consistent with the principle of non-discrimination to use a criterion based on the objectively measurable expenditure of effort necessary in carrying out the work or the degree to which, reviewed objectively, the work is physically heavy.

[15]   Even where a particular criterion, such as that of demand on the muscles, may in fact tend to favour male workers, since it may be assumed that in general they are physically stronger than female workers, it must, in order to determine whether or not it is discriminatory, be considered in the context of the whole job classification system, having regard to other criteria influencing rates of pay. A system is not necessarily discriminatory simply because one of its criteria makes reference to attributes more characteristic of men. In order for a job classification system as a whole to be non-discriminatory and thus to comply with the principles of the directive, it must, however, be established in such a manner that it includes, if the nature of the tasks in question so permits, jobs to which equal value is attributed and for which regard is had to other criteria in relation to which women workers may have a particular aptitude.

[16]   It is for the national courts to determine on a case-by-case basis whether a job classification system as a whole allows proper account to be taken of the criteria necessary for adjusting pay rates according to the conditions required for the performance of the various duties throughout the undertaking.

[17]   The answer . . . must therefore be that Council Directive 75/117 of 10 February 1975 on the approximation of the laws of the Member States relating to the application of the principle of equal pay for men and women does not prohibit the use, in a job classification system for the purpose of determining rates of pay, of the criterion of muscle demand or muscular effort or that of the heaviness of the work if, in view of the nature of the tasks involved, the work to be performed does require the use of a certain degree of physical strength, so long as the system as a whole, by taking into account other criteria, precludes any discrimination on grounds of sex.

HANDELS-OG KONTORFUNKTIONAERERNES FORBUND I DANMARK v DANSK ARBEJDSGIVERFORENING (FOR DANFOSS) (Case 109/88) [1989] ECR 3199, Court of Justice

Danfoss paid the same basic pay to employees in the same wage group. However, because of a system of pay supplements based upon mobility, training and seniority, pay within each wage group differed from individual to individual. It was established that in two particular wage groups men's average pay was higher than women's. Because it was not clear how the system of supplements was applied, workers were unable to compare the individual components of their pay with those of other workers in the same wage group. The Danish industrial arbitration board asked the Court of Justice whether, in these circumstances, it was for the employer to prove that its pay policy was not discriminatory. (Article 177 reference.)

[10]   . . . the issue between the parties to the main proceedings has its origin in the fact that the system of individual supplements applied to basic pay is implemented in such a way that a woman is unable to identify the reasons for a difference between her pay and that of a man doing the same work. Employees do not know what criteria in the matter of supplements are applied to them and how they are applied. They know only the amount of their supplemented pay without being able to determine the effect of the individual criteria. Those who are in a particular wage group are thus unable to compare the various components of their pay with those of the pay of their colleagues who are in the same wage group.

[11]   In those circumstances the questions put by the national court must be understood as asking whether the Equal Pay Directive must be interpreted as meaning that where an undertaking applies a system of pay which is totally lacking in transparency, it is for the employer to prove that his practice in the matter of wages is not discriminatory, if a female worker establishes, in relation to a relatively large number of employees, that the average pay for women is less than that for men.

. . .

[13]   It should next be pointed out that in a situation where a system of individual pay supplements which is completely lacking in transparency is at issue, female employees can establish differences only so far as average pay is concerned. They would be deprived of any effective means of enforcing the principle of equal pay before the national courts if the effect of adducing such evidence was not to impose upon the employer the burden of proving that his practice in the matter of wages is not in fact discriminatory.

[14]   Finally, it should be noted that under Article 6 of the Equal Pay Directive Member States must, in accordance with their national circumstances and legal systems, take the measures necessary to ensure that the principle of equal pay is applied and that effective means are available to ensure that it is observed. The concern for effectiveness which thus underlies the directive means that it must be interpreted as implying adjustments to national rules on the burden of proof in special cases where such adjustments are necessary for the effective implementation of the principle of equality.

[15]   To show that his practice in the matter of wages does not systematically work to the disadvantage of female employees the employer will have to indicate how he has applied the criteria concerning supplements and will thus be forced to make his system of pay transparent.

14.3   Indirect Discrimination

14.3.1   INDIRECT DISCRIMINATION AND OBJECTIVE JUSTIFICATION

ENDERBY v *FRENCHAY HEALTH AUTHORITY AND THE SECRETARY OF STATE FOR HEALTH* (Case C-127/92) [1994] 1 CMLR 8, Court of Justice

Within the National Health Service, speech therapists were paid at a lower rate than pharmacists. Speech therapy was overwhelmingly a female profession, whilst most pharmacists were men. Dr Pamela Enderby, who was employed by the Frenchay Health Authority (FHA) as a speech therapist, claimed that she was the victim of sex discrimination. Two of the questions referred to the Court of Justice by the Court of Appeal concerned the justifications advanced by the FHA in respect of the different rates of pay. In giving judgment, the Court proceeded on the assumption that the two jobs in question were of equal value. (Article 177 reference.)

[20]   . . . the Court of Appeal wishes to know whether the employer can rely as sufficient justification for the difference in pay upon the fact that the rates of pay of the jobs in question were decided by collective bargaining processes which, although carried out by the same parties, are distinct and which, considered separately, have no discriminatory effect.

[21]   As is clear from Article 4 of Council Directive 75/117 on the approximation of the laws of the member-States relating to the application of the principle of equal pay for men and women . . . collective agreements, like laws, regulations or administrative provisions, must observe the principle enshrined in Article 119 EEC.

[22]   The fact that the rates of pay at issue are decided by collective bargaining processes conducted separately for each of the two professional groups concerned, without any discriminatory effect within each group, does not preclude a finding of *prima facie* discrimination where the results of those processes show that two groups with the same employer and the same trade union are treated differently. If the employer could rely on the absence of discrimination within each of the collective bargaining processes taken separately as sufficient justification for the difference in pay, he could . . . easily circumvent the principle of equal pay by using separate bargaining processes.

[23]   Accordingly . . . the fact that the respective rates of pay of two jobs of equal value, one carried out almost exclusively by women and the other predominantly by men, were arrived at by collective bargaining processes which, although carried out by the same parties, are distinct, and, taken separately, have in themselves no discriminatory effect, is not sufficient objective justification for the difference in pay between those two jobs.

[24]   . . . the Court of Appeal wishes to know to what extent – wholly, in part or not at all – the fact that part of the difference in pay is attributable to a shortage of candidates for one job and to the need to attract them by higher salaries can objectively justify that pay differential.

[25]   The Court has consistently held that it is for the national court, which has sole jurisdiction to make findings of fact, to determine whether and to what extent the grounds put forward by an employer to explain the adoption of a pay practice which applies independently of a worker's sex but in fact affects more women than men may be regarded as objectively justified economic grounds . . . Those grounds may include, if they can be attributed to the needs and objectives of the undertaking, different criteria such as the worker's flexibility or adaptability to hours and places of work, his training or his length of service . . .

[26]   The state of the employment market, which may lead an employer to increase the pay of a particular job in order to attract candidates, may constitute an objectively justified economic ground . . . How it is to be applied in the circumstances of each case depends on the facts and so falls within the jurisdiction of the national court.

[27]   If, as the question referred seems to suggest, the national court has been able to determine precisely what proportion of the increase in pay is attributable to market forces, it must necessarily accept that the pay differential is objectively justified to the extent of that proportion. When national authorities have to apply Community law, they must apply the principle of proportionality.

[28]   If that is not the case, it is for the national court to assess whether the role of market forces in determining the rate of pay was sufficiently significant to provide objective justification for part or all of the difference.

14.4   Directive 76/207: Equal Treatment for Men and Women in Employment

14.4.1   SCOPE OF DIRECTIVE 76/207

COUNCIL DIRECTIVE 76/207/EEC OF 9 FEBRUARY 1976 ON THE IMPLEMENTATION OF THE PRINCIPLE OF EQUAL TREATMENT FOR MEN AND WOMEN AS REGARDS ACCESS TO EMPLOYMENT, VOCATIONAL TRAINING AND PROMOTION, AND WORKING CONDITIONS OJ 1976 L 39/40

[Preamble omitted.]

Article 1

1.   The purpose of this Directive is to put into effect in the Member States the principle of equal treatment for men and women as regards access to employment, including promotion, and to vocational training and as regards working conditions and, on the conditions referred to in paragraph 2, social security. This principle is hereinafter referred to as 'the principle of equal treatment'.

2.   With a view to ensuring the progressive implementation of the principle of equal treatment in matters of social security, the Council, acting on a proposal from the Commission, will adopt provisions defining its substance, its scope and the arrangements for its application.

Article 2

1.   For the purposes of the following provisions, the principle of equal treatment shall mean that there shall be no discrimination whatsoever on grounds of sex either directly or indirectly by reference in particular to marital or family status.

2.   This Directive shall be without prejudice to the right of Member States to exclude from its field of application those occupational activities and, where appropriate, the training leading thereto, for which, by reason of their nature or the context in which they are carried out, the sex of the worker constitutes a determining factor.

3.   This Directive shall be without prejudice to provisions concerning the protection of women, particularly as regards pregnancy and maternity.

4.   This Directive shall be without prejudice to measures to promote equal opportunity for men and women, in particular by removing existing inequalities which affect women's opportunities in the areas referred to in Article 1(1).

Article 3

1.   Application of the principle of equal treatment means that there shall be no discrimination whatsoever on grounds of sex in the conditions, including selection criteria, for access to all jobs or posts, whatever the sector or branch of activity, and to all levels of the occupational hierarchy.

2.   To this end, Member States shall take the measures necessary to ensure that:

(a)   any laws, regulations and administrative provisions contrary to the principle of equal treatment shall be abolished;

(b)   any provisions contrary to the principle of equal treatment which are included in collective agreements, individual contracts of employment, internal rules of undertakings or in rules governing the independent occupations and professions shall be, or may be declared, null and void or may be amended;

(c)   those laws, regulations and administrative provisions contrary to the principle of equal treatment when the concern for protection which originally inspired them is no longer well founded shall be revised; and that where similar provisions are included in collective agreements labour and management shall be requested to undertake the desired revision.

Article 4

Application of the principle of equal treatment with regard to access to all types and to all levels of vocational guidance, vocational training, advanced vocational training and retraining, means that Member States shall take all necessary measures to ensure that:

(a) any laws, regulations and administrative provisions contrary to the principle of equal treatment shall be abolished;

(b) any provisions contrary to the principle of equal treatment which are included in collective agreements, individual contracts of employment, internal rules of undertakings or in rules governing the independent occupations and professions shall be, or may be declared, null and void or may be amended;

(c) without prejudice to the freedom granted in certain Member States to certain private training establishments, vocational guidance, vocational training, advanced vocational training and retraining shall be accessible on the basis of the same criteria and at the same levels without any discrimination on grounds of sex.

Article 5

1. Application of the principle of equal treatment with regard to working conditions, including the conditions governing dismissal, means that men and women shall be guaranteed the same conditions without discrimination on grounds of sex.

2. To this end, Member States shall take the measures necessary to ensure that:

(a) any laws, regulations and administrative provisions contrary to the principle of equal treatment shall be abolished;

(b) any provisions contrary to the principle of equal treatment which are included in collective agreements, individual contracts of employment, internal rules of undertakings or in rules governing the independent occupations and professions shall be, or may be declared, null and void or may be amended;

(c) those laws, regulations and administrative provisions contrary to the principle of equal treatment when the concern for protection which originally inspired them is no longer well founded shall be revised; and that where similar provisions are included in collective agreements labour and management shall be requested to undertake the desired revision.

Article 6

Member States shall introduce into their national legal systems such measures as are necessary to enable all persons who consider themselves wronged by failure to apply to them the principle of equal treatment within the meaning of Articles 3, 4 and 5 to pursue their claims by judicial process after possible recourse to other competent authorities.

Article 7

Member States shall take the necessary measures to protect employees against dismissal by the employer as a reaction to a complaint within the undertaking or to any legal proceedings aimed at enforcing compliance with the principle of equal treatment. (Remaining provisions omitted.)

P v S AND CORNWALL COUNTY COUNCIL (Case C-13/94) [1996] ECR I-2143, Court of Justice

P had been dismissed by her employer, Cornwall County Council, and brought an action before the industrial tribunal against S (the Director of the establishment where she was employed) and the Council, claiming that she was the victim of sex discrimination. Although S and the Council maintained that the reason for P's dismissal was redundancy, the tribunal's reference to the Court of Justice indicated that the real reason was P's intention to undergo gender-reassignment. The tribunal asked the Court whether Directive 76/207 precludes the dismissal of a transsexual for a reason related to his or her gender-reassignment. (Article 177 reference.)

17.   The principle of equal treatment 'for men and women' to which the directive refers in its title, preamble and provisions means, as Articles 2(1) and 3(1) in particular indicate, that there should be 'no discrimination whatsoever on grounds of sex'.

18.   Thus, the directive is simply the expression, in the relevant field, of the principle of quality, which is one of the fundamental principles of Community law.

19.   Moreover, as the Court has repeatedly held, the right not to be discriminated against on grounds of sex is one of the fundamental human rights whose observance the Court has a duty to ensure . . .

20.   Accordingly, the scope of the directive cannot be confined simply to discrimination based on the fact that a person is of one or other sex. In view of its purpose and the nature of the rights which it seeks to safeguard, the scope of the directive is also such as to apply to discrimination arising, as in this case, from the gender reassignment of the person concerned.

21.   Such discrimination is based, essentially if not exclusively, on the sex of the person concerned. Where a person is dismissed on the ground that he or she intends to undergo, or has undergone, gender reassignment, he or she is treated unfavourably by comparison with persons of the sex to which he or she was deemed to belong before undergoing gender reassignment.

22.   To tolerate such discrimination would be tantamount, as regards such a person, to a failure to respect the dignity and freedom to which he or she is entitled, and which the Court has a duty to safeguard.

23.   Dismissal of such a person must therefore be regarded as contrary to Article 5(1) of the directive, unless the dismissal could be justified under Article 2(2). There is, however, no material before the Court to suggest that this was so here.

24.   It follows from the foregoing that the reply to the questions referred by the Industrial Tribunal must be that, in view of the objective pursued by the directive, Article 5(1) of the directive precludes dismissal of a transsexual for a reason related to a gender reassignment.

14.4.2   EQUAL TREATMENT AND RETIREMENT AGES

BURTON v *BRITISH RAILWAYS BOARD* (Case 19/81) [1982] ECR 555, Court of Justice

Employees of British Railways Board could take advantage of their employer's voluntary redundancy scheme from the age of 60 (for men) and 55 (for women). Mr Burton applied for voluntary redundancy but his application was turned down because he was only 58. He complained to an Industrial Tribunal of sex discrimination. The Employment Appeal Tribunal asked the Court of Justice whether the different age requirements amounted to discriminatory treatment within the meaning of Directive 76/207. (Article 177 reference.)

[9]   According to Article 5(1) of Directive 76/207 application of the principle of equal treatment with regard to working conditions, including the conditions governing dismissal, means that men and women are to be guaranteed the same conditions without discrimination on grounds of sex. In the context of the directive the word 'dismissal' must be widely construed so as to include termination of the employment relationship between a worker and his employer, even as part of a voluntary redundancy scheme.

[10]   In deciding whether the difference in treatment of which the plaintiff in the main action complains is discriminatory within the meaning of that directive account must be taken of the relationship between measures such as that at issue and national provisions on normal retirement age.

[11]   Under United Kingdom legislation the minimum qualifying age for a State retirement pension is 60 for women and 65 for men.

[12]   From the information supplied by the United Kingdom Government in the course of the proceedings it appears that a worker who is permitted by the Board to take voluntary early retirement must do so within the five years preceding the normal minimum age of retirement, and that he may receive the following benefits: (1) the lump sum calculated in accordance with the provisions of the Redundancy Payments Act 1965, (2) a lump sum calculated on the basis of the total length of his employment with the Board, and (3) 25% of the sum of the first two amounts. In addition he is entitled up to

the minimum retiring age to an early retirement pension equal to the pension to which he would have been entitled had he attained the minimum statutory retirement age and to an advance, repayable at the minimum retiring age, equal to the sum to which he becomes entitled at that age.

[13]   Council Directive 79/7/EEC of 19 December 1978 on the progressive implementation of the principle of equal treatment for men and women in matters of social security . . . which was adopted with particular reference to Article 235 of the Treaty, provides in Article 7 that the directive shall be without prejudice to the right of Member States to exclude from its scope the determination of pensionable age for the purposes of granting old-age and retirement pensions and the possible consequences thereof for other benefits.

[14]   It follows that the determination of a minimum pensionable age for social security purposes which is not the same for men as for women does not amount to discrimination prohibited by Community law.

[15]   The option given to workers by the provisions at issue in the present instance is tied to the retirement scheme governed by United Kingdom social security provisions. It enables a worker who leaves his employment at any time during the five years before he reaches normal pensionable age to receive certain allowances for a limited period. The allowances are calculated in the same manner regardless of the sex of the worker. The only difference between the benefits for men and those for women stems from the fact that the minimum pensionable age under the national legislation is not the same for men as for women.

[16]   In the circumstances the different age conditions for men and women with regard to access to voluntary redundancy cannot be regarded as discrimination within the meaning of Directive 76/207.

ROBERTS v TATE & LYLE INDUSTRIES LTD (Case 151/84) [1986] ECR 703, Court of Justice

Mrs Roberts was a member of the contracted-out occupational pension scheme set up by her employer, Tate & Lyle. The scheme provided for compulsory retirement with a pension at the age of 65 for men and 60 for women. Mrs Roberts was made redundant when Tate & Lyle closed its Liverpool depot. Under the severance terms agreed with the trade union, an immediate pension was paid to all members of the company's occupational pension scheme who had attained the age of 55. Mrs Roberts did not receive the pension because she was only 53 at the date of the redundancy. She complained of sex discrimination, pointing out that men who were made redundant received their pension ten years before retirement age, whereas women received their pension only five years before that age. One of the questions referred to the Court of Justice by the Court of Appeal concerned the compatibility of these redundancy pension arrangements with Directive 76/207. (Article 177 reference.)

[30]   The Court observes in the first place that the question of interpretation which has been referred to it does not concern the conditions for the grant of the normal old-age or retirement pension but the termination of employment in connection with a mass redundancy caused by the closure of part of an undertaking's plant. The question therefore concerns the conditions governing dismissal and falls to be considered under Directive No. 76/207.

[31]   Article 5(1) of Directive No. 76/207 provides that application of the principle of equal treatment with regard to working conditions, including the conditions governing dismissal, means that men and women are to be guaranteed the same conditions without discrimination on grounds of sex.

[32]   In its judgment in the *Burton* [*Burton* v *British Railways Board* (Case 19/81) [1982] ECR 555] case the Court has already stated that the term 'dismissal' contained in that provision must be given a wide meaning. Consequently, an age limit for the compulsory redundancy of workers as part of a mass redundancy falls within the term 'dismissal' construed in that manner, even if the redundancy involves the grant of an early retirement pension.

[33]   Even though the retirement scheme at issue does not *prima facie* discriminate between men and women with regard to the conditions for dismissal, it is still necessary

to consider whether the fixing of the same age for the grant of an early pension nevertheless constitutes discrimination on grounds of sex in view of the fact that under the United Kingdom statutory social security scheme the pensionable age for men and women is different. Under United Kingdom legislation the minimum qualifying age for a State retirement pension is 60 for women and 65 for men.

[34]   As the Court emphasized in its judgment in the *Burton* case, Article 7 of Directive No. 79/7 expressly provides that the directive does not prejudice the right of Member States to exclude from its scope the determination of pensionable age for the purposes of granting old-age and retirement pensions and the possible consequences thereof for other benefits falling within the statutory social security schemes. The Court thus acknowledged that benefits linked to a national scheme which lays down a different minimum pensionable age for men and women may lie outside the ambit of the aforementioned obligation.

[35]   However, in view of the fundamental importance of the principle of equality of treatment, which the Court has reaffirmed on numerous occasions, Article 1(2) of Directive No. 76/207, which excludes social security matters from the scope of that directive, must be interpreted strictly. Consequently, the exception to the prohibition of discrimination on grounds of sex provided for in Article 7(1)(a) of Directive No. 79/7 applies only to the determination of pensionable age for the purposes of granting old-age and retirement pensions and to the consequences thereof for other social security benefits.

[36]   In that respect it must be emphasized that, whereas the exception contained in Article 7 of Directive No. 79/7 concerns the consequences which pensionable age has for social security benefits, this case is concerned with dismissal within the meaning of Article 5 of Directive No. 76/207. In those circumstances the grant of a pension to persons of the same age who are made redundant amounts merely to a collective measure adopted irrespective of the sex of those persons in order to guarantee them all the same rights.

[37]   Consequently, the answer to the first question referred to the Court of Justice by the Court of Appeal must be that Article 5(1) of Directive No. 76/207 must be interpreted as meaning that a contractual provision which lays down a single age for the dismissal of men and women under a mass redundancy involving the grant of an early retirement pension, whereas the normal retirement age is different for men and women, does not constitute discrimination on grounds of sex, contrary to Community law.

MARSHALL v SOUTHAMPTON AND SOUTH-WEST HAMPSHIRE AREA HEALTH AUTHORITY (TEACHING) (Case 152/84) [1986] ECR 723, Court of Justice

Mrs Marshall worked as a dietician for the Southampton and South-West Hampshire Area Health Authority. The Authority had a general retirement policy laying down a retirement age of 65 for men and 60 for women. Mrs Marshall wanted to continue working until 65 but her employer, pursuant to this policy, dismissed her when she reached 62. Mrs Marshall's claim that her dismissal amounted to sex discrimination eventually came before the Court of Appeal, which made a reference to the Court of Justice concerning the interpretation of Directive 76/207. (Article 177 reference.)

[32]   The Court observes in the first place that the question of interpretation which has been referred to it does not concern access to a statutory or occupational retirement scheme, that is to say the conditions for payment of an old-age or retirement pension, but the fixing of an age limit with regard to the termination of employment pursuant to a general policy concerning dismissal. The question therefore relates to the conditions governing dismissal and falls to be considered under Directive No. 76/207.

[33]   Article 5(1) of Directive No. 76/207 provides that application of the principle of equal treatment with regard to working conditions, including the conditions governing dismissal, means that men and women are to be guaranteed the same conditions without discrimination on grounds of sex.

[34]   In its judgment in the *Burton* [*Burton* v *British Railways Board* (Case 19/81) [1982] ECR 555] case the Court has already stated that the term 'dismissal' contained in that provision must be given a wide meaning. Consequently, an age limit for the compulsory

dismissal of workers pursuant to an employer's general policy concerning retirement falls within the term 'dismissal' construed in that manner, even if the dismissal involves the grant of a retirement pension.

[35]   As the Court emphasized in its judgment in the *Burton* case, Article 7 of Directive No. 79/7 expressly provides that the directive does not prejudice the right of Member States to exclude from its scope the determination of pensionable age for the purposes of granting old-age and retirement pensions and the possible consequences thereof for other benefits falling within the statutory social security schemes. The Court thus acknowledged that benefits tied to a national scheme which lays down a different minimum pensionable age for men and women may lie outside the ambit of the aforementioned obligation.

[36]   However, in view of the fundamental importance of the principle of equality of treatment, which the Court has reaffirmed on numerous occasions, Article 1(2) of Directive No. 76/207, which excludes social security matters from the scope of that directive, must be interpreted strictly. Consequently, the exception to the prohibition of discrimination on grounds of sex provided for in Article 7(1)(a) of Directive No. 79/7 applies only to the determination of pensionable age for the purposes of granting old-age and retirement pensions and the possible consequences thereof for other benefits.

[37]   In that respect it must be emphasized that, whereas the exception contained in Article 7 of Directive No. 79/7 concerns the consequences which pensionable age has for social security benefits, this case is concerned with dismissal within the meaning of Article 5 of Directive No. 76/207.

[38]   Consequently, the answer to the first question referred to the Court by the Court of Appeal must be that Article 5(1) of Directive No. 76/207 must be interpreted as meaning that a general policy concerning dismissal involving the dismissal of a woman solely because she has attained the qualifying age for a State pension, which age is different under national legislation for men and for women constitutes discrimination on grounds of sex, contrary to that directive.

14.4.3   DEROGATION FROM THE EQUAL TREATMENT PRINCIPLE

14.4.3.1   Article 2(2)

COMMISSION v UNITED KINGDOM (EQUAL TREATMENT FOR MEN AND WOMEN) (Case 165/82) [1983] ECR 3431, Court of Justice

The Commission considered that the UK had failed adequately to implement Directive 76/207. (Article 169 proceedings.)

[12]   According to the United Kingdom, the exclusions from the prohibition of discrimination provided for in section 6(3) of the 1975 Act in the case of employment in a private household or in undertakings where the number of persons employed does not exceed five are justified by the exception provided for in Article 2(2) of the directive itself, according to which:

> This directive shall be without prejudice to the right of Member States to exclude from its field of application those occupational activities and, where appropriate, the training leading thereto, for which, by reason of their nature or the context in which they are carried out, the sex of the worker constitutes a determining factor.

[13]   It must be recognized that the provision of the 1975 Act in question is intended, in so far as it refers to employment in a private household, to reconcile the principle of equality of treatment with the principle of respect for private life, which is also fundamental. Reconciliation of that kind is one of the factors which must be taken into consideration in determining the scope of the exception provided for in Article 2(2) of the directive.

[14]   Whilst it is undeniable that, for certain kinds of employment in private households, that consideration may be decisive, that is not the case for all the kinds of employment in question.

[15]   As regards small undertakings with not more than five employees, the United Kingdom has not put forward any argument to show that in any undertaking of that size the sex of the worker would be a determining factor by reason of the nature of his activities or the context in which they are carried out.

[16]   Consequently, by reason of its generality, the exclusion provided for in the contested provision of the 1975 Act goes beyond the objective which may be lawfully pursued within the framework of Article 2(2) of the directive.

[17]   The Commission's third complaint relates to the fact that the 1975 Act ensures access to the occupation of midwife and to training for that occupation only within certain limits. This is said to entail discrimination based on sex.

[18]   The United Kingdom acknowledges the facts. By virtue of paragraph (3) of schedule 4 to the 1975 Act, until a day to be specified by order of the Secretary of State, men are granted access to the occupation in question and may be trained for that purpose only in certain specific places. This situation is due to the fact that in the United Kingdom the occupation in question is not traditionally engaged in by men. In a sphere in which respect for the patient's sensitivities is of particular importance, it considers that at the present time that limitation is in conformity with Article 2(2) of the directive. However, it adds that it intends to proceed by stages and keep the position under review, in accordance with the obligations imposed by Article 9(2) of the directive.

[19]   That provision requires Member States periodically to assess the occupational activities referred to in Article 2(2) in order to decide, in the light of social developments, whether there is justification for maintaining the permitted exclusions. They are to notify the Commission of the results of that assessment.

[20]   It is undeniable that in the area in question, as the United Kingdom acknowledges, the Member States are under an obligation to implement the principle of equality of treatment. It must however be recognized that at the present time personal sensitivities may play an important role in relations between midwife and patient. In those circumstances, it may be stated that by failing fully to apply the principle laid down in the directive, the United Kingdom has not exceeded the limits of the power granted to the Member States by Articles 9(2) and 2(2) of the directive. The Commission's complaint in that regard cannot therefore be upheld.

JOHNSTON v *CHIEF CONSTABLE OF THE ROYAL ULSTER CONSTABULARY*
(Case 222/84) [1986] ECR 1651, Court of Justice

The Chief Constable of the Royal Ulster Constabulary (RUC) decided that women officers in the RUC Reserve, unlike male officers, would not carry fire-arms or be trained in their use. Since general police duties frequently required the carrying of firearms, fewer women officers would be needed. Consequently, fixed-term contracts of female officers were not to be renewed. Mrs Johnston, a member of the RUC Reserve, challenged the Chief Constable's refusal to renew her contract and to give her training in the handling of fire-arms, claiming that this amounted to sex discrimination. Certain of the questions referred to the Court of Justice by the Industrial Tribunal concerned Article 2(2) and 2(3) of Directive 76/207. (Article 177 reference.)

[35]   As is clear from the Industrial Tribunal's decision, the policy towards women in the RUC full-time Reserve was adopted by the Chief Constable because he considered that if women were armed they might become a more frequent target for assassination and their fire-arms could fall into the hands of their assailants, that the public would not welcome the carrying of fire-arms by women, which would conflict too much with the ideal of an unarmed police force, and that armed policewomen would be less effective in police work in the social field with families and children in which the services of policewomen are particularly appreciated. The reasons which the Chief Constable thus gave for his policy were related to the special conditions in which the police must work in the situation existing in Northern Ireland, having regard to the requirements of the protection of public safety in a context of serious internal disturbances.

[36]   As regards the question whether such reasons may be covered by Article 2(2) of the directive, it should first be observed that that provision, being a derogation from an individual right laid down in the directive, must be interpreted strictly. However, it must

be recognized that the context in which the occupational activity of members of an armed police force are carried out is determined by the environment in which that activity is carried out. In this regard, the possibility cannot be excluded that in a situation characterized by serious internal disturbances the carrying of fire-arms by policewomen might create additional risks of their being assassinated and might therefore be contrary to the requirements of public safety.

[37]   In such circumstances, the context of certain policing activities may be such that the sex of police officers constitutes a determining factor for carrying them out. If that is so, a Member State may therefore restrict such tasks, and the training leading thereto, to men. In such a case, as is clear from Article 9(2) of the directive, the Member States have a duty to assess periodically the activities concerned in order to decide whether, in the light of social developments, the derogation from the general scheme of the directive may still be maintained.

[38]   It must also be borne in mind that, in determining the scope of any derogation from an individual right such as the equal treatment of men and women provided for by the directive, the principle of proportionality, one of the general principles of law underlying the Community legal order, must be observed. That principle requires that derogations remain within the limits of what is appropriate and necessary for achieving the aim in view and requires the principle of equal treatment to be reconciled as far as possible with the requirements of public safety which constitute the decisive factor as regards the context of the activity in question.

[39]   By reason of the division of jurisdiction provided for in Article 177 of the EEC Treaty, it is for the national court to say whether the reasons on which the Chief Constable based his decision are in fact well founded and justify the specific measure taken in Mrs Johnston's case. It is also for the national court to ensure that the principle of proportionality is observed and to determine whether the refusal to renew Mrs Johnston's contract could not be avoided by allocating to women duties which, without jeopardizing the aims pursued, can be performed without fire-arms.

. . .

[41]   In its fourth and fifth question the Industrial Tribunal then asks the Court for an interpretation of the expressions 'protection of women' in Article 2(3) of the directive and 'concern for protection' in Article 3(2)(c), which inspired certain provisions of national law, so that it can decide whether the difference in treatment in question may fall within the scope of the derogations from the principle of equal treatment laid down for those purposes.

[42]   In *Mrs Johnston's* view, those provisions must be interpreted strictly. Their sole purpose is to assure women special treatment in order to protect their health and safety in the case of pregnancy or maternity. That is not the case where women are completely excluded from service in an armed police force.

[43]   The *United Kingdom* states that the aim of the policy with regard to women in the RUC full-time Reserve is to protect women by preventing them from becoming targets for assassination. The expression 'protection of women' may cover such an aim in a period of serious disturbances. The *Commission* also takes the view that an exceptional situation such as exists in Northern Ireland and the resultant dangers for armed women police officers may be taken into consideration from the viewpoint of the protection of women.

[44]   It must be observed in this regard that, like Article 2(2) of the directive, Article 2(3), which also determines the scope of Article 3(2)(c), must be interpreted strictly. It is clear from the express reference to pregnancy and maternity that the directive is intended to protect a woman's biological condition and the special relationship which exists between a woman and her child. That provision of the directive does not therefore allow women to be excluded from a certain type of employment on the ground that public opinion demands that women be given greater protection than men against risks which affect men and women in the same way and which are distinct from women's specific needs of protection, such as those expressly mentioned.

[45]   It does not appear that the risks and dangers to which women are exposed when performing their duties in the police force in a situation such as exists in Northern Ireland are different from those to which any man is also exposed when performing the same duties. A total exclusion of women from such an occupational activity which, owing to a general risk not specific to women, is imposed for reasons of public safety is

not one of the differences in treatment that Article 2(3) of the directive allows out of a concern to protect women.

14.4.3.2   Article 2(3)

CRIMINAL PROCEEDINGS AGAINST STOECKEL (Case C-345/89)
[1991] ECR I-4047, Court of Justice

Criminal proceedings were issued against Mr Stoeckel, who was charged with employing women to work at night contrary to the French Labour Code. In this context, the Tribunal de Police referred to the Court of Justice a question concerning the interpretation of Directive 76/207. (Article 177 reference.)

[13]   . . . pursuant to Article 2(3), the Directive is to be without prejudice to provisions concerning the protection of women, particularly as regards pregnancy and maternity. In its judgment in *Johnston* v *Chief Constable of the Royal Ulster Constabulary* (Case 222/84) [1986] ECR 1651, at paragraph 44, the Court held that it was clear from the express reference to pregnancy and maternity that the Directive was intended to protect a woman's biological condition and the special relationship which exists between a woman and her child.

[14]   The French and Italian Governments submit that the prohibition of nightwork by women, which in any case is subject to numerous exceptions, is in conformity with the general aims of protecting female workers and with particular considerations of a social nature relating, for example, to the risks of attack and the heavier domestic workload borne by women.

[15]   As far as the aims of protecting female workers are concerned, they are valid only if, having regard to the principles mentioned above, there is a justified need for a difference of treatment as between men and women. However, whatever the disadvantages of nightwork may be, it does not seem that, except in the case of pregnancy or maternity, the risks to which women are exposed when working at night are, in general, inherently different from those to which men are exposed.

[16]   As regards the risks of attack, if it is assumed that they are greater at night than during the day, appropriate measures can be adopted to deal with them without undermining the fundamental principle of equal treatment for men and women.

[17]   As far as family responsibilities are concerned, the Court has already held that the Directive is not designed to settle questions concerned with the organization of the family or to alter the division of responsibility between parents (see the judgment in *Hofmann* v *Baimer Ersatzkasse* (Case 184/83) [1984] ECR 3047).

[18]   Thus, the concern to provide protection, by which the general prohibition on nightwork by women was originally inspired, no longer appears to be well founded and the maintenance of that prohibition, by reason of risks that are not peculiar to women or preoccupations unconnected with the purpose of Directive 76/207 cannot be justified by the provisions of Article 2(3) of the Directive which is referred to in paragraph 3 of this judgment.

14.4.4   PREGNANCY AND EQUAL TREATMENT

DEKKER v STICHTING VORMINGSCENTRUM VOOR JONG VOLWASSENEN PLUS
(Case C-177/88) [1990] ECR I-3941, Court of Justice

VJV's offer of employment to Mrs Dekker was withdrawn when it was discovered that she was pregnant. The employer gave as the reason for its decision that its insurer (the 'Risicofonds') would not reimburse the benefits which it would have to pay Mrs Dekker during her maternity leave. VJV would consequently be unable to afford a replacement during Mrs Dekker's absence and would be short-staffed. The national court asked the Court of Justice (*inter alia*) whether the employer directly or indirectly breached the principle of equal treatment contained in Directive 76/207. (Article 177 reference.)

[8]   It should be noted at the outset that the purpose of the Directive, according to Article 1(1), is to put into effect in the Member States the principle of equal treatment for

men and women as regards access to employment, vocational training and promotion, and working conditions.

[9] Article 2(1) of the Directive provides that '. . . the principle of equal treatment shall mean that there shall be no discrimination whatsoever on grounds of sex either directly or indirectly by reference in particular to marital or family status'. Under Article 3(1) 'application of the principle of equal treatment means that there shall be no discrimination whatsoever on grounds of sex in the conditions, including selection criteria, for access to all jobs or posts . . .'.

[10] Consideration must be given to the question whether a refusal of employment in the circumstances to which the national court has referred may be regarded as direct discrimination on grounds of sex for the purposes of the Directive. The answer depends on whether the fundamental reason for the refusal of employment is one which applies without distinction to workers of either sex or, conversely, whether it applies exclusively to one sex.

[11] The reason given by the employer for refusing to appoint Mrs Dekker is basically that it could not have obtained reimbursement from the Risicofonds of the daily benefits which it would have had to pay her for the duration of her absence due to pregnancy, and yet at the same time it would have been obliged to employ a replacement. . . .

[12] In that regard it should be observed that only women can be refused employment on grounds of pregnancy and such a refusal therefore constitutes direct discrimination on grounds of sex. A refusal of employment on account of the financial consequences of absence due to pregnancy must be regarded as based, essentially, on the fact of pregnancy. Such discrimination cannot be justified on grounds relating to the financial loss which an employer who appointed a pregnant woman would suffer for the duration of her maternity leave.

HANDELS-OG KONTORFUNKTIONAERERNES FORBUND I DANMARK v DANSK ARBEJDSGIVERFORENING (HERTZ) (Case 179/88) [1990] ECR I-3979, Court of Justice

Mrs Hertz was employed as a cashier by Aldi Marked. She had been absent from work for long periods because of a complicated pregnancy. After the birth, she once more took sick leave because of illness arising from the pregnancy and confinement. Aldi Marked dismissed Mrs Hertz, stating that her periods of absence were the reason for the dismissal and that it was normal practice to dismiss workers who were absent on account of illness. The Court of Justice was asked whether the dismissal was in breach of Directive 76/207. (Article 177 reference.)

[8] On the one hand it is claimed that the dismissal of a woman on account of pregnancy, confinement or repeated periods of absence due to an illness attributable to pregnancy or confinement is – irrespective of the time when that illness occurs – contrary to the principle of equal treatment, since a male worker is not subject to such disorders and hence cannot be dismissed on that ground.

[9] On the other hand it is contended that an employer cannot be prohibited from dismissing a female worker on account of her frequent periods of sick leave solely because the illness is attributable to pregnancy or confinement. Dismissal on that ground is insufficient proof of infringement of the principle of equal treatment. Such a prohibition, which would apply to an employer for many years after the confinement, would be liable to entail not only administrative difficulties and unfair consequences for the employers but also negative repercussions on the employment of women. Furthermore, although Article 2(3) of the Directive allows Member States to introduce provisions designed to protect women in connection with pregnancy and maternity, it gives no guidance as to the exact content of such provisions.

[10] It should be noted at the outset that the purpose of the Directive, according to Article 1(1), is to put into effect in the Member States the principle of equal treatment for men and women as regards access to employment, vocational training and promotion, and working conditions.

[11] Article 2(1) of the Directive provides that '. . . the principle of equal treatment shall mean that there shall be no discrimination whatsoever on grounds of sex either directly or indirectly by reference in particular to marital or family status'. Under Article 5(1) 'application of the principle of equal treatment with regard to working conditions,

including the conditions governing dismissal, means that men and women shall be guaranteed the same conditions without discrimination on grounds of sex'.

[12]   Article 2(3) of the Directive further states: 'This directive shall be without prejudice to provisions concerning the protection of women, particularly as regards pregnancy and maternity'.

[13]   It follows from the provisions of the Directive quoted above that the dismissal of a female worker on account of pregnancy constitutes direct discrimination on grounds of sex, as is a refusal to appoint a pregnant woman (see judgment of today's date in *Dekker* v *VJM-Centrum* (Case C-177/88) [1990] ECR I-3941).

[14]   On the other hand, the dismissal of a female worker on account of repeated periods of sick leave which are not attributable to pregnancy or confinement does not constitute direct discrimination on grounds of sex, inasmuch as such periods of sick leave would lead to the dismissal of a male worker in the same circumstances.

[15]   The Directive does not envisage the case of an illness attributable to pregnancy or confinement. It does, however, admit of national provisions guaranteeing women specific rights on account of pregnancy and maternity, such as maternity leave. During the maternity leave accorded to her pursuant to national law, a woman is accordingly protected against dismissal due to absence. It is for every Member State to fix periods of maternity leave in such a way as to enable female workers to absent themselves during the period in which the disorders inherent in pregnancy and confinement occur.

[16]   In the case of an illness manifesting itself after the maternity leave, there is no reason to distinguish an illness attributable to pregnancy or confinement from any other illness. Such a pathological condition is therefore covered by the general rules applicable in the event of illness.

[17]   Male and female workers are equally exposed to illness. Although certain disorders are, it is true, specific to one or other sex, the only question is whether a woman is dismissed on account of absence due to illness in the same circumstances as a man; if that is the case, then there is no direct discrimination on grounds of sex.

HABERMANN-BELTERMANN v *ARBEITERWOHLFAHRT BEZIRKSVERBAND* (Case C-421/92) [1994] ECR I-1657, Court of Justice

Mrs Habermann-Beltermann was engaged as a night attendant in a home for the elderly. Her contract, which was for an indefinite term, stipulated that she was to be assigned night-time work only. She subsequently discovered that she was pregnant and that the pregnancy had begun before her contract was signed. On being informed of Mrs Habermann-Beltermann's condition, the employer dismissed her, stating that legislation on the protection of mothers (the Mutterschutzgesetz), which prohibited night-time working by pregnant women, had the effect of rendering her contract void. The national court asked the Court of Justice for a ruling on the interpretation of Directive 76/207. (Article 177 reference.)

[15]   It is clear that the termination of an employment contract on account of the employee's pregnancy, whether by annulment or avoidance, concerns women alone and constitutes, therefore, direct discrimination on grounds of sex, as the Court has held in cases where a pregnant woman was denied employment or dismissed (see the judgments in *Dekker* v *VJV-Centrum* (Case C-177/88) [1990] ECR 1-3941 and *Handels-og Kontorfunktionærernes Forbund i Danmark* v *Dansk Arbejdsgiverforening* (Case C-179/88) [1990] ECR I-3979).

[16]   However, the unequal treatment in a case such as this, unlike the *Dekker* case referred to by the national court, is not based directly on the woman's pregnancy but is the result of the statutory prohibition on night-time work during pregnancy.

[17]   The basis for that prohibition, laid down by Paragraph 8(1) of the Mutterschutzgesetz, is Article 2(3) of the directive, according to which the directive is without prejudice to the provisions concerning the protection of women, particularly as regards pregnancy and maternity.

[18]   The question, therefore, is whether the directive precludes compliance with the prohibition on night-time work by pregnant women, which is unquestionably compatible with Article 2(3), from rendering an employment contract invalid or allowing it to be

avoided on the ground that the prohibition prevents the employee from doing the night-time work for which she was engaged.

[19]   According to the Arbeiterwohlfahrt, the Member States possess a wide and independent discretion in appraising the interests of workers, both male and female, and of employers and society. Excessive protection of mothers might lead to abuse by women and also to discrimination against men who do not have the same opportunity of being paid without having to work in return.

[20]   That argument must be rejected.

[21]   In the first place, so far as concerns the purpose of Article 2(3) of the directive, by reserving to Member States the right to retain or introduce provisions which are intended to protect women in connection with 'pregnancy and maternity', that article recognizes the legitimacy, in terms of the principle of equal treatment, first, of protecting a woman's biological condition during and after pregnancy and, second, of protecting the special relationship between a woman and her child over the period which follows pregnancy and childbirth (see the judgment in *Hofmann* v *Baimer Ersatzkasse* (Case 184/83) [1984] ECR 3047, paragraph 25).

[22]   As the Court has held (see the *Hofmann* judgment cited above, paragraph 27), the directive leaves Member States with a discretion as to the social measures which must be adopted in order to guarantee, within the framework laid down by the directive, the protection of women in connection with pregnancy and maternity and to offset the disadvantages which women, by comparison with men, suffer with regard to the retention of employment.

[23]   In this case, the questions submitted for a ruling relate to a contract for an indefinite period and the prohibition on night-time work by pregnant women therefore takes effect only for a limited period in relation to the total length of the contract.

[24]   In the circumstances, to acknowledge that the contract may be held to be invalid or may be avoided because of the temporary inability of the pregnant employee to perform the night-time work for which she has been engaged would be contrary to the objective of protecting such persons pursued by Article 2(3) of the directive, and would deprive that provision of its effectiveness.

[25]   Accordingly, termination of a contract for an indefinite period on grounds of the woman's pregnancy, whether by annulment or avoidance, cannot be justified by the fact that she is temporarily prevented, by a statutory prohibition imposed because of pregnancy, from performing night-time work.

WEBB v *EMO AIR CARGO (UK) LTD* (Case C-32/93) [1994] ECR I-3567, Court of Justice

Mrs Webb was employed under a contract for an indefinite term partly to replace another employee, Mrs Stewart, during the latter's maternity leave. It was envisaged that Mrs Webb would continue in that employment after Mrs Stewart's return. Shortly after commencing work, Mrs Webb discovered that she too was pregnant. She was dismissed. The House of Lords referred questions to the Court of Justice concerning the interpretation of Directive 76/207. (Article 177 reference.)

[19]   As the Court ruled in paragraph 13 of its judgment in *Handels-og Kontorfunkionærenes Forbund i Danmark* (Case C-179/88) [1990] ECR 1-3979 (hereinafter 'the *Hertz* judgment') and confirmed in paragraph 15 of its judgment in *Habermann-Beltermann* (Case C-421/92) [1994] ECR I-1657, the dismissal of a female worker on account of pregnancy constitutes direct discrimination on grounds of sex.

[20]   Furthermore, by reserving to Member States the right to retain or introduce provisions which are intended to protect women in connection with 'pregnancy and maternity', Article 2(3) of Directive 76/207 recognizes the legitimacy, in terms of the principle of equal treatment, first, of protecting a woman's biological condition during and after pregnancy and, second, of protecting the special relationship between a woman and her child over the period which follows pregnancy and childbirth (*Habermann-Beltermann*, cited above, paragraph 21, and *Hofmann* v *Baimer Ersatzkasse* (Case 184/83) [1984] ECR 3047, paragraph 25).

[21]   In view of the harmful effects which the risk of dismissal may have on the physical and mental state of women who are pregnant, have recently given birth or are

breastfeeding, including the particularly serious risk that pregnant women may be prompted voluntarily to terminate their pregnancy, the Community legislature subsequently provided, pursuant to Article 10 of Council Directive 92/85/EEC of 19 October 1992 on the introduction of measures to encourage improvements in the safety and health at work of pregnant workers and workers who have recently given birth or are breastfeeding . . . for special protection to be given to women, by prohibiting dismissal during the period from the beginning of their pregnancy to the end of their maternity leave.

[22] Furthermore, Article 10 of Directive 92/85 provides that there is to be no exception to, or derogation from, the prohibition on the dismissal of pregnant women during that period, save in exceptional cases not connected with their condition.

[23] The answer to the question submitted by the House of Lords, which concerns Directive 76/207, must take account of that general context.

[24] First, in response to the House of Lords' inquiry, there can be no question of comparing the situation of a woman who finds herself incapable, by reason of pregnancy discovered very shortly after the conclusion of the employment contract, of performing the task for which she was recruited with that of a man similarly incapable for medical or other reasons.

[25] As Mrs Webb rightly argues, pregnancy is not in any way comparable with a pathological condition, and even less so with unavailability for work on non-medical grounds, both of which are situations that may justify the dismissal of a woman without discriminating on grounds of sex. Moreover, in the *Hertz* judgment, cited above, the Court drew a clear distinction between pregnancy and illness, even where the illness is attributable to pregnancy but manifests itself after the maternity leave. As the Court pointed out (in paragraph 16), there is no reason to distinguish such an illness from any other illness.

[26] Furthermore, contrary to the submission of the United Kingdom, dismissal of a pregnant woman recruited for an indefinite period cannot be justified on grounds relating to her inability to fulfil a fundamental condition of her employment contract. The availability of an employee is necessarily, for the employer, a precondition for the proper performance of the employment contract. However, the protection afforded by Community law to a woman during pregnancy and after childbirth cannot be dependent on whether her presence at work during maternity is essential to the proper functioning of the undertaking in which she is employed. Any contrary interpretation would render ineffective the provisions of the directive.

[27] In circumstances such as those of Mrs Webb, termination of a contract for an indefinite period on grounds of the woman's pregnancy cannot be justified by the fact that she is prevented, on a purely temporary basis, from performing the work for which she has been engaged . . .

[28] The fact that the main proceedings concern a woman who was initially recruited to replace another employee during the latter's maternity leave but who was herself found to be pregnant shortly after her recruitment cannot affect the answer to be given to the national court.

[29] Accordingly, the answer to the question submitted must be that Article 2(1) read with Article 5(1) of Directive 76/207 precludes dismissal of an employee who is recruited for an unlimited term with a view, initially, to replacing another employee during the latter's maternity leave and who cannot do so because, shortly after recruitment, she is herself found to be pregnant.

14.5 Directive 79/7: Equal Treatment in Matters of Social Security

COUNCIL DIRECTIVE 79/7/EEC OF 19 DECEMBER 1978 ON THE PROGRESSIVE IMPLEMENTATION OF THE PRINCIPLE OF EQUAL TREATMENT FOR MEN AND WOMEN IN MATTERS OF SOCIAL SECURITY OJ 1979 L 6/24

[Preamble omitted.]

Article 1

The purpose of this Directive is the progressive implementation, in the field of social security and other elements of social protection provided for in Article 3, of the principle of equal treatment for men and women in matters of social security, hereinafter referred to as 'the principle of equal treatment'.

Article 2
This Directive shall apply to the working population – including self-employed persons, workers and self-employed persons whose activity is interrupted by illness, accident or involuntary unemployment and persons seeking employment – and to retired or invalided workers and self-employed persons.

Article 3
   1.   This Directive shall apply to:
     (a)   statutory schemes which provide protection against the following risks:
       – sickness,
       – invalidity,
       – old age,
       – accidents at work and occupational diseases,
       – unemployment;
     (b)   social assistance, in so far as it is intended to supplement or replace the schemes referred to in (a).
   2.   This Directive shall not apply to the provisions concerning survivors' benefits nor to those concerning family benefits, except in the case of family benefits granted by way of increases of benefits due in respect of the risks referred to in paragraph 1(a).
   3.   With a view to ensuring implementation of the principle of equal treatment in occupational schemes, the Council, acting on a proposal from the Commission, will adopt provisions defining its substance, its scope and the arrangements for its application.

Article 4
   1.   The principle of equal treatment means that there shall be no discrimination whatsoever on ground of sex either directly, or indirectly by reference in particular to marital or family status, in particular as concerns:
     – the scope of the schemes and the conditions of access thereto,
     – the obligation to contribute and the calculation of contributions,
     – the calculation of benefits including increases due in respect of a spouse and for dependants and the conditions governing the duration and retention of entitlement to benefits.
   2.   The principle of equal treatment shall be without prejudice to the provisions relating to the protection of women on the grounds of maternity.

Article 5
Member States shall take the measures necessary to ensure that any laws, regulations and administrative provisions contrary to the principle of equal treatment are abolished.

Article 6
Member States shall introduce into their national legal systems such measures as are necessary to enable all persons who consider themselves wronged by failure to apply the principle of equal treatment to pursue their claims by judicial process, possibly after recourse to other competent authorities.

Article 7
   1.   This Directive shall be without prejudice to the right of Member States to exclude from its scope:
     (a)   the determination of pensionable age for the purposes of granting old-age and retirement pensions and the possible consequences thereof for other benefits;
     (b)   advantages in respect of old-age pension schemes granted to persons who have brought up children; the acquisition of benefit entitlements following periods of interruption of employment due to the bringing up of children;
     (c)   the granting of old-age or invalidity benefit entitlements by virtue of the derived entitlements of a wife;

    (d)   the granting of increases of long-term invalidity, old-age, accidents at work and occupational disease benefits for a dependent wife;

    (e)   the consequences of the exercise, before the adoption of this Directive, of a right of option not to acquire rights or incur obligations under a statutory scheme.

    2.   Member States shall periodically examine matters excluded under paragraph 1 in order to ascertain, in the light of social developments in the matter concerned, whether there is justification for maintaining the exclusions concerned.

(Remaining provisions omitted.)

14.5.1   SCOPE OF DIRECTIVE 79/7

DRAKE v *CHIEF ADJUDICATION OFFICER* (Case 150/85) [1986] ECR 1995, Court of Justice

Mrs Drake, who had given up work in order to look after her invalid mother, applied for invalid care allowance. She was refused because, under the Social Security Act 1975, the benefit was not payable to married women living with their husbands. Two questions were referred to the Court of Justice by the Chief Social Security Commissioner. (Article 177 reference.)

Question 1

[11]   By his first question the Chief Social Security Commissioner seeks to know whether the right to the payment of a benefit to a person who cares for a disabled person constitutes part of a statutory scheme providing protection against the risk of invalidity to which Directive 79/7 applies under Article 3(1)(a) of that directive.

. . .

[20]   It must be pointed out first of all that according to the first and second recitals in the preamble to Directive 79/7, the aim of that directive is the progressive implementation of the principle of equal treatment for men and women in matters of social security.

[21]   According to Article 3(1), Directive 79/7 applies to statutory schemes which provide protection against, *inter alia*, the risk of invalidity (subparagraph (a)) and social assistance in so far as it is intended to supplement or replace the invalidity scheme (subparagraph (b)). In order to fall within the scope of the directive, therefore, a benefit must constitute the whole or part of a statutory scheme providing protection against one of the specified risks or a form of social assistance having the same objective.

[22]   Under Article 2, the term 'working population', which determines the scope of the directive, is defined broadly to include 'self-employed persons, workers and self-employed persons whose activity is interrupted by illness, accident or involuntary employment and persons seeking employment . . . [and] retired or invalided workers and self-employed persons'. That provision is based on the idea that a person whose work has been interrupted by one of the risks referred to in Article 3 belongs to the working population. That is the case of Mrs Drake, who has given up work solely because of one of the risks listed in Article 3, namely the invalidity of her mother. She must therefore be regarded as a member of the working population for the purposes of the directive.

[23]   Furthermore, it is possible for the Member States to provide protection against the consequences of the risk of invalidity in various ways. For example, a Member State may, as the United Kingdom has done, provide for two separate allowances, one payable to the disabled person himself and the other payable to a person who provides care, while another Member State may arrive at the same result by paying an allowance to the disabled person at a rate equivalent to the sum of those two benefits. In order, therefore, to ensure that the progressive implementation of the principle of equal treatment referred to in Article 1 of Directive 79/7 and defined in Article 4 is carried out in a harmonious manner throughout the Community, Article 3(1) must be interpreted as including any benefit which in a broad sense forms part of one of the statutory schemes referred to or a social assistance provision intended to supplement or replace such a scheme.

[24]   Moreover, the payment of the benefit to a person who provides care still depends on the existence of a situation of invalidity inasmuch as such a situation is a

condition *sine qua non* for its payment, as the Adjudication Officer admitted during the oral procedure. It must also be emphasized that there is a clear economic link between the benefit and the disabled person, since the disabled person derives an advantage from the fact that an allowance is paid to the person caring for him.

[25]   It follows that the fact that a benefit which forms part of a statutory invalidity scheme is paid to a third party and not directly to the disabled person does not place it outside the scope of Directive 79/7. Otherwise, as the Commission emphasized in its observations, it would be possible, by making formal changes to existing benefits covered by the directive, to remove them from its scope.

[26]   The answer to the first question referred by the Chief Social Security Commissioner must therefore be that a benefit provided by a Member State and paid to a person caring for a disabled person forms part of a statutory scheme providing protection against invalidity which is covered by Directive 79/7 pursuant to Article 3(1)(a) of that directive.

Question 2

[27]   Since Question 1 has been answered in the affirmative, it is necessary to examine Question 2, which concerns the issue whether discrimination on grounds of sex contrary to Article 4(1) of Directive 79/7 arises where legislation provides that a benefit which forms part of one of the statutory schemes referred to in Article 3(1) of the directive is not payable to a married woman who lives with or is maintained by her husband, although it is paid in corresponding circumstances to a married man.

. . .

[31]   It should be noted that Article 4(1) of Directive 79/7 provides that the implementation of the principle of equal treatment, with regard in particular to the scope of schemes and the conditions of access to them, means that there should be no discrimination whatsoever on grounds of sex.

[32]   That provision embodies the aim of the directive, set out in Article 1, that is to say the implementation, in the field of social security and between men and women, of the principle of equal treatment, a principle which the Court has frequently described as fundamental.

[33]   It follows from the foregoing that a national provision such as that at issue before the Chief Social Security Commissioner is contrary to the aim, as stated above, of the directive, which under Article 189 of the Treaty is binding on the Member States as to the result to be achieved.

[34]   The answer to Question 2 must therefore be that discrimination on grounds of sex contrary to Article 4(1) of Directive 79/7 arises where legislation provides that a benefit which forms part of one of the statutory schemes referred to in Article 3(1) of that directive is not payable to a married woman who lives with or is maintained by her husband, although it is paid in corresponding circumstances to a married man.

ATKINS (STANLEY CHARLES) v *WREKIN DISTRICT COUNCIL AND DEPARTMENT OF TRANSPORT* (Case C-228/94) [1996] ECR I-3633, Court of Justice

Mr Atkins considered that he had been discriminated against on the ground of his sex because, at the age of 63, he was refused travel concessions under Wrekin District Council's public transport scheme, which was operated under powers granted by s. 93 of the Transport Act 1985. A woman of the same age would have been entitled to such concessions. He brought proceedings before the High Court, which referred to the Court of Justice questions concerning the interpretation of Directive 79/7. (Article 177 reference.)

8.   By its first question the High Court asks essentially whether, on a proper interpretation of Article 3(1) of Directive 79/7, a scheme such as that provided for in s. 93(7) of the 1985 Act and implemented and operated by Wrekin District Council, under which concessionary fares on public passenger transport services are granted to certain classes of persons, in particular to certain elderly persons, falls within the scope of the Directive.

9.   According to Article 3(1)(a), the Directive is to apply to statutory schemes which provide protection on against the risks of sickness, invalidity, old age, accidents at work and occupational diseases, and unemployment. . . .

10. The Court has already held that, in order to fall within the scope of Directive 79/7, a benefit must constitute the whole or part of a statutory scheme providing protection against one of the specified risks, or a form of social assistance having the same objective (see, in particular, Case C-137/94 R v *Secretary of State for Health, ex parte Richardson* [1995] ECR I-3407, paragraph 8).

11. The Court has also stated that, although the way in which a benefit is granted is not decisive for the purposes of Directive 79/7, the benefit must, in order to fall within its scope, be directly and effectively linked to the protection provided against one of the risks specified in Article 3(1) of the Directive (*Richardson*, cited above, paragraph 9).

12. A benefit such as that provided for in s. 93(7) of the 1985 Act and granted under the scheme implemented and operated by Wrekin District Council does not meet those conditions.

13. It is true that, being provided for in a statutory provision, it forms part of a statutory scheme, albeit it is granted only pursuant to measures adopted by local authorities.

. . .

16. However, a benefit such as that provided for in s. 93(7) of the 1985 Act, consisting of concessionary fares on public passenger transport services which may be granted to various classes of persons, including persons who have reached statutory retirement age, certain young or disabled persons and any other class of persons to be determined by ministerial order, does not afford direct and effective protection against one of the risks listed in Article 3(1) of Directive 79/7.

17. The purpose of such a benefit is to facilitate access to public transport for certain classes of persons who, for various reasons, are recognized as having a particular need for public transport and who are, for the same reasons, less well off financially and materially.

18. Old age and invalidity, which are among the risks listed in Article 3(1)(a) of Directive 79/7, are only two of the criteria which may be applied to define the classes of beneficiaries of such a scheme of concessionary public transport fares.

19. The fact that the recipient of a benefit is, as a matter of fact, in one of the situations envisaged by Article 3(1) of Directive 79/7 does not suffice to bring that benefit as such within the scope of the Directive (see Joined Cases C-63/91 and C-64/91 *Jackson and Cresswell* [1992] ECR I-4737, paragraphs 18 and 19).

14.5.2 INDIRECT DISCRIMINATION

TEULING v *BEDRIJFSVERENIGING VOOR DE CHEMISCHE INDUSTRIE* (Case 30/85) [1987] ECR 2497, Court of Justice

Under Dutch social security law, a benefit amounting to 70% of the statutory minimum wage was available to persons who were unable to work because of incapacity. The benefit could be increased up to the full value of the minimum wage if a beneficiary had a dependent spouse or children. Mrs Teuling claimed that this system of calculating benefit was incompatible with Article 4(1) of Directive 79/7. (Article 177 reference.)

[14] . . . according to statistics provided to the Commission by the Netherlands Government a significantly greater number of married men than married women receive a supplement linked to family responsibilities. According to the plaintiff and the Commission, that results from the fact that in the Netherlands there are at present considerably more married men than married women who carry on occupational activities, and therefore considerably fewer women who have a dependent spouse.

[15] In such circumstances a supplement linked to family responsibilities is contrary to Article 4(1) of the directive if the grant thereof cannot be justified by reasons which exclude discrimination on grounds of sex.

[16] In that regard, the purpose of the supplements at issue must be considered. According to the Netherlands Government, the General Law does not link benefits to the salary previously earned by the beneficiaries but seeks to provide a minimum subsistence income to persons with no income from work. It must be observed that such a guarantee granted by Member States to persons who would otherwise be destitute is an integral part of the social policy of the Member States.

[17]   Consequently, if supplements to a minimum social security benefit are intended, where beneficiaries have no income from work, to prevent the benefit from falling below the minimum subsistence level for persons who, by virtue of the fact that they have a dependent spouse or children, bear heavier burdens than single persons, such supplements may be justified under the directive.

[18]   If a national court, which has sole jurisdiction to assess the facts and interpret the national legislation, finds that supplements such as those in this case correspond to the greater burdens which beneficiaries having a dependent spouse or children must bear in comparison with persons living alone, serve to ensure an adequate minimum subsistence income for those beneficiaries and are necessary for that purpose, the fact that the supplements are paid to a significantly higher number of married men than married women is not sufficient to support the conclusion that the grant of such supplements is contrary to the directive.

RUZIUS-WILBRINK v BESTUUR VAN DE BEDRIJFSVERENIGING VOOR OVERHEIDSDIENSTEN (Case 102/88) [1989] ECR 4311, Court of Justice

Under a Dutch system of invalidity benefits, full-time workers received a minimum subsistence income whereas part-timers received payments based upon their previous income. By virtue of the relevant social security legislation, payments to part-timers were necessarily lower than the minimum subsistence income. It was claimed that the system was incompatible with Article 4(1) of Directive 79/7 because most part-time workers in the Netherlands were women. (Article 177 reference.)

[15]   . . . a provision such as the one at issue leads, in principle, to discrimination against female workers in relation to male workers and must be regarded as contrary to the objective pursued by Article 4(1) of Directive 79/7/EEC, unless the difference of treatment as between the two categories of workers is justified by objective factors unrelated to any discrimination on grounds of sex (see the judgment of 13 July 1989 in *Rinner-Kühn* (Case 171/88) [1989] ECR 2743).

[16]   The only reason put forward in the main proceedings to justify the difference of treatment between persons who worked on a part time basis before the onset of their disability and other beneficiaries of the allowance in question, namely that it would be unjust to grant them an allowance higher than the income previously received, cannot objectively justify that difference of treatment since, in a substantial number of other cases, the amount of the allowance granted under the 1975 Law is higher than that previous income.

14.5.3   EXCEPTIONS

R v SECRETARY OF STATE FOR SOCIAL SECURITY, EX PARTE EQUAL OPPORTUNITIES COMMISSION (Case C-9/91) [1992] 3 CMLR 233, Court of Justice

The Equal Opportunities Commission sought a declaration that the UK State pension scheme unlawfully discriminated against men because it required men to pay contributions for 44 years and women for 39 years in order to qualify for the basic retirement pension. The High Court referred to the Court of Justice a question on the interpretation of Article 7(1)(a) of Directive 79/7. (Article 177 reference.)

[12]   By its question the High Court seeks to ascertain whether those forms of discrimination, which are in principle contrary to Article 4(1) of the directive, are nonetheless temporarily permissible by virtue of the power conferred upon Member States by Article 7(1)(a) to derogate from the directive by fixing different pensionable ages for men and women for the purposes of granting old-age and retirement pensions. The question therefore is whether that power of derogation merely allows men and women to be treated unequally with respect to the moment at which they become entitled to a pension or whether it also covers other legislative and financial consequences flowing from a different pensionable age such as the obligation to contribute until reaching that age.

[13]   Since the text of the derogation refers to 'the determination of pensionable age for the purpose of granting old-age and retirement pensions', it is clear that it concerns the moment from which pensions become payable. The text does not, however, refer expressly to discrimination in respect of the extent of the obligation to contribute for the purposes of the pension or the amount thereof. Such forms of discrimination therefore fall within the scope of the derogation only if they are found to be necessary in order to achieve the objectives which the directive is intended to pursue by allowing Member States to retain a different pensionable age for men and women.

[14]   In that regard it should be noted that the express purpose of the directive is to achieve the progressive implementation of the principle of equal treatment for men and women in matters of social security. The progressive nature of the implementation is reflected in a number of derogations, including the one provided for by Article 7(1)(a), and manifests itself by the absence of any precise time limit for their maintenance. Thus, Article 7(2) requires Member States periodically to examine matters excluded under paragraph (1) in order to ascertain, in the light of social developments in the matter concerned, whether the maintenance of the exclusions can be justified. Moreover, Article 8(2) requires Member States to communicate to the Commission *inter alia* the provisions adopted pursuant to Article 7(2) and to inform it of their reasons for maintaining any existing provisions on the matters referred to in Article 7(1) and of the possibilities for reviewing them at a later date.

[15]   Although the preamble to the directive does not state the reasons for the derogations which it lays down, it can be deduced from the nature of the exceptions contained in Article 7(1) of the directive that the Community legislature intended to allow Member States to maintain temporarily the advantages accorded to women with respect to retirement in order to enable them progressively to adapt their pension systems in this respect without disrupting the complex financial equilibrium of those systems, the importance of which could not be ignored. Those advantages include the possibility for female workers of qualifying for a pension earlier than male workers, as envisaged by Article 7(1)(a) of the directive.

[16]   In a system such as the one concerned in the main proceedings, whose financial equilibrium is based on men contributing for a longer period than women, a different pensionable age for men and women cannot be maintained without altering the existing financial equilibrium, unless such inequality with respect to the length of contribution periods is also maintained.

[17]   Consequently, any interpretation of Article 7(1) of the directive whose effect would be to restrict the scope of the derogations provided for in subparagraph (a) to that of allowing Member States to provide that men and women do not become entitled to a pension at the same time and to exclude discrimination with respect to contribution periods would lead to the financial disequilibrium of the pension schemes.

[18]   Interpreted in that way, the derogation laid down in Article 7(1)(a) would be rendered nugatory since the consequence would be that the Member States concerned would have been obliged, before the expiry of the six-year period laid down by Article 8 for the implementation of the directive, to undertake a general restructuring of the system of contributions and benefits and to alter substantially a financial equilibrium based on an obligation to contribute until pensionable ages that were different for men and women.

[19]   To exclude from the derogation discrimination concerning contribution periods, determined according to pensionable age, would thus be contrary to the very objective of Article 7(1). Article 7(1)(a) of the directive must therefore be interpreted as authorising the maintenance of different contribution periods for male and female workers under pension schemes such as the one concerned in the main proceedings.

14.6   End of Chapter Assessment Questions

1   Outline the role played by the Court of Justice in the extension of individual rights under Community sex discrimination law through its broad interpretation of the concept of 'pay' contained in Article 119 of the Treaty.

2   How did the Equal Pay Directive 75/117 'flesh out' the meaning of 'equal work' in Article 119 of the Treaty?

3   Assess the importance of *Jenkins* v *Kingsgate (Clothing Productions) Ltd* (Case 96/80) and *Bilka-Kaufhaus GmbH* v *Karin Weber von Hartz* (Case 170/84) in the development of the concepts of indirect discrimination and objective justification in Community sex discrimination law.

4   'From relatively modest beginnings, Community sex discrimination law has developed into a substantial body of law according extensive rights to individuals in employment and in matters of social security'. Discuss.

14.7   End of Chapter Assessment Outline Answers

(Unless otherwise stated, references in the following answers are to the Treaty of Rome.)

QUESTION 1

Article 119 of the Treaty, which establishes the principle of equal pay for equal work for men and women, defines 'pay' broadly as 'the ordinary basic or minimum wage or salary and any other consideration, whether in cash or in kind, which the worker receives, directly or indirectly, in respect of his employment from his employer'. This Treaty definition of pay has been interpreted generously by the Court of Justice. A wide range of payments and benefits have been held by the Court to fall within the scope of Article 119, including amounts paid by an employer directly into an occupational pension scheme and used in calculating gross salary (*Worringham*), a severance payment, even though this was made on termination of the employment (*Kowalska*) and a benefit in kind which an employer was not contractually obliged to grant (*Garland*).

The term 'pay' has also been interpreted by the Court of Justice to cover a range benefits and payments which might on first consideration be viewed as social security benefits rather than as pay but which were held by the Court to fall within Article 119 because employees were entitled to them by reason of the employment relationship. These included statutory sick pay (*Rinner-Kühn*), benefits under a supplementary occupational pension scheme funded solely by the employer and set up in accordance with statutory provisions (*Bilka-Kaufhaus*), and payments under a contracted-out occupational pension scheme and statutory redundancy scheme (*Barber*).

The Court of Justice's broad interpretation of 'pay' brings a wide range of payments and benefits within the scope of the equal pay principle and, more particularly, within the scope of Article 119 which, because it is both vertically and horizontally directly effective (*Defrenne (No. 2)*), can be invoked by individuals against both public and private employers. In the specific area of pensions, by classifying occupational pension benefits (under both contracted-out schemes (*Barber*) and supplementary schemes (*Moroni*)) as pay rather than as social security, the Court removed such schemes from the scope of the derogation in Article 7(1)(a) of Directive 79/7, which permits different pensionable ages for men and women for the purposes of granting old-age pensions in statutory social security schemes.

Because of concern about the impact of its ruling in *Barber* on the organisation of occupational pension schemes, the Court of Justice limited the effects of its judgment to entitlement to pensions from the date of the judgment, save where claims had already been initiated in the national courts. This limitation has been clarified in a Protocol annexed to the Treaty by the Treaty on European Union which provides that, save in the case of claims already initiated, benefits under occupational pension schemes are not to be considered as pay in so far as they are attributable to periods of employment prior to the date of the judgment (17 May 1990).

Although, since *Barber*, the Court of Justice appears to have retreated somewhat from its progressive broadening of the definition of 'pay' under Article 119 (*Neath*, *Coloroll* (transfer benefits and capital sums paid under a pension scheme in the event of redundancy held not to constitute pay)), the Court has to date played a very significant role in the extension of individual rights under Community sex discrimination law through its generous interpretation of 'pay' under Article 119.

QUESTION 2

Article 119 of the Treaty requires Member States to implement the principle of 'equal pay for equal work for men and women' and provides that equal pay without discrimination based on sex means equal pay for the 'same work' at piece rates or at time rates. The Equal Pay Directive 75/117 extended the principle of equal pay contained in Article 119 to 'work to which equal value is attributed'. The Court of Justice has held that the Directive defines the scope of Article 119 (*Jenkins*). Consequently, an individual is able to rely upon Article 119 rather than the Directive in order to pursue an equal value claim, thus avoiding any possible difficulties over the direct effect of the Directive.

QUESTION 3

In *Jenkins*, the Court of Justice extended the scope of Article 119 to indirect discrimination. This was an important development, for it broadened the scope of sex discrimination to include an employer's pay policy which was purportedly based upon criteria other than sex but which in fact resulted in inequalities of pay between men and women. However, the impact of this development was diminished by the introduction by the Court of the concept of objective justification. In *Jenkins*, the precise meaning of this concept was left unclear. In *Bilka*, the Court of Justice gave further guidance on the factors which constitute objective justification. Both *Jenkins* and *Bilka* concerned sex discrimination claims by part-time female workers.

In *Jenkins*, the Court of Justice was asked to consider whether a difference in the level of pay between part-time and full-time workers amounted to discrimination contrary to Article 119 of the Treaty when the part-time workforce was composed exclusively or predominantly of women. The Court's response was that the difference in pay did not breach Article 119 provided that the difference was 'attributable to factors which are objectively justified and are in no way related to any discrimination based on sex'. It went on to suggest that this might be the case where the employer, for economic reasons, is trying to encourage full-time work, regardless of the sex of the worker. It was for the national court to decide whether an indirectly discriminatory pay policy is justified.

Further guidance on the meaning of 'objective justification' was supplied by the Court of Justice in *Bilka*, in which the Court considered the exclusion of part-time workers from an employer's occupational pension scheme. The Court held that this policy would be contrary to Article 119 if it were found that, having regard to the difficulties faced by women in working full-time, its effects fell disproportionately on women and that the policy could not be explained by factors other than discrimination based on sex. The policy would be objectively justified if the employer could show that it corresponded to a real need of the business, was appropriate to the objective pursued and was necessary to achieve that objective. Again, the Court of Justice left it to the national court to determine whether the grounds of justification put forward by the employer constituted objective justification.

The concept of indirect discrimination, because it takes account of the disadvantageous effects of an employment policy which is not discriminatory on its face, has contributed significantly to the promotion of equality of pay and treatment for men and women. First brought within the scope of Article 119 in *Jenkins* and employed again by the Court in *Bilka*, this concept has been applied in later cases (see for instance *Rinner-Kühn*, *Nimz* and *Enderby*). However, its impact is undermined because it is open to an employer to justify a discriminatory policy provided the *Bilka* criteria for objective justification are satisfied. As the Court of Justice has reiterated on a number of occasions, whether an employer's policy is objectively justified in any particular case is a matter for the national court.

QUESTION 4

This question requires you to take an overview, focusing on the main legislative provisions and on the role played by the Court of Justice in promoting equal rights for men and women.

You might begin by outlining the reasons for the inclusion of the equal pay principle in the original Treaty, the scope of the equal pay principle contained in Article 119 and in Directive 75/117, the significance of the Court of Justice's broad interpretation of 'pay' and the importance of the direct effect of Article 119. It would be appropriate to use a summary of your answers to Questions 1 and 2 for this part of your answer.

You could then point out that the equality principle has been extended by secondary legislation beyond the limits of equal pay to include equal treatment for men and women in employment (Directive 76/207), equal treatment in matters of social security (Directive 79/7), equal treatment in occupational social security schemes (Directive 86/378) and equal treatment in self-employment (Directive 86/613). You should outline the main provisions and indicate how these have been applied by the Court of Justice. In particular, some reference should be made to dismissal and retirement ages (*Burton, Roberts* v *Tate & Lyle, Marshall (No. 1), Barber*), pregnancy (*Dekker, Hertz, Habermann-Beltermann, Webb*) and to derogation from the equal treatment principle in employment (*Johnston, Hofmann, Kalanke*) and in social security (*R* v *Secretary of State for Social Security ex parte EOC, Thomas*).

Your answer should deal with the distinction between direct and indirect discrimination and outline the role played by the Court of Justice in developing and applying the concepts of indirect discrimination and objective justification in relation to equal pay (*Bilka, Rinner-Kühn, Enderby*) and equal treatment in social security (*Teuling, Ruzius-Wilbrink*). This part of your answer might draw on the answer to Question 3.

It is important to point out that although Community sex discrimination law has developed substantially beyond the equal pay principle and has been interpreted liberally by the Court of Justice, which views it as a vehicle for the achievement of social as well as economic objectives, it is nevertheless confined within the employment context. This limitation is perhaps most prominent in the sphere of social security, where the right to equality under Community law does not constitute a general right to non-discrimination in matters of welfare but is a right granted only to the 'working population'. Further, whilst the Court of Justice has extended the scope of 'sex discrimination' to include discrimination based upon the gender-reassignment of an individual (*P* v *S*), it has held that discrimination on grounds of sexual orientation does not violate the principle of equality under Community law (*Grant*).

Finally, reference should be made to remedies, notably the obligation placed on Member States to do all that is necessary to give effect to Community law and, more specifically within the context of equal treatment for men and women in employment, to provide sufficient, real and effective remedies for the protection of individual rights.